# THE OXFORD HANDBOOK OF

# MOBILE MUSIC STUDIES

VOLUME 2

# THE OXFORD HANDBOOK OF

......................................................

# MOBILE MUSIC

# STUDIES

......................................................

## VOLUME 2

*Edited by*

SUMANTH GOPINATH

*and*

JASON STANYEK

OXFORD

UNIVERSITY PRESS

# OXFORD
UNIVERSITY PRESS

Oxford University Press is a department of the University of Oxford.
It furthers the University's objective of excellence in research, scholarship,
and education by publishing worldwide.

Oxford   New York
Auckland   Cape Town   Dar es Salaam   Hong Kong   Karachi
Kuala Lumpur   Madrid   Melbourne   Mexico City   Nairobi
New Delhi   Shanghai   Taipei   Toronto

With offices in
Argentina   Austria   Brazil   Chile   Czech Republic   France   Greece
Guatemala   Hungary   Italy   Japan   Poland   Portugal   Singapore
South Korea   Switzerland   Thailand   Turkey   Ukraine   Vietnam

Oxford is a registered trademark of Oxford University Press
in the UK and certain other countries.

Published in the United States of America by
Oxford University Press
198 Madison Avenue, New York, NY 10016

Library of Congress Cataloging-in-Publication Data
The Oxford handbook of mobile music studies, volume 2 / edited by
Sumanth Gopinath and Jason Stanyek.
v. cm.
Includes bibliographical references and index.
ISBN 978-0-19-991365-7 (alk. paper)
1. Digital music players—Social aspects.   2. Portable media players—Social aspects.
3. Digital music players.   4. Music—Social aspects.   5. Music trade.
I. Gopinath, Sumanth S.   II. Stanyek, Jason
ML3916.O95 2014
302.23—dc23
2012014154

1 3 5 7 9 8 6 4 2
Printed in the United States of America
on acid-free paper

# CONTENTS

## PART IV    DANCE AND DANCE MUSICS

## PART V    POPULAR MUSIC PRODUCTION

## PART VI    GAMING AESTHETICS

# PART VII  MOBILE MUSIC INSTRUMENTS

# Preface to Volume 2

It is a rather commonplace notion that the early twenty-first century is *the* era of "mobility." We are told, over and over, that the world is "on the move," that it is "in motion," and that it is perpetually "in flux." Indeed, the mobility trope is so pervasive that it has, arguably, ceased to function as a persuasive referent or descriptor, its specificity gobbled up by the vast range and innumerable instances of its employment.

Why "mobility" then? It is precisely the ubiquity of the term that provides an opening for research, allowing scholars to reframe and reimagine many kinds of inquiry. Such ubiquity, moreover, neatly dovetails with conspicuous, and even alarming, transformations in the material world. The so-called mobile device has become a basic fact and near necessity of contemporary modernity, and it is hard to imagine everyday life without some link to services or products that are deemed "mobile." All manner of human activity—the way we walk, talk, create, consume, love, listen—is increasingly tracked along and through various trajectories of movement and, indeed, is very often redefined by movement. The motion of humans is mirrored by and tethered to other forms of motion: that of informational signals via the telecommunications system, of bulky commodities threading value chains that crisscross the world's transportation networks, of social and political forms and practices born in one place and quickly adopted and adapted in others.

This, the second volume of the *Oxford Handbook of Mobile Music Studies*, takes as its starting point the idea that the mobilization of music and sound during the period between the late nineteenth and early twenty-first centuries produced crucial shifts in modes of musical/sonic performance and aesthetics. Here, we understand these two key terms—"performance" and "aesthetics"—rather broadly, thinking together self-consciously artistic production with the often (but not necessarily) unconscious performances of quotidian life. We note that there is not only a complex spectrum between these two points but also that they feed back and forward into one another in a variety of ways. Another observation that one may glean from this volume's many contributions is that "mobility" is not the same thing as actual "movement," and that this simple fact has ramifications for mobile performance, which does not necessarily depend on transit or directed human motion to produce the perception or signification of mobility. Indeed, various forms of *stasis* are central to much mobile performance. We should also mention that this volume focuses primarily on performative and aesthetic transformations occurring in the late twentieth and early twenty-first centuries, even though comparable transformations took place throughout the "long century" of mobile music discussed in Volume 1.

The twenty chapters in this volume, while not comprehensive (mobile music is too immense a theme to be encompassed even in two large volumes), do nevertheless provide a précis for thinking about a vast range of issues that concern scholars and general readers interested in tracking and parsing the performative and aesthetic shifts born under the sign of sonic and musical mobility. The volume's chapters coalesce around a few broad thematic areas: the shifting profile of *frequency range* in everyday life, brought about by compressed sound files and—stretching back to the nineteenth century—sirens; the role of the *sound vehicle*, from ice cream trucks to "boom cars" to commuter trains; the gestural and ambulatory *choreographies* of sound walks and everyday mobile device use; the transformations in *dance* and *dance music* in the era of the mobile DJ and peripatetic listener; the new values and techniques of *popular music production* that have occurred in the wake of the creation of new media such as flash drives and new sound-producing devices such as mobile phones; the range of unprecedented *gaming aesthetics* that have developed since the emergence of handheld video games in the 1980s; and the creation of new *mobile music instruments and ensembles* that began to transform musical practice at the turn of the millennium. Many of this volume's chapters, however, do not fit neatly into any single category and instead incorporate a number of different perspectives and orientations, including those just mentioned.

Our hope is that the chapters of Volume 2 be considered with their brethren in Volume 1. The project was originally conceptualized as a rather monumental whole but as the number of essays (and their concomitant word counts) multiplied, it became necessary to divide the contributions into two separate volumes. Nonetheless, Volume 2 can be read on its own and, given that much of this content will appear in Oxford University Press's online databases, we suspect—and, indeed, welcome—that many readers will produce their own maps of and paths through the wide-ranging material offered up by our contributors.

Many people and institutions contributed to the making of these volumes. First and foremost we'd like to express our heartfelt gratitude to Danielle Kuntz, who served as the primary assistant editor for both volumes of the *Handbook*. Without her help and diligence, this project simply would not have come to completion. We would also like to thank the other research assistants, Emily Lechner and Brian Schmidt, both of whom made absolutely essential contributions.

Two editors at Oxford University Press, Suzanne Ryan and Norman Hirschy, made this project possible in the first place, and they are due our immense gratitude. As lead editor, Norm repeatedly went above and beyond the call of duty when handling our numerous concerns, and we are eternally grateful for his efforts, patience, and hefty critical acumen. Several editorial assistants at the Press have been involved with the project over the years, and we'd like to thank them for their fastidious work: Katharine Boone, Caelyn Cobb, Adam Cohen, Lisbeth Redfield, and Madelyn Sutton. Our deepest thanks also go to Sujatha Karthikeyan and Sreejith Viswanathan at Newgen Knowledge Works in Chennai, India for their help in moving the volumes through production.

This *Handbook* emerged in part through a pair of conferences at which some of its contributions were developed and/or presented in embryo. First, Georgina Born and Tom Rice hosted the conference titled "Music, Sound, and the Reconfiguration of Public and Private Space" in April 2008 at Cambridge University's Centre for Research in the Arts, Social Sciences and Humanities (CRASSH), and invited us to present a talk (subsequently a chapter in Born's edited collection *Music, Sound, and Space*) that was inextricably bound up with the present project. Our paper on the Nike+ Sport Kit was perfectly placed on a panel entitled "Urban and Mobile Music/Sound," and we extend our gratitude to the panel's other participants: Michael Bull, Steven Connor, John Drever, and Byron Dueck. Second, Ali Momeni and Sumanth Gopinath received a generous grant from the Minnesota Futures Grant Program at the University of Minnesota and in May 2009 hosted a conference titled "Mobile Music for Everyday People," at which several of the our contributors presented versions of their chapters. Many thanks go to Katie Kuelbs and Ali Momeni for handling the logistics of that conference, to the University of Minnesota's Institute for Advanced Study, Department of Art, School of Music, Collaborative Arts Department, and College of Liberal Arts for providing further support for it, and to all of the faculty participants at the University of Minnesota who chaired panel sessions or participated in other capacities (including the contributions of Minneapolis Art on Wheels): Maria Damon, John Keston, Diyah Larasati, Scott Lipscomb, Ali Momeni, Jenny Schmid, Anna Schultz, Susannah Smith, David Steinman, and Andrea Steudel.

In addition, we would like to acknowledge the support we have received from our employers—the University of Minnesota (School of Music and College of Liberal Arts), New York University (Department of Music), and the Faculty of Music and St. John's College at the University of Oxford. Crucial funding was provided by an Imagine Fund grant from the University of Minnesota and from NYU's Department of Music. Lawren Young and Pauline Lum at NYU were particularly helpful at various crucial junctures. The Stanford Humanities Center also offered enormous support and special gratitude is due to specific members of the Center's staff: Robert Barrick, Zoe Bower, Nicole Coleman, Aron Rodrigue, Najwa Salame, Susan Sebbard, Beth Stutsman, and Matthew Tiews.

We would like to thank our interviewees and interlocutors, who aided in the writing of our own quasi-introductory chapters: Yuya Ozawa at Groundriddim, Shingo Annen, Lalya Gaye, and Aurelie Tu. Moreover, numerous friends, family members and colleagues allowed us to bounce ideas off of them at various stages of the project, and we cannot thank them enough for their involvement, love, and support—especially Beth Hartman, Daisy Hung, and our parents. Finally, we would like to thank our contributors for their excellent work and patience as the project took shape over the last few years: we hope that the end result is to their liking, but we take responsibility for any errors and deficiencies that remain.

# Contributors

**Sumanth Gopinath** is Associate Professor of Music Theory at the University of Minnesota. He is the author of *The Ringtone Dialectic: Economy and Cultural Form* (MIT Press, 2013). His essays, articles, and reviews on Steve Reich, Marxism and music scholarship, academic politics, the ringtone industry, Bob Dylan, and Benjamin Britten have appeared in scholarly journals including *Music Theory Spectrum, Journal of the Society for American Music,* and *First Monday,* and the edited collections *Sound Commitments, Highway 61 Revisited,* and *Music and Narrative since 1900.* He is working on a book project on musical minimalism and is doing research on sound in new and formerly new media, Bob Dylan's musicianship, the aesthetics of smoothness, and the music of James Dillon.

**Jason Stanyek** teaches at the University of Oxford where he is University Lecturer of Ethnomusicology and Tutorial Fellow at St. John's College. Before arriving to Oxford he was Assistant Professor at New York University, Visiting Associate Professor at Harvard University and External Faculty Fellow at the Stanford Humanities Center. He has published on subjects ranging from Brazilian hip-hop to Pan African jazz, from free improvisation to posthumous duets. His ethnographic monograph on music and dance in the Brazilian diaspora and a co-edited volume (with Frederick Moehn) on the history of bossa nova in the United States are forthcoming. From 2013 to 2018 he will serve as Reviews Editor of the journal *Twentieth Century Music.*

**Eliot Bates** is Lecturer in Ethnomusicology and Popular Music Studies at the University of Birmingham. He taught at the University of Maryland after completing his Ph.D. at the University of California, Berkeley. An ethnomusicologist, his work focuses on digital audio recording cultures, with a particular interest in the production of arranged folkloric music in Istanbul. His first book, *Music in Turkey: Experiencing Music, Expressing Culture,* was published by Oxford University Press in 2010. Eliot is a performer and recording artist of the 'ud (oud), and he currently collaborates with the Cornell Avant Garde Ensemble and the hallucinatory apocalyptic supergroup Current 93.

**Frauke Behrendt** is a Senior Lecturer at the University of Brighton and her research interests include the areas of digital cultures, sound studies, mobility, interaction design, sustainable transport and smart cities. She leads the 3-year RCUK funded 'Smart e-bikes' research project (http://www.smart-ebikes.co.uk) that developed an open-source fleet monitoring system with sensor integration. She was on the Steering Committee of the EU COST Action on Sonic Interaction Design and The International Mobile Music

Workshop Series. Previously, Behrendt held posts as Research Fellow at the Cultures of the Digital Economy Research Institute (CoDE) and as Assistant Professor at the Rhode Island School of Design (US). For publications, invited keynotes and other projects see www.fraukebehrendt.com

**Harmony Bench** is Assistant Professor of Dance at The Ohio State University. She researches the impact of media technologies on movement, gesture, and choreography—namely in social and screen media. Harmony's research interests include histories and theories of corporeality, digital media and its consequences for bodily experiences and dance practices, and critical theories of dance and performance. She is on the editorial board of the *International Journal of Screendance*, and she is working on a book tentatively entitled *Screen/Dance and the Politics of Mediality*.

**Justin D. Burton** is Assistant Professor of Music at Rider University. His work engages posthumanity, critical race theory, and hip hop. Recent publications appear in the *Journal of Popular Culture and the Journal of the Society for American Music.*

**Mark J. Butler** is a music theorist whose research addresses popular music, rhythm, and technologically mediated performance. He is Associate Professor and Coordinator of the program in Music Theory and Cognition in the Bienen School of Music at Northwestern University. He is the author of *Unlocking the Groove* (Indiana, 2006) and the editor of *Electronica, Dance, and Club Music* (Ashgate, 2012). His most recent book project is based on extensive fieldwork with internationally active DJs and laptop musicians based in Berlin. By examining relationships between technology and improvisation, he reveals how these musicians create dynamic, novel performances through the transformation of seemingly "fixed" prerecorded objects.

**Karen Collins** is Canada Research Chair in Interactive Audio at the Canadian Centre of Arts and Technology, the University of Waterloo, Ontario. Her work focuses primarily on sound and music in games, and explores how new technologies impact our audio experience. This research has included studies of sound on smart tables (horizontal computers), mobile phones, video games, and how sound is used in slot machines to manipulate players. She has published two books: Game Sound (MIT Press 2008), which was named in the Top 10 Big Ideas in Gaming at the Game Developers' Conference in 2009, and From Pac-Man to Pop Music (Ashgate 2008).

**Georg Essl** is Assistant Professor for Electrical Engineering and Computer Science and Music at the University of Michigan. He holds a Ph.D. in computer science from Princeton University. He has been affiliated with Deutsche Telekom Laboratories, MIT Media Lab Europe, University of Florida, and HyperWave. His current research focuses on mobile phones as musical instruments, sound synthesis, and tangible interactions. He founded and directs the Michigan Mobile Phone Ensemble (Michigan MoPho), is also co-founder and co-director of the Stanford Mobile Phone Orchestra (MoPho), and is founding director of the Berlin Mobile Phone Orchestra (Berlin MoPho).

**Miki Kaneda**  is a Ph.D. candidate in music with a designated emphasis in new media at the University of California, Berkeley, and a Mellon C-MAP Fellow (influence of the performative focus) at the Museum of Modern Art. Her dissertation explores changing senses of the everyday in postwar Japan through a historical and ethnographic study of intermedia art and experimental collectives in the 1960s.

**Kate Levitt**  is an accomplished DJ who has performed in venues throughout the United States, Mexico, and Europe. She is a doctoral candidate in communication at the University of California San Diego, where she works on the relationship between music, technology, and identity. Her research spans many different areas, including constructions of risk and security in urban nightlife, transnational flows of culture and policy between the United States and Latin America, and the contested ways in which society adopts new media. She holds a BA in political science from Barnard College and an MA in communication from UCSD.

**Wayne Marshall**  is an ethnomusicologist (Ph.D. 2007, University of Wisconsin-Madison), blogger (wayneandwax.com), and DJ whose work focuses on digital media and cultural politics across the United States, the Caribbean, and the wider world. A faculty associate at Harvard's Berkman Center for Internet and Society, he is currently teaching at Brandeis University while writing a book on grassroots creativity in the age of YouTube. He co-edited *Reggaeton* (Duke 2009) and has written for *The Wire* and the *Boston Phoenix,* as well as journals such as *Popular Music* and *Callaloo.*

**Andra McCartney**  is Associate Professor of Communication Studies at Concordia University, Montreal, Canada, where she teaches courses in sound production, research creation, media technology as practice, and sound theory. She is a soundwalk artist, leading public walks and creating gallery installations, recordings, performances, videos, and radio works. Her works can be heard on the internet, on CBC radio, and on CDs produced by Deep Wireless, Terra Nova, and the Canadian Electroacoustic Community. Her current FQRSC-funded research project, Soundwalking Interactions, investigates the ways that people listen through and engage with soundwalks and artworks made from soundwalks.

**Daniel T. Neely**  is an independent scholar (Ph.D. 2008, New York University) living in New York City. His research interests include the traditional musics of Jamaica and Ireland, sound theory, and the articulation of music and humor.

**Henri Penttinen**  was born in Espoo, Finland, in 1975. He completed his M.Sc. and Ph.D. (Dr. Tech.) degrees in Electrical Engineering at Aalto University (former Helsinki University of Technology) in 2002 and 2006, respectively. His main research interests are sound synthesis, signal processing algorithms, musical acoustics, and real-time audio applications in mobile environments. Dr. Penttinen was a visiting scholar at Stanford University (CCRMA), during 2007 and 2008. He is one of the co-founders, with Georg Essl and Ge Wang, of the Mobile Phone Orchestra of CCRMA 1.0. He is also the co-inventor, with Jaakko Prättälä, of the electro-acoustic bottle (eBottle).

**Benjamin Piekut** is Assistant Professor in the Department of Music at Cornell University. His research has appeared in *American Quarterly, Jazz Perspectives, Cultural Critique,* and *The Drama Review,* and his book, *Experimentalism Otherwise,* was published in 2011 by the University of California Press. He is co-editor (with George E. Lewis) of the *Oxford Handbook of Critical Improvisation Studies.*

**Alexander Rehding** is Fanny Peabody Professor of Music and Department Chair at Harvard University. He was editor of *Acta musicologica* and is editor-in-chief of the *Oxford Handbook Online* series in music. His main interests lie at the intersection of theory and history, and cover a wide spectrum from Ancient Greece to the Eurovision Song Contest. He is interested in the history of music theory, music-aesthetic questions, and issues of sound and media. Recent publications include *Music and Monumentality* and the *Oxford Handbook of Neo-Riemannian Music Theories.*

**Atau Tanaka**'s early inspiration came upon meeting John Cage during his Norton Lectures at Harvard, informing his re-creation of Cage's Variations VII, which has been performed across Europe. He creates musical instruments using bio-sensor interfaces and mobile technologies, and seeks out the continued place of the artist in democratized digital forms. His work has been presented at Ars Electronica, SFMOMA, Eyebeam, V2, ICC, and ZKM. He has been artistic ambassador for Apple, researcher at Sony CSL, artistic co-director of STEIM, and director of Culture Lab Newcastle. He leads a major European Research Council project on gesture and music at Goldsmiths, University of London.

**Chris Tonelli** received his doctorate at the University of California, San Diego in the Critical Studies and Experimental Practices in Music Program. He was Visiting Lecturer in Contemporary Music and Culture at the New Zealand School of Music at the Victoria University of Wellington and Visiting Assistant Professor of Ethnomusicology and Popular Music Studies at Memorial University of Newfoundland. His research interests include transnational flows of popular music between North America and Japan, extra-normal vocal performance, imitation, and the history of American popular music. He is currently a postdoctoral fellow for 2013–2014 with the Improvisation, Community, and Social Practice project.

**Ge Wang** is Assistant Professor at Stanford University in the Center for Computer Research in Music and Acoustics (CCRMA), and researches mobile and social music, programming languages and interactive software systems for computer music, and education at the intersection of computer science and music. Ge is the author of the ChucK audio programming language, the founding director of the Stanford Laptop Orchestra (SLOrk), and co-founding director of the Stanford Mobile Phone Orchestra (MoPhO). Concurrently, Ge is the Co-founder of Smule—reaching over 100 million users—and the designer of the iPhone's *Ocarina* and *Magic Piano.*

**Alexander G. Weheliye** is Associate Professor of African American Studies and English at Northwestern University, where he teaches black literature and culture, critical theory, social technologies, and popular culture. He is the author of *Phonographies: Grooves in Sonic Afro-Modernity* (Duke University Press, 2005). Currently, he is working on two projects: *Habeas Viscus: Racialization, Bare Life, and the Human* and *Modernity Hesitant: The Civilizational Diagnostics of W.E.B. Du Bois and Walter Benjamin*. His work has been published in *American Literary History*, *boundary 2*, *The Journal of Visual Culture*, *Public Culture*, and *Social Text*.

**Justin A. Williams** is Lecturer in Music at the University of Bristol. He received his BA in music from Stanford University, master's degree in music from King's College London, and a Ph.D. from the University of Nottingham. He completed an ESRC-funded Postdoctoral Fellowship to research a project on music and automobility at the Centre for Mobilities Research at Lancaster University. He is author of *Rhymin and Stealin: Musical Borrowing in Hip-hop* (University of Michigan press, 2013) and is currently editing the *Cambridge Companion to Hip-hop*.

**Christina Zanfagna** is Assistant Professor of Ethnomusicology at Santa Clara University. Her research focuses on the intersections of music, spiritual practice, and urban geography. In particular, she specializes in Black sacred and popular musics, especially soul music, hip-hop, and gospel rap. Christina's work has appeared in *Black Music Research Journal*, the *Pacific Review of Ethnomusicology*, and *Ballroom, Boogie, Shimmy Sham, Shake: A Social and Popular Dance Reader*. She has worked extensively with community arts organizations such as Afropop Worldwide and Mosaic Multicultural Foundation and currently dances flamenco throughout the Bay Area.

THE OXFORD HANDBOOK OF

# MOBILE MUSIC STUDIES

VOLUME 2

CHAPTER 1

# THE MOBILIZATION OF PERFORMANCE: AN INTRODUCTION TO THE AESTHETICS OF MOBILE MUSIC

SUMANTH GOPINATH AND JASON STANYEK

## THE MOBILIZATION OF PERFORMANCE

*The wealth of societies in which the capitalist mode of production prevails appears as an "immense collection of commodities"; the individual commodity appears as its elementary form. Our investigation therefore begins with the analysis of the commodity.*[1]

—Karl Marx, *Capital*, Volume 1

AND ours begins with a piece of rubber-sheathed plastic shoved deep in an ear canal, an immense speaker system bolted to a flatbed truck, a boombox swinging in a hand, or a transistor radio nestled close to a body under the covers in a darkened, late-night bedroom. Or perhaps it begins with some smartphone playlists accessed via satellite, DJ set lists on a laptop computer, broadcasts funded by and acting as advertisements— each entailing complex social and economic relationships between user, device, and built environments. In these examples, the commodity, however, does not appear as an "elementary form," but rather—to quote a Marx slightly younger than the one just summoned—as "sensuous human activity" (1970:121). To oversimplify: if the first volume of *The Oxford Handbook of Mobile Music Studies*, which focuses primarily on mobile music devices and markets and overarching theories about mobile music, might be said to deal with the commodity's exchange value and its myriad ramifications, our task in Volume 2 is to attend to use value, the particularities of how and why devices are used, and how they shape and participate in sensory experience. Ultimately, the commodity form does not provide us with the analytic we seek, and in this volume we instead start from the premise that the commodity's "elementary form" always emerges *in performance*, in its consumption, in its being used (and used up), in the work that it does and the work done to it and through it.[2] The commodity here is, therefore, not only social and economic, but also bound up with the senses and with the creative sensibility, whose harnessing by human agent, device, corporation, and infrastructure helps constitute an aesthetic of mobility. For our purposes, the sensory domain of greatest interest is that of hearing; that is, the commodity forms that principally concern us are *heard* (even if also seen and felt). At the core of the essays on mobile music that follow is an attentiveness to what the plastic-penetrated ear hears, to the listening public that is generated when a boombox is brought to circulate through the streets, or to what happens as the sound truck vibrates and resonates, buzzing with bootylicious bass lines.

Arranging their daily activities in coordination with a variety of mobile systems, large and small, mobile music users engage in individual performances and dedicated practices that emerge with, through, and because of sound and sound's articulations with other forms of sense data. A crucial link in the chain of relations between sound source and user is bodily comportment: indeed, *comportment*, whose root "port" is one of the most pervasive signifiers of mobility (as in "portability"), entails a repertoire of performance practices, behaviors, and etiquettes that produce and activate sound. This repertoire includes the percussive, rhythmic indexicality—or better, polexicality—of text-messaging and cell phone keypad use; the ubiquitous, close-to-the-ear auralities of headphone listening; newer practices of dragging and tactile manipulation of touch screens (and the audible traces that such practices produce); the transformations of vocality in response to voice recognition systems; forms of managed bodily entrainment, exercise, and less conscious gestural choreographies that are reliant upon, and coax into being, varied sonic worlds. Such recent practices, primarily involving mobile handheld devices, have emerged over the last two decades, but they do, of course, have important ancestors, some of which endure: the various forms of dialing associated with rotary, touch-tone telephones; the manipulation of knobs and antennae in the process of tuning portable radios and televisions; the transformation of automotive experiences through the presence of car radios, stereos, cassette tape players, and compact disc players; the practice of setting up relocatable sound and media systems, such as opening the lids of suitcase gramophones. (Mobility studies is primarily preoccupied with the feet and the seat, but the experience of mobile music often is decidedly hand-oriented.)

The sheer range of what we are calling "mobile performances" is obviously very wide, but are there common features that warrant uniting them together under a single rubric? Certainly, electrical and digital devices are extremely important, with many if not all tending to be relatively small, handheld or otherwise easily ported (the sound truck being a notable exception in device size). We might even go so far as to say that the inclusion of self-evidently mobile-musical devices such as iPhones, iPods, or laptop computers within this rubric is definitional. On account of their connection to the marketing term "mobile music," these small devices might seem to figure a kind of "ideal type" of mobile music performance—an idealization that would need to be deconstructed. Perhaps equally important is the role of headphones in these performances—used conspicuously by commuters, silent ravers, mobile video game players, participants in "walk" pieces—and the kinds of listening that they encourage or permit. But not all mobile performance is *headphoned* performance; there are all kinds of sonic mobilities—ones associated with sound vehicles or devices such as the boom box—whose principal use value resides in a relatively wide *propagation* of sound into the surrounding (but still limited) ambient space. Mobile music performances are often designated as such, not just through the presence of portable or movable devices, but also through the movement of human bodies, most often *horizontally*, through space. And yet, it becomes quite apparent from even a cursory examination of mobile performance practices, that many are not necessarily very mobile in a strict sense. Indeed, quite a few involve the equivalent of fourth-wall-based performances of fixed duration and, often, fixed seating, reproducing the conventional audience-performer relationships found in end-stage theatrical spaces. Even though many of the examples discussed in this volume highlight the use of electrical and digital devices, additional cases could be adduced that are mechanical or even corporeal in nature: an unmediated sound walk, a parade of singers or drummers, an ambulatory use of a music box. We might better understand the relation between these examples through flexible forms of categorization, such as family resemblances or through particular archetypes. Nonetheless, while none of the features just discussed seem to be *necessary* for classifying mobile performance, a few that follow may be *sufficient*.

The presence of mobile devices in performance is one obvious, but perhaps counterintuitive, example of these sufficient features. Indeed, there exists an entire class of mobile performance that does not involve any degree of movement, at least not any more than is typically found in the standard proscenium concert performance. One prime example would be the mobile phone orchestra, itself prefigured by John Cage's pieces with radios (for example, *Imaginary Landscape No. 4* from 1951). Usually these are tied to a single space, with relatively traditional performance boundaries kept intact. Regardless of whether performers move to any great degree, the expectation of or potential for bodily movement is present. The devices themselves serve as a kind of horizon orienting or framing performance. A foundational example illustrating this effect is *Dialtones (A Telesymphony)*, created in 2001 by Golan Levin, Gregory Shakar, and Scott Gibbons, among others. Seated in a square-shaped arrangement of chairs, audience members are entirely stationary. An LED held by an audience member lights up whenever his or her phone rings, and the entire audience is reflected in a massive mirror suspended above. Functioning as a sonic source indicated as a pixel on a grid, each audience member's *immobility* is highlighted *in extremis*.[3] As seems to be the case with many works like *Dialtones*, the mobile device is not only a means of performance; it also serves as a signifier of mobility, a part of the performance's communicative effect.

While mobile performance can be rather constrained spatially, there is another class in which bounded performances are *respatialized*. Such performances occupy unfamiliar spaces, thereby denying generic expectations and reproducing localized dynamics within a greater extensity. One conspicuous post-millennial example is the flash mob, whose networked organization situates performance in *public* or *already otherwise occupied* spatialities, its unapproved nature directly impinging on bystanders. We treat one class of flash mob performance—the silent rave—later in this chapter, but numerous examples abound, such as the seemingly impromptu flash mob dances and performances that take place in the celebrated *non-places* of airport and train terminals (Augé 2000). These heavily rehearsed performances feature unison choreographies, familiar cultural forms (such as musical theater), mobile sound systems, a large number of participants, and an exaggeratedly affected and mannered performing style—all necessary to stand out from the noisy bustle of a congregated public. Crucial to the effect, especially when documented on video, are the facial expressions of bewildered and amused onlookers.[4]

If respatialization is effectively a kind of defamiliarizing of a particular performance practice by placing it within a novel space and social context, new practices of performance also appear when performance behaviors are literally set in motion, or *mobilized*. Certainly, on the one hand, the mobilization of a performance can share features with performative respatialization—an impromptu, unexpected musical performance in a subway station is not, in this sense, very different from a similar performance that might take place within a moving subway train. But on the other hand, the conjunction of musical performance and experience with transit has created new kinds of performative behaviors such as commuting with a Walkman or iPod or driving while listening to the radio. These two examples are not unrelated: they bespeak a series of experiences that connect mobilized spaces—which can be as "small" as one's own headspace—to domestic spaces. The smooth, nearly seamless continuity between the home and the vehicle (or between the home and the mediatized ambulation away from home) is perhaps one of the momentous changes wrought by mobilization.

The consequences of these changes for the relationship between labor and leisure were treated in our introduction to Volume 1 as part of the discussion of the "anytime, anywhere" trope. This trope is more than just good advertising copy (although it was, and remains, that too); the trope forms an essential ideological foundation upon which the burgeoning entertainment market of the early twentieth century was built. The expectations of both capital and consumers began to be spatially and temporally stretched, and from this stretching a pliable aesthetic began to emerge, one that entailed a rather extensive colonization of time and space by a new ordering of the senses. Concomitantly, as the twentieth century progressed, novel forms of social behavior and experience emerged and were predicated on changes in, for example, bodily comportment and entrainment, gestural choreography, mapping between sound and data, and semiotics and symbolism of mobility. By the early twenty-first century, these novel forms of social behavior and experience coalesced into a rather replete set of aesthetic resources that have manifested in a wide variety of situations.

# AESTHETIC MUNDANITIES

Many of the examples of "mobile performance" described above fall into the domain of seemingly everyday, mundane behaviors. But mobile performance isn't only mundane; there is a whole series of designated artistic events that coagulate around mobilizations of the mobile. These encompass not only concerts, theatrical productions, dance recitals, and other familiar genres of artistic performance, but also include soundwalks, sound installations, and musical and sonic smartphone apps, as well as entire genres of musical and sonic production that defamiliarize the content of art while maintaining some elements of its means of presentation (chiptune music and mobile deejaying might be two examples).

Given the rather tenuous dichotomy of the mundane and the artistic (which also intriguingly recalls other dichotomies such as consumer/producer and amateur/professional), can we say that there is such a thing as a "mobile music performance?"[5] If we take an expansive view of the "performative"—and we do—we can answer this question with an unequivocal yes, but with a caveat that the range of performance types is heterogeneous and extensive. And therein lies a second caveat: the ubiquitous presence of mobile devices often leads to quotidian performances going unnoticed, obscured under the gauzy scrim of routine and habit.

Theorizing the everyday and the artistic under the rubric of performance creates a different conceptual partition than is typically found in discourses on mobile media. In mainstream journalism and mass-market publications, for example, the mobile device is featured as central, with mass usages of many stripes (everyday/mundane, humanitarian, profitable, entertainment-oriented) seen as a product of the devices (an obvious technological determinism) and simultaneously as a legitimization of those very devices. But if we instead think together mass usages with more rarified or specialized—and self-consciously aestheticized—ones under the domain of "performance," we effectively shift the weighting toward a heterogeneous range of practices rather than toward their most frequent instances. Correspondingly, we also focus the analytic lens away from the determinist imperatives of technological capital, at least for the moment. (These, like all repressions of course, return.[6])

What does it mean, then, to think about a boom car in tandem with a mobile phone orchestra? Or an ice cream truck with a Game Boy? Or a siren with a laptop DJ performance? We should note that one result of bringing such a range of performances together might be to raise the possibility of canonical performances in the everyday, as well as to problematize self-evident canonicity in sanctioned performance. Art and the everyday intersect and, in the last instance, are inseparable from one another. Two quick examples: The character Radio Raheem's performance in *Do the Right Thing* (1989) is a canonical instance of using a boombox, one that confirmed and reproduced an everyday experience. Or, Ge Wang's promotional video for the Ocarina app,[7] in which Led Zeppelin, Asian-guru/master fantasies, and the history of the long 1960s counterculture flow into the world of computer music, the app economy, and again into the further reaches of popular culture. Comparing these two examples, one might be tempted to align more mundane performances with the unscripted, and self-consciously artistic performances with the scripted. But, in fact, this not necessarily the case: for instance, iPod users unthinkingly draw on the social script of listening to music while commuting, whereas many apparently prescribed artworks incorporate a wide range of freely determined behaviors and contributions by participants.

The spectrum of the scripted and the unscripted may be a red herring when attempting to understand mobile music performances. Instead, by incorporating theorizations of genres and subgenres of human behavior into observations of *the consistency of form*, we might bypass problematic assumptions about the nature of art, about who creates and who does not. Indeed, the performances described in this volume of essays easily traverse such assumed reified divisions. What would an analysis of mobile performance that dispenses with these divisions look like? To offer a provisional answer to this question, we present three case studies that compare performances of a wide range: (1) a DJ duo takes the sneaker as an iconic apparel item—one that is almost the quintessence of mobility—and wields it as a musical instrument (2) a digital media artist creates a walking piece, incorporating a backpack-housed musical interface that senses a city's environmental features (3) flash mobbers assemble at a train station and dance to the music of their own, individualized iPods—participating in what has become known as a "silent rave." Our gambit in these case studies is to foreground three distinct approaches to the analysis of mobile music performance, each of which respectively emphasizes a different analytical register: the *material*, the *phenomenological*, and the *relational*. These registers are not discrete categories: each of the performances we discuss abounds with material resources, affords a variety of phenomenal experiences, and involves relational networks of actors. As such, these registers are layered into and through every mobile music performance, to varying degrees. With this in mind, the three case studies should not only be read sequentially; they should be allowed to resonate with each other and be understood as representing three dimensions of a single analytic and interpretive project.

## "WHEN A SHOE BECOMES A MUSIC INSTRUMENT" (OR, "IT'S A REALLY STRANGE INSTRUMENT . . . OR A SHOE")

*Shoes are the new turntables.*[8]

One would think that mobile music has something to do with mobility. And what more powerful symbol do we have of the "mobile" than the sneaker, the meeting point of uncountable histories: the asymmetric motilities of Euro-American colonialism (think rubber); the kinetics of athletic capitalism; the cosmo-portabilities of early twenty-first century urbanity? And the Nike Corporation, the world's top seller of athletic footwear, with its swoosh emblem bespeaking never-ending movement and flow, might be a candidate—along with Apple and Sony—for *the* lifestyle corporation of the mobile age. This is the company whose advertising campaigns brought us neutered revolutions and doing, not thinking;[9] whose malfeasance shone a light on the all too immobile class politics that inhere in global capitalism's extensive reliance on sweatshop labor; whose engineers developed technologies of support and form-fitting bounce; whose products can be found pretty much wherever people can be found, each moving on Nike's sole.

KEIZOmachine! and Juicy—aka Hifana—have their Nikes, and not just on their feet, but in their hands too.[10] The DJ duo is behind a table whose surface is cluttered with two mixing boards and six pairs of sneakers—fluorescent blue, pink, gray, green—the back sole of each fitted with an 1/8th-inch output that transmits MIDI and OSC data to computers. We see the musicians plugging in the sneakers, cables now connecting the footwear to the mixing boards (see Figure 1.1). Behind them are two large speaker cabinets made out of what appear to be Nike sneaker boxes, each with its own swoosh logo, all in the unmistakable orange of the Nike brand. *Sneaker* cabinets. There's a sound check, each sneaker from the table is flexed and bent, producing the noise of different instruments: a drum machine, a synthesizer (and we see that the cable connected to one sneaker is labeled "bass"). Monitoring the technical setup from the side are young men sitting observantly behind MacBook Pros—the presence of the Apple Corporation being crucial to the enhancement of Nike in its "Nike+" project (Gopinath and Stanyek 2013).[11] Finally, the performance begins. We recognize it immediately: it's Richard Strauss's *Also Sprach Zarathustra*, no longer just an emblem of nineteenth-century grandiosity, or even of the slow-motion, orbital futurity of the mid-twentieth-century counterculture. Here it's bedecked in the sonic rubber of hip-hop breakbeats, variably filtered bass synth lines, neo-African congas, a cowbell timeline/clave pattern, and a hi-hat layer, with each performed and looped live using a foot-controlled Boss RC-50 Loop Station. The feet that stomp on the pedals of the Boss are also wired in, creating multiple signal paths. But both musicians have other sets of feet, and these they manipulate with their hands. The six pairs of sneakers on the table are variably picked up, and twisted, flexed, bent: ghost feet that exist in the viewer's imagination, manipulated deftly by two hip-hop puppeteers. A few moves are particularly arresting, both visually and temporally. The sneakers go up *en pointe* and do pirouettes, mimicking ballet positions and thereby simultaneously evoking a kind of classicism, which is also signaled early on by the Strauss and KEIZOmachine! and Juicy's bodily reactions to the famous rush of orchestral sound answering *Also Sprach Zarathustra*'s iconic opening trumpet fanfare.[12]

The video of Hifana's performance serves as an advertisement for Nike, and in it the two DJs clearly insert themselves into a broader discourse that Nike has consistently capitalized on, one that has drawn attention to the balletic dimensions of professional athleticism.[13] In fact, Nike advertisements have often acted as staging grounds for meetings between representatives of "classical" and "popular" culture (as in the 1990 ad with

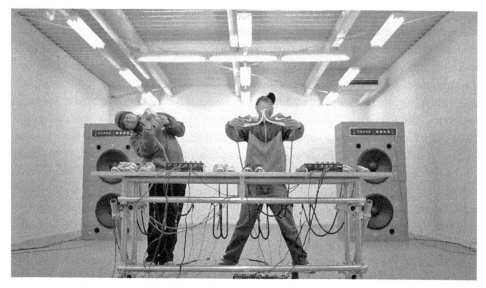

FIGURE 1.1 Hifana performs mobility. Screenshot by the authors.

basketball player David Robinson and Czech pianist Rudolf Firkušný, or a Russian Nike ad from 2007 featuring a ballerina and a hip-hop dancer).[14] Many of these advertisements also feature vast, neutral, and even anonymous spaces—abstracted basketball courts, cavernous gyms, dark warehouses, lofts—and in this respect the Hifana ad is no different. But the space here is particularly antiseptic and clinical, akin to a brand-new art studio or, more likely, some kind of light industrial environment used for manufacturing precision equipment. In this sense, the space is fitting, as it is the site of sophisticated musical experimentation, undertaken by Hifana's collaborators Seiichi Saito and Daito Manabe (of the digital design/architecture firm Rhizomatiks) and Tomoaki Yanagisawa (of the design research lab 4nchor5 la6). For the Nike ad, Saito served as the software engineer and Yanagisawa was responsible for the hardware design. Each sneaker was fitted with three flex sensors and an accelerometer, which were designed to use the open-source Arduino electronic prototyping platform to transform the twisting and flexing of the sneakers into MIDI and OSC data that could then be transmitted to a MacBook Pro. Once the data entered the computer, it could be sonified using Max/MSP and Ableton Live. At that point the audio signal could be sent back to the DJs (or, as Peter Kirn called them, the "Shoe-Js"[15]), who could then use the crossfaders on their mixing boards and their Boss loop machine to do one last set of manipulations of the sounds before outputting them to the speakers. A learning process was required for Hifana to become comfortable manipulating the shoes as instruments, which altered sound according to position in space, as well as to degrees of lateral bending and rotor twisting. As Daito Manabe commented on the performers' use of the shoes, "As expected, their bend rate while performing is different from mine. At times the difference was, like, *that much*?!"[16]

A key part of this story is that the musical experimentation undertaken by Rhizomatiks and Hifana on the "Nike Music Shoe" was commissioned by the Tokyo branch of the global advertising firm Wieden+Kennedy, the very agency that has been instrumental in creating Nike's (in)famous ads. (The Tokyo branch's purported goal is "…to create strong, provocative relationships between good companies and their customers."[17]) But, there's one more twist, or flex, here. Wieden+Kennedy has their own music label, W+K Tokyo Lab, and Hifana is one of their recording artists. The history of advertising and corporate-sponsored cultural production has for decades revealed a close relationship between experimental artists and large, often multinational firms—the days of oppositional, avant-gardist relationships between cutting-edge culture and capital being long gone, if they ever existed.[18] Hifana and Wieden+Kennedy represent an advance in the realm of incorporated possibility, not only in demonstrating such close proximity between advertiser and constituent cultural producer, but also to the point of developing an entire *incorporated aesthetic*, one here imagined as profoundly multimediatic but with sound artists playing a—arguably *the*—central role.[19]

The advertising relationship between Hifana and Wieden+Kennedy might partially account for the *materialistic* aesthetic of the performance under consideration, but what are the *material* aesthetics of a performance that has a common, not to say iconic, material object at its very core? A basic accounting of material objects would traverse one step toward such an understanding. This accounting might include *protocols* (MIDI [Musical Instrument Digital Interface], OSC [Open Sound Control]), *software platforms* (Ableton Live, Max/MSP), myriad *devices* in various states of alteration and assembly (sneakers, Boss RC-50 Loop Machine, Apple PowerBook, cross-fading DJ mixers, amplifier, large mixing board, PA system, sneaker cabinets), and *controllers* (flex sensors, accelerometers, touchpads/mouse interfaces). There are, of course, material objects that are more easily taken for granted, such as what we might call *tethers*, or linking elements within the chains of computation and sound production (cables, RFID chips, wireless links, solid-state circuit boards, etched wires on integrated circuits), not to mention the *built environment* making the entire performance possible (the warehouse-like building's drywall, concrete, beams, corrugated metal ceiling, piping, fluorescent lighting, electrical wiring, plumbing, telephone-internet infrastructure, as well as the A/C power grid, roads, ambient sound, and communications networks). One might even theorize a flattened *material substrate* of the performance, encompassing all of the performance's materials already mentioned (rubber, copper, plastic molding, silicon; the cotton, nylon, rubber, synthetic fibers, etc. of the apparel worn by the performers; electricity; the carbon-basis of organic life). Finally, there are the (perhaps) not-so-evident material domains (or *reserves*) of the *sonic* and the *gestural*: the sound files used to create the performance, including recorded samples of Strauss, percussion, Chinza Dopeness's voice, as well as synthesized sound; or the movement forms, vocabularies, and clichés drawn from popular imagery of classical ballet (pirouettes, going on point, arm positions/carriage [*Port de bras*]) and hip-hop dance/movement, among others.

Of course, at the center of this vast material network is the sneaker, which acts as a kind of nodal point for the performance in numerous ways. For example, the fact that it is connected via 1/8-inch jack and cable not only turns the sneaker into an instrument but also gives it instrument-like features, invoking a semiotics of *plugging in* that is crucial to the experience of setting up music gear. Additionally, this is no ordinary sneaker but a *Nike* sneaker and therefore a prized fetish object within many consumer markets—including those associated with hip-hop; it thereby gives the performance a symbolism of *materialism*, acting in tandem with the materiality of its numerous components. Furthermore, the sneaker motivates and organizes performance tropes, as well as the occasion of the performance more broadly. Hand-manipulated dance moves demonstrated through the sneakers and the balletic dance behavior of the two performers must be read through a kind of *shoe- and foot-centric* lens, wherein all such dance practices are understood through the fact of their podiality and the fact that many dance forms are associated with (if not having specifically developed) distinct types of shoes, including the sneaker in breakdance.

One modality of mobile performance places the device front and center and, in so doing, highlights its capacity to signify mobility, rather than merely demonstrate it. (The performance does seem to involve relatively relocatable and compact equipment, suggesting a mobility of repositioning.) Such a performance could have employed far more typical exemplars of sonic mobility, such as an iPhone, iPod, portable radio/boombox, etc., but the fact that a sneaker is used arguably drives the point home more directly: having a narrow range of prescribed uses, sneakers are indelibly linked to the movement of feet, to walking, or to running. The fact that the sneakers are allowed to retain their *sneakerness* is key here: although transposed into an apparently alien context, the sneaker is never disguised (at least visually) as anything other than what it is, and its movements, even when motivated by hand, remain familiar and recognizable to wearers (or viewers) of sneakers.

The matter-of-factness of Hifana's use of the sneaker extends to the whole of the performance, which relies upon an elegant simplicity, rather than an extremely complicated technical apparatus. For example, the programmers suggest that their Max patches (software programs made on Max/MSP) are extremely basic; the other pieces of equipment—computers, mixing boards, pedal controllers—likewise were not altered at all, with two major exceptions: the sneaker cabinets and the shoe-controllers. The latter involved a seemingly lengthy process of embedding flex controllers inside them, making the shoes' bends and twists legible as data for Max (transmitted via OSC). Thus, one way to evaluate the performance may be through what might be termed a dialectic of implementation and modification—the latter seemingly characteristic of much experimental cultural production—its "off-the-shelf" (not to say, consumerist) character would become readily apparent. On the other hand, experimental culture also involves forms of recontextualization and combination, which this performance exhibits in numerous ways. Hence, to reduce the performance to one or the other side of an implementation/modification binary would not do it justice.[20]

# PLAYING THE CITY

*Encounters, events, architecture, (mis)behaviours—all become means of interacting with or "playing the city."*[21]

For some modalities of mobile music performance, mobility as explicit human movement is central. The surest confirmation of this form of mobility is the subjective perception of movement through space: the ambulatory motion of the self-propelled, featherless biped. Here, the sneaker is not the central component, but the foot, which is the irreducible ground for such movement. If mobile music performance has a core repertoire, the "walking" piece would be one essential genre—one that ironically marries the fundamental motility of the human species with the latest trends in mobile, digital technologies. The theoretical underpinnings of that repertoire's aesthetic discourse is variegated but largely stems from the literatures on "everyday life" emerging during and in the wake of the long 1960s and its antecedents: Benjamin's *flâneur* is a crucial reference, de Certeau's "walking rhetoric" is another, and the Situationist *dérive* yet one more. Other theoretical, artistic, and ethnographic treatments of walking have been influential as well, perhaps the most notable being Bruce Chatwin's *The Songlines* (1987), a hybrid book that uses the indigenous Australian practice of the walkabout—a musicalized walking map—as one of its primary source materials.[22] While audio technology is not a prerequisite for the "walking piece," a number of composers and performance artists have employed various kinds of playback devices in the service of creating surrogate sonic worlds for walkers as they move through composer-determined environments.

By the turn of the millennium, portable devices could do much more than either record or emit prerecorded sounds—through new capabilities for digitized data conversion, devices could handle and produce complex inputs and outputs within a localized algorithmic computation system. One crucial precedent for this kind of practice is "wearable computing," catalyzed in varying degrees and at various technological levels through the widespread availability of microelectronics. A significant advocate for this practice was Steve Mann, whose work sutured apparel and computer, capitalizing on the development of backpack-mounted computers in the 1980s (Rheingold 2002:106–12; Mann and Niedzviecki 2001). The cyborgian implications of that work are self-evident and can be seen as part of a broader cultural formation that included key representations of the cyborg, such as in cyberpunk fictions like the iconic Ridley Scott film *Blade Runner* (1982) or William Gibson's novel *Neuromancer* (1984).

The cyborg imaginary might additionally be seen as an aesthetic tied to emergent practices of "interactivity," specifically, digital multimedia art forms in which—unlike earlier forms of computer-generated art, video, or music—both output and input data were collected, used, and processed during the performance itself, for the purpose of transforming the artwork itself in self-evident, tangible ways. Interactive art was also intertwined with pre-existing and contemporaneous efforts to produce new kinds of connections between artistic participants separated geographically, between different media ("multimedia art"), and between artists and audiences ("participatory art"). Interactive art's long history, also extending back at least to the 1970s, became married productively to the massification of digital technologies quite early on, but "[d]igital art made its official entry into the art world only in the late 1990s," and gained aesthetic legitimacy only relatively recently (Paul 2003:23). Nonetheless, the presence of self-proclaimed interactive art was widespread by the early 2000s, and by that time it had certainly made its way into experimental musical composition in Europe and North America. One means of varying the content of the work in real time is to transform non-sonic data into audio, in a process termed "sonification." Alvin Lucier's *Music for Solo Performer* (1965), which famously transformed the composer's own brainwaves into sound, might serve as a pre-digital effort at what would become much more common in the digital era (Charles Dodge's *Earth's Magnetic Field* from 1970 is a conspicuous early example).

The reference points mentioned above provide a context for what should be understood as one of the founding works of an experimental type of "mobile music."[23] In Göteborg, Sweden between 2002 and 2004, a multi-disciplinary team of researchers led by Lalya Gaye and Ramia Mazé at the Future Applications Lab (Viktoria Institute) and the PLAY Studio at the Interactive Institute developed an interface they called "Sonic City."[24] In the work, a headphoned user wears a host of sensors—a light-to-frequency converter, a microphone, a metal detector, an accelerometer, a temperature sensor, and a pollution sensor—that "map" a broad range of parameters: temperature, ambient sound, pollution level, lighting conditions, presence of metal, bodily choreographies (stopping, bending, running, jumping). The sensors are wired to a backpack loaded with a sound-processing laptop computer, helping to "create" *Sonic City* when the backpack, carried through the streets of Göteborg, produces subtle variations of looped beeps and bleeps (see Figure 1.2).

The creators of the project also documented their work in a video that serves as a useful entry point in understanding the technical underpinnings of *Sonic City* (although it is obviously by no means a comprehensive representation). The video opens with an excerpt from "Tamghra Nouchen" (Wolf Marriage), a drum and bass track with a world-music tinge recorded in 2002 by Naab (Nabil Hassoute), a French musician of Berber Moroccan descent.[25] Soon after the video begins, the song's propulsive groove—it has a bpm (beats per minute) of around 172—gives way to the more austere sonic world produced by the *Sonic City* interface. Laced with sounds iconic of academic computer music—pulses of synthesized tones, sharp interjections of white noise, and so forth—the pace and layering of bleeps and beeps varies according to time of day, ambient noise (especially passing automobiles), proximity to metal objects like gates, and data from other sensor inputs. In their trebly bleepiness, these sounds are also somewhat reminiscent of early 8-bit video-game music. But while the sounds of *Sonic City*—and, hence, the video's diegetic soundtrack—changes in accordance with each

FIGURE 1.2 Cyborgized *Sonic City* participant, walking through Göteborg. Photograph by Lalya Gaye. Used with permission of Lalya Gaye.

individual user's activities shown in the videorecorded sequences, "Tamghra Nouchen" recurs unchanged and serves as a kind of leitmotif during the video, helping to structure its form by appearing during intervening still-shot segments.

The contrast between the two sound worlds featured in the film is striking and implicitly indicative of *Sonic City*'s aesthetic aims. It's clear that "Tamghra Nouchen" is layered *onto* the built environment of the city, perhaps providing what Michael Bull calls a "filmic experience" (2000:86) and that aural figurations of *Sonic City* are perceived as emerging *out of* the interactions between body, interface, and city. The differing aesthetics between the non-diegetic film soundtrack and the sounds generated by *Sonic City* itself— between a resolutely urban and world-music inflected electronica track and a more variable computer-music/game-music sound world—reinforces the gap between pre-composed music and user-controlled, interactive music. If filmic experience is produced when ambulatory headphone listeners traverse space and create tightly looped, often synchronized correlations between sight and sound, these frequently depend on an intimate— indeed, *predictive*—knowledge of the track being listened to. In contrast, users have some control over the music in *Sonic City* but, as in a video game, this control is not absolute. Thus, when the creators of *Sonic City* speak of "playing the city," we're faced with a central conceit of this particular brand of mobile music performance, one that involves, simultaneously, the city functioning as locus of three forms of play: the playing of a newly designed musical instrument called "the city"; the playing of a video game whose name is "the city"; and playing with a competitor known as "the city."

These themes are borne out in the comments by D. R. and M. K., two *Sonic City* participants who were recorded as they traversed Göteborg:

> D. R. [*with traffic sounds in background*]: Here we're in the middle of the tune with a part with drums and a bass there...almost. Then you come back to the same part again, almost. Time to hit the dance floor here! [*walks*] There was a sound here that I...[*moves close to the brick face, and then blind-covered windows of an apartment building*] There is really a massive amount of sound here. This is fun! I try to affect it though, like here when I'm testing...I'm doing all I can to control the music. It's going quite well I think.
>
> M. K.: Now one notices that the music gets shakier when you get into the light and the cars also have a very [*sic*] impact. So it's more fun to walk here where things are happening with the music.

The foregoing quotes raise a broader problem central to *Sonic City*—that of *place*— which may initially seem antithetical to a work of *mobile* music. In the commentaries, D. R. and M. K. evoke place through manifold uses of the word "here." Specifically, whereas M. K. mentions that it's fun to "walk here" (here being the city, or the part of it encountered on her route), D. R. mentions specific locations in the musical flow as it transmogrifies before his ears, at one point invoking the "dance floor here," simultaneously speaking of the music and the potential transformation of the out-of-doors cityscape into an indoor club. The variability of the word "here" points to two different issues relevant for the study of *Sonic City* and, perhaps, mobile musical performance in general. On the one hand, mobile music that involves transit of some kind might be understood as musical performance occurring in successions of diverse emplacements, continuously transitioning *between* "places." The ecological concept of the "ecotone," which refers to boundaries of environment (defined by changes in species habitat) and which are often signaled by sonic shifts and overlaps, might be adapted to refer to (subtle) architectural and structural shifts in cities themselves, the crossings between places and the highlighting of transitions.[26] Indeed, *Sonic City*'s sensor system encourages attention to this sort of boundary point, as users often attempted to provoke changes in order to alleviate the boredom induced by unaltered musical looping—such as approaching and bending one's head closer to a metal gate, attracting both the proximity sensor and metal detector.[27]

On the other hand, most (if not all) such transit-oriented mobile musical performances seem to take place within what one might think of as a single "place," whether understood as a larger geographical or architectural entity (a city, a park, a street, a building, a room) or as the positional equivalent of a phenomenological "now." The notion of "moorings" (Urry 2007:54; Adey 2010:21–22)—spatially fixed supports or entities— that help to produce mobility (one might think of highways or railways for automobiles and trains, respectively) implies a more generally applicable dialectic in which mobility requires movement *through* a relatively static space (or between relatively static spaces).

Such static entities help determine both motion and position and, taken together, mobile and static elements comprise entire "mobility systems" (Urry 2007:12–16). Although one could identify practical limitations as the justification for "single-space" mobile performance—relatively localized performances are easier to stage—mobility in musical performance is often invoked to encourage exploration *of* a bounded space. Indeed, the very title *Sonic City* emphasizes the fact of geographical singularity: it is emphatically *not* called *Sonic Cities*.

At one level, the relationship between user and place invoked in *Sonic City* highlights the contrast between the user-as-mobile agent and the city-as-(mostly) static space or environment. In fact, one of the recurring terms in the literature on the piece is "duet" (as in the promotional video's description of the work as a "duet with the city").[28] This description, however, elides the fact that a third agent is present: the wearable computing apparatus donned by the user. That agent is, in fact, even more constant than the city itself, not primarily because of the city's own variable objects like traffic, pedestrians, etc., but mainly because users take different routes through it. Indeed, the "hereness" of the technical apparatus may be manifested not only in its physicality (its weight, tactile and haptic effects, etc., making it always "here" with the user) but also in the fact that it produces a (stereo) sonic space overlaid on top of the shifting auditory scene of the urban environment. This apparatus is undoubtedly a central partner in *Sonic City*, and is *arguably more important than the city itself.* As a thought experiment, we could imagine taking the same equipment and applying it to different cities, conurbations, or even less developed environments, and producing similar effects, whereas the same would not be true if one took an equally variable approach to the work's gear.[29] Thus, although the work would have to be understood as a "trio" in *Sonic City*, the primary players are the user and the interface, with the city acting as raw material for both.

If the performing trio in *Sonic City* is fundamentally constituted through human-nonhuman (and nonhuman-nonhuman) interactions—between user and city, user and backpack, and backpack and city—one way of analyzing the piece would be to prioritize the ways in which these interactions transform *both* the human sensorium *and* the transductive and co-constitutive capacities of machines during the course of a performance. Such a performance might be best understood through a kind of *phenomenological* aesthetics, subject to the caveat that phenomenology, as we understand it, does not solipsistically prioritize the human but rather is sensitive to interanimations of machine, human, and environment—one that encompasses a "phenomenology of the cyborg," in George Lewis's terms (Lewis 2009:462).[30] An aesthetics of this sort is one that might consider emplacement of the user-backpack dyad within the city, triadically understanding distances between humans and devices and structures in terms of *proxemics*.[31] Shifts in *body position* and *location*, particularly in relation to established and emergent *moorings*, would need to be considered, even across micro-ecological shifts in urban space or *ecotones*. Devices and humans are also understood proxemically, with problems of *portage, support,* and *load-bearance* inflecting performance. Performances themselves could be interpreted not only through mappings of urban space but a closer-grained reading of *movement patterns*—involving continuous movement, steady-state or constant movement, arrested movement, pausing, linearity and nonlinearity, circumambulation, and more. These movements are of course one result of a complex algorithmic system of processing and transduction, wherein human and device (backpack) together transform *inputs* and produce *outputs*, largely through a process of *sonification*. The multiple loops that feed forward and back help to shape a user's sense awareness and might be in part captured by degrees of *absorption* and qualities of *immersion*, as experienced within an *auditory headspace*. Mappings between these different dimensions—say, quadrangulating location, body position, headspace, and movement pattern—might then produce a sense of the flow of a single performance of *Sonic City*. Similar mappings of inputs and outputs onto city locations would likewise give a different sense of the piece's conditions of possibility.

The phenomenology of experiencing *Sonic City* might lead one to hastily slot the work into the familiar aesthetic category of *interactivity*, yet interpreting the work through an aesthetics of sonification might be more apropos. For if interactivity calls attention to the various forms of real-time relationships between the different entities making up the piece (urban environment, computer software and hardware, the "user"), *sonification* points up the particular translations that occur between sonic and non-sonic realms, with various forms of statistical data being made audible or transformed into sound as communicative information. While we might tend to associate the term sonification with the transformation of data-rich information into equally data-rich sound, it, in fact, exists on a continuum from the simplest mappings of data into sound, on one end, to highly complex sound-production translations, on the other.[32] In particular, *Sonic City* makes use of the irreducible gap between data input (sensor inputs) and data output (sonic emanations converted from the sensed data). The utopian zone of *Sonic City* could be characterized as a "flow experience" produced by the interaction of music and sonified biofeedback data; without this zone, this gap, performing *Sonic City* would be a mere process of data conversion.[33]

If data is being sonified in *Sonic City*, the questions still remain as to how that sonification takes place and what aesthetic effects result from that process. The coding system in the piece seems to privilege certain physical specifics and downplay others, including various cultural signifiers not detectable in the interface. One cannot, for example, produce prominent effects through raced aspects of bodies or historically contingent qualities of building facades. The attention toward certain physical qualities, proximities, and conditions have something to do with how the city is conceptualized: it is a *purified* city, stripped clean of its historically weighted, sedimented features. Instead of producing a semiotically replete city, and fostering a kind of historical consciousness during performance, we could say that the work encodes a kind of phenomenological ideology of urban experience, one that employs purification devices to sequester the user from the environment (almost as if the environment were something *separate* from the user, not something the user is a part of).

If the preceding discussion reads like a critique of *Sonic City*, this would only be the case if the experience of the city that it helps create were fundamentally distinct from all other urban experience. Of course, it is not, and in fact it shares a close kinship with a rather mundane form of "processing" the urban: "hearing" it through headphones via a portable music player or listening device. For is it not the case that headphoned music listeners also experience (and even "play") the city, undertake mood regulation, and reconstruct it quasi-cinematically, occupying the rather permeable bubbles that seem intended, in part, to inoculate them from potentially damaging or harmful urban soundscapes, indeed from urban spaces more generally? The feedback and feedforward loops between listeners, headphoned music, and urban spaces do not sequester the first two in a "warm" cocoon from the "chill" of the third; rather, the phenomenology of this experience, like that of *Sonic City*, is co-constitutive.[34] In both cases, sense and sensibility are inseparable, constructing and transforming subjectivity so that it is not the sole province of the human. As the blurb accompanying the *Sonic City* video on YouTube makes clear, the backpack system "creates electronic music based on *sensing* bodily and environmental factors" (emphasis ours). Clearly, the sensors of the *Sonic City* system *sense* both the bodies and environments networked with it. What the sensors lack is a sensibility that cognizes the urban environment as an alien entity to be managed and controlled. The aesthetic—the relationality of which multiplies exponentially with the linear increase of bodies and machines—is what makes that management possible.

## "Have Fun and No Riots"

*This is going to be huge.*[35]

Mobility, of course, is something experienced not only by individuals or through its signifying technologies, but also in collectivities, even those of substantial magnitude. Indeed, mobility studies often has as its locus of attention large-scale mobility systems, principally those facilitating the transit of sizeable numbers of people. In collective mobile performances, groups of mobilized individuals congregate in pre-arranged spaces—mobile *nodes*—with mobile devices providing information on place and time, and on the general anatomy of an event. The dynamics of mobility become much more complex, ranging from mobile equivalents of the two- and three-body problems to those understood as statistical aggregations. Such performances also contain the possibility of multiple angles of documentation—each participant carrying a multifunctional device that can both facilitate participation in an event and capture it in a multimedia format. The potential for a proliferation of traces of an event perhaps grows proportionally with the number of individual agents creating them. Moreover, the networking of these devices, a given in the case of mobile phones, wireless internet devices, and smartphones, means that they can be transmitted to other individuals in real-time or uploaded almost immediately to general-access sites like YouTube for wider sharing. Like begets like: viral generation and dispersion of information creates an often fleeting archive that needs to be sifted through, in order to stitch together some tangible sense of the past.

The political force of such viral transmissions is already well known. One could construct a canon of political rallies and gatherings made possible by mobile communications and social networking sites: consider the early People Power II text-message rallies in Manila (2001) or the protests in the wake of the 3/11 Madrid train bombings; the 2006 immigrants' rights protests in the US likewise were made possible in part by SMS and MySpace messages; the Arab Spring's efflorescence and intensification in Sidi Bouzid and Cairo were also initiated, at least in part, through Facebook.[36] Although such events are never the product of networking technologies alone—despite the "telecommunicative fantasies" that mystify them (Rafael 2003:399)—the political rally has quite clearly gained new contours in the age of mobile communication and computing. In part, it has been influenced by the emergence of networked congregations more generally ("smart mobs") and even especially absurdist, apolitical ones known as flash mobs.[37] Of course, the longer history of collective experiences of amplified sound and music—including political gatherings, concerts, and free-form dance events of the rock era and after—inform these new developments as well, although their apparently unplanned or spontaneous nature is certainly aided by the speed of access to and propagation of invitations ("invites").

One such invitation to a dance was sent out in January of 2009 by the "Liverpool Street Station Silent Dance" Facebook group administered by Crazzy Eve, a twenty-two-year-old Londoner. The group, which boasted over 14,000 members, updated its website before the event with the invitation shown in Figure 1.3. In response, thousands of people made their way into the station on Friday evening, February 6, 2009. In Crazzy Eve's words, "At a quarter to seven people just flocked into the station like someone opened a plughole and the water went out." He continued, "They just kept coming in like sheep. As it grew and grew, I just thought, 'This is going to be huge'" (CNN 2009). The City of London Police estimated the size of the crowd to be over 12,000 people. Just before 7:00 p.m., a collectively chanted 10-second countdown, facilitated by the clock on the station's departures board, formally inaugurated the event. At the turn of the hour attendees began to dance for about 25 minutes to their own headphoned music selections, to sing out loud and dance without headphones, and to stand by, watching and documenting the event as it unfolded. Among the highlights included crowdsurfing, mass dancing on the station's main floor, upper floors, and ersatz platforms, and, in one case, a man stripping naked to great applause.

After the event, Crazzy Eve explained to CNN how he thought up the idea: "I was watching TV and the T-Mobile advertisement came up and I thought, hm, let's get my friends down to Liverpool Street and do a little dance." The ad to which he refers had been filmed a few weeks before (January 15) in the same train station, featuring about 400 dancers performing a choreographed routine to a medley of various popular songs and pieces, encompassing a variety of styles.[38] The commercial—part of T-Mobile's "Life's for Sharing" campaign—begins with a wide-angle shot of the station's rather large waiting area, the general din of the commuters providing the only soundtrack. We hear an innocuous, generic voice on the station's loudspeaker system making an announcement—"the next train to depart from platform 17"—that is quickly cut off by Lulu's cover

FIGURE 1.3 Screen shot of the Facebook invitation to the Liverpool Street Station Silent Dance.

(with backing group the Luvvers) of the Isley Brothers' 1959 epochal anthem "Shout," Lulu's voice mimicking Ronald Isley's original melismatic opening. At first, only a few dancers begin their movements, slight perturbations in the general fabric of commuter choreographies that define the station's social imaginary. By the time the third song of the medley—the Pussycat Dolls' "Don't Cha"—is heard, it's quite clear that these are professional dancers, their tight synchronized movements betraying a significant amount of rehearsal. The commercial's mode of performance is accretive, with ever more dancers joining together in synchronous movements, an invocation of a flash mob spontaneously agglutinating. As Johann Strauss's "Blue Danube Waltz" ends—the dancers twirling to the climactic cadence, pausing to let Kool and the Gang's "Get Down on It" begin (to rapturous applause)—the dancers have quite clearly taken over the entirety of the space, filling not only the center of the station's main floor area but also the staircases around the outer edges of the inside of the terminal. When Millie's "My Boy Lollipop" begins, we are given a static shot of a rather bemused, unmoving young commuter who, quite clearly taken up in the wave of feel-good T-Mobilism, begins to throw his hands in the air, like he just doesn't care. We see quite clearly that part of the ad-hoc, documentary flavor of the spot is generated from shots of onlookers recording the event with their mobile phones (the style of the ad seems to suggest that we might even be watching one of these impromptu captures of quotidian life). But long before the Contours' "Do You Love Me" comes on to close the medley and hundreds of people clap together in unison, there's no mistaking that this is a polished, highly *scripted*—lavish, prepaid, and fully licensed—event.

On his "History Is Made at Night" blog, Neil Transpontine offered a nuanced historical reading of the original T-Mobile ad, alleging that "a choreographed telephone advert is a fake copy of something that has already been diluted" (2009a). Indeed, the flash-mob simulacrum on display here appropriated a longer history of impromptu performances and gatherings at the Liverpool Street Station itself: "mobile clubbing" events involving hundreds of people had hit the station in 2006 and 2008 and the station itself has been featured in films and music videos of some note. And there is even a round that ingeniously incorporates its name into a jaggedly hocketed texture ("The Liverpool Street Song"). Choosing its location wisely, T-Mobile's intervention was debated and praised in many circles; one UK advertising industry figure felt that "it was a blatant You Tube 'Improv Everywhere' rip-off with less charm than the original. It felt forced and a little fake. Everyone who I spoke to who worked in Advertising or Digital seemed to feel the same way." But, she also noted that the advertisement was quite successful with ordinary viewers:

> I stopped asking people's opinion who worked in the industry and started to listening to people outside of the industry. Every time that we went to the cinema and the T-Mobile ad came on the entire audience always seemed to be captivated, they laughed, in fact often there were little spatterings of applause. My mum loved it. My brother's girlfriend emailed it to me. My husband would stop what he was doing to watch when it came on TV. (Torode 2009)

One potential (and, perhaps, slightly dismal) reading of Crazzy Eve's gambit, then, is that it simply prompted a massive amount of people to provide unpaid labor for T-Mobile's marketing department. Facebook commenter Stuart Downs says as much (you can hear the sarcasm dripping from the screen): "YEAH LETS PLAY INTO THE HANDS OF A T MOBILE PR STUNT! YEAH LETS DO IT! WOOOOOOOO! OH YEAH I LOVE T MOBILES MARKETING DEPARTMENT! ITS SO COOL!!!!" (February 6, 2009 at 12:18 a.m.). Transpontine, in contrast, viewed the Silent Dance as a partial reclamation of the station after T-Mobile's advertising incursion, approvingly noting that "the advert may have had the effect of amplifying the real silent rave phenomenon" and proclaiming, "What we really need is somebody to turn up with a sound system on a truck to really take this to another level" (2009b).

But one of the defining differences between T-Mobile's ad and the Crazzy Eve event is precisely that the latter did not rely on a large, publicly audible sound system (or the kinds of public synchronizations that music played over such a sound system can engender). In this way, the Silent Dance—while clearly influenced by T-Mobile's commercial—departs radically from it. In place of meticulously rehearsed, unison movements and collective listening to what really amounts to a mix that could be heard at any wedding in the United States or United Kingdom, the Silent Dance harnessed—perhaps aestheticized is a better word—the quotidian practice of individualized mobile listening. Conversely, the event mundanized the usually heightened experience of free-form dancing by placing it in a public space (as can happen with parades and outdoor music festivals). On any given evening in Liverpool Station, thousands of commuters make their ways home with earbuds in their ears, their gaits entrained (in some way or another) to the sounds coming out of their portable music players.

Of course, the aestheticization on offer here was by no means uniform. Indeed, one of the strikingly *undisciplined* aspects of Crazzy Eve's event and silent raves more generally is that they are not necessarily all that silent. Indeed, the Liverpool Street Station crowd ranged from chattily buzzy to downright noisy, particularly when cheers were elicited by an occurrence visible to a large swath of the crowd. In general, the event was quite loud, especially when experienced from the ground floor—so much so that recordings of the event are typically distorted, with cell phone microphones overdriven by the high-amplitude signals. Additionally, the recordings are cluttered with transients caused by proximate motion (breathing, rubbing against clothing, quick movements). Leakage from headphones filled out the ambience as well, and frequent loud whistles and moments of individual singing punctuated the station's soundscape from time to time.[39] The reverberant acoustic of the cathedral-like station itself further raised the ambient decibel level and blended the whole into a swirling mix of incidental, accidental, and intentional sound, particularly for those on the upper level of the station. Collectively synchronized sounds were heard on occasion: the stripping dancer's efforts elicited a mass chant of "Off! Off! Off!" from a large number of dancers, and toward the end of the event, as the police began to break up the crowd, groups of people began to sing "We Shall Not Be Moved" in response.

In contrast to the aggregate sonic effect of the event, each individual's sonic experience remains by and large inaccessible to those seeking to study it. The Facebook comments say relatively little about the listening choices (or predilections) of the participants. What is said does, however, reveal something about how some participants were conceptualizing the sonic curation of the event (which, at its heart, was supposed to be about *individual control over the sonic headspace*). For example, entire musical genres are promoted by individual enthusiasts. Alessio Babolin's RSVP to the event states, "im so there skanking to some minimal tech" (February 5, 2009, 12:26 p.m.). Poppy Rose Császi likewise says, "HAPPPY HARDCOREE!! hahaha cant waitt" (February 3, 2009, 12:54 p.m.), and Teddy Hall notes, "I GOT MY FUNKY HOUSE TUNES PEOPLE WATCH OUT FOR THE DANCE MASTER DOING HIS TING LOL" (February 5, 2009 at 3:03 p.m.). In these cases, prospective participants mention musical subgenres of electronic dance music (minimal techno, happy hardcore, house), in keeping with expectations that the silent rave would approximate the contours of club/rave dance event. Moreover, some respondents mention individual songs that they intended to dance to during the proceedings. For example, two minutes after Leon Aj Arnelle Jenkins leaves this comment (at 12:24 a.m. on 6 February, the day of the event) "Head Shoulderz Knees n toez!!!!!!!! man dem lemmie see u keep it sho....!!! tuuuuuune!" (quoting the lyrics to K.I.G.'s 2008 track "Head, Shoulders, Kneez & Toez"), Richard The-Tank Campbell responds: "u done know that tune it gonna be on my play list" (Facebook, February 6, 2009 at 12:26 a.m.). And John Andrew Trimble uses Chris Brown's "Take You Down" as an enticement for potential participants to create a synchronized subgroup of dancers: "EVERYONE ADD MY GROUP 100 PEOPLE TO DO CHRIS BROWNS TAKE YOU DOWN TOMORROW ALL YOU NEED IPOD HIS SONG GET ON YOU HANDS AND KNEES AND TAKEEEE YOUR SELFF DOWN BABYY (February 5, 2009 at 10:58 p.m.).

These comments reveal an aesthetic—perhaps drawn from the standard practices of dance clubs—that privileges synchronized, collective movement or "keeping together in time," to use William McNeill's poignant phrase (1995). But, judging from the video documentation of the event, it seems unlikely that such desires came to fruition. Like the aspirational character of the flash mob more generally—which seeks, in the first instance, to take place, and then to be meaningful and have a lasting effect, despite its limited duration—members of the crowd of 12,000 sought to overcome the event's anarchical character and, with a few exceptions, failed. Perhaps inspired by the initiating T-Mobile event or the New York-based Improv Everywhere group's MP3 events (wherein thousands of people listen/dance to the same MP3 in public), such aspirations were not limited to producing what Benedict Anderson calls "unisonance"; also evident was the unrealized desire, of at least one participant, for a kind of *unisilence*. Ann Hoang articulated her dissatisfaction with the event when she mentioned,

> I imagined everything to be quiet and the only sound would be the "tch tch tch" from our mp3s and our feet though. :( (February 6, 2009, at 10:00 p.m.)
> What's the point of a SILENT dance with all the screaming and shouting. Now more and more are getting held but I bet every one of them will be full of screaming. Come on guys, it would be more funny dancing crazily without all the shouting! (February 7, 2009, at 10:42 p.m.)

One of the most striking forms of loud, collective vocal performance during the dance—and also one of the primary exceptions to the asynchronous nature of the event—was the group countdown from 10 seconds before 7:00 p.m., when the dance officially began. Indeed, countdowns seem to be characteristic of silent raves: In Lara Pellegrinelli's "Silent Ravers Dance 'Together, But Individually,'" a report for National Public Radio on a silent rave that took place in the summer of 2008 in New York's Union Square Park, the countdown can clearly be heard (though perhaps not as bombastically as the countdown that can be heard on the numerous videos circulating of the Liverpool Station event): "Ladies and Gentleman, Silent Rave New York will start in 15 seconds...Five, Four, Three, Two, One." As Pellegrinelli succinctly put it: "the music isn't synchronized, just the starting time," and the lack of a common pulse caused the "booty-wiggling, fist-pumping mob" to look "kind of rhythmically challenged in its attempts to dance together. More than a few toes got mashed by the spastic conga-line which wove reck-lessly in and out of the crowd."

What can we make of this aspiration—common to most "silent" performances—to synchronize in time? The countdown is, of course, a ritual of asserting a temporal collec-tivity familiar to many mass events—the New Year's Eve party, the ending of a sporting event, the pre-launch lift-off. The countdown is also one of the most public demonstra-tions of the temporal synchronization that has reshaped the world to the benefit of a relatively recent form of instrumental reason made possible through the standardiza-tion and increasingly precise quantification of global time. Perhaps the most striking aspect of the Liverpool Station countdown, however, was that it was defined by a clock typically used to coordinate the movement of trains and travelers within the station, many of whom are commuters going to and from workplaces; indeed, as we have seen, commuters were prevented from traveling by the disruption of the event itself. Arresting commuter mobility and transforming a conduit into a club, the event involved a radi-cal transformation of human mobility; in preventing or hampering mobility to or away from the station itself, it amplified it to a much greater extent *within* the station, the crowds notwithstanding.

The subversion of the commuting space, however, is not indelibly accompanied by the subversion of capitalist time. One possible reading of the event would emphasize its utility for the T-Mobile company itself. Although the creators of the original com-mercial did not necessarily predict that such events would take place, the company certainly understood that the experience economy is broad and malleable enough to incorporate large, relatively spontaneous performances of this sort. In fact, by mak-ing a highly popular commercial based on an already existing social phenomenon—the train-station flash mob—T-Mobile effectively claimed that phenomenon for itself; future events of this sort would have to contend with the company's intervention, if not acquiescing to it altogether.[40] One of these would include the mass appearance of imitation "T-Mobile dance" performances on YouTube, which thereby perpetuate the effect of the advertisement itself, even as it went out of currency. But to reduce 12,000 people to corporate lackeys might be missing the point. Given that capital can, at pres-ent, account for labor-power employment systems both highly synchronized (i.e., 9 to 5, workplace-based) and asynchronous (i.e., telecommuting, flexible work schedules, project-based employment), one could still assert that it is an achievement to bring together a sizable mass of individuals to a non-place like a mass transit station for the purpose of collective (if mostly sonically individualized) revelry.

The paradoxes of communality and solipsism that mark this type of event prompt an analysis that attends to the particularity of its *relational* qualities. What are the relational aesthetics of such a collective performance?[41] One possible way to summarize the Silent Dance narrated here would be to provide an accounting of the relational elements at play during that brief moment at Liverpool Station. Such an account may include consider-ations of sonic *leakage*, with surfeits of sound repeatedly perforating the boundaries of particular *enclosures*, especially those constructed through headphone space, and the social effects resulting from those breaches. Individual spaces are transformed through collectivities, which produce various kinds of social *warmth*—as might music itself, in a different way. Collectivities have different *densities*—witness the striking difference in human density in the T-Mobile ad (with its orderly columns of dancers and their partners) and the Silent Dance (two orders of magnitude greater in size)—which profoundly affect the possibilities for movement and action within spaces, and which condition the specific *topologies* that indicate the social morphologies of the event. Bodies keep together in time to varying degrees, of course, and a striking feature of the Silent Dance (in contrast to the T-Mobile ad) was the unruly lack of mass *synchronization* (smaller-scale synchrony may have appeared with greater frequency, however). Despite this asynchrony, the extremely dense congregation exhibited a significant degree of *control* over the contours of the performance; that said, various forms of control were also exerted by the police who oversaw and eventually shut down the event. With the ricocheting of sound off the station walls, generating a highly complex ambience, sounds also potentially produced *masking* effects, obscuring or confusing perception and/or communication. In a performance such as this, which privileges certain forms of *human interaction* at the expense of others, certain *social mores* are reinforced (such as the sanctity of individual space) and others transgressed (limits on the amplitude of collective vocalizations, or the unsanctioned collective occupation of a public space). The merging together and intersection of numerous *formations* (including material assemblages and constructions; social groups—revelers, police, commuters, station workers; and historical developments—including the recent one of the flash mob) helped to shape the events into a specific form, interpretable through competing *narratives*.

The most obvious of these narratives are polarized: those that make ambitious claims for the utopian power of the silent rave/flash mob/spontaneous performance, and those that critique such performances as reified, precorporated, and appropriable "free" labor that serves corporations like T-Mobile (Fisher 2009:9; Terranova 2000). Of course, neither pole is entirely correct, and both contain their truths: there is no way for a relational aesthetics to stand outside capitalist social relations, but a relational aesthetics can also not be reduced to those social relations, either. Perhaps the most useful interpretation of ephemeral events (and their residues) such as the silent raves would embark upon a comparison between these and another very celebrated series of gatherings: the Occupy movement (especially as manifested in the Occupy Wall Street encampments that initiated a widespread, international phenomenon, with a local variant in London itself). At first blush, the two appear rather different: the silent rave is an extremely ephemeral event with modest ambitions, a performance from which one may "go home," whereas the Occupy movement proposed to claim public space as a new, communal home, demanding radical (if often unspecified) social change all the while. Although it would be a simple matter to pit the Occupy movement as the authentic, political counterpart to the artificial, apolitical, and incorporated silent rave, the similarities between them are striking, even beyond their participants' common social locations and relatively disciplined comportments. One such similarity concerns a sonic technique specific to each. Both, of course, employed various kinds of collective chants, including the silent rave's countdown, as we have seen, and thereby amplified the power of the crowd into a voluble force, one that "tightens the space of relations," in Bourriaud's parlance (2002:15–16).[42] But the Occupy movement also made use of an unusual technique of sonic redistribution called "the human microphone," wherein strategically positioned individuals would physically rebroadcast speeches to listeners out of earshot, with the effect of unifying a spatially distributed crowd and orienting it toward someone at its "head." Although coalescences around central points of spectacle (such as the naked man) also were found in the silent rave, its basic sonic technique—individualized headphone music listening (with now and again, eruptions of synchronized vocality)—was fundamentally one of disunity, even if the listening and dancing practice itself was replicated by each participant. In its dialectical capturing of group and individual, does the silent rave pose a more powerful political model, at least in one small sense? Raising the question may be sufficient to spur a subtler appreciation of the varieties of utopian imaginings found in the forms of public and mobile performance that characterize much of the contemporary urban world.

# Mobile Aesthetics, Mobile Etiquettes

We can ask the question: Do the three case studies we just presented (Hifana, *Sonic City*, London Silent Dance) and the attendant aesthetics that we highlighted for each (*material, phenomenological*, and *relational*) coalesce into a broader aesthetics of mobile performance? Yes and no. The problem to address, in our view, is that each of the performances we discussed—and indeed all of the performances treated in both volumes of the *Handbook*—concern, in varying degrees, two registers that are fundamental to the experience and performance of mobile music, as well as mobile performance more broadly. These are the *device* (or technology more broadly) and the *human* (or performer, user, participant, experiencer).[43] It is our contention that a mobile aesthetics of the kind we propose here must engage, at least as an initial step, with this fundamental dyad—as well as its complications and myriad multiplications that arise in actual performances. The relationship between human and nonhuman, or user and device, is crucial, in that it allows for a clarification of the aesthetics that arise in one of two respective domains: specifically, the *aesthetics of design* in the device or technology (including the affordances of that technology and its raw sensory features) and the *aesthetics of form* in specific performances (including the temporal and sequential ordering of events, the range of gestures and acts defining those events, the constraints that bind and guide action arising from the circumstances of the performance). The relationship between design and form can be understood in terms of *loops* and their degree of *tightness* or *looseness*. Loops, or relations involving attentiveness, feedback, kinetic-tactile contact, sensory detection and material production, are not bubbles (to cite a well-trodden term in some writing on mobile music). Instead, they always involve an exceeding of their immediate geographic and/or networked confines. As such these loops provide the possibility of external audiences—though they may not be essential to the performance or even present at all. A performance may involve a single loop or multiple loops of varying tightness/looseness, with inputs, outputs, and various forms of propagation feeding into a sequential chain of events (no matter how short in duration) and/or occurring simultaneously and even synchronously. Hence, in this scheme, a performance involving the playing of a mobile game (with audio) may involve a relatively tight loop of user and device, with possible bystanders impinging upon the user's attention, whereas a staged performance of group device usage necessarily requires the divided attention of users—between device (or devices), other users/performers, and, if they are present, audience members or bystanders.[44]

The benefit of conceptualizing performance in such a way is that it allows us to imagine—as we started to do in the first section of this essay—what might be described as "everyday" performances and "art" (or "concert" or "theater") performances as being similar to one another, rather than giving in to the reification of the art/everyday binary. Moreover, this commonality mirrors an actual facet of mobile device usage; as Wolf-Dieter Ernst puts it, the aesthetics of mobile performances "blurs the boundary between use value and aesthetic value."

> If we imagine a smart phone in the place of the Game Boy, or an mp3-player, a camera, etc., we realise that all these objects make it difficult to decide whether to estimate their function in terms of usefulness or playfulness. Mobile aesthetics thus disrupts the conventional opposition between the realm of the quotidian and that of the aesthetic; it shifts aesthetic judgment into an area of micro-level everyday decision making. (Ernst 2011:66)[45]

Or, at least, it can do so. For mobile performance not only encompasses the tight "single loop" that is typical of how quotidian performances are understood (as in the ostensible "bubble" of mobile headphone listening); it also facilitates the possibility of "scaling up" into more complex, multi-user, or multi-device performances precisely because of their ease of use. Thus, the MP3-player transforms into the silent rave, the Game Boy into a multi-user gaming experience, the iPhone into a mobile phone orchestra, and so on.

We can cite a multitude of human/device relationships that might fall under the rubric of a mobile music aesthetics: four people listening to a car radio while driving in a convertible; a child playing a handheld video game; an adult listening to an iPod playlist via headphones while running; a group of youths—one holding a boombox—meandering noisily through a neighborhood; each member of a string quartet performing while flying in his/her own individual helicopter (with the audio of each performance sent to a speaker system in a stadium containing an audience).[46] The basics of the human/device relationship are relatively easy to describe. But what precisely is a loop? In asking this question, what we mean is that we have yet to define the *stuff* constituting the material routed through the loop—which is necessarily some sensory (or to-be-sensed) form. In the most basic system, involving a single user and device, the primary form of interaction is necessarily sensorial (or, to borrow Steven Connor's apt word, *intersensorial* [2004]): the pressure waves of sound, the visually processed photons emitting as electromagnetic radiation from a source, the force of two objects coming into contact, such as a human digit touching a plastic button. When the system becomes more complicated, a greater number of materialities (but not necessarily immediately perceptible forms) enter into the picture. Analog and digital electrical signals and electromagnetic radiation (in the form of radio or television broadcasts, Bluetooth bands, or satellite transmissions) now become part of the loop, rather than merely a part of any signal or information loops internal to the device or human. Of course, in all cases, the human/device dyad is never really autonomous or isolated—living and dead labor help to constitute the very being of both, and a great many devices are connected to broader communication systems of one sort or another (as we make clear in our three case studies).

The loops we study in this volume of essays are sonically saturated, with sound forming the primary condition for sensory attentiveness.[47] The tighter loops—a headphoned individual, a phone caller hearing a ringback tone—maintain a very close relationship (and, usually, proximity) between sound source and ear, or with listening devices (such as those involving voice recognition) including microphones and other inputs likewise usually physically close to their sources. Whereas tight loops will produce forms of leakage, given their non-hermetic structure, looser ones are more expressly designed to emanate and radiate sound outward and/or to likewise absorb and detect sound from a wider field of sources. When sound is projected outward, it gains a new capacity to transform and control space, territorializing it, if you will; the boombox and boom car are particularly celebrated examples of this effect, whereas more expressly violent forms of sonic control can be found in military contexts (such as loudspeakers on battlefields playing music or simulating entire fronts).[48] When loops include larger numbers of humans and devices, forming more complicated networks, sound can emerge and submerge with the greatest of ease, capable of being processed and reprocessed, converted, amplified, filtered, digitized, and more, pinged between different nodes so as to produce a more complicated effect—as might be the case, for example, in the activation of sound installations involving numerous mobile phones calling one another, instigated by a human prompt.[49] In such instances, audiences (which may or may not include humans participating within the loops) perceive sound not only as a single device's output, but also, even primarily, as an aggregate of sounds producing a cumulative effect, a cloud of standing and bouncing waves heard within a single, well-defined space... perhaps.

What distinguishes the preceding description of a musical or sonic performance from a mobile music performance, of course, is the presence of mobility, understood here in terms of the capacity for or incorporation of movement. Given that nearly all performance involves some kind of movement, the forms of movement we are imagining here are, as is common within the field of mobility studies, ideal-typically oriented around various enacted or potential forms of transit: walking, biking, driving, flying, and so forth. Sound has its own continuities and temporalities, and thus has the capacity not only to transform one's experience of traversing geographic expanses but also to remap these expanses durationally (for example in accord with the temporal frame of a single song). Moreover, the mechanisms of transit can come to be heard in polyphony with the device's emitted sound, thus producing a new sonic constellation specific to a particular auditory source and travel context (as in the conjunctions captured and mystified by Volkswagen's famous "Synchronicity" advertisement). Such conjunctions allow for a sonic reshaping (retuning, even) of the world. And yet, as we pointed out in the introduction to the first volume of the *Handbook*, the experience of mobile music is often, paradoxically, a static one within the velocity reference frame of motion, and as such it is often the small motions not constitutive of transit per se—the tapping of fingers and toes, breathing elevated to consciousness, fidgets and twitches—that engage in bodily choreographies and entrainments activated by listening.

From all this one might assume that there is a kind of archetype of a mobile music performance we have in mind. But this is not the case—such performances are extremely variegated, functioning for a range of ends. While it's clearly impossible to describe the full array of potential sonic mobilities, we can locate a spectrum of performance types that might provide conceptual ballast for a number of the chapters in this volume. In one instance we might call attention to the creation of a *continuous* sonic environment that persists through/within disparate locations or frames. Or we might cite how smooth mobile continuities fragment into *punctuated* usages, with the *on* of persistent sound rendered into an interposed *on/off*. The performance of mobile music has also revealed itself—especially since the emergence of the smartphone (but also for as long as radio waves have been capturable by portable devices)—through forms that are *connective*, with sonic access occurring across a range of locations, often synchronously. Another crucial mobile-music performative inheres in the simultaneity of sound and motion, with mobility being completely inseparable from its own sonic residues (that is, in these instances, sound proclaims and maps directly onto mobility). And sonic mobilities also have their ghosts—*pre-echoes* and *echoes*—announcing a motion that will, or has already, occurred.[50]

It should be clear from the foregoing discussion that the aesthetics of mobile music is not equivalent to an aesthetics of mere motion or movement. Instead, it involves a compounding of the looped, networked relations of human and device, a privileging of sound within the circuits of those loops and networks, and a foregrounding of mobility, rather than movement or motion per se. More directly: as we intimated earlier, mobility does not require actual motion or movement. If it did, even the mere positing of a "mobile aesthetics" would, by necessity, conjure a "static aesthetics," which it clearly does not. (Indeed, the notion of a static aesthetics seems patently absurd.) Instead, an aesthetics of stasis is not only produced by a mobile aesthetics but, paradoxically, encompassed by it; the opposite, on the other hand, cannot be said. Clearly, conjoining "mobile" and "aesthetics" together charges the aesthetic with a qualifier and a specific kind of valence—suddenly, the question of mobility becomes a *problem* for a musical and sonic aesthetics.

Why exactly is the question of mobility a problem for the aesthetics of sound and music? First, we must have an adequate sense of the relevance of aesthetics for our purposes, in the context of a discourse that largely avoids consideration of it. For if an aesthetic of music and sound, to oversimplify, concerns the forms of labor and attentiveness directed toward the ordering and reordering of the sensorium, with a particular emphasis on hearing and listening, then a mobile sonico-musical aesthetic must account for the effects that potential and actual spatial repositionings might have on sensory labor and attentiveness. We can imagine at least two such effects. First, the very focus of inquiry seems to transform as a result of any significant degree of movement: the space in which that movement takes place becomes all the more crucial to the performance that occurs within it. Second, the idea of mobility, signified for example by devices or networked communication systems, is sufficient to give rise to imaginaries of transportability, of routing and rerouting, and hence may become central to the basis for understanding, evaluating, and creating a performance.

As the regime of the mobile extends performance in space and time, we might further ascertain that the aesthetic transformations occurring during the long century of mobile music were not simply technological or even sonic (in terms of the sound worlds available to listeners, performers and creative musicians); rather, these changes were profoundly social and involved shifts in entire aesthetic imaginaries. These imaginaries are, of course, built out of myriad practices, some generative, others consumptive. But that dichotomy, while perhaps remaining partly relevant, falls apart when set in motion. This unraveling produces, perhaps, another dichotomy, one not between production and consumption, or even art and the everyday, but between aesthetics and etiquette. Whereas the tradition of aesthetics that was generated in conjunction with heroic romanticism, philosophical categories of contemplation, reason, and judgment might have had a vital (and necessary) pairing between aesthetics and ethics, our present concern with mobility peels away the outer crust of the ethical and leaves the softer core of civility, manners, and protocols.

So much of the discourse on capitalism, especially since the 1960s, has theorized the reproduction of production. Capital is reproduced not only through acts of exchange, but also through the reproduction of labor power. Yet the reproduction of labor power was historically a domain distant from the marketplace. (Re)introducing the marketplace and forms of exchange to the spaces, places, and temporalities of labor-power reproduction has been one of the major sources of new capital accumulation in the last half-century. Mobile music's ubiquity is entirely inseparable from this process. "Anytime, Anywhere"—a trope at the center of any *etiquette* of mobile music—thus becomes a kind of war of position between producer/marketer and consumer/laborer, with the former seeking to make incursions on the latter's "free" time. That such strategies were welcomed by consumers says much about the dialectical relationship between capital's methods of accumulation and its desire to produce consumers. The etiquette of mobile music that emerges out of the *experience* of "Anytime, Anywhere" is conditioned through a curious play between capital's accumulative/consumptive desires and the sensual attentiveness to the looped aesthetics we describe earlier.

Etiquette transforms radically as a result of ubiquity—social mores *must* accommodate themselves to the imperatives of exchange. As Shannon Winnubst puts it: "If etiquette is the proper comportment of the body, these social mappings of power should be readily legible in the codes of its practices" (2007:153). Consider this now ubiquitous example of mobile phone use: increasingly, it is acceptable to excuse oneself and/

or speak on the phone while in the presence of company. Often this has to do with workplace demands, as well as personal ones, which are designed to radically increase labor productivity. (This dynamic can be subsumed into the present-day regime of perpetual availability characterized by Luc Boltanski and Ève Chiapello as "the projective city" [2005:103–163].) Mobile music experience (say, the canonical example of the listening commuter) has much to do with the recuperation of unpaid labor time (transit labor), as well as the emotional/affective labor of mood management that makes labor (and labor-power's reproduction) possible. Increasingly, this particular form of mobile music experience is dependent on rentier capitalism's ubiquity through services such as Spotify and iTunes, in which forms of intellectual property are made always already available for any mobile user.

To conclude a treatment of aesthetics by raising the specter of etiquette may seem somewhat surprising, but it goes to the heart of our inquiry. The ubiquitization of musical performance may entail an inflation of the importance of etiquette, corresponding to the increasing role of utility in the aesthetics of mobility. Indeed, one might argue that a central effect of the mundanization of aesthetics is the emergence of a new sphere of etiquette, recalling art prior to its reification as an autonomous form, when it historically played a principally social role. If the incursions of the mobile can be registered anywhere with particular accuracy, it is the way in which social interactions, guided by etiquette, have undergone profound, if easily ignored transformations. Gluing together the cracks of social life, etiquette is ultimately indispensible not only for aesthetics but also ethics. As Karmen MacKendrik posits, "Ethics by itself is no way to live. Without etiquette, which is not ethics, no system of ethical rules can hold: ethics is about human behavior, and we cannot continue to interact without grace notes" (2007:205). Our only emendation to this claim might be that grace notes, not always especially graceful, occupy a particularly important place in the cacophony of melodies coursing through the worlds of mobile music.

# EPILOGUE

Does mobile music have a paradigmatic exemplar, one that could be taken as a kind of origination point for the studies in these volumes? Certainly, the ambulatory human body, shorn of instruments or devices, is already a complex, rhythmic system of sonic production, the periodicities of which have long encouraged sympathetic entrainments of various sorts produced by the walker herself. All things that move through the medium of air produce sound, and the human body is no different. But humans accompany the residual sounds of their movements with hums and whistles and pats and taps, with all manner of vocalizations and percussions. In more recent times, the image of the walking whistler, typically gendered male, stands as a synecdoche for one kind of modernity—flaneur, commuter, lurker—with all of its mobilities, possibilities, and even perversities. Like Deleuze and Guattari's humming child in their discussion of the "refrain," the whistler (and consciously ambulatory noisemaker more generally) asserts some control over space, re-territorializing it and, to a degree, making it over in their image (Deleuze and Guattari 1987:311). The walking whistler is potentially a dangerous figure (think of Peter Lorre's Hans Becket in the film *M* [1931]) or potentially an utterly wholesome one, creating the sense of safety and even "home" that Deleuze and Guattari mention (think of the theme song to *The Andy Griffith Show*; somewhere in between is the whistling soldiers' rendition of Kenneth Alford's "Colonel Bogey March" in *Bridge on the River Kwai*, in which sonic control over space is produced collectively [1957]).[51] The ramifications of such behavior are complex and certainly relevant to the contemporary world: witness the racial and class dynamics of the titular example Claude Steele gives in his book *Whistling Vivaldi*, of an African-American male (psychology researcher Brent Staples) whistling a classical music chestnut while walking in public to dispel white bypassers' stereotypes (and fears) of the dangerous black man (Steele 2010:6–7).

In the twentieth century, however, this paradigm must be articulated with and is even possibly supplanted by another: one involving a device and listener and not necessarily a demonstration of motion in a literal sense. The *sine qua non* of this conception of mobile music—as it is defined in the *Oxford Handbook of Mobile Music Studies*—might be, in the end, a highly static form of performance that became utterly ubiquitous in the more privileged enclaves of the First World almost as soon as the transistor was mass produced: teenagers listening to portable transistor radios in their rooms, under the covers, sequestered away from their parents and indeed the rest of the domestic sphere, but connected to the mobilities of the wider world through radio signals.

> So the TI [Texas Instrument] unit was way too expensive for your average, or even above average, sixteen-year-old. The Japanese units sold for a lot less. Now, the music could go with you anywhere. You could even get an earphone, so that no one else had to hear it—useful in class or in the bedroom after lights out. Many listeners heard Alan Freed's late-night shows while lying under the covers with an earphone in their ear. (Bordowitz 2004:82)[52]

We can mark the prior movements of the radio listener—how they came to be there in the dark, enveloped in a cave of sonic fabric—but these prior movements are insufficient and unnecessary to signal the mobility of this event. What is key, in this instance, is the condensed and congealed *capacity* for movement that the portable radio brings, and with it, an articulation to a vast system of capital that has found ever new ways to harness the value of mobility and perpetual availability—hence, the fecund use of "anywhere" in the quotation.

And yet, the relationship between that radio listener and media infrastructure—earpiece, transistor radio, radio program and genre, and broadcast personality—cannot simply be reduced to a system of capital accumulation alone, an exchange relation. Just as vital to the story is the use value of that relationship, one that vitally produces a number of different intimacies: the intimacy of *insertion* (earpiece in the ear); the intimacy of *enclosure* (the sonic bubble of the earphoned headspace and the womblike envelopment of the covers); the intimacy of the *human other* (the radio deejay, the voices of the singers); the intimacy of the *distributed collective* (listeners drawn together through the synchronic time engendered by radio technology). There is also, crucially, the intimacy of *the body with device*, that other entity beside and besides the listener. A multiplication of intimacies therefore produces a network of interrelated bonds that form communal relationships not only, or even primarily, structured by conscious or unconscious rational-choice evaluations.[53]

These experiences, as with communal relationships generally, cannot be produced by one-time interactions in the way that exchange relationships can. As a result, they transform into habits and rituals that therefore play a powerful role in the structuring of one's schedule and in temporal experience itself. Mobile music's constant availability—the "anytime"—involves a multiplication of moments available for listening, producing reiterations of the sensory and sensual experiences associated with music and sound. But mobile music is also in theory available "anywhere," thus entailing a multiplication of places and spaces as well. The calculus of the relationship between anytime and anywhere is what produces mobility, at least in the context of mobile music performance, and to reiterate an important theme articulated above and in our introduction to Volume 1, one effect of this calculus is that one doesn't need to be in motion to be "mobile."

The tendency for mobile music to encroach on all places at all times is unsurprisingly linked to everyday experience, and yet something crucially remains special about mobile music listening—a specialness that binds the spectrum of performances under consideration here. The everydayness of mobile music, even when habitual or ritualistic, is never merely routine: perpetual and omnipresent access to music and sound seemingly paradoxically creates unique, meaningful experiences and creative opportunities accessible in an ever-increasing array of places and spaces at increasingly differentiated points in time. If one result of mobile music's anytime, anywhere status is the production of new genres of art, the other is a suffusing of everyday life with a different and new kind of aestheticization: life is absorbed into art but art is also absorbed—as capacity—into life.

The art/everyday divide and its dissolution is a primary thematic for our study of mobile music, principally because one of our goals is to tease out the lineaments of the transformation of social life in the long twentieth century, an epoch whose outer edges may be marked by the development of new mobile products, many of which transform sensory experience and, in so doing, catalyze the emergence of new aesthetic forms. Our major claim is that there is a value to analyzing these new aesthetic forms, putting pressure on their varied provenances and the varied ambient spheres of their use values. To the extent that their effect radiates outward into other, established genres of artmaking—examples of which appear in some of the chapters that follow—our skepticism toward a putatively comprehensive taxonomy of such practices led us to focus on the primal scene of mobile music performance, as it were, and to allow case studies and descriptions of performance genres, including our own, to sit within a rich, if necessarily partial, constellation of phenomena and practices. We can characterize that scene in terms of the notion of *exceptionality*, in which the mobile performance announces itself as such, over and against the quiescence of non-exceptional existence. (Indeed, that the normative experience can never entirely lose its exceptionality is in part what makes the experience of mobile music so potentially powerful.) The long arc of mobile music's history has amounted to a shift on the sliding scale of what counted as *sonically* exceptional; in the present moment, the once-exceptional may increasingly be merely normative.

What we have presented here and in our introduction to Volume 1 is not a theory of mobile musical performance for all time but one that captures a state of mobile performance at a particular historical moment, albeit a long one. Although the reflexive understanding of mobile culture might locate its emergence coterminously with the rise of the digital, our goal in these two volumes has been to illumine a larger historical parcel and to suggest that capital's harnessing of mobility has, perhaps, distinguished a new mode of production and a correspondingly new sensory habitus. This new mode articulates with and, indeed, activates a series of comportments and etiquettes, which, when taken together, congeal into what we—and others—have called a mobile aesthetic. The studies in the pages that follow articulate, in very different ways, aspects of that aesthetic.

## NOTES

1. Marx (1977:125).
2. This expansive view of performance aligns with the work of a number of scholars in the field of performance studies, many of whom draw upon a distinct lineage stretching back to Erving Goffman, Victor Turner, and Richard Schechner. For one version of this history, see Schechner (2002).
3. For an extensive treatment of *Dialtones*, see chapter 4 of Gopinath (2013).
4. See, for example, the musical theater performance at Stansted Airport in London in 2008 at http://www.youtube.com/watch?v=8FMzWfeRy6o (accessed January 31, 2013).
5. Literature that explicitly theorizes mobile music performance includes Essl and Rohs (2009), Behrendt (2005), and Essl, Wang, and Rohs (2008).
6. Combining art and the everyday is in some ways rather similar to cultural studies' long-standing efforts to think through mass culture and the avant-garde together rather than separately.
7. The Ocarina video is available at http://www.youtube.com/watch?v=kfrONZjakRY (accessed January 31, 2013).
8. Kirn (2010).
9. One might imagine the conjunction of Nike and Apple (the latter signified by the "+," enhancing the former) as a combination of their most famous advertising slogans, respectively: "Just Do It" + "Think Different."
10. The following discussion references a performance occurring in a Nike advertisement available at http://www.youtube.com/watch?v=uS1exujG3cY& (accessed February 1, 2013). See also Ramirez (2010).
11. For a critical treatment of Nike+, see Gopinath and Stanyek (2013).
12. In an email to us on October 19, 2011, Yuya Ozawa—one of the producers working with the creative collective Groundriddim, which includes Hifana—further explained the samples used in the performance: "The vocal samples in this film were recorded by CHINZA

DOPENESS, another of our clients. The lyrics embedded in the sample are: 'One, Two, Gunyo Gunyo, Magaru' and 'One, Two, Gune Gune, Hashiru.' 'GUNYO GUNYO' & 'GUNE GUNE' is the same. They are imitation sounds of BENDING. 'MAGARU' is to BEND. 'HASHIRU' is to RUN."

13. Note, too, the way that at 0:42–0:43, one of the performers adopts a runner's or athlete's starting-line stance, possibly a reaction to the fact that he's wearing athletic shoes.

14. See the fall 2007 ad featuring Russian dancers Maria Vinogradova and Anastsiya Soboleva, available online at http://www.youtube.com/watch?v=0600GrzioKU (accessed February 1, 2013). The Robinson/Firkušný ad can be found at http://www.youtube.com/watch?v=vVKWBrVqCzs (accessed February 1, 2013).

15. For a detailed treatment of the video/performance's technical details, see Kirn (2010).

16. As cited in the W+K Tokyo Lab "making of" video, "Nike Free Run+: When a Shoe Becomes a Music Instrument," posted April 27, 2010 at http://www.youtube.com/watch?v=LlDBrVohXGE& (accessed February 1, 2013).

17. Cited from the W+K Tokyo Lab website at http://wktokyo.jp/ (accessed February 1, 2013).

18. On this point, see Wu (2002).

19. Regarding the nature of Hifana's collaboration with Wieden+Kennedy, see the response on the comments section of Kirn (2010). "As someone who does a lot of composing for advertising, I'm struck by this on a completely different level. Knowing how much time and energy are often spent in the process of original music creation with the agency hiring several different music companies to throw different ideas at the same piece, I think this is a great example of marketer and composer making a true commitment to partner up and build something seamlessly tailored to communicate a specific message. That's innovative in and of itself, and subverts a method that in my opinion, quite often devalues original music while confusing the process." Post by waveplant, on April 16, 2010, at http://create-digitalmusic.com/2010/04/bendable-musical-shoes-for-nike-and-how-they-were-made/ (accessed February 1, 2013). Also, see the programmatic statement about the W+K Tokyo Lab music label. "Wieden+Kennedy Tokyo Lab is a new music label concept launched by Wieden+Kennedy Tokyo in 2003. Embracing the concept of hybrid, our mission is to bring new experiences that can only be created in Tokyo [t]hrough a unique global mix of music, visuals, and other forms of creative expression through a DVD and CD. W+K Tokyo Lab is all about being in Tokyo now, using the power of the city to attract the most innovative creative collaborators from around the world. We are passionate about the development of new ideas with our creators and connecting them to a new audience. Simply put, it is about good music, fresh visuals, and new concepts of creative expression." Available at http://wktokyolab.com/blog/ (accessed February 1, 2013).

20. The dialectic of implementation versus modification should be understood as producing a continuum, with the outer conceptual edge of the former residing in tools fully formed, prescribed usages, protocols, and licensed adoptions and the latter ranging from modest forms of customization to an outer edge of radical retrofittings and experimental jimmy-ings. The implications of this continuum, from consumption to production, might help to link prescribed consumer uses of devices and objects to the most recondite forms of new object creation in artistic production. For one treatment of such issues as pertain to consumer audio systems and the customization end of this continuum, see Perlman (2003).

21. Gaye, Mazé, and Holmquist (2003:109).

22. Also see Ingold and Vergunst (2008).

23. Mobile music meant in this sense refers in part to the work of the composers and sound artists associated with the Mobile Music Workshops. See Kirisits, Behrendt, Gaye, and Tanaka (2008) and Goggin (2011:76–79).
24. A lengthy description of the piece is found at Gaye's personal website, http://www.lalyagaye.com/archive/?p=12 (accessed February 1, 2013).
25. "Tamghra Nouchen" appears on the album *Salam Haleikoum* (2002).
26. Our use of "ecotone" here bears some resemblance to Houben's notion of the "verge" (Houben 2005:111).
27. See discussions of this very problem in Gaye and Holmquist (2004).
28. Cf. the title of Gaye and Holmquist (2004) as well.
29. In the literature on *Sonic City* we've seen, no mention is made of the ways in which the technical system was attuned to the specific materialities or properties of urban Göteborg, and therefore we assume that "the city" is a more general figure, identified in form by object proximities, especially proximities to metallic materials.
30. Numerous other terms for the kind of aesthetics we're imagining have been offered up by a wide range of scholars in a diversity of disciplines: interactive aesthetics, distributed aesthetics, network aesthetics, prosthetic aesthetics, cyborg aesthetics, etc. These capture aspects of our aims that the traditional notion of the phenomenological does not. Many of these have certainly been discussed in print, including in Barker (2012), Munster (2006), and Galloway (2004).
31. Our invocation of this term derives from critical, non-essentialist applications of the work of Edward T. Hall (1963) to human-computer interaction (Olson and Olson 2000) and sound recording technology (Moore 2012:100).
32. On the complexities of data sonification, see Barrass, Whitelaw, and Bailes (2006).
33. For an exactly parallel analysis of the Nike+ Sport Kit, see Gopinath and Stanyek (2013:147).
34. See Bull (2000) and Bull (2007).
35. Crazzy Eve, cited in CNN (2009).
36. See, in part, Castells, Fernández-Ardèvol, Qiu, and Sey (2007:185–213).
37. See Rheingold (2002) and Todd and Scordelis (2009), for example.
38. The song sequence in the medley is "Shout" by Lulu & the Luvvers, "Don't Cha" by Pussycat Dolls, Johann Strauss, Jr.'s the "Blue Danube Waltz," "Get Down On It" by Kool & The Gang, "Since You've Been Gone" by Rainbow, "My Boy Lollipop" by Millie, and "Do You Love Me (Now That I Can Dance)" by The Contours.
39. A theory of "leakage" is presented more fully in Stanyek and Piekut (2010).
40. Indeed, the fact that the Liverpool Station Silent Dance seems not to have been repeated in that location may have something to do with T-Mobile's effective appropriation of it.
41. Relational aesthetics is, of course, most associated with the writings of Nicolas Bourriaud, who applies the term to performance and installation art involving various forms of social management and gathering that became especially common in the 1990s and after. See Bourriaud (2002).
42. See the discussion of "tight places" in Goldman (2010).
43. The relationship between device and user is, of course, not unique to the mobile devices featured in these volumes and discussed in our case studies. Indeed, one could describe the performance of traditional instruments in much the same way, although it would break down distinctions between concert performances, practicing, noodling, etc., in ways that seem especially apropos for the range and character of usage practices found with mobile music devices.

44. On feedback and the tightness of loops (and Gordian knots thereof), also see Gopinath and Stanyek (2013).

45. This quotation from Ernst signals a crucial distinction between our development of a mobile music aesthetics—one built around mobile music performance—and a more established (if still relatively recent) discourse on a broader "mobile aesthetics." Among the most insightful contributions in this discourse include the work of two Europe-based architects, Anthony Hoete (2003) and Francine Houben (2005), concerning the aesthetic relationships between architecture and mobility.

46. The last example is Karlheinz Stockhausen's *Helikopter-Streichquartett* (1995), from his opera *Mittwoch aus Licht* (1995–1997).

47. Sound's physical mobility (through air, esp.) per se is not, however, sufficient to undergird a mobile musical/sonic aesthetics. If it were, then all musical and sonic aesthetics would be a mobile music/sound aesthetics, which would be deeply and unnecessarily reductive—a kind of "vulgar mobilism," if you will.

48. The military examples are found in Chanan (2000:97); also see Goodman (2010).

49. Craighead and Thomson's *Telephony* is one such example; see chapter 4 in Gopinath (2013).

50. Apropos of this point, one might also consider the relationship between mobility and "mode" (and modes' multiplicity as characterizing the present). See Hoete (2003:11–13).

51. The apparently wholesome homosociality of these whistling soldiers, especially when imitated by children (even in juvenile parodies like "Comet-Vomit"), is belied by the unstated lyrics in *River Kwai* being those of a vulgar British anti-German parody of the march, "Hitler Has Only Got One Ball." See Schwabach (2001:75–78).

52. There are numerous accounts that depict under-the-bedcover transistor radio listening. One is narrated by the Beach Boys' Brian Wilson, who listened to R&B stations late at night in this way (Gaines 1995:253).

53. On exchange versus communal relationships, see Clark and Mills (1979).


## References

Adey, Peter. 2010. *Mobility*. Abingdon, Oxon: Routledge.

Augé, Marc. 2000. *Non-Places: Introduction to an Anthropology of Supermodernity*. London: Verso.

Barker, Timothy Scott. 2012. *Time and the Digital: Connecting Technology, Aesthetics, and a Process Philosophy of Time*. Hanover, NH: Dartmouth College Press.

Barrass, Stephen, Mitchell Whitelaw, and Freya Bailes. 2006. "Listening to the Mind Listening: An Analysis of Sonification Reviews, Designs and Correspondences." *Leonardo Music Journal* 16:13–9.

Behrendt, F. 2005. *Handymusik: Klangkunst und "Mobile Devices."* Onsabrück: Electronic Pub. Osnabrück. http://www.epos.uos.de/music/templates/buch.php?id=57 (accessed January 31, 2013).

Bordowitz, Hank. 2004. *Turning Points in Rock and Roll: The Key Events That Affected Popular Music in the Latter Half of the 20th Century*. New York: Citadel Press.

Bourriaud, Nicolas. 2002. *Relational Aesthetics*. Dijon: Les Presses du réel.

Bull, Michael. 2000. *Sounding Out the City: Personal Stereos and the Management of Everyday Life*. Oxford: Berg.

———. 2007. *Sound Moves: iPod Culture and Urban Experience*. London: Routledge.

Castells, Manuel, Mireira Fernández-Ardèvol, Jack Linchuan Qiu, and Araba Sey. 2007. *Mobile Communication and Society: A Global Perspective*. Cambridge, MA: MIT Press.

Chanan, Michael. 2000. *Repeated Takes: A Short History of Recording and Its Effects on Music*. London: Verso.

Chatwin, Bruce. 1987. *The Songlines*. New York: Viking.

Clark, Margaret, and Judson Mills. 1979. "Interpersonal Attraction in Exchange and Communal Relationships." *Journal of Personality and Social Psychology* 37(1):12–24.

Connor, Steven. 2004. "Edison's Teeth: Touching Hearing." In *Hearing Cultures: Essays on Sound, Listening, and Modernity*, ed. Veit Erlmann, 153–72. Oxford: Berg.

CNN. 2009. "Facebook Flashmob Shuts Down Station." *CNN.com*, February 19, http://www.cnn.com/2009/WORLD/europe/02/09/uk.station.flashmob/index.html (accessed February 1, 2013).

de Mul, Jos. 2005. "From Mobile Ontologies to Mobile Aesthetics." *Contemporary Aesthetics* 3, http://www.contempaesthetics.org/newvolume/pages/article.php?articleID=346 (accessed January 31, 2013).

Essl, Georg, and Michael Rohs. 2009. "Interactivity for Mobile Music-Making." *Organised Sound* 14(2):197–207.

Essl, Georg, Ge Wang, and Michael Rohs. 2008. "Developments and Challenges turning Mobile Phones into Generic Music Performance Platforms." In *Proceedings of the 5th International Mobile Music Workshop 2008*, 13–5 May, Vienna, Austria, 11–4. Vienna: Universität für Angewandte Kunst. http://www.uni-ak.ac.at/personal/kirisits/mmw2008/MMW_PDF/MMW_proceedings2008_web.pdf (accessed January 31, 2013).

Ernst, Wolf-Dieter. 2011. "Rimini Protokoll's 'Call Cutta' and the Performance of Presence." In *Moving Images, Mobile Viewers: 20th Century Visuality*, ed. Renate Brosch, Ronja Tripp, and Nina Jürgens, 65–74. Berlin: Lit.

Fisher, Mark. 2009. *Capitalist Realism: Is There No Alternative?* Washington, DC: Zero Books.

Fujimoto, Kenichi. 2005. "The Third-Stage Paradigm: Territory Machines from the Girls' Pager Revolution to Mobile Aesthetics." In *Personal, Portable, Pedestrian: Mobile Phones in Japanese Life*, ed. Mizuko Ito, Daisuke Okabe, and Misa Matsuda, 77–101. Cambridge, MA: MIT Press.

Gaines, Steven. 1995. *Heroes and Villains: The True Story of the Beach Boys*. New York: Da Capo Press.

Galloway, Alexander R. 2004. *Protocol: How Control Exists after Decentralization*. Cambridge, MA: MIT Press.

Gaye, Lalya, and Lars Erik Holmquist. 2004. "In Duet with Everyday Urban Settings: A User Study of Sonic City." In *Proceedings of the 2004 Conference on New Interfaces for Musical Expression (NIME04)*, 161–4. http://www.nime.org/archive/?mode=ylist&y=2004 (accessed February 1, 2013).

Gaye, Lalya, Ramia Mazé, and Lars Erik Holmquist. 2003. "Sonic City: The Urban Environment as Musical Interface." In *Proceedings of the 2003 International Conference on New Interfaces for Musical Expression*, 109–15. http://www.nime.org/proceedings/2003/nime2003_109.pdf (accessed January 31, 2013).

Goggin, Gerard. 2011. *Global Mobile Media*. Abingdon, Oxon: Routledge.

Goldman, Danielle. 2010. *I Want to be Ready: Improvised Dance as a Practice of Freedom*. Ann Arbor: University of Michigan Press.

Goodman, Steve. 2010. *Sonic Warfare: Sound, Affect, and the Ecology of Fear*. Cambridge, MA: MIT Press.

Gopinath, Sumanth. 2013. *The Ringtone Dialectic: Economy and Cultural Form*. Cambridge, MA: MIT Press.

Gopinath, Sumanth, and Jason Stanyek. 2013. "Tuning the Human Race: Athletic Capitalism and the Nike+ Sport Kit." In *Music, Sound and Space: Transformations of Public and Private Experience*, ed. Georgina Born, 128–48. Cambridge: Cambridge University Press.

Hall, Edward T. 1963. "A System for the Notation of Proxemic Behaviour." *American Anthropologist* 65(5):1003–26.

Hoete, Anthony, ed. 2003. *ROAM: A Reader on the Aesthetics of Mobility*. London: Black Dog.

Houben, Francine. 2005. "From Centre to Periphery: The Aesthetics of Mobility." In Esther Ruth Charlesworth, ed. *Cityedge: Case Studies in Contemporary Urbanism*, 102–17. Oxford: Architectural Press.

Ingold, Tim and Jo Lee Vergunst, eds. 2008. *Ways of Walking: Ethnography and Practice on Foot*. Aldershot: Ashgate Publishing Company.

Kirisits, Nicolaj, Frauke Behrendt, Lalya Gaye, and Atau Tanaka, eds. 2008. *Creative Interactions—The Mobile Music Workshops 2004–2008*. Vienna: Universität für Angewandte Kunst.

Kirn, Peter. 2010. "Bendable, Musical Shoes for Nike, and How They Were Made." *Create Digital Music* (blog), April 16, http://createdigitalmusic.com/2010/04/bendable-musical-shoes-for-nike-and-how-they-were-made/ (accessed January 31, 2013).

Lewis, George. 2009. "Interactivity and Improvisation." In *The Oxford Handbook of Computer Music*, ed. Roger Dean, 457–66. New York: Oxford University Press.

MacKendrick, Karmen. 2007. "Make It Look Easy: Thoughts on Social Grace." In *Etiquette: Reflections on Contemporary Comportment*, ed. Ron Scapp and Brian Seitz, 199–206. Albany, NY: State University of New York Press.

Mann, Steve, and Hal Niedzviecki. 2001. *Cyborg: Digital Destiny and Human Possibility in the age of the Wearable Computer*. Toronto: Doubleday Canada.

Marx, Karl. 1970 [1888]. "Theses on Feuerbach." Trans. C. J. Arthur. In Marx, Karl, Friedrich Engels, and C. J. Arthur, *The German Ideology: With Selections from Parts Two and Three, Together with Marx's "Introduction to a Critique of Political Economy,"* Part One, 121–3. New York: International Publishers.

——. 1977 [1867]. *Capital*. Volume 1. Trans. Ben Fowkes. New York: Vintage.

McNeill, William Hardy. 1995. *Keeping Together in Time: Dance and Drill in Human History*. Cambridge, MA: Harvard University Press.

Munster, Anna. 2006. *Materializing New Media: Embodiment in Information Aesthetics*. Hanover, NH: Dartmouth College Press.

Naukkarinen, Ossi. 2005. "Aesthetics and Mobility—A Short Introduction into a Moving Field." *Contemporary Aesthetics* 3, http://www.contempaesthetics.org/newvolume/pages/article.php?articleID=350 (accessed January 30, 2013).

Olson, Gary M., and Judith S. Olson. 2000. "Distance Matters." *Human Computer Interaction* 15:139–78.

Paul, Christiane. 2003. *Digital Art*. London: Thames & Hudson.

Pellegrinelli, Lara. 2008. "Silent Ravers Dance 'Together, But Individually.'" *All Things Considered*, NPR, September 18, http://www.npr.org/templates/story/story.php?storyId=94541066 (Accessed December 23, 2013).

Perlman, Marc. 2003. "Consuming Audio: An Introduction to Tweak Theory." In *Music and Technoculture*, ed. René T. A. Lysloff and Leslie C. Gay, 346–57. Middletown, CT: Wesleyan University Press.

Rafael, Vicente. 2003. "The Cell Phone and the Crowd." *Public Culture* 15(3):399–425.

Ramirez, Elva. 2010. "Deconstructing Nike's Music Shoe Video." *The Wall Street Journal*, "Speakeasy" blog, April 16, http://blogs.wsj.com/speakeasy/2010/04/16/deconstructing-ni kes-music-shoe-video/ (accessed January 31, 2013).

Rheingold, Howard. 2002. *Smart Mobs: The Next Social Revolution*. Cambridge, MA: Basic Books.

Schechner, Richard. 2002. *Performance Studies: An Introduction*. London: Routledge.

Schwabach, Aaron. 2011. *Fan Fiction and Copyright: Outsider Works and Intellectual Property Protection*. Farnham, Surrey: Ashgate.

Stanyek, Jason and Benjamin Piekut. 2010. "Deadness: Technologies of the Intermundane." *TDR (The Drama Review)* 54(1):14–38.

Steele, Claude. 2010. *Whistling Vivaldi: And Other Clues to How Stereotypes Affect Us*. New York: W.W. Norton & Company.

Terranova, Tiziana. 2000. "Free Labor: Producing Culture for the Digital Economy." *Social Text* 18(2):33–58.

Todd, Charlie, and Alex Scordelis. 2009. *Causing a Scene: Extraordinary Pranks in Ordinary Places with Improv Everywhere*. New York: HarperCollins.

Torode, Ameila. 2009. "New T-Mobile 'Flash Mob' Ad in Trafalgar Square," *Life Moves Pretty Fast* . . . (blog), May 1, http://ameliatorode.typepad.com/life_moves_pretty_fast/2009/05/new-tmobile-flash-mob-ad-in-trafalgar-sqaure.html (accessed February 1, 2013).

Transpontine, Neil. 2009a. "Pseudo Flashmob at Liverpool Street Station." *History Is Made at Night* (blog), January 17, http://history-is-made-at-night.blogspot.com/2009/01/pseudo-flashmob.html (accessed February 1, 2013).

——. 2009b. "Liverpool Street Closed by Silent Dance." *History Is Made at Night* (blog), February 7, http://history-is-made-at-night.blogspot.com/2009/02/liverpool-street-closed-by-silent-dance.html (accessed February 1, 2013).

Urry, John. 2007. *Mobilities*. Cambridge: Polity.

Winnubst, Shannon. 2007. "Make Yourself Useful!" in *Etiquette: Reflections on Contemporary Comportment*, ed. Ron Scapp and Brian Seitz, 151–62. Albany, NY: State University of New York Press.

Wu, Chin-Tao. 2002. *Privatising Culture: Corporate Art Intervention since the 1980s*. London: Verso.

# PART I

# FREQUENCY-RANGE AESTHETICS

# CHAPTER 2

·······························································································

# TREBLE CULTURE

·······························································································

## WAYNE MARSHALL

We've all had those times where we're stuck on the bus with some insuf-
ferable little shit blaring out the freshest offerings from Da Urban Classix
Colleckshun Volyoom: 53 (or whatevs) on a tinny set of Walkman phone
speakers. I don't really find that kind of music offensive, I'm just indifferent towards it but every time I hear something like this it just winds me up
how shit it sounds. Does audio quality matter to these kids? I mean, isn't
it nice to actually be able to hear all the different parts of the track going
on at a decent level of sound quality rather than it sounding like it was
recorded in a pair of socks?

—A commenter called "cassette"[1]

. . . do the missing data matter when you're listening on the train?

—Jonathan Sterne (2006a:339)

AT the end of the first decade of the twenty-first century, with the possibilities for
high-fidelity recording at a democratized high and "bass culture" more globally present
than ever, we face the irony that people are listening to music, with increasing frequency
if not ubiquity, primarily through small plastic speakers—most often via cellphones
but also, commonly, laptop computers and leaky earbuds.[2] This return to "treble culture," recalling the days of transistor radios or even gramophones and scratchy 78s, represents a techno-historical outcome of varying significance for different practitioners
and observers, the everyday inevitability of "tinny" transmissions appearing to affirm a
preference for convenience, portability, and publicity, even as a variety of critical listeners express anxiety about what might be lost along with frequencies that go unheard
(and, in the case of bass, unfelt). From cognitive and psychological studies seeking to
determine listeners' abilities to distinguish between different MP3 bitrates to audiophiles and "bass boosters" of all sorts lamenting not only missing frequencies but also
the ontological implications thereof to commuters complaining about noisy broadcasts
on public transport, there has already been a great deal of ink spilled over today's trebly
soundscapes.

Beyond obvious differences in preferred or dominant frequency ranges, what I am calling "treble culture" differs from what others have celebrated as "bass culture" in ways that deserve some explication.[3] While a number of scholars and enthusiasts have waved the banner of "bass culture," it remains underspecified. In general, the term describes a preference for and permeation of musical life by low-end frequencies, a set of aesthetic priorities pioneered by reggae producers and grounded in the centrality of massive sound systems to the genre. As ethnomusicologist Ken Bilby bears witness, recalling an experience in a small Jamaican bar which, despite its size, boasted a powerful set of speakers: "It was the loudest music I had ever heard—louder even than the overdriven Marshall amplifiers of a hard-rock concert, but with one main difference: the loudness was concentrated in the all-enveloping rumble of the bass rather than in the searing treble of live guitar-driven rock" (1995:148). For many observers and practitioners, the cultivation and experience of such rumbling bass force has crucial phenomenological effects. Michael Veal, in his book on dub, situates Jamaican music's remarkable and consistently expanding low-end bias in the context of entrepreneurial and competitive practices, as well as the power of the musical experience it produces: "Ever since the R&B and ska years, when sound system operators pushed their bass controls to full capacity in order to *thrill and traumatize* their audiences and have their sounds heard over the widest possible outdoor distances, the electric bass had grown in prominence in Jamaican music" (2007:32, my emphasis). And Steve Goodman, a lecturer in Music Culture at the University of East London (also known as DJ and producer Kode9), extends this idea to argue that the deployment of bass and sub-bass frequencies, particularly in sound system contexts, represents an exercise in "fear activated deliberately to be transduced and enjoyed in a popular musical context" (2009:29).

While their philosophical implications remain up to debate, these preferences and practices have migrated through and beyond the reggae diaspora, into hip-hop and kindred electronic popular dance genres, and such bass-ful experience might be said to constitute a "culture" at least insofar as people have developed and sought out sound systems capable of delivering these frequencies in such ordinary contexts as cars, homes, and movie theaters. Indeed, one could contend that recent trends in the "treblification" of audio culture are paralleled, if not dwarfed, by a more longstanding process of "bassification," including the increasing availability of subwoofers in consumer-grade stereo systems or headphones with frequency ranges that dip down to 20 Hz. It is precisely the coexistence of these parallel trends that makes the sudden (re)ascension of trebly listening practices so striking. This chapter thus poses "treble culture" as a suggestive foil to "bass culture" in order to think through contemporary debates around emerging mobile musical practices, but I don't mean to suggest that "treble culture" is any sort of *fait accompli*. Unlike in "bass culture," few people seem to consciously fetishize the trebleness of sound, instead tolerating and using it as part of a portable music culture. Nevertheless, whether or not current trends in "treblification" constitute something akin to way of life, it is telling that observers, especially of a critical persuasion, often employ the term *culture* when discussing such phenomena as kids listening to music on their mobile phones.[4]

This chapter examines recent trends in "treble culture" in the context of twentieth-century precedents as it attends to new practices emerging with digital devices, as well as to the debates around them: among others, the class issues and racially tinged discourses around public projection of mobile sound (or "noise"), the socialization of personal mobile technologies via communal listening, the aesthetic shifts initiated by new modes of listening, and the novel representational strategies on the part of producers and engineers to compose music that "works" through such devices. Focusing in particular on the paradox of filtering bass culture through treble culture, but also taking a broader view of the phenomenon, this chapter traces the cultural and historical contours of treble culture in three parts: (1) an ethnographic overview of the everyday and public dimensions of treble culture; (2) an historical narrative placing treble culture in the context of a century of sound reproduction; (3) an appraisal of the aesthetics informing and emerging from today's treble-some predicament.

## From Ghetto Blasts to Sodcasts

when I went to brasil 2 winters ago
I was really enthused by the fact I could hear funk everywhere in Rio
even though it was supposed to be more marginal
or at least that's what the newspapers were saying
Funk in the street, funk at the ice cream van
and more precisely
funk on the beach at Posto 9
on cell phones
loud cell phones[5]

Sodcasting (verb)—The act of playing music through the speaker on a mobile phone, usually on public transport. Commonly practiced by young people wearing polyester, branded sportswear with dubious musical taste.

*Delia was exposed to hip hop for the first time last Wednesday, when, on the 75 bus to Catford, a youth was sodcasting from the back seat.*[6]

Welcome or not, it has become an everyday experience, a commonplace the world over, especially in cities: a teenager, or a group of young people, broadcasting a tinny slice of pop in public.[7] From London to Stockholm, Boston to Bamako, today's mobile treble culture permeates urban soundscapes. For some, these thin transmissions add but another layer of noise to the daily din, and, though this is not always the case, such assessments do often politicize particular sounds and sonic practices in the ways that "noise" sometimes entails (Attali 1985; Rose 1994; Biddle 2007). When played to captive audiences on a bus or train, cellphone broadcasts can be perceived as annoying, even threatening. Critiques of such mobile music frequently express anxieties about the social order, about unruly, unsophisticated "chavs" and "sods," bringing class and race

and age either implicitly or explicitly into the debate. Others hear in treble culture a reclamation of public space and an impulse toward communal musicking (Hancox 2010).

Whether framed as social or anti-social activity, however, what seems beyond dispute is the utter ubiquity of treble culture today. Remarkably, for all its omnipresence,
the practice remains relatively undocumented. When I sought out examples of public
discussions of the cellphone as mobile sound system, I was able to find relatively little
in print, even as the subject seemed something of a settled matter, a cliché even. One
UK-based music journalist replied to my query, via Twitter: "all i can offer for now is the
'cliche' london kids listening to grime on their phones on the bus."[8] And, indeed, one of
the earliest print references I could locate documenting the practice was a significantly
neutral, if not mildly celebratory, article about the resourceful use of mobile phones
among London youth participating in the grime scene:[9]

> The success of a U.K. music genre known as grime, championed by the likes of Dizzee
> Rascal, has made rapping to mobile phones a popular pastime for a lot of British
> young people.
> On the street, cell phones enable impromptu rapping, or "spitting," over music
> played through speaker phones.
> If MCs or rappers want to try out their "bars," or rhymes, they can "flow" over
> beats played over the speaker phone. (Biddlecombe 2005)[10]

It is revealing that, at this point, the focus falls on the enthusiastic young users of the
technologies themselves, rather than on the beleaguered greater public, who, as I explore
later in this chapter, have increasingly become the louder voices in the current conversation about treble culture.

In the interest of offering more documentation than I could find in print, I polled
friends, colleagues, and readers of my blog and Twitter feed for anecdotes about cellphones as mobile sound systems.[11] Allow me to share a small sampling to give a sense of
the widespread nature of the practice, audible across the so-called developed and developing worlds alike, in rural and urban settings, and with positive, negative, and neutral
valences for participants and observers. One friend, living in Mali, emailed the following report:

> The cellphone is by far the most ubiquitous personal music player—I think I've seen
> maybe one iPod here so far, and very few walkmen or portable CD players. Many
> young men (and some women) walk (or drive, on moto-scooters) around with ear-
> buds in or hanging over their ears, in some cases just headphones for listening to
> music from their phones, in other cases earphones/microphones, for both phone
> calls and music. Small groups of people sitting on a corner drinking tea, or in a room
> waiting for dance rehearsal, will often be listening to music from someone's cell-
> phone, the tiny speakers straining (and often distorting) as they tinnily reproduce
> the sounds of Nahawa Doumbia, Oumou Sangare, Aaliyah, etc. Though iPhones
> and Blackberries are extremely rare, a large percentage of cell phones here can
> serve as MP3 players, and have bluetooth connections—generally someone trans-
> fers songs from computer to phone via bluetooth (at a cyber cafe), and the tracks are

then shared from one phone to another via bluetooth.  Not surprisingly, one thus also hears all kinds of amusing snippets as ring tones—usually Western songs, even though the full songs people play from their phones are more often by Malian artists. A fair number of phones here also pick up radio and/or television (with extendable antenna) or play videos—more trebly, tinny reproductions.[12]

In contrast, a colleague in New York shared a more ambivalent account, one which subtly and not so subtly touches on issues of race, class, and age:

> In the subway, I feel tortured. Since I was a teen I've been pretty good at tuning out subway noise—preachers, boomboxes etc. But I find it harder to tune out the music leaking out of people's nasty little earbuds.
>
> I can pick individual songs out! Or at the very least the genre—the insistent high hats and cymbal smashing of speed metal, the exasperating dembow of reggaetón, the electronic loops of T-Pain voiced pop, the plink of bachata guitar. I never seem to be bothered by singer-songwriter stuff, or shoegaze rock or classical. Is it because of the tones or because those people never crank it up to 11?
>
> Worse, because it seems like a deliberate invasion of soundspace, is people listening to music on their cellphones in the subway. One, what exactly is it that people HEAR through those eeny meeny speakers? To me, it sounds just short of AM radio static. And then, because of the subway, people have to crank it up, further distorting whatever they're listening to. If I actually LIKE the song, it just ruins it for me. If I don't, it's enough to drive me to subway rage.
>
> I know that some of this is old-lady "dag-nab kids" complaining, but even with lots of punk and Motorhead concerts under my belt, I keep thinking, isn't this messing up their hearing? And why oh why do I need to hear the most piercing notes from ten speed metal songs in a row? Sometimes, it's not even the guy next to me, but the girl like ten feet away. If I can hear that, what the heck are they hearing?[13]

Although one might expect such sonic leakage on the subway, trebly emissions have become so commonplace that one encounters them even in contexts when greater sonic definition would seem desirable. Producer Ghislain Poirier admits that, unlikely as it would seem, laptops have become the new "boomboxes" in the bass-centric music circles in which he travels. As a result, a fair amount of guesswork infuses the listening process today, including the sort of specialist listening practiced by keen-eared DJs and workers in the recording industry:

> It's common in my circle to judge music, bass music I should say, through laptop speakers, even if we don't hear the bass. We just guess where it is. I've seen that with DJs, producers and labels peoples. Primarily because the laptop is right there in your face, it's the main object you work with…. When you travel and meet people on the road, the laptop is the boombox.[14]

And yet despite how it suffuses urban experience, today's treble culture is by no means restricted to cities. As cellphones and laptops have become everyday listening devices everywhere, they can be heard wanly but effectively propelling group activity in rather unlikely circumstances, especially when hi-fi alternatives are not available. One colleague wrote to share a story about a family reunion in a remote part of Wyoming:

> We traditionally have a dance when we get together. This time we were in cabins in Nowhere, Wyoming sans electricity. Folks hadn't really thought out the music piece of this beforehand. My youngest sister was in charge of the jams and pulled out her laptop. Those inclined to dance hung around her in a tight circle, trying to stay close enough to reasonably hear the not-booming built-in speaker.[15]

These stories affirm my own everyday experiences over the last several years, in meatspace and cyberspace, witnessing a sort of treble culture in full bloom whether via dance videos on YouTube where the soundtrack is clearly provided by a tinny device or in mundane encounters on the streets and subways of Cambridge and Chicago.[16] I recall, among other notable examples, watching a trio of dancers take a break from the powerful sound system of a Boston nightclub by gathering outside around an iPhone playing a Bee Gees song, possibly streaming from a YouTube video (and hence with added degrees of bass attenuation, as I will discuss in the next section). And a remarkable percentage of teens I pass on the sidewalks of Cambridge—especially, but not exclusively, when in groups or pairs—include at least one person broadcasting a trebly slice of hiphop, r&b, reggae, or reggaeton. Given the apparent lack of attention to whatever song is playing, the practice sometimes seems to serve an ambient function, maintaining pop's presence in their lives (and, whether I like it or not, mine), especially by keeping the latest hits in the air. In doing so, these "expressive youth," as Christian Licoppe would call them, also project a sense of selfhood, neighborhood, or even nationhood, the blasting cellphone serving as an important if often unremarked bit of accompaniment, marking them as hip or brash much as a particular ringtone might or—via visual cues—a fresh fitted cap or a pair of trendy jeans.[17] Like the bass-riddled rattling of car trunks, which, amidst and against treble culture, maintain a strong sonic presence in the streets of my city and many others, these distorting pieces of plastic serve as announcement, accompaniment, and accessory alike.

More than their affront to high fidelity, however, it is these devices' ability to call attention to themselves, to bleed outward from the immediate group (or individual) into shared social spaces, which most raises the ire of certain observers. For a variety of reasons, including population density, diversity, and relative levels of development and privilege (i.e., broad access to mobile electronics), the UK—and London in particular—has been the site of a great deal of hand-wringing over treble culture, as well as celebration of it. In the debates that have ensued, questions of class and race frequently come to the fore. An article in *The Guardian* about commuting, for instance, contains a complaint from a bus-rider who not only imagines a violent response to any requests to turn the music down but seems to racialize the threat as well:

> Jennifer van Schoor, a freelance graphic designer in London, says endless roadworks have made her consistently late for work in the past few months. "Often I get off the

bus and have to walk, but I resent having to do that because I've paid £90 a month for my travelcard."

A recent increase in aggression and noise pollution on buses hasn't helped. "Either I'm listening to someone talking on her mobile about how she's broken up with her boyfriend, or I've got some little pipsqueak next to me who's playing some 'doosh-de-de-doosh' music. If I say anything, who knows—maybe he's going to stab me." (Viney 2008)

Affirming this sentiment, some London commuters based in the borough of Enfield began a "Music Free Bus Campaign," calling for a total ban of music on buses, motivated by fears that direct complaints to treble-casting kids about public noise could result in physical or verbal violence. One of the organizers of the campaign shared his frustration with a local newspaper, conjuring a gang of teenagers in order to set an intimidating scene: "People think they can sit on a bus and blast music out, and when you ask them to turn it down you get the abuse, especially from teenagers. I am not surprised people do not say anything because if I saw a group of seven or eight people playing music I would not go up to them, but if TfL [Transport for London] advertised it on the bus, we could point to the sign to show them it is not permitted."[18]

Although sometimes couched in subtle or euphemistic language, the conversation about trebly transmissions on public transport frequently opens into debates about race and class. Consider, for example, an exchange at drownedinsound.com, a UK-based music webzine and forum, which recently hosted a discussion of contemporary sound quality and, inevitably, of "music on buses." One commenter explicitly connects the "chav's [sic] walking around playing music through their phone's [sic] speakers" to earlier figurations of race, space, and noise, opining that today's cellphone-infused soundscape "is really no different to the eighties when people used to walk around with a 'ghetto blaster' on their shoulder."[19] Whether race or class is implicitly or explicitly invoked, however, the valence is not always necessarily negative. As another commenter added to the same discussion thread, "I like kids playing tunes off their mobiles":

> Where I live they mostly play Grime, Funky or Dancehall so its [sic] actually a good way to keep up with new tunes. I think sound quality does still matter to a lot of people, but of course it depends on context and financial circumstances. Playing music on the bus is about showing off, not actually listening so it doesn't really matter how it sounds.[20]

It is telling that the genres named here are all associated with London's black underclass. For the defenders of so-called "sodcasting," a condescending pun which journalist Dan Hancox calls "a pretty horrible, New Labour-esque neologism," part of the appeal of today's trebly public soundings is, at least in part, due to their militant projection of music that carries a certain charge in a postcolonial, multicultural society. For Hancox, the practice represents "much more than anti-social territorialism"; rather, for him, given the context of legal and technological enclosure whereby the Metropolitan Police Service of Greater London single out "black music" as the target of their actions, "sodcasting represents a vital, politicised re-socialisation of public culture, through the collective enjoyment of music."[21]

UK-based author and blogger Owen Hatherley appears to agree with Hancox, at least in part and in spirit. In February 2008, he mounted a "(partial) defence" of sodcasting on his blog. Hatherley's sympathetic account is motivated by a recognition of a kind of inherent communality that works against the grain of individualized, isolated musical experience, as well as by an aversion to the barely veiled racism at the heart of so much criticism of the practice:

> That [i.e., "sodcasting"] being the apparent neologism for the recent phenomenon of bus passengers, usually young and in the euphemism of the day 'urban', playing music from their phones or iPods out loud rather than on headphones.... By all means, the chap with Newham Generals [a local rap group] blaring out at the back of the bus will be enormously irritating to most folk without interest in such things. Yet: doesn't this go against so many of the trends in how music is listened to and consumed (*iPod*, *My*Space, etc etc)? The aforementioned public broadcaster *wants everyone else to hear the music*. It would actually sound more powerful, more bass-heavy, more audiophile to listen to it on the headphones rather than screeching out of a tiny, tinny speaker. It's not for his own benefit, it's for everyone else. Sure, there's a fuck-you, anti-social element to that, which is the only element anyone seems to have noticed. But isn't there also an attempt, doomed obviously to failure, to make the music public again, to have it listened to outside, in groups? You can see a hint of that when it's a group, rather than one person, listening together to the bleeps coming out of the mini-speakers over the rickety roar of the bus.[22]

Notably, some of the comments on Hatherly's post reenact the very prejudices that he assails as "euphemistic." Take, for instance, two successive comments, one apparently issuing from the UK (note the disparaging reference to "West Midlands"), the other from Ontario (and hence explaining the use of the term "aboriginal," rather than, say, "urban"):

> a very public sociologist said...
> Music played off mobile phones sounds incredibly naff. In my experience the kids who play always seem to insist upon those really irritating urban grooves that feature munchkins on the vocals. Is this just a West Midlands thing? Do fans of a particular genre of music have a propensity toward exposing us to their taste?

> cain_devera said...
> Yes they do, or at least where I live; rap is almost exclusively the music that people play loud and 'obtrusively' on buses, which also happens to be played mostly by poorer teenagers, usually aboriginal.

For all the casual racism and class prejudice that creep into the pubic debate, not all complaints and worries about being assaulted by teenagers asked to turn their music down are groundless, though, again, I have found little beyond anecdotal evidence to confirm such claims. Commenting on Dan Hancock's post about sodcasting, Tan Copsey frames the practice as "a means of creating confrontation": "I've seen it used as a prelude to threats of both normal and sexual violence. Can be especially nasty for women who dare complain." Finessing his point to address the question of reclamation of public space celebrated by the likes of Hancox and Hatherley, Copsey adds:

> Public spaces like this have to be negotiated not reclaimed. Sadly in my experience most people playing music do not respond well to requests to turn off their music from others. I think if another member of the public asks you to you have a responsibility to take their concerns seriously. In my experience most people don't seem to and on a number of occasions this has resulted in pretty nasty verbal threats from those playing music.[23]

Obviously context is crucial. Other anecdotes attest to the community-building effects that can emerge from making due with the trebly resources at hand. Gabriel Heatwave, a London-based reggae DJ, left a comment on my blog describing a recent scene in which his phone stood at the center of a communal, social moment:

> I was at a festival recently, and about 4 in the morning when the stages were shutting down, we ended up sitting round listening to tunes on my mobile phone. Someone showed me that if you put the phone in a paper/plastic cup it amplifies the speaker output and gives it more bass. It made a big difference, though it wasn't Stone Love [a popular Jamaican sound system] or anything still. We called it rave in a cup:-)[24]

As this vignette reminds us, occurring immediately after some serious immersion in bass culture, few people listen to music exclusively in trebly circumstances. Rather, as my attempts at ethnography seem to illustrate, a range of life contexts determine the degree of low or mid-range frequencies audible and present.

What emerges as salient across all these accounts is the insistent, if not insurgent, importance of portability—frequently trumping fidelity—to the ways we listen to and share music. As much as we seem to want our music rich in frequencies and full of dynamics, we also clearly want it to be mobile. These competing desires draw us into a basic dialectic of the history of the recording industry, or—more broadly even—of the history of recording and transmitting sound. Indeed, reaching back to the dawn of sound reproduction, we can observe a steady, alternating march between what Greg Milner calls "perfecting sound forever" and making music mobile (often by making it trebly). As early as the 1910s, Milner notes, when choosing between Thomas Edison's cylinders and his competitors' discs, "the typical music buyer was willing to forgo some elusive sonic pedigree for the convenience and lower cost of discs" (2009:47).

# A Brief History of Fidelity versus Portability

> The history of sound reproduction in the twentieth century is not, as sales literature might suggest, a story of ever increasing fidelity, and it may very well also not be a history of audiences who really care about greater fidelity. Even the quite notable increases in sonic definition are really a side-story. Recording has both space- and time-binding characteristics. And the more remarkable story of sound reproduction in the last hundred years is a spatial story, about how recorded and transmitted sound became more portable and suffused an ever growing segment of people's everyday lives, both during hours of waking and during hours of sleep.
>
> —Jonathan Sterne (2006a:345)

Media scholar Jonathan Sterne's contention that portability has mattered as much as fidelity in the history of sound reproduction is instructive if we seek to put today's treble culture into context. Rather than representing the embrace of compressed digital audio and tinny mobile devices as an aberration, scholarship on the history of sound reproduction bears witness to a longstanding if not fundamental dynamic between making music as big and rich and full as possible (whether guided by ideals of sonic realism or studio-abetted surrealism) and making music more easily transmitted. Given contemporary anxieties over "treble culture," whether concerned with public noise (as detailed in the previous section) or with ontological and phenomenological loss (as I'll discuss in the next), it seems crucial to recount the various ways that music, in its ongoing dance with production and transmission technologies, has become trebly over the course of the last century. One might go so far as to contend that the history of recorded sound to date, especially at the so-called "consumer" end, is one in which treble predominates. So, how did we get here? Let us count the ways.

Before discussing technologies of sound reproduction per se, we might begin with the humbling fact that our ears themselves are, in present day lingo, "lossy." This recognition can be traced back at least to sound reproduction pioneer Thomas Edison, himself hard of hearing, who would literally sink his teeth into the wooden bodies of his phonograph prototypes in order to better "hear" what they were playing. As Greg Milner relays, "[Edison's] research had convinced him that the three small bones in the ear that convey sound waves from the middle ear to the inner ear were strikingly inefficient. 'There is a good deal of lost motion in those bones,' he said. 'Part of every sound wave that enters the ear is lost before it reaches the inner ear'" (2009:40). Edison's teeth remind us that, regardless of the various sorts of loss occurring throughout the sound reproduction process (not to mention the biological and psychoacoustic dimensions of listening), people have a remarkable ability to naturalize what they hear as possessing fullness and depth, never mind verisimilitude, despite how frequency-impoverished a recording, or listening experience, may be.[25] To take another early example, when Valdemar Poulson, the "Danish Edison," unveiled his telegraphone in Paris in 1900, "People heard its tinny, fragile sounds, and remarked on how natural they were" (109). The tendency for audiences at "tone test" concerts in the early days of phonographs and gramophones to be gleefully "tricked" into being unable to distinguish between a live performer and a recording serves as testament to the commonplace acts of self-deception or auto-correction inherent to the listening process. Notably, such reactions are not limited to the dawn of the era of sound reproduction. As Milner recounts in *Perfecting Sound Forever* (2009), such scenes play out over and over again throughout the twentieth century—beginning with demonstrations by the likes of Edison and Poulson, continuing with Bell Labs and electrical recording in the 30s, Ampex and magnetic tape in the 50s, and up through the debut of compact discs in the 80s—and indeed, we might see recent tests of college students' perception of MP3 compression rates as but the latest instance of our abiding interest in the ability to appreciate audio fidelity (Salimpoor et al. 2007; Pras et al. 2009; Spence [Berger] 2009).

We might proceed then from the acknowledgement, perhaps surprising to some, that access to audible, never mind palpable, bass frequencies via sound recordings is, really, a relatively recent development and perhaps remains as much a luxury today—requiring powerful equipment and thus, typically, a trip to a club or concert venue—as it always has been. Along these lines, another basic point to bear in mind, as Fletcher and Munson proved in the 1930s, is that lower frequencies actually need to be louder than higher ones in order to sound equally loud to a listener. Some playback equipment compensates in this manner, using Fletcher-Munson curves—think of the "bass boost" button on a Walkman or a home or car stereo system. Magic buttons or no, this sonic principle reminds us how important volume—and hence context—can be in determining the overall balance between treble and bass. Today's commonplace personal listening scenarios can often mean that "real" bass—the sort that produces palpable, not just audible, vibrations—is a rarity. Listening to low bitrate MP3s on cellphones is, however, only the latest scenario. Frequency attenuation has been a recurring issue in the history of musical media—sometimes due to limitations of recording or reproduction technology, sometimes as a choice on the part of people who prioritize portability. "Every time the signal got clearer," Sterne reminds, "artists, musicians and engineers sought out new methods of distortion. And every time the bandwidth grew, engineers looked for new ways to make recorded or transmitted sound more mobile, more flexible and more ever present" (2006a:345). To put a fairly fine point on it, he continues: "The history of digital audio is only partly a story about the definition of sound. It is also a history of transmission" (345). This contention motivates the present section of this chapter, an attempt to sketch out the intertwined histories of definition and transmission in sound reproduction technologies and the degree to which we have always lived in a certain state of "treble culture." As such, we will take into account recording technology (from acoustic to electric to digital), sound media (records, cassettes, CDs, MP3s, etc.), and listening devices (e.g., radios, hi-fi—and lo-fi—home stereo systems, walkmen, iPods, cellphones and laptops).

That trebly emissions are a longstanding phenomenon, predating the digital by decades, is probably not news to many. Indeed, a contemporary notion of "treble culture" only makes sense in reference to the more recent rise of "bass culture" (especially since the rise of home and automotive hi-fi systems). Cylinders, 78s, and other early sound media are well known for their tinny qualities. That such media initially carried only acoustically produced recordings, prior to the advent of electrical means in the 20s (i.e., microphones and amplifiers), only further muted any semblance of bass. Fewer recognize that 33rpm LPs and even 45rpm singles are themselves subject to physical limitations on the amount of bass they encode (an irony given how the 45 was, for decades, reggae's primary medium—not to mention acetate "dubplates"). It was not until the appearance of the 12" single in the 70s—a development informed by, and encouraging, the practice of disco DJs—that a record's grooves were wide enough to accommodate a dynamic range permitting a level of bass presence that did not require additional amplification per se. Because deep grooves were difficult to manage prior to the 12" and because a stylus has inherent difficulty picking up sounds in the mid-to-high range, records were often purposely made more trebly. Interestingly, foreshadowing today's debates about aesthetics in the age of "sizzling" MP3s (as we will explore in the next section), audio equipment expert E. Brad Meyer (1996) argues that these frequency-response errors end up "crucial" to the LP's very "musicality":

> Many links in the recording chain, including the microphones, were designed with LPs in mind, so many master tapes are too bright in the upper midrange and lower treble. The LP system tends to tame that hardness. Otherwise, the sound is always mildly irritating, and the listener is slightly but constantly repelled, making it very hard to relax and enjoy the music. (quoted in Milner 2009:229)

Due to such technical constraints, even when electrical equipment made it possible to record and amplify bass frequencies, producers would continue to push high frequencies while reducing lows, and playback equipment compensated by boosting bass via a built-in amplifier (or "pre-amp"). Gronow and Saunio, historians of the record industry, explain how this procedure could, nevertheless, serve to improve dynamics and sonic definition:

> With the advent of electrical recording, the record company engineers began consciously manipulating the recording characteristics of their equipment. Strong bass notes, which could now be captured with the microphone, could easily destroy the groove of the recording. On the other hand the surface noise of a record is strongest in the high frequencies, which the improved amplifiers were now picking up. It was thus necessary to attenuate the low frequencies in recording, and boost the treble. When the record was played, the amplifier performed the same operation in reverse. Thus it was possible to improve the dynamics of the records and reduce background hiss. (1998:56)

The rise of the bassier record pre-amp notwithstanding, the tendency to produce trebly recordings was exacerbated in the age of transistor radios, especially during the 1960s.

Sensitive to consumers' primary listening contexts, popular producers such as the UK's Joe Meek, Phil Spector (of "Wall of Sound" fame), and Berry Gordy of Motown pushed treble further to the fore. As Greg Milner describes it:

> One of the keystones of this new consumer youth culture was the emergence of the portable transistor radio. And Meek and Spector's blatant quest for hits led both of them to make music that sounded like it belonged there. Their music, and indeed most of the pop music of the era, was purposefully produced to sound optimal on an AM station as heard through a tiny speaker. That's why so much of the music sounds excessively tinny to us today.... Meek and Spector embraced this new world as individual auteurs, but if there was one label that collectively institutionalized a radio-ready aesthetic, it was Motown. (2009:154–55)[26]

This techno-historical moment calls attention once again to the give-and-take between high fidelity and portability; in particular, it reminds us of the central role that so-called consumers—or perhaps consumer electronics manufacturers—have played in affecting the very process of recording and the aesthetics of popular music. It also moves us toward a consideration of the dialectics between a particular historical moment's popular listening technologies and its range of aesthetic positions, a dynamic we will consider in greater detail with regard to today's treble culture in the next section.[27]

The importance of radio in pushing music further into the treble range brings us back to the crucial question of what happens to sound at the listener-end of the process—that is, how sound which has been recorded and rendered to media again becomes audible. At various points in the chain from producer to receiver, a recording might be mediated by a variety of transmission channels, media, and playback devices, all of which can have effects on the sound. Radio, including both AM and FM, introduces a variety of its own technical limitations, not to mention the distorting effects—especially with regard to dynamic range—of various kinds of compression (especially, in recent years, a la the "loudness war").[28] These effects extend to other popular broadcast media: television, of course, and more recently a host of "streaming" sites and services via the Internet. Not only do such broadcast technologies frequently impose their own degree of compression to keep levels even, but the equipment used to receive them—whether a TV set, a portable radio, a home stereo-system or boombox, computer speakers (including, in particular, those built-into laptops), or mobile devices (especially phones) and their leaky earbuds—also tend to feature, with the exception of "hi-fi" systems, less-than-impressive speakers, introducing additional layers of attenuation to the playback process. In the case of laptops and their built-in speakers, which increasingly mediate a great swath of everyday musical experience (at least for the laptopped classes), bass suffers particularly. In the age of streaming audio via the Internet and smartphones, moreover, listeners are as likely to listen to a song via a site such as YouTube or MySpace (which also further compress audio content). Compression and attenuation compound, over and over again, and the more mobile music becomes, typically the more trebly too.[29]

This brings us, finally, to the import of digital audio to treble culture. Here we should return to the work of Jonathan Sterne, who again offers a historical corrective that may seem more persuasive in light of the time line noted previously: "Audiophiles may consider digital audio—especially in its compressed form—as a giant step backward in a story of ever increasing sonic definition, but that story of progress never really quite happened" (2006a:345). Instead, Sterne offers an altogether different orientation with regard to digital audio: "Regardless of whether potential definition is increased or compromised in a particular form, digital audio is incredibly mobile and incredibly social" (346). Moreover, for all the complaints about the lossy qualities of compressed digital audio, it is important to note that MP3s and their ilk do not necessarily privilege treble over bass. Rather, both low and high frequencies—and plenty in between—can be removed during the encoding process, which uses what Sterne calls three "psycho-acoustic acoustic tricks" to reduce the size of the files. Sterne's lucid explanation of these three procedures, what he calls "auditory masking, temporal masking and spatialization," is worth quoting at some length as he helpfully demystifies a little understood but ubiquitous technology:

> Auditory masking is the elimination of similar frequencies, based on the principle that when two sounds of similar frequency are played together and one is significantly quieter, people will hear only the louder sound. Temporal masking is a similar principle across time: if there are two sounds very close together in time (less than about five milliseconds apart, depending on the material) and one is significantly louder than the other, listeners can only hear the louder sound. The third principle is spatialization. While it is very easy to locate the direction of sounds in the middle of the audible range when they are played back in stereo, it is close to impossible for people to locate very low or very high sounds. To save more dataspace, the mp3 encoder saves sounds at either end of the frequency spectrum only once for both channels, rather than twice and plays them back as mono files. Since most human adults cannot hear above 16khz, some mp3 encoders also throw out all the data from 16–20khz to save even more space. Psychoacoustically, the mp3 is designed to throw away sonic material that listeners supposedly would not hear otherwise. (2006b:834–85)

To illustrate the rather incredible bag of tricks this is, Greg Milner notes that "between 80 and 90% of the music is simply discarded" (2009:357) in the conversion to MP3 (or AAC, the iTunes default, as well as other compressed formats). For Sterne, the MP3 thus contains in its very code "a whole philosophy of audition" which exploits or even celebrates "the limitations of healthy human hearing" (2006b:828). But again, a lot of the so-called "loss" that results from the encoding process is inconsequential—a point which no doubt rankles the same audiophiles who might bemoan the loss of transients or "presence" in moving from vacuum tubes to solid state or 16 tracks to 24.[30] "The key point," argues Sterne, "is that while traditionally, sound reproduction technologies have been theorized in terms of their relation of absolute fidelity to a sound source, the human ear is not capable of such fine distinctions. In fact, people can lose most of the vibrations in a recorded sound and still hear it as roughly the same sound as the version with no data compression. This is the principle upon which the mp3 rests" (2006b:834).

What this underscores about the MP3 is that its very design dovetails with the preference for portability and with the diverse, often "imperfect" listening contexts that have come to define everyday musical experience in the first decade of the twenty-first century. And yet, as with previous patterns in this give and take between fidelity and portability, we find plenty of detractors among the critical observers of contemporary audio design. John Atkinson, editor of *Stereophile*, a magazine devoted to high fidelity sound and the expensive equipment that makes it possible, expressed his frustrations with this pendulum swing toward portability in a February 2005 newsletter:

> One of the factors that has increasingly marginalized the high-end audio industry is the lack of attention paid to sound quality in the music industry: If there's no more quality to be retrieved from an overcompressed, overequalized, overprocessed, underdithered, underperforming MP3 than can be obtained from playback on a computer via a pair of pitiful plastic PC speakers, then why should anyone bother with putting together a high-performance audio system?[31]

Atkinson is quite clearly at odds with Sterne's central contention that the MP3's design favoring "easy exchange, easy storage and maximum portability" is not an aberration in the history of recorded sound but rather that such a product "has been a long-term goal in the design of sound reproduction technologies" (2006a:345). Then again, Sterne's argument is precisely that the MP3 was designed not with a hi-fi setting in mind but "to be heard via headphones while outdoors, in a noisy dorm room, in an office with a loud computer fan, in the background as other activities are taking place and through low-fi or mid-fi computer speakers" (2006b:835).

Interestingly, Atkinson's audiophile aversion to the MP3 finds shared skepticism among unlikely allies. Steve Goodman, author of *Sonic Warfare* (2009), contends that, "just as there is 'expert decision' making going on behind the supposedly psychoacoustic criteria involved in perceptual coding of mp3s that favors certain average frequencies over others... there is a politics of frequency that permeates the whole technical ecology of sound recording, storage and playback devices."[32] Rather than audiophilia, however, Goodman's comments are motivated by a studied distrust of the intersections between the military-industrial complex and sound reproduction technologies. If our present moment of treble culture can be characterized as one of "ubiquitous music," Goodman fingers corporations such as Muzak for initiating, "our submersion into a generalized surround sound culture, the insidious purr of control and the digital modulation of affective tonality that smoothes the experience of the ecology of fear" (2009:144). As a producer working in and across genres that privilege bass frequencies, Goodman's suspicious take on contemporary "politics of frequency" is directly connected to his immersion and participation in bass culture.

Notably, as it has provided a locus for a great deal of conversation and contestation over the public nature of treble culture, the United Kingdom—and London in particular—has also, as a crucial node in the Jamaican diaspora and reggae industry, long served as a central site in global bass culture. Over the last decade, playing to what Greg Milner calls our "twenty-first-century ears" (2009:11), producers from London and the greater United Kingdom—and, of course, in musical metropoles the world over—have been among those who have embraced both the possibilities and limitations of contemporary treble culture, squeezing and filtering and creatively representing bass "weight" through today's commonplace technologies of circulation and listening.

# Blog House, Ringtone Rap, and Bass Imagination

> Constant copying erodes data storage, degrading image and sound, overwhelming the signal of media content with the noise produced by the means of reproduction.... In this way, piracy creates an aesthetic, a set of formal qualities that generates a particular sensorial experience of media marked by poor transmission, interference, and noise.
>
> —Brian Larkin (2004:190–91)

> The odd angles and eerie spaces in productions by Mannie Fresh or Mr Collipark were flattened out, replaced by portentous digi-synth fanfares and lumbering beats, a brittle bass-less blare that seemed pre-degraded to 128kbps to cut through better via YouTube and mobile phone ("ringtone rap", some called it).
>
> —Simon Reynolds (2009)

Regardless of the codec or medium in question, ultimately all sound must be processed by our ears, our bodies, and our brains, all of which entail physiological and enculturated processes. Jonathan Sterne's provocative contention that the MP3 "plays its listener" (2006b:835) offers a stark acknowledgement of all the work that goes on in our heads when we listen—and how much of that work might be done for us before the act of listening even begins. But an attention to the act of listening (never mind dancing) to MP3s, or to any music emanating from the tinny speakers of a laptop or cellphone, extends beyond psychoacoustics and into the realm of culture and aesthetics. As popular practice bears witness and as several studies have shown, plenty of people have happily accepted the ubiquity of the MP3 (Salimpoor et al. 2007; Pras et al. 2009; Spence [Berger] 2009). Indeed, some—including musicians and other "expert" listeners—actually prefer the telltale "sizzle" of (relatively) low bitrate digital audio, recalling how their peers with 1960s ears gravitated toward Motown's radio-ready sound. Moreover, following in the footsteps of producers like Berry Gordy and Phil Spector, and their many acolytes over the years, contemporary producers sometimes explicitly work with today's trebly media in mind, transposing "bass" lines into higher octaves or shaping synthesizer patches so that they seem to come to life when broadcast from a thin piece of plastic. Listening to bass culture through treble culture at the close of the first decade of the twenty-first century, we can behold a set of aesthetic preferences and procedures bridging the wide worlds of hip-hop and r&b, reggae and dubstep, techno and house, and a wide variety of contemporary genres and styles—some of which, like "blog house" or "ringtone rap," have acquired snarky monikers describing their sonic profiles and primary listening contexts. Tracing the contours of this feedback loop between producers and listeners, our exploration of aesthetics in today's treble culture will consider two main questions and their implications: 1) the resurgent concern with quality or fidelity and, in particular, of the audibility (or not) of digital artifacts; 2) how producers appear to be working with new listening technologies and contexts, rather than struggling against them.

Let's begin with an entertaining and instructive conversation between New Yorker music critic Sasha Frere-Jones and Radiohead guitarist Jonny Greenwood:

SASHA FRERE-JONES:   Is the MP3 a satisfactory medium for your music?

JONNY GREENWOOD:   They sound fine to me. They can even put a helpful crunchiness onto some recordings. We listened to a lot of nineties hip-hop during our last album, all as MP3s, all via AirTunes. They sounded great, even with all that technology in the way. MP3s might not compare that well to a CD recording of, say, string quartets, but then, that's not really their point.

SFJ:   Do you ever hear from your fans about audio fidelity?

JG:   We had a few complaints that the MP3s of our last record wasn't [sic] encoded at a high enough rate. Some even suggested we should have used FLACs, but if you even know what one of those is, and have strong opinions on them, you're already lost to the world of high fidelity and have probably spent far too much money on your speaker-stands.

SFJ:   Do you think any of the MP3 generation—ten- to twenty-five-year-olds—want a higher quality experience?

JG:   No. That comes later. It's those thirty-something men who lurk in hi-fi shops, discussing signal purity and oxygen-free cables and FLACs. I should know—I was very nearly one of them.

SFJ:   What are your feelings about the various audio formats?

JG:   Sonic quality is important. I'd feel frustrated if we couldn't release CDs as a band, but then, it only costs us a slight shaving of sound quality to get to the convenience of the MP3. It's like putting up with tape hiss on a cassette. I was happy using cassettes when I was fifteen, but I'm sure they were sneered at in their day by audiophiles. If I'm on a train, with headphones, MP3s are great. At home, I prefer CD or vinyl, partly because they sound a little better in a quiet room and partly because they're finite in length and separate things, unlike the endless days and days of music stored on my laptop. (Frere-Jones 2009)

What I would like to highlight here is the guitarist's attention to specific listening contexts and, in particular, his mention of a "helpful crunchiness" offered by MP3s. Figuring the MP3 in this manner, as a format with distinctive and even preferable timbral qualities, underscores how the MP3 has become an object of aesthetic value in its own right, embodying a particular moment in techno-historical time, a periodized sound. In this sense, one might appreciate the "crunchy" qualities of an MP3 alongside its predecessors in musical media. Listeners have, of course, long enjoyed—and even fetishized—the sound of a particular medium. The crackle of a dusty record, for instance, is prized by vinyl lovers and became a signpost of authenticity among hip-hop producers in the 1990s (Marshall 2002, 2006), and in recent years even cassette hiss has found its nostalgists and recuperators (Link 2001; Keenan 2009).

For the MP3 generation—and it is telling that Greenwood and Frere-Jones make explicit reference to age in their conversation (not to mention gender)—the audible artifacts of bitrate compression can add a bit of desirable "crunch" or "sizzle" to recordings. Through the wonders of habituation, such timbral effects, however subtle, have rapidly been naturalized as downright constitutive of the sound of music today. In other words, the very things that may be anathema to "those thirty-something men who lurk in hi-fi shops" are the same qualities which have engendered an actual aesthetic preference for many. Notably, while some studies have demonstrated that listeners from a variety of backgrounds—in particular, "expert" listeners (i.e., people with years of musical training or practice)—are not only able to distinguish but indeed prefer "CD quality" audio to low bitrate MP3 files (up to 192kbps), others have suggested that this preference can swing in the other direction, especially among young people (i.e., college students).[33] Testing and polling his students over an eight year period by playing them different encodings of the same song, Stanford music professor Jonathan Berger found "not only that MP3s were not thought of as low quality" but that "over time there was a rise in preference for MP3s" and, more specifically, for what Berger calls their telltale "sizzle" or "metallic" sound (quoted in Spence 2009).

Since the naturalization of MP3 "sizzle" and the widespread adoption of "tinny" listening devices, musicians and producers have had to grapple with this predicament.[34] For those who see no choice but to embrace music's contemporary technological circumstances, opportunities for tailoring music to treble culture arise both during the production phase—with regard to the type of sounds used and frequencies foregrounded—and in mastering (i.e., the stage at which loudness and particular frequency bands can be boosted and refined). Among other anecdotes, I was told of engineers being asked by the bands they recorded to master the music not necessarily *for* MySpace but in order to sound *like* MySpace.[35] And Steve Goodman / Kode9 affirmed, from his perspective as head of the Hyperdub label, that "tracks get EQd and mastered with [treble culture] in mind, to make the tracks brighter than you might think is necessary or comfortable to listen to in the studio."[36] In this way, contemporary producerly practices recall the radio-friendly approaches of Spector and Gordy in the 1960s, not to mention the legion of producers who have continued to mix and master for automotive stereo systems and other everyday listening contexts.[37] Studio equipment manufacturers have themselves gotten into the game, marketing products to producers that offer, as in the case of Avantone MixCubes, "the ability to hear what your mixes will sound like on bass-challenged real-world systems such as computers, televisions, car stereos, and iPod docking stations." Such products acknowledge in their pitch that listening contexts in the "real world" are far from the ideal audio environments in many studios: "Mini reference monitors, like the MixCubes, give you an idea of what your mix will sound like in real-world listening situations—like stock TV and computer speakers, and basic car stereos, and earbuds. If you want to create a professional-sounding mix that will translate everywhere, you've got to give it the real-world test."[38]

Of course, while some producers have actively mixed their music for MP3 players, MySpace, and mobile phones, others eschew altogether any attempt to tailor—never mind distort—their productions to meet current expectations or for inferior media. In the notes for a recent release, for example, Robert Henke, aka electronic producer Monolake, makes explicit that: "The music on this album has not been compressed, limited or maximized at any production stage." Henke's explanation for his decision to depart from convention blames trebly technologies, old and new, for destroying any room for dynamics, and he is rather frank about the limitations of cellphones as listening devices—shortcomings that, at least for this particular project, would not suit the detailed textures of his music:

> Radio, and more recently mp3 players and laptop speakers influenced the way popular music is composed, produced and mastered: Every single event has to be at maximum level all the time. This works best with music that is sonically simple, and music in which only a few elements are interacting. A symphony does not sound convincing thru a mobile phone speaker, and a maximized symphony does not sound convincing at all.[39]

Going a step further, producer Stephen Street, who has worked with such popular rock groups as the Smiths and Blur, dismisses mobile music players altogether: "I'd hate to think that anything I'd slaved over in the studio is only going to be listened to on a bloody iPod" (Spence 2009). This sense of disgust and dismay, no doubt echoed in high-end studios around the world, recalls *Stereophile* editor John Atkinson's lament that the days of high fidelity are over, but although it seems unlikely that one would inspired by today's treble culture to assemble a costly hi-fi, people's desire to hear the latest and greatest, wherever they may be, has hardly diminished. And so these very "deficiencies" in contemporary audio culture have led producers, as always, to seek new ways of optimizing musical effects for popular playback technologies.

Beyond the tricks of mastering a mixed-down track, we can point to a number of ascendant sonic qualities or representational techniques in today's treble culture—the stuff of "blog house," bassline, and grime, to name a few. Because such genres largely circulate and are played through laptop computers, MP3 players, and cellphones, their very aesthetics are bound up with the sounds of low bitrate compression and ringtone-like (if not ringtone-derived) bloops and bleeps—that is, sounds which, like ringtones themselves, are able to cut through the din of public life. Take, for example, the following passage from Dan Hancox's blog post about sodcasting and note in particular how Hancox names a variety of technologies—from filesharing software Limewire to mobile phones—and the way their traces seem to issue from the crunchy timbres and impoverished (bass) frequencies of the music itself, qualities which have come to peri-odize these recordings for the author and his cohorts:

> While road-rap may hold sway on the buses now, it's grime which has the best fit for the context—clear in grime's low-bitrate, badly-mastered early incarnations, which carried that rawness and DIY energy of punk, as Alex Bok Bok and I argued in [a previous] post:
>
>> Tracks like the insane, taut Ruff Sqwad anthem R U Double F—one of the few vocal tracks we've included [in the mix]—is a 64kbps, straight-off-Limewire, never-released work of genius. It's an mp3 dubplate, and the grooves have been battered into submission by repeated compression: we've included many low-bitrate tracks in this mix, because for us fucked-up sounding mp3s were a massive part of listening to music from this era.
>
> Grime suits mobile phone speaker technology, or lack thereof, perfectly. The glo-rification of treble culture in grime reached a peak of forthrightness with the Slix Riddim 'No Bass', rinsed by the likes of Ruff Sqwad, Bossman, and scores of mobile phone DJs throughout 2005/6.[40]

Although bass may seem largely absent from such tracks, at least as heard through a cell-phone or laptop, one interesting development across some of the genres named earlier is the use of particular synthesizer shapes that seem well poised for trebly playback, as well as, sometimes in conjunction with such standout waveforms, the transposition of bass lines into higher octaves, often doubling the bass melody in a more audible, reproducible range. Both sonic strategies emerged as hallmarks of the (sub)genre known as bassline (or bassline house), an offshoot of UK house and garage initially based in Sheffield. Commenting on an article about bassline by Mark Fisher (2008a), author Dominic Fox zeroes in on these techniques while tying them to the well-noted phenomenon of young people playing music on buses, recalling the discussion in the first part of this chapter:

> Couple of things I've noticed:
>
> i) Use of filtered square waves in the bass lines. These sound dated, 8-bit, BBC-micro-ish, but also (because of the filter envelope, which gives it a sort of duck-like quack) round and phat. They also transpose well out of the normal bass range into higher tones—you hear synth melodies that are basically bass figures pitched up an octave or two. I haven't listened to enough stuff closely enough to tell whether bits of tune migrate between bass and melody in the same song, but it wouldn't surprise me.
>
> ii) In spite of the bass-heaviness of it, it's also clearly designed to sound good com-ing out of tinny little portable mp3 player speakers. This is in fact how I've heard nearly all the bassline house I've heard over the past month (that and the occasional visit to 1Xtra): teenagers in the bus station crowded round someone's phone or player listening to the stuff. It's like the return of the portable transistor radio (with similar connotations of public nuisance—I've seen kids get kicked off buses for playing their music too loud), and a complete breakout from the iPhone personal-music-space

mentality. It turns out that peer-to-peer file copying isn't the only way people like to share music, after all.[41]

And, indeed, one of the more well-known producers working in the bassline genre, Dexplicit, seems to confirm this frequency drift at the stage of production, though his observations remains rather conjectural: "A lot of producers nowadays are building their tunes around a strong synth riff, as opposed to a distinctive bassline being the integral part of the song. Maybe this is a result of their audiences becoming more accustomed to mid-range music via their iPods? Or maybe they are just toning down the bass to get more radio airplay?" (Hancox 2010).

Critic Simon Reynolds also tries to connect this overriding aesthetic quality to contemporary listening practices, hearing in bassline—and in "blog house," a somewhat jokey umbrella term including the French acts to which he alludes—a kind of "flat" quality that seems tailor-made for plastic laptops: "Bassline seems much more in your face and to my ears has something of the 'flat' sound I associate with Justice and all those French disko-roque type outfits (which really leap out at you through computer speakers but I can only imagine is supremely grating through a big system)."[42] Further, this connection between production aesthetics in the 00s and computers as primary listening stations echoes in the words of sound engineer Dan D'Errico, for whom a recent album by London-based producer Zomby seemed to sound better when listened to via "inferior" equipment: "I can't help but feel that it plays better through the speakers on my laptop than through my nice studio monitors. It has a lot more life to it when listened to that way. It takes on less of the uber-compressed sound and opens up a bit more."[43]

Among other aesthetic phenomena connected to today's trebly zeitgeist is the trans-genre style that has come to be called "wonky" (after an influential article by critic Martin Clark, who also produces under the name Blackdown).[44] "[T]he mid-range is being hijacked by off-kilter, unstable synths," wrote Clark in April 2008, "[c]rossing hip-hop, hyphy, grime, chip tunes, dubstep, crunk, and electro." An era in which bass is hardly heard outside club contexts has given rise, to Clark's ears, to a great deal of "music that uses the middle interestingly."[45] This approach includes the doubling or transposition of bass lines into mid-range registers in bassline house, but it goes further: not content simply to represent bass lines in more audible ranges, producers embracing the "wonky" aesthetic—many of whom, it should be noted, also infuse their tracks with plenty of bass—have zeroed in on the mid-range as the primary register of sonic salience. Although Clark was skeptical when I asked him about the relationship between contemporary listening technologies and the wonky aesthetic, he did offer that "the MP3 is definitely to blame to an extent" and affirmed that, for young people in particular, and especially those without access to expensive and powerful audio equipment, "mobiles are the new boomboxes—except with defacto hi pass filters."[46] Steve Goodman / Kode9, on the other hand, who has himself produced and released some "wonky" music, more readily recognized a kind of "feedback from a youth culture used to hearing their music as purely in the mid-range of frequencies," pointing in particular to "the brittle production of grime," though he was quick to add that grime is "still a very bass heavy music"—an important reminder that bass culture perhaps paradoxically sustains itself as such even when the music is, in many cases, experienced as bassless.[47]

Whether or not we can posit a causal connection between MP3s, mobile devices, and the emergence of wonky and other styles that exploit mid-range frequencies, it is clear that this constellation nevertheless animates a great deal of discourse (especially of the hand-wringing sort) around the effects of treble culture on bass culture. Take, for instance, a comment from a Jamaican observer bemoaning the trebly turn in reggae, bass music *par excellence*:

> We've been having this debate a lot recently in Jamaica—bass is gone from dance-hall and even so-called "one drop" riddims are more about the guitar motif than a heavy bass line. A lot of people are saying this is a big reason behind the drop-off in dancehall popularity outside of Jamaica and the diaspora—it's no fun to dance to anymore....
>
> Most of the young and new producers are at home mixing their stuff on computer speakers or maybe a pair of low-end 6" Roland or M-Audio speakers at best. There's no mastering, no one's going to Mixing Lab or Arrows or wherever to have a real engineer give it the magic touch. The production chain in Jamaica is now Fruity Loops/Acid/Reason/Nuendo > mp3 > MySpace/Facebook/email all your friends (and not even a good mp3 encoding).[48]

Note the attention to the software-dominated "production chain" and how it affects sound—not to mention the connection drawn between bass and dancing, to which we will return in a moment. And yet, on the other hand, we would be remiss to overlook the other side of the aesthetic coin: in an era of treble culture, treble-centric genres have thrived. Perhaps the best example is regional Mexican music, an estimated 85% of which—in terms of digital sales—is now purchased and listened to on cellphones (Kun 2009). As Josh Kun recounts in a recent article for the *New York Times*, regional Mexican artists have found remarkable success reaching audiences via the mobile market, and although this has as much to do with the mobility of the audience itself and the ease of access cellphones offer (as opposed to the expense of home computers and broadband connections), Kun also noted via personal correspondence, that Mexican regional music was treble-centric prior to today's treble culture and hence the lack of bass presents no impediments to its popularity (not that there is any evidence that hip-hop, reggae, or other bass-centric genres have suffered in this regard, at least in terms of soundscape presence).

In contrast to the easy marriage between treble-inclined genres and mobile technologies, the particular and sometimes painful ironies of filtering bass culture through treble culture clearly produce anxieties among certain practitioners and stakeholders. The concern is not simply that attenuated bass leads to impoverished musical experience, strictly sonically speaking; rather, the lack of bass in contemporary audio culture, for some, opens into other kinds of loss. In such discourse, we behold how aesthetics pertain not simply to issues of form and content but also to the phenomenological, even ontological, effects of music and sound. For certain critical observers, less bass means less dancing, less embodiment, less profundity. Don Letts, a British musician and film-maker of Jamaican parentage, recently expressed some acute worry about how con-temporary technologies—once again, figuring young people on buses—are "ruining" bass culture, with serious implications for, among other things, gender balance among audiences. "It's disturbing when I see kids on buses, listening to music on their phones, and it's just going: tsk, tsk, tsk, tsk, with no bass," Letts told *The Guardian*, "Bass cul-ture is Jamaica's gift to the world and technology is, kind of, ruining that. Bass is sexy. Women respond to bass" (*The Guardian* 2009). Regardless of whether this strikes some as sexist or paternalistic, Letts's sentiments echo elsewhere. Returning to the Jamaican commenter on my blog quoted earlier, we get a similar sense that today's bass paucity, increasingly built into actual productions themselves as opposed to simply filtered out via lossy tech, has direct connections to the ways music engenders movement, especially inter-gender dance: "There is no more rub-a-dub in actual dances here—daggering is the only male-female contact, and that's not a bass-induced movement (unless you count the fact that have to climb up on top of the subs to leap off of to do it)."[49]

Sometimes this sense of loss and anxiety about treble culture registers as an incom-pleteness to the music in question, or to musical experience itself. In an article for *Fact Magazine*, British critic and theorist Mark Fisher (aka K-Punk) discusses the club con-text as a privileged, but also crucial, place for accessing the special sense of spatiality that certain music, especially genres nodding to or influenced by dub reggae, can create. "Both dubstep and minimal techno only achieve their full potency," he argues, "when played on a club soundsystem. The subtle pressure of sub-bass, the way it moves the very air itself, the hypnotic pulse of the drums, not to mention the role of the dancing crowd itself: none of this can be replicated at home, still less on iPod headphones" (2008b). Beyond a certain phenomenological lack, the absence of such "potency" and "subtle pressure" can have profound ontological implications, not least of which being a certain forgetfulness about how our bodies themselves are objects on which music operates. Steve Goodman takes this idea to a somewhat far-out, if intriguing, extreme:

> What gets lost is a certain sensual relation between the dancer and their body, the sense of the materiality of their bodies, that they are just another vibrating object in the room. What I think is conceptually powerful about bass culture is that it reminds the arro-gant human race that they are really mostly composed of non-organic matter, are not self-enclosed individuals but permeable membranes through which forcefields can pass and interfere with your insides. I think there is an extent to which bass culture edu-cates dancers about their bodies, literally vibrating parts they didn't know they had.[50]

Notably, Goodman is not so much concerned with bass poverty in mobile listening contexts but rather with the unavailability of sub-bass frequencies even in music ven-ues that theoretically have the power to project them.[51] His position, however, stands in contrast to other expressions of dismay about the aesthetic effects of treble culture on a generation of habituated youth. "How wretched would a world without bass be," asked one commenter on Dan Hancox's post about sodcasting, adding, "I can't get excited that a generation are becoming used to listening to music like this."[52] But, from another perspective, to worry so much about treble culture is not only paternalistic and, as I hope I have demonstrated, historically short-sighted, it may also be premature—not to mention utterly projected (that is, uninformed by ethnographic evidence).[53]

On the contrary, the aesthetics of treble culture may well include, if not impel, a certain kind of active listening—an engagement with music that is far from impoverished, at least with regard to imagination and even embodiment. Replying to the commenter who asked, in fairly typical fashion for detractors, "isn't it nice to actually be able to hear all the different parts of the track going on at a decent level of sound quality rather than it sounding like it was recorded in a pair of socks?" another contributor to the same forum offers: "A kid listening to the same tune the next day on the bus is more than likely aware that it sounds like tosh, but is probably thinking about how awesome it sounded the night before!"[54] Indeed, affirming this contention, a handful of commenters on my own posts about treble culture insisted that they imagine bass—or remember it, which is a kind of imagining—even when it is not audible.[55] They sway and shake as they might otherwise, an imagined embodiment of bass (which becomes a sort of "real" embodiment as soon as one moves). They "hear" lines that are not actually present. In other words, they reserve some psychoacoustic space for the missing bass. Or, it is not only the MP3 which plays the listener, we listeners also play ourselves. Riffing on this idea of intentional—as opposed to automatic—psychoacoustic labor, one commenter at my blog, a hip-hop producer named Canyon Cody, argued that listening in digital treble culture is, therefore, actually a creative act, a form of participatory culture even: "In contrast to analog listening, we are always imagining sounds to fill the space in all digital music—an unconscious blurring of the interstitial space between bits—but I think there's a higher level of agency in our participation with treble culture."[56]

## CONCLUSION: SONIC CULTURE IN TRANSITION, PUBLIC CULTURE TOO?

For all the optimism if not outright utopianism that pervades discussions of digital technologies, dissenting voices offer some temperament as we charge forward into the brave new world of mobile culture. British cultural historian Paul Gilroy, for one, is wary about how such new technologies (as well as their analog predecessors) impose a layer of mediation that bypasses the powerful, face-to-face, real-time musical encounters that he likes to think of as the "electric church." Speaking specifically to the experiences of black Britons in the 1970s and 80s, and emphasizing the importance of "bass culture" to an oppositional epistemology, he argues:

> Musical culture and the elaborate social relations that eddied around it, at least until the digital revolution changed the game, created that locus [of healing and autonomy] and invested it with a precious democratic energy in which audiences and performers could interact and collaborate.... First pirate radio then the anti-social

cultures of mobile privatization replaced the ancient authority of the electric church with something shallower and more consumer-friendly.... That world of sound celebrated here was specified hesitantly but repeatedly in the same vernacular code as something like a 'bass culture.' It was shaped by a fundamental awareness that as far as understanding the predicament of these sufferers was concerned, vision was not the master sense and words alone could not be a stable or trustworthy medium of expression and communication. (2003:388–89)

In the paragraph that follows, however, Gilroy registers some ambivalence about the fact that the image of black Britons he romanticizes may well be one of people standing in front of a DJ and a stack of speakers. And yet he also notes that there are important redemptive and connective possibilities embodied by the mobility of recorded sound:

> The preference for recorded rather than live performance was an interesting and disturbing feature of the soundscape of the period, which did not reveal an absolute enthusiasm for music made and heard in real time. The aesthetic and anti-aesthetic codes that governed this economy of pleasure, escape, transcendence, and desire specified instead that the highest value was to be placed on and invested in art that spoke to the immediate circumstances in which it appeared but relied upon processes of intermixture and combination that made elsewhere audible. (389)

Clearly, the contested sociality of public sound reproduction remains at the heart of the debate over both mobile culture and treble culture. But couldn't perhaps today's noisy (and often black) "kids on buses," as well as their interlocutors and opponents, constitute another kind of interactive, collaborative listening public? Other, more celebratory narratives of pirate radio and mobile music in London push against this interpretation, arguing for their constitutive role in creating and maintaining community.[57] Is mobile, treble culture a matter of privatization, or publicization? Are new audiences, listening publics, public spheres even, capable of being engendered by mobile culture in a manner that once again holds some promise of "a precious democratic energy," of debates and discussions and of collective expressive and interpretive practices? Why should we privilege the mobile sound systems of the mid-to-late twentieth century over the mobile sound systems of the twenty-first? Is it just a matter of missing bass? Or are certain critics, so to speak, missing the bus?

Although a marked concern with the loss of high fidelity—and in particular, a paucity of bass—permeates the discourse around today's treble culture, conjuring specters of ontological and phenomenological poverty, even the bass boosters of the world can hear potential—the opening of new social, cultural, and political possibilities—in sound's newfound portability. While these possibilities may remain to be seen or heard or realized, attending to treble culture without the blinders of bass fetishism might prove a more productive strategy. Steve Goodman—a dedicated futurist, hence hesitant to rope off possible scenarios through critical foreclosure—offers an important reminder that focusing on frequencies, as much as that may reveal about our aesthetic and cultural priorities, can risk missing the forest for the tress:

> I think something much more interesting is going on with kids using mobile phone speakers as mobile sound systems. The potentials of young people carrying sound

reproduction (and increasingly production) devices around with them at all times is more significant than the fact that they are trebly. The becoming trebly of mobile culture is perhaps part of the cost of sound's ubiquity—bass is heavy—i.e., it's not so portable. I think that sonic culture is in transition right now, and this kind of ubiquity is going somewhere quite unpredictable and I don't think you get half of that picture by just complaining about lack of bass, as much as I do generally complain about that.[58]

By hearing today's treble culture in the *longue durée* of sound reproduction provided by Jonathan Sterne, Greg Milner, et al.—that is, in the historical context explored in the middle section of this chapter—we can appreciate, on the one hand, how well today's technologies and practices fit into an overarching dynamic whereby engineers and producers have increased sound's portability alongside innovations in sonic definition and "fidelity" (to what, of course, is another question in an era of synthesized and sampled music made on computers). On the other hand, as Goodman's attention to the "unpredictable" qualities of today's sonic culture implies, there does seem to be something genuinely new and unprecedented in the contemporary portability and ubiquity of sound reproduction technologies. Not everyone carried around a transistor radio, despite their popularity, but it is becoming increasingly difficult to find people without cellphones, even in the underdeveloped world or among the disadvantaged in rich countries. (Indeed, across both of the latter populations, access to mobile phones is remarkably widespread and steadily on the increase.[59]) As mobile devices, especially phones, make sound reproduction—however trebly—more commonplace and perhaps more social than ever before (hotly contested as that sociality or sociability may be), we can only wonder about, as we try to take stock of, the effects on listening as a private and a (counter?) public activity, not to mention the implications thereof (Warner 2002).

Imagining unheard bass calls attention to the active possibilities in treble culture. And indeed, as perhaps my own narrative offers, a lot of the dyads through which the public debate plays out—active versus passive, progressive versus regressive, public versus private, sociable versus individualistic—might be easily enough flipped depending on one's perspective. This reconcilability suggests that treble culture, especially in its contemporary form, offers what writer and artist Jace Clayton (aka DJ /Rupture) calls a "strategy for intimacy with the digital" (2009). In the ongoing dance between people and technology, treble culture opens a space where imaginary bass can move us as much as tinny blasts of noise. As participants in today's treble culture attest, the MP3 may play its listener, but people imagine a lot more than missing bits when they listen. Ironically, the techno-historical convergence that Gilroy mourns, in which "community and solidarity, momentarily constituted in the very process, in the act of interpretation itself" (2003:388)—a lament which issues also from the anxious discourse around today's treble culture—may yet find some resuscitation thanks to trebly audio technologies. For what do such acts of interpretation require if not listening together? And isn't listening, perhaps more now and more collectively and publicly than ever, what treble culture is all about?

## NOTES

1. Posted to a message board at *Drowned in Sound*, a UK-based music webzine with an active discussion forum. The particular conversation thread was titled "Is sound quality really important any more?" and can be found here: http://drownedinsound.com/community/boards/music/4201236# (accessed January 4, 2010).

2. London-based Jamaican artist and critic Linton Kwesi Johnson popularized the term "bass culture" on a 1980 album of politically charged spoken word reggae, or dub poetry. It later served as the title for a popular history of reggae by Lloyd Bradley, *Bass Culture: When Reggae Was King*, published in the United States as *This Is Reggae Music: The Story of Jamaica's Music*. According to legions of reggae diasporists—or, depending who you ask, imperialists—reggae's worldwide spread and its formative influence on popular dance music from hip-hop to house, drum'n'bass to dubstep, means that bass culture has truly "gone global" (to employ a catch phrase from advertising and reggae alike). Insofar as Jamaican style sound systems are now an international staple, never mind how reggae aesthetics—with particular regard to the role of bass—have informed the production of modern pop (see, e.g., Veal 2007:220–48), claims to a more widespread bass culture than ever before would seem to have some merit.

3. To be clear, when discussing "treble" or "tinniness" in this chapter, I am generally referring to frequencies between 6 and 20 kHz, whereas "bass" indexes the frequencies on the lower end of the audible spectrum (e.g., 20–250 Hz, including what is known as "sub bass"). The actual frequency ranges for the bass or treble registers might differ depending on how much "mid" or "upper" bass one wishes to include in the low end, or conversely, how much "upper midrange" in the high end.

4. Take, for example, a recent interview with London-based producer Mark Lawrence (aka Mala), who works mostly in dubstep, a genre deeply informed by reggae's predilection for bass. Recounting a series of music workshops he offered, Mala shuddered to think about the aesthetic feedback loop produced by the rise of mobile phones as primary listening devices: "Most of the youngsters were listening to music mostly on their mobile phones. So you have to think that you have producers trying to recreate music and music's made for this bandwidth and they only understand music sonically on that bandwidth. So actually *this whole culture* of compressed files and bad sound quality, is, to some extent having a knock on effect" (Franco 2010: n.p., emphasis mine).

5. Guillaume Decouflet, email message to author, September 3, 2009. Decouflet is a DJ and blogger by way of France/Canada.

6. http://www.urbandictionary.com/define.php?term=Sodcasting# (accessed January 4, 2010).

7. Although teens appear to be the figures most often fingered in treble culture discussions, I do not mean to imply that adults and children are not also active, noisy participants. See, for instance, Tyler Bickford's chapter in *The Oxford Handbook of Mobile Music Studies, Volume 1*, "Earbuds Are Good for Sharing," for an account of how kids in primary school are engaging in treble culture by using maxed-out earbuds as miniature speakers, among other practices. Moreover, writing for *The Guardian*, Dan Hancox observes that the practice is not so easily consigned to a particular age-group: "On London buses, I've seen middle-aged gay couples playing South American pop on a wet Saturday afternoon, moody raver mums sodcasting acid house from their glory years; it's not just the preserve of teenagers with attitude problems" (2010).

8. http://twitter.com/laurent_fintoni/status/3689580497 (accessed January 4, 2010). Allow me to offer my thanks here to Laurent and to all the other helpful interlocutors who responded to my queries on Twitter and my blog. These contributors—my collaborators, really—are too numerous to mention here, but I want to express my deep gratitude for all the feedback this project has received. Researching treble culture with the help of online social networks has proven, if I may, to be the most successful bit of "crowdsourced" scholarship I've had the pleasure to co-produce.

9. Grime is a genre that emerged in London just after the turn of the millennium, drawing together influences from UK garage and other club music, hip-hop, and dancehall reggae, with a marked aesthetic preference for sounds recalling video games and cellphones.

10. The appearance of the article in *Wired* magazine, known for its optimistic take on technology matters, is perhaps one explanation for its celebratory rather than critical tone.

11. The following blog post served as a call, and it returned a large number of anecdotes and opinions, which I imagine will continue to trickle in: http://wayneandwax.com/?p=2332 (accessed January 4, 2010).

12. Alex Helsinger, email message to author, October 29, 2009. Helsinger has long worked in the media industry (in particular, with musical meta-data); when we corresponded, he was living in Bamako while his partner, a graduate student in anthropology, conducted field research for her dissertation. Ethnomusicologist Ingrid Monson, who has been doing research in Mali for several years, told me after presenting this chapter as a work in progress that the phenomenon is really quite new, noting that such phones were nowhere to be seen or heard as late as 2007.

13. Carolina Gonzalez, email message to author, June 17, 2008. Gonzalez is a longtime music and culture writer, blogger, and, in her words, "cultural studies academic." Of course, there is a slight difference between a trebly device (one that doesn't have the capacity to reproduce certain frequencies) and the apprehension of sonic "emanations" that sound trebly. In the case of Carolina's subway example, trebliness is not a product of the frequency response of headphones but is more an effect based on a differential relationship to the sound source. Nevertheless, such incidental broadcasts obviously enter into public perceptions of and debates around mobile music and "treble culture."

14. http://wayneandwax.com/?p=2332#comment-10796 (accessed January 4, 2010).

15. Andrew Clarkwest, email message to author, September 4, 2009. Clarkwest is a Harvard trained sociologist now working outside academia.

16. See, for example, "frederic tecktonic," a brief video in which a young man dances outdoors to a beat seemingly provided by a rather trebly device: http://www.youtube.com/watch?v=8Ot—qcl3aM (accessed January 4, 2010). It is worth noting, as well, that the trebly quality of a great many YouTube videos also arises from recording devices (especially cellphones, small cameras, and other everyday mobile technologies) that simply cannot capture large frequency ranges. This effect seems to be a critical part of the attenuated sonic culture of a wide swath of YouTube videos, particularly live recordings made with consumer-grade devices.

17. In a study of mobile phone practices, and in particular the use of ringtones, Licoppe contrasts "intimists" ("mostly women"), who seek to minimize "public exposure of personal features," with "expressive youth," who use their mobile phones "as a way to assert and make public various identity claims." For Licoppe, musical ringtones constitute "a resource for distinguishing oneself by making one's tastes visible in the public sphere, usually in relation with some form of collective and recognizable identity claim, either with respect to an

actual peer group (friends) or an imaginary one (everyone who likes a particular type of music)" (2008:146–47).

18. See *Enfield Independent* 2006. Thanks to Dan Hancox for this reference, as mentioned in his interesting and helpful blog post on "sodcasting": http://dan-hancox.blogspot.com/2009/10/on-buses-sodcasting-and-mobile-music.html   (accessed   January 4, 2010).

19. http://drownedinsound.com/community/boards/music/4201236#r4919350   (accessed January 4, 2010).

20. http://drownedinsound.com/community/boards/music/4201236#r4919401   (accessed January 4, 2010).

21. Again, Hancox's blog post can be accessed here: http://dan-hancox.blogspot.com/2009/10/on-buses-sodcasting-and-mobile-music.html; see http://news.bbc.co.uk/1/hi/entertainment/8309690.stm for the article describing a kind of racial profiling on the part of the Metropolitan Police.

22. Hatherley's "In (Partial) Defence of 'Sodcasting'" can be accessed here: http://nastybrutalistandshort.blogspot.com/2008/02/in-partial-defence-of-sodcasting.html (emphasis in original, accessed January 4, 2010).

23. http://dan-hancox.blogspot.com/2009/10/on-buses-sodcasting-and-mobile-music.html?showComment=1256826252856#c6495460244025346915; see also, a series of related tweets from Copsey, recounting bad bus experiences ("conversations in our flat post-incidents") to confront Hancox's assertions about treble culture and community: "nastiest involved man threatening woman 'i'll cut out your eyes'" (http://twitter.com/tancopsey/status/5235651020); "when asked to turn off crap tinny music. he moved behind her and kept up threats. community destroyed at these moments." (http://twitter.com/tancopsey/status/5235695791).

24. http://wayneandwax.com/?p=2332#comment-11055 (accessed January 4, 2010).

25. See Stephen Connor's article, "Edison's Teeth" (2004), for a theoretical consideration of the inventor's belief in his superior sense of "hearing" resulting from his "wonderfully sensitive inner ear" receiving sounds and overtones far more accurately via his teeth and jawbones than from "normal ears."

26. Moreover, with regard to bass we should add that, according to Gronow and Saunio, "The secret of the Motown bass sound was that the label's studio was the first to record the electric bass directly from the pick-up of the instrument without a separate microphone" (1998:160).

27. I don't have the space to explore it here, and the extant literature seems lacking, but the connections between popular playback technologies and production aesthetics would—despite being driven by US-based music industry—no doubt emerge more clearly in comparative, global perspective. Nilanjana Bhattacharjya notes, for instance, that "Indian lo-fi cassette recorders and radios favor the treble, so for a long time (and arguably still) many music producers master their recordings toward that end." Email message to author, September 14, 2009.

28. For more on the "loudness war," see Milner's chapter 7 (2009:237–92) or any number of articles that have been published on the subject (e.g., Southall 2006; Levine 2007).

29. I qualify this sentence because it is likely that before long we will witness a swing in the other direction as lossless compression schemes, cheaper storage, and greater broadband access make it possible for music to remain portable without affecting audio quality as much. Or as mastering engineer Jonathan Wyner puts it, recognizing the difference between the

high fidelity world and that of "standard practice": "We'll be able to store CD-quality files, transmit them across the next-generation Internet, and see higher fidelity creep into standard practice" (Anderman 2007). Moreover, it is important to remember that some of the most bass-ful experiences of the twentieth century were provided by mobile equipment, whether Jamaican sound systems, Colombian picós, Brazilian trios elétricos, or Trinidadian tractor trailers.

30. For those who prize sonic definition above all, we could identify a host of issues of concern. And yet, while the following innovations served to increase or decrease sonic definition, they did not tend to affect the audibility of treble over bass, per se. Nevertheless, certain listeners locate a loss of "depth" or "presence" in the transition, around 1970, from vacuum tube powered recorders to those that relied on solid-state transistors, as well as in the shift from sixteen to twenty-four track consoles—a decrease in bandwidth that led to the loss of certain "transients" or "the very high and low frequencies that," at least for certain engineers and audiophilic ears, "fleshed out the sound" (Milner 2009:160–61)—a complaint eerily echoed in discussion of MP3s. Along these lines, in the 1980s audiophiles complained about crude early CD standards (44.1 kHz) as well as early AAD transfers to CD—that is, recorded and mixed in analog, transferred to digital—which often did not account for the (analog-era) bass boost in record-player pre-amps discussed earlier. Given a concern with such sonic minutiae, hi-fi's defenders might take heart in a movement away from portability as an overriding ideal, at least among some listeners. "Bad sound on an iPod has had an impact on a lot of people going back to vinyl," fifteen-year-old high school sophomore David MacRunnel recently told a reporter from *Time* (Dell 2008). Then again, a good number of MacRunnel's 1000-plus LPs were likely to have been recorded, mixed, and mastered with digital technology.

31. The newsletter is excerpted and reprinted at http://he-japu.blogspot.com/2005/06/meta-audiophile-recordings-and-sacddvd.html; see also, Atkinson (1999).

32. Steve Goodman, email message to author, September 17, 2009. I published excerpts of this email exchange to my blog (http://wayneandwax.com/?p=2365), where it generated further discussion.

33. In a paper prepared for the 2009 Audio Engineering Society Convention, Pras et al. found that test subjects "significantly preferred CD quality to mp3 files up to 192 kb/s for all musical genres" (2009:1), although it is remarkable—and, in my opinion, regrettable—that the genres in question ("Pop," "Metal Rock," "Contemporary," "Orchestra," and "Opera") did not include any drawn from bass culture or electronic dance music. Because "high frequency artifacts were the most selected criterion" by test subjects discerning a difference in audio quality, the researchers conclude that "mp3 compression introduces audible artifacts, and that listeners' sensitivity to these artifacts varies as a function of musical genre and listeners' expertise" (6). The researchers acknowledge, if perhaps somewhat dismissively, Stanford professor Jonathan Berger's study (see, e.g., Spence 2009), one of the more widely cited in the press and the genesis of "sizzle" as a distinctive and preferred timbral quality of MP3s, as "an informal study where young listeners preferred compressed formats to CD quality" (7).

34. It is interesting that commonplace adjectives such as "tinny," referring to metal rather than plastic, locate the discourse around treble culture in outmoded but obviously still resonant technological terms, affirming again a continuity across the various trebly moments in the history of recorded sound.

35. Michael Bell Smith, direct message to author via Twitter, September 1, 2009: "I've heard anecdotes of young bands wanting engineers to mix/master songs so they sound more like 'myspace'–LBR [low bitrate] aesthetics."

36. Steve Goodman, email message to author, September 17, 2009. Of course, it is worth noting that hot mastering can also offer a "semblance of low end" on "mediocre sound systems" (Milner 2009:248) because of the simple but profound fact that, listened to loud, more low frequencies are audible. So, ironically, even as compression in the age of "loudness wars" decreases dynamic range, favoring the more easily audible, higher frequencies, it can also boost a sense of bass.

37. Along these lines, I witnessed a recording engineer at a Jamaican studio in 2004 mixing back and forth between large studio monitors and a small radio, making sure that, as he put it, "the man on the street" would also hear the bass.

38. http://www.sweetwater.com/store/detail/MixCubesAct/ (accessed January 4, 2010). Thanks to Jesse Kriss for bringing this to my attention.

39. http://www.monolake.de/releases/ml-025.html (accessed January 4, 2010).

40. http://dan-hancox.blogspot.com/2009/10/on-buses-sodcasting-and-mobile-music.html (accessed January 4, 2010); the previous post to which this quotation refers, a description of a DJ mix featuring lots of low bitrate grime tracks, can be found here: http://dot-alt. blogspot.com/2002/10/blogariddims.html (accessed January 4, 2010).

41. http://k-punk.abstractdynamics.org/archives/010014.html (accessed January 4, 2010).

42. http://blissout.blogspot.com/2007/11/emerging-from-miasma-of-work-excursion.html (accessed January 4, 2010).

43. http://wayneandwax.com/?p=2365#comment-11260 (accessed January 4, 2010).

44. http://pitchfork.com/features/grime-dubstep/6840-grime-dubstep/ (accessed October 10, 2011); for further thoughts on timbre, texture, and melody in "wonky," see http:// rougesfoam.blogspot.com/2009/06/loving-wonky.html (accessed January 4, 2010).

45. Martin Clark, email message to author, May 1, 2008.

46. Ibid.

47. Steve Goodman, email message to author, September 17, 2010.

48. http://wayneandwax.com/?p=2365#comment-11249 (accessed January 4, 2010).

49. http://wayneandwax.com/?p=2365#comment-11249 (accessed January 4, 2010). "Rub-a-dub" is a well-worn Jamaican term for close partner dancing, whereas "daggering" describes a recent dance trend that could be described as a kind of cartoonish sexual pantomime in overdrive.

50. Steve Goodman, email message to author, September 17, 2010.

51. "My problem is not with tinny playback devices in situations where there traditionally there was never much bass playback. My problem is more with the squeezing out of bass in music performance venues/clubs/festivals, etc." (ibid.).

52. http://dan-hancox.blogspot.com/2009/10/on-buses-sodcasting-and-mobile-music.html ?showComment=1258642671936#c5348073059544751240 (accessed January 4, 2010).

53. I say "premature" because, given the way technology tends to work, it is quite possible, probable even, that cellphone and laptop speakers will get better and bassier, within physical limitations of size, of course. Regarding ethnography, I regret that beyond my readership on Twitter and at wayneandwax.com, I did not have an opportunity to talk with more young people immersed in public treble culture. It is certainly an important place for further research, and the work of Tyler Bickford (see, for instance, chapter 15 in Volume 1 of *The Oxford Handbook of Mobile Music Studies*), among others, will help to flesh out the phenomenological implications of today's treble culture. It is all too telling that the concerns over "kids these days" and their trebly music are primarily voiced by older observers.

54. http://drownedinsound.com/community/boards/music/4201236# (accessed January 4, 2010).
55. Thanks to Michael Heller for reminding me that Robert Walser notes a parallel listening practice in his study of heavy metal, wherein listeners imagine the music not with greater bass presence but with high volume: "Even when it is heard from a distance, or even sung softly to oneself, metal is imagined as loud, for volume is an important contributor to the heaviness of heavy metal" (1993:45).
56. http://wayneandwax.com/?p=2352#comment-11095 (accessed January 4, 2010).
57. Again, see the blog posts on "sodcasting" by Dan Hancox and Owen Hatherle: http://nastybrutalistandshort.blogspot.com/2008/02/in-partial-defence-of-sodcasting.html; http://dan-hancox.blogspot.com/2009/10/on-buses-sodcasting-and-mobile-music.html (accessed January 4, 2010). See also, Hancox's follow-up article in *The Guardian* (2010).
58. Steve Goodman, email message to author, September 17, 2009.
59. Among other indicators, see, e.g., the following articles: *CBC News* (2009); Arnquist (2009); Bellman (2009); Contreras (2009).

## REFERENCES

Anderman, Joan. 2007. "Ever Lower Fidelity." *Boston Globe*, March 14.

Arnquist, Sarah. 2009. "In Rural Africa, a Fertile Market for Mobile Phones." *New York Times*, October 5.

Atkinson, John. 1999. "Mp3 and the Marginalization of High End Audio." *Stereophile* (February):22.

Attali, Jacques. 1985. *Noise: The Political Economy of Music*. Minneapolis: University of Minnesota Press.

Bellman, Eric. 2009. "Cellphone Entertainment Takes Off in Rural India." *Wall Street Journal*, November 23.

Biddle, Ian. 2007. "Love Thy Neighbour? The Political Economy of Musical Neighbours." *Radical Musicology* 2:49 pars, http://www.radical-musicology.org.uk.

Biddlecombe, Elizabeth. 2005. "Cell-Phone Rappers Spit Grime." *Wired*, July 25.

Bilby, Kenneth. 1995. "Jamaica." In *Caribbean Currents: Caribbean Music from Rumba to Reggae*, ed. Peter Manuel, 143–82. Philadelphia: Temple University Press.

Bradley, Lloyd. [2000.] 2001. *This Is Reggae Music: The Story of Jamaica's Music*. New York: Grove. [Originally printed in Great Britain as *Bass Culture: When Reggae Was King* by Penguin Books Ltd., Harmondsworth, Middlesex, England].

*CBC News*. 2009. "Developing world embraces mobile phones: UN report." March 2, http://www.cbc.ca/technology/story/2009/03/02/un-telecommunications.html (accessed January 4, 2010).

Clayton, Jace. 2009. "Pitch Perfect." *Frieze Magazine* 123, May, http://www.frieze.com/issue/article/pitch_perfect/ (accessed September 30, 2011).

Connor, Steven. 2004. "Edison's Teeth: Touching Hearing." In *Hearing Cultures: Essays on Sound, Listening, and Modernity*, ed. Veit Erlmann, 153–72. New York: Berg.

Contreras, Felix. 2009. "Young Latinos, Blacks Answer Call of Mobile Devices." *NPR*, December 1.

Dell, Kristina. 2008. "Vinyl Gets Its Groove Back." *Time*, January 10.

*Enfield Independent.* 2006. "Music Free Bus Campaign Finds Hundreds of Friends." October 20.

Fisher, Mark. 2008a. "Bassline House and the Return of 'Feminine Pressure.'" *Fact Magazine,* January, http://www.factmagazinearchive.co.uk/da/67961 (accessed January 4, 2010).

——. 2008b. "Rebellious Jukebox (06/08)" *Fact Magazine,* June 25, http://www.factmagazine. co.uk/index.php?option=com_content&task=view&id=676&Itemid=52 (accessed January 4, 2010).

Franco, Mónica. 2010. "Mala: It's all about the space." *PlayGround,* September 15, http:// www.playgroundmag.net/entrevistas/14101-mala-its-all-about-the-space-monica-franco (accessed September 30, 2011).

Frere-Jones, Sasha. 2009. "Dithering: Jonny Greenwood." *The New Yorker,* September 2.

Gilroy, Paul. 2003. "Between the Blues and the Blues Dance: Some Soundscapes of the Black Atlantic." In *The Auditory Culture Reader,* ed. Michael Bull and Les Back, 381–96. Oxford: Berg.

Goodman, Steve. 2009. *Sonic Warfare: Sound, Affect, and the Ecology of Fear.* Cambridge: MIT Press.

Gronow, Pekka, and Ilpo Saunio. 1998. *An International History of the Recording Industry.* Trans. Christopher Moseley. London and New York: Cassell.

*The Guardian.* 2009. "Is This It?" April 4.

Hancox, Dan. 2009. "On the buses: sodcasting and mobile music culture." *Dan Hancox* (blog), October 23, http://dan-hancox.blogspot.com/2009/10/on-buses-sodcasting-and-mobile-m usic.html (accessed September 30, 2011).

——. 2010. "Mobile Disco: How Phones Make Music Inescapable." *The Guardian,* August 12.

Hatherley, Owen. 2008. "In (Partial) Defence of 'Sodcasting.'" Sit down man, you're a bloody tragedy (blog), February 6, http://nastybrutalistandshort.blogspot.com/2008/02/ in-partial-defence-of-sodcasting.html (accessed September 30, 2011).

Keenan, David. 2009. "Hypnagogic Pop." *The Wire* 306:26–31.

Kun, Josh. 2009. "Mexican Bands Hear Success Calling." *New York Times,* April 3.

Larkin, Brian. 2004. "Degraded Images, Distorted Sounds: Nigerian Video and the Infrastructure of Piracy." *Public Culture* 16(2):289–314.

Levine, Robert. 2007. "The Death of High Fidelity in the Age of MP3s." *Rolling Stone,* December 27.

Licoppe, Christian. 2008. "The Mobile Phone's Ring." In *Handbook of Mobile Communication Studies,* ed. James E. Katz, 139–52. Cambridge: MIT Press.

Link, Stan. 2001. "The Work of Reproduction in the Mechanical Aging of an Art: Listening to Noise." *Computer Music Journal* 25(1):34–47.

Marshall, Wayne. 2002. "Producing the Real: Hip-hop Music and Authenticity." MA Thesis, University of Wisconsin-Madison.

——. 2006. "Giving Up Hip-hop's Firstborn: A Quest for the Real after the Death of Sampling." *Callaloo* 29(3):868–92.

Meyer, E. Brad. 1996. "The Romance of the Record." *Stereo Review* (January):67–70.

Milner, Greg. 2009. *Perfecting Sound Forever: An Aural History of Recorded Music.* New York: Faber and Faber.

Pras, Amandine, Rachel Zimmerman, Daniel Levitin, and Catherine Guastavino. 2009. "Subjective Evaluation of MP3 Compression for Different Musical Genres." Proceedings of the 127th Audio Engineering Society (AES) Convention, New York, October 9–12.

Reynolds, Simon. 2009. "Notes on the Noughties: When Will Hip-Hop Hurry Up and Die?" *The Guardian,* November 26.

Rose, Tricia. 1994. *Black Noise: Rap Music and Black Culture in Contemporary America*. Hanover, NH: Wesleyan University Press.

Salimpoor, Valorie, Catherine Guastavino, and Daniel Levitin. 2007. "Subjective Evaluation of Popular Audio Compression Formats." Proceedings of the 123rd Audio Engineering Society (AES) Convention, New York, October 5–8.

Spence, Nick. 2009. "iPod generation prefer MP3 fidelity to CD says study." *MacWorld*, March 5, http://www.macworld.co.uk/ipod-itunes/news/?newsid=25288 (accessed September 30, 2011).

Sterne, Jonathan. 2006a. "The Death and Life of Digital Audio." *Interdisciplinary Science Reviews* 31(4):338–48.

——. 2006b. "The MP3 as Cultural Artifact." *New Media and Society* 8(5):825–42.

Southall, Nick. 2006. "Imperfect Sound Forever." *Stylus Magazine*, May 1, http://www.stylus-magazine.com/articles/weekly_article/imperfect-sound-forever.htm (accessed September 30, 2011).

Veal, Michael. 2007. *Dub: Soundscapes & Shattered Songs in Jamaican Reggae*. Middletown, CT: Wesleyan University Press.

Viney, Melissa. 2008. "Commuter Pursuits." *The Guardian*, February 9.

Walser, Robert. 1993. *Running with the Devil: Power, Gender, and Madness in Heavy Metal Music*. Hanover, NH: University Press of New England.

Warner, Michael. 2002. *Publics and Counterpublics*. New York: Zone Books.

Youngs, Ian. 2009. "Police Target Hip-Hop Nightclubs." *BBC News*, 16 October, http://news.bbc.co.uk/2/hi/entertainment/8309690.stm (accessed September 30, 2011).

# CHAPTER 3

························································

# OF SIRENS OLD AND NEW

························································

## ALEXANDER REHDING


## PITCH AS BLISS

·············································································

No sooner do we encounter the sirens, in Book 12 of Homer's *Odyssey*, than they spell trouble.[1] We recall that in that episode the sorceress Circe warns Odysseus against the mythical creatures that enchant all passers-by with their beautiful singing. No mortal, she explains, can resist their powerful charms; the alluring music causes listeners to lose all will power and control over their bodies (*Od.*,12.39–54). The question of what it was in this siren song that had such extraordinary powers on the human psyche has long captivated the minds of musical thinkers. Some have shown remarkable dedication to finding a scientific answer to this question, not withstanding the mythical origin of these creatures.[2] Meanwhile, any endeavor to understand the siren song better is made more difficult by the troubling circumstance, as Circe's report continues, that the sirens use their powers to bring death to the humans unfortunate enough to fall for their singing.

The story of the sirens is in many ways an archetypal tale of music and mobility. In ancient Greek epic there are only two accounts of heroes making it past the sirens and surviving to tell the tale. The first, and best known, is of course from the *Odyssey* itself. Circe advises Odysseus that the only way to hear the song of the sirens and to save himself at the same time is to have himself tied to the mast by his companions. He can listen but not act upon their powerful musical charms. The companions, meanwhile, must close up their ears with beeswax—a "honey-sweet" substance to match the dangerous "honeyed voices" (Segal 1994:100)—to resist the sirens by not even being tempted. They can act but not listen. In other words, there are two ways to pass the sirens unharmed: by being deaf or immobile; in combination, this form of division of labor is invincible.

In fact, as we learn later in Book 12, this is exactly how it happens (*Od.*,12.158–200). The winds die down as Odysseus's ship approaches the sirens' flowery meadows. So the crew has to start rowing to keep moving across the seas permeated by the sirens' song. When Odysseus, tied securely to the mast, is overcome by irresistible desire and urges his crew to release him, two of his men, with safely sealed ears, come up to him and tie

FIGURE 3.1 A stamnos, an ancient Greek storage jar, depicting Odysseus' ship and three sirens. Odysseus is tied to the mast, the deafened companions are rowing. The two sirens at the top of the image sit with open mouths, apparently singing, while a third siren is hurling herself into the sea, as their victims escape. © The Trustees of the British Museum.

his shackles more tightly.[3] As they leave the sirens' meadows behind, the companions untie him from the mast and take the wax plugs out of their ears.

The aspects of mobility and stasis that are so prominent in this scene are epitomized structurally by emblems of verticality and horizontality (Dougherty 2001:71–73). The *Odyssey* as a whole is quintessentially a narration about mobility—the adventurous journey home across the oceans—whereas the sirens' only task is to stop the travelers from moving ahead, to draw them in by means of their music. The enforced upright verticality of Odysseus tied to the mast, shown beautifully in image depicted in Figure 3.1, serves to emphasize his inability to move on. It is only thanks to the deafened companions rowing—remaining, as it were, in the horizontal plane—that Odysseus does not fall prey to the murderous sirens and continues on his journey.

The other ship that made it past the sirens in the ancient world is found in the *Argonautica* of Apollonius of Rhodes, dating from the third century B.C.E. This epic relates the adventures of Jason and his men, who tried another tack: Jason is advised by his mentor, the centaur Chiron, to take Orpheus on his voyage (*Arg.*,4.891–919). As soon as the travelers hear the sirens' voices, Orpheus in turn strikes his lyre and starts singing. His singing neutralizes and drowns out the sirens. Only one of Jason's men can hear them—sharp-eared Boutes—and hurls himself into the sea. He is saved, however, by the benevolence of Aphrodite who brings him back to the ship unscathed and before any harm could be done. This single near-victim is the result of a certain logic of mythological necessity because it is said that the sirens themselves would die if they were unsuccessful, so they are spared a tragic fate in this instance.[4]

We know deplorably little about the physical nature of the sirens. Homer is noticeably tightlipped about them. From grammatical details in the *Odyssey*, the repeated use of dual forms, we can gauge that Homer counted two sirens (*Od.*,12.52,167). For Apollonius, by contrast, there was already a whole chorus of them. Homer barely tells us what sex the sirens are, nor does the text reveal anything about their appearance. In the *Odyssey*, the sirens are nothing but disembodied voice. Apollonius gives us more about their background: they are the daughters of the muse Terpsichore and the River God Achelous; the Apollonian sirens live on the lovely island of Anthemoessa—not on the Homeric meadows—and they were once in the entourage of Demeter's daughter Kore, who became Persephone once she was abducted by Hades. In Apollonius' account, the sirens assume the appearance of half-birds, half-females (*Arg.*,4.895–98). In some later versions, they were turned into these figures by Demeter as punishment for not having saved her daughter. Others claim that their birdlike nature is the source of their enthralling singing. It is in this shape that we often see them in ancient and modern representations. The ancient Greek storage jar in Figure 3.1 in effect conflates the two myths: it shows a depiction of Odysseus and the sirens, whereas the representation of the sirens is not based on Homer, but takes its cue from the tradition to which Apollonius' *Argonautica* belongs and which, admittedly, poses less of a challenge to the painter.

The uncertainties of the sirens' physical appearance complicate the question of their musical allure somewhat. As nineteenth-century studies, which tend to approach this question with the seriousness and the literalism so characteristic of that age, have pointed out, it is unlikely that the avian shape of the sirens would necessarily mean that their singing also resembled birdsong: the human voice is much more likely as a communicating device for both emotions and auguries (Kastner 1858:84).[5] In fact, the third major source from classical antiquity, Ovid's *Metamorphoses*, corroborates this suspicion (*Met.*,5:551–63).

Still, it would be wrong to think that there is anything approaching consensus, among the many different ancient sources and the different traditions they represent, about the physical appearance of the siren. Just as often as they appear as feathered (and sometimes bearded) bird-women creatures, they are also depicted as mermaids (Holford-Stevens 2006:29). It is no coincidence that in many Romance languages the word for mermaid and siren is identical. The critical question of the sirens' complex bodies, in a word, remains contentious.

This does not mean, however, that the search for their voices is doomed right from the start. Let's adopt, for the sake of the argument, the exuberant style of the nineteenth century with its ebullient faith in the explanatory power of science and its tendency to take ancient mythology literally in hopes of finding the kernel of truth buried in it. From this perspective, there is one point we can extrapolate from Apollonius's account with some certainty: the sirens' voices must, in all likelihood, have been female. This is due to the simple acoustical effect of simultaneous auditory masking, where due to the physiological specifics of the inner ear lower frequencies are much more efficient at drowning out higher frequencies than the other way round (see for instance, Gelfand 2004). Orpheus is in effect nothing but a portable noise-maker, and his male voice would have been at a natural advantage here.[6]

An obvious disadvantage in Jason's approach to overcoming the sirens is that, because of the sheer noise this ancient battle of mythical singing superheroes must have produced, no one—save, perhaps, Boutes—heard what it was that the sirens sang. The *Odyssey* is a little more reliable in this respect. Homer's account of this episode at least reports the words that the sirens sang. It is possible that at one point we also knew the melody, but ever since the *Odyssey* changed from oral transmission to its written form, this crucial, musical part of their charms has been lost. The hexameters they sang are as follows:

> Come hither, much-praised Odysseus, great glory of the Acheaens, draw up your ship, that you may hear the voice of us two. For no one yet has passed this way in his black ship before hearing the honeyed voice from our mouths, but he goes home having rejoiced and knowing more. For we know all the things that in broad Troy the Argives and Trojans endured by the will of the gods; and we know all things that happen on the many-nurturing earth. (*Od.*,12.184–91)

We have to assume that their claims of omniscience must be true—after all, the sirens only address Odysseus, by name even, and not his men, as though to underline their awareness that the companions would not be in a position to appreciate their song anyway. But we can also sense that, on one level, the allure of the sirens in the *Odyssey* works in a fundamentally different way than the ones Jason has to contend with. The promises that the Homeric sirens make apparently offer the reward of knowledge: the sirens possess knowledge of the past and the future; they promise greater self-awareness. Their lure is the prospect of memory and of self-consciousness—in short, *kleos*, or renown, the sung praise that is the hero's greatest reward, and that, needless to say, interacts in complex ways with the epic of the *Odyssey* as a whole (Segal 1994:85–109; Nagy 1979). At the same time we know, thanks to Circe's warning, that the sirens are lying: in fact, no one has gone home from their shores, which are instead littered with the rotting flesh and bones of other unfortunate passers-by. The putrescent reality of their seemingly luscious meadows shows exactly the opposite of what the sirens falsely promise (Segal 1994:100–5). This is not the glorious death of a hero, who is survived by the ever-lasting tales of his bravery, but an ignoble death in anonymity, forgotten by posterity. In other words, immobility—giving in to the sirens—means death twice over: physical death and oblivion.

In fact, the fascinating details of the Homeric siren song give away much about their multi-layered significance of their promises. As has been pointed out, style and rhythm of their song is noticeably closer to the tone of the *Iliad* than anything else in the *Odyssey*: the sirens quite literally threaten to derail the independence of the epic by falsely aligning it with its older counterpart, from which it is constantly at pains to set itself apart.[7] Yielding to the sirens' song would therefore inevitably mean an end to the independence of the *Odyssey*: a fate that is the poetic equivalent to the anonymous bodies of failed heroes decaying on the sirens' shore.

As classicists have argued, the concept of *kleos*, the hero's sung glory, is noticeably absent from this episode. Similarly, all descriptions of the sirens (in Book 12 and later in Book 23, when Odysseus finally tells his wife Penelope of all his adventures) carefully avoid all mention of *kleos*. The verb that features notably instead is the very general verb *akouein*—material hearing, closely related to our word "acoustics," not the hearing of praise, *kluein* (Segal 1994:105). Similarly, what Odysseus heard in the siren song is not *phone* or *tonos*—words that describe sound with a flavor on the human voice that feature elsewhere in the *Odyssey*. For the sirens, instead, the *Odyssey* reserves the bland and more abstract term *phthongos*—best translated as "pitch."[8] The danger and allure of the sirens, it seems, is located purely in the acoustical realm.

Despite the difference in the details between the Apollonian and Homeric accounts, the music in both cases has an immediate psychological and physiological effect—we should call it erotic—on the seamen. In the case of the *Argonautica*'s Boutes, this erotic appeal was so strong that he was moved to jump into the water to swim ashore, even though he had been made aware of his impending doom. And the physiological effects caused by Homer's cognitively savvy sirens were similarly dramatic. Let's imagine, for a moment, what the spectacle must have been like from the perspective of Odysseus' deafened companions: of course, they could not hear the sirens' false promises, all they knew was how dangerous it was to hear their voices. How would they have known when they were out of danger? The cues the crew had were purely visual: Odysseus at the mast must have been writhing and wriggling—so much so that they had to tie him up more firmly. (Homer's text details that Odysseus was "nodding with his brows" [*Od.*,12:194].) Only when the ship had moved out of their acoustical reach and the siren song had become inaudible, did Odysseus become calm again.

Not least owing to the foundational position of the *Odyssey*, there is no shortage of critical commentary on the sirens. Perhaps Max Horkheimer and Theodor W. Adorno's reading of Odysseus' encounter with the sirens as an allegory of the birth of art in bourgeois culture is the most famous among the ones dating from more recent times (1981, especially "Excursus I: Odysseus or Myth and Enlightenment"). For Horkheimer and Adorno, Circe's plan is based on a proto-capitalist division of labor where Odysseus' men are condemned to row and cannot hear the beauty of the siren song—they only know of its dangers. It is the lordly Odysseus alone who is in a position to listen to the siren song, but only by taking the precaution of rendering himself impotent to act on their erotic allure. In this position, Horkheimer and Adorno conclude, music itself becomes impotent (66–67). And only as such does it become art, an object of contemplation, as opposed to unmediated erotic appeal. It is beauty rendered powerless. In denying the sirens' allure, art is now split up into cognition (*Erkenntnis*) and sensuous pleasure, and the sensuous part is rejected along with the sirens. What remains is "mere art."[9]

What I am interested in here is the other side of the equation. In this momentous mythical act that gives birth to art—or rather, to "mere art"—what happens to the parts of the siren songs, and its significance for the formation of the modern self, that falls by the wayside? What about the physiological effects of the siren songs on the body? The erotic appeal of art never quite goes away: it is merely banished in modern society (that is, in Adorno's European high-brow bourgeois modernity) so that the aesthetic realm can open up as a source of cognition and knowledge.[10] In this essay, I am hoping to debarrass music of the whole apparatus of art, of beauty and the philosophy that has been imposed on it—or at least pry them apart temporarily—in order to see where the sonic magic went.[11]

In other words, what I want to look at is a kind of aesthetics in the Greek sense of *aisthesis*, or perception. Since I am not interested here in questions of consciousness, of selfhood, of cognition and knowledge, but rather in their absence—one could even say I am interested the parts of the sirens' music that may help to weaken our resolve, shut down our self-awareness and might even make our selves do things against our will—the term "anaesthetics" is apropos. The German philosopher Wolfgang Welsch explains what he means by this term:

> Anaesthetics emphasizes the elementary basis of aisthesis. "Aisthesis" is, of course, an ambiguous term, it means sensation or perception, feeling or knowledge. And while aesthetics in its traditional form likely goes back to stressing the cognitive pole in the end, anaesthetics...is primarily related to sensation. This is not only the case in philosophy but also in medicine: anaesthetics switch off our ability to perceive sensations—and the loss of higher cognitive [*erkenntnishafte*] perception, of apperception, is its immediate consequence. In this sense, anaesthetics problematizes the basic level of the aesthetic, its conditions and limitations (1990:11).[12]

In the following I want to explore this aesthetics that also includes its opposite.[13] What is particularly appealing in this concept is the implication of dulling the senses—of rational alertness and self-control—that is such an important aspect in the part of the sonic world that we are going to explore. Odysseus' men have "anaesthetized" themselves in a rather literal way, by putting "honey-sweet wax," as Homer specifies, into their ears; Odysseus himself, meanwhile, still allowed this basic form of sensation to be processed. He is, quite literally, "all ears." His anaesthetic of choice hindered himself from acting upon the siren song. What happens to their non-artistic sound in the modern world? If this primordial division split up the siren song into its various components and in this way isolated a musical art that was neither dangerous nor erotically appealing, where did these other parts go?

## PITCH DISENCHANTED

In the modern age, the alluring song of the sirens has turned into a deafening scream. In 1819, two and a half millennia after the sirens' demise in their encounters with Jason and Odysseus, the French scientist Charles Cagniard de la Tour presented the world with a new noise-making device, which called the "sirène"—an unhappy appellation, as some later commentators felt (Robel 1891, I:12).[14] French speaker that he was, Cagniard evidently thought of sirens as mermaids, and his apparatus had the advantage of working under water just as well, and at the same pitch, as in air (1819:171). Ironically, the alarm function that the siren has in contemporary consciousness could not have been further from his French inventor's mind: the acoustic instrument that came to be known as the siren was first and foremost a device to produce a pitch and measure its frequency exactly, something that could not be done with the monochord, the traditional acoustical experimental apparatus of choice.

As with its ancient cousins, questions about the quality of tone were also at the forefront in Cagniard's conception of the siren. What had particularly piqued Cagniard's interest was the novel sound production of this apparatus. He explained at the outset of his publication:

> If, as physicists believe, instrumental sound is principally based on the regular succession of multiple impulses [chocs] passed on to the atmosphere by means of their vibrations, it seems only natural to think that with a mechanism put together so as to stir the air with the same speed and the same regularity, one could give rise to sound generation. (1819:167–68)[15]

Figure 3.2 shows the apparatus that he constructed. A bellows is attached to the chamber at the bottom of the device (marked A and B in the images). Air is forced up and through the metal disk that sits at the top of the air chamber. The disk (shown in the two smaller diagrams on the right) has holes in regular intervals, which are drilled diagonally through the metal so as to set the disk rotating (see bottom right diagram). As the air pressure increases, the sound rises in both pitch and volume. Later sirens disconnect the air mechanism from the rotation mechanism in order to decouple volume from frequency modulation.

What made the mechanism of the siren so controversial was the fact that it challenged conventional theories about the nature of sound (Seebeck 1841:417).[16] Its mechanism was radically different from traditional instruments, which all produced steady-pitch sounds by means of plucking strings or blowing pipes, and which were all known to vibrate in a more or less complex sinusoidal waveform, which would produce its characteristic sound. No such vibration patterns could be shown for the sound production of the siren: it really was no more than a short "on" impulse, followed by a longer "off" period. The siren, like its Homeric cousins, has no body that could be set into vibration, and it was in this disembodied sound that its revolutionary potential resided. Its sound derived out of a succession of interruptions, in a mechanism that can only be described as "digital" *avant la lettre*.

The venerable experimental acoustician Ernst Chladni may have been the first to realize the revolutionary potential inherent in the siren.[17] Chladni argued that as a consequence of the siren the very conception of what a "tone" is must be expanded, as it does not require "a standing vibration from a sounding body" but may, more broadly,

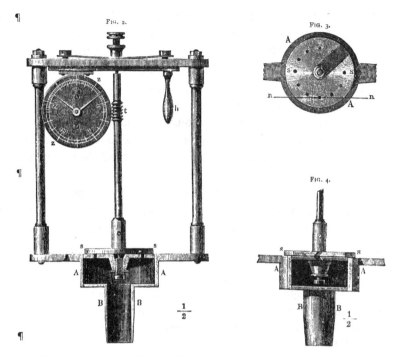

FIGURE 3.2 The mechanism of Cagniard's siren, from Helmholtz, *On the Sensations of Tone*. Reproduced with permission from the Eda Kuhn Loeb Music Library of the Harvard College Library.

be thought of as a series of "sufficiently strong and rapid impulses" which are "in some way communicated across the surrounding medium to the ear" (1826:464).[18] In other words, in the siren it was not the regular alternating rarefaction and compression of the air around an assumed zero point of normal pressure, corresponding to a sinusoidal soundwave, that caused the sensation of sound in the ear, but the mere effect of a regular pressure change that sufficed to generate sound. In marked distinction to the Leibnizian scientific axiom, *natura non facit saltus* (Nature does not make leaps), the siren suggested the possibility that discrete mechanical events could give rise to a fused sonic phenomenon.[19]

A generation after Cagniard's presentation of the siren, an experimental and a theoretical physicist, August Seebeck and Georg Simon Ohm, fought out this paradigmatic battle over the significance of this device.[20] Seebeck, on the one hand, took up the challenge and argued that the generation of sound through a pulsation of air puffs in the siren contradicted the idea that all sounds are based on sine waves. He argued, consequently, that information about pitch was given to the ear by means of a pulsation, and argued that the sinusoidal form of the wave, which had traditionally been assumed to be crucial, was in fact not an essential part of sound generation.

Ohm, on the other hand, held with Joseph Fourier that all complex waves can be analyzed into their sinusoidal components of various frequencies and amplitudes

corresponding to multiples of the fundamental frequency. A violin string or an air column typically vibrates in multiple modes simultaneously to produce a more complex
waveform and a rich timbre. A well-trained ear, Ohm's assumption continued, was capable up to a point of breaking down the complex waveform into its constituent frequencies. In other words, by picking out not only the fundamental frequency but also some
of the upper partials of a musical sound, the ear was assumed to be able to perceive,
decompose and analyze the multiple modes of vibrations that had produced the sound
in the first place. The siren, he concluded, with its discrete "on" and "off" periods and its
near-rectangular wave form was no exception from this rule—all it was was a somewhat
more complex sinusoid.[21]

Seebeck's invitation to Ohm to visit him in Dresden and to inspect the experimental
setup himself—and his whimsical hope that Ohm would "not seal his ears before the
song of his siren" (see Turner 1977:22)—fell on deaf ears. After a formal, somewhat testy
response to Seebeck in the same journal (Ohm 1844), Ohm never returned to the matter.
In the 1840s the dispute seemed to have been settled in Seebeck's favor. It was up to the
important scientist Hermann von Helmholtz a decade later to solve the dispute between
them. Helmholtz introduced a distinction between *Klang*, the physical impression of
the periodic movement of air molecules that constitute the soundwave, and *Ton*, the
perceptual impression of the periodic vibration in the ear (see also Robel 1891, I:32):

> Seebeck contends that Ohm's definition of a tone is too narrow, that besides the wave
> motion corresponding to the fundamental pitch other elements of the Fourier spec-
> trum can reinforce the sensation of the fundamental pitch. This is quite correct if he
> understands by tone that which we have just called "sonority" (*Klang*) and which for
> an ear schooled only by everyday usage is the sensuous whole, while Ohm's defini-
> tion of the tone indeed seems to denote that which is the most basic element in the
> activity of the auditory nerves (Helmholtz 1856:527).[22]

In truly solomonic fashion, Helmholtz relocated the battleground away from the modes
of production and toward the physiology of the ear, where he found it possible to reconcile ideas of both and still managed to give the crown to the Ohm, who had nearly been
slighted by the history of acoustics.[23]

Besides the protracted controversy about the physics of sound generation, in the
end, the siren came into focus for its ability to demonstrate one other point that had
previously been a theoretical possibility but not practical reality. It showed that, on a
perceptual level, the dimensions of pitch and rhythm were not sharply differentiated
but existed on a continuum. Let's revisit the mechanism of the siren: when the disk
rotates at slow velocity, individual air puffs form a continuous pulsating rhythm, but at
a frequency of around 20 Hz, that is to say at a rotation speed of 1/20 sec between each
impulse, the rhythm turns into a continuous sound. In other words, a series of short
individual sounds gave rise to the sensation of one continuous sound, the pitch of which
depended on the frequency of the periodic impulses. The discrete impulses with which
the sound was produced would merge into one overriding acoustical phenomenon, and
the siren would begin to wail and scream.

Musicians were fascinated by the potential inherent in this discovery. An anonymous series of "Acoustical letters" published in the *Neue Zeitschrift für Musik* (1852) gave the most vividly poetic description of this effect.[24] In reading this passage with its luxurious imagery (whose none-too-subtle eroticism is brought out particularly in English translation), it is useful to bear in mind that the type of siren he describes is very different from the types before. Designed by the German physicist Heinrich Wilhelm Dove, this siren is not based on a disc but a vibrating rod. The letter writer narrates:

> In the center of a large, darkened room there is a rod, which under certain conditions is set to vibrate. And every care need be taken that the vibrations are in regular succession and that their velocity can be continually increased. I step into the dark room … at a time when the rod makes but few vibrations. Neither ear nor eye tells me anything about the presence of this rod. But I *feel* its vibrating; my hand can sense its throbbing when it touches the rod. The vibrations become faster. They reach a certain number and now I perceive a noise. It is individual beats or thumps that I can discriminate with my ear; small explosions, whose rapid succession I can barely follow. The vibrations of the rod increase relentlessly. The explosions follow one after another in more and more rapid succession, they become ever stronger. There is one moment where my ear cannot discriminate any longer; in my mind they merge into one; I only perceive a whirring noise—and suddenly a low bass tone strikes my ear. It is of such stunning intensity that no other sound—not my voice, not a musical instrument, not even the sound of an organ— could be heard at all. This tone continually rises in pitch. It passes through the entire medium range up to the shrillest high-pitched sound that pierces our ear with unbearable intensity. But now everything falls back into dead silence. Still astonished by what I heard, I suddenly feel a pleasant warmth radiating from the very point where just now the sounds died away, as cozy as a fireplace. But everything around me is still plunged into darkness. Meanwhile, the vibrations become faster still. A weak red light emerges; it becomes more and more intensive, the rod is glowing. First red, then it turns yellow, then blue. It passes through all the colors until, after violet, everything sinks back into the night.… That is the siren of our century, which in its characteristic effect can well measure up to the one that once lured Odysseus. (Anon. 1852:73–74)[25]

Here the poetic description runs the whole gamut of vibrations: from individual pulses, to continuous pitch, to heat, to colors and beyond that presumably into what is now used as the radio and microwave ranges. The sensuous voluptuousness of the description is likely not matched by any realistic experiment but it wonderfully illustrates the continuity of sensation across our perceptual categories.[26]

What mattered most, however, as the anonymous letter writer was quick to add, was the transition from regular throbbing to steady pitch—perhaps because these two sensations related to the same perceptual organ, or perhaps simply because this was the only transition that stood a chance of actually being observed in practice and not being part of a nineteenth-century flight of fancy. (Helmholtz [1863] 1954:174, for one, explained that he could not bring his siren to a high enough speed to figure out at what frequency human pitch perception would end.) But even at this relatively low range of the register the implications of this fantastical experiment are nothing short of miraculous. It means no less than that the two realms of rhythm and pitch are not the perceptually discrete categories as which we treat them.

We see this every day in conventional musical notation, which uses distinct systems of signification for rhythms and pitches: durations are indicated by a relatively complex system of noteheads, stems, and flags, while pitches are indicated by the position of the notehead on the stave. Of course, very large organ pipes—bottom C is around 20 Hz— can produce similar phenomena: we tend to hear more of a pulsation than a real pitch. But it was only with the invention of the siren and its variable frequency that the boundary between the two apparently discrete dimensions could be transgressed. In the sonic reality that Cagniard's siren made possible, the two parameters become a continuum— one can be transformed into the other.

## PITCH/RHYTHM RATIONALIZED

Musicians were eager to exploit this new scientific insight. The astronomer and amateur music theorist Friedrich Wilhelm Opelt began as early as the 1830s to use the siren as the cornerstone of an all-encompassing theory of music, and developed his own siren type in the process (Opelt 1834, 1852).[27] Using his multi-voiced siren, Opelt showed how the interval of the fifth (the ratio 2:3) corresponded to the rhythmic pattern ♫♫ ♫♫ (Opelt 1834:32). In this way, he reconstructed rhythmic equivalents to complex harmonic patterns. However, since Opelt's work in music theory did not meet with the resonance he had hoped for, it took almost a century for this phenomenon to be appreciated in its entire momentousness.

The coordination of rhythmic and pitch-related features was of considerable interest in the American experimental tradition, especially in the circle surrounding Henry Cowell.[28] His *Quartet Romantic* and *Quartet Euphometric* (1915–17 and 1916–19) were based on the idea of a "demonstrable physical identity between rhythm and harmony" (Cowell 1976:preface). The rhythmic structures of the pieces are based, not dissimilar from Opelt's "harmonic rhythms," on ratios corresponding to an underlying "conceptual" (and inaudible) chordal progression. Figure 3.3 shows the opening of Cowell's *Quartet Romantic* and indicates the relationship of its pulsating rhythms to the ratios of the overtone series, which add up to a "rhythmic major harmony."[29]

In his book, *New Musical Resources*, begun around the same time and published in 1930, Cowell explained more generally how "time [is] translated, as it were, into musical tone." In that context he made explicit the relation of this idea to mechanics of the siren:

> There is a well-known acoustical instrument which produces a sound broken by silences. When the silences between the sound occur not too rapidly, the result is a rhythm. When the breaks between the sound are speeded, however, they produce a

FIGURE 3.3 The coordinated rhythms of Henry Cowell's *Quartet Romantic* correspond to the ratios of the overtone series. The opening, shown here, spells out the same ratios as a four-voiced major triad.

new pitch in themselves, which is regulated by the rapidity of the successive silences between the sounds. There is of course nothing radical in what is thus far suggested. It is only the interpretation that is new; but when we extend this principle more widely we begin to open up new fields of rhythmical expression in music." (Cowell [1930] 1996:50–51)

Eventually Cowell commissioned the musical inventor Leon Theremin to build a machine that was capable of playing several periodic rhythms based on these overtone ratios simultaneously, at a level of exactitude and complexity that surpassed human capabilities. The electrical "Rhythmicon," the result of Cowell's and Theremin's efforts, is something of a precursor to the modern drum machine. In the early 1930s Cowell composed a number of works for the Rhythmicon, with which he was hoping particularly to have performed in Europe. The device only had one problem; as Cowell's supporter, the composer and conductor Nicholas Slonimsky, noted many years later: "Like many a futuristic contraption, the Rhythmicon was wonderful in every respect, except that it did not work" (Slonimsky 1988:151).[30]

Here the idea clearly went far ahead of the technological possibilities. Another composer who became fascinated a few years later by the effect that Opelt had theorized was

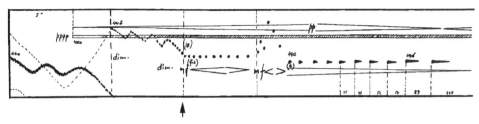

FIGURE 3.4 The performance score of Stockhausen's *Nr. 12 Kontakte* represents graphically a section in which pitch is turned into rhythm. The short excerpt (at rehearsal fig. X) shows how a meandering line of closely notated dots, at the arrow, changes into a more widely spaced row of dots. This graphic representation corresponds to a line of sounds that are heard as a glissando of changing pitches turning into a rhythm of discrete attacks of indeterminate pitch. Reproduced with permission from Universal Edition.

none other than Karlheinz Stockhausen in the 1950s. He described a thought he had while on retreat in a remote village in the Swiss Alps:

> I started to compose sounds in a new way around 1956. I recorded individual pulses from an impulse generator, and spliced them together in a particular rhythm. Then I made a tape loop of this rhythm, let's say it is tac-tac, tac, a very simple rhythm—and then I speed it up, tarac-tac, tarac-tac, tarac-tac, tarac-tac, and so on. After a while the rhythm becomes continuous, and when I speed it up still more, you begin to hear a low tone rising in pitch. That means this little period tarac-tac, tarac-tac, which lasted about a second, is now lasting less than one-sixteenth of a second, because a frequency of around 16 cycles per second is the lower limit of the perception of pitch and a sound vibrating at 16 cycles per second corresponds to a very low fundamental pitch on the organ. The timbre of this sound is also an effect of the original rhythm being tarac-tac rather than, say, tacato-tarot, tacato-tarot, which would give a different tone colour. You don't actually hear the rhythm any more, only a specific timbre, a spectrum, which is determined by the composition of its components. (1989:91–92)[31]

Composing in the age of tape recording, Stockhausen had greater chances of realizing this effect in composition than Cowell had had a few decades previously. Stockhausen put this principle to use in the important electronic composition *Kontakte*, where a complex timbre is slowed down gradually until becomes recognizable as a series of impulses. The graphic notation Stockhausen developed for the score of *Kontakte*, represented in Figure 3.4, shows how the line traverses a pitch space meandering from high to (eventually) low and finally breaks off into a series of discrete dots. The arrow indicates the moment when the pitch sequence turns into individual rhythmic impulses.

From the isolation of the Swiss Alps, Stockhausen tried to develop this principle into an all-encompassing system with which he hoped to lead Darmstadt serialism into new territories (Stockhausen 1996:183, 1989:44–45). In a word, Stockhausen noted the dependency of both musical pitch and musical duration on temporal aspects and decided to place them in relation to one another, where note values would be a kind of "macrocosm" to the "microcosm" of pitch. Since Stockhausen—and, by extension, European avant-garde musical discourse as a whole—had at that time given up any sense of a traditional tonal hierarchy in favor of the serial organization of the musical material, he sought ways of organizing note values in equivalent ways.

We do not need to go through all of Stockhausen's calculations here. Suffice it to note that he rejected the conventional durational hierarchies, based as they are on the basis of duple proportions. A better equivalency to the equal-tempered chromatic tone reservoir could be found, he went on to argue, in a logarithmic system, where each pair of temporal units was different by a factor of the twelfth root of two. In analogy with the twelve-tone principles of pitch, no duration was to be repeated until all twelve had been used. In the end he settled for a metric system that used conventional note values to denote the equivalent of octaves in pitch, and indicated fine-tuned differences within these "durational octaves" by means of metronome marks. To be sure, Stockhausen used the rhythm-pitch continuum more as inspiration than as a technically well-founded theory. The edited version of his essay "...wie die Zeit vergeht..." is furnished with an elaborate body of footnotes, a running commentary by a physicist, Georg Heike, correcting Stockhausen's scientific blunders. None of this, however, stopped the inspiration this insight afforded him.

For Stockhausen this serialization of temporal relations paved the way out of a compositional impasse into a new age of music. His essay concludes: "For it seems unproductive to remain stuck in a contradiction between on the one hand materials, instruments, that have become pointless, and the compositional imagination on the other. Instead of fighting windmills or building a whole work on a compromise, many a composer"—by which he meant himself—"attempts to bring his craft into alignment with a new musical time." (Stockhausen is punning here: this could also mean "into alignment with a new musical era.") "Then he need no longer fear rules and prohibitions, systems, theories, or constraints of any kind; for he lives in this temporal order, and his music knows how to respond to the nature of sound as it appears before him: when he begins to sense it..." (Stockhausen 1963:139).[32]

Stockhausen was convinced that he had discovered a natural law of music. Of course, he tended to adopt a certain grandiloquence, and his compositions of the time, *Zeitmaße, Klavierstücke V-XI* as well as the important *Gruppen für Orchester*, which in many ways is an exemplification of the ideas expounded in the essay, show that for him this principle may indeed have solved some important compositional issues. It is also true that this principle helped him rationalize apparently distinct musical parameters along the same lines. Students of serialism hailed the essay as a landmark.[33] Whether, however, this principle really responds to something inherent in the nature of sound is more questionable, as Stockhausen was widely criticized at the time.[34]

Stockhausen's peroration in "...wie die Zeit vergeht..." appealed in the final instance to a sense or premonition (*Ahnung*) rather than hard-nosed knowledge. From the perspective of "anaesthetics" it seems that the comprehensive rationalization of the musical material that he advocated would take us in the wrong direction: Stockhausen's argument is a compositional poetics, and as such it may be the furthest anyone has ever taken the principle of the siren. It constitutes perhaps the boldest attempt of the twentieth century to unite diverse musical parameters (Metzger and Riehm 1981:4). It contains nothing, however, in the way of the perceptual dimensions that were so central to the interest in the modern siren, beyond boundless faith in the "nature of sound."

## PITCH/RHYTHM AS DANGER

In terms of the anaesthetic aspects of the sirens, Stockhausen's discovery did little more than to put Opelt's harmonious siren on an electrical footing and in this way to introduce it to the complexities of the modern world and modern music. Sirens had in fact become electric in 1885 (Weber 1885:671–80), as shown in Figure 3.5. This allowed them to emit the wailing warning screams that distinguished them from their ancient cousins at sufficient loudness levels, and finally turned them into the alarm devices that now characterize the modern soundscape like no other noise. The composer Edgard Varèse iconically captured its newly found status in art music in his composition *Ionisation* in 1931.

It is here that the curtain finally rises for the story of the modern siren as mobile music. Mounted as alarms on fast-moving vehicles—police cars, fire engines, and ambulances—or instructing large collectivities of hearers to move out of oncoming dangers—air raids or tornadoes—the siren's deafening warning sound has become an integral part of the soundscape of our modern lives.[35]

In marked contrast to the siren's supreme importance within modern life, there is a certain irony in the fact that the rise of the siren as an alarm is all but a footnote in its history, which began, inauspiciously enough, as something of a glorified kettle whistle.

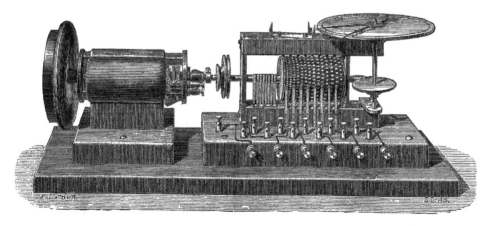

FIGURE 3.5 A Weber Electric Siren, from *Scientific American* 1885. Reproduced with permission from the Cabot Science Library of the Harvard College Library.

Following a suggestion by Christian Doppler, a mechanical siren was used as a controlling device to check the pressure level of steam engines to prevent explosions (Doppler 1850).[36] It was only when popular electrical sirens such as the Decot or the Sterling came onto the market in the early years of the twentieth century that the alarm siren was set on its path to become the hallmark of the modern soundscape. After World War I, it was widely agreed that, "once heard, the 'note' of the Sterling electric siren can never be forgotten" (Anon. 1921:441).

With the electrification of the siren, however, the principle of the pitch-rhythm continuum it espoused also became exposed to new realms of inquiry. In the electric age, the siren was not merely a device warning of approaching dangers, but the mechanism that it liberated began to represent a distinct danger in its own right. At the same time as Stockhausen's thought experiments in remote Switzerland, the secret services of all major states were busy researching the part of the acoustical world below the auditory pitch threshold, to which the mechanism of the siren had initially drawn such attention, with the hope of developing sonic weapons that operate in what is known as the "infrasound" range.[37] The international researchers—spearheaded by the exiled Russian Vladimir Gavreau (born Gavronsky), who worked at a French lab in Marseille—took Ohm's sinusoidal line to sound and were interested in sinewaves with a frequency lower than 20 Hz (Gavreau 1968). Unlike the pulsating sound of the siren or the temporal periodicity in Stockhausen's theoretical framework, however, a pure sine wave—as could be imagined, at least theoretically, as being emitted by a gigantic tuning fork—would be completely inaudible, at most it could be felt as a vibration.[38] In the mechanical world, infrasound can be picked up by seismographs, as earthquakes, tsunamis, volcanic eruptions and the like operate in a similar frequency range, but conventional microphones do not react to infrasonic waves at all. Infrasonic waves have an extremely low absorption rate, which means that they are capable of traveling very long distances without being stopped by obstacles. Moreover, Gavreau found, much to his surprise, that infrasound had the atypical behavior of not being radiated in all directions, like normal sound, but of being unidirectional. This was obviously beneficial to developing the properties of infrasound as a sonic weapon. In such a scenario, such trumpets of Jericho would not even have to be audible to blow down the proverbial city walls.

Whether this plan of infrasound as a weapon ever bore fruit is still a matter of some contention: researchers in the respectable science journal *New Scientist*, always attuned to current affairs, calculated in 1972 that in order to produce fatal injury at some 800 ft (250m) distance, an infrasonic source would need an intensity of 198 dB. This could only be achieved with a sound source of 3500 ft (1100m) in diameter (Bryan and Tempest 1972:396). The likelihood of building such a large sonic cannon, or rather deploying such a device effectively, is extremely slim. Obviously, any reliable information would be hampered by the seal of confidentiality under which labs involved in military research operate. In 1973 the British government announced cryptically: "There may be some high-wattage American sound equipment of a type used in Vietnam lying around in a store unused—but it's not our policy to discuss any weaponry that we haven't used" (Rodwell 1973).

So urgent and so real did the threat of a military application of the frequency range below 20 Hz appear that the Hungarian state produced a report for the United Nations in 1978 trying to summarize the reliable knowledge of the state of research on infrasound, which it suspected was being developed into a new kind of weapons of mass destruction (Anon. 1978). The Hungarian UN paper even found alarming pathological effects including throat spasms, breathing disorders, the induction of epileptic fits and lethal injuries to internal organs (407–8). Other studies were more cautious in their findings, including discomfort, dizziness, irritation and fatigue. Some of these effects may be attributed to the sense of balance being located in the middle ear, but Gavreau and his team initially also reported "painful resonances within the body" which disappeared after three hours.[39] Other researchers found that their subjects experience physiological effects such as "moderate chest pain vibration, a sensation of gagging, a blurring of vision and amplitude modulation of speech" (Bryan and Tempest 1972:393). Gavreau himself reported:

> I was so intrigued by the effects of the infrasound emitted by our defective ventilator that I decided to experiment with myself as a guinea pig. I wanted to find out whether it was true infrasound and whether it acted only through the ears or directly on the body. The effects were certainly unpleasant, producing a characteristic throbbing in the head and making the most simple intellectual task impossible. Perhaps this was due to the particular frequency involved? Seven Hertz is the medium frequency of the "alpha waves" of the brain which corresponds to an absence of any kind of intellectual work. (1968: 386)

This speculation is most vehemently rejected later (Broner 1978:418). The idea of such trumpets of Jericho seem to be the largely product of science fiction. At least, so far none of these weapons of mass destructions have surfaced.

But perhaps if killing people is not the main objective, unpleasant effects might be enough. It seems that this goal was much easier to reach. In 1973 the *New Scientist* reported about anti-crowd weapons that operated at 15 Hz, in an infrasound range that would produce an unpleasant throbbing sensation in the crowds without an obvious source and that would cause the crowds to panic and disperse—or so the theory goes (Anon. 1973b:726). While the device was classified as a "non-violent weapon" it was feared that the mechanism could induce epileptic fits in about 5 per cent of people exposed to this frequency. The final purpose, as in all these crowd-control devices dating from the 1970s, was to cause panic so as to wrest control away from any potential leaders of the mob.

The "Curdler," or people repeller, shown in Figure 3.6, was another anti-riot weapon that produced two very loud, high-pitched sounds at 16,000 and 16,002 Hz respectively (Applegate 1981:279–80; Goodman 2009:19). The beating pattern between the two resulted in a separate frequency of 2 Hz, in other words in the infrasound range. As the caption of the image reproduced in Figure 3.5 makes clear, there are two kinds of pulsations going on at the same time: where the infrasound disperses the crowds, the rhythms of the protesters unify the throng. But if the hand-clapping rhythms really unify and hypnotize the mob, as the illustration suggests, can infrasound itself be all that bad?

**HPS-1 SOUND SYSTEM WITH CURDLER ATTACHMENT**
The Curdler blasting 350 watts of piercing, penetrating, pulsating shrieks (comparable to standing behind a jet fighter during take-off), is an extremely effective anti-riot weapon designed to
break up the slogan-shouting, chanting, hand clapping beat that unifies and hypnotizes a mob.
   By breaking up the unifying cadence of organized agitation, mob leaders lose control and law
enforcement agencies take command. At close range, the Curdler's penetrating dissonant sound
is so piercing that it forces would-be rioters, advancing on the sound source, to turn away and
discard their weapons, banners, signs, etc., in order to free their hands to cover and protect their
ears. In confined areas such as in narrow streets or alleys, the effects are greatly magnified; at
night, the sound many times arouses panic instincts.

FIGURE 3.6 "The Curdler," an anti-riot sonic weapon. Reproduced from *Riot Control* (1981)
by Col. Rex Applegate with permission from Paladin Press.

# RHYTHM AS BLISS

After all, the rhythmic pulse is nothing but another form of infrasound—produced, as
in Cagniard's siren, not as a complex sinusoid but as a periodicity of pulses. This idea is
less outlandish than it may sound at first. In non-Western musics, we find many forms of
trance-inducing music—think of Whirling Dervishes or Siberian Shamans—and many
of them using rhythmic forces as the main constituent.[40] In the West, similar effects
are perhaps best realized in Electronic Dance Music. One commentator remarks succinctly: "Techno makes the body vibrate" (Böpple and Knüfer 1996:180).[41]
   In fact, a palpable physiological effect seems to be the measure of success of most
forms of Electronic Dance Music. Here is a German DJ trying to capture in words what
makes good techno music:

> Any techno party should not only be "extremely swingy," but it must also bring with
> it "profound changes of physical, linguistic and other probabilities [sic]." At least
> afterwards one should have the feeling of being "pummeled by God."...When you
> feel the bass line tickle your organs, when DJ Hell, in his "Jump from the clouds,"

raises the bass just a little more, when the ravers start screaming—then you'll understand. (Böpple and Knüfer 1996:155)[42]

One point of consensus in techno criticism is that it is not about the musical qualities
in any traditional sense—the subtlety of the composition, the beauty of the material, or
the refinement of harmonic modulation—but rather the physiological effect this music
elicits in the ravers. A lot of this is dependent on the sheer volume at which the music
is played, but another important factor is the speed of the basic pulse. Some styles of
techno, mostly from the hardcore or gabber styles that were flourishing in the 1990s,
are extremely fast: they can go up to 500 bpm, that is, beats per minute (Volkwein
2000:407). The track "Thousand" (for 1000 bpm) by Moby entered the Guinness Book
of Record as the fastest rhythm on record. In other words, these pieces can have a pulse
of 16.6 Hz, which falls well into the infrasound range. In fact, this is close to the auditory
range, where the beat of "Thousand" at its peak rate could almost be perceived as a pitch
in its own right. Most serious techno aficionados consider this track a gimmick, which
was merely produced for the sake of being the fastest on record.

   In fact, it by far overshoots the goal, certainly if the goal of the techno experience, as
the literature states repeatedly, is to bring the heartbeat into alignment with the pulse
of the music.[43] Some critics argue that this is the reason extremely fast styles of techno
could not become mainstream because they exceed the capacity of the heartbeat to
adjust to rhythms at such high velocity. The mean of techno music in the 1990s seems to
be a little slower around 150 bpm, or 2.5 Hz.

   There is good reason to remain skeptical about this reasoning. The idea that music
and heartbeat really become one contains a good dose of romantic imagination. So far,
it seems, no studies have confirmed the correlation between music and heartbeat. It is,
of course, undeniable that the heartbeat increases significantly—under the influence of
the loud music, the sheer physical exercise and, at least at times, considerable drug consumption. Other commentators therefore state more cautiously: "In an ideal case, the
music imitates and regulates the heartbeat. The body takes up the attacks of the music
from both ends with both ears and feet. The music has to flood the entire body, as in an
electric massage. The feeling to be all body, a being-in-the-world, is the experience of
bliss.... Ecstasy is caused by monotonous beats" (Böpple and Knüfer 1996:159–61).[44] The
music becomes not merely audible but physically palpable.

   All ravers agree that the effect of techno is based on the repetitive rhythms of the
music. This was also known to the British authorities, who after all had experience with
the dangerous potential of infrasound. In 1994 the British Government under Prime
Minister John Major announced a Criminal Justice and Public Order Act. Part V, section 63, conferred on the police "Powers to remove persons attending or preparing
for a rave." In order to delimit these powers clearly, concepts such as "rave" and, critically, "music" had to be (re-)defined: "Music," the new law specified, "includes sounds
wholly or predominantly characterised by the emission of a succession of repetitive
beats." This definition—and the danger identified in repetitive music—drew both ire
and ridicule from most commentators. One electronic music group responded to this

law by producing a dance track—Autechre's "Flutter" on the album *Anti EP*—that was absolutely safe, because its complex rhythm track contained no repetitive beats whatever.[45]

The mechanism of the modern siren pulls us in two directions at once. The use of infrasound in sonic warfare seems at first to be a far cry from the principles underlying the beats of electronic dance music, but in the final analysis both sides converge in their focus on the body, of which the British 1994 law is emblematic. Both sides intersect in two dimensions: on the one hand, fear, and on the other, loss of the self. It is no coincidence that both have been identified as markers of modernity.

# CONCLUSION

One musicologist comments: "Techno is the music of absolute immediacy and pure physicality" (Poschardt 1996:314).[46] Although used in a different context, this verdict makes an appropriate point for our own small Odyssey into the sound world of non-art music into which the tragic demise of the sirens has led us. It brings us back to the question of "anaesthetics," the aesthetic inquiry specifically into the sensuous parts of sound, with which we started. If there is one realm where the erotic desire, the physical immediacy and the danger of the sirens' song come together in a new form of anaesthetic music—devoid of cognition (in the philosophical sense) but full of bodily desire—then it would be in the form of electronic dance music.

This is not the place to engage in the complicated question of the (an)aesthetics of techno, but we can nonetheless glean, more broadly, from Horkheimer and Adorno a critique of a sensory experience that does not serve any philosophically cognitive ends, that does not, in other words, support the formation of the self. They view such a phenomenon in a distinctly Freudian vein:

> The effort to hold itself together attends the ego at all its stages, and the temptation to be rid of the ego has always gone hand-in-hand with the blind determination to preserve it. Narcotic intoxication, in which the euphoric suspension of the self is expiated by deathlike sleep, is one of the oldest social transactions mediating between self-preservation and self-annihilation, an attempt by the self to survive itself. The fear of losing the self, and suspending with it the boundary between oneself and other life, the aversion to death and destruction, is twinned with a promise of joy which has threatened civilization at every moment. (2002:26)

Horkheimer and Adorno are referring here to the lure of the music of the Homeric sirens, but one can see how their judgment could be applied without too many adaptations to the field of electronic dance music, with its urge to leave behind individual selfhood and become one with the dancing community.[47] The dance floor allows the formation of an alternative kind of identity, not one based on individual selfhood in the manner of traditional aesthetics, but one in which the repetitive rhythms unify the dancing bodies anonymously into one collective organism. Rave culture sometimes celebrates the ecstasy of the dance floor as its very own kind of Stendhal's *promesse du bonheur*.[48] But, certainly as far as Horkheimer and Adorno are concerned, this withdrawal from public order is in itself a highly political move that comes at a price: the desire to relinquish selfhood presents no less than a threat to the fabric of civilization.[49]

With this in mind we can begin to retrace our steps across the various parts of our Odyssey. Most centrally, of course, the question has often been raised about how the modern sirens relate to their ancient cousins. Cagniard de la Tour, as we saw, struck a poetic pose in christening his invention "sirène," though in highlighting the amphibian existence of both noisemakers, he homed in on an aspect that has turned out to be less central than its inventor may have imagined. Philipp von Hilgers, by contrast, has elegantly argued (2003:104) that in ancient times travelers used to be warned *against* the sirens, whereas in our modern age we are warned *by* the sirens themselves. With a view specifically to mobility, it is further noticeable that the old sirens hindered seafarers from moving on, whereas modern sirens induce the public to move more quickly.

It seems, however, that the most important point that connects old and new sirens is in the common awareness of the fact that we do not merely listen with our ears but with our whole body. The modern sirens, specifically, have unlocked the barrier that had divided the sonic world above and below 20 Hz, into the seemingly separate domains of pitch and rhythm. In this anaesthetic mode of perceiving the song of the sirens, our cognitive capacities are reduced to their basics, to a level where pleasure and pain are connected. Both old and new sirens elicit responses that may be alluring or threatening. With their immediacy and physicality, they effortlessly bring together ecstasy and danger.

It seems that against this new form of siren song even Platonic and Aristotelian admonitions to ban certain modes from the ideal state would be ineffectual: its allure is not based on pitches, scales or modes, but on rhythmic power. Karl Bücher, the influential materialist thinker who tried to bring together music and labor, concluded: "Everybody knows how strongly rhythmic music affects our nerves, how it elicits movements of the head, the arms, or the feet, or how, at any rate, we sense a strong desire in these limbs to accompany march and dance music with bodily motions" (1897:333).[50] And even Nietzsche knew: "Rhythm is coercion. It induces an irresistible desire to yield, to join in; not only the step of the feet, the soul itself follows the beat—probably, or so one concluded, even the soul of the gods" (1990:93).[51]

It may appear as if our short Odyssey through the realm of tones has ended up in a somewhat different place than where we set out. To be sure, those who would want to argue that the ancient sirens lured Odysseus and his men onto their shores with seductive repetitive rhythms are few in number.[52] But the lesson of the sirens—their modern cousins, to be precise—is that those repetitive rhythms are not a million miles away from their ancient original *phthongoi*. Both held their charms, above or below 20 Hz, on either side of the threshold that our hearing imposes on the soundwaves.

## Notes

1. Thanks must go to Joseph Auner, Giulio Boccaletti, Bevil Conway, David Elmer, Branden W. Joseph, Thomas Y. Levin, and John Durham Peters for their expertise in the many different fields touched upon in this essay.

2. The most impressive attempt is perhaps found in George Kastner's large-scale exploration *Les sirènes* (1858), which ends, as was Kastner's wont, with an original composition on the subject, *Le rêve d'Oswald ou les sirènes*. More recently Friedrich Kittler (2006) has taken up the question of the sirens again.

3. The sexual imagery—the sirens' flowery meadows and Odysseus' phallic mast—has been much commented on. For feminist critiques see Peraino (2006) and Comay (2000).

4. Modern readers might wonder whether in principle the sirens should not have long been dead, at least since the time Odysseus got away some five hundred years previously, but the complex temporality of Greek mythology is not much inhibited by mundane questions of chronological succession. See Holford-Stevens (2006:20).

5. "Mais quel était, en general, le caractère du chant des Sirènes? Etait-ce une plainte amoureuse doucement modulée par des voix humaines ? Etait-ce un simple chant d'oiseau ? Qui peut le dire ? C'est là une difficulté d'autant plus insoluble qu'elle se rattache, d'une part, au problème de la forme des Sirènes dans l'*Odyssée* ; d'autre part, à la question de savoir si, lorsque les anciens avaient sous les yeux des oiseaux représentés avec des têtes de femme, ils leur attribuaient un organe humain ou bien un gazouillement semblable à celui des habitants de l'air. Ce qu'on peut décider, par analogie, c'est que l'organe humain doit avoir eu dans leur pensée la préférence, car c'est la voix de l'homme, qu'empruntent en général les oiseaux devins et prophètes qui, dans les cultes de l'Orient ou dans les religions du Nord, rendent des oracles et communiquent avec les mortels."

   (But what was the song of the sirens like? Was it an amorous lament, gently modified by human voices? Was it plain birdsong? Who could say? This issue is all the more unsolvable in so far as it is connected, on the one hand, to the problem of the shape of the sirens in the Odyssey, and on the other, to the impossibility of knowing whether, where the ancients imagined birds with women's heads, they would also attribute to them a human voice or twittering similar to that of the inhabitants of the air. What can be said, though, on the basis of analogy, is that they must have thought the human organ preferable, for in the cults of the Orient and the religions of the North, the augural and prophetic birds, which made oracular pronouncements and communicated with mortals, borrowed the voice of the human.)

6. At the same time, to take this speculation further, it seems that Gluck's decision to revise Orfeo's countertenor role as a tenor for Orphée in the French revised version of his opera *Orfeo ed Euridice/Orphée et Eurydice* was a choice that acousticians could only applaud.

7. See Segal (1994:101–5); Holford-Stevens (2006:17).

8. The term *phthongos* enters music-theoretical literature with the writings of Ptolemy in the second century C.E.

9. The term itself is from Wellmer (2000:7, 9), but see also Horkheimer and Adorno (1981:41). (The German has: "ihre Lockung wird zum bloßen Gegenstand der Kontemplation neutralisiert, zur Kunst.") No wonder, then, that modern listeners in the concert hall hearing Debussy's third *Nocturne*, with a wordless female choir vocalizing the *Sirènes*, have no desire to run up to the stage, but rather sit quietly until the end and then clap dutifully to express their enjoyment. See also Kramer (2006).

10. The German word *Erkenntnis*, a key term in Kantian and post-Kantian philosophy, is typically translated as "cognition." *Erkenntnis* carries a stronger sense of concept-based insights than the English term and is more closely related to insight and knowledge. Despite these connotative differences, I am retaining the standard translation and try to clarify its knowledge-related context wherever possible.

11. In fact, Horkeimer and Adorno themselves hint at that possibility, see (1981:40).

12. "Dabei betont Anästhetik die Elementarschicht der *aisthesis*. 'Aisthesis' ist ja ein doppeldeutiger Ausdruck, kann Empfindung oder Wahrnehmung, Gefühl oder Erkenntnis, sensation oder perception meinen. Und während die Ästhetik in ihrer traditionellen Ausformung meist doch wieder nur den kognitiven Pol betonte, bezieht sich Anästhetik...primär auf die Empfindung. Das ist nicht erst in der Philosophie, sondern schon in der Medizin so: Durch Anästhesie schaltet man die Empfindungsfähigkeit aus— und der Wegfall des höheren, des erkenntnishaften Wahrnehmens erweist sich als bloße Folge davon. Anästhetik problematisiert also die Elementarschicht des Ästhetischen, seine Bedingung und Grenze."

13. "Anaesthetics" is only one term for what is in fact a wider movement within aesthetics that is fairly prominent in Germany and that seeks to reorient aesthetics by questions of sensation. Böhme (2001); Barck et al. (1990); as well as Kittler (2006) should be mentioned here. Buck-Morss (1992) develops a more literal notion of "anaesthetics" out of the work of Walter Benjamin.

14. There is some dispute as to whether the Scottish scientist John Robison should count as the inventor of the siren, as he had developed a similar mechanism before Cagniard de la Tour. For our purposes, it is worth bearing in mind that it is only Cagniard's apparatus that carries the name siren.

15. "Si le son produit par les instrumens est dû principalement, comme le croient les physiciens, à la suite régulière des chocs multipliés qu'ils donnent à l'air atmosphérique par leurs vibrations, il semble naturel de penser qu'au moyen d'un mécanisme qui serait combiné pour frapper l'air avec la même vitesse et la même régularité, on pourrait donner lieu à la production du son."

16. "Dabei darf allerdings nicht vergessen werden, dass die von jenen Apparaten ausgehenden Wellen nicht ganz von derselben Natur sind, wie die durch stehende Schwingung eines elastischen Körpers erzeugten Wellen zu seyn pflegen" ("We must not forget that the waves emanating from these apparatuses are not quite of the same nature as the waves created by means of standing vibrations of elastic bodies tend to be.") And stronger in Seebeck 1843: "der einfache Ton $m$ [muss] nicht nothwendig von der Form $a.ccos(mt+\theta)$ seyn." ("The simple tone $m$ does not necessarily have to correspond to the form $a.ccos(mt+\theta)$.") (479). Ohm responds vehemently in an article of 1844.

17. See Robel (1891, II:3).

18. "Aus alle dem...ist zu ersehen, dass man den Begriff von *Ton* in etwas weitläufigerem Sinne nehmen muß, als es gewöhnlich geschieht, indem nicht allemal (stehende) Schwingungen eines tönenden Körpers dazu erforderlich sind, sondern es im Allgemeinen darauf ankommt, daß hinreichend starke und schnell auf einander folgende Stöße auf irgend eine Art dem umher befindlichen Medium und durch dieses dem Gehöre mitgetheilt werden."

19. See Hilgers (2003).

20. Key texts in this controversy include Seebeck (1841, 1843, 1844) and Ohm (1843, 1844).

21. In Ohm (1844:12), the physicist countered that "zur Erzeugung eines Tones von der Schwingungsmenge m/2l nur das eine Glied der Reihe (A.), welches dieselbe

Schwingungsmenge in sich trägt, beitragen kann" ("only the one member of the series
(A.), which carries in it the same vibration set, can contribute to the generation of a
tone of the vibration set m/21"). As Ohm cannot come up with a continuous wave—his
approach does not account for the periods between impulses, as he is well aware—he
continues: "Es könnte daher wohl geschehen, und das Daseyn der Combinationstöne
leistet im Grunde Gewähr dafür, dass die folgenden Glieder der Reihe (A.) den im
ersten Gliede enthaltenen Ton durch solche unregelmäßige Successionen zu verstärken
im Stande wären" ("It could happen—and the existence of combination tone in principle warrants it—that the following members of the series (A.) are capable of reinforc-
ing the tone contained in the first member by means of such irregular successions")
(1844:14). Helmholtz (1856) then reduced and focused their dispute on the question of
combination tones.

22. "Seebeck behauptet, daß Ohm's Definition des Tones zu eng sey, daß außer der dem
Grundton entsprechenden einfachen Wellenbewegung auch noch andere Glieder der
Fourier'schen Reihe die Empfindung des Grundtons verstärken könnten. Dies erscheint
ganz richtig wenn er unter Ton das versteht, was wir eben mit dem Namen Klang bezeich-
net haben, und was für die nur durch die Uebung des gewöhnlichen Lebens geschulte
Aufmerksamkeit allerdings ein sinnliches Ganze ist, während die Ohm'sche Definition
des Tons in der That das zu bezeichnen scheint, was in der Thätigkeit des Gehörnerven das
einfachste Element ist."

23. Helmholtz's suggestion is certainly a useful distinction that brings clarity to the complexities of the debate: Seebeck had argued that Ohm's theory cannot convincingly show why
the fundamental is so much stronger than the upper partials. Following Ohm's calculations—even after their correction by Seebeck—upper partials would have to be much
stronger than they usually are. Ohm argues that this is merely a problem of perception,
not of mathematical accuracy. Seebeck counters, very effectively, by pointing out that the
decision of what is essential tone, what is incidental noise, can only be made by the ear. For
a detailed discussion of the dispute, see Turner (1977) and Vogel (1993).

24. The last letter is signed by the author, Richard Pohl, and the letters in their entirety were
later published as a book, where the author is identified (Pohl 1853). Thanks go to David
Trippett for identifying the author.

25. "In der Mitte eines großen, finsteren Zimmers befinde sich ein Stab, der unter gewissen
Voraussetzungen in Schwingungen versetzt wird. Es sei dafür gesorgt, daß die Schwingungen
regelmäßig aufeinander folgen, und daß ihre Geschwindigkeit fortwährend vermehrt
werden kann. Ich trete in den dunklen Raum . . . in dem Augenblick, wo der Stab nur wenige
Schwingungen macht. Weder Auge noch Ohr sagt mir Etwas von dem Vorhandensein
diess Stabes. Aber ich *fühle* seine Schwingungen, denn die Hand empfindet seine Schläge,
wenn sie ihn berührt. Die Schwingungen werden schneller. Sie erreichen eine gewisse Zahl
und nun vernehme ich ein Geräusch. Es sind einzelne Schläge oder Stöße, die ich mit dem
Ohr unterscheide; kleine Explosionen, deren Aufeinanderfolge ich kaum zu trennen vermag. Die Schwingungen des Stabes vermehren sich aber fort und fort. Die Explosionen
erfolgen rascher und rascher, sie werden immer stärker. Es tritt ein Moment ein, wo sie
mein Ohr nicht mehr zu trennen vermag; sie fließen im Bewußtsein in Eins zusammen;
ich vernehme nur noch ein Sausen—und plötzlich schlägt ein tiefer Baßton an mein Ohr.
Er ist von so betäubender Intensität, daß weder von meiner Stimme, noch von dem Tone
irgend eines musikalischen Instrumentes, selbst nicht von dem der Orgel, das Geringste
gehört werden könnte. Dieser Ton erhöht sich fortwährend. Er durchläuft alle Mittelstufen,

bis zum höchsten schrillenden Ton, der in unser Ohr mit unerträglicher Intensität ein-schneidet. Aber nun sinkt Alles in die vorige Grabesstille zurück. Noch voll Erstaunen über das, was ich hörte, fühle ich plötzlich von der Stelle her, an welcher der Ton verhallte, eine angenehme Wärme sich strahlend verbreiten, so behaglich, wie ein Kaminfeuer sie aus-sendet. Aber noch bleibt Alles dunkel. Doch die Schwingungen werden noch schneller. Ein schwaches rothes Licht dämmert auf, es wird immer lebhafter, der Stab glüht. Erst roth, dann wird er gelb, dann blau. Er durchläuft alle Farben, bis nach dem Violett Alles wieder in Nacht versinkt... Das ist die Syrene unseres Jahrhunderts, welche an Eigenthümlichkeit der Wirkung sich wohl mit jener messen kann, die einst Odysseus lockte."

26. This text could pass as a scientific-poetic transcription of the *Rheingold* Prelude, as Rena Mueller pointed out to me. This is no coincidence: the anonymous author, Richard Pohl, is one of Wagner's most vociferous advocates.

27. See also Fink (1834); Becker (1835).

28. I am very grateful to Joseph Auner for pointing out the importance of American Experimentalism to me.

29. The underlying principles of Cowell's rhythmic-harmonic compositions are explored in Nicholls (1990:140–54). It is an open question to what extent precisely Cowell's ideas were based on the teachings of his teacher Carl Seeger, which were published in the lengthy study "Tradition and Experiment in (the New) Music." See Seeger (1994: esp.103).

30. To be fair to Theremin and Cowell, they did eventually succeed in producing a function-ing Rhythmicon. One of these instruments survives in the Smithsonian Institution. The mathematically inclined music theorist Joseph Schillinger was particularly taken by this device, and describes it in his late treatise *The Mathematical Basis of the Arts* (1948:665–67). He calculates that the Rhythmicon can combine 65,535 rhythms and if each combination is played for 10 seconds, a complete cycle will take 455 days, 2 hours and 30 minutes.

31. The fact that Stockhausen operates with 16 Hz, where most other researchers specify 20 Hz, is a negligible difference.

32. "Denn es scheint wenig fruchtbar zu sein, in einem Widerspruch zwischen dem sinnlos gewordenen Material, den sinnlos gewordenen Instrumenten einerseits und der komposi-torischen Vorstellung andererseits steckenzubleiben. Statt gegen Windmühlen anzuren-nen oder die ganze Arbeit auf einem Kompromiß aufzubauen, versucht manch einer lieber, sein Handwerk in Einklang mit einer neuen musikalischen Zeit zu bringen. Dann braucht er keine Regeln und Verbote, kein System keine Theorie und keinen Zwang mehr zu fürchten; denn er lebt in dieser Zeitordnung, und seine Musik gibt Antwort auf die Klangnatur, wenn sie sich ihm auftut: wenn er ahnt..."

33. See Blumröder (1993:117).

34. See, for instance, Fokker (1968); Backus (1962).

35. See Thompson (2001).

36. It is disappointing that Doppler missed the chance to exemplify his eponymous effect—surely a milestone in the history of moving music—by using the siren. The Doppler Effect had first been introduced in 1842, as a hypothesis to explain the different hues of the stars (see Doppler 1842). It was left to the Dutch physicist Christoph Buys-Ballot to transfer this effect to the acoustical realm three years later. Buys-Ballot first tested the acoustical Doppler effect using trumpet players on a passing train that he compared with the sound of a station-ary trumpet. Surprisingly perhaps, this experimental setup produced the desired results.

37. The role of music as torture has been probed in a pioneering article by Cusick (2006). See also Cusick and Joseph (2011). Many of the scientific texts drawn on in this section are compiled in the anthology Swezey (1995).

38. A review article in the English medical journal *The Lancet* (Anon. 1973:1368) points out that infrasound can be audible, but only at much higher levels of loudness: the audibility threshold at 10 Hz is 100 dB, and 120 dB at 3 Hz. Note also Broner (1978:413), who points out that von Békésy's 1936 calculations hold. He describes the sensation of infrasound as a "chugging," "rough" or "popping sound" while arguing that these may be due to upper harmonics generated by distortion of the middle and inner ear.

39. Again, *The Lancet* (Anon. 1973:1368) contradicts Gavreau in this point: "There is no hard evidence that infrasound below the threshold of hearing is detected by the body through any other receptor."

40. See for instance Becker (2004); Rouget (1985).

41. "Beim Techno vibriert der Körper mit." The most extensive study of the rhythms electronic dance music in English is Butler (2006).

42. "…jede Technoparty [sollte] nicht nur 'extrem swinging' sein, [sondern] auch 'tiefgreifende Veränderungen körperlicher, sprachlicher und sonstiger Wahrscheinlichkeiten' nach sich ziehen…Zumindest sollte man danach das Gefühl haben, von 'Gott durchgenudelt' worden zu sein…Wenn dich die Bassline an deinem Organen kitzelt, wenn DJ Hell bei seinem Track 'Sprung aus den Wolken' den Baß noch ein bißchen anhebt, die Partyleute dann dazu schreien—dann verstehst du."

43. For an inquiry into the aesthetic questions of techno see Volkwein (2003).

44. "Im Idealfall imitiert und reguliert sie [die Musik] den Schlag des Herzens. Von den Endpunkten, den Ohren und Füßen, nimmt der Körper die Attacken der Musik auf. Die Musik muß den ganzen Körper durchströmen, wie bei einer elektrischen Massage. Das Gefühl, Körper zu sein und 'dazusein', ist die Glückserfahrung…Ekstase wird durch monotone Beats erzeugt."

45. The album was sealed with a sticker that says: "Warning. *Lost* and *Djarum* contain repetitive beats. We advise you not to play these tracks if the Criminal Justice Bill becomes law. *Flutter* has been programmed in such a way that no bars contain identical beats and can therefore be played at both forty-five and thirty-three revolutions under the proposed new law. However we advise DJs to have a lawyer and musicologist present at all times to confirm the non-repetitive nature of the music in the event of police harassment. Important. By breaking this seal, you accept full responsibility for any consequential action resulting from the product's use, as playing the music contained within these recordings may be interpreted as opposition to the Criminal Justice and Public Order Bill."

46. "Techno ist die Musik absoluter Unmittelbarkeit und reiner Physik."

47. See Böpple and Knüfer (1996).

48. Böpple and Knüfer (1996), based on interviews within the techno community, comes close to providing an anthropologically based aesthetics of techno as "mass ecstasy" (162). See also, much more broadly, McNeill (1995).

49. We do not, of course, have to take Horkheimer and Adorno as the ultimate authorities on techno. One can endlessly debate whether cultural phenomena such as the German Love Parade constitute political events or not. (This question has gained renewed currency in light of the tragedy at the Duisburg Love Parade in 2010.) More recent scholars, such as Tia DeNora (2000) or Steven Connor (1996), may have better models of identity-formation in sonic phenomena, and post-Adornian philosophers, such as Jacques Rancière 2004, may have more up-to-date models for bringing together aesthetics and politics. What makes Horkheimer and Adorno interesting here is primarily their close relationship to the notion of "anaesthetics."

50. "Jedermann weiß, wie stark rhythmische Musik auf unsere motorischen Nerven einwirkt, wie sie Bewegungen des Kopfes, der Arme, der Füße hervorruft, oder wie wenigstens in diesen Gliedern ein starker Drang empfunden wird, Marsch- oder Tanzmusik mit Körperbewegungen zu begleiten."

51. "Der Rhythmus ist ein Zwang; er erzeugt eine unüberwindliche Lust, nachzugeben, mit einzustimmen; nicht nur der Schritt der Füße, auch die Seele selber geht dem Tacte nach,—wahrscheinlich, so schloß man, auch die Seele der Götter!)."

52. For completeness's sake, it should be mentioned that there is at least one author who comes close to arguing just that. Classicist William Harris [no year] writes in an online publication: "It should also be noted that the word 'Siren' means in Greek 'twinkler,' if it is correctly derived from the rare verb 'seriazein' 'to twinkle.' (The word is also applied to the planets after the notions of the Pythagorean school.) Perhaps it was the 'twinkling' or accelerated beats of the music that seem so absorbing to the Greeks, much in the way that the musical third-interval, which produces about twenty beats per second, seemed un-calming and frenzied to fourteenth century Church officials, who outlawed it from official church use."

# REFERENCES

Anon. [Richard Pohl]. 1852. "Akustische Briefe." *Neue Zeitschrift für Musik* 37:1–3, 13–15, 21–24, 35–36, 41–47, 73–76, 85–88, 185–87, 193–96, 249–51, 261–64.

——. 1853. "Akustische Briefe." *Neue Zeitschrift für Musik* 38: 25–28, 33–37, 65–67, 73–74.

Anon. 1885. "Weber's Electric Siren." *Scientific American* 53:82.

Anon. 1921. "The Siren as Fire Alarm." *The American City*, August 8 (25):441.

Anon. 1973a. "Infrasound." *The Lancet*, December 15 (302): 1368–69.

Anon. 1973b. "Anti-crowd Weapon Works by Causing Fits." *New Scientist*, March 29:726.

Anon. 1978. "Working Paper on Infrasound Weapons." In *AMOK Journal: Sensurround Edition* (1995):405–9.

Apollonius Rhodius. 1912. Ἀργοναυτικά/*Argonautica*. Trans. R. C. Seaton. Cambridge, MA: Harvard University Press.

Applegate, Col. Rex. 1981. *Riot Control: Materiel and Techniques*, 2nd ed. Boulder: Paladin Press.

Backus, John. 1962. "*Die Reihe*: A Scientific Evaluation." *Perspectives of New Music* 1:160–71.

Barck, Karlheinz, Peter Gente, Heidi Paris and Stefan Richter, eds. 1990. *Aisthesis: Wahrnehmung heute oder Perspektiven einer anderen Ästhetik*. Leipzig: Reclam.

Becker, C. F. 1835. [Review of Opelt 1834]. *Neue Zeitschrift für Musik* 3:121–23.

Becker, Judith. 2004. *Deep Listening: Music, Emotion and Trancing*. Bloomington: Indiana University Press.

Blumröder, Christoph von. 1993. *Die Grundlegung der Musik Karlheinz Stockhausens*. Stuttgart: Franz Steiner Verlag.

Böhme, Gernot. 2001. *Aisthetik: Vorlesungen über die allgemeine Wahrnehmungslehre*. Munich: Fink.

Böpple, Friedhelm, and Ralf Knüfer. 1996. *Generation XTC*. Berlin: Volk und Welt.

Broner, N. 1978. "The Effects of Low Frequency Noise on People—A Review." *Journal of Sound and Vibration* 58. Reprinted in *AMOK Journal: Sensurround Edition* (1995):410–16.

Bryan, Michael, and William Tempest. 1972. "Does Infrasound Make Drivers Drunk?" *New Scientist*, March 16. Reprinted in *AMOK Journal: Sensurround Edition* (1995):393–98.

Bücher, Karl. 1897. *Arbeit und Rhythmus*. Leipzig: S. Hirzel.

Bucks-Morss, Susan. 1992. "Aesthetics and Anaesthetics: Walter Benjamin's Artwork Essay Reconsidered." *October* 62:3–41.

Butler, Mark. 2006. *Unlocking the Groove: Meter, Rhythm and Musical Design in Electronic Dance Music.* Bloomington: Indiana University Press.

Cagniard de la Tour, Charles. 1819. "Sur la sirène, nouvelle machine d'acoustique destinée à mesurer les vibrations de l'air qui constituent le son." *Annales de la physique et la chimie* 12:167–71.

Chladni, Ernst F. F. 1826. "Ueber Töne bloß durch schnell auf einander folgende Stöße, ohne einen klingenden Körper." [*Poggendorffs*] *Annalen der Physik* 84:453–60.

Comay, Rebecca. 2000. "Adorno's Siren Song." *New German Critique* 81:21–48.

Connor, Steven. 1996. "The Modern Auditory I." In *Rewriting the Self: Histories from the Renaissance to the Present*, ed. Roy Porter, 203–23. London and New York: Routledge.

Cowell, Henry. 1976. *Quartet Romantic, Quartet Euphometric.* New York, London, Frankfurt: Edition Peters.

——. [1930] 1996. *New Musical Resources*, ed. David Nicholls. Cambridge: Cambridge University Press.

Cusick. Suzanne. 2006. "Music as Torture/Music as Weapon." *Revista Transcultural de Música./ Transcultural Music Review* 10, http://www.sibetrans.com/trans/trans10/cusick_eng.htm.

Cusick. Suzanne and Branden W. Joseph, 2011. "Across An Invisible Line: A Conversation About Music and Torture." *Grey Room* 42:6–21.

DeNora, Tia. 2000. *Music in Everyday Life.* Cambridge: Cambridge University Press.

Doppler, Christian. 1842. "Ueber das farbige Licht der Doppelsterne und einiger anderer Gestirne des Himmels." Vienna: Borrosch & André.

——.1850. "Über die Anwendung der Sirene und des akustischen Flugrädchens zur Bestimmung des Spannungsgrades der Wasserdämpfe und der komprimierten Luft." *Wiener Berichte* 6:206–14.

Dougherty, Carol. 2001. *The Raft of Odysseus: The Ethnographic Imagination of Homer's Odyssey.* Oxford: Oxford University Press.

Fink G[ottfried] W. 1834. [Review of Opelt 1834]. *Allgemeine Musikalische Zeitung* 36:cols. 785–89.

Fokker, Adriaan D. 1968. "Wherefore and Why." *Die Reihe* 8:69–79.

Gavreau, Vladimir. 1968. "Infrasound." *Science Journal* 4. Reprinted in *AMOK Journal: Sensurround Edition* (1995):379–89.

Gelfand, Stanley A. 2004. *Hearing: An Introduction to Psychological and Physiological Acoustics*, 4th ed. New York: Marcel Dekker.

Goodman, Steve. 2009. *Sonic Warfare: Sound, Affect, and the Ecology of Fear.* Cambridge, MA: MIT Press.

Harris, William. [no year]. *Euhemerism: The Greek Myths*, http://community.middlebury.edu/~harris/GreekMyth/Chap12LandAndClimate.html (accessed on June 18, 2009).

Helmholtz, Hermann von. 1856. "Ueber Combinationstöne." [*Poggendorffs*] *Annalen der Physik und Chemie* 99:523–29.

——.[1863] 1954. *Die Lehre von den Tonvorstellungen.* Reprint as *On the Sensations of Tone*, trans. Alexander Ellis. New York: Dover.

Hilgers, Philipp von. 2003. "Sirenen: Lösungen des Klangs vom Körper." *ZwischenRäume* 6:103–21.

Holford-Stevens, Leofranc. 2006. "The Sirens in Antiquity and the Middle Ages." In *Music of the Sirens*, ed. Linda Phyllis Austern and Inna Naroditskaya, 16–51. Bloomington: Indiana University Press.

Homer. 1919. ’Οδύσσεια/*Odyssey*. 2 vols. Trans. A. T. Murray. Cambridge, MA: Harvard University Press.

Horkheimer, Max, and Theodor W. Adorno. 1981. *Dialektik der Aufklärung*. Frankfurt am Main: Suhrkamp. Trans. Edmund Jephcott (2002) as *Dialectic of Enlightenment*. Stanford: Stanford University Press.

Kastner, Georges [Johann Georg]. 1858. *Les sirènes*. Paris: G. Brandus et S. Dufour.

Kittler, Friedrich. 2006. *Musik und Mathematik* I/1. Munich: Fink.

Kramer, Lawrence. 2006. "Longdyingcall: Of Music, Modernity, and the Sirens." In *The Music of the Sirens*, ed. Linda Phyllis Austern and Inna Naroditskaya, 194–214. Bloomington: Indiana University Press.

McNeill, William H. 1995. *Keeping Together in Time: Dance and Drill in Human History*. Cambridge, MA: Harvard University Press.

Metzger, Heinz-Klaus, and Reiner Riehm, eds. 1981. *Karlheinz Stockhausen: . . . wie die Zeit verging . . . MusikKonzepte* 19.

Nagy, Gregory. 1979. *The Best of the Achaeans*. Baltimore: Johns Hopkins Press.

Nietzsche, Friedrich. 1990. *Die fröhliche Wissenschaft*. Leipzig: Reclam Leipzig.

Nicholls, David. 1990. *American Experimental Music 1890-1940*. Cambridge: Cambridge University Press.

Ohm, Georg Simon. 1843. "Ueber die Definition des Tones, nebst daran geknüpfter Theorie der Sirene und ähnlicher tonbildender Vorrichtungen." [*Poggendorfs*] *Annalen der Physik und Chemie* 59: 497–565.

——. 1844. "Noch ein paar Worte über die Definition des Tones." [*Poggendorffs*] *Annalen der Physik und Chemie* 62:1–18.

Opelt, Friedrich Wilhelm. 1834. *Über die Natur der Musik*. Plauen/Leipzig: Hermann und Langbein.

——. 1852. *Allgemeine Theorie der Musik auf den Rhythmus der Klangwellenpulse gegründet*. Leipzig: Johann Ambrosius Barth.

Ovid [Publius Ovidius Naso]. 1951. *Metamorphoses/Metamorphoses*. 2 vols. Trans. Frank Justus Miller. Cambridge, MA: Harvard University Press.

Peraino, Judith. 2006. *Listening to the Sirens: Musical Technologies of Queer Identity from Homer to Hedwig*. Berkeley: University of California Press.

Pohl, Richard 1853. *Akustische Briefe*. Leipzig: B. Hinze.

Poschardt, Ulf. 1997. *DJ Culture*. Hamburg: Rogner & Bernhard.

Rancière, Jacques. 2004. *The Politics of Aesthetics*. Trans. Gabriel Rockhill, with an afterword by Slavoj Zizek. London: Continuum.

Robel, Ernst. 1891. *Die Sirene*. 4 vols. Berlin: R. Gaertner.

Rodwell, Robert 1973. "Army Tests New Riot Weapon." *New Scientist*, September 20. Reprinted in *AMOK Journal: Sensurround Edition* (1995):399–401.

Rouget, Gilbert. 1985. *Music and Trance: A Study of the Relation between Music and Possession*. Chicago: University of Chicago Press.

Schillinger, Joseph. 1948. *The Mathematical Basis of the Arts*. New York: Philosophical Library.

Seebeck, August. 1841. "Beobachtungen über einige Bedingungen der Entstehung von Tönen." [*Poggendorffs*] *Annalen der Physik und Chemie* 53:417–36.

——. 1843. "Ueber die Sirene." [*Poggendorffs*] *Annalen der Physik und Chemie* 60:449–81.

——. 1844. "Ueber die Definition des Tones." [*Poggendorfs*] *Annalen der Physik und Chemie* 63: 353–80.

Seeger, Charles, 1994. *Studies in Musicology II: 1929-1979*, ed. Ann M. Pescatello. Berkeley and Los Angeles: University of California Press.

Segal, Charles. 1994. *Singers, Heroes, and Gods in the Odyssey*. Ithaca: Cornell University Press.

Slonimsky, Nicholas. 1988. *Perfect Pitch: A Life Story*. Oxford: Oxford University Press.

Stockhausen, Karlheinz. 1963. "…wie die Zeit vergeht…" In *Texte zur Musik 1*, ed. Dieter Schnebel, 98–139. Cologne: Dumont.

——. 1989. "Four Criteria of Electronic Music." In *Stockhausen on Music: Lecture and Interviews*, ed. Robin Maconie, 88–111. London: Marion Boyars.

——. 1996. "Wille zur Form und Wille zum Abenteuer" (Stuttgart, 8. Januar 1978). In *Karlheinz Stockhausen: Einführung in das Gesamtwerk, Gespräche mit Stockhausen*, ed. Rudolf Frisius. Mainz: Schott.

Swezey, Stuart, ed. 1995. *Amok Journal: Sensurround Edition*. Los Angeles: Amok Books.

Thompson, Emily. 2001. *The Soundscapes of Modernity*. Cambridge, MA: MIT Press.

Turner, Stephen. 1977. "The Ohm-Seebeck Dispute, Hermann von Helmholtz, and the Origins of Physiological Acoustics." *British Journal for the History of Science* 10:1–24.

Vogel, Stephan. 1993. "Sensation of Tone, Perception of Sound, and Empiricism: Helmholtz's Physiological Acoustics." In *Hermann von Helmholtz and the Foundations of Nineteenth-Century Science*, ed. David Cahan, 259–87. Berkeley: University of California Press.

Volkwein, Barbara. 2000. "130 beats per minute: Techno." In *Musik in der Zeit—Zeit in der Musik*, ed. Richard Klein, Eckehard Kiem, and Wolfram Ette, 399–409. Weilserwist: Velbrück.

——. 2003. *"What's Techno?": Geschichte, Diskurse und musikalische Gestalt elektronischer Unterhaltungsmusik*. Osnabrück: Universität Osnabrück.

Weber, Robert. 1885. "Die elektrische Sirene." *Annalen der Physik* 640:671–80.

Wellmer, Albrecht. 2000. "The Death of the Sirens and the Origin of the Work of Art." *New German Critique* 81:5–19.

Welsch, Wolfgang. 1990. *Ästhetisches Denken*. Stuttgart: Reclam.

# PART II

## SOUNDING TRANSPORT

....................................................

# CHAPTER 4

# "CARS WITH THE BOOM": MUSIC, AUTOMOBILITY, AND HIP-HOP "SUB" CULTURES

....................................................

## JUSTIN A. WILLIAMS

I think men's minds are going to change in subtle ways because of automobiles.

—Eugene Morgan in *The Magnificent Ambersons*
(quoted in Lewis 2000:19)

We're conforming to the way machines play music. It's robots' choice. It used to be ladies' choice—now it's robot's choice.

—Donald Fagen, producer and Steely Dan frontman
(quoted in Levine 2007)

The music is just in me now, you know...and I know what people like to play in their cars.

—Dr. Dre, producer/rapper (quoted in Gold 1993:41)

THE automobile represents one of the most important mobile technologies of the twentieth and twenty-first centuries, transforming time, space, "the everyday," mass production, as well as urban and emotional geographies. While the automobile has been discussed and theorized as the "quintessential manufactured object" of the twentieth century (Urry 2005:26), little has been written on the cross-influences among recorded music, technology, and automobility. This chapter begins to outline the intersections between music and the automobile by surveying the history of car audio, contemporary car audiophile subcultures (including the phenomenon known as "boom cars"),[1] and investigating the role of the automobile in popular music production, namely, the hip-hop production style of Dr. Dre (Andre Young). Dr. Dre's creation of a style labeled

"G-funk" in the early 1990s, according to him, was created and mixed *specifically* for listening in car stereo systems. As borrowing, sampling, and other forms of intertextuality are central to hip-hop's ethos, Dr. Dre's production reflects how musical materials become re-used for a new space, updated and customized for the automotive listening experience.

# A Brief History of Car Audio in the United States

Media theorist Michael Bull, one of the few scholars to investigate sound and automobility, reminds us that "While the 20th century is sometimes interpreted as both the century of the automobile and of the moving image, it is also the century of mechanically reproduced sounds" (2005:248). Early anecdotal evidence suggests that car audio experimentation occurred soon after the turn of the twentieth century. Marconi had installed a radio in his steam-powered car in 1901, but the size of the radio made it too impractical (Fitch 2008).[2] In the 1920s, some motorists used their own home radios in the car, but the driver had to turn the engine off in order to listen to it. As early as 1922, Chrysler offered the first factory-unit car radio, but few were purchased, and production was soon discontinued (McCartney 2004:138). William M. Heina formed a car radio company called the Heinaphone Corporation in 1926, which was soon bought out by the Philco Radio & Television Corporation, and it began making car radios at the rate of twenty per day in 1927.[3] These early experiments were impractical and largely unsuccessful for a number of reasons, including high price tag, difficulty of installation, ignition interference, dependence on a large battery, and inability to hear the sounds above engine and road noise.

Galvin Manufacturing Company built the first commercially successful car radio in the early 1930s, known as the Motorola 5T71, an amalgamation of the words "Motor"-car and "Victrola" (Figures 4.1 and 4.2). (The company would later change their name to that of their most successful product.) Paul Galvin, Elmer Wavering, and William Lear successfully invented a system of voltage conversion so that the radio could rely on the car's electrical system rather than a battery (McCartney 2004:138). The first price of the 5T71 was $120, a large percentage of the cost of an automobile which, at the time, could be purchased for $650. As the business expanded, the price of the radio dropped to $55 by 1934 (2004:138; Petrakis 1991:92–100).[4] According to a *Time* magazine article in 1936, car radio sales rose to 34,000 in 1930, and by 1935, sales were up to one million units (*Time* 1936).

After World War II, advances in technology and increased popularity of radio led to an expansion in the number of radio stations and in the variety of programming. For example, from 1946 to 1948, the number of AM radio stations doubled (Widmer 2002:67). The "Top 40" radio format was beginning to emerge around this time, and the

FIGURE 4.1 Reproduction of Motorola's first car radio, 5T71, which included (left to right) a radio receiver, tuning control, and speaker. Courtesy of Motorola, Inc.

FIGURE 4.2 Detail of the tuning control of Motorola's first car radio, 5T71. Courtesy of Motorola, Inc.

invention of the transistor in 1947, first introduced in 1953, made radios more portable, more mobile, and increased their reliability (Smith 1999:123; also see Wall and Webber's chapter in *The Oxford Handbook of Mobile Music Studies*, Vol. 1). The year 1953 also included another important advance in this history of popular music, the electrification of the guitar (Widmer 2002:67). The advances in recording technology with magnetic tape gave studios the ability to record lower frequencies and capture other details. The use of drums and amplified guitar in popular music was arguably more "phonogenic" for automotive listening than other instruments, and as radio stations began to put their sounds through a compressor that made the signal sound louder, the better the result for the needs of this listening demographic.[5] Though technology such as the LP (introduced in 1949) increased record playing time, pop musicians and producers became more conscious of shorter song duration for radio (Smith 1999:123–25).

As the population of twenty to twenty-four-year-olds increased by 50% throughout the 1960s, products began to be marketed to teenagers and young adults on an unprecedented scale including both popular music and automobiles such as the 1964 Ford Mustang (the "Car of Young America"). And perhaps not surprisingly, 80% of Mustang buyers had a car radio installed in their vehicle (1999:123–25). Car radios eventually became the norm for most automobiles. In 1952, automobile radios were in just over half of America's cars. By 1980, the start of a decade which saw the rapid growth of both the car audio aftermarket and hip-hop music, that percentage had increased to 95% (McCartney 2004:139).

The radio, of course, was not the only sound system to appear in automobiles. In 1956, around the same time as FM (frequency modulation) radio began to grow in popularity,[6] the Chrysler Imperial featured an underdash 16 2/3 rpm record player intended to play 7-inch microgroove records provided by Columbia Records. Developed by Peter Goldmark for the CBS Electronics Division, the "Highway Hi-Fi" lasted only a few years in Chrysler luxury models (1956–61; see Figures 4.3 and 4.4).[7] In 1963, Earl "Madman" Muntz had fully developed his "Stereo-pac" which was a four-track cartridge to be used in automobiles (Sanjek and Sanjek 1996:391). William Lear and his collaborators, who developed the Lear Jet and the earliest car radios for Motorola, improved upon the Stereo-pac in a number of ways including doubling the duration of playback material. Developed with Ampex and to be used with RCA Victor Cartridges, Motorola sold the first eight-track players ("Stereo 8") for Ford Motor Company's 1966 higher-end automobiles. GM, Chrysler and American Motors subsequently included the player as an option in their 1967 models. Lear's success was aided by a 60 million dollar advertising campaign, and the "eight-track" was popular well into the early 1970s (Sanjek and Sanjek 1996:392, 549; Coleman 2003:157; *Time* 1965, 1966). Mark Coleman has written that the success of the eight-track "must be attributed to the automobile. Convenient for drivers owing to its size and shape, an 8 track tape could be inserted and removed with one hand while driving. Tellingly, this awkward format never caught on outside the car-crazed United States" (2003:159).

The compact cassette, developed by Philips in 1963, would eventually outperform the Stereo 8 in popularity (in part, because of its smaller size and ability to be rewound),

FIGURE 4.3 1956 Chrysler advertisement in *The Post* (courtesy of Lee Exline).

becoming the preferred magnetic tape-based playback option into the late-1970s and 1980s (Sanjek and Sanjek 1996:416, 551). The compact disc was released in 1982 by Sony, and in-car CD players started to appear around 1985, but still had a relatively high price tag (in 1989, in-car CD players were $800–900) (Fantel 1989). A 1989 *New York Times* article tells of a new feature in a Philips DC085, a compressor circuit that automatically raised the dynamic level when the music became soft, presumably an attempt to solve the issue of road and engine noise overwhelming quiet passages of music (Fantel 1989). As the compact disc began to replace the cassette as playback software of choice, automobile compact disc players became more common in the late 1990s. As with virtually all car audio technology, new developments originated as an exclusive option in select luxury cars, and later broadened its user spectrum depending on its popularity, increased production and lowered price, and functionality.

Two terms crucial to car audio discourse are "stock equipment" (what comes with the car, a.k.a. Original Equipment Manufacturer or OEM), and "aftermarket equipment" (items bought and installed after the automobile purchase). Sound quality as a result of the "high-fidelity" era has been popular with home audio systems since at least the 1950s, but the market for car stereo quality arrived later in the early to mid-1980s (Yoder 2000:96). In 1983, GM offered Bose-branded car audio systems in three of its luxury

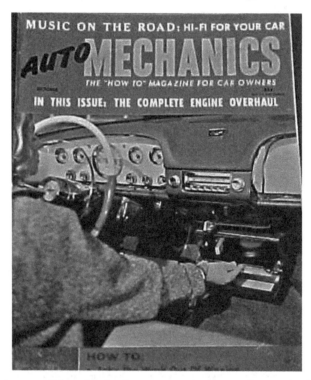

FIGURE 4.4 1956 cover of *Auto Mechanics* magazine (courtesy of Lee Exline).

vehicles. This began a trend for luxury cars to include high-quality sound systems, with Bose, JBL and Infinity dominating stock brands into the 1990s (Newcomb 2008:18). Car audiophiles became interested in sound quality and clarity, frequency response, and the "extended bass response" provided by subwoofers. There is currently a seemingly unlimited range of aftermarket car audio products, including head units that include CD, MP3s, and iPod players, USB ports, satellite radio, as well as audio/visual accessories such as GPS navigation and DVD players. Magazines such as *Car Audio and Electronics* and *Car Sound Magazine* offer information and advertising about the latest products, and catalogs provided by consumer electronics companies like Crutchfield have extensive car audio selections. In the past two decades or so, electronic stores in the United States such as Best Buy and Circuit City have sections devoted entirely to automotive stereo systems, and in many cases, most cities have one or more stores devoted entirely to the "mobile audio" market.[8] In 2007, sales of in-car consumer electronics were over $10 billion, not a surprising statistic considering the degree to which many drivers spend time in their automobiles ("CEA" 2008).[9]

Like those inhabiting custom car cultures before them, car audio enthusiasts form a community with shared interests, while expressing a sense of individuality. The design intensity and niche marketing of the car audio "aftermarket" can be said to participate in the so-called post-Fordist society; the fact that *The Car Audio and Electronics Buyer*

*Guide* had 3195 different speakers available in just one year (1998) attests to this (Yoder 2000:168). But many forget that the emblematic symbol of Fordism, the Model T, had over 5,000 accessories available in its lifetime, suggesting that the desire to customize the car is as old as automotive mass production itself (Marsh and Collett 1986:36).[10] Rather than invoke discourses of Fordism, perhaps it is more useful in popular music and other forms of production to acknowledge the influence of Sloanism, named after General Motors president Alfred Sloan, the creator of the "annual model," who produced different car models in a stylistic hierarchy and led the first separate design division for a car company in the 1920s (led by Harley Earl for over thirty years) (Gartman 1994:68–75).[11] Hip-hop music for example, with its heavy use of borrowing and sampling, adds surface features to old frameworks in some ways analogous to Sloanist production methods, and functions within a constantly shifting subgeneric hierarchy of cultural products.

It is important in any study of technology to avoid the "technological determinism" or "hard determinism" viewpoint that machines have unavoidable consequences for users and society (Katz 2004:3).[12] Mark Katz concludes from his study of how recording technologies shape music that "the value of any tool depends ultimately on its users," and that "Just as the technology shapes the activities of its users, their activities shape the technology" (190).[13] The use of the car stereo system is multifaceted; The music can be used for individual or collective listening while driving, or function like a boom box (hence the term "boom car"), to accompany and create a space of socialization such as a block party, or it may territorialize (and/or terrorize) the surrounding sonic environment.

"Boom cars" have been a source of both intense competition and neighborhood frustration. The International Auto Sound Challenge Association (IASCA) was formed in the late 1980s and regularly holds competitions for the loudest and highest quality car sound systems, competitions referred to by enthusiasts as "sound-offs," "crank-it-up competitions," or "dB Drag Racing."[14] Others see the boom-car pastime as using sound as a weapon, as activist groups in the United States who consider themselves "victims of audio terrorism" have pressed for legislation to decrease legal decibel levels in cars.[15] The multiplicity of car audio uses demonstrates its interpretive flexibility, and that technology and society influence each other in complex ways. What "boom cars" show more specifically is that the notion of a "good"/pleasurable or "bad"/harmful technology not only differs with users, but also with those who are directly or indirectly affected by a given technology.

# A Brief Overview of Car Audio Technology

The main components in a custom car audio system include the head unit, amplifier(s), loudspeakers, and the wiring that connects them (Figure 4.5). Car audio enthusiasts often think about sound in terms of frequencies, additionally installing equalizers to manipulate frequency intensities, and crossovers that control which frequencies are directed to which loudspeakers. Car audio discourses involve (not necessarily agreed upon) specialized language and well-defined parameters of value criteria, including "clarity," "dynamic range" (the ability to reproduce the correct dynamics), "frequency response" (how much of the frequency spectrum the speaker can produce), "timbre" (as "the system's ability to recreate sound as it was intended to be heard"), "tonal accuracy" (fidelity to the recording), and "staging and imaging" (the ability of a system to recreate the illusion of a stage and its performer(s)) (Newcomb 2008:23–25).[16] As one might expect from these definitions, opinions regarding these parameters vary widely across the car audio community, and many of these will depend on what type of recordings are used, and how one listens to them.

The "head unit" is the central panel that delivers the signal to the rest of the system. It can be found on the dash, and may have a tuner, CD, cassette player, or more advanced features. The head unit contains a built-in amplifier that powers the delivery of the signal to the loudspeakers. The main purpose of an amplifier is to take the low-level audio signal from a head unit and turn it into a high-level signal for the speakers (Newcomb 2008:111; Pettitt 2003:42). In a custom system, amplifiers are bought separately which can power a given range of speakers.

Dynamic loudspeakers (a.k.a. "speakers" or "drivers") are what turn the electronic signal into sound waves (Pettitt 2003:59). The loudspeaker is a transducer that converts the electrical energy from the head unit signal into acoustic energy, powered by an amplifier.[17] The importance of the loudspeaker to twentieth- and twenty-first-century musicking cannot be overstated. David Moulton has written that the loudspeaker should be considered as a musical instrument in itself with distinctive sound-generating qualities. To make one comparison, the directivity of acoustical instruments vary widely at all frequencies, but traditional loudspeakers "have a comparatively distinctive pattern of directivity... a pattern generally unlike almost all acoustical instruments" (2003:9). In addition to directivity, they also differ in frequency range and minimum and maximum sound-pressure levels (volume). And unlike many musical instruments, loudspeakers do not produce overtones by themselves. Moulton also compares live performances with loudspeaker performances, noting that we listen to most loudspeakers in private spaces (home, car, walkman) and that over the past century, loudspeaker music has "almost entirely displaced 'non-loudspeaker music'" (11).

Speakers come in a wide variety of shapes and sizes: from the smallest tweeters (one inch in diameter or smaller) that reproduce sounds in the 4 kHz–20 kHz range, to woofer/midrange speakers (400 Hz–5000 Hz), midbass (100 Hz–500 Hz), and subwoofers (125 Hz and lower). In terms of power, tweeters usually consume 5% of a system's power, while subwoofer amps traditionally use 40% of total system power (Yoder 2000:168). A crossover, sometimes called a filter, is a circuit that limits the frequencies given to the different loudspeakers. The frequency levels are called "crossover points" and can be adjusted in custom systems. For example, if a subwoofer has a crossover point of 90 Hz, the signal would be blocked at any frequency above 90 Hz (Newcomb 2008:207). These crossover points for any given speaker are variable and adjustable, largely dependent on the practicalities of the technology and tastes of listeners and manufacturers.

Because hip-hop music forms the central case study of this chapter, it is important to describe in more detail the primary object which connects the "boomy bass" of hip-hop to the automotive soundscape—the car subwoofer. Available in the car-stereo aftermarket since the early 1980s,[18] the subwoofer is a large, enclosed loudspeaker, 8 to 18 inches in diameter (Pettitt 2003:59). The subwoofer specializes in producing the lower-frequency waves in the sound spectrum (roughly 20–125 Hz), omni/nondirectional sensations of sound perceived as an amalgamation of pitch recognition and a feeling of pressure

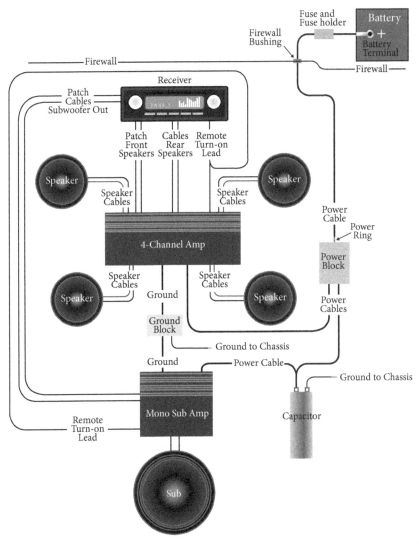

FIGURE 4.5 Car audio amplifier wiring diagram. (Diagram courtesy of Crutchfield Corporation © 2003)

(as sound measured in decibels is also known as Sound Pressure Level or SPL) (Anet 2003:60–62). In other words, the lower the frequency, the greater possibility that one will begin to "feel" the sound.[19] Without the subwoofer, other noises can cancel the lower frequencies in the music, frequencies which require so much power that one requires a separate amplifier for them. [20] Most road noise is in the 100–200 Hz range, and will cancel out this band of a recording's audio spectrum, therefore one function of the subwoofer is to bring out the lower frequencies in the music (Yoder 2000:96). A custom system creates a division of auditory labor in speaker types, with higher frequencies supported by tweeters, middle frequencies by mid-range speakers, and lower frequencies by the woofers and subwoofers (as exemplified in Figure 4.5). In choosing these and other types of speakers, one has to think of qualities such as "resonant frequency," the frequency that the speaker naturally wants to vibrate, and "transfer function": "a measure of how the volume of an enclosure, such as room or a car, effects the way a speaker sounds" (Polk Audio; Pettitt 2003:60). The attention given to specific technology such as loudspeaker types (and their qualities) and to the character of specific playback spaces are elements important to car audiophiles, and could be a fruitful lens with which to consider and analyze music production and recordings.

## THE AUTOMOBILE AND MUSIC PRODUCTION

The automobile sound system has been an important listening reference in many styles of music production since at least the 1960s, with the advent of Top 40 radio and the car's role in youth cultures. Steven Pond writes, "Bowing to the importance of radio airplay, pop producers up to the late 1960s routinely calibrated their final mixes to cheap car speakers, which could accommodate only a limited frequency range" (2005:132). Perhaps appropriately given their location in the car manufacturing Mecca of Detroit, Motown Records were attentive to this new listening market, as by 1963, fifty million automobiles had car radios. Suzanne Smith writes:

> At Hitsville Studios the proliferation of the car radio was not overlooked but capitalized on. Both the musical form and the audio fidelity of Motown hits such as "My Girl" and "Shop Around" were well suited and often produced with a car radio audience in mind. Some of the first critical commentary on the Detroit sound noted that "Motown's light, unfussy, evenly stressed beat, its continuous loop melodies, [are] the ideal accompaniment for driving." (Morse, quoted in Smith 1999:123)

Motown made their singles extra short to help ensure radio play and tested them for compatibility on car radio speakers. They were also aware that the majority of these car radio listeners were the baby boomer teenage market they were trying to attract. As producers would tailor their mixes to the car stereo, the needs of automotive listening influenced the timbre and volume of the music produced. As Warren Belasco has written, "The greatest success in rock'n'roll usually goes to those whose music suits the hyperkinetic formats of the Top-40 stations that transmit primarily to car radios and transistor receivers" (1980:264).

Radio stations since the 1960s heavily "compress" (i.e., use dynamic range compression) the sounds coming through the airwaves, as compression decreases the overall range of the dynamics to make music sound louder without increasing peak amplitude. Television commercials often compress their sound, which is why commercials often sound louder than the show that one is watching. One reason to utilize this "loudness" effect from compression was for competition with rival radio stations, to sound more exciting and keep the listener's attention; but another reason was to produce a consistent dynamic level that could be heard over the road and engine noise of an automobile. Music producers also use dynamic compression in their mixing for a number of reasons: to compete with other "loud" albums, but also when albums are expected to be played in loud environments such as bars, shopping malls, restaurants, and automobiles.[21]

Automotive listening, particularly listening to stock systems, demands a high level of dynamic consistency; listening to Berlioz's *Symphonie Fantastique* or Schubert's *Unfinished Symphony* in a stock system without a compressor can prove to be frustrating. Like earlier technologies of the phonograph record that influenced the length of music composed, the car stereo influenced other elements, such as the timbre of popular music recordings.[22] Furthermore, the ability to record bass, synthesizer and other sounds by DI ("direct injection" to the mixing console, rather than put microphone to an amplifier) seems to provide greater flexibility in altering the sounds once they are recorded.[23] As recording technology improved, so did the ability to tailor music to particular listening spaces.

Many music producers speak positively of the automotive listening space. When asked by an interviewer what the ideal listening environment for a minisystem was, producer and artist Stewart Copeland commented, "I've already got one: the car stereo—which is the first and best minisystem if you think about it. You're in this cocoon where you can have a really big sound in an enclosed environment." He continued to say, "When I record an album, I spend months listening to it in the studio. I listen to it every day going back and forth in my car. I check it out on tiny systems. And then I hear it coming out of the radio, so I know what it sounds like" (quoted in Baber 1997).

The "car test" or "car check" was and still is used in record mixing, as the car is often the first place that a mix is heard outside the studio.[24] California sound engineer Patrick Olguin states, "If I'm mixing 'unassisted' I'll check the mix in my stock system in my truck, and also check it in my custom system in my Mercedes."[25] Olguin ensures that his mix works for the majority of car owners (stock systems) as well as for the greater clarity, improved frequency response, and bass extension of a custom aftermarket system. He also mentions that "most hip-hop producers have upgraded car systems, so that would definitely be the first acid test for a mix after leaving the studio."[26] Studios normally have a number of sets of speakers for different instances of listening, selectable at the flip of a switch; and some studios (such as Sony Studios in New York City) have or have had a car speaker system built into the studio as part of their reference speaker configurations.[27]

Olguin also has a wireless system, to listen to mixes through the car radio by using a radio transmitter that delivers the signal to the parking lot, in order to hear the mix as it would go through a radio station.

In addition to the car's now serving as the producer's listening reference, producers have also become more conscious of the idea that a recording is intended to fill a particular space, rather than to reproduce accurately a performance. Adam Krims notes a trend in new classical music recordings that have shifted their aim from "concert realism" to an "abstract soundstage" that considers particular playback spaces. In hip-hop, the "star producer" will be valued for how his/her music fills a space, such as a car or jeep, rather than what s/he can do in live performance (Krims 2007:161).[28] The trademarked producer will be advertised on albums, assuring listeners that the product that they buy will fill space in a particular way (160).

Consideration of the relatively small space of the car interior in production and mixing affects elements such as dynamic compression, how frequencies are equalized, and, in particular, the sound quality of low frequencies (both the aural and tactile sensations produced by subwoofer playback). While the opinions of music producers are far from homogeneous, testing music mixes in the car (both stock and custom) has been a rarely acknowledged standard practice; and if we then consider both the playback spaces and speakers involved, we can better analyze the ecology of how a music recording interacts with the listener in particular environments.

## HIP-HOP CULTURES AND THE AUTOMOBILE

As hip-hop music began from playing records through large loudspeakers at block parties in the early 1970s Bronx, it is still largely characterized by its high volume and attention to the low frequencies in the sound spectrum (Rose 1994:75).[29] Many of these "beats" are intended for listening in car soundsystems, preferably custom aftermarket systems with subwoofers.[30] In mainstream hip-hop culture, cars and car accessories such as "rims" and grills become cross-marketed in a way that suggests "lifestyle" marketing, together with television shows like *Pimp My Ride* and *Rides* magazine.

The automobile and hip-hop culture form, in a certain sense, a nexus of status symbols (e.g., rims, subwoofers, and car brands) with an accompanying soundtrack. The high status that an upmarket or customized automobile provides to members of the African American community, according to Paul Gilroy, helps to compensate for the disenfranchisement and propertylessness experienced in African American history (2001:84).[31] Gilroy notes that auto-autonomy is a means of empowerment and resistance for African Americans with a history of coerced labor, and that the custom car is an ongoing process that may be "gesturing their anti-discipline to power even as the whirlpool of consumerism sucks them in" (97). African Americans, as of 2001, spent $45 billion on cars and related products, representing 30% of the automotive buying public; yet this demographic only consists of 12% of the US population (85). Race-specific marketing by no means suggests that these accessories are bought solely by the race to which it is targeted, but it projects a certain form of "blackness," real or imagined, that enters the cultural consciousness. Gilroy writes that the automobile is "at the very core of America's complex negotiations with its own absurd racial codings" (84). Others have suggested that the importance of the car harkens back to religious imagery, the chariot metaphor symbolizing the promise of freedom from slavery for the Hebrews and subsequently for antebellum African Americans (Demers 2003:84).

The automobile has been a central object in hip-hop music videos and album covers, ranging from the gangsta rap of Ice-T, Too $hort, and Dr. Dre to the "Bling Bling" era of Puff Daddy and Mase, and more recently, in the Southern "crunk" music of Lil' Jon and David Banner. The automobile (and its powerful sound system) is an object central to the boasting traditions in rap music and earlier African-based art forms such as toasting, as Daz Dillinger raps in "My System": "Cruzin' down the block/And my system bangin' out about a million watts/All these suckers wanna stare and jock/And hear my shit subbin' down the block."[32]

In the 1980s, in automobile-centric Miami, Florida, there emerged a subgenre of rap known as "Miami bass." This genre was pioneered by DJs emphasizing powerful low-end frequencies, as Miami DJs had direct links to Caribbean soundsystem culture that privileged *feeling* the music as much as listening and dancing to it. Miami groups such as 2 Live Crew made a direct connection with bottom-heavy music and bottom-heavy women on their album covers and music videos ("Miami bass" was sometimes referred to as "booty music" or "booty bass.").[33] By the late 1980s, the Miami bass scene began to intersect with subcultures of car audio. Advances in car audio technology coincided with the popularity of Miami bass, and in the words of Roni Sarig, was the moment "when producers very consciously started pushing the levels of low end further and further. Inevitably, those who liked the visceral experience of booming bass discovered that it was all the more intense when confined inside a car" (2007:30). One hit song by the Miami female rap duo L'Trimm rapped of their love of "boom cars," as they chanted "They're always adding speakers when they find the room, Cuz they know we like the guys with the cars that go boom."[34] Bass music, as popularized largely by 2 Live Crew, expanded in the early 1990s with hits such as "Whoot, There it is" by Jacksonville's 95 South in 1993, "Whoomp! (There it is)" by Atlanta's Tag Team in the same year, and "Tootsie Roll" by Jacksonville's 69 Boyz a year later.

Car audio bass became popular in areas of the South, Texas, and California where youth cultures were reliant on cars. "Drop the Bass" (1989) by Miami's DJ Magic Mike became popular in car stereos, and people used to slow the song's tempo for lower bass effects. DJ Magic Mike responded, "I hated hearing my song like that, it kind of made me mad. So I went to the studio and designed a song that, if they slowed the bass down, it would tear the speakers up. It was done pretty much as a joke" (quoted in Sarig 2007:31). The song was entitled "Feel the Bass (Speaker Terror Upper)" and became a hit with car audio enthusiasts. As Sarig notes, "It was, essentially, the first track created specifically for use in cars, a practice that would soon launch an entire industry" (31). These popular car audio bass albums include *Bass Computer* (1991) by Techmaster

P.E.B. and *Techno-Bass* (1992) by Beat Dominator, as well as numerous other bass music compilations.

More recently, St. Louis-based rapper Jibbs has boasted about the quality of his car soundsystem in "King Kong," as the chorus opens (in a lowered-pitch, slowed down voice) "If you hear me before you see me, I got King Kong in the trunk."[35] In fact, one could interpret the power of a car sound system as a metaphor for sexual prowess, just as early blues musicians used the car as an extended sexual metaphor.[36] Guest Chamillionaire raps on "King Kong": "I got plenty speakers up in my trunk and I turned it up/And all the ladies loving how it be bumping." Jibbs's music video includes rapping in front of customized sound systems with numerous subwoofers, driving down streets typical of ghetto representations in reality rap videos, and images of other customized cars in the neighborhood including low riders and monster trucks. Women pose with cars during the video, both consistent with certain genres of rap music video and magazines like *Lowrider* that consistently feature a scantily clad woman with an automobile on the cover. Much of this now conventional imagery of the automobile in rap music video arguably first reached large-scale exposure in the early 1990s with the mainstream success of Dr. Dre's *The Chronic*.

# DR. DRE AND "G-FUNK"

Dr. Dre (Andre Young), the "chief architect of West Coast gangsta rap," was born in Los Angeles (Gold 1993:40). He was a club DJ, then producer and rapper with groups The World Class Wreckin Cru and N.W.A. (Niggaz with Attitude). After leaving N.W.A., he spent all of 1992 producing his first solo album, *The Chronic*. What emerged was a sound that he christened "G-funk"(G for "gangsta"), inspired by the P-funk of George Clinton, but also borrowing from Leon Haywood, Isaac Hayes, Curtis Mayfield, and Donny Hathaway, as well as utilizing vocoder-esque effects similar to those of 1970s electro-funk groups like Zapp and Cameo.[37] What results is a highly layered effect, a mix of (often high-pitched) synthesized sounds, live instruments such as guitar and bass, and an added emphasis on low-end frequencies.[38]

One example of this style is the layers of the "basic beat"[39] in Dr. Dre's "Nuthin' But a 'G' Thang" from *The Chronic* (Figure 4.6):[40] The high synthesizer riff, derived from Leon Haywood's "I Wanna do Something Freaky to You," has become (in both timbre and melody) an important signifier of Dr. Dre, Southern California, and more widely, of the gangsta rap or "West Coast rap" subgenre. For example, as New York MC Mims raps of different geographical regions in "This Is Why I'm Hot" (2007): "Compton to Hollywood/As soon as I hit L.A./I'm in that low, low/I do it the Cali way," the riff from "'G' Thang" accompanies the stanza.[41]

As opposed to East Coast hip-hop producers at the time, Dr. Dre would rarely sample directly from a record itself. He might use a 1970s record for ideas (a melody, beat, or riff), but had live musicians re-record the sounds that he wanted. After equalizing

FIGURE 4.6 Basic beat from Dr. Dre, "Nuthin' But a 'G' Thang" from *The Chronic* (1992).

and sculpting particular sounds, he then can choose to put the sounds through a sampler. He often takes pre-existing drum sounds from recordings, loops them, and gradually replaces each drum part with new ones. Subsequently, a bass player often records a track over the drums, and other musicians may re-record or improvise, based on various tracks. In re-recording all the material live, in addition to avoiding high copyright costs,[42] Dr. Dre has greater control over all of the individual tracks: he can de-tune, add more "low end" frequency, apply dynamic compression, add effects, make it sound "dirty," or equalize to his tastes.[43] He often uses a Minimoog synthesizer to boost the bass, and other keyboards such as Wurlitzer, Fender Rhodes, Clavinet, and Vox V-305 organ, as well as a Roland TR-808 drum machine, employed by many hip-hop producers for its kick drum bass "boom" sound.[44] This flexibility was important to Dre, often labeled a perfectionist in the studio.[45]

Dr. Dre will often utilize a number of musicians to "orchestrate" various sounds that he wants, as producer Scott Storch recounts:

> Sometimes [Dre will] have a vision for a record where he'll program a drum pattern and tell musicians such as myself what to play verbatim, and we'll emulate for him, through him. He's capable of doing a lot of the stuff, like playing piano. But he creates a little band. He's orchestrating his little orchestra. And sometimes, I'll be at the keyboard noodling, and he'll be at the drum machine noodling and we'll find each other in that way—all of a sudden, *boom,* there's a record. (Quoted in Swenson 2006)

Jonathan Gold also writes of Dre's compositional process in the making of *The Chronic*:

> Listening to a Dre beat take shape in the studio is like watching a snowball roll downhill in a Bugs Bunny cartoon, taking on mass as it goes, Dre may find something he likes from an old drum break, loop it and gradually replace each part with a better

tom-tom sound, a kick-drum sound he adores, until the beat bears the same relationship to the original that the Incredible Hulk does to Bill Bixby.

A bass player wanders in, unpacks his instrument and pops a funky two-note bass line over the beat, then leaves to watch CNN, though his two notes keep looping into infinity. A smiling guy in a striped jersey plays a nasty one-fingered melody on an old Mini-Moog synthesizer that's been obsolete since 1982, and Dre scratches in a sort of surfadelic munching noise, and then from his well-stocked Akai MPC60 sample comes a shriek, a spare piano chord, an ejaculation from the first Beastie's record—"Let me clear my throat"—and the many-layered groove is happening, bumping, breathing, almost loud enough to see.

[Rapper] Snoop [Doggy Dogg] floats into the room. He closes his eyes as if in a dream and extends both hands toward Dre, palms downward. Dre holds out his hands, and Snoop grazes his fingertips with a butterfly flourish, caught up in the ecstasy of the beat....

Dre comes in from the lounge, twists a few knobs on the Moog and comes up with the synthesizer sound so familiar from *The Chronic,* almost on pitch but not quite, sliding a bit between notes... (1993:40)

Though these journalistic sources often portray information in highly stylized ways, they nevertheless are useful in mapping out Dre's compositional tendencies as producer. While Dre's production is a collaborative process, he most certainly has creative control over the final product.

*The Chronic* went on to become the best-selling hardcore rap album in history at the time, and Dre helped his next production credit, Snoop Doggy Dogg's *Doggystyle,* to become the first rap album to debut at number one on the *Billboard* charts.[46] This synthesized "post-funk" or "post-soul"[47] sound would characterize what is known as the "G-funk era" from 1992 to 1996, emblematic of a "West Coast Rap" aesthetic still influential in hip-hop production. *The Chronic* is often described as a crossroads in hip-hop historiography, the point when rap music became less about the rap itself (accompanied by unobtrusive beats), and more about how well the rapper incorporated him or herself within the producer's beats.[48] Snoop Dogg's laid back rap style, for example, arguably "fits" the music that Dr. Dre produces in terms of timbre, pacing, pitch, and rhythm.

Examples of media reception of *The Chronic* indicate both attention to the character of specific sounds and extra-musical discourses which may have influenced these interpretations. Robert Marriott wrote that G-funk was "haunted P-Funk laced with synthesized vice," and that "Dre and his collaborators gave body to the laid-back tension that characterizes the life in Los Angeles ghettos. It was depraved gospel" (Marriott 1999:321). Jan Pareles notes that *The Chronic* was

The album that defined West Coast hip-hop with a personalized style, G-Funk, that's simultaneously relaxed and menacing. The bottom register is swampy synthesizer bass lines that openly emulate Parliament-Funkadelic; the upper end is often a lone keyboard line, whistling or blipping insouciantly. In between are wide-open spaces that hold just a rhythm guitar, sparse keyboard chords and perhaps a singalong chorus between a rapper's unhurried rhymes. It's a hermetic sound, sealed off from street noise as if behind the windows of a limousine or a jacked-up jeep; it's the sound of the player, enjoying ill-gotten gains but always watching his back. (1999)

The legacy from 1970s funk music forms one recognizable influence, but the imagery from 'hood films and gangsta-rap music videos (from *The Chronic*, and earlier videos from N.W.A. such as 1988's "Straight Outta Compton") also helped solidify the relationship of synthesizers and bass extension to a "dirty" sound said to represent the ghettos of Los Angeles.[49] *The Chronic* was advertised in 1992 in hip-hop magazines like *The Source* with Dr. Dre standing prominently in front of his 1964 Impala, firmly establishing the link between the album and the prominence of the automobile in G-funk imagery even before the music was released.

As the preceding quotations suggest, media reception of Dr. Dre's production often made the link between the wide-open spaces of the West Coast and the development of G-funk. To quote Michael Eric Dyson, "West Coast hip-hop tailored its fat bass beats and silky melodies for jeeps that cruise the generous spaces of the West" (2004:421). Ideologies of "The West" helped to create a dichotomy between G-funk's "somatic" sound (often linked with automotive listening) to the allegedly more "cerebral" East Coast sound. One writer includes pop rap artist MC Hammer (from Oakland, California) in this West Coast aesthetic, and suggests that his sound and implied listening spaces are more conducive to mainstream success:

> In no uncertain terms, West Coast rap spelled out the acceptable and unacceptable ways to court mainstream success. On the East Coast, however, it was still just courting. New York rap often seemed deeply insular—the tricky wordsmith pyrotechnics and cryptic references of innovators like Gang Starr, Poor Righteous Teachers, and early Tribe Called Quest was much to be played on Walkmans while riding on the subway or cut up by DJ Red Alert in sweaty afterhours underground clubs. Also, much of it was interior—just listen to Rakim go back to the womb on 'In the Ghetto'—as well as spiritual, frequently laden with the insider-only rhetoric of Muslim sects like the 5% Nation. West Coast hip hop, in contrast, was driving music, ready-made to blare out of car windows and share with the world. And as Hammer found out with the gargantuan sales of *Please Hammer...*, there are more pop-friendly car drivers in America than subway-riding New York rap ideologues. (Diehl 1999:129)

This bifurcation between East and West, influenced in part by the sounds of the recordings, would have a profound influence on 1990s hip-hop.[50]

These connections between the *sounds* of "G-funk" and their implied listening spaces merit further explanation. Dr. Dre envisioned that the primary mode of listening would be through car stereo systems. He explained in a 1992 interview with Brian Cross:

> I make the shit for people to bump in their cars, I don't make it for clubs; if you play it, cool. I don't make it for radio, I don't give a fuck about the radio, TV, nothing like that, I make it for people to play in their cars. The reason being is that you listen to music in your car more than anything. You in your car all the time, the first thing you do is turn on the radio, so that's how I figure. *When I do a mix, the first thing I do is go down and see how it sounds in the car.* (Quoted in Cross 1993:197, emphasis added)

For Dr. Dre, the automotive listening space represents an idealized reference because it is reflective of what he perceives to be the way people listen to his music.[51] The centrality of the car to his lifestyle can be seen in a number of Dr. Dre's music videos from *The Chronic.* Dre's music video for "Nuthin But a 'G' Thang" also featured the car prominently as a crucial part of a day in the life of Compton's black youth.[52] The video opens with a close-up of Dr. Dre's car radio with a voiceover from "DJ Charmaine Champagne" (actually a pornographic film star) introducing the track. During the voiceover, the camera zooms out in a crane shot similar to the famous opening of Orson Wells's 1958 *Touch of Evil* (which also featured the automobile prominently). The camera eventually shows Dr. Dre exiting his car to pick up his friend Snoop Doggy Dogg at home. During the music video, there is a twenty second sequence that shows Dre and friends in their cars, driving on the freeway from the picnic they attended to a party later that night. In addition to Dre's own 1964 Chevrolet Impala (fitted with hydraulics), the video included many other lowrider cars, as Jonathan Gold recounts:

> Chugging, smoke-spewing old relics burnished to a high shine, bounding and rebounding higher and higher, tossing their passengers about like so many extremely urban cowboys. If you peek into the trunk of any of these cars, you will see 14 car batteries hooked up in series and a row of hydraulic motors mounted where you'd expect to see the spare tire, but you'd better get out of the way when it starts to jump. (1993:41)

The video concludes with Dr. Dre being dropped off in the same car at the same house which began the music video, creating a bookend image of the house and the automobile. Multiple gangsta rap music videos at this time began to show the car's prominence in the Southern Californian ghetto world, such as Dr. Dre's "Let Me Ride," Ice Cube's "It Was a Good Day," Nate Dogg's "G Funk," and Warren G's "Regulate." Associations of rap music with the automobile became so ingrained that it grew to be the source of parody and humor, such as the opening of the 1999 film *Office Space* (dir. Mike Judge). As we are introduced separately to the film's protagonists commuting to work in bumper-to-bumper traffic, one white, middle-class male character seems to be the only one enjoying himself in his car. He raps along blissfully to Scarface's "No Tears" in his automobile until he sees a African American man on the side of the freeway selling flowers. The white man, ironically named Michael Bolton, then sheepishly lowers his volume and locks his car door, a commentary on the stereotype of the "threatening" black man, and that the discovery of a white man engaging with gangsta rap, more specifically, rapping along to lines such as "You gotta realize somethin' nigga, you fuckin' wit the very best," might anger him. Another variation on this theme is an early 2000s Avis/XM Satellite

Radio commercial that featured three middle class men in suits commuting to work listening and rapping along to Lumbajac's "2 Gs." The lyrical topic of the song ("Make that money man...I gotta stack cheese"[53]) fit the men appropriately, but the commercial (and *Office Space*) subverted the imagined audience for the genre of music, usually presented in myriad representations as lower class African American youth. These scenes also represent the automobile as a private space, either for bonding with friends/co-workers and/or as a personal outlet of emotion and pleasure.

The geography of California is important, here, as one half of Los Angeles is dedicated to spaces designed specifically, and often exclusively, for the automobile (i.e., freeways, roads, parking lots) (Urry 2005:30). Southern California is the site of numerous car culture births (e. g., hot rods, lowriders, GM's Harley Earl, the pinstriping of George Barris and Von Dutch, the car audio aftermarket), helping to incorporate numerous car-inspired or car-dependent inventions into American life such as the drive-in, the suburban shopping mall, "cruising," the motel, drag racing, fast food, and trademarked modes of hip-hop production such as those from Dr. Dre. Adam Krims has noted that "One could certainly argue some specificity to the history of rap music in this case: Los Angeles car culture nurtured the so-called 'Jeep beats,' tracks mixed specifically for playback in car audio systems" (2007:161). California also played a crucial role in car customization cultures and the development of the subwoofer.[54] Marsh and Collett in their study of the psychology of the automobile, acknowledge: "The West Coast of America has spawned more auto cults than any other part of the world" (1989:85). The car cultures that arose in Los Angeles became mediating cultural practices that helped shape Dr. Dre's music production techniques.

Like the car customization cultures of Southern California, Dr. Dre takes old parts, and puts new features on old frameworks. Through his "replays" (Dre's term) or interpolations, he is customizing the music for an idealized imagined community that listen to his music in cars. His production style has been described as perfecting a "gangsta pop formula,"[55] the "pop" aspect most likely alluding to his use of the (usually simple) verse-chorus form and the repetitive "hooks" in those choruses (whether by synthesizer in "Dre Day" and "Nuthin' But a 'G' Thang," or by the voice in "Gin and Juice," for example).[56] The notion of G-funk as "gangsta pop" was not only influenced by song structure and chorus material, but also by the commercial success that *The Chronic* enjoyed, demonstrating that rap music could be successful in the popular music mainstream, what hip-hop historian Jeff Chang calls the "popstream."[57] Dr. Dre's production will often craft verse-chorus forms more familiar to non-funk-based popular music by using musical material from funk songs that do not follow this form.[58] The finished recorded product, like the automobile, appears as unified object but in actuality originated from numerous disparate sources. The automobile has over 10,000 parts, and like many other products of capitalist modernity, car designers attempt to create the illusion of unity from their inner working parts. Like Alfred Sloan, Dr. Dre updates the sounds of 1970s funk, similar to what Vance Packard referred to as the "upgrading urge" of the annual model (Basham and Ughetti 1984:40).

In addition, the interplay between human and machine in the driving experience may enlighten an analysis of hip-hop (and other) recordings that embrace the hybridity of their "human" sounds (e.g., the voice) and their "synthesized" ones (e.g., drum machine, synthesized keyboards). Rather than situate these recordings as reflecting a large-scale shift from "the human" to "post-human" in society as Katherine Hayles (1999) has suggested, it is more productive in this case to analyze how much of contemporary recorded music is a mix of the human, the synthesized, the acoustic (e.g., strings, guitar, drum kit), and other electromechanical instruments that are so deeply ingrained in cultural consciousness that we give little thought to their status as "technological artifacts" (e.g., electric guitar, electric bass) (Auner 2003:99).[59] G-funk, like many rap subgenres, espouses a notion of "realness." Rather than present a case of post-human ventriloquism by way of cyborg-like voices (Radiohead's "Fitter, Happier," for example), the technology used here is derived from a funk-based lineage ("connecting machines and funkiness" [Goodwin 1990:265]) that emphasizes the humanness, the *realness,* of the rapper.[60] I would argue further that Dr. Dre's emphasis on not digitally sampling the material helps contribute to this particular sense of realness as well.

An example typical of Dr. Dre's early 1990s production that demonstrates this hybridity of material and suitability for automotive listening is the Dr. Dre-produced single "Who Am I? (What's My Name?)," the debut single from Snoop Doggy Dogg's *Doggystyle* (Table 4.1) (1993). The synthesized sounds include a Roland TR-808 drum machine and a Moog synthesizer bass line derived from Tom Browne's "Funkin' for Jamaica" from the album *Love Approach* (1979). The basic beat is repeated throughout the song and changes texturally in terms of layering rather than in dynamic range, as it is likely that heavy dynamic compression was used in production to elevate the volume over the road and engine noise of a car (see waveform in Figure 4.8). The "Snoop Doggy Dogg" line,

---

**Table 4.1 "Who Am I? (What's My Name)?"—song structure**

(0:00–0:06) "Guitar intro" (2 measures)
(0:07–0:26) Chorus—m. 3—Basic beat begins (4 measures) +
    Vocal line 1 (4=2+2 measures)
(0:27–0:56) Verse 1 (12 measures)
(0:57–1:15) Chorus 2—Vocal line 1 (4=2+2 measures) +
    Vocal line 2 (4 measures)
(1:16–1:46) Verse 2 (12 measures)
(1:47–2:05) Chorus 3—Vocal line 1 (4 measures) +
    Vocal line 3 (4 measures: "Bow wow
    wow yippieyoyippie yay" from "Atomic Dog")
(2:06–2:35) Verse 3—(12 measures)
(2:36–3:14) Chorus 4 (Double chorus)—Vocal line 1 (8 measures) +
    Vocal line 2 (8 measures)
(3:15–4:05) Coda—Twenty measures of female vocalist singing
    "Snoop Doggy Dogg"

Table 4.2 "Who Am I? (What's My Name)?"—source material

| Musical Phrase | Derived from |
| --- | --- |
| Moog bass line | Tom Browne's "Funkin' for Jamaica" (1979/1980) |
| Vocal Line 1 | George Clinton's "Atomic Dog" (1982) |
| Vocal Line 2 | Parliament's "Tear the Roof off the Sucker (Give up the Funk)" (1976) |
| "Talk box" (vocoder-esque) | Zapp (1978–80s funk band) |
| Low vocal effects and | "Atomic Dog" (1982) |
| Vocal Line 3 | |

collectively sung in the intro, is from Parliament Funkadelic's "Atomic Dog" and the second vocal line is from Parliament's "Tear the Roof off the Sucker (Give up the Funk)," melodically virtually the same, but placed on a different harmonic backdrop/frame/chassis. Vocal line three is a quotation of vocal effects from "Atomic Dog": "Bow wow wow yippie yo yippie yay."[61] What I label the "guitar intro" is a sample from The Counts's "Pack of Lies" from the album *What's up Front that Counts* (1971), a two measure excerpt with guitar and saxophones. (See Table 4.2 for a list of source material.) Foregrounded lyrical textures travel among Snoop Dogg's laid back verses, singing in the chorus, and Zapp-like vocal effects (as Zapp frontman Roger Troutman was known largely for his use of the "talk box"). The track ends with vocals from an uncredited female voice, who sings improvisational-sounding melismas on the name "Snoop Doggy Dogg."

After the two measure "guitar intro," the basic beat begins (as shown in Figure 4.7). The three verses are primarily rapped by Snoop Doggy Dogg, although Dr. Dre recites a few lines at the end of verse one. The lyrical topics of the song focus on his debut as a solo artist, bragging about his lifestyle, locality of Long Beach, and his collaborations with Dr. Dre.[62] Interestingly, in the music video for "Who Am I" (directed by rapper Fab 5 Freddy), Dre's portion of the rap includes a visual of him standing next to a white car in front of a house similar to the one in " 'G' Thang." Though the narrative of the music video has little to do with the automobile, "Who Am I?" still demonstrates the centrality of the automobile to Dr. Dre's lifestyle and status. In the song, each chorus always contains at least one, four-measure iteration of vocal line one (consisting of the repeated, two measure phrase), but each chorus is slightly different, mixing multiple elements from the George Clinton songs that Dr. Dre interpolates. As characteristic of his production style at this time, Dr. Dre borrows from multiple different songs and constructs a verse-chorus form with them. It is a "simple verse-chorus" form, in that the harmony does not change between verse and chorus, and it is noteworthy that he was able to tailor material with relatively static harmonies into a repeating four-chord pattern (bm, bm/A, G, F#7).

While drum sounds and beats from funk were used since the earliest days of digital sampling in hip-hop, these were usually drawn from the earlier funk of James Brown (e.g. "Funky Drummer") and other recordings from the late 1960s and early 1970s such

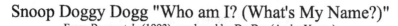

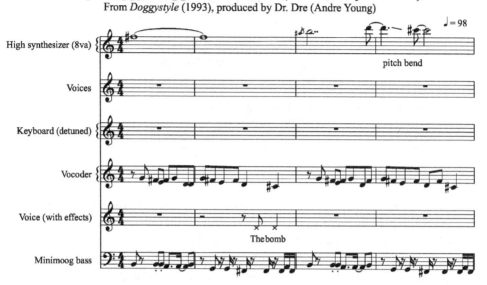

FIGURE 4.7 Basic Beat of Snoop Doggy Dogg's "Who Am I? (What's My Name?)" from *Doggystyle* (1993), produced by Dr. Dre.

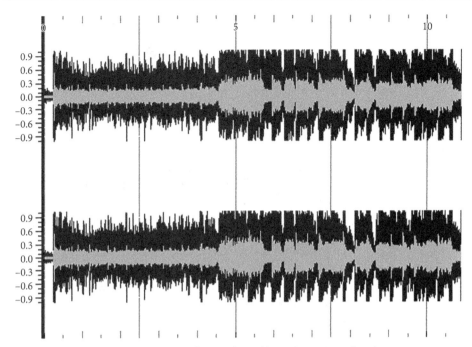

FIGURE 4.8 Opening of "Who Am I?" Waveform (from Sonic Visualizer).

as the Incredible Bongo Band's version of "Apache" (1972). Dr. Dre, in contrast, borrows funk music from a decade later, largely from the late 1970s and early 1980s in this example, reproducing stylistic characteristics such as synthesizers and vocal effects.

The decision to open with an early 1970s sample ("Pack of Lies") which never returns in the song may be demonstrating a conscious shift in funk sources, as Dr. Dre has expanded the hip-hop sound palette to reflect later funk developments for the rest of the song's duration. The song opening with a digital sample, quickly yielding to an un-sampled basic beat in a way authenticates this conscious shift. Richard Dyer, in his book on pastiche, includes a chapter on pastiche works within works of art. He cites the newsreel footage in *Citizen Kane* (film within a film) and the play "Murder of Gonzago" within *Hamlet* (play within a play). Dyer writes that the "effect of the inner pastiche is to authenticate the outer form" (2006:80). In a way, though the "inner pastiche" occurs at the opening of the song, the purpose of the sample is to contrast with, and authenticate, the realness of the entire song.[63]

As can be heard in the contrast between mm. 1–2 and mm. 3–4, the "basic beat" of the song appears stretched so that it fills the extreme ranges of its amplitude, something that would be ideal for loud environments such as the rumbling noises of an automobile. The graphic representation of the audio signal in the waveform in Figure 4.8 shows the differences between the "intro" and the "basic beat."

In the waveform, the x-axis represents time and y-axis represents the amplitude levels of the audio output. The waveform signal shows that the overall amplitude appears

George Clinton "Atomic dog" from *Computer Games* (1982)

Snoop Doggy Dogg "Who am I?"

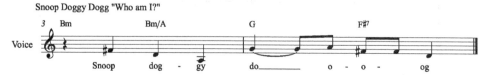

FIGURE 4.9 Comparison of Vocal Line 1 from "Who Am I?" (1993) with George Clinton's "Atomic Dog" (1982) from *Computer Games*.

expanded compared to the intro, and suggests the use of dynamic range compression on the basic beat. The effect is that measures 3 to the end of the song sound "louder" and more "filled out" than the intro section, consistent with Dr. Dre's desire to fill the automotive listening space.

By re-recording vocal lines from pre-existing sources, Dr. Dre can change the harmonic framework of the phrases and adapt them to any given harmony. In vocal line 1 in Figure 4.9, for example, the original version contains a harmonic backdrop of D for the duration, whereas the new version has a bass line that arguably becomes darker and more menacing with the minor mode descending tetrachord pattern (bm, bm/A, G, F#7). The effect is one of less static harmonic motion, including relatively strong movement to the dominant before returning to the tonic every two measures. This progression also has echoes with Latin music, as the descending progression has been associated with Phrygian-modal music in the Spanish-language world for centuries (Manuel 2002). Despite the harmonic differences, the melodic line is similar enough that the allusion to "Atomic Dog" can still easily be recognized. In the Snoop Dogg version of vocal line 1, there is a group singing the melodic line, a quotation that directly signifies the Parliament-style, collectively sung choruses. Both versions repeat the two measure phrase as well. Lyrically, Dr. Dre takes advantage of the dog/Dogg connection by quoting dog references from "Atomic Dog" at multiple points in "Who Am I?"

A similar tailoring occurs with vocal line 2. Once again, the original from George Clinton's Parliament includes a characteristic funk groove over just one chord, this time, an E7 (Figure 4.10). There are multiple voices singing in both examples (both shift from monophony to homophony), and the harmonies have changed to reflect the implied harmonies of the new bass line.

The contrast between the high and low synthesizer frequencies in "Who Am I?" and other examples in that style are particularly effective in aftermarket car sound systems, where the highly directional tweeters can exclusively support the high end frequencies, and the power of the subwoofer(s) produce the corporeal sensations from the bassline.

Parliment "Tear the roof off the sucker (Give up the Funk)" from *Mothership Connection* (1976)

"Who am I?" Second Vocal Line

FIGURE 4.10 Comparison of Vocal Line 2 from "Who Am I?" (1993) with Parliament's "Tear the Roof Off the Sucker (Give Up the Funk)" (1976) from *Mothership Connection.*

The "human" sounds (e.g., Snoop's rap, collective voices, and female at the end), their locus in the frequency range easiest for humans to hear (3 kHz–7 kHz), will be supported by woofers/midrange speakers which require much less power than a subwoofer.

The female voice that closes the song is particularly conspicuous, as Adam Krims has noted that any substantial female presence of any sort had been rare in "harder" rap genres before G-funk (2000:86). Stylistically, the singing is derived from "softer" styles such as contemporary R&B (e.g., R. Kelly, Mariah Carey), another "human" element perhaps in contrast with the vocal effects used exclusively for male voices.[64]

The styles utilized in G-funk (including late 70s/early 80s P-Funk, R&B, and simple verse-chorus form), largely pioneered in rap music by Dr. Dre and his collaborators, spread its influence over a number of subsequent groups. One example of a rap song that shares timbral style to Dre's "G-funk" is the song "Thuggish Ruggish Bone" by Bone Thugs-n-Harmony from their album *Creepin On Ah Come Up* (1994), which uses a mix of high synthesizer, low bass, and the singing of Shatasha Williams. Though G-funk was considered a "West Coast" style, it was also used by artists said to represent the East coast. For example, The Notorious B.I.G.'s "Big Poppa" (1994), produced by Chucky Thompson and Sean "Puffy" Combs, used a high-pitched synthesizer riff derived from The Isley Brothers' "Between the Sheets" in the style of Dr. Dre's production.

Synthesized sounds, dynamic range compression, and prominent bass frequencies are but three elements that seem to be most compatible with the automotive soundscape. The experience of automotive listening is a synthesis of musical technology and automotive technology that must co-exist with each other to be successful; I would argue that a certain aspect of popular music recordings can be analyzed through this particular, historically specific compatibility. Like the car-driver/driver-car relationship, hip-hop recordings are a mix of "human" elements and technology, a mix of man and man-made machine. Consideration of a particular listening space, and the transfer function of loudspeakers and their resonant frequency, should be acknowledged as an important component of subject position in the listening experience.

As we consider the automotive soundscape in hip-hop recordings, we should allow for alternatives to traditional analysis that accommodate the way that music producers and car audio enthusiasts think of sound (in terms of frequency rather than, or in addition to, pitch in a Western notational sense).[65] Frequency, playback spaces and speakers, and the hybrid human-machine element of recordings are all undertheorized facets of popular music production and the automotive listening experience.

# CONCLUSION

As a product of place- and space-specific urban car cultures, Dr. Dre's production techniques reflect a desire to customize and tailor sounds for the automotive soundscape. Automobile production, geographical specificity, and other mediating cultural practices such as car customization cultures have shaped Dr. Dre's and other producers' music production techniques. Perhaps car audio, like the streamlined outer appearance of many automobiles, provides the illusion of unity, sonically suturing the inconsistencies or ruptures in the fragmented bodies of culture, ideology, and subjectivity; like hip-hop music, the automobile is a unique (almost paradoxical) hybrid: both public (on the road) and private (owned), a site of mastery and womb-like comfort, human and machine, symbolizing freedom and dependence (on petroleum), at times transcendent and other times suffocating, a fantasy object (e.g. *The Fast and the Furious)* and the cause of trauma and nightmare (e.g. Stephen King's *Christine*), an object-cause of desire and a cause of stress (e.g., traffic jams and road rage), a "symbolic sanctuary" (Bull 2003:371), and the cause of numerous fatalities.

Jonathan Bell, in writing of the car's influence on architecture, comments that "our experience of the city, and hence our response to architecture, is almost exclusively conducted through the medium of the automobile: the car defines our space whether we are driving, being driven, or avoiding being driven over" (2001:11). Marsh and Collett write that "It is because the car has so much personal value that we have been, and are still, prepared to alter radically the environments in which we live in order to create societies in which the automobile can feature so centrally" (1986:4). The automobile has had a tremendous amount of influence on multiple realms of experience, and if the car does indeed define the spaces in which we live, and the automotive space is largely experienced in terms of sound, then one could say that sound (as mediated through the automobile) and our sense of space mutually shape each other.[66]

There are numerous levels by which one could investigate the automobile's impact on the world's soundscapes, such as the individual experience of car-drivers, the influence of the car on music production, car audio subcultures, and larger national and transnational trends.[67] In 2005, it was estimated that there were over 700 million cars on the world's roads (Urry 2005:25); this statistic suggests that automobility will continue to be a pervasive force in the decades to come, continuing the ever-shifting social, economic and political forces that shape the automobile, and the object's influence on multiple realms of societies. This chapter presents a model of the exchange between a given mobile technology and cultural production that acknowledges the centrality of sound and music to the experience of that technology, and has potential application to newer playback technologies such as the iPod. It encourages analysis of particular modes of listening, modes that have in turn inflected the way music recordings are produced.

# Acknowledgments

I would like to thank Adam Krims, David Metzer, Mervyn Cooke, Tim Hughes, Katherine Williams, and John Urry who kindly looked at drafts of this chapter at various stages of its development. Special thanks to Pat Olguin and Hank Shocklee for providing useful information for this project, and to Motorola Inc., Lee Exline, and the Crutchfield Corporation for providing diagrams and pictures. Later stages of this chapter were supported through a grant from the Economic and Social Research Council, United Kingdom.

# Notes

1. "Boom cars" are cars with customized sound systems, normally with a high attention to the low end frequencies by way of a subwoofer or subwoofers. Car audio enthusiasts can purchase a wide range of products for their automobile and either have a system installed by a specialist shop or the consumer can install it themselves. These cars are often called "boom cars" because they function in a similar way to boom boxes of the 1980s; a driver can roll the windows down and emanate sound throughout neighborhoods and other spaces.
2. According to David McCartney, one of the earliest known car radios was built in St. Louis, Missouri in 1904 (2004:138).
3. Heinaphone was first taken over by a group called the Automobile Radio Corporation (ARC) when it was subsequently bought out by Philco (*Time* 1936; Lamm 2000).
4. McCartney stresses the fact that the car radio evolved through a period of time rather than through one single breakthrough; The Galvin Manufacturing Corporation changed its company's name to Motorola in 1947. The company also had success in inventing the walkie-talkie during World War II and later in cellular phone technology (Petrakis 1991:91–100). The first US patent for the car radio was filed on August 3, 1931 (no. 1,944,139) by William P. Lear and approved January 16, 1934. *United States Patent and Trademark Office,* http://www.uspto.gov/index.html (accessed July 18, 2008).
5. For a discussion of "phonogenic" instruments in the context of early jazz recordings, see Katz (2004:81).
6. FM radio had a shaky start commercially from 1945 to 1957, and began to expand in 1958, and has continued to increase into the twenty-first century (Sterling 2002:602–8).

7. The Highway Hi-Fi was used in Chrysler automobiles from 1956–61. RCA Victor had their own car phonograph which played standard 45s, and was introduced in November 1960. Philips/Norelco created the Auto Mignon which also played 45s. The interest in car phonographs quickly waned at the onset of the four-track and eight-track cartridges (Miller 1997; see also Goldmark 1973).

8. To provide an example, in my former residence of Nottingham, England, I could visit a number of stores dealing almost exclusively with car audio and electronics, including Audio One, Audio Vision, Car Electronics, In Phase International, and Secure Audio. This is not to mention the large online mobile audio market in the United States, United Kingdom, and all over the world: www.mobileaudio.com, www.mobile-audio.net, www. dealercostcaraudio.com, and www.mobileaudioconcepts.com are a few sites with links to numerous mobile audio dealers (all accessed February 17, 2010). In the United Kingdom, mobile audio is more often referred to as ICE, or In Car Entertainment.

9. Though there are a number of varying statistics on time spent in the car in the United States, the most comprehensive account is from the 2000 Census which states that the average one-way work commute time is 26 minutes, and that 87.9% of all workers travel by car, truck, or van. The census also stated that of the 128.3 million workers in the United States, 97 million drove alone to work (75.5%) as opposed to carpooling, using public transport, motorcycle, walking, cycling, or working from home (Reschovsky 2004:1–5).

10. Before the automobile, coach builders would customize carriages for the rich, as a tailor would do for clothes. It was not uncommon for celebrities in the early automotive era to hire custom designers for their automobiles. What Harley Earl and General Motors President Alfred Sloan did in the late 1920s was simply to bring the look of customization to the wider public. Hollywood-born Earl, before leading the first Art and Color division of a major automobile manufacturer, was a custom car designer for celebrities such as Fatty Arbuckle and Cecil B. DeMille (Marsh and Collett 1986:31; Gartman 1994:211).

11. The term "Sloanism" was used in Marling (2002:355). Sloan hired Earl in the mid-1920s to compete with Ford's Model T. GM's La Salle, from the Cadillac division in 1927, was the first mass-produced car planned bumper to bumper by one man (Earl). Earl was also the first to put trademarked tail fins on a 1949 Cadillac, inspired by the P-38 lightening pursuit plane (Gartman 1994:75, 148).

12. Katz cites Smith and Marx (1994) and Kline and Pinch (1996) as critiques of technological determinism.

13. Kline and Pinch, in their study of the automobile in the rural United States, use the SCOT (Social Construction of Technology) model, which emphasizes "interpretive flexibility" of an artefact and its possible "closure" and stabilization when certain products become the dominant form of technology (1996:765–66). One could say that the Motorola car radio had a level of "closure" in the market, and more broadly speaking, that the car radio by the 1980s had a level of stabilization in that it was the dominant apparatus for automotive listening.

14. For more information, see the IASCA website: www.iasca.com; see also Hoffmann and Bailey (1991:71–72).

15. See The National Alliance Against Loud Car Stereo Assault, www.lowertheboom.org; anti-boom car legislation is not the first case of communities' seeking legal action for noise pollution associated with car culture, as some citizens as early as 1935 were fighting for laws against the noise pollution stemming from the then-new phenomenon known as drive-in theatres (Seagrave 1992:26).

16. As a musicologist, I cannot help but see the striking difference in meaning of words like "tonal" and "timbre" as used by car audio writers. Rather than simply dismiss the terminology as "inaccurate," I place more interest on how other audio cultures describe and think about sound in contrast to my own academic discipline.

17. A transducer converts mechanical, magnetic or acoustic energy into electric energy and vice versa.

18. One of the first successful car audio subwoofers was called the "Kicker," built in 1980 by Stillwater Designs in Stillwater, Oklahoma. Over twenty years later, Kicker's subwoofers could be added to vehicles as a factory- or dealer-installed option in Dodge and Chrysler cars. A number of car audio brands are now contracted with car companies to provide their products as stock system rather than in the aftermarket (Newcomb 2008:19).

19. There now exist products called "bass transducers" or "tactile transducers" that use the low frequencies in the music to vibrate the chassis of the vehicle more deliberately. One example of this is the Aura Bass Shaker (Rumerich 2005:130). An example of headphones as tactile transducer is the Panasonic Brain Shaker Extreme—RPHS900.

20. Subwoofers normally need to produce 80dB SPL to be heard or felt (Pettitt 2003:60).

21. Robert Levine writes, "Rock and pop producers have always used compression to balance the sounds of different instruments and to make music sound more exciting, and radio stations apply compression for technical reasons. In the days of vinyl records, there was a physical limit to how high the bass levels could go before the needle skipped a grove.... Intensely compressed albums like Oasis' 1995 (*What's the Story) Morning Glory?* set a new bar for loudness; the songs were well-suited for bars, cars and other noisy environments" (2007).

22. For examples of how the phonograph changed music composition, see Katz (2004): "When Igor Stravinsky composed his Serenade for Piano in 1925, he wrote the work so that each of the four movements would fit the roughly three-minute limit of a ten-inch, 78-rpm record side" (3).

23. For example, producer Elliot Schneider says that he uses a DI for the bass guitar because "the amp signal just doesn't have enough definition; it just contributes a lot of low end" (quoted in Massey 2000:60); Of course, other producers may want heavier low end, such as many hip-hop music producers.

24. A cinematic example of this practice can be found in the film *Once* (2006, dir. John Carney); after the band records their demo, the engineer takes them out for a drive to hear the mix.

25. Patrick Olguin, email correspondence with author, June 3, 2008. Olguin has worked with a number of commercially successful groups and artists, such as Papa Roach, Black Eyed Peas, rapper E-40, and Cake.

26. Patrick Olguin, email correspondence with author, September 19, 2008.

27. Hank Shocklee of the hip-hop production team The Bomb Squad recounted to me the existence of a custom car audio system in New York's Sony Studios. Hank Shocklee, interview with author, Wuppertal, Germany, March 8, 2009.

28. Krims writes that some popular music genres "help to provide a soundscape for design-intensive urban interiors, and they do so, arguably, just as classical recordings do, by targeting a soundscape to the design or desired ethos of the private playback space" (2007:157).

29. Rose also notes similarities with Caribbean musics such as Jamaica's talk over and dub.

30. In hip-hop parlance, the term "beat" refers to the entire sonic accompaniment to a rapper, composed by a producer, and usually recorded previous to the rap in a studio.

31. "It raises the provocative possibility that their distinctive history of propertylessness and material deprivation has inclined them toward a disproportionate investment in particular forms of property that are publicly visible and the status that corresponds to them" (Gilroy 2001:84).

32. Daz Dillinger "My System," *R.A.W.* (2000).

33. An early 2 Live Crew hit, the 1986 "Throw the D," included a B-side entitled "Ghetto Bass." Member Luke Skyywalker (Luther Campbell), a DJ from Miami's Liberty City neighbourhood and son of a Jamaican immigrant, started his own record label in 1986 called Luke Skyywalker Records to promote other Miami groups (Sarig 2007:12–19).

34. L'Trimm "Cars with the Boom," *Grab It!* (1988). See also Sarig (2007:30).

35. Jibbs, "King Kong" *Jibbs Featuring Jibbs* (2006). The opening line of the chorus is paraphrased in Bone Thugs-n-Harmony's "Bumps in the Trunk": "Cuz Niggas can hear me before they can see me." Bone Thugs-n-Harmony, "Bumps in the Trunk" *Strength and Loyalty* (2007).

36. One of the most well-known examples of the car as metaphor for sex in early blues is Robert Johnson's "Terraplane Blues" (recorded in 1936): "I'm bound to check your oil.... I'm on get deep down in this connection, keep on tangling with your wires."

37. This link between Dr. Dre's music and that of the 1970s is a formidable one, particularly in the borrowing of elements from 1970s funk, and imagery and characters from 1970s blaxploitation film. See Demers (2003).

38. While the use of drum machine was already common in hip-hop production, Dr. Dre's conspicuous use of synthesizers was not. The synthesizer has been a prominent feature of popular music for over forty years (including 1970s groups and artists from disparate backgrounds such as Yes, Wendy/Walter Carlos, Parliament Funkadelic, Sun Ra, Stevie Wonder, Kraftwerk, Genesis, Herbie Hancock, and ABBA). Anxieties toward the synthesizer were expressed, particularly in the 1970s, as they were susceptible to cultural assumptions that electronic instruments were "cold" and "inhuman," perhaps because the sounds produce fewer overtones than other instruments (Dickinson 2008:124). Though keyboards had a mixed reception in the 1970s, Andrew Goodwin points out that a generation of 1980s popular music artists and producers grew up with the synthesized sounds of the 1970s. Goodwin writing in the late 1980s comments that, "pop musicians and audiences have grown increasingly accustomed to making an association between synthetic/automated music and the communal (dance floor) connection to nature (via the body). We have grown used to connecting machines and *funkiness*" (1990: 263, 265). One can now, in hindsight, make a distinction between the sound and reception of analogue 1970s synthesizers as warm (e.g., Stevie Wonder, Parliament) as compared to digital synthesizers from the 1980s as more "robotic" (e.g., Kraftwerk, Gary Numan, and Devo). See also Cateforis (2011:151–181).

39. The "basic beat" in a given hip-hop song are the core layers of the musical complement that change little for a significant duration of the song. The concept of a "basic beat" is strongly indebted to Adam Krims's *Rap Music and the Poetics of Identity*, in particular, his discussion of layering and analysis of Ice Cube's "The Nigga Ya Love to Hate" (Krims 2000:93–122).

40. All transcriptions are by the author.

41. The riff, and other snippets from the single, is used in a number of international rap singles, as the G-Funk era was often the first experience that countries other than the

United States had with rap music. As Dre and Snoop reached mainstream success in the United States, they were able to secure international distribution on a larger-scale. One example is the Spanish rap group Arma Blanca, on their track "El Musicólogo," which samples from a number of American hits and DJ Tomek's "G Thang 2008" from Berlin. Ben Folds's cover version of Dr. Dre's "Bitches Ain't Shit" (from *The Chronic*) uses a high-pitched synthesizer in the middle eight similar to one that Dre might use. The Folds cover is characteristically representative of his piano/singer-songwriter style, but the inclusion of the synthesizer adds another layer of musical signification not normally found on his recordings.

42. It is important, here, to draw the distinction between publishing fees and master recording (or mechanical) fees. When Dr. Dre re-records songs, he only has to pay the publishing fees and not the mechanical fees in addition to the publishing, as would be the case if he digitally sampled the sounds. Kembrew McLeod writes, "When clearing a sample taken from a record, two types of fees must be paid: publishing fees and master recording (or mechanical) fees. The publishing fee, which is paid to the company or individual owning a particular song, often consists of a flexible and somewhat arbitrary formula that calculates a statutory royalty rate set by Congress" (2001:91). See also Schloss (2004:175).

43. "Control is Dre's thing. Every Dre track begins the same way, with Dre behind a drum machine in a room full of trusted musicians. (They carry beepers. When he wants to work, they work.) They'll program a beat, then ask the musicians to play along; when Dre hears something he likes, he isolates the player and tells him how to refine the sound. 'My greatest talent,' Dre says,' is knowing exactly what I want to hear' " (Tyrangiel 2001).

44. Kurtis Blow says, "The 808 is great because you can *detune* it and get this low-frequency hum. It's a car speaker destroyer. That's what we try and do as rap producers—break car speakers and house speakers and boom boxes. And the 808 does it. It's African music!" (quoted in Rose 1994:75).

45. Most accounts portray Dr. Dre as a "studio work-horse." One journalist notes, "Dre works in spurts. This week he's had three studio sessions of 19 hours or more. Last week he did a marathon 56-hour session. If he didn't go to the parking lot for the occasional car-stereo listening test, he'd have no idea whether it was night or day" (Tyrangel 2001). Dre has said he likes to use four or five (MPC3000) samplers at one time, to each have different drum sounds and one to sequence the keyboard ("Interview with Dr. Dre" 2005). Referring to Dr. Dre, Snoop Dogg has said, "I went and did a song with the nigga, the nigga made me do each word, word for word, until I got it right. See what people don't understand is, when you dealing with Dr. Dre, you dealing with a perfectionist. It's like if you dealing with God. So you have to be perfection when you do a record with him, because his sound is right, his direction is right. Everybody ain't prepared for that!" (Nima 2006).

46. Born Calvin Broadus Jr., rapper Snoop Doggy Dogg changed his stage name to "Snoop Dogg" in 1998 when he left Death Row Records for No Limit Records. I use the two interchangeably throughout the chapter.

47. Eithne Quinn labels the G-funk era as "post-funk" (2005:143), echoing Nelson George's book *Post-Soul Nation* (2004).

48. For a compelling argument of this, see Sanneh (2004:230).

49. Josh Tyrangiel has written about Death Row Records president Suge Knight's ability to understand the importance of MTV airplay in promoting his artists. Tyrangiel stated

that "By the summer of 1993, the popularity of gangsta rap was no longer debatable. With alternative rock already on the decline, MTV sensed it was missing something big and dipped its tow back in playing videos from Dr. Dre's solo debut on Death Row Records, *The Chronic*. The response was tremendous. The video for 'Nuthin' But a 'G' Thing' was a players' party, with Dre and his reed-thin protégé Snoop Doggy Dogg acting as the governors of good times, West Coast-style. The song was bangin', and because the MTV audience hadn't seen it or heard anything like it, they flipped out" (1999:141).

50. Artists and media eventually became involved in a so-called "war" between the two coasts, culminating in the deaths of two of rap's young icons: Tupac Shakur in 1996 and The Notorious B.I.G. in 1997.

51. Rapper Ice-T also expressed an association of his ideal listeners with the car stereo sound system when he said, "I pretty much record every record in a matter of a month, maybe two at the most....We did *Power* in L.A....The board was connected to the biggest system we could build that resembled a car stereo system, so we could check how it sounded when real people who would buy our tapes listened to that shit. Big woofers and all that" (quoted in Coleman 2007:249).

52. The importance of the automobile to Snoop Doggy Dogg has also been recorded in interviews: "One of the first things I did with my profits was to buy myself a car, a '77 cutlass supreme four-door I got off one of the homeboys from Compton for three hundred dollars. It didn't drive for shit, and every time you hit the brakes you could hear it squealing like a bitch in heat, but I loved the lines of that car and the way I looked sitting behind the wheel..." (quoted in Gilroy 2001:81).

53. "Stack cheese" is urban slang for making money.

54. Though the subwoofer was the product of a number of developments by a number of inventors, Los Angeles was crucial to its development and distribution. In the late 1960s, Ken Kreisel teamed up with Jonas Miller (of Jonas Miller Sound in Beverly Hills) and created M&K Sound in 1974, in which the second floor of the shop was devoted to subwoofers. Kreisel's advancements with subwoofers in the early 1970s originated from a desire to reproduce successfully the low frequencies that he heard from the bass of pipe organs in Los Angeles. He went to Harvard, MIT and Bell Labs to collaborate on acoustical research which greatly benefited his innovations and products (Phillips 1997).

55. "*The Chronic* became to gangsta rap what Bob Marley's *Legend* was to reggae—the record that started a mainstream fan on the true path. Dr. Dre perfected the Gangsta Pop formula with Snoop Doggy Dogg's *Doggystyle*—pop songs with the hardcore aura intact, rendered broadcast-ready by radio edits that, somehow, didn't castrate the groove"(Coker 2003:143).

56. "Simple verse-chorus form" is defined as song form in which the verse and chorus share the same harmonic progression, in opposition to "contrasting verse-chorus form" in which the chord progressions differ between verse and chorus.

57. "Just as the gang peace movement desired to mainstream hardcore bangers into civic society, *The Chronic* wanted to drive hardcore rap into the popstream" (Chang 2005:420).

58. I hesitate to overstate the case that Dre used entirely new materials in his production. After all, many of the keyboards in his productions were used by Parliament and other 1970s groups. Perhaps the success of the eight-track cassette in automotive listening in the United States had some influence on the use of keyboards and other electronic instruments in the 1970s that would have been most compatible to the contemporary technology, as well. What *was* new about Dre's style of hip-hop production was the re-recording of materials, attention to verse-chorus popular music forms, and the flexibility with which he was able to alter the musical elements and textures of the recording.

59. This echoes the statement from Auner that "in no aspect of our lives has the penetration of the human by machines been more complete than in music … we no longer even recognize complex devices such as a piano as technological artefacts" (2003:99).

60. Auner (2003) discusses Radiohead's "Fitter, Happier" and Moby's "Porcelain" as examples of post-human voices. For an example of the use of the vocoder as an example of empowering femininity in Cher's "Believe," see Dickinson (2001). Unlike these examples, Snoop Dogg's voice is far from that of a cyborg-esque post-human ventriloquism. In contrast, the humanness of his voice is supported and framed by the synthesized sounds, male vocal effects, group singing, and the female voice of the coda. In addition to this particular brand of realness, the notion of the human in this context is linked with notion of the subhuman, the amoral characters of gangsta rap as a product of inhuman social conditions.

61. This line from "Atomic Dog" is also quoted (without effects) in "F--- wit Dre Day" on *The Chronic*, a song similar in harmonic structure and instrumentation to "Who Am I?"

62. It is noteworthy that "Who Am I?" was Snoop Doggy Dogg's official debut single; emphasizing his realness, in the context of a gangsta rap authenticity, would be especially important to ensure future success. Dr. Dre has produced a number of protégés since, including Eminem, 50 Cent, and The Game.

63. Of course, sample-based hip-hop can suggest realness as well, explicated in Krims's discussion of The Bomb Squad's production on Ice Cube's "The Nigga you Love to Hate" (2000:93–102). "Who Am I" may reflect shifting sonic representations of "realness" within the reality/gangsta rap music subgenre, partly influenced by Dre's shift away from sample-based production.

64. Alexander G. Weheliye (2002) considers the melismatic and "soulful" voice of R&B as representing a different form of posthumanism than those described by Hayles and Haraway.

65. Evidence of this in hip-hop production may be found in the phenomena of "de-tuned" layers; if certain layers of sound do not correspond to exact notes in the well-tempered chromatic scale, then this supports the idea that producers think of sound in terms of frequency, rather than in terms of Western pitches. For example, Dr. Dre's "F—wit Dre Day" is in a key somewhere between c minor and c# minor. For more on "de-tuned" layers, see Krims 2000. Not all rap songs are de-tuned, however; for example, "Who Am I? (What's My Name)?" and "Thuggish Ruggish Bone" are closer to traditional keys than not.

66. Bull writes that "Sound engulfs the spatial, thus making the relation between subject and object problematic." (2003:361); Both Urry and Bull have acknowledged that drivers experience inhabiting the car rather than inhabiting the road or street on which one drives.

67. This framework is adapted from the tripartite framework provided by Mimi Sheller in her study of emotion and automobility. Her framework outlines the (1) micro-level: preferences for individual drivers; (2) meso-level: specifically located car cultures; and (3) macro-level: regional, national and transnational emotional/cultural/material geographies (2005:222).

## REFERENCES

Anet, Christopher. 2003. "An Insight into Subwoofers." *Resolution Magazine* 2(7):60–2.

Auner, Joseph. 2003. "'Sing It for Me': Posthuman Ventriloquism in Recent Popular Music." *Journal of the Royal Musicological Association* 128(1):98–122.

Baber, Brendan. 1997. "The incredible shrinking sound system." *Interview*, http://findarticles. com/p/articles/mi_m1285/is_n9_v27/ai_20227116/?tag=content;col1 (accessed July 21, 2008).

Basham, Frances and Bob Ughetti. 1984. *Car Culture*. London: Plexus.

Belasco, Warren. 1980. "Motivatin' with Chuck Berry and Fredrick Jackson Turner." In *The Automobile and American Culture*, ed. David C. Lewis and Laurence Goldstein, 262–79. Ann Arbor: University of Michigan Press.

Bell, Jonathan. 2001. *Carchitecture: When the car and the city collide*. London: Birkhäuser.

Bull, Michael. 2005. "Automobility and the Power of Sound." In *Automobilities*, ed. Mike Featherstone, Nigel Thrift, and John Urry, 243–59. London: Sage.

Bull, Michael. 2003. "Soundscapes of the Car: A Critical Study of Automobile Habitation." In *The Auditory Culture Reader*, ed. Michael Bull and Les Back, 357–74. Oxford: Berg.

Cateforis, Theo. 2011. *Are we not New Wave?: Modern Pop at the Turn of the 1980s*. Ann Arbor: University of Michigan Press.

"CEA predicts Sales of In-vehicle Electronics will Grow to $12.8 Billion." 2008. *Carsound. com,* http://www.carsound.com/artman2/publish/news/CEA_PREDICTS_SALES_OF_IN-VEHICLE_ELECTRONICS_WILL_GROW_TO_12_8_BILLION.shtml (accessed: March 13, 2008).

Chang, Jeff. 2005. *Can't Stop Won't Stop: A History of the Hip-Hop Generation*. London: Ebury Press.

Coker, Cheo Hodari. 2003. *Unbelievable: The Life, Death, and Afterlife of the Notorious B.I.G.* New York: Three Rivers Press.

Coleman, Brian. 2007. *Check the Technique: Liner Notes for Hip-hop Junkies*. New York: Random House.

Coleman, Mark. 2003. *Playback*. Cambridge, MA: Da Capo Press.

Cross, Brian. 1993. *It's not about a salary...Rap, Race, and Resistance in Los Angeles*. London: Verso.

Demers, Joanna. 2003. "Sampling the 1970s in hip-hop." *Popular Music* 22(1):41–56.

Dickinson, Kay. 2001. "'Believe'? Vocoders, Digitised Female Identity and Camp." *Popular Music* 20(3):333–47.

Dickinson, Kay. 2008. *Off Key: When Film and Music Won't Work Together*. Oxford: Oxford University Press.

Diehl, Matt. 1999. "Pop Rap." In *The Vibe History of Hip Hop*, ed. Alan Light, 121–25. New York: Three Rivers Press.

Dyer, Richard. 2006. *Pastiche*. London: Routledge.

Dyson, Michael Eric. 2004. "We Never Were What We Used to Be: Black Youth, Pop Culture, and the Politics of Nostalgia." In the *Michael Eric Dyson Reader*, 418–42. New York: Basic Civitas Books.

Fantel, Hans. 1989. "Car Stereo in High Gear." *New York Times*, June 4. Available at: http://www.nytimes.com/1989/06/04/arts/sound-car-stereo-in-high-gear.html (accessed August 20, 2013).

Fitch, Charles S. 2008. "Radio has Special Place in the Car." *Radio World Newspaper Online*, http://www.rwonline.com/pages/s.0053/t.10995.html (accessed June 27, 2008).

Gartman, David. 1994. *Auto Opium: A Social History of American Automobile Design*. London: Routledge.

Gilroy, Paul. 2001. "Driving While Black." In *Car Cultures*, ed. Daniel Miller, 81–104. Oxford: Berg.

Gold, Jonathan. 1993. "Day of Dre." *Rolling Stone*, September 30. Available at: http://www.rollingstone.com/music/news/day-of-dre-19930930 (accessed August 20, 2013).

Goldmark, Peter. 1973. *Maverick Inventor: My Turbulent Years at CBS*. New York: Saturday Review Press.

Goodwin, Andrew. 1990. "Sample and Hold: Pop Music in the Digital Age of Reproduction." In *On Record: Rock, Pop, and the Written Word,* ed. Simon Frith and Andrew Goodwin, 258–74. London: Routledge.

Hayles, Katherine. 1999. *How we Became Posthuman: Virtual Bodies in Cybernetics, Literature, and Informatics.* Chicago: University of Chicago Press.

Hoffmann, Frank W., and William G. Bailey. 1991. "Boom Cars." In *Sports & Recreation Fads,* 71–2. Philadelphia: Haworth Press.

"Interview with Dr. Dre." 2005. *Scratch Magazine,* http://www.dr-dre.com/info/interview_scratch_dr_dre.php (accessed July 21, 2008).

Katz, Mark. 2004. *Capturing Sound.* Berkeley: University of California Press.

Kline, Ronald and Trevor Pinch. 1996. "Users as Agents of Technological Change: The Social Construction of the Automobile in the Rural United States." *Technology and Culture* 37:763–95.

Krims, Adam. 2007. *Music and Urban Geography.* London: Routledge.

Krims, Adam. 2000. *Rap Music and the Poetics of Identity.* Cambridge: Cambridge University Press.

Lamm, Michael. 2000. "Radio Hits the Road." *American Heritage* 15(4), http://www.american-heritage.com/articles/magazine/it/2000/4/2000_4_18.shtml (accessed July 21, 2008).

Levine, Robert. 2007. "The Death of High Fidelity." *Rolling Stone,* December 27. Available at: http://www.rollingstone.com/news/story/17777619/the_death_of_high_fidelity/print (accessed August 20, 2013).

Lewis, Lucinda. 2000. *Roadside America: The Automobile and the American Dream.* New York: Harry N. Abrams.

Manuel, Peter. 2002. "From Scarlatti to 'Guantanamera': Dual Tonicity in Spanish and Latin American Musics." *Journal of the American Musicological Society* 55(2):311–36.

Marling, Karal Ann. 2002. "America's Love Affair with the Automobile in the Television Age." In *Autopia: Cars and Culture,* ed. Peter Wollen and Joe Kerr, 354–62. London: Reakton Books.

Marriott, Robert. 1999. "Gangsta, Gangsta: The Sad, Violent Parable of Death Row Records." In *The Vibe History of Hip Hop,* ed. Alan Light, 319–26. New York: Three Rivers Press.

Marsh, Peter and Peter Collett. 1986. *Driving Passion: The Psychology of the Car.* London, Jonathan Cape.

Massey, Howard. 2000. *Behind the Glass: Top Record Producers Tell us How They Craft the Hits.* San Francisco: Backbeat Books.

McCartney, David. 2004. "Automobile Radios." In *The Encyclopedia of Radio,* ed. Christopher H. Sterling, 138–39. New York: Taylor and Francis.

McLeod, Kembrew. 2001. *Owning Culture: Authorship, Ownership, and Intellectual Property Law.* New York: Peter Lang.

Miller, Chuck. 1997. "Highway Hi-Fi: Chrysler's 1950s Car Phonograph Add-On," *Ook: Observing Obscure Kulture,* http://ookworld.com/hiwayhifimill.html (accessed March 03, 2009).

Moulton, David. 2003. "The loudspeaker as musical instrument: an examination of the issues surrounding loudspeaker performance of music in typical rooms," *Moulton Laboratories,* http://www.moultonlabs.com/more/loudspeaker_as_musical_instrument/ (accessed March 11, 2009).

Newcomb, Doug. 2008. *Car Audio for Dummies.* New York: Wiley Publishing.

Nima. 2006. "Interview with Snoop Dogg." *Dubcnn.com,* http://www.dubcnn.com/interviews/snoopdogg06/part1/ (accessed July 21, 2008).

Pareles, Jon. 1999. "Still Tough, Still Authentic. Still Relevant?" *New York Times,* November 14. Available at: http://query.nytimes.com/gst/fullpage.html?res=9F03E6DF103A F937A25752C1A96F958260 (accessed August 20, 2013)."

Pettitt, Joe. 2003. *How to Design and Install High-Performance Car Stereo.* North Branch: Car Tech.

Petrakis, Harry Mark. 1991. *The Founders Touch: The Life of Paul Galvin of Motorola,* 3rd Edition. Chicago: J. G. Ferguson.

Phillips, Wes. 1997. "Audio Odyssey: Ken Kreisel of M&K." *Stereophile,* http://www.stereophile. com/interviews/136/ (accessed July 21, 2008).

Polk Audio. "Tips, Tweaks and Common Sense About Car Audio." Baltimore: Polk Audio, http://www.polkaudio.com/downloads/12vhndbk.pdf (accessed July 23, 2008)

Pond, Steven. 2005. *Head Hunters: The Making of Jazz's First Platinum Album.* Ann Arbor: University of Michigan Press.

Quinn, Eithne. 2005. *Nuthin But a "G" Thang: The Culture and Commerce of Gangsta Rap.* New York: Columbia University Press.

Reschovsky, Clara. 2004. "Journey to Work: 2000." U.S. Census Bureau: Economics and Statistics Administration, http://www.census.gov/prod/2004pubs/c2kbr-33.pdf (accessed 16 March 2010).

Rose, Tricia. 1994. *Black Noise.* Middletown: Wesleyan University Press.

Rumerich, Mark. 2005. *Car Stereo Cookbook.* 2nd Edition. New York: McGraw Hill.

Sarig, Roni. 2007. *Third Coast: OutKast, Timbaland & How Hip-Hop Became A Southern Thing.* Cambridge, MA: Da Capo Press.

Sanjek, Russell and David Sanjek. 1996. *Pennies from heaven: The American Popular Music Business in the Twentieth Century.* Cambridge, MA: Da Capo Press.

Sanneh, Kelefa. 2004. "Rapping about Rapping: The Rise and Fall of a Hip-hop Tradition." In *This is Pop,* ed. Eric Weisbard, 223–32. Cambridge: Harvard University Press.

Schloss, Joseph G. 2004. *Making Beats: The Art of Sample-Based Hip Hop.* Middletown, CT: Wesleyan University Press.

Seagrave, Kerry. 1992. *Drive-In Theaters: A History from their Inception in 1933.* London: McFarland and Company...

Sheller, Mimi. 2005. "Automotive Emotions: Feeling the Car." In *Automobilities,* ed. Mike Featherstone, Nigel Thrift, and John Urry, 221–42. London: Sage.

Smith, Merritt Roe, and Leo Marx, ed. 1994. *Does Technology Drive History? The Dilemma of Technological Determinism.* Cambridge, MA: MIT Press.

Smith, Suzanne E. 1999. *Dancing in the Street: Motown and the Cultural Politics of Detroit.* Cambridge: Harvard University Press.

Sterling, Christopher H. 2002. "FM Radio," *The Encyclopedia of Radio,* ed. Christopher H. Sterling, 602–08. New York: Taylor and Francis.

Swenson, Kylee. 2006. "Captain Contagious" *Remix Magazine,* June 1, http://www.remixmag. com/artists/remix_captain_contagious/index.html (accessed July 21, 2008).

*Time.* 1936. "Radio Boom." April 27.

——. 1965. "Carnegie Hall on Wheels." April 30.

——. 1966. "In a Merry Stereomobile." August 5.

Tyrangiel, Josh. 1999. "Hip hop Video." In *The Vibe History of Hip Hop,* ed. Alan Light, 135–43. New York: Three Rivers Press.

Tyrangiel, Josh. 2001. "In the Doctor's House," *Time,* September 15, http://www.time.com/time/ magazine/article/0,9171,1000775,00.html (accessed July 21, 2008).

Urry, John. 2005. "The 'System' of Automobility." In *Automobilities*, ed. Mike Featherstone, Nigel Thrift, and John Urry, 25–39. London: Sage.

Weheliye, Alexander. 2002. "'Feenin': Posthuman Voices in Contemporary Black Popular Music." *Social Text* 71:21–47.

Widmer, E.L. 2002. "Crossroads: The Automobile, Rock and Roll and Democracy." In *Autopia: Cars and Culture*, ed. Peter Wollen and Joe Kerr, 65–74. London: Reakton Books.

Yoder, Andrew. 2000. *Auto Audio*. 2nd Edition. New York: McGraw Hill.

## CHAPTER 5

# DING, DING!: THE COMMODITY AESTHETIC OF ICE CREAM TRUCK MUSIC

DANIEL T. NEELY

Well now, ice cream man, upon my street
I heard your truck outside, it's really neat.
Ice cream man, upon my block
Your little chimes, they reel and they rock.
> —Jonathan Richman and the Modern Lovers, "Ice Cream Man"

Hey, ice cream boy…you wanna turn that goddamn noise off? Don't nobody wanna hear that shit this time of morning.
> —Richard Pryor, *That Nigger's Crazy*

FOR many, the heralding sounds of ice cream trucks play to "the sweet melody of simple hearts."[1] They attract attention and business, and they have helped ice cream truck music become a symbol of that which is to be consumed—ice cream, frozen novelties, and other assorted sweets. Some say that this music is Pavlovian, that it is a conditioned stimulus that elicits a reflex response in people to want ice cream. However, the desire for ice cream is not conditional on hearing chime music, nor does the music's sound necessarily increase one's interest in having it. What I suggest is that the music is intended to play on anamnesis, more specifically a kind of anamnesis that is conditioned on the recognizability of a specific product through sound. On the road, vendors hope their music's tune and timbre will link perception to memory and lead to nostalgia—for childhood, for sweetness, or for the Main Street of the American imaginary.[2] But because anamnesic effect is determined by how a listener apprehends sound, ice cream truck music's tune and timbre may work against a vendor's best intentions and provoke negative reactions that sometimes lead to complaints or abatement efforts.

In this chapter, I examine ice cream truck music from several perspectives to explore what the system of automobility's role was in its use, why technology developed around timbre, and the responses and interpretations of those it has touched. My intention is to provide new insight into a music and its sound that although ubiquitous and easily recognizable have been historically neglected and intellectually untried.

## AUTOMOBILITY

The end of the nineteenth century marked the beginning of the modern era of the ice cream trade. As economic turmoil stabilized, industrial changes allowed new businesses to develop and hasten economic growth. This led to a new discourse about what constituted the good life and helped redefine the visual and aural expectations of popular culture. Access to new technologies—devices for making, storing, and serving ice cream, for example—became more universal and increasingly automated as a tendency toward ease of use permeated most industries. With this, America began to turn away from a "producer ethic" to a "mythology of consumerism"—especially in novelties and entertainments associated with the ice cream trade—that favored "effortless recreation, leisure, and immediate gratification" (Théberge 1997:29). If the new era's promise became apparent to American entrepreneurs at the 1893 Chicago World's Exhibition, its promise was fully realized at the Louisiana Purchase Exposition in St. Louis in 1904, where the ice cream cone became a national sensation (Rydell 1984:155). The business of selling ice cream was poised for dramatic growth.

The automobile would become an important part of this growth. Automobiles increased access to goods and services, and reduced the scale of long distances because they helped extend the radius of metropolitanism, or "the geographic configuration of a consumer society" in which car travel was a necessity (Interrante 1983:90–91).[3] They also satisfied the need for transportation brought on by new social and spatial cultural patterns at the beginning of the twentieth century. As a *system*, however, automobility reoriented and decentralized urban areas and reorganized and centralized rural space because it drew these often disparate territorialities into a closer and more interdependent relationship. In general, this helped businesses grow.

An upward trend in motor car use in the twentieth century ensured the mobile ice cream industry's growth. Automobility allowed for the more efficient shipment of wholesale product, and the reorganized rural and urban environment it provided meant that mobile retail sale was possible on a much larger geographic scale. Expanding metropolitanism and road-dependency aided this by organizing social networks around roads, which centralized cultural meaning on an ideological level and decentralized economic opportunity. An automobile also conferred an elevated status on drivers because they were seen as modernizing an old-fashioned model.[4] By the middle of the twentieth century, automobile-based point-of-sale vending became a dominant force in the industry, and began to subordinate other methods of retail sale including foot and pedal driven carts and probably also brick-and-mortar establishments.

Automobility also offered vendors important temporal advantages. Vendors who adapted to this new system had an edge on other street sellers because they could now travel farther before their product melted. Further, drivers could come or go in an instant, *lingering* where business was strong and disappearing from where it was not. This sort of temporal and spatial flexibility allowed automobile-based vendors to establish their brand with a wider network of consumers and to take greater advantage of the social and economic networks automobility's "peculiar combination of flexibility and coercion" locked in (Urry 2004:27). However, because street vending was—at best—a minimally scheduled activity from a consumer's perspective, the perception of automobility's influence on the form was minimal and the form retained a sense of old-fashionedness.[5]

Temporal and spatial freedom were important allowances for a product as acutely ephemeral as ice cream. While these freedoms were keys to mobile vending's growth, automobility had other implications. In this modernized form, mobile street vending became an element in a complex of social interlinkages with other industries that not only included the dairy and ice cream trades but others as well: drivers needed proper delivery vehicles (see Whitby and Earnshaw 1999; Earnshaw 2005), parts for these vehicles, gasoline, good roads and in time, refrigeration and, eventually, sound to maintain their business investment and guarantee solvency.

Within this system, sounds played from an ice cream truck helped reinforce this new spatiality and affirmed the social and economic changes automobility introduced. Sound's role in mobile vending has always been important. If there is one uniting theme in ice cream vending's history, it is the documented use of sound in attracting business. Virtually every nineteenth-century account includes some aspect of aurality, be it how vendors used sound to peddle their wares or how people reacted to them. For example, an 1828 issue of the *National Advertiser*, listed "I Scream, Ice Cream" as one of New York City's common street cries (Dickson 1972:25). Another slightly later nineteenth-century description comes from Philadelphia:

> The country man . . . sells an excellent article. . . . The loudest criers . . . are the coloured gentlemen who carry the tin cans containing [ice cream] about the streets on their shoulders. They sing a most laughable, but scarcely intelligible song in praise of their lemon ice cream and vanilla too. (Quoted in Funderburg 1995:72–73)[6]

Within automobility, the use of sound helped extend mobile vending's already increased influence. It allowed a vendor to surround and penetrate the ears of potential customers from a distance. Because the right sound could draw people to the roadside, the beaconing sound of an ice cream truck became a herald for the new automobile-based consumerism (Figure 5.1). Vendors knew this sound would have to be cheap, project well and yet somehow evoke the product it was being used to sell. At first, bells were the answer. Later on, however, the sound most adopted was technologically and timbrally similar to bells *and* musical amusements, in particular the music boxes of nineteenth-century ice cream parlors and soda fountains.

FIGURE 5.1 Patrons at an ice cream truck in New York City during the Northeast Blackout of 2003. Photo © 2003, John Osborne.

## Tradition and Technology

Emerging in 1874, the ice cream soda was an immediate hit with consumers. In the following decades, a zealous economy developed around the manufacture of ice cream soda fountains, and sound soon joined visuality as an important component in ice cream sales. According to one 1877 industry publication, "to please the palate, you must appeal to the eye." Another, in 1892, quoted a fountain owner as having said "it is the grossest error imaginable to suppose that there is any economy in having a small and unpretentious [fountain] apparatus."[7]

By 1893, soda fountains thrived as the ice cream soda became so popular that some hailed it as America's "national beverage" (Dickson 1972:62; cf. Funderburg 1995:100–7). While late 19th century accounts juxtaposed visuality with the palate, in-store aurality had become an equally important part of the soda fountain experience.[8] Drawn by the popularity of the ice cream soda (and, most likely, by ice cream in various other guises, like the milkshake and the sundae), customers grew used to seeing and hearing automata of various sorts in the stores that served ice cream. One of the most important of these automata were music boxes. In the nineteenth-century, these devices were unique in that they were common, could play familiar (or even not-so-familiar) pieces and were often musically, mechanically and decoratively ambitious (Chapius 1980:287; Tallis 1971:37, 41; cf. Hoover 1971).

In 1896, the Wurlitzer company became the first business to outfit music boxes (manufactured mainly by the American *Regina* company) with a device to make them coin-operated. Most of these boxes were used in saloons, soda fountains, and ice cream parlors and played adaptations of contemporary popular songs and light classical pieces (Roehl 1968:20). Shortly thereafter, *Regina* marketed an automatic changing device into its larger boxes that allowed listeners to select from a number of different tunes, each on a separate disc (28–29). These innovations made music boxes cheaper and more profitable. As such, they were visual and sonic draws and represented an important revenue stream for business owners (DeWaard 1967:107–8; Thompson 1995:13).

At the turn of the twentieth century, the phonograph devastated the music box industry, passing through it "like a virulent blight" (Ord-Hume 1973:287). However, an association between the sound of music boxes, the visuality of soda fountains and the taste of ice cream had already been forged in ice cream parlors and soda fountains. The emergence of more convenient forms to package and store ice cream allowed companies to increasingly use motorcars for wholesale delivery, and eventually as retail outlets. When this happened, they would take their visual and aural cues from nineteenth-century retail ice cream establishments and become the basis for how ice cream trucks would look—and more importantly, sound—for years to come.

In 1920 a man named Harry Burt in Youngstown, Ohio found inspiration in the success of the "I-Scream," the chocolate-covered ice cream bar Christian Nelson invented in 1919 that was renamed the "Eskimo Pie" in 1921. A confectioner and ice cream parlor operator by trade, Burt wanted to replicate Nelson's success and went to work on his own frozen novelty. The result was an ice cream bar on a stick. Because he believed that "the humors of the mind were regulated by those of the palate" (Dickson 1972:77), he named his product the "Good Humor" bar, evoking the nineteenth-century synesthetic visuality of soda fountain manufacturing, and began selling them from a truck.

Building upon this sense of synesthesia, Burt brought a clean visual sensibility to his business. Good Humor trucks were white with an illustration of a Good Humor bar on their sides; their drivers, who adhered to a rather strict code of courtesy and behavior, always wore white uniforms consistent with the truck's appearance (Jakle and Sculle 1999:182–83). To match this visual imagery in sound, Burt fitted his trucks with small bells. The first rack he used was taken directly from his family's bobsled. He doubtlessly saw these bells as a pleasing and cost effective way of announcing his truck's presence in a neighborhood, and a way of affecting a certain naïveté resonant with that evoked in nineteenth-century soda fountains.

Although long used by pushcart vendors, the choice of bells as ice cream truck vending's new sonic herald was significant because it tapped into and adapted bell ringing's larger history. Others have noted how larger bells once impelled a sense of regular daily rhythm by calling laborers to mealtime, signaling the beginning or end of a work day, or marking the scheduled departure of a train (Corbin 1998:x–xi; Smith 2001:34, 57–58). In street vending contexts, bell ringing had always also called people to specific (albeit irregular) action, but Burt's choice of small bobsled bells for his ice cream trucks was significant because it both recalled the familiar timbre of coin operated soda fountain automata and signified a *wintry* sound that conveyed ice cream's relieving coldness in hot weather. In addition, the delicate sound of small bells and their frequent association with juvenescence tapped into a rapidly changing consumer culture of the time, especially as it was directed toward children.[9] In her work on the modern consumer ethic and childhood, Susan Matt shows how attitudes toward envy as a moral and behavioral concern in children changed in the period 1890–1930. Discouraging material deprivation as a way of controlling envy not only supported the expansion of the consumer economy, but fostered in children "an emotional style which encouraged consumer activity" (Matt 2002:284). A positive response in both parent and child to a vendor's bells, then, could be justified as an object lesson in social meaning.

In this sense, Good Humor trucks had a kind of coercive power. As sonic pastiche, the synesthetic experience of Burt's small, twinkling bells appealed to people's sense of innocence and nostalgia, and its relationship to food (and specifically, a comfort food like ice cream) gave it an important role in the construction of social memory (Sutton 2001:73–102).[10] Because they were easily apprehended and (regardless of volume) quickly recognized, however, they *imposed* this mood and character onto the communities in which Good Humor's trucks operated. Using this pleasing sound to summon people to the roadside for a frozen treat helped turn Good Humor's trucks into a spectacle to be heard, then seen and patronized. It also extended the acceptance of some kinds of public sound. Bell ringing from an automobile could now be viewed positively and even advocated as a bit of nostalgia, even though bells added a layer of itinerant noise to an increasingly crowded soundscape. More importantly, the pealing bells helped centralize consumer ideology around the system of automobility further as a proxy for modern consumerism (Truax 2001:125, 210; Attali 1996:31).

Once sound became an identifiable part of the Good Humor company's brand, several years passed before it was elaborated, automated, and amplified to reach acoustic spaces beyond a bell's reach. When Burt died in 1926, a group of businessmen from Cleveland bought the rights to the Good Humor name, established the *Good Humor Corporation of America* and sold franchises for a down payment of $100 to entrepreneurs in Detroit, Chicago, Miami, Pittsburgh, and New York (Jakle and Sculle 1999:182–83). The company diversified further in 1929 after stock speculator Michael Meehan invested in the Cleveland group. With this, the company licensed Good Humor manufacturers in Los Angeles, Tulsa, Miami, and Dallas (*Time Magazine* 1935). Drivers in all of these markets learned quickly how automobility allowed them to target and move between popular roaming grounds to maximize sales.

During the Great Depression the mobile ice cream trade thrived. One of the most successful businesses was Good Humor of California, established in 1929 by a Los Angeles-based businessman named Paul Hawkins. Although a savvy businessman, Hawkins's success was in part due to his replacing the bells on his trucks with amplified mechanical music.[11] The device he used was manufactured by the small, California-based West Coast Organ Company and played a Polish folk tune called "Stodola Pumpa."[12] Housed in a small, rectangular plywood box, its musical works consisted of "a tiny 10-key carillon, operated by a rotating wood cylinder with steel pins to lift the mallets. Each mallet [was] powered by a piano-wire spring. Behind every steel chime bar [was] a magnetic pickup coil much like that for an electric guitar" (Rhodes 2006).

Although these units were mechanically complicated and prone to breaking, they were amplified (most likely through inexpensive coil-driven trumpet-horn loudspeakers mounted under the hood), which enabled a much larger potential market than non-amplified methods.[13] The choice of a single, simple melody was effective because it anchored an easily remembered sonic brand in the ears of consumers. While certainly not a perfectly phonogenic reproduction, this technological mediation preserved a level of timbral intimacy that allowed the chimey, bell-like timbre of West Coast Organ boxes to *sound* like music boxes should over a long distance. Most important, their sound evoked the aurality of nineteenth-century soda fountains more effectively than a rack of bells ever could, and helped reinforce the sense of pastiche that Good Humor had earlier established. In addition, the mood ice cream trucks now imposed on communities was better defined musically. It had an even more concrete, positively viewed cultural association that did a better job of negating arguments against its use. This gave Good Humor of California an important competitive edge during the depression; it continued manufacturing chime music boxes into the late 1950s and probably stopped shortly after Louis Bacigalupi, the likely owner (see footnote 12), died in 1959.

Hawkins's approach to sound *and* automobility helped extend his influence in other ways. He made sure that his trucks were parked outside movie studios and radio stations. In those locations, music helped attract actors and performers who gave him free publicity by talking about his "Good Humor" products on the air. He even sent trucks to on-location shoots up to 75 miles away as a way of keeping his company's name in good standing with members of the film industry (Harris 1949:96). Hawkins's success with sound on the road and, in turn, over the airwaves inspired others in the trade, especially after World War II (96).[14]

In late 1940s, for example, John Ralston was a driver for the Los Angeles-based Swelltime Ice Cream Company, one of Good Humor's competitors. Ralston had once worked for Hawkins at Good Humor and was aware of the commercial advantages music offered. In 1947, Swelltime's trucks had no music so Ralston decided to experiment and built a sounding apparatus using a toy cylinder-based music box works and an army surplus carbon microphone. He taped the mic to the works, taped the works to his steering column, attached a Distler toy car motor to drive the works, and played his new apparatus through a tube amplifier powered off the truck's battery. As Ralston told me, "It worked."[15]

Then, in early 1948, Ralston brought his idea to the Nelson Company for development. With the help of Bob Nelson, several changes were introduced that led to the commercial production of chime boxes for ice cream trucks. The first of these replaced the Distler motor Ralston used with a dynamotor, a small motor-generator that produced 240 volts off the truck's 6-volt battery and let the apparatus run more efficiently. The second replaced the Ralston's toy works with a Thorens AD-30, a comb-based movement that played six-inch interchangeable metal discs in a way that resembled a record player. With this, drivers could choose from hundreds of well-known popular, religious, and kiddie tunes.[16] By late 1949, ice cream truck bells were beginning to be replaced by music boxes that played tunes like *Strawberry Blonde, Little Brown Jug,* and *Sidewalks of New York* (Harris 1949:96). Amplified music had become a symbol of organizational strength, progress, and prosperity (Bijsterveld 2008:36–37).

Nelson, who later merged his outfit with the Stromberg-Carlson company, was the first to mass-produce chime music for ice cream trucks, but others followed. Huffein and Koditek were electronic technicians based out of California who manufactured disc-type boxes for a short period of time in the late 1940s and early 1950s. Another was Schulmerich Electronics, a company that developed its own comb-based chime music box in the early 1950s, originally intended to be a surrogate for church bells (they later manufactured boxes for Mister Softee). However successful these companies were in diversifying the kinds of sounds drivers had available to them, their products did little more than provide a range of options for choosing a melodic brand. None seemed to address the major problem facing drivers, that being how to balance the advantages amplification permitted with the technical limitations a gasoline-powered truck fitted with a refrigerator presented.

The most significant change in the use and manufacture of ice cream truck music happened in 1957. While refinements such as the dynamotor improved the effectiveness of chime music apparatuses, the amplifiers necessary for its use put a significant stress on a truck's battery and limited the amount of time music could be played. So, in 1957, John Ralston (who had continued to experiment with different chime music devices throughout the 1950s) approached Bob Nichols, an electrical engineer from Minneapolis, Minnesota, for help. Nichols had experience with emergent transistor-based technologies and responded first by improving the transduction method used in music boxes being used and then by building that into a transistorized amplification system.[17] These changes put a significantly lighter stress on the truck's battery (by 1956, most auto manufacturers had switched to a 12-volt system that made electrical components run more reliably) and gave drivers the option of playing music all the time. In doing so they could, in theory, attract more business on the road.

Nichols went into business under the name Nichols Electronics. In the early days, his units primarily used the Thorens AD-30 movement, but by 1962, he had switched over to a Thorens-manufactured cylinder works that was cheaper to work with and maintain. When Thorens halted production of these works in 1975, these movements came from the Japanese Sankyo company. While Nichols continued to service the AD-30-based boxes well into the 1970s and the cylinder-based works for much longer, in 1985 he began to manufacture boxes that mimicked chime music through chip-based waveform synthesis. Early versions of these electronic boxes featured one song; later models, including the still-popular industry standard *Digital II*, played eight, and one of Nichols's more recent models, the *Omni*, includes a selection of 32 tunes to choose from. As a special option, Nichols will also program boxes with custom renditions of popular public domain melodies from an in-house list. (Nichols's custom tune list is far, far smaller than that of the AD-30, but they are clearly related.) Distributing his product to mobile vendors throughout the Americas, Europe, and Asia, Nichols Electronics is rightly considered the largest and most important manufacturer of chime music in the world.[18]

Despite several innovations, the changes Nichols has made to his product line over the years have been remarkably conservative, emphasizing timbre over other considerations. In developing his electronic, computer chip-based system, Nichols's priority was to maintain a chime sound timbrally consistent with earlier analog movements. In this he was largely successful—the timbre of the new boxes was different from that of the old ones, but not unrecognizably so. He took the small number of early complaints he received from vendors about the new boxes not sounding "the same" with some sympathy, but there was nothing to suggest that the differences vendors noticed meant anything to the consumers they served, because the new boxes were as effective at drawing attention and, for many of an older generation, at provoking nostalgic discourse as the older models. Because the new technology was also more electrically efficient, the new boxes could be played loud with even less battery usage than earlier models. Further, because the new models contained no moving or user-serviceable parts, they proved more durable than their predecessors and represented a superior value.

While Nichols's knowledge of mobile vending's technological needs are reflected in the changes he—and others—introduced over the years, ultimately little about the sounds associated with ice cream has changed since the nineteenth century. The timbre vendors favored, and that manufacturers worked around, played on a mechanical technology whose ease of use mapped well onto the new consumerism at the end of the nineteenth century. Made mobile, it urged and in fact propagated a cultural formation, based on sound, between the taste of ice cream and the places that sold it.

## Tune and Timbre

Tune and timbre have been critical to individual success throughout ice cream vending's history. Tune, because many identify individual vendors or vending companies by the tune they play; timbre, because it is a powerful agent in evoking memory through anamnesis. In combination, these two elements elicit a visceral nostalgia for an idealized past that attracts attention and promotes business.

The tunes vendors typically favor are almost always bright, upbeat, and melodically simple; rarely are they in a minor key. Many include basic contrapuntal parts for harmonic effect and some today even include an end-of-loop vocalization ("Hello!") to help attract attention. In the industry, these tunes are referred to as "kiddie tunes." Because they are a factor in product recognition, vendors typically pick one tune and stick with it for a long time.

Today's best-known ice cream truck tune is probably Mister Softee's. Founded on St. Patrick's Day in 1956 in Philadelphia, Pennsylvania, by two brothers, William and James Conway, Mister Softee has since grown substantially and as of 2010 had 350 franchise dealers operating 600 trucks in 15 states. Its proprietary jingle is extremely well known throughout the United States and is a common reference in popular culture.[19]

"Mister Softee (Jingle and Chimes)" was written by Philadelphia-based jingle composer Les Waas and is an excellent example of how important tune and timbre are in marketing ice cream truck music. In 1958, shortly after the Conways moved Mister Softee's business operation from Philadelphia to Runnemede, New Jersey, they hired the small Philadelphia agency where Waas worked to compose a radio jingle.[20] In a move reminiscent of Paul Hawkins's marketing technique, company representatives asked that the sound of the bell they used on their trucks be incorporated somewhere in their advertisement to evoke the in-neighborhood aural presence of their trucks. Waas remembered that the bell Mister Softee provided him was heavy, about 12 inches tall, and had a built-in clapper. He carried it to New York City, where the jingle was recorded, and used it at the advertisement's beginning, to attract the attention of a group of children: "(Ding! Ding!) Here comes Mister Softee, the soft ice cream man!" (Figure 5.2):

> (Kids voices):
> The creamiest, dreamiest soft ice cream
> You get from Mister Softee.
> For a refreshing delight supreme,
> Look for Mister Softee.
>
> (Deep, pleasant male voice):
> My milkshakes and my sundaes and my cones are such a treat,
> Listen for my store on wheels, ding-a-ling down the street.
>
> (Kids again):
> The creamiest, dreamiest soft ice cream,
> You get from Mister Softee.
> For a refreshing delight supreme,
> Look for Mister Softee.
> S-o-f-t double "E," Mister Softee!

The jingle was successful in several local markets. But the bell ringing helped make it effective, I suggest, because it not only drew the in-ad children's attention to the Mister Softee truck, it also attracted the ear of radio listeners (most of whom likely already identified a ringing bell with mobile ice cream vending) to the ad itself. Mister Softee could (and later, did) build on the increased publicity this ad generated by adding chime music to its trucks in imitation of Waas's recorded jingle.[21] In the context of mobile vending, the timbre of the redone "Mister Softee (Jingle and Chimes)" granted the company's new on-the-road sonic herald a sense of historical authenticity. This legitimacy helped make the Mister Softee tune—for better or for worse—known to millions of people and a cultural icon throughout the United States.

Although tune is important, timbre is the crucial factor in how ice cream truck music accrues meaning. In cinema, for instance, ice cream truck music's timbre can be the basis of comedic parody, as in Sacha Baron Cohen's 2006 film *Borat,* where the music attracts hopeful kids to an ice cream truck's window where they are surprised to find

FIGURE 5.2  "(Ding! Ding!) Here comes Mister Softee, the soft ice cream man!"

an adult brown bear instead of a traditional vendor. Or it can be naiveté's foil. The horror genre has satirized ice cream truck music's innocence in such films as *Maximum Overdrive* (1986), *Killer Klowns from Outer Space* (1988), and *Ice Cream Man* (1995), and in the "We All Scream for Ice Cream" episode of the *Masters of Horror* TV series (2007), by playing on the incongruity between its timbre and that of screams of bloody murder.

Timbre's role in ice cream truck music's historical identity makes it the overwhelming basis upon which contemporary artists and musicians creatively re-imagine the music. For example, 8bitpeoples is a bitpop/chiptune artists collective founded in 1999. Its members make new music based on 8-bit digital technology, the same technology found in the music boxes Nichols Electronics began to manufacture in 1985.[22] In July 2007, 8bitpeoples member Richard Alexander Caraballo (aka "minusbaby") launched *WHY ICE CREAM, OR: WHY SCREAM?*, a project that invited other members to write "imaginary ice cream truck music in a chip music style."[23] In addition to sharing thirty-four tracks by thirty-three artists on the project's webpage, Caraballo posted a loop of New York City street sounds that could be played concurrently with the recordings to help give them life. Although most were effective, the project's most convincing submissions (including Bubblyfish's "Strawberry Flavor Green Frog," Bud Melvin's "Sherbertful Penis Lilt," Dotdummy's "Mr. Ding-a-Ling," Naruto's "Fantastic Sweetness Trucks," m_036's "Mario's Ice Cream," Peter Swimm's "Mi Heladero, Mi Salvador," and

Tugboat's "Frozen Ice Cream Pops in the Shape of a Tugboat") utilized (and in some cases, manipulated through signal processing) ice cream truck music's familiar 8-bit chime timbre to work both within and against the themes of innocence and nostalgia commonly associated with the genre.[24]

Another who explored ice cream truck music's timbre is sound artist and member of the Brooklyn, New York-based art collective *e-Xplo*, Erin McGonigle. In 2003, McGonigle received a Brooklyn Arts Council grant to re-imagine the ice cream truck's musical repertory by composing alternatives. Her goal was to underscore the role form and timbre have in creating context, location, and social identity through sound in public space.

She travelled with two drivers from Brooklyn's Kool Man Ice Cream Company along their daily route to better understand how music articulated with the community (McGonigle 2004). After several ride-alongs, she had gathered ideas about what effective alternatives might sound like and eventually produced eleven pieces that explored how timbre and repetition might be manipulated to reflect a driver's relationship to the community. Some of these were electroacoustic transformations of traditional ice cream truck music. One such piece removed the rhythmic pulse and melodic character of a toy music box by sampling and rearranging its melody into a non-melodic sequence and processing the result through echo; it became an exercise in pure timbre. Another placed a high frequency hiss over a backward sample of a calliope. Other pieces explored timbres with legitimate but not-so-obvious childhood associations. One interspersed the sound of white noise into the sound of marbles swirling in a metal bowl; another made church bells and fireworks the basis for a repeating ambient Carnivalesque texture. Some of McGonigle's more challenging pieces examined cultural and socio-economic differences by exploring ideas of spatiality. One such piece evoked an inner city housing project by juxtaposing the sound of a crackling fire, hard-heeled steps in a reverberant hallway, a surveillance helicopter, and gun fire into a repeating sonic collage; others played on neighborhood cultural boundaries by repeating and deconstructing samples of Cuban and Brazilian music.

Later that year, I saw McGonigle play her pieces on compact disc from a Kool Man ice cream truck in Williamsburg, Brooklyn. As the truck drove through the neighborhood, her pieces had varying degrees of immediate effectiveness. Of them all, the one that seemed to have the best response was a fairly straightforward field recording she made of Brooklyn's Hungry March Band rehearsing "Turkey in the Straw." Although the lively (if somewhat sloppy) brass band rendition veered far astray from chime music in sound, the sense of old-time nostalgia it struck helped underscore the efficiency and value of a chimey timbre. Chime boxes rely on a cheap, mass produced technology to convey in timbre what this recording achieved by other means, but only through sophisticated technological intervention.

As compact disc and, now, electronic media players become more common, such technological intervention represents a better value and creates space for musical innovations that work within ice cream truck music's traditional timbral boundaries. For example, after noticing the lack of musical variety on ice cream trucks in 2006, Brooklyn-based composer, multi-instrumentalist, writer, and producer Michael Hearst began to compose musically sophisticated alternatives that could *in theory* be played from a truck. Following several months of work, he released *Songs for Ice Cream Trucks* on his own Urban Geek Records label in early 2007.

A founding member of the eclectic indie "lit rock" band One Ring Zero, Hearst's goal with the project was to write familiar-sounding music that would "make sense" as ice cream truck music. To achieve this he began with simple, monophonic tunes:

> I wanted to write melodies that could stand on their own without chords and coun-
> terpoint, and then add to them, layer them with some other sounds. I wanted it to be
> an album that you would actually want to listen to, which was more of a challenge.
> Nothing but chime melodies by themselves is not something I would want to listen
> to over and over again. I wanted to somehow take what we know of already as ice
> cream truck music and the sound of these chimey simple melodies, and make it into
> something that fits in with our generation, maybe even has a slight hip quality to it.[25]

Timbre had a formative conceptual role in this. In many cases, Hearst first imagined these melodies through the sound of glockenspiel; in these early stages, he composed "in terms of high register"; "percussive, quick, short, sharp notes" were key. As he arranged, he chose instruments that would complement this sound. Instruments including clav-iola, a cheap chord organ, a small Casiotone keyboard, melodica, glockenspiel, and a small, high-pitched percussion instrument called "Space Crickets," lent themselves to the form well and were consistent with the stylistic direction in which he was headed. Eventually, Hearst found additional inspiration in a number of related musical styles (e.g., carnival/circus music, Muzak, calliopes, the works of composer Danny Elfman), each of which has its own nostalgic sensibilities that resonate well with a generational cohort that grew up in the 1970s and 1980s.

A few months after its initial release, the Brooklyn-based BAR/NONE record label re-released the album, which greatly increased its distribution both as a compact disc and as an MP3 download. (It is currently available through every major downloading site.) Reaction to *Songs for Ice Cream Trucks* was overwhelmingly positive.[26] Critics praised the album's musicality as well as how it maintained a traditional ice cream music aesthetic. Writer and literary critic John Hodgman, for example, wrote that Hearst "transformed one of the most overlooked, yet most insidiously infectious forms of American popular song into a rumination on summertime, innocence, and the music that lurks almost inaudibly in the margins of our lives."[27]

Although encouraged by its commercial success, Hearst's music's practical success revealed itself once he heard his music played from a truck. This happened shortly after the album's release, when Matt Allen, aka *The Ice Cream Man*, visited Brooklyn and asked Hearst to help with installing a new loudspeaker on his truck.[28] As they drove around playing *Songs for Ice Cream Trucks* later that afternoon, Hearst observed how the timbres he chose helped his music propagate correctly and attract attention. "Oh my God, it works," he remembered thinking. "It *sounds* like ice cream truck music when you hear it a block away." Through an ice cream truck's speaker, Hearst's music had a stylistic accuracy and an authority he had not anticipated.

This authority, however, was not lost on ice cream vendors. In May 2007, Hearst knew of eight using it; by spring 2009 there were at least 50, including individual trucks in North Carolina, Wisconsin, Georgia, and California, as well as an entire fleet of trucks in Portland, Oregon. One driver in North Carolina even commissioned a custom track for his own truck. Many vendors are thankful for an alternative that actually *sounds* like traditional ice cream truck music. The ease of plugging a compact disc or MP3 player loaded with *Songs for Ice Cream Trucks* into a loudspeaker has meant that vendors are more likely to use it.

# NOISE

Thus far I have focused on the mostly positive and nostalgic elements that motivated ice cream truck music's technology and sound aesthetic, but I have said little about the negative aspects of its use. While many hear this music nostalgically and reflect on it as a cherished part of childhood, others revile its sound as cloying and its use annoying. Many see it as a public health concern. For this latter group (and sometimes *even* for the former), ice cream truck music is nothing more than vaguely defined "noise," its banal repetitiveness an intrusion that epitomizes the redundancy of compelled consumption. Calls for its regulation and abatement are common and figure prominently into the music's political history, often dictating how and when it can be used. Further, mobility plays a major role in how people experience an ice cream truck's music. Although its timbre, form and delivery are determined by tradition and past use, the details of music's propagation are less predictable.[29]

In discussing ice cream truck music and abatement, then, one is faced with a fundamental question: what makes it noise? Barry Truax provided one interpretation, arguing that it is any manner of aural disturbance "that loosens the contact the listener has with the environment...works against effective communication [and] allows more noise to proliferate unprotested and unnoticed" (2001:94–95). In this view, ice cream truck music is a cognitive disruption that promotes less attentive listening. Because it focuses on how a sound articulates with an environment and not solely on its loudness or intensity, noise's consequences go beyond subjective concerns.

For example, an apprehension about ice cream truck music's deleterious effects on aesthetics was among soundscape researcher R. Murray Schafer's objections to it. He lamented that "almost all" the synthesized tunes played from ice cream trucks "contain at least one melodic inaccuracy, due...to the tin ear of the engineer who programmed them. In this way the 'fake' transmogrifications of well-known melodies are rendered 'real' for countless millions of people the world over so that the real tune, if ever heard again, will sound *wrong;* and engineers with no musical ability whatsoever become musical arrangers of incredible influence" (1993:121–22). From this perspective, ice cream truck music weakens what in Schafer's mind are objective musical values.[30]

Others, however, see more grave—and coercive—cultural implications. Jacques Attali argued that background sounds like ice cream truck music channel people toward consumption and are a powerful factor in leveling class differences, driving consumer integration, and abetting cultural homogenization (cf. Radano 1989; Sterne 1997). This happens largely through repetition, an element in music's commodification that Attali suggested dilutes its meaning. Although he was talking about music as a commodity-object, ice cream truck music draws out his point because it is *literally* repetitive in its commodification of sweets: in neighborhood after neighborhood, kiddie tunes play repetitively and (some might argue) *oppressively* from a truck that returns on a daily, weekly, seasonal, or annual basis. A stalwart—and basically welcome—neighborhood presence, the music ultimately "slips into the growing spaces of activity void of meaning and relations, into the organization of our everyday life … it signifies a power that needs no flag or symbol: musical repetition confirms the presence of repetitive consumption, of the flow of noises as ersatz sociality" (1996:111; cf. Fink 2005).

If coercion is one of this music's effects, silencing is another. While ice cream truck music's mere presence—regardless of intensity level—is enough to attract and polarize attention, even in a crowded soundscape, the music's repetitiveness obstructs communication and silences organized dissent about its use.[31] One reason for this, Truax suggested, is that the music is amplified and therefore carries a particular kind of power:

> Amplified messages, whether political, commercial or public service, when broadcast from vehicles moving through the streets, have the ability to command more attention than most other forms—with little scope for response. Some ice cream vendors even advertise their wares by repeatedly broadcasting an amplified electronic version of the traditional bell from their trucks, thereby driving the neighborhood to distraction for many blocks! This practice has been banned in some communities. Amplification automatically confers an aura of authenticity on any message, and puts the recipient at an immediate disadvantage. (2001:209)

Although timbre is perhaps ice cream truck music's most recognizable trait, it was amplification that enhanced the music's commercial potency at different points in its development. It was also one of the main reasons efforts are so commonly made to limit or ban its use.

In all these analyses, ice cream truck music is a disruption aggravated by automobility. "A symbol of individualized power" (Attali 1996:123), the automobile helped consolidate ice cream truck music's effects along the networks of roads, but also allowed it to be a presence that worked against abatement efforts. Since the twentieth century, efforts to attenuate traffic noise have included "traffic regulation, alternative pavements, new transportation constructions, and city planning," which have helped canalize traffic and create "new forms of order, integration, and enhanced predictability—a new smooth and controlled rhythm, so to speak—in city life" (Bijsterveld 2008:92–93). These visual and spatial considerations, however, seem to have focused discourse about traffic noise in ways that either fail to take more objective analyses into account or to justify it in particular ways.

Indeed, the most common arguments against ice cream truck music are ideologically driven and based on subjective or emotional criteria that lead to rationalizations ignorant of how sound works. Such "deaf spot" (Truax 2001:98–103) arguments hold, for example, that sound is not noise when one can grow accustomed or desensitized to it (habituation); that a sound is not noise if it is no louder than the sounds around it; that sound is not noise—and therefore acceptable—when it is not loud; and that noise may be excused when it is part of industry or economic progress. Ice cream music brings other, similar, arguments to bear. Many suggest that limiting the music will somehow disappoint children, or that doing so infringes upon one's right to free speech. Because these deaf spot arguments generally articulate definitions of noise poorly, they help perpetuate a logical inconsistency about what noise is by positioning abatement concerns against ideas about sentimentality, cultural meaning, and nostalgic effect.

Three hundred ninety noise complaints about ice cream truck music were lodged in New York City in July and August 2003; in the same period in 2004 there were 572 (243 in the month of May alone) and 410 in 2005 (*New York Times* 2005; Ramirez 2004). For many cities throughout the United States, ice cream truck music is a serious concern; legislative efforts to limit or ban its use are common annual events. Ever since bells and mechanical devices were first used on trucks to sell ice cream, mobility has made the enforcement of noise legislation difficult. A 1932 *New York Times* article, for example, not only pointed out that early noise laws were difficult to know because they were distributed haphazardly through the Code of Ordinances, but that most of the codes used in that era were passed "before the inception of the most important noise makers—the truck, the horn, the riveter, and the loudspeaker" (cf. Attali 1996:123).

New York City's current noise code literature explicitly acknowledges the difficulties mobility presents in enforcement.[32] Less obvious is how ice cream truck music's status as "noise" has exacerbated the enforcement challenges automobility presents. This began in the 1930s, when notions of what constituted traffic noise began to change. Karin Bijsterveld has shown how abatement efforts in cities like New York streamlined the system of automobility by introducing new kinds of order, integration and, predictability, and pioneered new ways of measuring sound, which led to alternative ideas about how loudness and "traffic noise" were defined. The "*chaos* of unwelcome sounds produced by badly behaving *individuals*" had become a blended hum that created "*levels* of unwanted sound" from a *collective* source (2008:93). Although the noise legislation that accompanied these advances addressed the problem of ice cream truck vehicular noise, it did so in a way that laid a heavy, and for many, unwarranted, hand on the music and its use. As modern abatement efforts threatened to silence this cherished old-fashioned form, a discourse about sound emerged that de-emphasized objectivity and anticipated new forms of legislation.

Today, typical noise legislation imposes temporal and spatial limitations on ice cream truck music's use to address loudness. In 1965, for example, New York City prohibited the use of ice cream truck music after 9 p.m. and provided that it could be no louder than four decibels at ten feet; further, operation was prohibited on certain restricted streets and "within 25 feet of a street corner" (*New York Times* 1965); in the 1970s, vendors could only play music "10 seconds at a time, and only once every 10 minutes when parked" (*New York Times* 1972). Sometimes, these restrictions can even more specific. For example, the noise ordinance passed in Chicago in 1962 stipulated that "a peddler using a vehicle... can travel any specific block only twice a day; stop not to exceed 30 minutes in any one block; operate only from 10 a.m. To 11 p.m.; must not park within 200 feet of any licensed shop selling the same merchandise; can sell only from the curbside; and, can use musical or noise making devices no louder than 6 decibels [audible about half a block] and play them only 30 seconds at a time and only from 10 a.m. To 9 p.m." (*Chicago Daily Tribune* 1962c).

However, legislation is only as effective as far as ice cream truck music is considered noise. For example, it is not known what effect—if any—New York's early 1930s efforts to ban "the operation of any musical instrument, radio, phonograph or other mechanical or electrical sound-making device on motor vehicle, airplane or dirigible the noise of which shall disturb the peace and quiet" (*New York Times* 1932) had on ice cream truck music's use in the City, but it would not appear that noise codes were always worthy of enforcement. In 1935, for example, the Mayor of Pelham, New York lifted a ban on ice cream truck chimes in Pelham's business district because they "were more soothing than the noise of hundreds of auto horns" (*New York Times* 1935). The Los Angeles City Council made a similar argument in 1960. It refused to ban the music outright after limiting music box operation to the hours between 9 a.m. and 9 p.m. because "the normal sound of music boxes on ice cream trucks is not loud enough to be a public nuisance" (*Los Angeles Times* 1960).

Legislation to restrict ice cream truck music often draws resistance that links child welfare with common sense nostalgia.[33] In Los Angeles in 1933, for example, a noise ordinance was introduced to restrict the use of "advertising loud-skeapers [sic] and ballyhoo wagons" (*Los Angeles Times* 1933b). Although the measure eventually passed (*Los Angeles Times* 1933c), a contemporary Los Angeles Times report played on an emotional connection to the sounds of street vending by threatening that the measure's passage would *eliminate* "the tinkling bell of the ice cream vendor that made dad dig, many evenings, for his spare nickels" (*Los Angeles Times* 1933a). This argument was echoed in 1953 in Trenton, New Jersey, where a member of the City Council came out against a local Magistrate who had ordered a vendor to remove his bells: "it cannot possibly be urged that the tinkling of the ice cream bell to notify little Mary or Johnny that they should commence to annoy and harass mother for a coin has become a crime. You must let the bells ring" (*New York Times* 1953). Here, abatement's intent is to "take a smile off a child's face" (Corbett 2007) in an effort to "traumatize" kids (Hu 2005). Such arguments, however, do little more than prejudice rational discussion about noise.

Popular resistance to abatement often leads to legislation based on compromise, which strikes a delicate balance between anti-noise concerns and the needs of small businesses. For example, in response to a 1947 investigation into the use of bells and amplified music on ice cream trucks called by the Los Angeles City Council's Public Health and Welfare Committee, one of its members convened a group of ice cream company owners to work out a set of provisions for its use that all parties could find mutually acceptable. The agreement they reached required vendors to "cease street selling at

9 p.m. and turn off their sound equipment. Tone volume generally is to be reduced and the call of the ice cream cone entirely muted around schools, churches, and hospitals" (*Los Angeles Times* 1947a; 1947b).[34] A similar deal was struck in 2004 when New York Mayor Michael Bloomberg proposed a strict new noise code that would require ice cream vendors to replace their music with bells (Steinhauer 2004). Mister Softee President Jams Conway argued that vendors "need the jingle," that it is "a New York institution" (Ramirez 2004), and ultimately hired a lobbyist to work with the city on a compromise (Barry 2004). The result was the 2007 noise code that prohibited vendors from using music unless their truck was in motion (New York City Department of Environmental Protection).

Very often, however, resolution is reached only after legal action. When the city of Chicago began to enforce an ordinance that banned "noise making" street vendors like ice cream trucks in 1962, for instance, Mr. Softee of Illinois, Tastee-Freez, and Freezefresh Inc. filed suit, alleging that the ordinance's enforcement discriminated against vendors because it had not been prosecuted in thirty-five years. After the vendors won a court injunction to prevent the ordinance's enforcement, the City Council's Committees on Health and Licensing responded by implementing the stringent noise ordinance I mentioned earlier (*Chicago Daily Tribune* 1962a, 1962b, 1962c). A more recent example involved Jeffrey Cabaniss, an ice cream truck driver based in Stafford Township, New Jersey known for playing "Turkey in the Straw." When the Township voted to ban ice cream truck music 1998, Cabaniss filed a lawsuit in federal court, which held that a ban on commercial speech would violate his First Amendment rights. He ultimately lowered the volume of his music (of his own volition), but only after a court injunction prompted the Township council to rescind the ban (Nieves 1998; see also Gordon 2002 and Zielbauer 2002).

There are many different ideas about what makes ice cream truck music noise. They are all, in essence, correct. But legislation to control this music has taken many forms and often tends to downplay how noise functions as sound in balancing abatement efforts with commercial interests. Local anti-noise efforts typically limit when, where, and how loud this music may be played and are often framed as a public health concerns. In instances when legislation becomes too ambitious, abatement is sometimes seen as a cultural threat; in these situations, ice cream truck music becomes more important because of the perceived (if, perhaps, imagined) dire consequence of a world without it. Ice cream truck music is tricky. Outside of an outright ban, it retains the chance ability to slip into the blank spaces of the acoustic community and be noticed. Regardless of abatement efforts, it remains an extremely effective way to sell ice cream.

# CONCLUSION

Most writing about ice cream truck music either plays on its nostalgic quality or its saccharine invasiveness (Neely 2005). These common approaches, however, miss the point that the music is effective largely because of how its sound works. Ice cream truck music's influence is indeed based on its representational power. When Harry Burt used bells on his trucks to sell ice cream, he wanted to evoke the taste of this popular Victorian-era comfort food by playing off an expectation about what such comforts should sound like. Music box-based devices built on this association—while a chimey timbre still represented the product, melody enabled consumers to distinguish one business's truck from another. In cooperation, tune, timbre, and technology recalled the sound of nineteenth-century soda fountains and ice cream parlors, and are the basis for the nostalgia many ascribe to the music.

But the *experience* of nostalgia (or noise) in ice cream truck music is achieved anamnesically. Each of the technical innovations outlined in this chapter was intended to improve the music's propagation in various ways. Some of these changes improved timbral reproduction, others more reliable amplification; but timbre remained a constant because it compels people's attention and draws them to the roadside so well. While few would find interest in listening to chime music on its own, from a moving truck this stilted, old-fashioned mechanical music becomes fluid and dynamic as its sound filters through different spatial configurations. The context of its reception influences how people determine the music's value and meaning, and becomes the basis for how nostalgia and noise are experienced.

It seems simple—perhaps even unworthy of inquiry—but ice cream truck music is a highly specialized and refined form, and its discourse should no longer be restricted to debates about nostalgia or noise. Made mobile, its sound organizes social networks of consumers while its timbre accrues ideological meaning through collective memory. Although some have experimented with these issues creatively, my hope is that this chapter will inspire new inquiry into how this and other heralding musics work. While many will doubtlessly still hear it as noise, there is much to contemplate in the "ding, ding" of the ice cream truck.

## NOTES

1. Here I am paraphrasing what Swiss writer Cecile Lauber once wrote about music boxes (quoted in DeWaard 1967:9). Although he was not talking about ice cream trucks in specific, the quote suggests a historical continuity in technology and in timbre that I follow throughout this chapter.
2. Following Augoyard and Torgue, anamnesis is "an effect of reminiscence in which a past situation or atmosphere is brought back to the listener's consciousness, provoked by a particular signal or sonic context. Anamnesis, a semiotic effect, is the often involuntary revival of memory caused by listening and the evocative power of sounds" (2006:21). My ideas about music's role in evoking the "friendly sites of junction, assembly, and encounter" of Main Street USA are inspired by Gage Averill's work on nostalgia in barbershop singing (Averill 2003).
3. Interrante borrows this word from a 1933 Hoover Commission report that in essence defined metropolitanism as a "reorganization of the physical and social urban and rural environments which changed people's need for transformation."

4. Funderburg (1995:72, 74–75) has suggested that in the nineteenth-century street vendors tended to be individuals who were then considered socially marginal or otherwise unemployable, including ugly women, the handicapped, the elderly, and midgets. As mobile vending changed and became a more profitable endeavor with twentieth century automobility, the image of the mobile vendor improved substantially, especially with the success of companies like Good Humor.

5. Oral history and written records show that during the nineteenth and early twentieth centuries, ice cream vending—usually from push or goat-drawn carts—had been accompanied by shouting, bell ringing, harmonica playing and even barrel organ music. Between this earlier period and point-of sale automotive vending, there was a moment where the wholesale delivery of ice cream took place from horse-drawn carts and early trucks. Although a related practice, because this delivery was wholesale and usually did not involve sound, it lies outside this chapter's purview.

6. Similar accounts came from the Caribbean as well. Nicholas Slonimsky, for example, remarked that "the symphony of pushcart tenors is particularly rich and varied. The *fiorituras* that a Havana knife-sharpener performed on his mouth harmonica reminded me of the neo-Grecian modes of Debussy's *Flûte de Pan* from *Chansons de Bilitis*" (1945:40). In Cuba, the songs of street vendors are called pregón and are the basis of popular song. Similarly, Granville Campbell, a classically trained Jamaican singer, arranged a *Jamaica Potpourri* entitled *Piano Fantasia on 5 (Some) Kingston Street Cries* in the 1930s; it was based on melodies collected by Jamaican musicologist Astley Clerk.

7. Quoted in Funderburg (2002:40), quoting from an October 1877 article entitled "Soda Water Apparatus," in *Carbonated Drinks*: 10; the second again comes from Funderburg (1995:95), quoting from June 15, 1892 article entitled "Soda Water in Chicago," in *Pharmaceutical Era* 7:409–14.

8. Mark Smith (2001:261–64) has done an excellent job articulating the relationship between aurality and visuality to show the tendency for historical accounts to favor the latter over the former. His work, along with that of Jonathan Sterne (2003:14–16), emphasizes the importance of aurality as a counterpoint to visuality in histories of the senses.

9. The most explicit and likely best-known authority on timbral association was Berlioz, who codified many in his *Treatise on Instrumentation*. He noted, for example, that the glockenspiel's sound is "soft, mysterious, and of extreme delicacy" while that of the high bells is "more serene in character; it has something rustic and naïve about it" ([1855]1991:338, 385, respectively).

Although Berlioz's commentary was likely the synthesis of a variety of creative sources and opinions of his day, there may also be a physical reason that ties this kind of timbre to a particular psychology. In *The Audible Past*, Jonathan Sterne cites Helmholz, who suggested that "sounds [can] best be distinguished from one another by their upper partials, that is through their higher frequencies" (Sterne 2003:64–65). Whether a culturally determined association between these frequencies and childhood was ever assumed is not known, but the physical phenomenon he describes seems open to this sort of analysis and deserves further inquiry.

10. My use of pastiche here follows Frederic Jameson's use as "the imitation of a peculiar or unique style [...] a neutral practice of [...] mimicry, without parody's ulterior motive, without the satirical impulse, without laughter, without that still latent feeling that there exists something *normal* compared to which what is being imitated is rather comic. Pastiche is blank parody, parody that has lost its sense of humor" (1983:114).

11. It is unclear when this happened. Old time Los Angeles-based driver John Ralston told me he thought it was circa 1929. Chime box manufacturer Bob Nichols believes it was probably the early to mid-1930s.

12. Yaras (2005) suggests that West Coast Organ was probably owned by Louis Bacigalupi, an organ builder specializing in barrel organs, who was also a professional wrestler, actor, and amateur herpetologist. For more on the use of barrel organs in nineteenth and early twentieth century America, see Zucchi (1992).

"Stodola Pumpa" was proprietary to Good Humor of California until 1962, when the company's assets were brought under new ownership and the music changed to "Danny's Dream," written by the company's new owner, Dan Tropp. However, "Stodola Pumpa" had already become an iconic part of southern Californian culture. For example, it was the basis for "Come and Get It," a 1963 single recorded by a Beach Boys side project called the "Tri-Five"; later that year, it was used again for "The Rocking Surfer," an instrumental included on the Beach Boys' *Surfer Girl* album.

13. The speakers were likely located under the hood to protect them from the elements. Anecdotal photographic evidence suggests that externally mounted loudspeakers did not emerge until the 1960s/1970s.

14. During the War, ice cream's availability was limited by the scarcity of ingredients and by truck tire rationing. Afterward, however, there was a drastic increase in street vending and sales. 1946 was an especially good year for ice cream. In 1948, sales reached a plateau that remained more or less constant for at least three decades.

15. John Ralston, telephone interview with author, 1999.

16. Kevin Johnson, who runs a website about the AD-30, has identified nearly 1,700 on-disc titles made for this music box model since its introduction in the 1920s. For this list, as well as detailed information about the different styles of AD-30, see http://www.thorensad30.com/.

17. Bob Nichols, telephone interview with author, 1999.

18. For more about the Nichols Electronics company, see http://www.nicholselectronicsco.com/.

19. For example, Eddie Murphy sings the melody in his 1983 stand-up comedy special *Delirious*; thrash metal band Nuclear Assault plays it on their 1986 album *Game Over*; it is the melodic basis for the acoustic duo Drink Me's 1995 recording "Song of the Ice Cream Truck"; it is the basis for Jed Distler's String Quartet #1, the "Mister Softee Variations, which premiered in 1999; it is played from the ice cream truck Bernie Mac's character is operating at the end his 2004 film *Mister 3000*; and, a toy piano-electro version appears on Twink's 2007 CD *Ice Cream Trucking*. When I talked about ice cream truck music with others, it is mentioned far more often than any other tune.

20. Les Waas, telephone interview with author, May 1, 2009.

21. Waas composed over 900 jingles and is not sure when this happened, although it occurred long before he found out about it. It seems to have been sometime in the 1960s or early 1970s (Broadcast Pioneers of Philadelphia). According to Bob Nichols of Nichols Electronics, which began manufacturing Mister Softee boxes in 1975, they were first manufactured by Schulmerich Electronics.

22. 8-bit sound is a synthesized digital technology that produces music via simple waveforms using a very low sample rate. It has a peculiar (and characteristic) lo-fi electronic sound. This format rose to prominence in the period 1970–1990 and found many commercial applications, especially the video game industry, where music was simple and very often

repetitive (as on ice cream trucks). This technology was capable of recreating frequencies that roughly mimicked the chimey sounds traditionally used by ice cream vendors on their trucks.

23. Project website can be found at: http://icecream.8bitpeoples.com (accessed April 20, 2009).

24. Jeffrey Lopez and Lauren Rosati, members of the Brooklyn-based artist collective suite405, initiated a similar project in 2007 called "Ice Cream Headache" (Smith, "We All Scream for New Ice Cream Song"). It invited sound artists to remix and reinterpret ice cream truck music to come up with a better alternative. The winner would have its music played from a rented ice cream truck over Memorial Day Weekend. Although they received more than 40 submissions, the organizers were not able to secure an ice cream truck and ultimately cancelled the event.

25. Michael Hearst, interview with author, February 12, 2009.

26. For example, Hearst appeared on the Today Show, on National Public Radio's "Fresh Air" program, and was interviewed for several influential pop culture blogs, including *Boing Boing*, *Gothamist*, and *Wired*.

27. For more on this project, see the MySpace page for "Songs for Ice Cream Trucks" at http://www.myspace.com/songsforicecreamtrucks; see also Heart's site at http://www.songsforicecreamtrucks.com/. Quote available at: http://www.bar-none.com/michael-hearst.html (accessed March 1, 2012).

28. Originally from Long Beach, California, Matt Allen drives around the country handing out free ice cream as *The Ice Cream Man*. Allen became an ice cream vendor in 2004 in Ashland, Oregon. Toward the end of the summer, he began to give his inventory away at pre-planned ice cream socials. Well-attended and widely publicized, these events inspired Allen to tour the country in his 1969 Chevy step-van, giving away free ice creams; his goal is to give away half a million. He funds this enterprise through advertising, sponsorship, promotional tie-ins, and merchandising. Hearst says the track of his that Allen plays most often is "Where do ice cream trucks go in the winter?"

29. A case can be made here for "aleatoric hearing," as opposed to conventional musical aleatory which involves compositional procedure (which this music typically does not). Here, chime music's propagation and how a listener hears it are contingent on many chance variables, including but not limited to the physical details of a vendor-in-motion's environment, where the vendor and the subject are positioned in relation to one another, and the subject's general state of mind at the moment of recognition.

   To better illustrate this point, a comparison can be made with John Cage's "empty" piece, *4'33"*. Using silence, Cage controverted the idea of the work of art by forcing the ear of the listener to hear music in the world of natural sound, often prompting the question "is it music?" (Campbell 1992). While ice cream truck music's prosaic commerciality lays aside any notion of it being a work of art, it similarly forces one to hear music in the world of natural sound in a literal sense albeit prompting the question "is it noise?" The qualitative difference between these two examples is that the former is bracketed by the pretense of a concert space while the latter is not.

   If one accepts the notion that Cage's critical success lay in his failure to undermine the musical work-concept by maintaining institutional control in the performance of *4'33"* (see Goehr 2005:264; cf. Campbell 1992), one might argue that chime music presents a far more successful challenge to the notion of art because its commercial success is so heavily dependent on circumstance and chance. The polarizing and often contradictory attitudes that result become compelling evidence to suggest that aleatory is a basic strategy behind ice cream truck music's success.

30. Although Schafer's point is well taken, mechanical boxes still greatly outnumbered boxes capable of playing "synthesized" tunes at the time this quote was published. The kinds of "inaccuracies" Schafer refers to are likely due to old or poorly maintained music boxes. As mechanical boxes get older, cylinder teeth and comb tynes break, thus eliminating notes and producing melodic gaps in the music. Further, as the metal of the comb tynes becomes fatigued, the pitch of certain notes will change slightly, leading to the effect Schafer describes.

31. This point generally speaks to silencing discourse about consumption, but it has other (sometimes amusing) implications as well. In 2010, for example, ice cream truck music was used to silence and disperse a group of rioting teenagers in Belfast, Northern Ireland (Kelly 2010; Henry 2010). Although chime music was an effective deterrent, however, the officer who used it came under scrutiny because its use was considered humorous and therefore not "appropriate" in this situation.

32. In New York City's *Noise Code Guide*, the section "Food Vending Vehicles and their Jingles" reads as follows:

> Ice cream is a refreshing summer treat and ice cream trucks traveling on city streets are important summer traditions, but their repetitious jingles create a community nuisance and disrupt the lives of nearby residents.
>
> To alleviate this problem, the new noise code prohibits the playing of jingles while any type of food vending vehicle is stationary. Jingles may only be played when vehicles are in motion, traveling through neighborhoods.
>
> **Enforcement**
>
> Because ice cream trucks travel from neighborhood to neighborhood, enforcement can be difficult. To decrease the need for enforcement, DEP works closely with the Department of Consumer Affairs, the City licensing agency for the vendors, to produce informational materials reminding drivers of their responsibilities under the new noise code. (New York City Department of Environmental Protection 2007:7)

33. In one notable instance, support for ice cream truck music focused not on an emotional link with children, but with veterans: "Don't forget that the drivers of the ice cream vehicles were heroes on the beach heads. God bless them one and all" (*Los Angeles Times* 1948b). Such examples, however, are unusual.

34. In this case, the compromise was not without controversy. Because the Councilman acted independently of the full City Council—and perhaps in the full interest of business owners—the provisions were not adopted.

## REFERENCES

Attali, Jacques. 1996. *Noise: The Political Economy of Music.* Minneapolis: University of Minnesota Press.

Augoyard, Jean-François and Henry Torgue. 2006. *Sonic Experience. A Guide to Everyday Sounds.* Montreal & Kingston: McGill-Queen's University Press.

Averill, Gage. 2003. *Four Parts, No Waiting.* New York: Oxford University Press.

Barry, Dan. 2004. "As Jingle Plays, Resistance is Futile." *New York Times*, June 23: B1, B4.

*Belfast Telegraph*, 2010. "'Ice Cream Music' Policeman Rapped," May 27. Available at http://www.belfasttelegraph.co.uk/breakingnews/breakingnews_ukandireland/ice-cream-music-policeman-rapped-28538244.html (accessed Aug. 16, 2013).

Berlioz, Hector. [1855] 1991. *Treatise on Instrumentation*. New York: Dover.

Bijsterveld, Karin. 2008. *Mechanical Sound. Technology, Culture, and Public Problems of Noise in the Twentieth Century*. Cambridge, MA: MIT Press.

8bitpeoples, "WHY ICE CREAM, OR: WHY SCREAM?" http://icecream.8bitpeoples.com (accessed April 20, 2009).

*Broadcast Pioneers of Philadelphia*, "Les Waas," http://www.broadcastpioneers.com/waas.html (accessed March 20, 2009).

Campbell, Mark Robin. 1992. "John Cage's 4' 33": Using Aesthetic Theory to Understand a Musical Notion." *Journal of Aesthetic Education* 26(1):83–91.

Chapius, Alfred. 1980. *History of the Musical Box and of Mechanical Music*. Summit, NJ: The Musical Box Society International.

*Chicago Daily Tribune*. 1962a. "Sue to Prevent Silencing of Vendor Trucks," July 17: B3.

——. 1962b. "Rules Trucks Can Ring Again for Ice Cream." July 27: B11.

——. 1962c. "Council Unit Votes Rein on Street Sales." September 18: A5.

*Chicago Tribune*. 1966. "Ice Cream Man Melts Good Will of Cool Customer." May 8: T1.

Corbett, Rachel. 2007. "...As Ice Cream Trucks Tune Up with Songs that Madden or Gladden." *New York Times*, May 20: 7(L).

Corbin, Alain. 1998. *Village Bells: Sound and Meaning in the 19th-Century French Countryside*. New York: Columbia University Press.

DeWaard, Romke. 1967. *From Music Boxes to Street Organs*. Translated by Wade Jenkins. New York: Vestal Press.

Dickson, Paul. 1972. *The Great American Ice Cream Book*. New York: Atheneum.

Earnshaw, Alan. 2005. "The Cool Chimes of Summer." *Vintage Roadscene 19*, no. 85 (September/October) 5–10.

Fink, Robert. 2005. *Repeating Ourselves: American Minimal Music as Cultural Practice*. Berkeley and Los Angeles: University of California Press.

Funderburg, Anne Cooper. 1995. *Chocolate, Strawberry, and Vanilla: A History of American Ice Cream*. Bowling Green, OH: Bowling Green State University Popular Press.

——. 2002. *Sundae Best: A History of Soda Fountains*. Bowling Green, OH: Bowling Green State University.

Goehr, Lydia. 1992. *The Imaginary Museum of Musical Works: An Essay in the Philosophy of Music*. New York: Oxford.

Gordon, Jane. 2002. "The Battle to Get Us to Pipe Down: When Civility Fails, Towns Step In." *New York Times*, July 21: CT1, 4, 5.

Harris, Eleanor. 1949. "The Pied Pipers of Ice Cream." *The Saturday Evening Post*, August 20: 36.

Henry, Lesley-Anne. 2010. "Police Stop Rioters with Ice Cream Van Music." *Belfast Telegraph*, May 28. Available at http://www.belfasttelegraph.co.uk/news/local-national/police-stop-rioters-with-ice-cream-van-music-28538357.html (accessed August 16, 2013).

Hoover, Cynthia A. 1971. *Music Machines—American Style: A Catalog of Exhibition*. Washington D.C.: Smithsonian Institution Press.

Hu, Winnie. 2005. "That Jingle of Mr. Softee's? It's the Sound of Compromise." *New York Times*, December 14: B1, B4.

Interrante, Joseph. 1983. "The Road to Autopia: The Automobile and the Spatial Transformation of American Culture." In *The Automobile and American Culture*, ed. David Lanier Lewis and Laurence Goldstein, 89–104. Ann Arbor: University of Michigan Press.

Jakle, John, and Keith Sculle. 1999. *Fast Food: Roadside Restaurants in the Automobile Age.* Baltimore: Johns Hopkins University Press.

Jameson, Frederick. 1983. "Postmodernism and Consumer Society." In *The Anti-Aesthetic: Essays on Postmodern Culture*, 111–25. Seattle: Bay Press.

Johnson, Kevin. "Thorens AD-30," http://www.thorensad30.com (accessed February 15, 2009).

Kelly, Dara. 2010. "Police use ice cream music to embarrass teen rioters in Belfast." *Irish Central,* June 8, http://www.irishcentral.com/news/Police-use-ice-cream-music-to-embarrass-teen-rioters-in-Belfast-95103964.html (accessed August 31, 2010).

*Los Angeles Times.* 1933a. "Ban on Noises Being Sought." July 28: A8.

——. 1933b. "Noise Curb Ordinance Ordered." August 24: A8.

——. 1933c. "Noise Still Annoys." August 27: 16.

——. 1935. "Noise Vote Stirs Town." January 6: 31.

——. 1947a. "Ice Cream Bells Queried." August 11: 5.

——. 1947b. "Bells Now Toll With Bad Humor." August 21: A1.

——. 1948a. "Sunday Noises." May 20: A4.

——. 1948b. "Music That Cheers." May 28: A4.

——. 1958. "City May Put Soft Pedal on Vendors' Tunes." September 28: SG10.

——. 1960. "Music Boxes on Ice Cream Trucks OKd." October 4: 2.

Matt, Susan J. 2002. "Children's Envy and the Emergence of the Modern Consumer Ethic, 1890–1930." *Journal of Social History* 36(2):283–302.

McGonigle, Erin. 2004. "The Koolman Repertoire, Reenvisioned." Radio interview on *Radiolab*. WNYC, January 2.

MySpace. "Songs for Ice Cream Trucks." Available at http://www.myspace.com/songsforicecreamtrucks (accessed May 3, 2009).

Murphy, Eddie. [1983] 2007. *Delirious.* DVD. Beverly Hills, CA: Entertainment Studios Home Entertainment

Neely, Daniel. 2005. "Soft Serve: Charting the Promise of Ice Cream Truck Music." *Esopus* 4:23–28.

New York City Department of Environmental Protection. 2007. "Have You Heard: New York City Has Overhauled Its Noise Code!" New York City Department of Environmental Protection, http://www.nyc.gov/html/dep/pdf/noise_code_guide.pdf (accessed April 20, 2009).

*New York Times.* 1932. "Bill to End City Din Ready for Walker." May 10: 23.

——. 1935. "Ice Cream Wagon Chimes Preferred to Auto Horns." June 3: 19.

——. 1940. "Noise Abatement Week." October 20: 12.

——. 1953. "No Law Against Tinkling: Trenton Ice Cream Vendor Wins City Backing for Bells." Special to the New York Times. August 8: 14.

——. 1965. "Vendors of Ices Told to Mute Bells at 9 P.M." May 6: 41.

——. 1972. "Ear-Splitters Under Attack." July 2: E10.

——. 2005. "For Ice Cream Trucks, A Little Less Noise." August 21: 32.

Nieves, Evelyn. 1998. "Savoring Legal Success, an Ice Cream Vendor Calls the Tune." *New York Times,* May 7: B1.

Ord-Hume, Arthur. 1973. *Clockwork Music: An Illustrated History of Mechanical Musical Instruments from the Musical Box to the Pianola From Automaton Lady Virginal Players to Orchestrion.* New York: Crown Publishers.

Pryor, Richard. 1974. *That Nigger's Crazy.* LP. Reprise MS 2241.

Radano, Ronald M. 1989. "Interpreting Muzak: Speculations on Musical Experience in Everyday Life." *American Music* 7(4):448–60.

Ramirez, Anthony. 2004. "Mister Softee May Fall Under Cone of Silence." *New York Times,* June 8: B4.

Rhodes, Robbie. 2006. "Bacigalupi Player Carillon for Ice Cream Truck," http://www.mmdigest.com/Archives/Digests/200606/2006.06.10.03.html (accessed March 26, 2009).

Richman, Jonathan and the Modern Lovers. 1987. *The Beserkley Years.* CD. Rhino R2 75889.

Roehl, Harvey N. 1968. *Keys to A Musical Past.* New York: Vestal Press.

Rydell, Robert W. 1984. *All the World's a Fair: Visions of Empire at American International Expositions, 1876–1916.* Chicago: University of Chicago Press.

Schafer, R. Murray. 1993. *Voices of Tyranny, Temples of Silence.* Ontario: Arcana Editions.

Slonimsky, Nicolas. 1945. *Music of Latin America.* New York: Thomas Y. Crowell Company.

Smith, Mark. 2001. *Listening to Nineteenth Century America.* Chapel Hill: University of North Carolina Press.

Smith, Robert. "We All Scream for New Ice Cream Song," National Public Radio, *All Things Considered,* http://www.npr.org/templates/story/story.php?storyId=9945901 (accessed May 1, 2009).

Steinhauer, Jennifer. 2004. "Bloomberg Seeks To Toughen Code for Noise in City." *New York Times,* June 8: A1, B4.

Sterne, Jonathan. 1997. "Sounds Like the Mall of America: Programmed Music and the Architectonics of Commercial Space." *Ethnomusicology* 41(1):22–50.

——. 2003. *The Audible Past: Cultural Origins of Sound Reproduction.* Durham: Duke University Press.

Sutton, David E. 2001. *Remembrance of Repasts: An Anthropology of Food and Memory.* New York: Berg.

Tallis, David. 1971. *Music Boxes: A Guide for Collectors.* New York: Stein and Day.

Théberge, Paul. 1997. *Any Sound You Can Imagine: Making Music/Consuming Technology.* Hanover, NH: Wesleyan University Press.

Thompson, Emily. 1995. "Machines, Music and the Quest for Fidelity: Marketing the Edison Phonograph in America, 1977–1925." *The Musical Quarterly* 79(1):131–71.

*Time Magazine.* "Good Humor." Sept. 30, 1935, p. 23.

Truax, Barry. 2001. *Acoustic Communication. 2nd ed.* Westport, CT: Ablex Publishing.

Urry, John. 2004. "The 'System' of Automobility." *Theory, Culture & Society* 21(4/5):25–39.

Whitby, Stuart and Alan Earnshaw. 1999. *Fifty Years of Ice Cream Vehicles.* Cumbria, CA: Trans Pennine Publishing.

Yaras, Thom. 2005. "Louis Bacigalupi (Bacigalupo): Organ Builder, Wrestler, Actor, Herpetologist," March 12, http://www.mmdigest.com/Pictures/bacigalupi1.html (accessed March 26, 2009).

Zielbauer, Paul. 2002. "Judge's Finding is Music to Mister Softee's Ears." *New York Times,* August 3: B5.

Zucchi, John E. 1992. *Little Slaves of the Harp: Italian Child Street Musicians in Paris, London, and New York.* Buffalo: McGill-Queen's University Press.

CHAPTER **6**

# THERE MUST BE SOME RELATION BETWEEN MUSHROOMS AND TRAINS: ALVIN CURRAN'S *BOLETUS EDULIS—MUSICA PENDOLARE*

BENJAMIN PIEKUT

THE term *Boletus Edulis* is a fancy way of saying "porcini mushroom," and *Musica Pendolare* is Italian for "commuter music." Composed for a train line in Northern Italy in 2008, Alvin Curran's *Boletus Edulis—Musica Pendolare* was thus a double homage and commemoration of John Cage, who in addition to being a well known mushroom lover, had in 1978 organized a large-scale happening on train lines in the same region of Emilia Romagna. Although Cage's *Alla ricerca del silenzio perduto* (also known as *Il Treno di John Cage*, or simply "prepared train") has been the focus of some critical attention, this chapter will describe Curran's event and elucidate a few of the key differences between this later work and the Cage composition it was intended to commemorate.

Curran's use of the term "commuter music" is more than a cheeky reference to the workers who pile into the train every morning and evening on the way to or from their jobs in Bologna and the surrounding area. What do we do when we commute? The train schedule is rigid, but our movement through and with it is not: we might walk a different route in the station, sit in a different car, or occupy ourselves differently while awaiting our arrival. This openness extends to that other important component of commuting—we are always with others, working with (and sometimes against) our fellow passengers. Commuter music could therefore be considered the sonic result of improvisations with other people.

These two aspects of commuter music—improvisation within structure and working in concert with large groups of people—have been long-time interests for Curran.

While living in Rome in 1975, Curran received a request for help from students who had occupied the National Academy of Theatre Arts. Perplexed, he visited the scene of the occupation and improvised a participatory vocal exercise for "two hundred sweaty revolutionaries," as he later recalled. "I think what happened was I got them to intone a unison at a certain point and then I said, 'Okay, let's keep this going, and now everyone freely from this first tone that we are singing, sing a second tone, freely.' And before you know it, the whole place exploded into song" (quoted in Tortora 2010:170). (Curran's facility with amateur performance had already been cultivated during his years in Musica Elettronica Viva, a radical electro-acoustic improvisation group that frequently encouraged audience participation.)[1] He was soon hired as professor of vocal improvisation, and the classroom activities he developed gradually led him to his first large-scale environmental performance, *Maritime Rites* (1979–), a monumental work that has taken various forms in performance over the years, from choreographed rowboat-based improvisations, to ship-horn blast symphonies, to a large public radio piece in 1985 involving field recordings, interviews, and improvisations down the Eastern seaboard of the United States.

Other works in this vein followed in the 1980s, including *Monumenti* (1982), a large environmental work that positioned instrumentalists in and around various spaces in the Alte Oper in Frankfurt; *Unsafe for More Than 25 Men* (1983), set at the foot of the Brooklyn Bridge, and in the words of John Rockwell, "performed by a shifting assortment of downtown singers, instrumentalists and tape-cassette players wandering about the space" (1983); and *A Piece for Peace* (1985), in which a mixed chorus, soloists, and other instrumentalists performed conventionally notated music and improvisations in three separate locations (in Holland, Germany, and Italy), mixed live and broadcast on the radio.

In recent years, Curran has produced *Beams* (2005), for 35 ambulatory members of the Zeitkratzer Ensemble in Berlin, and *Nora Sonora* (2005), another environmental concert featuring 100 musicians at an archeological site in Sardinia. But his most ambitious piece has been *Oh Brass on the Grass Alas*, commissioned by the Donaueschingen new music festival and performed in October 2006. Written for over 300 brass-band musicians, the work combined structured improvisations and choreography on a massive scale—it was performed in a pasture the size of three football fields. Curran divided the piece's forty minutes into a series of vignettes, each exploring a technique or sound world familiar to devoted listeners of his music. There are sections devoted to quiet unisons, trills, honks and car horns, random chords formed by blaring long tones, a slowly descending chromatic scale played as a melody, and a sloppy march.

The success of *Oh Brass* depended entirely on the participation of local bands in the Bad-Württemburg area. Curran writes, "With such a vital musical resource culturally excluded from the traditionally elitist three-day festival, I thought, let's invite this local treasure directly into the home of the new music aliens" (2007). The composer's faith in amateur musicians betrays a complex relationship to non-"elitist" traditions, which Curran clearly loves, but which also provide the raw fuel for his peculiar, puckish modernism. In the past, he has written that collaborations like these create "very real musical situations with a large creative potential [that] is surely greater than one finds in most of the overfed solemnity of conventional concerts of new or classical music" (Curran 1985). Amateurs, then, can create provocative or unexpected sonic textures, but function in this regard as the means to familiar modernist end: original, complex sounds. "[T]he entropy of huge scale not only makes 'soup' happen but causes it to happen in heavenly and dysfunctional random tunings," Curran writes of *Oh Brass* (2007).

But in these large-scale environmental pieces, movement is not merely a formal or statistical parameter of composition, but always a movement through human space—spaces that are inhabited, cultivated, and traversed in the course of everyday life. In *Maritime Rites*, for example, the acoustical magic of sounds glinting across open water is surely a big draw, but it is the specific folkways of maritime culture that attracts Curran to harbors, rivers, and ports—this is a piece concerned with human activity, history, and, yes, movement, in these natural seascapes. Likewise, in *Boletus Edulis*, Curran sought to return his listeners to a quotidian life-on-the-move by following the example set out by Cage thirty years before. There were important differences between the two works, however, differences that are plainly encapsulated in the titles: while Cage's work was primarily based around *Il Treno* itself, *Boletus Edulis— Musica Pendolare* was addressed to commuters and the spaces they move through on a daily basis.

Indeed, for Cage, the train was the main attraction, and it ran on three different lines during the course of the three-day event—the Bologna-Porretta Terme (June 26), the Bologna-Ravenna (June 27), and the Ravenna-Rimini (June 28) lines.[2] Each of the cars contained two loudspeakers, one amplifying the signals from microphones on the exterior of the car and one amplifying the signals from microphones on the interior of the car. A control in each car allowed passengers to switch between the two sources freely. This sound system operated during any times the train was in motion. Once the train stopped at a station, these speakers were shut off, and the action shifted to another pair of loudspeakers on the roof of each car. One of these received signals from a large reservoir of cassette players, which played back recordings of the sounds of the station gathered by Walter Marchetti and Juan Hidalgo. The other amplified a different set of cassette recordings, "prepared by [Marchetti and Hidalgo] from recordings of the region local to the stop representing the people living there, their work, their music, and the noises and sounds, musical or not, of their daily life weekdays and Sundays." The public was free to change any of these cassettes.

Each of these station stops was something of a celebration. Cage proposed that as many television sets as there were existing channels be installed above eye level, and as many live performing groups as could be afforded played music. "These groups should be genuinely of the neighborhood of the station, representing the culture of the place," Cage wrote. "The station itself should present an exhibition of the arts and crafts of the people who actually live in that town or part of town." He also suggested that food and drink be made available at each station along the way. The station's public address system would announce the imminent departure of the train, and the change from stasis to motion was signaled sonically by an abrupt switch in sound sources (from cassettes to microphones) and in loudspeakers (external to internal). In the event that any of the performers from the community board the train while still singing, playing, or dancing, Cage notes, they would be welcomed. Photographs and film footage of the event that were published many years later reveal several performing groups on the train (a pair of flutists, a string quartet, a pianist in a special car, etc.). He also requested that buses and taxis be made available to anyone who missed the train or needed to be elsewhere before the conclusion of the event.

Tito Gotti had proposed this project in a letter to Cage, dated March 5, 1977 (though he had already broached the topic in person in Paris some weeks earlier). Ideologically opposed to traditional concert presentations, Gotti envisioned something on the order of a "musicircus" in motion, to be presented that summer along a train line in Bologna. "[W]e want to create a relationship among a musical event, a people and a territory," he wrote, "meaning both the territory seen by the travelers of the train and the territory inhabited by the people of the places where the train will stop; besides, a relationship between the latter and the travelers, who will be able to join the others during the journey, and so on...."[3]

Cage, however, had a number of prior commitments, and his reply to Gotti points out that the proposal was more than a musicircus, since it involved moving and stopping. He suggested that they seek out the young composer Robert Moran, a Mills College graduate who had made a name for himself composing massive works for the musical forces of an entire city. "He has a good deal of experience in urban festivals and circumstances involving mobility and music," Cage wrote, "both in this country and in Europe."[4]

But Gotti was persistent, enrolling the help of his friend Marcello Panni, who was also friendly with Cage. In a letter to Cage of March 25, Panni offered his own ensemble for the Bologna event that summer, and also assured the American that he could gain him further performance opportunities in Rome should he agree to the Italian excursion.[5] In his reply, Cage reiterated that he had not agreed to come to Bologna, though he still had pleasant memories of Mrs. Panni's cooking, which he had experienced on a previous trip.[6] In his missive to Cage on April 12, Gotti expressed regret that the 1977 event would not be possible, but suggested that the following summer would also be an option, a possibility to which Cage agreed soon thereafter.[7] His "score in the form of a letter" was written and delivered to Gotti some months later.[8]

Although the ostensible reason for Cage's initial abstention that summer was prior commitments, he indicated his general state of mind during this period in the letter to Panni. Seemingly by way of explanation, he wrote, "I am not very well, cannot drink any wine! Or eat any cheese or meat!"[9] Indeed, the spring and summer of 1977 were something of a crisis for Cage, whose health problems (numbness in the feet, arthritis, various pains) were getting out of control and would only be ameliorated by the macrobiotic diet he soon began (Revill 1992:256–59).[10] For a lifelong heavy drinker and smoker otherwise devoted to the haute cuisine of Julia Child, this was a cataclysmic change.

Food seems to have been woven into this story from the outset in a number of ways. Cage wrote the following mesostic on the name of the event organizer:

> There must be
> some relatIon
> beTween
> mushrOoms and trains:
> otherwise you'd never have thouGht
> Of asking me
> To
> wriTe
> componiIbile 3.[11]

And though that mysterious relation between mushrooms and trains wouldn't become perspicuous until 2008, there was at least one other connection between gustation and transportation in 1978: the small spiral notebook in which Cage drafted his "score in the form of a letter" for *Il Treno* contained one other item: early drafts of the poem "Where Are We Eating? and What Are We Eating?"[12]

Curran's *Boletus Edulis* was commissioned by the AngelicA International Festival of New Music, under the direction of Massimo Simonini, who had been in charge of the organization for nineteen years. These kinds of outdoor works enrolling masses of people require enormous political preparation, and the constituencies involved in this particular production also included the region of Emilia Romagna, the Provincia di Bologna, its capital of Bologna, the Rete Ferroviaria Italiana (the national rail network), the Museo d'Arte Moderna di Bologna (MAMbo), local musicians in the towns along the route, and Curran's select group of improvisers.

Curran's composition was the centerpiece of a three-day festival, organized by Simonini with Oderso Rubini, which also included two concerts of the music of John Cage (performed by the Bologna-based FontanaMIXensemble); an inaugural concert featuring Curran, Joan La Barbara, and Philip Corner; an exhibition at MAMbo of photographs, film footage, documents, and recordings of the 1978 event; and a performance by and for children at the Bologna Museo della Musica of Cage's work. As the musical director of this festival, Curran offered the title "Take the Cage Train," a name that slyly extended the frame of reference for most Cageans to include a few of Curran's own predilections: Ellington, jazz improvisation, and popular song.

While Cage's *Alla ricerca del silenzio perduto* took place on three train lines in three days, *Boletus Edulis* was restricted to a single line (the Bologna-Porreta Terme line) on two days (the weekend of May 31–June 1).[13] The piece began with a fifteen-minute prelude in Bologna's Central Train Station, where a group of ten to fifteen musicians (and nonmusicians) greeted the audience with an ambulatory amuse-bouche. Equipped with a harmonica and two blocks of wood, each musician followed the choreographic instructions of the composer: "Walk, stop, play. Walk, stop, play." Deep breaths in and out on the harmonicas were framed by pauses lasting three to ten seconds, while quadruple-*forte* claps on the wood blocks punctuated this breezy murmur at irregular intervals (also of three to ten seconds). At the close of this prelude, the performers led the audience to the platform where the departing train awaited, trading their wood and steel for plastic: corrugated plumbing tubes, to be specific, which they swung in fast circles to produce a different kind of ghostly susurrus (see Figure 6.1).

Upon arrival at the platform, the tubes were put to rest. Here the composer himself played the shofar in a quartet with vocalist Vincenzo Vasi, accordionist Luca Venitucci, and saxophonist Eugenio Colombo. They each played or sang five to seven very long, single tones (separated by pauses), before transitioning into a melodic improvisation that grew in intensity toward its point of culmination: a "FREAK OUT TOTALE!!!" (as the score has it) that lasted about two minutes (the quartet played for seven to ten minutes in toto). All the while, the Banda Roncati, an anarchist musicians' collective based in Bologna, played festive songs, such as "Roll out the Barrels," to see the piece, its performers, and its audience off to their next stop in Sasso Marconi.[14]

Before Sasso Marconi, however, came nearly twenty minutes on the train itself. The first five of these were enjoyed in silence—or, rather, in the ambient sounds of the train and its passengers. This relative quietude was soon broken, however, by the sounds of Curran's "Symphony of Train Sirens," an audio collage the composer prepared with recordings of train horns from around the world. Unlike the case of *Maritime Rites*, the "Symphony of Train Sirens" was not a result of the composer's own travels and site-specific recordings. Rather, he gathered his source recordings from the most obvious place: the internet. ("Isn't that what it's for?" he later asked with a chuckle.)[15] Portable stereos in each train car relayed the "Symphony" to its audience, while Venitucci and Colombo strolled from opposite ends of the train sounding very loud, horn-like bursts of their own.

This honking texture continued until the train arrived in Sasso Marconi, where there sat, on the platform, the cellist Tristan Honsinger, seemingly oblivious to his new audience. Honsiger improvised for about ten minutes as the audience stepped off the train and surrounded him, soon to be joined by Curran on shofar. Meanwhile, Curran's traveling troupe of improvisers—many of them wind players—had set themselves up in a nearby tunnel passageway, through which they led the audience into the town piazza. Sitting in the middle of this piazza was a baby grand piano, along with the pianist Marco Dalpane, who innocently entertained himself at the instrument in apparent ignorance of the audience who filtered in around him. The performance culminated with Curran, Honsiger, and the wind musicians surrounding Dalpane for a group improvisation. (Although Curran's score indicates that he intended the pianist to break away from this activity and lead a group of children playing small radios—an homage to Cage's *Imaginary Landscape No. 4*, but clearly not a "proper" performance of that composition—this ensemble never materialized for logistical reasons.)

After about twenty minutes in Sasso Marconi, the audience once again boarded the train and continued on to Riola, with a brief stop at Marzabotto to pick up the female chorus, Gruppo vocale Calicante, who sang resistance songs from the Second World War. (Marzabotto was a noted pocket of resistance against the Germans near the end of the war.) Once back on the train, the main musician group (of 10–15 players) split up into

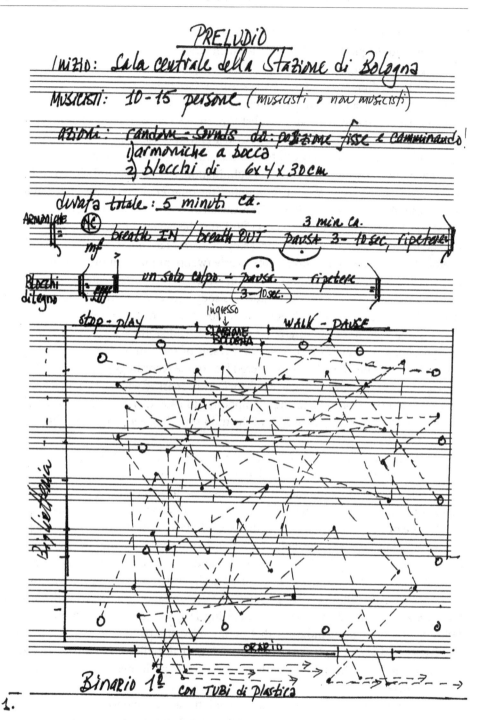

FIGURE 6.1 Alvin Curran, *Boletus Edulis—Musica Pendolare*, p. 1, used by permission of the composer.

groups of two or three per car, playing staccato, punchy patterns out of seven four-pitch aggregates supplied by the composer. The composer recalls that the intention was to create a minimalist sensibility using somewhat random means. Each aggregate sounds out roughly a triad with one added pitch—a lowered second (in cells 2 and 4), a lowered sixth (in cells 1 and 3), or a mixed-modal third (in cells 5 and 7). Harmonically, Curran generally favors sonorities centered on F (augmented, major, and minor triads) and B-flat (augmented and major). In terms of raw pitch content, the pitch-classes F and D occur with the greatest frequency (six and four times, respectively), though every pitch-class appears at least once (with one exception: G). After some time, Curran asks the musicians to select only two notes out of this mix, and to create "a personal improvisation" of figures and repeated notes, fragmented but with occasional legato sections. During this part of the journey, accordionist Venitucci and saxophonist Colombo again moved from car to car, in opposite directions, playing freely with the other musicians in each car.

The forty-five minutes spent in the town of Riolo presented some of the work's most spectacular moments. Upon arrival, the audience and musicians departed the train and walked a few minutes to the setting of the next musical episode, an austere yet luminous church designed by Finnish modernist Alvar Aalto in 1966 and built in the late 1970s.[16] The festivities began in the piazza, where two local brass bands, numbering a total of seventy or so musicians, performed material from some of Curran's recent compositions, most prominently *Oh Brass on the Grass Alas*.[17] They began by wandering freely around the site for five minutes, playing long, loud tones (with pitches specified by Curran) in a *sostenuto* cacophony—a return to the composer's "walk, stop, play" texture of the prelude. This activity transitioned into a four-minute version of another Curran standby, *Klaxon*, which is meant to approximate the sound of car horns in a traffic jam; the band's forces were divided into two choirs that traded bleeps and honks over a bed of softer trills. Following a three-minute percussion ad lib solo, the bands settled on a sustained drone, clustered around D-flat, which the performers carried into the church with their audience trailing behind. Awaiting them there was a women's chorus *in medias res*, already singing the same unison in anticipation of everyone's arrival.[18]

The church's interior is a massive, soaring space. "The acoustics in there are quite spectacular, as you might expect with a huge volume of space and all reflective surfaces of stone and cement and glass and so on," remarks Curran. "And so I really wanted to use that." This architecture was integral to the acoustic mixing and interpenetration of instrumental and vocal forces that began the next section of *Boletus Edulis*. Following a cue from their director, the band then dropped out to leave the chorus singing their unison alone, which they soon augmented with long tones on other pitches for about five minutes, getting increasingly softer. Curran then directed them to begin adding melodic shapes to this soft murmur, and Vasi served as an obbligato soloist with his voice and theremin simultaneously. This texture was brought to a frenzied finish via a several-minutes-long crescendo. Curran created this complex effect with minimal means:

This improvised chorus wasn't so improvised—they had very clear gestures describing how to make continually thickening textures. I all but wrote out all the notes, knowing that there was no time to study them, nor could this kind of group sing that kind of, let's call it 'Ligeti-esque masses of sound.' They're not trained, they're not professionals. But—if you ask them to *do* something like that, they do it beautifully. Not all groups can, but groups that want to brush their selves against some sort of contemporary essences, as it were, those people who are really interested in doing that, will really give it everything. And they can be even more interesting than professionals. Absolutely.

Just as the chorus was sonically "discovered" within the church upon the band's entrance at the beginning of this section, so too did the band "reappear" underneath the singers during their fortissimo sound masses. The composer directed these instrumentalists to add a "carpet" of accompanying sound by choosing pitches from a grand chord provided in the score (roughly, B-flat major with semitonal saturation in the upper partials to approximate the overtone series). The chorus then dropped out in accordance with a strictly timed cut-off, and the band continued to play while leading the audience back to the train.

This exit music, like the introductory fare leading into Aalto's church, was more or less strictly defined by Curran. First came five minutes in the piazza, with all musicians sounding long tones, loudly, in a somewhat limited range of specified pitches. After another brief percussion solo, the group moved through a series of cued passages in a section of the piece that may have appeared to be the most clearly organized: first, five more minutes of walk-stop-play, back to the platform, with more frantic and angular pitch material supplied by Curran; next, an ad libbed "staccatissimo" texture of two minutes; a unison D-flat for one to two minutes; another short passage of trills; a short percussion solo; and finally a cut off for everyone. Back on the train.

Once in place on their familiar means of travel, Venitucci and Colombo entertained the audience with such old chestnuts as "Besame Mucho" and "Around the World." The sonic texture wasn't all pleasing tunes, however, as Curran had also prepared a CD mix that combined the sounds of train horns and brakes screeching. To this noisy soundscape, Curran added the sounds of Italian pop hits from 1978 in a nod to popular taste at the time of Cage's original event.

For the journey's penultimate stop at Porretta Terme, Curran organized a "proper" concert (on a stage, with little movement, with audience members seated in chairs, and so on) that began with a reprise of the ambulatory prelude from Bologna—all knocks of wood, exhalations through harmonicas, and overtone whistles from plastic tubing. Curran's lead musicians (Honsinger, Dalpane, Colombo, Venittuci, Vasi, and others) improvised for about fifteen minutes onstage while other musicians strolled around the theater bouncing basketballs in casual punctuation. (This portion of the journey also offered an unintended tribute to the premiere of Cage's *Imaginary Landscape No. 4*. Written for twelve radios, *Imaginary Landscape* was performed at the end of a very long concert at Columbia's McMillin Theater in 1951. At that late hour, no radio stations were still broadcasting, so the work proceeded in near silence. In Porretta Terme, Curran's intention to begin the concert with three whistling tea kettles across the front of the stage was thwarted by hot plates that refused to provide enough heat to boil water.)

Poretta Terme is home to a thermal spa and famous for its porcini mushrooms, so for the hour following this mini-concert, the musicians, tech crew, and entire audience (up to 400 listeners) enjoyed a meal of polenta drenched in a porcini mushroom sauce, local cheeses, red wine, and cake. Prepared by a local branch of army retirees and their families, the meal was both an homage to Cage's love of mushrooms and a celebration of the gustatory offerings of the surrounding area. The veterans were members of the Bersaglieri, a celebrated infantry corps from the region who also maintained a rich choral tradition. Their brief performance concluded this chapter of the piece.

For the 75-minute trip back to Bologna, Curran directed the musicians to play and sing a "grande sostenuto UNISONO" on the pitch B-flat, a pitch that was also emanating from the portable stereos in each car. At the end of the day's performance, the composer reasoned, everyone would welcome the chance to be quietly escorted back to their point of origin on a single note, "like a magic carpet." This isn't exactly what occurred, however, since many of the musicians couldn't hold back.

> They started to key in to the drone, but, you know, improvisers of a certain kind sometimes, when they feel the calling, when something tells them, 'Nah, nah, I gotta go somewhere else,' then they just do it. And of course, that started a kind of contrapuntal story in the different cars, and different people were coming into the drone, and doing improvisational things around it, and they just made it up, basically.

As gifted an improviser as he is a composer, Curran couldn't really object. "They took the music into their own hands, as real anarchists would. . . . It was just beautiful."

Curran's reference to "real" anarchism seems to pose a subtle challenge to Cage's brand of hands-off musical anarchism and provides an opportunity to briefly consider the political history that lay beneath the surface of Cage's event in 1978. *Il Treno* was staged at the height of a fourteen-year span of turmoil known as the *Anni di piombo*, "years of lead" or "years of the bullet," during which period (1969–1983) over 12,000 acts of terrorism or politically motivated violence were perpetrated (Antonello and O'Leary 2009:1). The majority of these incidents took the form of bombing attacks in public spaces, the primary weapon of neofascist groups that sought to discredit the left and to create confusion and fear among the public (and thus, they hoped, generating a desire for an authoritarian, centralized state apparatus). For example, on August 2, 1980, less than two years after the performance of *Alla ricerca del silenzio perduto*, the central train station in Bologna was rocked by a massive explosion that claimed 85 lives and left 200 wounded. The consequent legal machinations that began in 1987 and continue to this day have revealed a tangled web of far-right extremist groups and shadowy governmental and Masonic organizations with a hand in the bombing (Bull 2007:21–22). It is widely believed that the right's "strategy of tension" during the 1970s was supported and funded in part by the US and British secret services, who had established "stay-behind" counterinsurgency forces in Western Europe following World War II in the event that a nation like Italy moved far to the left (as indeed it did—see Bull 2007 and Nuti 2007).

Although Curran and Cage were focused on anarchism in their musical processes, it was the communists who wielded power on the Italian left. Following astonishing electoral gains in the local elections of 1975 and the general election of 1976, the Partito Comunista Italiano forged a "historic compromise" with the ruling center-left coalition of the Christian Democrats. This compromise was shattered when the Second Red Brigades, a militant Marxist-Leninist organization critical of the compromise, kidnapped and subsequently killed the president of the Christian Democrats' National Council, Aldo Moro, in the spring of 1978. (Moro had also served as the Italian Prime Minister from 1963 to 1968 and from 1974 to 1976.) According to historian Donald Sassoon, Moro was the most senior politician to be assassinated by terrorists in Europe since the 1920s (1997:250–51). His body was found in Rome just over a month before the staging of Cage's *Il Treno*.

There are three salient differences in the ways that Cage and Curran approached the idea of music on a train; each of these differences sounds a variation on the theme of human agency in the musical drama of sound and motion. First is the status of non-elite musical traditions, which never held much attraction for Cage. In *Alla ricerca del silenzio perduto*, the songs of the people are only important to the extent that they added to the general noisiness of unimpeded, interpenetrating sounds. In this regard, I do not agree with Daniel Charles's reading of this piece as "ethnological or ethnographic" (1987–88:115). From my perspective, *Il Treno* shows no "ethnographic" interest in the people of Bologna other than as stochastic sound producers. (But Charles is nonetheless correct to describe Cage's resolutely materialist piece as "nothing abstract, nor theoretical.") Indeed, as Giampiero Cane has reported, the crowd only began spontaneously to sing Verdian tunes once *Il Treno* was finished for the day—on the journey back to Bologna, after the electronic equipment had been shut off and the train fell "silent." As Cane notes, these singers—like all participants in the event—were free from the beginning to produce any sounds they desired to contribute. "But they could not (or would not) do it in front of the art that imposed itself on their folklore, which only now [once the event was over for the day] could become *musique d'ameublement* and conquer the train's silence" (Cane 2008:25).

For Curran, however, vernacular musics are part of the lived sonic history of the region, and thus are included in *Boletus Edulis* as reminders of a world outside of the somewhat narrow concerns of the avant-garde. Regarding his tape mix of radio hits from the late 1970s, Curran comments, "The Italians particularly appreciated that, because it had that sense of humor, irony and tenderness, of really recalling history not through the avant-garde, but through the popular culture." Because he had lived in Italy since late 1964, Curran enjoyed a certain familiarity with Italian culture that Cage did not. He later remarked, "My advantage in being an adopted Italian is that I was really able to communicate with musicians and public in a very warm and familial way." Curran's mix of radio hits therefore seems to have resulted directly from a respectful decision *not* to allow his "art" to impose itself on his audience's "folklore." Nonetheless, the tradition of Italian *musica popolare* to which Curran referred is a complex one marked by ideological struggle, particularly after 1960, when Nuovo Canzoniere

Italiano emerged as a major cultural movement on the left (Bermani 1997). Curran may not have been aware of the many associations of the term *musica popolare* (which in the 1960s and 1970s meant "music of the people" in a leftist sense—folk songs, communist tunes, and music of the proletariat broadly construed—rather than Anglophone radio hits), but in the end it may not have mattered: the tape mix was not compiled by Curran, but rather by his friend, Oderso Rubini, who had been an important producer in the Italian post-punk scene and who also happened to have attended the original 1978 performance.

Another difference between these two works was the extent to which electronics were employed. *Il Treno* was undoubtedly the more impressive technological feat (can we imagine such a massive undertaking these days?)—impressive enough, perhaps, to dissuade Curran from even trying to compete. "I just wanted to keep it to people and acoustics. [That was] complicated enough," he remarks. Although Curran did place a few portable stereos throughout the train in order to present his "Symphony of Train Sirens" and mix of popular tunes, most revealing was an idea that was *not* included in the final version of *Boletus Edulis*. "I wanted to place an electronic keyboard in the train that the audience could play, and it would activate a number of real train horns placed on the train itself, outside," Curran explains. "So as we went through the countryside or into a station, somebody or anybody could sit at this keyboard and be playing these powerful, different kinds of train horns." Although scuttled by train authorities for reasons of safety and acoustic ecology, the idea for a train-horn keyboard envisions a kind of audience interaction that places greater weight—and, in the end, responsibility—in the hands of the listener-performers than is imaginable in Cage's *Treno*.

A final difference between Curran and Cage turns on the place of improvisation in their aesthetics. Curran articulates this difference along the lines of structure and spontaneity: "The fundamental difference is—and this is a generational one, it's an ideological one, and at the end of the day, it's a truly musical one—John was the ultimate structuralist. I'm an anti-structuralist. The kinds of chaos that I generate are sloppy, imprecise, *truly* unpredictable—and desirably so. John would never permit that...." By using chance to deny musicians recourse to their memories and egos, Cage sought to guarantee a stochastic sonic texture that bubbled and scraped with the shaky rhythms of indeterminacy. Curran explored a different route to these sloppy, unpredictable textures, one that began *precisely* from the position that Cage wanted to erase:

> I'm embracing the raw, emotional power of people unleashing themselves in sound and through sound. Not in a ragged and unreasoned, illogical, and primitive way, as it might be thought, but in what I consider to be a very labored evolution of a language in which accidental collisions of sounds and tones and densities will produce inevitably exciting moments in which the protagonists, the musicians themselves, can act on freely. This cannot happen in John's music. He was an anti-improvisational.... John's music is also totally spontaneous, taken from a certain perspective, but it's obedience to the rigor of time and instruction and commitment to that precision. It's like Swiss clockwork.

Although their methodologies proceeded in such different directions, Curran's homage to his mentor and friend stops far short of repudiation. And how could it not? As many have noted, the sheer audacity of works like the 1978 happening opened up the musical playing field for Cage's successors, Curran included. By the time of *Il Treno*, Cage was a world-class celebrity, and he loved it. On the surface, the piece was a multi-channel celebration, but it celebrated its author above all. Curran is no less partial to the position of genius-creator that Cage was, but, as works like *Boletus Edulis* make clear, he holds a deep affection for the little guy. "[T]he guiding principles still remain the same," he remarked of the range of his compositions, "that all human beings are not only potentially but virtually musical beings" (Curran 1985).

# Acknowledgments

I would like to thank Alvin Curran, Susan Levenstein, Massimo Simonini, D. J. Hoek, and Jennifer Ward for their assistance with this chapter.

## Notes

1. See Beal 2009.
2. The following account of the event is based on Cage (1977). The score is reprinted, with beautiful photographs, sound recordings, and a short film on DVD, in Gotti et al. (2008).
3. Tito Gotti to John Cage, March 5, 1977, John Cage Correspondence, Northwestern University Music Library (hereafter "JCC"). Giacomo Manzoni clarified Gotti's antipathy for traditional concert presentations (whether for new or old compositions) in a conversation with me on January 15, 2011.
4. Cage to Gotti, March 12, 1977, JCC.
5. Panni to Cage, March 25, 1977, JCC.
6. Cage to Panni, April 10, 1977, JCC.
7. Gotti to Cage, April 12, 1977, JCC. I cannot locate Cage's letter to Gotti agreeing to the summer 1978 performance, but Gotti refers to this document (dated April 20) in a letter of August 2, 1977.
8. Cage to Gotti, December 2, 1977, JCC.
9. Cage to Panni, April 10, 1977, JCC.
10. See also Cage (1979).
11. Undated mesostic, JCC, box 2, folder 2. The final term "componibile 3" was used as an informal title for Cage's piece, which was the third in a series of pieces written for Gotti's Feste Musicali in the 1970s. The Italian word describes something consisting of discrete parts that can be assembled into a whole; it is typically used in the context of modular kitchens, or "cucina componibile."
12. See Cage (1979); this text dates from Cage's pre-macrobiotic days in 1975.
13. The following account of *Boletus Edulis* is based on Curran, interview with author, October 17, 2008; Curran, telephone interview with author, August 30, 2009; the manuscript of

the score (in author's possession); video documentation of the event on Curran's website, www.alvincurran.com; and photo documentation in Casanova (2008).

14. See the band's Facebook page: https://www.facebook.com/pages/BANDA-RONCATI/308780495297.

15. Curran, interview with author, October 17, 2008. All subsequent Curran quotations are drawn from this interview.

16. This episode in Aalto's church only occurred on one of the two days of performance. On the other day, the bands continued to play in the piazza in front of the church for an extended time before returning to the train.

17. The first of these bands, the Banda Bignardi di Monzuno, was directed by Alessandro Marchi; the second, directed by Claudio Carboni, was an amalgamation of three smaller groups: Banda Giuseppi Verdi Riola; Banda Giuseppi Verdi Poretta; and Corpo Bandistico Gaggese.

18. The chorus was Coro Arcanto, directed by Gloria and Giovanna Giovannini.

## REFERENCES

Antonello, Pierpaolo, and Alan O'Leary, eds. 2009. *Imagining Terrorism: The Rhetoric and Representation of Political Violence in Italy 1969–2009*. London: Modern Humanities Research Association and Maney Publishing.

Beal, Amy C. 2009. "'Music is a Universal Human Right': Musica Elettronica Viva." In *Sound Commitments: Avant-garde Music and the Sixties*, ed. Robert Adlington, 99–120. New York: Oxford University Press.

Bermani, Cesare. 1997. *Una Storia Cantata, 1962–1997: Trentacinque Anni di Attività del Nuovo Canzoniere Italiano/Istituto Ernesto de Martino*. Milan: Jaca.

Bull, Anna Cento. 2007. *Italian Neofascism: The Strategy of Tension and the Politics of Nonreconciliation*. New York: Berghahn Books.

Cage, John. 1977. *Alla ricerca del silenzio perduto*. John Cage Music Manuscript Collection, New York Public Library, JBP 94-24 Folder 543.

——. 1979. "What Are We Eating? and Where Are We Eating?" In *Empty Words: Writings '73–'78*, 79–80. Hanover, NH: Wesleyan University Press.

Cane, Giampiero. 2008. "On the Tracks of the Imaginary." In *Alla ricerca del silenzio perduto*, Gotti et al., 20–25. Bologna: Baskerville.

Casanova, Claudio. 2008. "Take the Cage Train—terza e ultima parte." *All About Jazz*, July 2, http://italia.allaboutjazz.com/php/article.php?id=2951 (accessed October 29, 2009).

Charles, Daniel. [1978] 1987–1988. "Alla ricerca del silenzio perduto: Notes sur le 'train de John Cage.'" *Revue d'Esthétique* (new series, nos. 13–15), 111–21.

Curran, Alvin. 1985. "Making Music with People You Have Never Seen Before and Will Likely Never See Again." Available at Curran's website, www.alvincurran.com (accessed October 29, 2009).

——. 2007. "Oh Brass on the Grass Alas." *The Score: Four Innovative American Composers Sound Off* [blog], *New York Times*, March 27, www.nytimes.com (accessed July 17, 2009).

Gotti, Tito, et al. 2008. *Alla ricerca del silenzio perduto: Il Treno di John Cage: 3 escursioni per treno preparato*. Bologna: Baskerville.

Nuti, Leopoldo. 2007. "The Italian 'Stay-Behind' Network—The Origins of Operation 'Gladio.'" *Journal of Strategic Studies* 30(6):955–80.

Revill, David. 1992. *The Roaring Silence*. New York: Arcade.

Rockwell, John. 1983. "Concert: Curran's Music and Burckhardt's Films." *New York Times*, July 22.

Sassoon, Donald. 1997. *Contemporary Italy: Economy, Society and Politics since 1945*. 2nd ed. London: Longman.

Tortora, Daniela Margoni, ed. 2010. *Alvin Curran: Live in Roma*. Milan: Die Schachtel.

# PART III

# WALKING AND BODILY CHOREOGRAPHY

CHAPTER 7

························································

# CREATIVE SONIFICATION OF MOBILITY AND SONIC INTERACTION WITH URBAN SPACE: AN ETHNOGRAPHIC CASE STUDY OF A GPS SOUND WALK

························································

FRAUKE BEHRENDT

THIS chapter explores how mobile media and sound are experienced and in particular how locative technologies such as GPS can be used for the creative sonification of mobility. This is realized by examining *Aura—the stuff that forms around you* (hereafter *Aura*), a 2007 artwork by Steve Symons. In this work, participants equipped with headphones and a GPS-enabled backpack explore a city while listening to generative sounds that depend on their movement and location, as well as on how many people have been in the same location before. *Aura* was premiered at the "Enter_Unknown Territories" (hereafter "Enter_") festival in Cambridge (United Kingdom) in April 2007.[1] The piece adds an invisible digital sound layer to the existing architecture of Cambridge. It forces you to move, as standing still produces increasing "noise." Because earlier participants have already left behind a trail of "noise," you are "forced" to move onto un-walked territory. *Aura* changes your perception as you pay attention to a different architecture, to the sound art layer added by the artist. The experience provokes you to reexamine your senses and makes you think about the use of space and about the sharing of space. One participant recalls her experience as follows:

> I was deliberately trying to find places where I didn't think people had been before. The sound was horrible when I first put it on. It was very loud; I had to pull the headphones away from my ears. Very urban and gritty sounding. And then, as I walked towards the trees it just fell silent, and it was really lovely hearing, something that was really mad suddenly became silent.[2]

This account by an *Aura* participant gives us a first-hand impression of how people experienced and described the piece. I conducted semi-structured interviews with participants after they returned from their *Aura* walk (all names have been changed), observed participants, and took photographs and video. I also conducted an hour-long interview with the artist Symons on site and participated in *Aura* myself. The interviewees proved to be very articulate in discussing their sonic, embodied, and mobile experiences. This chapter discusses the themes that were articulated in the interviews with participants and the artist in light of de Certeau's arguments developed in *The Practice of Everyday Life* (1984) about spatial practices in urban space—such as the distinction between views from above and maps as *reading* and the embodied mobility of walking paths as *writing*.

## THE GPS SOUND PIECE *AURA*: SONIFYING MOBILITY

At the "Enter_" festival premiere of *Aura*, the main festival area was located on Parker's Piece (a park in the center of Cambridge), consisted of various tents, and had no entrance fee (Figure 7.1). The *Aura* checkout station was located in one of these tents (Figure 7.2), alongside various other media and sound pieces, many of which invited the audience to explore the urban environment. The fine weather on this spring weekend enabled most festival visitors to enjoy the sun outside and not spend much time inside the tents.

Parker's Piece was a busy public space. People walked on their own and in groups, some with children or dogs, either "going for a walk in the park" or just crossing the green on their way through the town. Many people also spent a considerable amount of time in the park, where all sorts of activities took place: picnics, football games, people watching, cricket practice, children's games, and so forth. Each of these groups occupied their own chosen section of the park, marking football goals with bags and coats, using trees for shade, putting down blankets as tables, and so on. This existing busy outdoor setting formed the backdrop for several of the mobile media pieces that were part of the "Enter_" festival, including *Aura*.

The "Enter_" festival was one of events taking place in the park, although in a more organized and permanent manner than the others. It consisted of a group of white tents housing a reception area, a café, and exhibitions of artworks. The festival area was intended to be open to attract a wide audience. However, given that many artworks relied on specific (and, in some cases, expensive) technology and equipment, the camp was surrounded by fences (and there were also several security guards), and thus did not look as inviting as I would have imagined. The lack of an entrance fee was intended to make it inviting to passers-by. But in fact, the vast majority of people I observed and talked to in the camp came explicitly for the event.

The tents forming the camp had a special dome shape, which was visually appealing, but due to being inflated (much like a bouncy castle) they were sonically challenging

FIGURE 7.1 The main "Enter_" festival area on Parker's Piece, Cambridge (United Kingdom), 2007.

environments. The fans inflating the tents produced a constant background noise that interfered with the overall sonic experience. While *Aura* and several other mobile pieces were meant to be experienced within the broader environs of the park, participants first needed to enter the tents to access each piece's "base station." Here, they familiarized themselves with the requirements of each piece (see Figure 7.2). This set-up influenced the kinds of participants *Aura* had, and, therefore, my interviewees. They were not "everyday" people walking through the park, happening to stumble upon the festival and the piece. The interviewees were people already interested in media art who had decided to attend the festival, and *Aura* was one of the pieces they experienced there.

 *Aura* is described as a "multi-layered soundscape immersive game" on the festival website (Enter_). The artist labels it as a "located sound project" on his website and explains that *Aura* "explores notions of consumption and ownership within a space by allowing users to leave an audio trail as they move within the Real World." He chooses to describe the piece further by using a visual metaphor:

> Imagine a playing field after a fresh falling of snow. The snow lies evenly and untrod-den. This represents an empty *Aura* sound world and, if you wore an *Aura* backpack, would sound like soft white noise. Someone walks across the field leaving footprints,

FIGURE 7.2 Inside one of the festival tents, staff (on the right) is explaining *Aura* to festival visitors at the "base stations" (far right) that double as checkout point.

> the snow is sullied, eroded; the walker has left a patina in the world. In the *Aura* world this patina is represented by filtering applied to the soft white noise. So a user walking with an *Aura* backpack will hear soft white noise (virgin snow) then lower tones will emerge as they cross the path left previously by another *Aura* user. (Symons, "artworks/ aura")

In the interview I conducted, Symons further explains his motivation for creating *Aura* and talks about the technology behind it. It is interesting to note how he uses visual (painting) metaphors in his account:

> It's about consumption.... The interest in the idea that there is only a certain amount of art work out there and it gets consumed. So each user makes a path-, should make a permanent effect on it.... So the start of everything is blank. and it's my virgin, pure world which sounds hüüa or eee or chichi, depending. And as soon as the GPS starts reading it starts painting on this world.... This consumption is shown in terms of that the sounds change, they get more distorted.... Because people are coming out of the back of our domes.... This is all consumed. So people have to walk further and further.... Little spots emerge which haven't been consumed. So you get little deposits of value.[3]

The whole *Aura* system consists of stationary base stations (Figure 7.3) and mobile back-packs (Figure 7.4) and is designed to be self-sufficient, to function without the artist's supervision. The base stations are located in one of the festival tents and serve as check-out desks for the backpacks. Screens located in the base stations also visually display previous participants' paths. The backpacks contain a custom-built computer attached to large, binaural headphones. The sound of the piece is not prerecorded; it is gener-ated in real-time, depending on the participant's movement and on prior "consump-tion" of sounds by others. *Aura* is a custom-made, open-source surround-sound system. Symons explains the system design of *Aura*, outlining the development of the backpacks and the software:

> The backpacks are bespoke systems; they are the worlds first solid-state Linux sur-round sound systems.... As far as I know. Six channel Linux. It's all using open source software.... I have used Java.... And for the sound I have used Supercollider.... Plus there is associated hardware for compass and GPS, and then there are battery issues, recharging. And what happens when you plug it in. Then it has to talk to the server, so there is a network.[4]

The technical side of this piece is complex and utilizes an approach different than that of other mobile sound artists, who often use off-the-shelf solutions like mscape.[5]

Although *Aura* is a sound work, it also has a visual aspect: the trails of people's walks are displayed on the base stations (Figure 7.3). In our interview, the artist noted that he was not happy with the audience reaction to this visual aspect of the piece: "I'm a bit upset, everyone is obsessing over seeing their map. And that's the last thing I want them to do.... I want people to walk." I asked Symons to explain how he came to incorporate this visual aspect, especially as his earlier *Aura 1* from 2004 did not feature any screens. He replied:

> Two things. One, they need to have a recharge point. And two, *Aura 1* the galler-ies were going: what's in my gallery when *Aura* is out? Bags? ID? And people were like: "Oh, not very..." And I get little tables in the corner, and people put all their coats on there 'cause they'd see all my backpacks. So it got a bit like, ok I need to work in installation more.[6]

The artist is not entirely comfortable about the piece's visual mapping and I share his unease. Symons explains how the relation between walking and the visuals were negoti-ated in the design of the piece:

> There was this massive designing to work out what goes on at these base sta-tions.... so there's the base station [he is drawing while talking], walking, so listen-ing, and then,... returning to base station. If these base stations are too satisfying, too interactive, they're not gonna walk. And it's the walk that I want people to do. The art is walking. It's not here. This is just a practical lure. Ok, it looks nice, a nice box.[7]

This distinction between the visual mapping at the base stations and the embodied walk-ing out in the park resonates with de Certeau's theory of strategies and tactics, wherein

FIGURE 7.3 Two of the *Aura* base stations in one of the tents. The screens were supposed to display the visualizations of previous participant's paths, and headphones would allow listening to the corresponding sounds.

walking is understood as tactical, mapping as strategic. For de Certeau, strategies belong to the sphere of institutions and power structures, while tactics are in the realm of everyday actions by ordinary people. The reception of de Certeau's concepts has often focused on the potential of resistance in the tactical realm. Mapping involves "flattening-out," to use de Certeau's term: "time and movement are thus reduced to a line that can be seized as a whole by the eye and read in one single moment, as one projects onto a map the path taken by someone walking through a city" (de Certeau 1984:35). The ease and pleasure of appropriating temporal activity in one glance, as opposed to the effort of walking and listening, is what makes both Symons and me feel critical about the visual part of his work—and explains why galleries and curators are so attracted to it. From the artist's statements given above we can understand how Symons was ambiguous about the path visualization of *Aura*: While it satisfies the quick gaze of the passing festival visitor and has a more robust presence in the gallery, the "real" piece is in the act of walking, away from the screens (Figure 7.5).

De Certeau has been discussed in the context of mobile art and hybrid spaces but not with reference to sound (Kraan 2006; Kluitenberg 2006; Altena 2006; Souza e Silva 2004). One of those considerations of de Certeau is by Tarkka, who notes that "The

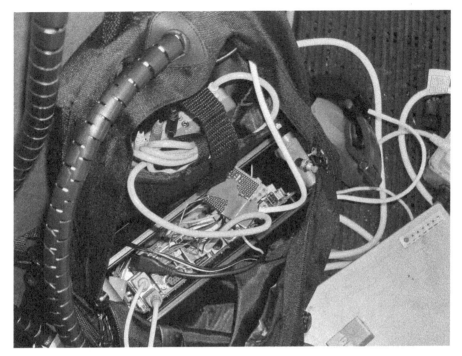

FIGURE 7.4 Custom-made hardware and software inside one of the *Aura* backpacks.

'locative gaze' conflates a god's eye view—the frozen military 'view from nowhere' of satellite vision and atomic clocks—with the situated, embodied 'pedestrian perspective'...coincid[ing] with Michael de Certeau's distinction between strategy and tactic" (2005:17). Tarkka elaborates: "The participatory annotation of urban space fits well into de Certeau's description of tactical practice—for what else is annotation than a writing in the margins, a commentary which is never taking the space over in its entirety?" (20).

De Certeau is very aware of the spatial component of practice, and this is productive for understanding mobile media: "In the technocratically constructed, written, and functionalized space in which the consumers move about, their trajectories form unforeseeable sentences, partly unreadable paths across space" (1984:xviii). Whereas space is often understood as an abstract concept and place as a lived-in space with some sort of meaning attached to it, in de Certeau's conceptualization the meanings are inverted. De Certeau divides space into viewed space and experienced space (which is process), and links this to his concept of tactics and strategies: "To walk is to lack place" (103). A principal aspect of the piece *Aura* is that the artist wants "people to walk" because "the art is walking" as he states in the interview.[8] During a public presentation of the piece at the festival he added that walking is also "very instinctive" (Symons 2007). Even though walking is instinctive, it is still work: the labor of walking and the attention the participants need to pay while walking and listening to *Aura* are asking more of the audience than most traditional pieces of visual or sound art.

FIGURE 7.5 An *Aura* participant (centre) is walking out of the festival area into the park, where other people are going for a walk (left) among many other activities.

De Certeau draws our attention away from city planning and toward actual situated activities, the space-making practices of the inhabitants of a city that make do with the planned space in various different ways, in "swarming activities of these procedures" (1984:96). It is interesting to pay attention to how these swarming procedures have changed with ubiquitous mobile media use. A close look at *Aura* allows us to do this. De Certeau believes that "the spatial practices in fact secretly structure the determining conditions of social life" (96). And our spatial practices are mediated ones. He aims to "follow out a few of these multiform, resistant, tricky, and stubborn procedures that elude discipline without being outside the field in which exercised and which should lead us to a theory of everyday practices, of lived space, of the disquieting familiarity of the city" (96). The present chapter is doing something similar: finding disquieting familiarities in the sonic world created by the participants of mobile art; discovering how space is lived in ever more commercialized and privatized urban spaces, with technology designed by the telecommunications industry to secure ever greater profits; locating resistant and creative practices while avoiding any romanticizing of these. *Aura* is one manifestation of creative space-making practices, pushing away from totalizing views, and toward the very activity of inscribing movement into space via sound.

De Certeau suggests that we try "to locate practices that are foreign to the 'geometrical' or 'geographical' space of ... visual, panoptic, or theoretical constructions" (1984:93). For me, this sounds like a call for giving priority to the auditory but, for de Certeau, this other spatiality, these "practices of space" are a specific way of operating "an opaque and blind mobility" (93). He juxtaposes the "planned and readable city" with this other city that is made up of spatial practices, "a migrational, or metaphorical city" (93). He switches from totalizing vision to the movement of bodies.

The way GPS coordinates are often used in mobile and locative art projects can resonate with de Certeau's totalizing vision from the World Trade Center (1984:93).[9] The way one "sees" the movement of the city at once from a distance and from color-coded GPS traces suggests that it is possible to grasp the city and the mobile movements it is made from with one glance. Often it is forgotten or marginalized that the actual experience of these urban journeys—these movements of bodies through the city with their idiosyncratic, subjective, multi-sensory layered experiences—are complex and cannot be grasped in one fell swoop. This experience is reflected in the following account of David, one of the *Aura* participants: "I did feel slightly odd for the fact that I was walking around in circles but I was trying to get away from the sound."[10]

In *The Practice of Everyday Life*, de Certeau rarely makes sound productive in his descriptions. His accounts of everyday observations are strangely silent. For example, he talks about the "mute silences of memories." However there are few instances where he is attuned to the sounds of the world; for example he contradicts his "silent memories" by recounting "a walk though the night, alive with sound" (1984:15). He is talking about a visit to Brazil; and from the same trip he remembers "the songs of the Brazilian *saudade*" (15). Elsewhere, he discusses reading and talks about "grumblings, tics, stretchings, rustlings, unexpected noises, in short a wild orchestration of the body" (175). De Certeau's attention to sound seems to be connected with internal, bodily and private realms, with foreign cultures and with technologies (see the train description below) but not with everyday or Western culture. The public realm of the Western city is especially silent in his accounts.

Even when describing footsteps—as making up the city in their multiplicity of movements, weaving places together by this space-making practice of walking—his is a mute account. There is no sound to the footsteps in de Certeau's descriptions, no heels clicking, no trainers being dragged, no polyphony of feet running down stairs. He is concerned with the temporality and the movement, but not with the sound. I argue that sound is a good reminder of temporality and spatiality: the echo of our footprints in the under-path is gone within fractions of a second while we are one step ahead already. The only time de Certeau mentions sound in connection with walking, he resorts to metaphor: "Walking affirms, suspects, tries out, transgresses, respects etc., the trajectories it speaks. All the modalities *sing a part in this chorus*, changing from step to step, stepping in through proportions, sequences, and intensities which vary according to the tie, the path taken and the walker" (de Certeau 1984:99; my emphasis). This focus on walking bodies and their trajectories is productive for mobile sound art: "The ordinary practitioners of the city live...they walk—an elementary form of this experience of the city; they are walkers, *Wandersmänner*, whose bodies follow the thicks and thins of the urban text, they write without being able to read it" (de Certeau 1984:93; author's emphasis).

De Certeau understands walking as a form of (tactical) writing and looking down on the city (the totalizing views as he describes them from the top of the World Trade

Center) as a form of (strategic) map reading. So, to walk is to write, to look is to read. Therefore, you cannot read the city while you are in it, you can only write it, because the map is an authored work. For him, paths are what you walk through "blind," trajectories you push out with your body, and they do not necessarily have to follow roads (even if they do). The fact that you take a meandering path, or the fact that you always walk *these* steps and not *those* steps, is the process of writing your own trajectory. This trajectory is not known exactly to others before you actually perform it.

This distinction that takes "views" as reading and "embodied movement" as writing is a rather visual one. If we follow de Certeau's suggestion to "[e]scap[e] the imaginary totalization produced by the eye" (1984:93) we should ask how reading and writing can operate in sonic ways too. What is the auditory equivalent of a view from above, of a map, of a path? For sonic reading you might have to be in the midst of the city, as listening from above or from a distance gives you a faint din, and possibly a few soundmarks, but no "overview" or map-like view of a city. To "read" the sounds of a city, there is no soundmap; you need to be in the streets, walking, listening to the city: to cars before crossing the road, the train pulling into the station, the busker in the park, a conversation on a mobile phone, music spilling out of a shop, the wind howling around the corner. Listening and walking might have features of both writing and reading. The temporal effort of listening and writing also suggest this connection, whereas the scopic snapshot from above is an effortless one.

In many mobile or locative art pieces, the participants need to walk in order to experience the work.[11] The choices each participant makes in terms of direction, length of the walk, and time spent in specific locations, determine the participant's experience of the piece. Each audience member makes his or her own version, and walking becomes remixing. Galloway and Ward, for example, describe how this practice allows "for multiple readings" of "narrative fragments [fixed] in physical space" (2006).

Hight (2006) also contributes to the understanding of walking as remixing in a text that focuses on locative narratives (especially those with a historic context) or, what he terms "Narrative Archeology."[12] His insistence on prioritizing the role of the situated experience of a walking audience is key for my understanding of mobile sound art. The participant determines the timeline of the experience: the order of the locations, the time spent at each location or in each sound zone, the pace, direction and duration of their walk. For his own narrative pieces Hight observes that:

> In a sense, the ultimate end-author in locative narrative is the movement and patterns of the person navigating the space. The narrative is dictated by their choices, aesthetic bias in the physical world toward certain sections, buildings or objects to move toward and investigate and their duration and breadth of movement. The narrative is composed in sections, but is edited by the movements of the person with the locative device. (2006:3)

Walking is intrinsically temporal—and the same is true for sound. Therefore, mobile sound art experience is difficult to reduce to a point or line on a map, a link, a database entry. The embodied mobility of walking, especially as articulated in public space, is a key aspect of mobile sound art.

In mobile sound art works such as *Aura*, the audience writes sound into space, but also simultaneously reads the existing soundscape as well as the added "virtual" sound layer. I argue that the distinction between reading and writing becomes less clear cut in an auditory context, where embodied trajectories might be able to do both: read and write.

# FRICTION

One of the *Aura* participants I interviewed was twenty-seven-year-old Ben who lives in London and works for a theater company. He came to Cambridge for the festival to "get some ideas" for a project he was working on. Ben recalls his *Aura* experience: "I kind of felt a bit detached from where I was. So that the place where I was wasn't as important as what I was hearing."[13] By focusing his attention on the auditory layer of the piece, Ben felt "detached" from his surroundings. His comment prioritizes the auditory space over the physical environment, in a manner similar to Bassett (2003:348), who describes how mobile telephony is constantly shifting between "attention" and "inattention" and often "prioritizes the auditory at the expense of the embodied and visual world." I suggest that de Certeau offers another metaphor that is useful for describing the economy of these different spaces we inhabit in the hybrid city. As discussed earlier, footsteps are silent in De Certeau's descriptions of the city–whereas his account of traveling by rail is all about sound:

> Only the partitions make noise. As it [the train] moves forward and creates two inverted silences, it taps out a rhythm, it whistles or moans. There is a beating of the rails, a vibrato of the windowpanes—a sort of *rubbing together of spaces* at the vanishing points of their frontier. These junctions have no space. They indicate themselves by passing cries and momentary noises. These frontiers are *illegible*; they can only be heard as a single stream of sounds, so continuous is the tearing off that annihilates the points which it passes. (1984:112–13; my emphasis)

De Certeau describes the mobile technology of railway travelling as "rubbing together of spaces" and this metaphor can also be productive for contemporary mobile technologies of mobile phones, iPods, and mobile art. If the "rubbing together of spaces" cannot be read, I suggest listening to it instead. *Aura* provides an opportunity to explore virtual and geographic, sonic, and imagined spaces "rubbing together." The artwork seems to allow for an alternative spatial experience: "in a way . . . it forces you to think about how you're walking through a space in a completely different way," as Ben described.[14] I argue that we can conceptualize this "different way" of walking through space, the sensation of "feeling a bit detached," as various "spaces rubbing together." Such a conceptualization allows us to think about the kind of friction that is generated by all these different media, sound, social and physical layers rubbing together in our encounters with (and within) contemporary urban spaces. By participating in *Aura*, a new hybrid sonic architecture is produced, one that is temporal and embedded and embodied. It is not commercial but an art space, with a different economy of power; for example, participants are allowed to fail, to take off the headphones, to invent their own path, to do it in their own time.

## Sound and Control

With *Aura*, interaction with other participants happens over time. In theory, several of the backpacks could be out on a walk simultaneously. (Although at the "Enter_" festival this did not happen as only one was working and charged at a time.) You can detect traces of previous walkers, the trails of noise they left behind. Most mobile art projects work with the idea of "positive" traces, of leaving behind something "nice" or "interesting," such as messages for others, audio snippets, colorful trails (Behrendt 2012a). For *Aura* the opposite is the case: you leave behind something undesirable, you do not want to go where others have been, you want to find the un-consumed areas, the pleasant white noise, unexplored space, as indicated by "nice" sounds. Others have left behind trails of noise before, taking away choice from us; they have consumed some of the pleasant sounds already. This equates to a great deal of sonic control in *Aura*, as the noise makes people walk, forces them to explore virgin sonic territory. The artist had to negotiate these issues of control when he designed *Aura*. His account is ambivalent:

> I can't, you can't make the audience do anything. I've realized. [laughing] Although I really want to make a maze. [laughing] That's a real control of it. I want to control them. They will do what I tell them. [laughing] ... But even then, if you make a maze, with sound, where the walls are made of sounds, you know, you have to keep in the quiet bit, people will just walk over them. So you can't.[15]

The artist realizes that he has no means to control the audience trajectories:

> You just have to try not to, I have decided. I make the system; I make it as flexible as I can. I set the direction of it ... and then let the users do their thing. 'Cause if I try to anticipate everything ... I mean they can, like 500 meters square, they can walk in any direction, at any speed ... there's nothing I can do about that [laughing].[16]

These claims suggest that participants can "walk in any direction" but if we take his above comments into consideration, it becomes clear that those areas that are already "consumed" by previous participants are so unpleasant that they force subsequent participants to walk elsewhere. The system the artist developed does control the audience trajectories by sonic means.

Another aspect of sonic control—in addition to the nice sounds vs. noise—revolves around volume. According to David: "there is this noise you can't get away from. Mmmm, other than taking off the headphones."[17] As I recall from my own experience of *Aura*, the piece was very loud. While I was walking around the park, I tried to find the volume control on the device. Even though I had been told that there was none, I still couldn't resist searching for one. This issue of volume control is also illustrated in the audio recording of my own experience, in a conversation between a festival helper (Mary) and myself Mary advises me: "You may need to pull it away from your ears a bit as you go out here because it's noisy, it's quite loud."[18]

The issue of control of sound adds to the discussion around mobile media and music in urban space (Kirisits et al. 2008) and how people aim to control the experience of urban environment and their moods with mobile music (Bull 2000, 2007). *Aura* has an ambiguous relationship to sonic control: Participants do control the sound by inscribing a path of noise, but unlike with the use of a portable media player, they are not able to choose the sounds they hear. And, further, they have no control over their encounters with the trails of noise left by other participants.

# FEELING SELF-CONSCIOUS

Another theme that consistently came up in interviews had to do with the participants feeling "self-conscious." In relation to their everyday mobile media use, this is remarkable. In everyday life, mobile media has becomes increasingly invisible and non-self-conscious (as illustrated by the spread of the mobile phone). Nowadays, having a mobile phone with you is the default position; one is only is conscious of it in its absence, as Ben's statement illustrates:

> I was really conscious of it [*Aura*] in a way that I'm not particularly conscious of my phone anymore. Although that's always a weird one, isn't it? 'Cause if I ever leave my phone, then I'm very conscious of not having it... and I remember when I first got one feeling very much like I was connected to something, something new and something else... and... yeah, so I think there is definitely something akin to that early feeling of when I first got a mobile phone.[19]

In *Aura*, participants try to locate this self-consciousness in the actual technology. Ben continues:

> I think, it's quite weird because you're kind of walking around feeling expectant of something to happen, and my focus was definitely on the fact that I had this thing, this equipment with me and also, you do get a few strange looks from people with this weird thing on top of your head and people are not quite sure what to make of you.[20]

David—a filmmaker from Cambridge in his late twenties who is "quite intrigued by…all sorts of installations…sound installations"—also felt self-conscious. In our interview, he first mentions the equipment and then realizes that he is not the only one equipped like this.[21] His next explanation is that his movement in space made him feel self-conscious, as this did not match more common forms of walking around the park.

> It was kind of an unusual experience because it wasn't like you stand out wearing a headphones and a backpack, 'cause many people wear headphones and a backpack. I did feel slightly odd for the fact that I was walking around in circles but I was trying to get away from the sound.[22]

David tried to inscribe his name onto the space, claiming territory, using the virtual space to claim physical space, to make the hybrid space his own by walking his name—and again feels watched, self-conscious.

> And the other thing which I realized that you could do with the GPS was that you can, once that's traced, you could write letters and things like…I was trying to spell my name out on Parker's Piece, so that was probably something else that people might have been watching me. Sort of "what the hell is he doing." Kind of walking around in sort of strange shapes.[23]

Emma is from Norfolk but "used to live near Cambridge." She is thirty-three and works with her "husband in a[n] artist collaboration."[24] Emma is somewhat self-conscious about her media use in general, and also about mobile media use in public. Not fitting in with the crowd, her unusual mobile media behaviors (such as stopping while everyone is walking) make her feel uncomfortable, even vulnerable. This unease also applies to her *Aura* experience: "But also because you've got this big thing on your head you know that people, you're looking different, you're not blending in like you normally do [laughing]."[25] Later on in the interview she tries to explain her awareness of other people by her changed sense of hearing: "I think I was just really aware of all the people on Parker's Piece. I had to sort of negotiate a football game. And I felt like I was more likely to be kicked by a football because I couldn't, I didn't have my own hearing. You know what I mean. I was locked into this."[26]

Wearing the small *Aura* backpack and the headphones does not make you look much different than music aficionados you meet in the city. Still, the participants felt self-conscious about walking around with the *Aura* equipment, as we can see in the above comments. I suggest that the unease has not much to do with what the participants look like with the *Aura* equipment. Rather, I argue that it is located around the perception of self and others, and this perception is shaped by the content, i.e., my own music on the iPod, the artist's sounds and noises, an unexpected phone call. I suggest that the feeling of self-consciousness, of feeling different, is also located in the altered experience of space, an alteration conditioned by participating in an art work and perceiving the world in a different way through exploring the sounds generated by oneself and others. Feeling self-conscious is not only about the devices, it is also about an altered sense perception.

How the participants of *Aura* feel self-conscious is also partly explained by the fact that it is a "discomfort walk," during which you hear noise if you cross a previous participant's path. This makes people feel as if they are not doing the "right" thing. The park where *Aura* takes place is full of "noise" in many places already. Additionally, the park is also full of all the "normal" park visitors that are walking around, having picnics, playing football, and so forth. Inside the park you have to negotiate this busy physical space, making sure not to step on other people's feet, cross into their paths, or avoid being hit by balls. Inside the art space of *Aura* you are also trying to avoid treading on someone else's path to avoid the "noise." This double navigation of "spaces rubbing together" required by the audience also contributes to the feeling of self-consciousness.

In *Aura*, the senses are not mobilized in an ordinary way. This departure from "normality" can then be used to pinpoint this very normality. In everyday life we multitask, whereas this artwork focuses us on doing one thing at the time. I argue that mobile sound art reexamines our senses in playing with everyday patterns and rhythms of sense perception—while at the same time working with our everyday (mobile) media skills. The *Aura* headphones act as a kind of auditory picture frame for our senses.

## MOMENTS OF BREAKDOWN

Digital media artworks (almost) always include moments when they do not function as intended or as expected. This section focuses on these relevant moments when media expectations break down. As *Aura* is a sound piece, one would expect an experience of "breakdown" would be associated with "silence," with no sound coming out of the headphones. For example, if you walk too fast, the system is unable to keep up with the GPS readings, and this results in the sound cutting out. Symons is aware of this: "When I see people walking a little too quickly . . . I know it will jump. A bit like an LP jumping . . . the GPS works a bit slow and you might be better if you go slower."[27] Ben describes how he was uncertain of what to do when he experienced this cutting-out of the sound:

> Well, I was sort of confused when the sound kind of cut out at a few points and it cut out with a bit of a crackle. And so, and it sounded like the noise when wires have lost their connection. And I wasn't quite sure that's what happened. . . . And then I was like "shall I carry on walking?" "Shall I take it back?"[28]

In this quote "not working" is indeed associated with the sound cutting out, the headphones falling silent. This supports my suggestion that for a sound piece like *Aura* to be experienced as not working one would expect complaints about silent headphones. However, for some people, the opposite seems to be true: silent headphones still give the impression that the piece is working fine. Some people went for a walk with an *Aura* backpack that was not working at the time (e.g., the battery was flat). The artist recalls that some people still enjoyed the experience:

> But then people would still be coming back and be like "Oh wow, I heard all these wonderful noises." But then…part of the work is, it does amplify, it is designed to amplify the real world as well.… They would just walk around with non-functioning headphones and say this was an amazing experience.[29]

For these participants the *Aura* headphones functioned as "auditory picture frames" for their senses, even when they were not working as intended. It did make the participants listen and appreciate their soundscape as "beautiful." A different (almost opposite) experience of *Aura* not working is reported by John. For him, the main experience is failure—even though *Aura* works perfectly fine when he takes it out: "The trouble is that, that it didn't work.…I got what I call noise…What is the purpose of the exercise."[30] His account is interesting because the interviewee is very critical, even hostile toward the piece. John is forty to fifty years old, lives just north of Cambridge, and is a mathematician, engineer, and musician. He has deep interest in media.[31]

> One of my students there, he tells me that it didn't work yesterday, or something, or they got it to work. So, I mean, it's a bit embarrassing because I always like to support things like this, you know. But I had to sort of question their favorable gloss on it. It's a shame really. At least I hope I understood what the goal of the exercise was.[32]

For John, "failure" is not about silence, it is about noise. He does not seem to be able to make sense of this intervention into familiar soundscapes, to make sense of the noise. One explanation for John's experience of breakdown could be that he does not have the mobile media skills required: he is not experienced with iPods and mobile phones in the way the other interviewees were. He uses his mobile more like a "proper" telephone, or, in other words, only to make phone calls. He is not very aware that most people also use it for many other purposes, as the interview reveals.

If we return to de Certeau's notion of paths as writing and maps as reading, we could extend this to the "roadmaps" of expectations we might have toward mobile sound art (with the pieces as "reading maps," and the actual experience of them as "writing paths"). There is a genre expectation in locative art (and more generally in interactive media art) that the sound one contributes is additive and somehow positive (for instance, in adding my voice to a tapestry).[33] In *Aura* however, the participants add and encounter unpleasant "noise." Arguably, in John's head, there was already a roadmap of sound art as "adding nice sounds," a cliché genre expectation of how mobile sound art operates. This means that this genre expectation, John's roadmap, has become a strategy, rather than a tactic. The map already in his head did not fit while writing his path during the actual experience of the piece.

It is not only the audience that experiences unexpected and unplanned aspects of *Aura*. Symons also had to make do with challenging conditions in developing the piece.

Working in public space and working with digital media is always a process of adjusting to ever-changing contexts, especially when working within the economic constraints of art on the fringe. Symons' original plan was to encourage people to walk around a larger area in the city center of Cambridge where the artist mapped several zones with different sounds:

> 'Cause it's a city-wide thing and I was looking at the political, how much you can move within spaces, and what spaces have been used for...and I talked to people and found out the University areas and then I mapped that with a mixture of tourist map.... [I was looking] for areas which are closed off. Or areas which are used in different ways. Not physically, but on that conceptual cartography level. So I was just looking for social zones....I made about...seven big zones of space which are the colored map on the screen. And I made different sounds, there are different sounds that operate in each of those spaces.[34]

The planned trajectory of walking though the city was supposed to be encouraged by the scattered locations of *Aura* base stations.

> In theory there is a nice line where you've got Parker's Piece, Market, and Kettles' Yard [the three locations originally planned] at the top. And then that is a two-kilometer-square space. And there's the main artery there. So people will naturally want to walk down there but that will get consumed quite quickly so you know there will be, they'll start doing other walks.... That was the theory anyway, wasn't it?[35]

However, during the development phase of the piece funding was cut in half. Also, the custom hardware and software system developed by the artist is very complex.[36] Therefore, Symons had to adjust to the changing conditions and make do with the local environment. Two changes were made. First, only one backpack and base station were working and charged at any one moment in time (not the intended four). Second, the area of the piece was shrunk from city center to park-size. After resizing the area to Parker's Piece, *Aura* only works within this "playing field." If you walk outside this area, it will not work; there will be no sound on the headphones. For the audience and the artist there have been different moments of the piece breaking down that have provided us with an insight into how different these moments of sonic media breakdown can be experienced and articulated.

## AMBIGUOUS MOBILE MEDIA EXPERIENCES

This last section of the chapter is concerned with the participants' everyday use of mobile media. People walk the city in an aestheticized sound environment in their daily lives, e.g. with mobile phones and MP3 players. In his study of how iPod users aestheticize their urban journeys, Michael Bull argues that both mobile phones and MP3 players are warming up urban space for the user, but at the same time they are making urban space chillier for everybody else (2007:12ff.). I am interested in the link between everyday and art experience, how they can speak to each other and inform each other. After discussing their *Aura* experiences, I also asked the interviewees about their experiences with everyday mobile and sonic media. This chapter shows that art experience can open up a participant's senses, and, in this regard, asking people to reflect upon their everyday mobile media practices directly after having participated in a work of sound art can be productive. The *Aura* headphones act as a form of acoustic picture frame that enables participants to see and reflect upon their everyday mobile media use. Everyday mobile media experience such as mobile phone use is made conspicuous by the art experience.

One of the most striking findings of the interviews is how ambivalent the participants felt toward their mobile phones, as illustrated by Ben's comment: "You know there is something really useful about having a phone but at the same time there's a burden that goes with it 'cause you can't just go: 'I'm just gonna go off now. Leave everything behind.'"[37] Paul also feels ambivalent about mobile phones as we can see in the following two comments:

> I use an MP3 player every day. I commute to London, so I use that to listen to music. It can play video but I don't tend to use it for that, I just use it for music. I've got a mobile phone which I tend to use very little, as little as possible [laughing]...I like them you know and I like to be able to be contacted. They are very useful but I find them a bit intrusive and a bit annoying at times....I just find that they take people's attention away from wherever, from whatever they are doing at that time.[38]

Both Ben and Paul first stress the usefulness of mobile phones before admitting to also find them "intrusive," "annoying," and "a burden." Bull identifies a major difference between MP3 player use (such as iPods) and mobile phone use in terms of control and continuity. Music listeners choose their music and have a continuous experience whereas receiving a phone call is beyond people's control and disruptive. According to Bull, "[t]he two technologies represent two distinct, and largely contradictory, modes of relating to the management of time, space and 'otherness' in urban life: the *continuous* and the *discontinuous*" (2007:67; my emphasis). This is reflected in Paul's comment above, where he states that mobile phones are "intrusive" and "take attention away."

The more continuous experience of being in a "bubble" of sound surfaces in my interview with David. His iPod use is interesting because he feels ambivalent about it and his description switches between his own use and that of "others." His account oscillates around pleasure and danger:

> I use an iPod from time to time...everybody is becoming more and more obsessed with these things and...it's kind of weird 'cause it's all, in your own kind of bubble. When you start noticing you are doing it itself, if you are doing any activities or you're cycling and you've got the headphones in, just...cycling with headphones, I'm slightly uncomfortable. So I just feel like quite sort of dangerous....From time to

time, you know if I'm going for a long cycle ride, it's quite good fun. To have some good tunes and just ride the road, it's good.[39]

Bull reports that iPod users express "ambivalence toward their [mobile phones]" (2007:67), whereas their accounts of iPod use do not show ambivalence. In David's account we can see this ambivalence is also felt toward MP3 players. In my interviews, the mobile phone accounts oscillated between "useful" and "annoying;" this iPod comment is torn between the "danger" and the "fun" of listening to mobile music.

In addition to these ambiguous feelings toward their mobile devices, interviewees also reported many creative ways of using mobile media. One of them is Ben's use of voice mail. There is an interesting tension between the playful and creative way Ben uses technology and how he thinks of himself as being too shy to use features of his mobile phone. I asked him about any musical or sonic use of mobile technology and he replied:

> A couple of weeks ago I did in fact sing happy birthday down the phone to a friend of mine. . . . I [am] often actually bored of leaving just ordinary messages on the phone 'cause I'm a sort of theater person I suppose, I often . . . just make up characters and leave stupid voices and stupid messages on the phone. . . . Little improvisation sessions. To while away the minute. But I think other than that I tend to use things pretty much for how they are designed. And actually a bit shy of using my phone to do all the things it can do. I'm not, not sure why it can do all the things it can do.[40]

Despite his creative use of telephones (such as making up characters and stories, as well as singing) he describes his telephone use as following certain standards, and even as shy. Using mobile phones for creative practices such as making music has been increasingly common over the last decade or so, especially with the rise of app culture (Behrendt 2012b).

Finally, from these "everyday use" sections of my interviews, I mention an account from Emma that contradicts our "multi-tasking" expectations of media activities being carried out while doing something else:

> Well, I use my mobile phone. . . . I use the computer. But I'm very dyslexic so I find it quite hard to navigate the Internet or respond to emails. You know, I do it a little bit, but I feel I have a disadvantage because I can't read very well. What other technology? I use a camera. [Me: So you more likely to use an maybe an iPod or listen to music?] Yeah, no, I don't. And I don't listen to very much music. [laughing] . . . I find it hard to multitask. So I never have music on in the background when I'm doing something else.[41]

If we return to the earlier argument that I built on de Certeau's comment regarding "spaces rubbing together," for Emma the "rubbing together of different spaces" (for example the auditory space of an iPod and her surroundings), might produce too much friction to bear. Discussing these everyday mobile media experiences after the *Aura* experience has allowed me to access emotional and creative responses that are often difficult to uncover in interviews.

# Conclusion

*Aura* is an articulation of creative space making practices that allows us to shift our attention from the often totalizing views and "flattening-out" of maps toward the activity of inscribing sound into space via movement (de Certeau 1984:35). In *Aura*, as the stream of GPS data is fed into the generative audio software, the very movement through space generates sound—what I have defined as "sonified mobility" elsewhere (Behrendt 2010). There is also sound if you do not move, a static GPS signal is programmed to generate increasing noise, to encourage you to walk. *Aura* could be regarded as symptomatic of contemporary urban space or even privatized space—where it is possible to move around, but often increasingly difficult to stop, to rest, to sit down, to linger, if it is not for a commercial reason.

Mobile sound art platforms are often concerned with adding "nice" sounds and similarly in "sonified mobility" contexts the movement or trajectory is often sonified in "pleasant ways" (Behrendt 2010, 2012a). In *Aura* people's trajectories are sonified as "noise" whereas previously un-walked territory is experienced as "pleasant" sounds. In discussing the experience of the piece with some of its participants, I identified the key issues of friction, control, self-consciousness, ambiguity, and "break-down." These themes manifest themselves in various ways in each audience member's experience of the piece, in some cases producing discomfort and dissonance.

The form of the encounter is in the sensory register rather than in the rational one (as is the case with mobile sound art where the audience is invited to send text messages to interact with a piece, for example). While I argue that other artworks such as "smSage" by Redfern and Borland (2007) aim to enable communication to make (and break) transient micro public spheres in public space (Behrendt 2010), this chapter has been about co-existing in spaces in a way that is painful and difficult, where participants are (almost) stepping over people and falling over an artwork. The polyphony of the piece makes it dissonant; it is a visceral dissonance of sharing public spaces in asynchronous ways. *Aura* is not about rational forms of communication; it is about a visceral experience. In *Aura*, art space and everyday space co-exist in the same park in Cambridge, and the tensions of this co-existence—the friction between these spaces—is what has allowed insight into the sensory media experience of its participants.

The social aspect of *Aura* evolves over time, and happens without the direct interaction of its participants with one another. The idea of having some sort of shared social space without having to interact directly with other people might be typical of hybrid space, illustrating the ambivalence of wanting some social contact, while staying in the secure state of not having to communicate with strangers. There might be a desire to warm up more than your own space, or a desire to not cool down the urban environment by warming up your space (Bull 2007). *Aura* provides an opportunity to explore virtual and geographic, sonic and imagined spaces "rubbing together" via sound, as de Certeau might put it.

## Notes

1. The festival topic was "Unknown Territories," and its website advertises it as "exciting festival of interactive and playful public art events, live performances, a conference, workshop and club nights taking place throughout Cambridge" (Enter_).
2. Sarah, interview with author, April 28, 2007.
3. Steve Symons, interview with author, April 28, 2007.
4. Ibid.
5. Mscapes is developed by Hewlett-Packard. For a discussion see Behrendt (2010).
6. Steve Symons, interview with author, April 28, 2007.
7. Ibid.
8. Ibid.
9. Of course, de Certeau wrote this before database or street surveillance, so he understands vision as "the thing that sees," whereas in the age of CCTV (visual surveillance) and GPS (database surveillance) your body itself and its trajectory though space becomes "seen." See Andrejevic (2009).
10. David, interview with author, April 27, 2007.
11. Many texts that deal with the relationship of sound, space, and the body do not consider walking (Ouzounian 2006; Brown 2006), but some mention it (Harris 2006). Walking has been discussed in relation to other art genres, but mainly with a focus on the artist(s) walking, not the audience (Careri 2001; Araya 2004).
12. Hight's text gravitates around his own piece "34 North, 118 West" (2002, with Knowlton and Spellman), which delivers the narrative via headphones while also relying on the screen of the device for displaying maps.
13. Ben, interview with author, April 27, 2007.
14. Ibid.
15. Steve Symons, interview with author, April 28, 2007.
16. Ibid.
17. David, interview with author, April 27, 2007.
18. Frauke, interview with author, April 28, 2007.
19. Ben, interview with author, April 27, 2007.
20. Ibid.
21. David, interview with author, April 27, 2007.
22. Ibid.
23. Ibid.
24. Emma, interview with author, April 28, 2007.
25. Ibid.
26. Ibid.
27. Steve Symons, interview with author, April 28, 2007.
28. Ben, interview with author, April 27, 2007.
29. Steve Symons, interview with author, April 28, 2007.
30. John, interview with author, April 28, 2007.
31. Ibid.
32. Ibid.
33. For example "Urban Tapestry" (Silverstone and Sujon 2005).
34. Steve Symons, interview with author, April 28, 2007.
35. Ibid.

36. As of 2009 no comparable system has been developed or made publicly available—the artist is still gathering funding to do so, so as to benefit the mobile sound and music community with a public release version.
37. Ben, interview with author, April 27, 2007.
38. Paul, interview with author, April 28, 2007.
39. David, interview with author, April 27, 2007.
40. Ben, interview with author, April 27, 2007.
41. Emma, interview with author, April 28, 2007.

## REFERENCES

Altena, Arie. 2006. "Publishing Everywhere and Anywhere: Droombeek in Enschede." *Open. Cahier on Art and the Public Domain* 11:134–139.

Andrejevic, Mark. 2009. *Ispy: Surveillance and Power in the Interactive Era (Cultureamerica).* Lawrence: University Press of Kansas.

Araya, Kinga. 2004. "Walking in the City: The Motif of Exile in Performances by Krzysztof Wodiczko and Adrian Piper." PhD diss., Concordia University.

Bassett, Caroline. 2003. "How Many Movements?" In *The Auditory Culture Reader,* ed. Michael Bull and Les Back. Oxford: Berg.

Behrendt, Frauke. 2010. "Mobile Sound: Media Art in Hybrid Spaces." PhD diss., University of Sussex.

——. 2012a. "The Sound of Locative Media" *Convergence: The International Journal of Research into New Media Technologies* 18(3): 283–295.

——. 2012b. "Playing the iPhone" In *Moving Data: The iPhone and the Future of Media,* ed. Pelle Snickars and Patrick Vonderau. New York: Columbia University Press: 287–295.

Brown, Nicholas. 2006. "The Flux Between Sounding and Sound: Towards a Relational Understanding of Music as Embodied Action." *Contemporary Music Review* 25 (1/2):37–46.

Bull, Michael. 2000. *Sounding Out the City: Personal Stereos and the Management of Everyday Life.* Oxford: Berg.

——. 2007. *Sound Moves: Ipod Culture and Urban Experience.* London: Routledge.

Careri, Francesco. 2001. *Walkscapes: Walking as an Aesthetic Practice (Land & Scape).* Barcelona: Gustavo Gili.

De Certeau, Michel. 1984. *The Practice of Everyday Life.* Berkley: University of California Press.

Enter_. Aura-the Stuff That Forms Around You—Steve Symons, http://www.enternet.org.uk/enternet/unknownterritories/event.acds?instanceid=2682312&context=2659815 (accessed January 13, 2008. No longer available online)

Enter_. Enter_ Unknown Territories. http://www.enternet.org.uk/enternet/unknownterritories/home.acds?context=2659795 (accessed January 13, 2008. No longer available online)

Galloway, Anne, and Matt Ward. 2006. "Locative Media as Socialising and Spatializing Practice: Learning From Archaeology." *Leonardo Electronic Almanac* 14 (3). http://www.leoalmanac.org/wp-content/uploads/2012/07/Locative-Media-As-Socialising-And-Spatializing-Practice-Learning-From-Archaeology-Leonardo-Electronic-Almanac.pdf

Harris, Yolande. 2006. "Inside-Out Instrument." *Contemporary Music Review* 25 (1/2):151–162.

Hight, Jeremy. 2006. "Views From Above: Locative Narrative and the Landscape." *Leonardo Electronic Almanac* 14 (07–08). http://www.leoalmanac.org/wp-content/uploads/2012/09/09_JHight.pdf

Kirisits, Nicolaj and Frauke Behrendt, Lalya Gaye, Atau Tanaka, eds. 2008. *Creative Interactions – The Mobile Music Workshops 2004–2008*. Vienna: University of Applied Arts. Available at http://tinyurl.com/jwbfu72 (accessed September 2011).

Kluitenberg, Eric. 2006. "The Network of Waves. Living and Acting in a Hybrid Space." *Open. Cahier on Art and the Public Domain* 11:6–16.

Kraan, Assia. 2006. "To Act in Public Though Geo-Annotation. Social Encounters Though Media Art." *Open. Cahier on Art and the Public Domain* 11:38–47.

Ouzounian, Gascia. 2006. "Embodied Sound: Aural Architectures and the Body." *Contemporary Music Review* 25 (1/2):69–79.

Silverstone, Roger, and Zoetanya Sujon. 2005. "Urban Tapestries: Experimental Ethnography, Technological Identities and Place." *MEDIA AT LSE Electronic Working Papers 7*.

Souza e Silva, Adrianna Araujo de. 2004. "From Cyber to Hybrid. Relocating Our Imaginary Spaces Through Mobile Interfaces." PhD diss., Federal University of Rio de Janeiro.

Symons, Steve. "artworks/ aura: the stuff that forms around you." http://stevesymons.net/aura2 (accessed September 2011).

——. 2007. "Artist's Talk." Paper at Enter_ Festival: Cambridge.

Tarkka, Minna. 2005. *Labours of Location: Acting in the Pervasive Media Space*. London: Diffusion eBook series.

........................................................................................................

# CHAPTER 8

# SOUNDWALKING: CREATING MOVING ENVIRONMENTAL SOUND NARRATIVES

........................................................................................................

## ANDRA MCCARTNEY

SOUNDWALKING is a creative and research practice that involves listening and sometimes recording while moving through a place at a walking pace. It is concerned with the relationship between soundwalkers and their surrounding sonic environment. The term was first used by members of the World Soundscape Project under the leadership of composer R. Murray Schafer in Vancouver in the 1970s. However, this group was not the first to orient themselves to an area by sound and to record the sounds of the environments that they walked through. This chapter documents some earlier examples of works produced by walking while audio recording, and situates soundwalk research and creation in relation to soundscape studies. It then explores several contemporary approaches to the practice of soundwalking, and includes an analysis of variations on a soundwalk in Queen Elizabeth Park, Vancouver—a site that is important, since it was the subject of Hildegard Westerkamp's early article on soundwalking.

Decisions about the location, style, content, and montage of sound in a soundwalk have political, social, and ecological consequences. Soundwalks take place in urban, rural, wilderness, and multiply mediated locations. A soundwalk can be done individually or in a group. It can be recorded or not. It can be resituated in the same location or translated into other media forms with little or a great deal of sound processing. Soundwalk artists maintain differing attitudes toward the place in question, sounds recorded, processes used, audience of the walk itself, and the audiences of interpretive pieces based on soundwalks. Their intentions may be aesthetic, didactic, ecological, political, communicative, or some combination of these. This chapter attempts to tease out the characteristics of these proliferating contemporary approaches to soundwalking.

In this chapter, soundwalking is distinguished from other kinds of mobile listening and field recording practices that are not so closely linked to the act of walking, which is a particular kind of movement through a place. The practice of listening while walking has a long history in philosophies of walking (Thoreau 1862; Schaub 2005), as well as practices of walking meditation, in which attention to listening figures prominently (Thich 1996).[1] Soundwalking can be situated in relation to long-standing artistic, philosophical, and political concepts that theorize through the practice of walking, such as haiku poets' use of daily walks as a creative structure, writing about the figure of the flâneur and the situationist concept of the dérive, as well as the approaches of conceptual artists, such as those in the Fluxus movement.

Since the term *soundwalking* focuses on the act of walking, it could be understood to exclude those who are not able to walk and require wheelchairs or strollers. While some walks are planned to allow access to such conveyances, this is not always the case. Wilderness hiking trails are particularly exclusive in this respect. This is not the only exclusion fostered by a choice of such a location. When soundwalks are planned in remote locations that require participants to use individual transport to get there, such choices have political implications: as Alexander Wilson (1998) points out, access to wilderness parks is the privilege of the middle class who have cars. He notes that in some cases, roads to parks were designed with bridges that exclude public transport, a move that explicitly excluded those who do not have cars; while in many others there are no public buses or trains that will take people directly to parks. Because of the association of soundwalks with the World Soundscape Project and the northern pastoralism of its founder, R. Murray Schafer, wilderness parks have been a favored location for soundwalks. However, in recent years, there has been an increase in public walks and soundwalk research projects planned in accessible locations associated with music festivals and urban sonic research groups.

A walking pace (andante, 75 beats per minute (bpm), like that of a relaxed and active heartbeat) is slow in musical terms, slower than the pace of the sound cyclist, the sound tourist, the sound safari; it is a reflective pace. While recording, even slower movement—andante grazioso, 60 bpm—is often necessary to reduce wind on the mic. The walk is slow movement, where stillness is only temporary and motion is more or less audible. In many soundwalk recordings, it is possible to hear sounds of the recordist, traces of breath, gait, touch, and presence that are more often effaced in still recordings. This emphasis on slowness, human movement and a focus on particular places brings attention to the presence of the soundwalkers and their ways of interaction in that place; also it can be considered an ecological act in its reduction of carbon and acoustic footprints to local and accessible places. However, this depends on decisions about where to do the walk. If someone plans walks in their own neighborhood, this can facilitate a focus on local concerns and politics.

The focus on the everyday noises of a place and their "wild" interaction, as well as the inclusion of traces of the moving presence and perspective of the recordist, goes against the grain of early ideologies of sound recording, which developed around the sound studio (or sound lab). In the studio approach, sounds are isolated from each other and from the outside world, in order to provide a favorable signal to noise ratio and to make sounds easier to control and edit (Thompson 2002:7). In the studio, noise is considered a problem to be baffled, and in everyday life, noise is something to be avoided, blocked

FIGURE **8.1** Sonic memory walk with David Graham in Dollar, Scotland with soundscape researchers of the project Acoustic Environment in Change, Heikki Uimonen (right) and Helmi Järviluoma (who took the photo) in 2000.

out or ignored. In soundwalks, noises and their relationships can be the focus of attention and participants can be asked to consider their place in the soundscape and their cultural significance in that context. This ideology of considering all sounds, including those usually discounted as noise, is similar to that of John Cage, who said that the use of electrical instruments "will make available for musical purposes any and all sounds that can be heard" (1961:4).

Soundwalks take the everyday action of walking, and everyday sounds, and bring the attention of the audience to these often ignored events, practices, and processes. Figure and ground can be shifted, in a way that is potentially paradigm-shifting as well. It is important to note that many of the major figures in the field of soundwalking are women, unlike with many other areas of electroacoustic sound art and research, indicating possibilities for changing gender dynamics in relation to sound and technology. Some soundwalks shift power relationships between artists and audiences, acknowledging the varied listening experiences and knowledge of audience members. A tradition of public group soundwalks is now associated with many music festivals and conferences, and these are sites for group listening and discussion that are often unusual in their openness and accessibility. In discussions following the walks, audiences can be encouraged to express a wide range of responses, including musical elements of the sound environment heard, comments on who controls the sounds, the history of that particular sound environment, and associations with other sound environments. People who may feel they are not entitled to speak about contemporary music since they lack musical training seem more likely to engage in such wide-ranging discussions, and audiences remark on what they learn from others' responses (McCartney 2008). Some soundwalk artists have extended this communicative approach that can be considered mutually conscientizing (Freire 1994) to interactive installation work and other forms that emphasize artist-audience communication. Soundwalking has been translated across media for radio, gallery installations, and the internet. Recently, the concept of soundwalking has expanded into several variations on the idea, such as shadow walks, electrical walks, blind walks, audio walks, tourist walks and listening walks, each of which are discussed later in this chapter. In addition, the value of soundwalking as a method of research creation is now understood in areas such as social work as well as in contemporary art and soundscape research (Figure 8.1).

# Early Mobile Listening and Sound Recording Practices

Practices of walking narratives have been used as methods of orientation and cultural knowledge-making for eons. Bruce Chatwin's *The Songlines* discusses oral walking narratives that the Aboriginal Australians linked to routes through the landscape to orient themselves physically and spiritually, continually singing the world into existence (1987:2). Prior to the invention of sound recording technologies, literary perspectives on aural landscapes could occasionally be found in diaries, letters and creative writing. However, it takes significant research to find and collate literary sources for a particular location throughout history. In the 1970s, the World Soundscape Project received substantial research grants from the Donner Canadian Foundation, the Canada Council and UNESCO, to do soundscape research. This funding allowed them to provide a historical perspective on changes in the Canadian and European sound environments in times prior to sound recording, for instance in the Vancouver Sound Diary (Schafer 1977a). The works of literary flâneurs in nineteenth century Europe documented changes in daily life during industrialization through a method of walking through cities. While these documents were primarily from a visualist perspective (Gleber 1999), occasional references were made to sound. Clues about the sound environment in different historical periods can also be found in visual art pieces. A thoughtful link between sound and visuality is made in the Paris Soundwalk: The Louvre by the World Soundscape Project, in which listeners are advised to listen to paintings. The documentation of this walk includes reproductions of the paintings along with questions for the listener about how the activities depicted in them would sound (Schafer 1977b:86–91).

The invention of sound recording technologies at the end of the nineteenth century opened up the possibility of doing audio recording during walks. As noted earlier, sound recording is primarily undertaken as a studio practice isolated from environmental sounds that are considered problematic noise. Early instances of sound recorded outside the studio include dialogue recording for film, and ethnological recordings, although usually the latter were still recordings made with portable equipment, not moving recordings. The most common use of sound recording with movement was during a tracking shot in a film shoot. It is not surprising then that an early example of mobile sound recording was done with a film camera, while another involved recordings made for Folkways, whose primary holdings are ethnological.

Walter Ruttman used a film camera to do the field recording for the sound piece "Weekend" in 1930, in which urban sounds are montaged. His interest in exploring the rhythms of urban life in sound owes much to his earlier, rhythmically edited silent film documentaries such as Berlin: Symphony of a Great City (1927).

Radio producer and theorist Tony Schwartz recalls the difficulty of recording with a portable tape recorder in 1946 and how he met that challenge. Having been given funding by a benefactor to take on a sound project of his choosing, he decided to devote a year and a half to the study of life in his postal zone, New York 19:

> The New York 19 project was to be a documentation of sounds and songs in the natural environment. So I did not want to bring a vegetable vendor or street musician into my studio in order to record him. But in 1946 there were no portable recorders. If a sound could not be brought into the studio, a sound effect was created to substitute for reality. I developed a portable recorder specifically for the New York 19 project. It was battery-operated, could be used while walking or running, and weighed about fourteen pounds. Once I was free of Mr. Edison's cables, I could explore the beauty of language in everyday situations and the sounds of life around us. (Schwartz 1974:xiii)[2]

Schwartz was then asked by Folkways Records to produce a number of albums devoted to the sounds of everyday life: "My material enabled a listener to experience actual sounds—sounds that served vital communicative functions in people's lives" (xiii). Most of these recordings were made within a few blocks of Schwartz's home in New York, maintaining an emphasis on a local neighborhood that is echoed in the work of some contemporary soundwalk artists.

The Fluxus movement has used scores for walks, although these are not specifically marked as soundwalks.[3] It is more difficult to find recorded examples of sound-oriented walks created by conceptual artists. Adrian Piper's early conceptual sound work Streetwork Streettracks I–II (1969) began with a sound recording of a walk along a city street in New York. Then the following week during a festival she did a simultaneous recording of a walk along the same route, during which she engaged with the public while playing back the earlier solo walk at double speed, bringing attention to the technology and creative process while inviting dialogue in the new recording.

Prior to the introduction of light, portable sound recording technologies such as the Walkman, the act of recording soundwalks while moving through a place was relatively cumbersome, as Tony Schwartz notes (1974:xiii). Until the 1970s, there was no practice defined as soundwalking as such: practitioners came from such fields as audio documentary (such as Schwartz), film (Ruttman) or conceptual art (Piper). In the 1970s, prepared by the artistic work and political ideologies of the Fluxus movement in New York and the Situationist movement in France, both of which emphasize a focus on art from everyday life, two major research groups began more sustained work in researching and recording sound environments, providing more possibilities for collaboration, exchange and publication.

# EARLY SOUNDWALK RESEARCH

In the 1970s, sustained attention to walking in a research project, as well as the interdisciplinary study of sound in environments, was established through the work of Jean Francois Augoyard at the research center CRESSON, in Grenoble, France. Also beginning in the 1970s, soundwalking and the study of the soundscape were investigated by R. Murray Schafer, Hildegard Westerkamp, and other researchers at the World Soundscape Project in Vancouver, Canada.

CRESSON is the *Centre de recherche sur l'espace sonore et l'environnement urbain,* a laboratory founded in 1979 in Grenoble, expanding on work begun earlier that decade by J. F. Augoyard and others. Their interdisciplinary research interests include acoustic architecture, urban acoustics, anthropology of space, the sonic environment, urban sociology, and theories of architectural and urban ambiances. Augoyard is a philosopher and musicologist, and was director of the institute for several years. His doctoral dissertation, originally published in 1979 as *Pas a Pas: Essai sur le cheminement quotidien en milieu urbain,* is a methodological and theoretical consideration of ways of walking in an urban environment, focusing on a specific location (the Arlequin neighborhood in Grenoble, France) and referring directly to the testimonies of inhabitants in order to develop a rhetoric of walking, an early example of reflexive research methodology in which the ideas and experiences of research subjects were acknowledged within the research enterprise. Augoyard was a good friend of Michel de Certeau, whose influential theoretical essay "Walking in the City" (from *The Practice of Everyday Life,* 1984) benefitted greatly from the insights developed by Augoyard during his project about walking, including the consideration of the rhetorical figures of synecdoche and asyndeton as they are configured by walkers in urban space. Augoyard's ground-breaking work has only recently been translated into English (Augoyard and Torgue 2005; Augoyard 2007). In more recent years, research on experiences of sound and other ambiances in urban environments is carried out by a growing team of CRESSON researchers including notably Pascal Amphoux, Jean-Paul Thibaud, Nicolas Tixier, and Rachel Thomas. An evolving collaborative research website (http://www.ambiances.net/) includes writings in both French and English.

The World Soundscape Project (WSP) began at Simon Fraser University in Vancouver, Canada in the early 1970s. This project, founded and directed by composer R. Murray Schafer, and including other composers such as Barry Truax, Howard Bloomfield, Peter Huse, Bruce Davis, and Hildegard Westerkamp, began their work with concerns about noise pollution, and received extensive private and public funding in the wake of Canada's Centennial celebration, to undertake major research projects of soundscapes in cities and villages of Canada and Europe. This work resulted in several research and educational books and articles about soundscapes by members of the research team, as well as a range of soundscape radio works that were broadcast on CBC radio in Canada, and archived on tape in the holdings of the WSP at Simon Fraser University in British Columbia, Canada. The WSP researchers used soundwalks for orientation when they first encountered a new sound environment, and soundwalks were included in their publications with instructions for listeners to follow routes and pay attention to their sonic features (Schafer 1977a, 1977b). However, the soundscape pieces featured on radio by the group were the result of still recordings, and soundwalks were considered primarily for their educational potential. Hildegard Westerkamp took the concept further in her Vancouver community radio show, *Soundwalking*.

## Soundwalking Score and Radio: Hildegard Westerkamp

The *Soundwalking* radio show at Co-op Radio in Vancouver was based on ideas about soundwalking that Westerkamp developed while working with the World Soundscape Project. Prior to beginning this show, Westerkamp wrote an article that discusses her approach to soundwalking, and uses an example of a soundwalk in Queen Elizabeth Park, Vancouver as a kind of score, describing aspects of the park environment and suggesting questions for a soundwalker to consider while doing the walk.

> A soundwalk is any excursion whose main purpose is listening to the environment.... The intention of soundwalking is listening. Soundwalks can take place in the mall, at the doctor's office, down a neighbourhood street or at the bus stop. The focus on listening can make this a meditative activity, sometimes shared in silence with others. A soundwalk can be ... done alone or with a friend (in the latter case the listening experience is more intense and can be a lot of fun when one person wears a blindfold and is led by the other one through several different and interesting acoustic environments). It can also be done in small groups.... The first soundwalk can be done anywhere, at any time, and as often as desired. For the sake of intensity it may be wise to limit the walk initially to a small area.... In each case it depends on how long it takes to remove the initial hearing barriers, how deep the involvement is and how much fascination can be found in such an exploration. (1974:18–19)

The article that Westerkamp writes about soundwalking establishes an imaginary dialogue with the audience through describing different areas of Queen Elizabeth Park, and asking direct questions to the reader that are not just focused on sound but extend to all the senses. For instance, when discussing the Conservatory, Westerkamp asks: "When you walk into the conservatory, you are entering an artificially created, tropical environment...Does it look and smell and feel tropical? Does it sound tropical?" (21). The article grounds Westerkamp's ideas about soundwalking through a specific site that the audience is encouraged to explore in their own ways, with her suggestions and questions as guides. The article then functions as a kind of score for potential soundwalkers. Like a Fluxus score (Friedman 2009) it provokes the audience and suggests that they engage in certain activities, in this case listening and analyzing as they walk through a place, or making sounds by activating surfaces. However, it is more elaborated and didactic, with much longer discussions than the usually terse Fluxus score.

The *Soundwalking* show at Co-op Radio gave Westerkamp a forum to further explore some of her ideas about sound ecology.

> I was attempting to make radio a place of environmental listening by broadcasting the soundscapes that listeners experienced in their daily lives....My own first attempt to create radio that listens was called Soundwalking....Produced in 1978 and 1979, Soundwalking took Co-op Radio listeners into the soundscape of Vancouver and surroundings....I went to a shopping mall, park, zoo, factory, residential area located under a flightpath and the streets of Vancouver. (Westerkamp 1994:88–89)

As with the article "Soundwalking," her intention with the *Soundwalking* radio show was to take listeners to various locations not far from their homes, in the Vancouver region, then to play back the sounds of these environments to listeners, framing and contextualizing them through on-air commentary. Sometimes, as in a program about Lighthouse Park, she would read excerpts of others' writings (in this case, Emily Carr). The radio shows often had a political point made acoustically. For instance, the show "Silent Night" contrasts the name of the Christmas carol with the reality of acoustically crowded reverberant urban shopping malls in the weeks before Christmas, juxtaposing cash registers and holy music; "Under the Flightpath" repeats the words of residents saying they don't hear the planes any more, with the roaring of jets overhead.

Westerkamp notes that the radio show gave her experience in field recording in a wide variety of different sound environments, as well as experience in communicating with the radio listener from the recording location. These soundwalks use various techniques to reach the radio listener. She includes commentary on inaudible aspects of the environment, in order to maintain contact with the radio audience and situate the soundscape. "Sort of like a sports announcer, I was the link between the audience and the radio station. But it was much more slow-motion than being a sports announcer, it was more contemplative, meditative, depending on which environment I was in."[4] Westerkamp remembers that she gained technical competence through producing many shows, not only about the equipment, but also about interacting with environmental sounds, and talking with people.

> What would my microphone pick up if I do this, and how do you play with environment and voice at the same time, live, while you're out there? How do you deal with people who approach you? So I developed a fairly passive style of

recording. Very different from the radio journalist. I would just stand some-place and record. Then people who were familiar with that environment would approach me, I would not approach them. And as a result I got some very interesting conversation.[5]

At least part of the reason that Westerkamp develops a non-intrusive style of recording at this point is that she is very aware of her position as a newcomer to Canada, since she immigrated from Germany in 1968. Renato Rosaldo (1988:85) describes immigrants to North America as bobbing and weaving between assimilation to the new culture and allegiance to their original one, creating for themselves a border zone which resembles both, yet is part of neither. The immigrant's experience necessarily includes a sense of displacement, one in which there is rarely any permanent return to the place of birth, and therefore there is a need to become part of the chosen culture. At the same time, the immigrant's formation in the home culture invites comparisons between the cultures in order to understand how to fit. So the immigrant swings between the two poles of home and chosen culture, bringing together aspects of both in their experience. As she learns about the Canadian soundscape with an immigrant's displaced ears, Westerkamp is at once inside this new soundscape and outside it, able to hear with a fresh perspective. But perhaps more importantly, her experience as an immigrant leads Westerkamp to the use of the microphone as a tool of access, and the development of a dialogic approach to field recording and production that would become a significant part of her style, bridging cultures in sound. She uses the microphone, with the justification of a radio show, to go into situations that she may not otherwise have entered, allowing her to learn about a new culture through listening.

Entitlement to explore public places through sound technology is important to consider in relation to other processes besides migration. It is notable that many of the best-known practitioners of soundwalking and related practices, such as Westerkamp, Corringham, Cardiff, and Kubisch, are women. This is unusual in electroacoustic soundmaking practices, which tend to be dominated by well-known male figures.

The question of gender arose in a soundwalk project that I directed at Concordia University 2000–2003, in which soundwalks by women researchers drew attention to the way a woman's movements through public space are marked and regulated, and at the same time how access to recording technologies can act as a kind of security device to shift gender dynamics. Doing a soundwalk at night, research assistant Sandra Gabriele was approached by a passing cyclist who doubled back and asked her to turn off her recorder so he could say something to her. When she refused, saying she was doing research, he left. Gabriele says:

> The microphone, as a means of recording, as a technological barrier that stands between me, my body and this man, ultimately marks my body as being off limits. By refusing to stop recording, reclaiming the agency I normally feel while recording, I shift the dynamics between us, forcing him to get back on his bike and ride away quickly. Linda McDowell (1999), a feminist geographer, insists that a woman's

presence on the streets, particularly at night, is always complicated by her gender. This gendered position always marks her visibility, making the notion that a woman can observe quietly, detachedly almost impossible. (Quoted in McCartney and Gabriele 2001)

Soundwalk work is far from detached. The recordist's perspective is written into the recording, into the listening, touching, experiencing and moving through the space, so that soundwalkers are simultaneously flâneurs and not flâneurs. As wandering explorers and documenters of city life, soundwalkers seem like flâneurs. But a recording sound-walker is at the same time an intensely engaged listener, connected by a phonic umbili-cus to the surrounding world. At the moment that Gabriele met this passing cyclist, he asked her to stop recording, to stop inscribing her sonic presence in this context. Her refusal and the agency she insists on by continuing to record are important parts of the soundwalk recording experience, and the sense of entitlement access to such technol-ogy can provide.

# Listening Walks: Wagstaff

The aims of a recording soundwalk by an individual soundwalker are often different from the aims of public group walks. Acoustic ecologist Gregg Wagstaff (2002) distin-guishes between soundwalks, in which participants are actively encouraged to make sounds during the walk, and listening walks, during which participants are asked to stay as quiet as possible. In common practice, the term soundwalk is often used rather than listening walk to refer to a silent public walk, often given free of charge at festivals and conferences, which is led by a guide with the intention of encouraging active listening among a wide audience to the surrounding sound environment. Participants in such a walk often are asked to stay silent for a number of reasons. The ear hears the frequency range of the human voice most clearly, and will focus on voices to the exclusion of other sounds. Culturally, people are predisposed to focus on languages that we understand, which leads to less available attention for other sounds. Also, a silent group has a kind of presence that is remarkable, drawing attention of others to the listening activity as it happens. Group silence in such cases is followed by conversation: these public walks are followed by reflective discussions that are wide-ranging in subject and tone, and can be used in the design of future soundwalk experiences. In the research group in Montreal we have begun recording soundwalk discussions for research purposes, because of important insights about soundwalks by participants that can be connected with sound theory. For instance, some walkers find the silence to be an unacceptable constriction of personal agency, resulting in the development of walks that include smaller and larger group work with varying degrees of silence and discussions at several points. In another discussion, after a recent urban walk, comments consistently referred to the vital-ity of a noisy street shopping area as a favorite part of the walk, which reminded me of

Kreutzveld's (2006) discussion of the work of urban theorist and activist Jane Jacobs, and her writing about urban vitality as an important theme.

# BLIND WALKS: FRANCISCO LOPEZ

Though not central to his acoustic practice, Francisco Lopez's blind walks cultivate relationships and listening strategies that change power relationships between sighted and unsighted people (Figure 8.2). Performed under the theme of "Invisible Cities" for Champ Libres International Symposium, City Art Technology 2006, these soundwalks allowed for sighted participants in Montreal to be guided through the city by someone who is blind. Afterward participants would also enter an art installation space where they remained blindfolded and continue actively listening to distorted audio recordings of local soundscapes.

Participants signed up in the atrium of the library, where they would be blindfolded and assigned a unsighted guide who would proceed to lead them through the vibrant Latin Quarter district surrounding the site. Where Wagstaff is concerned with the presence of the silent group in public, here the focus shifts to the interpersonal relationship developed between individuals of two very different listening groups, and how they

FIGURE 8.2 Derek Lang's photo of a blind listening walk led by Nadene Theriault of Sound Travels in Toronto in August 2007, presented by New Adventures in Sound Art.

acoustically relate and communicate in this public space. Lopez states that "it works as a piece/experience that explores the possibility of transferring apprehensions of the world through the interaction of people living in different perceptive universes and through the direct exposure to real and virtual sound environment" (2006).

By blinding the participants and having them guided by unsighted experts on acoustic orientation Lopez highlights the ocular-centric experience of even active listening for most people. The practice also hints at such adages as "the blind leading the blind", which often have derogatory connotations and biases. Here, assumptions that may even subconsciously exist about such listening groups as the blind, are challenged and reworked for the participant.

# DISLOCATED SOUNDWALKS: ON THE WEB AND IN PERIPATETIC INSTALLATIONS

Westerkamp's Soundwalking show was always connected directly with the place of recording. The radio listeners lived in Vancouver, where the recordings were made. During or after listening to a show, they could do a soundwalk in the same site and hear how it sounded. Soundscape theorist Murray Schafer was concerned about how the mediation of sounds as they are dislocated from their source make them schizophonic (a term invented by him that means sound split from its source, that can also imply schizophrenia and mental disassociation). However, schizophonia can also lead to schismogenesis, or the birth of new perspectives, as Steven Feld points out (1994). Putting interpretations of soundwalk experiences into different historical and geographical contexts can lead to further insights. After reading Westerkamp's 1974 article on soundwalking, I asked her to repeat that soundwalk with me in 1997. I then listened to the recording from the 1997 walk, and wrote about that soundwalk in relation to the original article, focusing on historical changes. A number of decisions were made in the design of this walk and its subsequent presentations. First, location: it is at Queen Elizabeth Park, which Westerkamp wrote about, and which is therefore accessible for comparison and analysis. Second, recording technology: a DAT recorder for clarity (the best quality portable recording in 1997) and a large, visible shock-mounted microphone. Two still cameras were used for photographic documentation of the walk. Third, style of walk: two listeners, one recording audio (Westerkamp) and the other doing photographic documentation (McCartney), occasionally conversing with others or announcing the date and weather, but mostly silent; moving through the areas of the park identified by Westerkamp in the article. Fourth, form of presentation: an interactive gallery installation, website, and short radio pieces using sound and images from the walk that were transformed using asyndeton and synechdoche to produce short (one to three minute) multimedia works and inviting commentary from the audience.

The areas of the park delineated in Westerkamp's article are the parking lot, the lookout, the conservatory, the quarry garden and the creek. Even though we discussed these areas as if they were discrete, in the recording there are segues or border regions rather than the rigid boundaries that appear on a map: walking down from the lookout into the quarry of the sunken garden, for instance, the acoustics subtly change over time becoming more enclosed, the sound of the waterfall gradually increases and the sound of the drummers diminishes.

The approach to production with the soundwalk was different from Westerkamp's approach in her radio show.[6] While her radio pieces maintain the timing and flow of an original walk with very little editing, in this case the work interprets and condenses the walk, with the intention of making shorter pieces that would suit the memory restrictions of interactive and online venues, using asyndeton and synechdoche as compositional strategies. Asyndeton is "the deletion from the perception or memory of one or many sound elements in an audible whole" (Augoyard and Torgue, 2005:26). It is a matter of not hearing, or forgetting parts of a sonic whole. It is a complementary process to synechdoche, in which one specific part of the soundscape is valorized by selection (123). The processes are complementary because in order to valorize one part, a listener has to forget about or pay less attention to others. While these processes are both important to memory and perception, they are also involved in sound production, and were used to structure the Queen Elizabeth Park pieces created for the installation, website, and radio works. Ellipsis is used: short sections of sound are selected through time and cross-faded together to create shortened versions of a walk through an area (twenty minutes becomes two minutes). Particular moments are valorized because of their sonic potential, and highlighted using pitch-shifting, frequency filtering, panning and amplitude changes to create more abstract work. No attempt is made to re-situate the recordings or to provide a paced audio guide to the park.

A copy of the soundwalk tape was given to artist P. S. Moore. He began producing a series of drawings, paintings, and sculptures, based on his listening to the soundwalk and to abstract compositions based on it. The images were related to each of the sound files by referring to James Tenney's ideas about music and gestalt perception. Significant changes in the tempos, timbres, pitches and harmonies of the sounds determined how the images in the installation would change over time. For instance, in the Sunken Garden area, while approaching the waterfall, timbral density and amplitude both increase. The associated imagery becomes increasingly layered, with concentric rings that allude to the regular rhythm of the drums, and excerpts from photographs of the water that emphasize its quality of timbral or textural complexity. Both imagery and sounds reflect on listening, through abstraction, based on the experience itself. Finally, each composition was completed and connected to a map on the computer screen, which was based on the map from Westerkamp's article. Audience responses were collected and displayed on a computer in the gallery space.

Installation of this work took place in 1998, in Toronto and Kingston, Canada and New York, United States. Comments derive from written responses by students and gallery visitors. Several noted that the installation heightened their listening experience.

Tara says: "the sounds were quite clear, and made you stop and realize how often you don't pay attention to those sounds." Some visitors focused on the relationships between sound and images, and how the drawings and sculptures in the gallery were integrated with the digital imagery. JD says:

> I appreciate your recognition of the space around you, not only within your multi-media exploration, but of your occupation of the gallery space itself. The connection of the objects, images and studies which you have introduced into the 'environment', and their evidence on the walls in markings, etc., serve to heighten the levels of interaction and communicative exchange on levels which refer back to and heighten and expand those issues of space, landscape, experience and communication addressed in the video and multi-media work. I am far less isolated in the space than I expected to be.

Tara says that the installation "made you feel as if you had really visited Vancouver and the park." Several people at both the York University and the New York versions of the installation said that it reminded them of visits that they had previously made to Vancouver. Marcia's comment is interesting: she says that she would like to visit the park some day "to see how my perceptions of the second visit differ from the first." Here, she is explicitly referring to her visit to the installation as a visit to the park itself. Wendy makes an important point when she describes this as "a unique experience of a day at a park...that enables the viewer to be there with her." This construction of Queen Elizabeth Park is one based on a particular recording made at a certain time on a soundwalk by two individuals. The recordist's perspective influences how a soundwalk recording will be created and transformed, and how it will sound to the audience. The interpretation of that experience depends on each audience member, and their memories and experiences. Some other audience members write about the installation as futuristic. John describes it as portraying "a normal and serene setting in a particularly futuristic manner...you can experience what it feels like to be in a place without really being there." He continues by adding "This idea bothered me a little." Although John does not elaborate about why this idea bothered him, perhaps it could be because virtual worlds can seem a replacement for physically going somewhere. At the same time, Michelle suggests how this could be enabling: "someone who isn't able to travel could view the sights and listen to the sounds on the computer." Audience responses to this work voice some important questions, such as how gallery installations are related to the environments that inspired them, how hearing recorded sounds and pieces based on them leads to reflection on the significance of daily sounds that are often ignored otherwise, and how technology facilitates and constrains the documentation and representation of an experience.

As well as the interactive installation, a didactic website was produced (McCartney 2000) that compared the two walks (1974 and 1997) with the intention of developing both historical and geographical dimensions, discussing the soundwalk as it had changed over time and the park as an example of an urban post-industrial park (it was originally a quarry). This included short pieces that excerpted and cross-faded short sections of the walk. The pieces were kept short for greater public access since many people do not have high-speed internet. This website was later used by the British Educational Communications Technology Association as a resource for music education at the public school level (BECTA 2003). Students and teachers at the schools read about soundwalks on the website, listened to the excerpted pieces, and then designed and performed soundwalks around their school areas. The wide reach of this activity was supported by significant government funding and infrastructure in the United Kingdom.

Early in this century some attention began to be given to the range of approaches used in soundwalk work. A soundwalk website was developed by the Canadian Electroacoustic Community, bringing together the recorded walks and ideas about soundwalks of several authors, such as Steven Feld, Dallas Simpson, Victoria Fenner, Hildegard Westerkamp, and others (EContact! 2002). At the same time, practices based on walking and involving sound began to emerge from the visual arts and from music performance. These are not called soundwalks by the artists or musicians, yet some of these approaches are often grouped with soundwalks in discussions of the work.[7]

# Electrical Walks: Christina Kubisch

It could be argued that Christina Kubisch's electrical walks are not really soundwalks at all, since they deal with a kind of wave that cannot be heard because it is outside the range of human hearing: electricity. However, these walks transform electrical waves into sounds that can be heard and articulated, so that parking meters and neon lights each have a characteristic sound that can be a focus of listening through the headphones provided, a focus of attention, a focus of critique. A map of the area is marked with interesting electrical characteristics, and the listeners move freely throughout the space rather than on a prescribed or commented walk. The walks developed out of a technical challenge associated with her earlier installations based on electromagnetic induction. As Kubisch says:

> The magnetic headphones with their built-in coils respond to electrical fields in the environment. At first I tried to filter the soft hum of the electrical wires out of the headphones. Then, in 2003, the constant increase and spread of "unwanted," electrically produced sounds triggered a new cycle of works: Electrical Walks. With special, sensitive headphones, the acoustic perceptibility of aboveground and underground electrical currents is thereby not suppressed, but rather amplified. The palette of these noises, their timbre and volume vary from site to site and from country to country. They have one thing in common: they are ubiquitous. (2009)

Kubisch draws attention to the ubiquity of electricity by making it audible, an approach that is a bit different from the noise awareness activities of sound ecologists in its focus on the inaudible, but similar in its attention to contemporary waveform pollution.

## SOUND PILGRIMAGE: OLIVER SCHROER

Camino is a performative sonic pilgrimage and the aural record of a 1000 kilometer walk by violinist Oliver Schroer, his wife and two friends, in May and June of 2004. They walked the Camino pilgrim trail through France and Spain, and Schroer played his violin in churches along the way. The pilgrims carried a portable recording studio. Since permission to play in these spaces was often tenuous, Schroer always felt he could be stopped at any moment. Playing sometimes for several people and sometimes for a single listener, each space lent a different character to the performance: "The sense of place is strong here— pilgrims praying, children playing, birds, bells, footsteps, passing snatches of conversation, the sounds of the buildings themselves. Each space has its own distinct character and resonance" (Schroer 2005). Mixed around and between the violin tracks on the CD of the Camino experience are soundscape pieces that move between different spaces: "Moissac Bellswirl. On this day in Moissac an organ was playing in the cathedral and the bells were ringing outside. With my microphone I moved between these two places, the interior billowing with waves of mighty organ, and the outside alive with the sounds of the square, its bells, bicycles and birds, the sonorous shuffle of people living their lives" (Schroer 2005). Here, the instrumental performances in different locations form a series of stopping points along the way, reminiscent of the type of punctuated daily structure developed in the travel journals of the famous haiku poet Basho (2005). The sound pilgrimage forms a bridge between soundwalking practice and instrumental performance.

## SHADOW WALKS: VIV CORRINGHAM

English musician and sound artist Viv Corringham combines listening and walking with sung vocal improvisation. She documents her walks with audio recordings, accompanies them with objects found at the site (inspired by the work of British walking artist Richard Long), and creates other related artwork such as handmade books, photographs, textual work, and what she refers to as psycho-geographic maps. Psychogeography is a term that is associated with the Situationists and the concept of the dérive. "In a dérive one or more persons during a certain period drop their relations, their work and leisure activities, and all their other usual motives for movement and action, and let themselves be drawn by the attractions of the terrain and the encounters they find there" (Debord [1958] 2006). Unlike the flâneurs of the nineteenth century, the dérivistes often did their excursions as a group, and women were included although the main Situationist figures were men. Debord's writing about psychogeography and the concept of the dérive suggests an ecology of the senses:

> The ecological analysis of the absolute or relative character of fissures in the urban network, of the role of microclimates, of distinct neighborhoods with no relation

to administrative boundaries, and above all of the dominating action of centers of attraction, must be utilized and completed by psychogeographical methods. The objective passional terrain of the dérive must be defined in accordance both with its own logic and with its relations with social morphology. ([1958] 2006)

Corringham links her work as well with the long tradition in Britain of rural walking as a public right of way.[8] Paths are maintained that cut across private lands, providing access for walkers throughout the country. In her project "Shadow walks," Corringham asked people to show her walks that were personally meaningful. She would walk with the person and record their conversation during the walk, then go back along the same route alone, attempting to get a sense of the place they had walked through. Then she would sing what she felt using wordless improvisations. The sound pieces produced from this process integrate singing, narration and the sounds of the place. The relationships of shadows to subjects mirror the links between songs and spoken words, environmental sounds and the people who hear them, and present walks with earlier iterations. Corringham takes a number of approaches to the showing of this work: "Shadow-walks have been disseminated as audio-walks through which other people could follow the route and add their own traces and memories, as listening posts at public spaces in a town, or in an art gallery via headphones, along with objects found on the street while walking" (2010).

After this project, Corringham moved to Rochester in the United States. She found in that city there were very few people walking on the streets, and discovered that they were walking at the mall. She has continued her shadowing project in this kind of location, trying to understand the process of mall walking through participating in it and creating sound work out of that experience.

## Audio Walks: Janet Cardiff and George Bures Miller

The term audio walk is used by artists Janet Cardiff and George Bures Miller to describe their guided narratives inspired by film noir. While some writers refer to these narratives as soundwalks,[9] this term is not used by the artists themselves, who link their work more with audio production than with sound. Audio walks share with soundwalks their emphasis on sonic experiences of particular places, but there are some significant differences in conceptualization and practice. Cardiff and Miller's first audio walk was Forest Walk, completed while Cardiff had a residency at the Banff Centre for the Arts in 1991, where many Canadian sound artists including Hildegard Westerkamp have also worked, so they were likely aware of soundwalk practices. But in the monograph *The Walk Book*, written by Miriam Schaub (2005) in collaboration with the pair and giving a detailed introduction to their work, audio walks are situated in relation to museum and tourist tours rather than to soundwalks or soundscape art. The focus of audio walks is not acoustic ecology but rather the creation of a directed narrative using environmental sounds as a base or ambient track, as in a film soundtrack. There are frequent references to film culture in writing about audio walks. Schaub refers to the work as physical cinema, and says that Cardiff "creates a soundtrack for the real world" (25). This emphasis on the created or imaginary world superimposed over real world sounds differs from acoustic ecologists' desire for listeners to pay attention to the sounds of the environment for their own intrinsic qualities and social meanings.

In audio walks, sounds recorded on site are layered with a dramatic monologue by Cardiff which is forefronted in the mix (again like a film soundtrack) and accompanied by sound effects and music related to the narrative. Listeners walk through the site wearing headphones. The walks encourage slippage between the real environment that the listener walks through and the imaginary environment created and directed by Cardiff and Miller. The relationship with the audience is one of intimacy and direct authority, since Cardiff tells audience members exactly where to walk, controls pacing by asking listeners to match her footsteps, directs attention to particular visual and haptic features of the location, and suggests lines of thought or inquiry. Environmental sounds feature prominently at times in the soundtrack but the main focus of attention is the voice and its narrative flow. The audio walks have the flavor of murder mysteries, speaking of missing persons and murders, thus sometimes inducing a state of anxiety in the listener. These walks also include references to local history and contemporary news, as in the New York Central Park walk, Her Long Black Hair, which asks listeners at one point to consider Cardiff's interpretation of a news photo of an Iraqi father whose three daughters were killed by a bomb. Marla Carlson describes how this strategy works with cultural memory during the audio walk: "Cardiff has shifted us a step further, from memories of a single, historical act of violence with broad cultural resonance to the ongoing, wide-ranging violence of the war in Iraq that many of us screen out in order to proceed with everyday life" (2006:404). Carlson writes evocatively of how at this moment, other images and memories of reported war and murder come together in her experience of the walk. Another walker-writer comments on how Cardiff's walk integrates experience by synesthetically calling on all the senses (Gagnon 2007). By its emphasis on audio production of a directed and multi-layered narrative, the audio walk leads the listener into an imaginary world in which real sounds and architectural features blend into a mysterious narrative, drawing on that place.

## AUDIO GUIDES AND LISTENING GUIDES

The website soundwalk.com originated as a commercial venture, intended to give tourists to New York audio guides to specific areas of the city, narrated by local residents, with tips on good places to shop, eat, and dance. The site then expanded to include audio guides to other cities, and more recently has featured a section on art projects created by the team. Now, the Wikipedia oracle has a disambiguated fork for the term *soundwalk*, in which one fork is associated with sound ecology and the second with the soundwalk. com site, indicating the ubiquitous association of the term with this kind of guide. Like the audio walks of Cardiff and Miller, these are walks intended to be heard through headphones, are timed to the footsteps of the narrator, are densely layered and are represented as a particularly cinematic experience. However, rather than always having the same narrator, here the narration is provided by a range of different people depending on the location. In the case of the Ground Zero memorial created by soundwalk.com, the voices of several artists are mixed with 911 calls and other more public discourse. Marla Carlson (2006) points out that even though the group does not explicitly position itself as an artistic group, the narrative about Ground Zero refers to artistic ideas about the site. Research assistant Marc Griebel went to New York and experienced the Ground Zero walk, having been asked to keep in mind aspects such as communication with the audience, treatment of the environment, and overall aesthetics:

> The Ground Zero Sonic Memorial Project, developed by soundwalk.com in collaboration with NPR's *All Things Considered,* is an award winning audio work that allows tourists to be personally guided through the area of Lower Manhattan where the World Trade Centre used to stand. Beginning at the front of St. Paul's chapel it directs participants along the southern half of the site, ending behind the World Financial Centre Plaza. Over the course of just under 45 minutes one is asked to follow the voice of the narrator, author Paul Auster, as he leads one through cemeteries, busy streets, construction sites, corporate buildings, and urban parks. Along the way these environs are transformed for the audience by incorporating a variety of seamlessly edited and densely layered narratives, archived recordings, music, and environmental sounds that contextualize the area's history and memories. Described as a "sonic memorial soundwalk" this audio guide is intended to function as a way to cultivate specific cultural and collective memories around the atrocities which occurred at the site on September 11, 2001.
>
> I took the Ground Zero Sonic Memorial in the early spring of 2010 with two friends, Beth and Dan, in order to glean a deeper understanding of both the site, as well as how the audio work functioned as a soundwalk. No one in the group had ever been to New York, and all of us were curious about how this experience may better inform our conception of the events surrounding 9-11 as well as the current state of the site. We had bought the MP3 from the soundwalk.com website and experienced it by listening through an iPod and headphones.
>
> At the beginning of the guide Paul Auster thanks the participants for "joining (him) on this Sonic Memorial Soundwalk," an interesting choice of words considering the form, content, and relationships that are developed through the audio. One of the first qualities of the work to be noticed by all three of us was the pacing, which was 70–75 beats per minute. The pace was often acoustically timed out by a metronome that accompanied much of the music and would set a sense of rhythm for the site. The problem here was that it did not leave enough beats, or steps, to completely traverse from one point to another in an attentive manner. With such a lack of time between the points of interest we found ourselves continually rushed to keep up with the instructions, walking against the beat provided, while often reaching the

"soundwalk locations" 10 to 15 seconds too late. This made for a sense of mild anxiety and frustration for everyone in the group, as we had to often rush forward and passively listen while navigating the space rather than be attentive to the new environment surrounding us.

The content of the instruction had a deep impact on the experience of the place as well. Whereas many soundwalk practices include discussions at the beginning of the walk in terms of etiquette and various strategies for active listening, the instructions for this work come through the narration and commanded the participant as to where they can go and when, binding them into the piece, and demanding their attention the entire walk in order for the work to be executed properly. This affects the individual's experience of the place as they are not open to informing their own understandings of the environment, but are consistently told what to think.

The effects of this narrative may also be understood in relation to how pronouns are incorporated to address the audiences relationship to the work and the space. When delivering a personal story about the WTC, the storytellers always uses the personal form of "I." The narrator introduces guests as "they," puts in his own experiences, and will make statements involving a "we." One of the few examples of this "we" is right at the beginning of the walk when Paul Auster states: "We came together after September 11th, 2001; radio producers, artists, construction workers, bond traders, secretaries, archivists, widows, fire fighters..." but nowhere does he mention the participants current "coming together" with the work, events, and space. At the end of the work he also states "we all knew this could happen, we have been talking about the possibility for years..." Again, one could ask if Auster is including the audience as part of this "we", or if it is a specific type of New Yorker, which the audience as tourist is most likely not. The only time that the participants are actually addressed is when they are given explicit instructions on where to go and when. It should be mentioned that this is not the way that all audience members have experienced the piece. Marla Carlson states that the Ground Zero Soundwalk: "...is one of a number of ways to actively remember and restage this locale.... The Soundwalk gave me new memories of a place for which I never had any particular fondness" (2006:414). For Carlson the engagement of the audience with these narratives in the space where the event took place allows for us to understand others memories while creating our own. I would tend to wonder what the quality of these experiences actually are. Though this audio work does engage the audience with others memories, I found that it allowed little space for the participant to reflect on their understandings of the tragedy surrounding 9-11, let alone any contemporary conception of what the site may be able to communicate to us about what these memories may mean to us today.

A listening guide is similar to an audio guide in its use of headphone delivery and regulated pacing. But the emphasis shifts from audio production values to a focus on listening strategies. Lisa Gasior's "Sounding Griffintown: A Listening Guide of a Montreal Neighbourhood" incorporates soundscape recordings with interviews of former Griffintown residents and imagined sounds of the past to create a sense of the competing claims of history through everyday story-telling.[10] This former residential neighborhood was changed to an industrial area in the 1960s and the listening guide gives an eerie sense of the residential past in the industrial present. The listening guide draws attention to conflicting ideas of truth and the workings of memory. The voice of the narrator (Gasior) stays in the background as the histories and mythologies of the area are recounted by former residents. The focus of narrative voices shifts from that of experts to competing claims on truth and memory, where different voices contradict each other. This approach to soundwalking can be situated in between art and documentary in its consideration of ideas about truth, memory and representation in the oral histories of the former residents. While voices are central to an understanding of the Griffintown listening guide, Gasior asks the listener to maintain contact with the sound environment by pausing the narrative at street corners, and telling the listener to remove the headphones from time to time in order to listen more closely to contemporary sounds of the environment, forming a bridge between history and current concerns.

Another contemporary approach to online place-telling with sound is through the development of sound maps with instructions for public uploading, which have been established for several areas including New York city, Berlin, Aberdeenshire, Montreal, Toronto, Cologne, Minnesota and many other sites. These sound maps are often linked to pages describing the approaches of soundwalking, psychogeography and Situationism, as well as practical guides to working with GPS systems.[11] Sound maps provide access points for people interested in field recording to upload sound experiences to a common interface, providing the possibility for exchange and collaboration without the gate-keeping of gallery sites. Soundwalk recordings and pieces made from them are included on these sites which also include examples of other types of field recording.

The practices discussed here take very different approaches to communication with audiences, style of delivery, methods of audio production and dissemination, and overall intention. Each soundwalk structures the experience of participants through the way the location is presented and the kind of dialogue that is facilitated. Westerkamp directs questions to her audience and asks them to reflect on their own experiences and understandings. The approach of Lopez challenges the perceptual understandings of sighted soundwalkers who must give up their ocular privilege and submit to the acoustic leadership of an unsighted companion. Throughout the Ground Zero soundwalk, the audience hears specific narratives by citizens and experts directly impacted by the collapse of the World Trade Center and is told what this site meant for others, more than asked what it might currently mean for them. Janet Cardiff maintains a playful, seductive tone to her interactions with the audience, including reflective moments such as the one mentioned by Marla Carlson about the Iraqi family's loss, but also instructions to walk backward or wet the finger, or not to turn even while sonically being followed. In Viv Corringham's shadow walks, the participants are asked to remember a personally meaningful story, and to recount it. This recounting, combined with Corringham's vocalizations and the objects she gathers from the site, provides several layers of meaning and possible reflection to gallery visitors, who are encouraged to walk the route themselves gathering objects and reflecting. The fact that the objects collected are often trash adds a layer of environmental awareness that extends beyond the sonic.

There are also a number of questions raised by these divergent practices about the relative importance of different sound sources in the soundwalk experience and the way it is produced for audiences. More recent walk experiences, such as Cardiff's audio walks, Gasior's listening guide, and the soundwalk.com downloads, all integrate environmental sounds into a soundtrack about the place that is densely layered, often includes music, has a specific pace, and is directed by a vocal narrative. In the case of memorial soundwalks, this narrative is strongly emotional, drawing the attention of the walker even further. These walks are all intended to be listened to on headphones, which creates a sonic bubble around the listener, giving them the privilege of privacy and anonymity. Where tour groups often make tourists an obvious outsider in the spaces they visit, the audio guide, once purchased for download and accessed with the accompanying iPhone application, can be consumed personally, not drawing attention to the individual. This allows for the participant to blend into the environment that they are led through. At the same time headphones insulate and isolate the participant from the actual sound environment. There can be less concern for the sound environment where the walk is taking place. Whereas Gasior and Cardiff include moments for the audience to interact directly with the sound environment, there are no points of silence within the Ground Zero walk to listen to the present sound environment. The continual narrative, often contextualized with archived material and music, make the site a place of history, but does not focus on its present incarnation for the participant. This allows for the audience to become aware of the tragedy of the area, but limits reflection about current issues that may be occurring. By cutting off the acoustics of the space from the individual, and replacing it with post-production works layered with narrative, music, and foley, the experience of the space becomes more cinematic, taking it closer to the realm of entertainment or a simulacrum, with a focus on the walker as consumer of a packaged experience. While contemporary soundwalking practice includes highly produced soundwalks such as these, other recent approaches include sites such as the New York sound map and other websites devoted to soundwalking methodologies which leave the responsibility of choice of location, design of the walk, and style of recording and production practices completely up to the participant. Installation work is a third stream of soundwalk practice that includes evocative productions as well as suggestions about soundwalking methods, and is often linked with public soundwalk events.

Soundwalking retains its dual roles in artistic creation and research. Contemporary work on soundwalking as a research methodology is being carried out at several international sites. At CRESSON, Nicolas Tixier, in collaboration with Nicolas Boyer and under the direction of Jean-Francois Augoyard, has developed an approach that he describes as "qualified listening in motion." In this method, participants in urban settings are recorded walking through an area that they know well while commenting on the sounds that they hear. Tixier notes that this research method encourages a particularly fluid and open relationship between soundscape researcher and participant (Tixier 2002).

Soundwalking is being used as a primary research method by an interdisciplinary group at the University of Salford in the United Kingdom, under the name Positive Soundscapes. This group considers soundwalking a useful approach to bring professionals of different disciplines together in a common activity, in which information can be shared with less disciplinary boundaries. This group notes the importance of successive

FIGURE 8.3 Tia Kramer's photo of Antarctic recording soundwalk led by Andrea Polli.

soundwalks as a way to develop a map with acoustic features. This historical approach of developing an ongoing soundwalk practice, with possibilities for sustained methodological research, is being investigated in other research creation projects as well. The Vancouver New Music Society has instituted a regular season of soundwalks as part of the new music offerings in that city. As a result, the Vancouver Soundwalk Collective has formed in Vancouver, who are meeting on a regular basis to explore and produce various approaches to soundwalking, thinking about issues such as collaborative leadership. Andrea Polli has integrated soundwalks into her geosonification work, most recently in Antarctica (2009) (Figure 8.3). In Montreal, the Journées Sonores: canal de Lachine project used the recording of individual soundwalks and commented walks by local residents, as well as public walks followed by reflective discussions, and the development of an interactive installation, as research methods to think about the changing sonic environment in an urban area over a time of significant change, as a disused industrial canal formerly known as the birthplace of Canadian industry was re-opened to public recreational traffic (McCartney 2005).

Soundwalking has established a substantial role in contemporary sound research as well as artistic practice. The influence of soundwalking also extends beyond sonic research into suggested methodologies for the social sciences. A recent article in

Qualitative Inquiry suggests soundwalking as a method to initiate contextually sensitive interviews (Hall et al. 2008).

As an artistic practice, contemporary soundwalking has been interpreted in a number of different ways, many of which have been discussed in this chapter. However, because these practices are proliferating widely and broadly, there are likely many other approaches to soundwalking. The reader is encouraged to use the sites and readings listed in the text and in the following references as starting points for soundwalks of their own devising.

# Acknowledgments

The author wishes to thank the Quebec FQRSC–Fonds de recherche sur la société et la culture for their support of this research. Thanks to the readers and editors of this work for their close reading and incisive editorial suggestions, and to Hildegard Westerkamp, Ellen Waterman, Nimalan Yoganathan, Rainer Wiens, David Paquette, Samuel Thulin, and Andrea Polli for commenting on early drafts of this chapter. The assistance of Marc Griebel was invaluable at the editing stage.

## Notes

1. See also http://www.egreenway.com/walking/walk9bib.htm. Accessed Jan 23, 2011.
2. See also http://www.tonyschwartz.org/#audio. Accessed March 16, 2011.
3. See for instance Fluxus walk 1962–2002, http://www.mail-archive.com/fluxlist@scribble.com/msg10417.html. Accessed March 5, 2011.
4. Hildegard Westerkamp, interview with McCartney, April 1993.
5. Ibid.
6. For an example, listen to Lighthouse Park Soundwalk (1977), http://cec.concordia.ca/Radio/Long/Westerkamp.html. Accessed Jan 12, 2011.
7. See for instance LaBelle 2006 and Licht 2007.
8. See also Whitehead 2006.
9. See for instance LaBelle 2006 and Licht 2007.
10. Available at www.griffinsound.ca.
11. For a particularly good list of resources, see http://www.nysoundmap.org/.

## References

Augoyard, Jean Francois. 2007. *Step by Step: Everyday Walks in a French Urban Housing Project.* Trans. David Ames Curtis. Minneapolis: University of Minnesota Press.

Augoyard, Jean-Francois, and Henry Torgue. 2005. *Sonic Experience: A Guide to Everyday Sounds.* Trans. Andra McCartney and David Paquette. Montreal: McGill-Queen's Press.

Basho, Matsuo. 2005. *Basho's Journey: The Literary Prose of Matsuo Basho*. Trans. David L. Barnhill. Rochester, NY: State University of New York Press.

British Educational Communications and Technology Agency (BECTA). 2003. *ICT Advice: Using web-based resources in primary music: Soundwalk*. Coventry, UK. http://www.mmiweb.org.uk/publications/webprimary/music.pdf (accessed March 2010).

Cage, John. 1961. *Silence*. Cambridge, MA: MIT Press.

Carlson, Marla. 2006. "Looking, Listening and Remembering: Ways to Walk New York After 9/11." *Theatre Journal* 58:395–416.

De Certeau, Michel. 1984. *The Practice of Everyday Life*. Trans. Steven Rendall. Berkeley: University of California Press.

Chatwin, Bruce. 1987. *The Songlines*. London, UK: Pan.

Corringham, Viv. 2010. "Shadow Walks," http://vivcorringham.org/shadow-walks; and http://www-fofa.concordia.ca/econtact/11_4/corringham_shadowwalks.html (accessed March 29, 2010).

Debord, Guy. [1958] 2006. "Théorie de la dérive." In *Situationist International Anthology*, Rev. Ed. Trans. Ken Knabb. Available at http://www.bopsecrets.org/SI/2.derive.htm (accessed December 8, 2008).

Feld, Steven. 1994. "From Schizophonia to Schismogenesis..." In *Music Grooves*, ed. Charles Keil and Steven Feld, 257–89. Chicago: University of Chicago Press.

Friedman, Ken. 2009. "Events and the Exquisite Corpse." In *The Exquisite Corpse: Chance and Collaboration in Surrealism's Parlor Game*, ed. Kanta Kochhar-Lindgren, Davis Schneiderman, and Tom Denlinger, 49–82. Chapel Hill, NC: University of Nebraska Press.

EContact! 2002. 4.3 Promenade Sonore/Soundwalk. Canadian Electroacoustic Community. Text, still images, sound. http://econtact.ca.

Freire, Paulo. 1994. *Pedagogy of Hope: Reliving Pedagogy of the Oppressed*. New York: Continuum.

Gagnon, Monika. "Janet Cardiff." *Senses and Society* 2(2):259–64.

Gleber, Anke. 1999. *The Art of Taking A Walk: Flanerie, Literature and Film in Weimar Culture*. Princeton, NJ: Princeton University Press.

Hall, Tom, Brett Lashua, and Amanda Coffey. 2008. "Sound and the Everyday in Qualitative Research." *Qualitative Inquiry* 6(14):1019–40.

Kreutzfeld, Jacob. 2006. "Ishibashi Soundscape: Investigating the Soundscape of Urban Japan." *Studies in Urban Cultures* 8:88–99.

Kubisch, Christina. 2009. "Works with Electromagnetic Induction," http://www.christinakubisch.de/english/klangundlicht_frs.htm (accessed March 3, 2009).

LaBelle, Brandon. 2006. *Background Noise: Perspectives on Sound Art*. New York: Continuum.

Licht, Alan. 2007. *Sound Art: Beyond Music, Between Categories*. New York: Rizzolli.

Lopez, Francisco. 2006. "Blind City." Champs Libres, Montreal. Invisible City, http://www.champlibre.com/citeinvisible/uk/participants/pagetype.php?rubrique=inst&ssrub=1&fiche=063 (accessed March 26, 2010).

McCartney, Andra. 2000. "Sounding Places with Hildegard Westerkamp." Electronic Music Foundation. http://www.emf.org/artists/mccartney00/ (accessed March 30, 2009).

McCartney, Andra, and Sandra Gabriele. 2001. "Soundwalking at Night." Paper presented at *Night and the City*. McGill University, Montreal, QC, March 15.

McDowell, Linda. 1999. "In Public: The Streets and Spaces of Pleasure." In *Gender, Identity and Place: Understanding Feminist Geographies*, 148–69. Minneapolis: University of Minnesota Press.

Piper, Adrian. "Streetwalk/Streettracks I–II (1969)," Adrian Piper archive, http://www.adrian-piper.com/art/sound.shtml (accessed August 18, 2008).

Polli, Andrea. 2009. "Sonic Antarctica: Soundscape, Geosonification and the Social Geography of Global Climate Change." Paper presented at World Forum for Acoustic Ecology conference, Mexico City, March.

Rosaldo, Renato. 1988. "Ideology, Place, and People without Culture." *Cultural Anthropology* 3(1):77–87.

Schafer, R. Murray, ed. 1977a. *Vancouver Sound Diary*. Vancouver: ARC Publications.

——. 1977b. *European Sound Diary*. Vancouver: ARC Publications.

Schaub, Mirjam. 2005. *Janet Cardiff: The Walk Book,* ed. Thyssen-Bornemisza. Koln: Koenig.

Schroer, Oliver. 2005. *Camino* [liner notes]. Borealis Records. Available at www.oliverschroer.com.

Schwartz, Tony. 1974. *The Responsive Chord.* New York: Doubleday.

Thich, Nhat Hanh. 1996. *The Long Road Turns to Joy: A Guide to Walking Meditation*, rev. ed. Berkeley, CA: Parallax Press.

Thompson, Emily. 2002. *The Soundscape of Modernity: Architectural Acoustics and the Culture of Listening in America, 1900–1933.* Cambridge, MA: MIT Press.

Thoreau, Henry David. 1862. *Walking.* Bedford, MA: Applewood.

Tixier, Nicolas. 2002. "Street Listening. A Characterisation of the Sound Environment: The 'Qualified Listening in Motion' Method." In *Soundscape Studies and Methods*, ed. Helmi Jarviluoma and Gregg Wagstaff, 83–90. Turku: Finnish Society for Ethnomusicology.

Wagstaff, Gregg. 2002. "Soundwalks." *Radio Art Companion.* Toronto, ON: New Adventures in Sound Art.

Westerkamp, Hildegard. 1996. *Transformations.* CD. Montréal: empreintes DIGITALes.

——. 1974. "Soundwalking." *Sound Heritage* 3(4):18–27. Republished in *Autumn Leaves, Sound and the Environment in Artistic Practice*, ed. Angus Carlyle (2007). Paris: Double Entendre.

——. 1977. "Lighthouse Park Soundwalk." *EContact! 2002 Soundwalk Issue.* Canadian Electroacoustic Community, http://cec.concordia.ca/Radio/Long/Westerkamp.html.

——. 1994. "The Soundscape on Radio." *In Radio Rethink*, ed. D. Augaitis and D. Lander. Banff, Alberta: Walter Phillips Gallery.

Whitehead, Simon. 2006. *Walking to Work.* Abercych, Pembrokeshire, Wales: Shoeless.

Wilson, Alexander. 1998. *The Culture of Nature: North American Landscape from Disney to the Exxon Valdez.* Toronto: Between the Lines.

CHAPTER 9

# GESTURAL CHOREOGRAPHIES: EMBODIED DISCIPLINES AND DIGITAL MEDIA

HARMONY BENCH

IT began with a simple drag. My friend's daughter was playing with an iPhone. A year and a half old, she had grown tired of what had recently been her favorite application, one in which noisy farm animals hide behind red barn doors that open when tapped. She had begun to master puzzles, dragging shapes from the corner of the iPhone to their corresponding outlines in the center of the small screen. As she dislodged each shape, it made a suctioning sound, as though it was attaching to her body. As she pulled her finger away from the screen, the puzzle piece snapped into place. Watching her delicately position each shape, moving her tiny pointer finger slowly and purposefully so as not to lose contact with the image (see Figure 9.1), I began to think about my own screen-oriented gestures. I began to notice all the people around me on their hand-held devices: the ways their bodies curved into supportive architectures with which they cradled touch-screens and tried to cocoon electronic pinging, firing, and splatting sounds with their bodies (see Figure 9.2); their techniques for walking and texting, their button-pressing falling in and out of sync with the uneven rhythms of their feet on the pavement (see Figure 9.3); and their impromptu feats of multitasking negotiating the multiple information streams of screens, sounds, gestures, text, and other data (see Figure 9.4). I wondered how these bodies emerged and what sensorial knowledge was already in place to accommodate the requirements of digital and mobile media. As I watched the toddler next to me, I further wondered at the role technologies play in bringing into being the bodies that can use them. At what point in my own bodily history did a tap-and-drag motion cease requiring concentration and become habit, thus installing itself, through repetition, in a set of bodily movements that seemed "natural" because I no longer had to think about them? What was it about electronic sounds

FIGURE 9.1 A toddler plays a puzzle game on a first-generation (2G) iPhone. Note the facility with which she holds the phone in her left hand and uses her right pointer finger to grab and drag the onscreen images. Photo by Harmony Bench.

that spurred me to mute all sound-based notifications and alarms on my digital devices, silencing all auditory feedback, while my friend sought to amplify every possible sonic function, from her custom ringtones to the noisy racket of her retro typewriter touch screen keyboard? Through what experimental processes had the little girl beside me begun to distinguish the functions and limits of her tapping, the efficacy of which was demonstrated both visually and sonically (and sometimes haptically) on a touch screen but not on a television, and which netted altogether different results when used on her mother or her dog? In response to what complex of gestures and sounds are digital devices designed, and what alternate gestural and sonic configurations do they produce through their imitation and reworking of human perceptual faculties?

Not being a psychologist or neurologist, I am unprepared to answer these questions, nor can I pretend to accurately reconstruct my own process of acquiring the physical skills of computing and media operation that reach back to my own childhood of pressing buttons, maneuvering joysticks, and, much later, typing on a computer keyboard. What I attempt to do in this essay is to demonstrate how the movement vocabularies of gestural computing, much of which occurs on mobile media platforms, layer bodily techniques cultivated across media and technologies, establish these movements as interface-based choreographies of sound and gesture, and move computational gestures from the terrain of communication into that of information manipulation. A "tap" is a

FIGURE 9.2 A college student plays a game on his smartphone while riding the bus. Note the curvature of his body and downward focus. Also note the way he holds the device close to his body and slightly wings his elbows outward to compensate for the phone's proximity, enabling him to manipulate the screen's contents with his left thumb and right fingers. Photo by Harmony Bench.

bodily technique, a form of physical training. Each gesture that a user performs in order to navigate information rehearses these digital bodily techniques and interface-based choreographies, at once cultivating and performing the body that has been imagined in programming code and hardware design.

## CULTIVATING CORPOREALITIES

How we know our bodies and therefore know how to use them is increasingly articulated in relation to the digital technologies that surround us. Philosopher Giorgio Agamben observes, for example, that in Italy, "the gestures and behaviors of individuals have been reshaped from top to toe by the cellular telephone" (2009:15–16). Now that a majority of the global population uses a cell phone (*Associated Press* 2009), the same could be said almost anywhere in the world—and most certainly those residing in the media-saturated United States are shifting their corporeal and social arrangements to accommodate the ubiquitous presence of cell phones and other digital

FIGURE 9.3 A woman walks down the sidewalk while texting. She cradles the phone in her hands and presses its buttons with her thumbs. Her downward focus is interspersed with occasional glances at her environment, but for the most part she looks at the text(s) she is composing on her phone while walking. Photo by Harmony Bench.

media devices. A Horowitz Associates study conducted in 2008 showed that among internet-using 15- to 17-year-old Americans, 86% owned a handheld device, whether a cell phone or smartphone, personal digital music player, or portable gaming device.[1] According to an April 2009 study by the NDP Group, it is not only teenagers and adults who own such items. They found that 30% of American youths 4 to 14 years old currently own a personal digital music player and 37% own a portable gaming device. Howard Rheingold, writing for the technology magazine *Wired*, reports that even Amish communities in Pennsylvania, long known for their rejection of electronic technologies, have incorporated cell phones and computers into their business operations, if not into their home lives (1999). So-called "digital natives" are thus not the only ones for whom ubiquitous computing profoundly impacts sociality, culture, and physicality. Adopted at whatever point in one's life, the daily uses of cell phones, digital music players, GPS navigation and mapping technologies, email, and word processing find their places in a growing inventory of bodily techniques and disciplinary technologies. Digital media not only demand a new form of physical education, they are themselves the mechanisms for that education. Moreover, this physical education takes place not only in the muscles and joints, but in the apprehension of sound as well.

FIGURE **9.4** A preteen is captured in full multi-tasking mode: talking on a wireless landline phone, operating her Nintendo DS with a stylus, and surfing the Web on a home computer. Photo by Alisa Wakefield. Used with permission.

Media create the bodies that use them. Analyzing alphabetic writing as a media technology, cultural theorist Brian Rotman argues that alphabetic writing "engages directly and inescapably with the bodies of its users. It makes demands and has corporeal effects. As a necessary condition for its operations it produces a certain body...by imposing its own mediological needs on the body" (2008:15). At school, children are taught to hold their writing utensils in a manner deemed "correct," and they eventually discipline scribbles and scrawls into legible letters or characters. With the help of teachers and parents, children fill out worksheets of letters, following dotted lines before making any unguided attempts of their own, practicing, repeating, memorizing the motions required to produce each letter, duplicating lines and curves to the best of their abilities, noting how the strokes of an "i" differ from those of an "s," not only in their shapes, but in the sounds they create on paper: the perfunctory line of the "i" and its staccato dot, the changing pitch of the "s" as it rounds its long curving sweep. With each exercise, students trace the movement and neural pathways that form linkages between thoughts and written words, thereby facilitating future translations of ideas, images and sounds onto the page.

For media theorist Ellen Seiter, it is the young musician rather than the young writer who forms a contemporary parallel with computer users and gamers. She argues that the current rate of computer and internet usage in homes mirrors the spread of pianos throughout Europe in the eighteenth century. As "instruments of modern education" (2008:47), pianos and computers are markers of middle class identities and their mastery acts as a form of cultural capital. Seiter delineates shared requirements of musical and digital literacy, noting in particular that "learning is time consuming, with time spent practicing rewarded by qualitatively different levels of mastery" (33). Like the rote repetitions required to learn a musical instrument, practicing scales and working through tunes until they can be played with ease, increased time spent at the computer or playing videogames results in increased competence. Musicians fine-tune finger movements and bowing techniques, adjusting the pressure they exert to coax different sound qualities from their instruments (or their unconventional sound-making objects). Computer and media operators train their bodies to use their computational instruments, increasing their typing speeds, learning keyboard shortcuts, creating spatial relationships among pieces of information scattered across a screen, responding to auditory cues (the crumple of electronic trash or the startling plunk of a disallowed action) and navigating by manipulating a mouse or performing finger-sized calisthenics on a trackpad or touch-screen.

In games such as Activision's *Guitar Hero*, available on the palm-sized Nintendo DS as *Guitar Hero: On Tour*, finger movements are loosely associated with playing chords on a guitar. As a song plays, a gamer strums and presses the color-coded fret buttons that correspond to gems cruising down the onscreen highway, which resembles the neck of a guitar. The objective is to strike the strum bar and press the fret buttons as the gems pass a threshold indicating when the notes are played in the song. Although the *Guitar Hero* games encourage gamers to tune in to a song's rhythmic structure, they do not offer instruction in playing guitar, or, for that matter, in music composition and innovation. The skills of playing *Guitar Hero* are non-transferable, in part because, in Rotman's words, the "mediological needs" of a guitar and a videogame controller or of music and videogames differ substantially, even when one approximates the other.

Like writing and musicianship, digital technologies demand a corporeal training that impacts operators' experiences of their physicality, often in relation to sound. Almost from the beginning of computer and videogame design, sound has been a crucial component of the gaming experience, establishing the mood of gameplay, subconsciously adding to the pressure a gamer feels when confronting a particularly challenging game situation and marking a gamer's jumping or shooting commands with "boings" and "bangs." But sound also plays a role in a gamer's physical education; as media users repeat certain gestures over and over, working them into the body as a gestural repertory, they respond to and produce sonic feedback. Just as students learn to write by repeatedly practicing the same finger, hand, wrist and arm motions to produce legible letters, young gamers, texters and computer enthusiasts develop a muscle memory of keystrokes, button combinations, and abstract motions that produce desired onscreen outcomes. These bodily motions and onscreen results have material and auditory effects.

Courses in computer literacy, for example, begin, as did the courses that first taught use of the typewriter, by teaching students to type without looking at the keyboard.

Students sit in front of computers learning the placement of "home keys" by tapping each letter according to a pattern onscreen: ffff jjjj dddd kkkk, etc. For the WIMP (windows, icons, menus, pointing device) user interfaces that have predominated in desktop and laptop computing environments, hands and wrists find themselves next to one another on the keyboard, closer than the shoulders' width that anatomically separates them. Fingers curl down mimicking a relaxed position—neither stretched nor retracted but poised over the keyboard. Letters and numbers appear onscreen with the fingers' downward motions, with which their tips press the appropriate keys firmly but gently, a consistent clattering of keys that sheds the harder striking force required for typewriters and "hunt and peck" typing—a style that betrays one's lack of training. The thumbs, meanwhile, are given the odd job of spacing from a sideways position.

Although each finger is assigned a unique set of keys, the positions of which are fixed in muscle memory through rote repetition, it is not the case that typists orient their bodies to a computer keyboard exclusively through the tactility of hardware interfaces and the repetitive gestures associated with them. The standardized (variable by linguistic region) spatial arrangements of keys, the raised bump on "f" and "j" on QWERTY keyboards are joined by the sounds of the keys, grouped into categories of function and frequency of usage, to inform typists of where their fingers sit on the keyboard. Because of their different shapes and sizes, each set of keys has its own inflection. The larger command keys on the far sides of the keyboard and especially the spacebar beneath have a different sonic range than the smaller letter and number keys, each resisting a finger or thumb's downward push and reverberating according to its size.

The use of a mouse adds to this repertory of keyboard movements and sounds. Fitting nicely in the palm of one's hand, the mouse summons a vocabulary of pointing and clicking to select text or menu options, and grabbing and dragging to move icons and other visual representations within the screen space. Because the field of mouse movement is contained, either by the reach of a cord or the size of a mouse pad or trackpad, it is common to brush a mouse multiple times in a single direction, scraping along the surface where the mouse sits or stroking a smooth touch-sensitive trackpad, to reach some far corner of the screen. Selection occurs with a dull, quiet thump on a trackpad or the two-part click and release of a mouse button—sounds that, like computational gestures, have become so familiar that they cease to consciously register.

The price of this automaticity is time. The cultivation of computing skills requires a time investment, much of which occurs outside official learning environments or surreptitiously within them, and which is especially oriented toward amusement. Often, young people begin their digital physical education prior to formal training in a classroom by playing video and computer games, and as they get older, they continue that training without the presence of an instructor through such diverse activities as social networking, peer-to-peer file sharing, gaming, chatting, texting or surfing the Internet. Perhaps because these activities are associated with leisure and are viewed by some as a waste of time rather than a time investment, the physical training and bodily knowledge required to operate digital media remains invisible as such. Parents may think their children have a "knack" for computing by virtue of having been born into a media-saturated environment, but as anthropologist Marcel Mauss remarks, "a manual knack can only be learned slowly" ([1934] 1992:457). Furthermore, computing skills must constantly be cultivated and updated as operators adapt to user interfaces and programmed behaviors that change frequently and sometimes radically, as, for example, with the release of new computer operating systems or new game controllers. Digital media therefore require constant practice to develop and maintain the physical skills that accompany technical savvy.

As Seiter observes in her comparison of computing and musical skills, "practicing for large blocks of time results in a physical orientation to the piano or PC, so that the relationship of the body to the object becomes automatic rather than conscious" (2008:34). For the well-trained, those who have committed the requisite number of hours to the mastery of digital media, this automaticity hides the technical object or tool behind the work and play it enables. And indeed, this disappearance is desirable from a product design perspective—physical or cultural awareness of computing detracts from both work and play, which drives the marketability of media technologies. Physical disorders such as the 1990s phenomenon of "nintendinitis," the current need for occupational therapists to address symptoms of carpal tunnel and cubital tunnel syndromes, or the recently reported increase in hearing loss among American teenagers (*Medical News Today* 2010) shift awareness away from the task at hand and refocus it on the sometimes detrimental effects of constantly fitting bodies into the spaces carved out by technologies. Though the persistent ideal is one of a seamless interface between body and technology, media, from pianos to MP3 players, place a burden of activity on body parts not anatomically equipped to assume such roles. In response, bodies rebel against the limits of technologically determined corporeal organizations; physical competence may result in injuries of overuse. When interfacing with digital media becomes difficult, the complex choreographies that govern media operation and the physical training and skill they necessitate are most apparent. Physical habits and motor pathways must be unlearned and bodies reoriented in order to recover from or prevent further injury, while attempts to shut out environmental noise with earphones may lead to irreversible damage to the ear.

Even though doing so may cause physical discomfort or even injury, digital media operators attune their bodies to the standards, protocols and dimensions of their devices, assuming what ergonomics specialist Robin Mary Gillespie politely describes as "sustained and awkward postures" (2002:249). Cell phone users on busy streets contort their bodies into sound barriers—ears clamped, shoulders hunched. Or else they become human antennas, desperately grasping at bits of meaning, pacing and stretching to amplify a weak signal, like spiritualists coaxing a disembodied voice across the ether with great physical effort. Working on laptop computers, students and businesspeople align their gaze with the angle of their screens by slouching or "turtle-necking"—leaning ever closer to the sights and sounds of a screen, jutting out the chin, breaking the curve of the spine as if their proximity to a screen could compensate for the diminutive size of its contents. These postures then work themselves into the bearing, gait and bodily comportment of media users; near constant engagement with screen technologies causes media operators to move differently.

In response to the pervasiveness of computing and the rigorous corporeal education digitality demands, ethno-techno-phenomenologist Ingrid Richardson has encouraged researchers to consider mobile technologies' "techno-corporeal or *technosomatic* attributes" in order to analyze how media "work on and modify the body" (2005: n.p.). Richardson notes that scant attention has been paid to the "corporeality of mobile phones…or to the phenomenological impact of physical mobility on game play and new media consumption/deployment" (2007:205). Like many theorists bringing phenomenological accounts to bear on computational and mobile media, Richardson is influenced by French phenomenologist Maurice Merleau-Ponty's theorization of an elastic corporeal schema able to incorporate tools into its body-image. In her analyses of how media operators habituate themselves to their cell phones and mobile devices, memorizing the placement of keys and making bodily sense of their ever-present technologies, Richardson emphasizes a "medium-specific mode of embodiment" by which users reshape the structure of their bodies (206). The mechanisms by which content is created, delivered and received impact corporeal arrangements. In a later essay, Richardson and coauthor Ian MacColl argue that every electronic interface presents its own "corporeal and communicative effects," which summon different sets of "attitudes, postures, motility, and body-space relations" (2008:101, 103). Although I agree with Richardson and MacColl that every user interface interpellates media operators into distinct corporeal configurations insofar as they afford certain actions and not others, their analyses do not account for crucial developments in the fashion and frequency with which bodies interact with digital technologies.

First, the number of hardware devices and software applications any one person might use on a daily basis, combined with pressure from an electronics industry for consumers to routinely upgrade their phones, gaming consoles and computers every two to five years, ensures that no single device and its specific corporeal arrangement predominates. In the course of a single evening, for example, a typical American high school or college student might review handwritten class notes, read printed textbook chapters, listen to music, conduct Web-based research, text or telephone friends, watch television, and engage in social networking. Each medium vies for attention—the ding of an instant message or a text and its promise of distraction easily pulls a student away from homework, while music playing in the background helps focus a busy mind by establishing a rhythm to work to. The relative silence of print texts in such environments does not easily compete with the noise-filled immediacy of electronic devices. Even so, users move between and combine different media interfaces, platforms and content, toggling among distinct, even contradictory bodily and mental priorities suggested by each medium. A treatment of media's effects on users' bodies cannot, therefore, be limited to a single platform but must allow that corporeal vocabularies manifest and coalesce around collections of media tools and devices. These vocabularies may also build upon a family of movement pathways established by previous technologies upon which contemporary designs are based (e.g., a pen-like stylus), or which are nostalgically re-presented in digital form (e.g., electronic book pages on e-readers). Media operators, therefore, perform accumulations of recycled and remediated corporeal schemas.

Second, while Richardson emphasizes the bodily incorporation of new media tools, she suggests only that people expand their bodily awareness to accommodate the presence of such devices. She remarks that this incorporation results in an aggregate experience of vision coupled with "variable and oscillating modes of somatic involvement" (2007:208–9). One gets a hint of networked bodies imbricated within systems of technological relations and economic exchanges from which they cannot be extricated emerging from Richardson's account, but her phenomenological vocabulary stops short of the processes of corporeal and ideological disciplining upon which technological embodiment relies. She does not offer a critical analysis of how hardware and software interfaces imagine the bodies of their operators (or how designers program and build models of computing bodies) and how media devices compel users to move in specific ways in order to accomplish their computational goals. As articulated earlier, this body is achieved by implementing the bodily techniques associated with computing. Insofar as these techniques establish movement patterns, particularly those that are utilized across platforms or devices, they disclose digital media's choreographies.

## Digital Choreographies

Media establish the means of accessing and manipulating their content, whether scanning a printed text and turning the pages of a book, sitting on a couch with a remote control watching television, or discovering which button combinations lead to successful outcomes in a videogame. In order to produce desired outcomes on a screen, an operator must perform gestures that are recognizable to the computer system. Occasionally the range of acceptable input is quite liberal—I have seen young children enjoy much success as singers in the Harmonix videogame *Rock Band* by simply screaming into the microphone, a source of much resentment for those around them. In most cases, however, there are strict parameters within which operator input can be recognized; information that falls outside these parameters will be ignored or might produce an error message or sound. When playing a game on Nintendo's Wii platform, for example, one must remain within range of the Wii sensor bar, beyond which a player's, or more specifically, the remote's motion cannot be tracked. Or as another example, attempting to access a computer file while a message box is open or trying to delete an image in a program that requires you to drag it to the trash produces a sound letting the user know that the action is prohibited. Digital media offer material and organizational structures that stipulate gestural choreographies for their users. In order to operate their media devices, whether digital or analog, users submit to the spatial limitations, gestural vocabularies, and movement pathways established by their interfaces. Users, in other words, perform the choreography of the medium.

Media additionally enforce cultural values in how they display information and determine what types of user input will be recognized. Setting forth specific choreographies embedded in hardware designs, user interfaces, and even in the concept of mobility, a medium's choreography is inextricably linked to ideology. Because machines cannot intuit user intent (as close as search engines may come), the user has to adapt to the machine. The digital choreographies that accompany the spread of computing technologies and mobile devices have a global reach. Adopted all over the world, such technologies interpellate their users into a similar bodily configuration, promoting and cultivating gestural homogeneity among consumers and operators. Perhaps they even contribute to the articulation of a global (cosmopolitan) physicality and the emergence of a global (cosmopolitan) "imagined community," in anthropologist Benedict Anderson's words ([1983] 1991), predicated on a shared physical vocabulary shaped by contemporary media technologies.

In her 2002 study of mobile phones usage commissioned by Motorola, feminist media theorist Sadie Plant suggests that as a result of global distribution and usage of digital media, particularly mobile phones, a globally recognizable body language has begun to emerge. From her research in centers of global industry and capital, including Tokyo, London, Dubai, and Hong Kong, among other cities, Plant concludes that mobile media users have developed a distinct set of user responses to the physical and psychological demands that such technologies present:

> People have introduced new stances, gestures, and bodily movements to their everyday behavior, changing the ways in which the body, the fingers, the thumbs, the hands and the eyes are used while making and taking mobile calls or sending and receiving mobile messages. Many of these actions and positions have become familiar to observers all over the world, and it is possible to articulate some of the more marked and conspicuous elements of this new body language.[2] (2002:51)

As communications technologies allow individuals to maneuver through informational and material worlds simultaneously, their postures and movement vocabularies, gestures and behaviors incorporate the presence of mobile media. "In Tokyo," Plant notes, "people are expert navigators of busy city streets, railway platforms, and subways while keeping an eye on their *keitai*. In Beijing, the new skill is more likely to involve riding a bicycle while making and taking mobile calls" (2002:50). Commenting on his own dangerous habit of texting while driving, writer Rob Getzschman quips, "Done right, it's a thing of natural beauty, a ballet of manual and technical dexterity" (2009). Although specific skills sets arise in relation to predominant modes of transportation, Plant notes that the body language that results from the use of communications technologies is recognizable the world over. For this reason, some scholars insist that the adoption of digital media devices is not as simple as acquiring a physical skill. For these authors, the demands of global media usage might more appropriately be considered a form of corporeal colonization.

In their analysis of cell phone use during the 2004 Indian Ocean tsunami, for example, Wendy Robinson and David Robison consider the cell phone as a tool of Western imperialism. Technologies, from cars to televisions to mobile phones, they argue, "carry with them considerable Western baggage," from the infrastructure required to support these technologies, to socioeconomic structures of credit and financing, to attitudes toward the environment and disposability (2006:96). "Electronic mobility," they go on to argue, "is not value-neutral; the use of these devices carries an ideological kernel..." (96). Though cell phones and other forms of mobile media superficially appear to be purely functional and therefore benign, they are implicated in the spread of ideologies embedded in the technologies' infrastructural and socioeconomic underpinnings—the scaffolding of what sociologist Manuel Castells calls "informational capitalism" ([2000] 2009), without which digital technologies cannot function. Like Robinson and Robison, Anandam Kavoori and Noah Arceneaux argue that cell phones are "a cultural technology, intimately connected with issues of global capitalism and cultural hegemony" (2006:5). Their hegemonizing force does not remain at the level of language or symbolic systems as an intellectual process. Instead, the ideologies embedded in technological systems are brought into physical contact with those who use them, rubbing against their flesh and penetrating their ears, or in the case of biomedical technologies, reaching under their skin. Digital and mobile media can thus be read as mechanisms of corporeal discipline and colonization.

In *Mobile Communications and Society*, however, Castells and his coauthors argue that mobile communication does not impose norms, but is rather "adopted, adapted, and modified by people to fit their own practices, according to their needs, values, interests, and desires. People shape communications technology, rather than the other way around" (2007:125). Plant also argues that while mobiles "are introducing some common patterns of behaviour to very varied regions of the world, there is no homogenous mobile effect" (2002:77). As people adapt to their technologies, they find innovative and often unintended uses for them. Thus mobile media can have anti-hegemonic implications as well, some of which can appear to threaten state control. In 2008, for example, videos of China's military response to Buddhist monks protesting in Tibet were uploaded to YouTube before Chinese officials could suspend internet service and block YouTube. In 2009, videos of beatings and riots around Uighur and Han ethnic conflicts were similarly posted and subsequently censored. Also in 2009, the social media site Twitter helped mobilize protestors in Thailand, Moldova, and Iran, the respective governments responded by restricting internet services. Even as digital media impose a choreography that some would describe as "Western," they can also support local radical politics. The cultural importance and narratives surrounding cell phones and other portable technologies vary, as the social and political significance of mobile media is defined locally. Entering into social spaces with preexisting norms and expectations, the potential uses of digital tools do not necessarily coincide, therefore, with the choreographies of digital interfaces, which are universalizing in their mass production and global distribution. There is a difference, in other words, between the operative gestures a device requires and the uses to which that device may be put. The globalized digital economy allows for only minimal modifications to products shipped worldwide; hardware is only minimally responsive to differences of ideology or culture, and few consumers have the knowledge or desire to physically alter their devices with mods or add-ons. The Amazon Kindle e-reader, for example, now offers support for non-Latin scripts such as those used in Russian, Chinese, Japanese, and Korean, but only for personal documents (i.e., not electronic books), and menu items and the dictionary remain English-only. iPhones allow users to choose their language preference, but they cannot substantively alter the device without violating the terms of service. Similarly, the Apple iPad is shipped with a choice of languages and keyboard layouts such that few components, such as those relating to electric voltage, vary among models sold around the globe.

A priority of programming and interface design is thus developing common visual-aural-gestural languages that can provide global support structures for local and individual uses—a lexicon of digital interfaces shared beyond the confines of geographically or linguistically defined cultures. Personal computers have long utilized standard hardware designs to support word processing in both Latin-based and non-Latin-based scripts, accommodating entirely different language systems and patterns of character strokes with similar physical architectures. For example, because of their sheer number, Chinese characters cannot be "typed" in the same way that letters are, so computer users begin typing in *pinyin*, a phonetic transliteration system, and then select the appropriate character from a dropdown menu. When working with Chinese characters the activity of writing foregrounds menu-selection, but the gestures available to computing bodies remain the same regardless of language because the platform remains unchanged.

Tools for creating digital content, whether by writing source code or compositing and editing images, similarly draw from a shared vocabulary of icons and functions such that creative labor, in addition to language, becomes uniform in its gestural vocabularies of input. As new media theorist Rita Raley argues in her analysis of machine languages and Global English, these common languages of digital interfaces are invested in "universality, neutrality, and transmittability" and are "presumably context- and value-free when they are at their premium" (2003:305). However, because the majority of programming languages use English keywords, the English language functions as the means of expressing this ideal of neutrality. The predominance of English does not only affect programming languages, however. Asian languages such as Japanese, Chinese, and Korean have shifted the vertical orientation of written characters to horizontal, first from right to left and then from left to right. The latter shift occurred in part as a response to the directional limitations of word processing programs, requiring that readers of these languages modify their gestures even on an ocular level.[3] The gestures for writing and creating or working with real-world objects are rechoreographed for digital environments in such a way as to appear universal and unbiased, yet the visual icons, sounds, programming languages and gestures of manipulation that construct the vocabularies of an international digital culture are already mediated by anglicized computational and cultural codes.

As the gestures associated with communications technologies expand beyond rudimentary deictic—pointing and locating—motions that have been a primary feature of navigating graphical user interfaces to include operational gestures with parallels in the physical manipulation of real world objects, they reference preexisting cultural metaphors. For example, while Kindle users press buttons located on either side of the e-reader screen to navigate forward and backward through a novel's electronic pages, those who use iBooks on the Apple iPad swipe the touch-sensitive surface to turn a page, a gesture that references the arc one traces in space when turning the page of a book, but flattens it for a screen. These movements link digital choreographies to operational commands through a culturally determined chain of signification. Though the movements that form the basic vocabularies of gestural computing are naturalized, associated with a mental construct of what human bodies quintessentially are and do, they involve a corporeal training by which bodies become versed in computational choreographies.

# GESTURAL RHETORICS

The founders of FingerWorks, a company acquired by Apple in 2005 as part of the latter's development of the multi-touch iPhone and laptop trackpads, state on their FAQ page their belief that "in this century, people will seamlessly weave gesture and speech together to form a tight and efficient link between them and their computer."[4] The availability of increasingly accurate dictation software coupled with the recent explosion of touch interfaces and gestural computing with popular videogame platforms such as the Nintendo Wii, smartphones such as the Apple iPhone and the 2010 release of the iPad tablet, suggest that although we have not yet witnessed a fusion of speech and gesture, the FingerWorks founders' instinct was correct. Speech recognition, which allows users to write without typing on a keyboard or keypad, and motion recognition, which enables users to bypass pointing devices such as a mouse or stylus, are on their way toward revamping computing bodies. Together, they create a space for linguistic and manual dexterity in computing environments, particularly those associated with everyday communication.

In addition, the constant increase in computing power and the current proliferation of touch-screen and motion recognition technologies have allowed phone, computer and videogame designers to program a growing array of behaviors associated with gestures. These gestural vocabularies do not require familiarity with the programming languages upon which devices rely, nor do they require much knowledge about the black-boxed devices themselves, in order to interact with visual representations of data or to trigger a coded behavior with bodily movement. Digital devices present a discrete but expanding repertory of codified gestures designed for gameplay and computing. Far fewer gestures are recognized, however, than verbal commands, in part because dictation software has enjoyed a longer history of development. Although dictation systems lose vocal qualities such as intonation or prosody in their translation of speech to text, speech is not limited to giving a computer commands, as gesture tends to be (with the exception of artistic experimentation): move left, go here, play/pause, zoom, display, toggle, etc.

As I have mentioned, computational gestures must be performed within a strictly delimited field in order to be effectively recognized by computational systems. Such gestures are thus highly choreographed, propagated through an ongoing process of physical training that aligns bodily movement with the cultural ideologies of corporeality embedded in touch and motion sensitive devices in order to render motion significant within a computational context. Users must perform the body whose gestures have been imagined and inscribed in code. With their bodies thus conscripted, users' gestures assume specific computational functionality.

Mobile media, particularly smartphones, have been at the forefront in expanding users' physical vocabularies for operating digital media. Adding to the pressing of buttons on a game controller, typing on a keypad or texting on a number pad, all of which frame the dexterity of the thumbs, the current touch-interface smartphone repertory of choreographies for fingers includes scrolling, dragging, flicking, tapping and double-tapping. With forefinger and thumb users can also pinch and expand to zoom in or out on the screen's contents. Tilt, rotate and shake are hand and wrist gestures that work on devices with accelerometers, which include the iPhone 3G, LG Dare, BlackBerry Storm and Palm Pre. Each of these gestures is tied to one or more functions, taking advantage of both the ambiguity of gesture, which makes it a flexible mode of input, and its ability to signify, which enables programmers to establish correlations between gestural input and media output based on cultural metaphors that link meaning with motion. Shaking an iPhone, iPod Touch or iPod Nano that is playing music stored on the device, for example, shuffles song playback. Yet shaking as a physical action is associated with any number of meanings. One can shake one's head "no," shake a fist in anger, shake hands in greeting or congratulations, shake with fear, shake one's "booty" and so forth. Yet the shuffle function attached to shaking an iPhone or iPod Touch does not refer to any of these rapid to-and-fro motions collectively designated as shaking. The shaking that shuffles songs more closely resembles shaking dice in games of chance or mixing the contents of a container, for example when pulling names out of a hat. The gesture's functionality presumes a cultural knowledge of the relationship between shaking and random ordering, a bodily knowledge that the device itself transmits as a part of users' digital physical education.

Shaking can also have much more violent connotations, as is found, for example, in the "Baby Shaker" application, which Apple pulled from its App Store in April 2009. Using the same gesture as randomizing and decision-making applications such as the restaurant-finder "Urbanspoon," "Baby Shaker" uses Shaken Baby Syndrome, the brain damage and even death caused by a frustrated caregiver shaking a crying child, as its premise. A sketched drawing of a baby appears onscreen along with the sounds of fussing and crying. Shaking the device vigorously "kills" the onscreen baby—two red Xs appear over the baby's eyes and it stops crying—and the next baby takes its place to be shaken, silenced and killed. Like the physical link between shaking and randomness that allows users to change a song on an iPod, the "Baby Shaker" application exploits the very specific connection between the shaking and silencing/death of children.

Media and game theorist Alexander Galloway describes operative gestural vocabularies as "grammars of action" that human operators pantomime with their controllers, particularly when playing videogames (2006:4). However, pantomimic "gestural grammars" (4) are largely reserved for game-specific controllers, such as the "guitar" used for *Guitar Hero* and guns used in first-person shooters, or platforms that include motion recognition such as Nintendo Wii or Xbox 360 with Kinect. While console game designers can afford to proliferate the number and types of controllers associated with specific games, mobile game platforms necessarily restrict the amount of space allotted to gameplay. Portable devices such as the Sony PSP and Nintendo DS thus continue to utilize a traditional game control layout, which maintains a large conceptual and physical gap between the gestures performed by the videogame player and those appearing onscreen. Arrows and numbered and lettered buttons on standard controllers can produce flips, jumps, kicks, flight or gunfire when pushed in their appropriate combinations, or, like the Konami code, increase an avatar's number of lives.[5] Whether gamers deduce the efficacy of particular attacks from hours of gameplay or find "cheats" that give them extra lives or ammunition, all manner of movements, from walking to martial arts and weapons handling, are rechoreographed as the timely and clever execution of button sequences. Practiced gamers keep their bodies remarkably still and reserve virtuosic movements for their thumbs and fingers as their avatars perform gravity-defying feats under the purview of manual manipulation.

Games designed for smartphones incorporate their touch-screen capabilities, allowing users to interact with images directly on the display where they appear rather than via a mouse, trackpad, stylus or button scheme. Such devices and the applications built for them rework and in some cases seem to collapse the distinctions between user input and onscreen output, enlarging choreographies for fingers and thumbs beyond the act of button-pushing. As the number of recognizable gestures and motions continue to expand, computing will continue to transform operators' physical relationships to their digital media devices. Digital media theorist Lisa Nakamura cautions against an uncritical embrace of gestural computing, however. She contends that in doing away with keyboards and mice, gestural interfaces "meld vision and gesture," but that, as with previous hardware designs, "the manual labor of interface manipulation becomes laborious soon enough" (2008). This process can be detrimental, as with the computing-related injuries noted earlier, but it also contains the possibility of realizing embodiment in new ways. By assigning specific commands to gestures such that gesture is articulate without the accompaniment of speech, and replacing human interlocutors with electronic addressees as the primary audience for users' gesticulations, choreographies of digital interfaces repotentialize gesture as a medium of communication, navigation and operation.

Some gestural commands are delivered through the press of a button or button combinations, while others utilize gesture recognition to spatially describe the desired operation. On a multi-touch surface, one can scroll by sliding a finger along a vertical or horizontal line, or eschew linear movement and drag the desired text or image into view from any direction. One can pinch to zoom out or "reverse pinch" to zoom in, as though describing the screen's contents becoming larger or smaller. Such gestures, which are becoming codified and standardized across devices—a process slowed but not halted by attempts to secure proprietary rights over gestural commands—tie movements to specific operations. Gesture recognition transforms gestures from bodily movements that convey meaning or describe impressions into movements that act. Gesturing thus moves from a descriptive and conversational domain into a computationally performative one.

In computing, performative gestures enact the conditions for the speech acts of code,[6] triggering the behaviors linked to those motions. Performative gestures are both commands addressed to the technological apparatus and the execution of those commands; they are an expression of an intention directed at a device and its realization on that device. The performance of a pinch gesture on an iPhone screen is temporally coincident with the resizing of the screen's contents, which can also be repositioned in the frame by dragging a finger across the screen.

And thus we return to the gesture with which I began this essay: a simple drag. But this drag, as it should by now be clear, is not simply a drag. A tap is not a simple tap, a shake is not a simple shake when performed on a computational device. These and other gestures are choreographies that enact computing's bodily techniques. As such, they must conform to the bodily configuration that has been imagined in hardware design in order to be recognizable to a platform and, further, must conform to the gestures inscribed in code in order to be recognizable to an application. In other words, with their movements, users must follow and fulfill the choreography of an interface. Gestures that have no programmed behavior associated with them will produce no result or unintended results. Gestures performed incorrectly or for too short a duration will likewise be ignored or misinterpreted. Media choreographies thus require technique.

As an assurance of correct performance or an indicator of incorrect performance, sound helps to situate a body in relation to a screen. Computer keys clatter as they are struck, guns fire and coins ding in response to video-game play, and notifications and alarms remind busy people of what they are forgetting. Both computational gestures and sounds fade from awareness as we incorporate and naturalize their occurrence, not thinking through the requisite layers of bodily training that are employed each time we reach for a digital device when it chimes.

Users rehearse the bodily configurations, responsiveness, and cultural logics upon which computational gestures are founded, aligning their bodies with an imagined and encoded counterpart. Repeating some movement pathways while allowing other movement possibilities to diminish, a media operator cultivates his or her body into the one designers and programmers have conceived—a universal body, literate and articulate in movement, but only when achieved through and directed at digital technologies.

## Notes

1. "According to Horowitz Associates' *Broadband Content and Services 2008(TM) Report*, young, multicultural consumers are on the leading edge, embracing new media platforms; especially video-enabled handheld devices. The study found that nearly nine in ten (86%) of 15- to 17-year-old internet users have a handheld device, whether it is a cell phone (69%), an iPod or other MP3 player (66%), a PSP (31%) or a smartphone (12%). According to the study, one quarter (26%) of 15- to 17-year-old internet users pay for internet access on their cell phone, compared to 11% of 35- to 49-year-old internet users. Similarly, one

quarter (24%) of 15- to 17-year-old internet users watch video on their handheld devices on a monthly basis" ("Cable TV, Advertising and Program Executives Tackle Audience Trends" 2009: n.p.).

2. Plant delineates some of these postures and attitudes, including what she calls the extro-verted "speakeasy" and introverted "spacemaker," the "firm grip" and "light touch" with which users grasp their mobile devices, the scan and the gaze as alternate visual modes, and the "phone tap" and "gentle touch" with which users input information—the former describing the use of the pointer finger and the latter the use of thumbs (2002:51–53). Plant also relates differences in making and taking calls to personality more than differences of culture or sex, identifying a number of characters that read like an Aesop's Fables of mobile phones. She compares modes of using and displaying phones to hedgehogs and foxes (2002:62, 78), and no fewer than six bird species, including sparrows, peacocks, and starlings (2002:66–67).

3. Should the Kindle finally support e-books written in languages read from right to left, it will be interesting to see whether or not that capability is reflected in the Kindle's design, for example with equally sized back and forward buttons or with one button on either side of the device. Currently, there is a small back and larger forward button on both sides to facilitate single-handed operation.

4. Fingerworks, "Frequently Asked Questions," http://www.fingerworks.com/faq.html (accessed October 15, 2009).

5. The Konami code is the button sequence "up up down down left right left right B A start," which, when pressed during a Konami videogame's title screen, would reward a player with extra lives.

6. New media theorists have compared the function of the performative utterance to the function of computational code. In her analysis of Neal Stephenson's novel *Cryptonomicon*, literary and digital media theorist N. Katherine Hayles notes, for example, that "perfor-mative code operates as instructions to the machine and therefore initiates action in the world" (2005:126). More simply, she states, "Performative code makes machines do things" (127). Similarly, Inke Arns argues that "program code is characterized by the fact that here 'saying' coincides with 'doing.' Code as an effective speech act is not a description or a representation of something, but, on the contrary, it directly affects, and literally sets in motion—or even 'kills' a process" (2004:9).

## REFERENCES

Agamben, Giorgio. 2009. "What Is an Apparatus?" In *What Is an Apparatus? And Other Essays*, trans. David Kshik and Stefan Pedatella, 1–24. Stanford: Stanford University Press.

Anderson, Benedict. [1983] 1991. *Imagined Communities*. London: Verso.

Arns, Inke. 2004. "Run_Me, Read_Me, Execute_Me: Software and Its Discontents, or: It's the Performativity of Code, Stupid!," http://www.projects.v2.nl/~arns/Texts/Media/Arns-Article-Arhus2004.pdf (accessed May 3, 2009).

*Associated Press.* 2009. "6 in 10 People Worldwide Have Cell Phones." March 2, http://www2.tbo.com/content/2009/mar/02/6-10-people-worldwide-have-cell-phones/news-money911/ (accessed August 30, 2009).

"Cable TV, Advertising and Programming Executives Tackle Audience Trends and Opportunities at 9th Annual Horowitz Multicultural Forum." 2009. *News Blaze,* February

18, http://newsblaze.com/story/20090218065302o0004.pnw/topstory.html (accessed July 31, 2009).

Castells, Manuel. [2000] 2009. *The Rise of the Network Society*. 2nd ed. Oxford: Blackwell.

Castells, Manuel, Mireia Fernández-Ardèvol, Jack Linchuan Qiu, and Araba Sey. 2007. *Mobile Communication and Society: A Global Perspective*. Cambridge, MA: MIT Press.

Galloway, Alexander R. 2006. *Gaming: Essays on Algorithmic Culture*. Minneapolis: University of Minnesota Press.

Getzschman, Rob. 2009. "I cn txt n drv btr thn u." *Christian Science Monitor*, August 3, http://news.yahoo.com/s/csm/20090803/cm_csm/ygetzschman (accessed August 7, 2009).

Gillespie, Robin Mary. 2002. "The Physical Impact of Computer and Electronic Game Use on Children and Adolescents, a Review of Current Literature." *Work* 18:249–59.

Hayles, N. Katherine. 2005. *My Mother Was a Computer: Digital Subjects and Literary Texts*. Chicago: University of Chicago Press.

Kavoori, Anandam, and Noah Arceneaux. 2006. "Introduction." In *The Cell Phone Reader: Essays in Social Transformation*, ed. Anandam Kavoori and Noah Arceneaux. New York: Peter Lang.

"Kids' Use of Consumer Electronics Devices such as Cell Phones, Personal Computers and Video Game Platforms Continue to Rise." 2009. *NDP Group*, http://www.npd.com/press/releases/press_090609a.html (accessed January 3, 2010).

Mauss, Marcel. [1934] 1992. "Techniques of the Body." In *Incorporations (Zone 6)*, ed. Jonathan Crary and Sanford Kwinter, 455–77. Cambridge, MA: MIT Press.

MacColl, Ian, and Ingrid Richardson. 2008. "A Cultural Somatics of Mobile Media and Urban Screens: Wiffiti and the IWALL Prototype." *Journal of Urban Technology* 15(3): 99–116.

*Medical News Today*. 2010. "Hearing Loss Among US Teenagers Increases by 31%." August 17, http://www.medicalnewstoday.com/articles/198055.php (accessed 10 September 2010).

Nakamura, Lisa. 2008. "What Steven Wants: Gestural Computing, Digital Manual Labor, and the Boom! Moment," http://mediacommons.futureofthebook.org/imr/2008/03/11/what-steven-wants-gestural-computing-digital-manual-labor-and-boom-moment (accessed January 5, 2010).

Plant, Sadie. 2002. "On the Mobile: The Effects of Mobile Telephones on Social and Individual Life," www.motorola.com/mot/doc/0/234_MotDoc.pdf (accessed August 15, 2009).

Raley, Rita. 2003. "Machine Translation and Global English." *Yale Journal of Criticism* 16(2):291–313.

Rheingold, Howard. 1999. "Look Who's Talking: The Amish are famous for shunning technology. But their secret love affair with the cell phone is causing an uproar." *Wired* 7.1, http://www.wired.com/wired/archive/7.01/amish_pr.html (accessed December 1, 2009).

Richardson, Ingrid. 2005. "Mobile Technosoma: Some Phenomenological Reflections on Itinerant Media Devices." *Fibreculture* 6, http://www.fibreculture.org/journal/issue6/issue6_richardson.html#1 (accessed November 15, 2009).

———. 2007. "Pocket Technospaces: The Bodily Incorporation of New Media." *Continuum* 21(2):205–15.

Robinson, Wendy, and David Robison. 2006. "Tsunami Mobilizations: Considering the Role of Mobile and Digital Communication Devices, Citizen Journalism, and the Mass Media." In *The Cell Phone Reader: Essays in Social Transformation*, ed. Anandam Kavoori and Noah Arceneaux, 85–103. New York: Peter Lang.

Rotman, Brian. 2008. *Becoming Beside Ourselves: The Alphabet, Ghosts, and Distributed Human Being*. Durham: Duke University Press.

Seiter, Ellen. 2008. "Practicing at Home: Computers, Pianos, and Cultural Capital." In *Digital Youth, Innovation, and the Unexpected*, ed. Tara McPherson, 27–52. Cambridge, MA: MIT Press.

# PART IV

# DANCE AND DANCE MUSICS

CHAPTER 10

# (IN)VISIBLE MEDIATORS: URBAN MOBILITY, INTERFACE DESIGN, AND THE DISAPPEARING COMPUTER IN BERLIN-BASED LAPTOP PERFORMANCES

MARK J. BUTLER

ELECTRONIC dance music (EDM) is a quintessentially global musical style. The musical lingua franca of nightclubs around the world, it evokes urbanity in a tongue of abstract sophistication: wordless, synthesized, rhythmic. Moreover, it has long been at the forefront of the digital developments currently revolutionizing the ways in which we obtain, experience, and share music; well before anyone ever emailed an MP3 to a friend, EDM artists were using digital sampling as a formative compositional technique. Small wonder then, that the style has been celebrated for its "immateriality" and "hyper-mobility" (Born 2005:25).

Yet EDM is also resolutely local and material. Its origins and characteristic genres continue to be strongly associated with particular places: Detroit techno, Chicago house, Baltimore breaks, and now Berlin minimal.[1] It is a "high-tech" style distributed on twelve-inch vinyl and played back on analog turntables. It is produced on artist-run labels, sold in small record stores, and often pressed in local plants.

Tensions between these tendencies have intensified in recent years as performance approaches have diversified. In addition to the standard DJ set, musicians now commonly perform with laptop computers and a variety of affiliated technologies. Often described as "live," the laptop set appeals to musicians partly because of mobility; performers can now easily transport huge numbers of tracks, along with much of their recording studio. Yet even as performance networks proliferate across Europe and the world, certain cities continue to function as real and imagined centers for EDM producers and consumers. Berlin is the prime example: cheap rents and an unrestricted club scene have made it the focus of an unprecedented techno migration, the new home of numerous leading EDM artists from around the world, and a principal site of pilgrimage for "techno tourists." From Berlin, musicians such as Robert Henke and Gerhard Behles—creators of the performance software "Live," a key component of the laptop revolution—disperse sounds and performance approaches across the world.

The trend toward laptop sets, however, has reinvigorated certain long-standing concerns surrounding musical performance. The proliferation of recording and playback technologies within the twentieth century fostered a reactive desire to experience performance as "live"—as direct and unmediated. Introducing computers into performance has only increased anxieties around liveness: these devices are associated primarily with nonmusical pursuits, and their small and nonspecific control elements make it difficult to perceive connections between physical gestures and sonic results.

This chapter traces the emergence of this distinctive form of mobile performance in Berlin. In the first half I explore the movement of EDM to, from, and within the city. After delineating the origins of EDM in America and the paths it followed to Europe, I turn to three exemplary instances of musical flows in which Berlin has been central: the club and record label Tresor, the recurring event known as the Love Parade, and the recent phenomenon of techno-based immigration and tourism. The second half of the chapter then develops a more oblique notion of mobility: one concerned less with the physical movement of humans (and their music) through the world than it is with certain musical practices that have developed in conjunction with geographic and socioeconomic mobility. In particular, I trace the issues at stake in the rise of the laptop set and the ways in which musicians have responded to these concerns. In this context, mobility reveals itself in the ways in which performers move through or navigate hardware and software interfaces, which may be conceived of as "environments" or "ecologies" affording particular modes of creative interaction. Movement also emerges in a temporal sense, as practices previously associated with preserving music via recording enter the real-time world of performance. As a result of these metaphorical extensions, I consider a number of different "spaces" in which music is created and performed— not only clubs and cities, but also software interfaces and arrays of equipment on performance tables. Rather than seeking to resolve the disjunctures that inevitably arise between different instances of mobility, I wish to ask instead what the tensions at work might say about the ways in which music flows through these kinds of spaces.

# EDM in Motion, I: From the Midwest to Berlin (and Back Again)

The origins of electronic dance music are characteristically traced to three American cities: Detroit, Chicago, and New York.[2] In Chicago, during the late disco era, African

American gay men began congregating at a club called the Warehouse, where DJs such as Frankie Knuckles blended soulful, vocally oriented disco tracks with the electronic sounds of simple Japanese drum machines and bass-line generators. As with disco and hip hop before it, and many of the EDM styles that followed it, "house music" developed first on the dance floor, through the visionary ways in which disc jockeys combined and transformed records from a variety of genres. The unique sound that they fostered was eventually imitated and transformed through studio production, but not until several years into the phenomenon; the first house releases only began to appear on vinyl in 1983.[3]

Near Detroit in the early 1980s, a group of high-school friends in the suburb of Belleville formed a DJ collective, which they nicknamed "Deep Space." These musicians—Juan Atkins, Eddie Fowlkes, Derrick May, and Kevin Saunderson—had been enculturated into dance music through a network of DJed parties organized by African American teenagers in the northwest of the city. They were also exposed to electronic music from outside of Detroit through an influential local radio show. Within a few years they each began to release their own records. Though initially regarded as house music that had been made in the Motor City (just three hundred miles to the east of Chicago), the emerging Detroit sound was eventually labeled "techno." While clearly related to house, Detroit techno featured starker, more purely electronic sounds, with less emphasis on "human" elements such as swung rhythms and sung vocals.

In their earliest days house and techno were distinctly local phenomena, developing in specific subcultures within their respective Midwestern cities. In New York City during this era, relationships between club music and mainstream culture were more complex and oppositional. The most significant contributions of America's largest city to the future of dance music had actually occurred earlier in the 1970s, when a set of emerging cultural practices—dancing for long periods of time to recorded music, played continuously at high volumes and a constant tempo, in locations designed expressly for this purpose—coalesced and transformed into the mass-cultural phenomenon known as disco. Due to the cultural and economic importance of New York, disco's promulgation via the music industry had immediate and far-reaching effects on a wide range of musical and social practices, not only in New York but also in the rest of the United States and many other locations. By the late 1970s, however, the popularity of disco had declined rapidly, accompanied by the homophobic backlash of the "disco sucks" movement.[4] In New York City, dancing to continuous, beat-oriented recorded music in clubs returned to the underground, where the communities who had originally cultivated the practice—gay men, particularly those of color—continued it with fervor. The phase of dance music that followed from this development bears an especially strong association with the Paradise Garage, a club in SoHo that operated between 1977 and 1987. Like the Warehouse in Chicago, the Garage gave its name to a genre, although garage is also frequently described, tellingly enough, as "underground." The sound of garage might best be situated somewhere between disco and Chicago house. Although some tracks did incorporate electronic elements such as drum-machine percussion and studio effects, the recordings identified as "classics" typically emphasize gospel- or R&B-tinged vocals and live instrumentation. Garage is also intimately linked to its most famous DJ, Larry Levan.[5]

By the mid-1980s, then, the foundations of EDM had coalesced in these three local scenes. Each city had developed its own institutions for the production and performance of its music: in Detroit, for instance, techno records were pressed in local plants, while Chicago house and New York garage were each connected in originary ways to a particular club. These sites strengthened and focused the sense of place associated with these genres, as they came to be rooted not only within certain cities but also in specific locales within them.

Although musicians and recordings did circulate between Detroit, Chicago, and New York to a certain extent, the sounds of techno, house, and garage remained largely confined to their hometown scenes during these formative years. This situation did not last for long, however. The music gradually began to flow to other parts of the world. It did not do so in an even, systematic way (as for example we might imagine a pop hit originating in a particular place and then being spread through the American "market" via radio play throughout the country). Rather, its distribution was initially spotty, taking place in fits and starts. Records were scattered toward Europe like seeds, and in some places they began to take root. One of the most widely documented points of entry was the United Kingdom, where cities such as Manchester and London played especially important roles. Techno and house sounds also made their way to Amsterdam, Belgium, and various German cities. In the local scenes that sprang up in these places, EDM played a central role in the formation of new kinds of musical-social practices, which gradually spread across the continent and subsequently throughout much of the world. In England, for instance, house music became the basis for raves, a distinctive type of event that developed there and became widespread during the late 1980s. When party promoters in the United States began to throw raves following the English model during the early 1990s, EDM was reimported into its original home, becoming popular on a much larger scale than before. As most Americans were unaware of the small but vibrant EDM traditions that had developed within their country, EDM came to bear strong European associations, to the extent that many casual listeners associate its beginnings with Europe even today.

Questions of origins aside, in the present moment Europe does function as a center for producing, consuming, and distributing EDM. While many cities within Europe have played significant roles in the development of the genre—and most locations of any size have substantial EDM followings—Berlin in particular has risen to the forefront in recent years. Its club culture is exceptionally well-developed and vibrant, and it is home to more leading EDM musicians and performers than any other city in the world. Accordingly, the rest of this chapter focuses on a number of key musical developments within Berlin. In addition to the historical information featured in the following section, I also discuss the performance approaches of five internationally active musicians who live and work in Berlin: Pole (Stefan Betke), Robert Henke, Pacou (Lars Lewandowski), DJane Aroma/Discopunk (Aroma P. Schmidt), and Henrik Schwarz. Information on these artists derives from fieldwork trips in 2005, 2006, and 2007; during these years

I lived in the city for periods ranging from one to four months, interviewed these and many other musicians about their work, and observed and filmed performances for close analysis.

# EDM in Motion, II: Border-Crossing and Flows in/to Berlin

Like their UK counterparts, Berliners first began to encounter American electronic dance music during the mid- to late 1980s. Berlin's emergence as a prime location for EDM began slightly later, however, and its musical development subsequently went down a rather different path due to the unique culture of the city and the historical events that followed. In 1988, the year of the "Second Summer of Love" in England, West Berliner Dimitri Hegemann founded an EDM-oriented club called UFO, as well as a label, Interfisch Records, which focused on house, acid house, techno, and industrial sounds. On the ninth of November 1989, portions of the Berlin Wall began to be opened, and East Germany (the "Deutsche Demokratische Republik" or DDR) was officially dissolved on October 3, 1990. At the same time as this political reconfiguration, the city was beginning an equally dramatic spatial transformation, one that had powerful ramifications for life, work, and play alike.

In 1990, the UFO club closed due to financial problems. When Hegemann had opened the venue, the city was divided, and he had chosen a space in Kreuzberg, a West Berlin neighborhood that was well known as a center of counterculture. Now, in search of a new space, Hegemann looked to the former East Berlin. Newly opened to the West, it was teeming with buildings in various states of disrepair, many of which had been abandoned since the division of the city. The East German government had addressed housing needs primarily with new construction (most famously with the "Plattenbauten" developments built from prefabricated concrete), leaving older housing stock such as that found in the historic Prenzlauer Berg neighborhood to fall into disrepair. The architecture of Berlin's most central district, known as Mitte, was neglected as well. This was in large part due to the Wall: not only did it divide the city, it also left it without a center, for the barrier and the no-man's-land that accompanied it ran right through the former heart of Berlin. And the space that Hegemann eventually chose for his club could hardly have been closer to the center. Tresor, as it came to be called, was located on Leipzigerstraße 126a, less than one block east of the former Wall. Prior to World War II, the area was the site of two large squares, Potsdamer Platz and Leipziger Platz. Razed by the construction of the Wall and death strip, they have since been rebuilt in their original locations (albeit with entirely new buildings).[6]

The building that housed Tresor had originally been home to Wertheim, a business that in its heyday was the largest department store in Europe. The name Tresor (a noun meaning "safe" or "vault" in German) referred to the location of the main dance floor, which was situated underground in an area that had housed the store's vaults. Tresor's website describes the aesthetic in evocative terms:

> The club's rough, apocalyptic atmosphere ruled above all: condensation dripped down the raw concrete walls of the old vault rooms; rusty steel bars separated visitors from the bar; several hundred forced-opened safe-deposit boxes lined the walls that spoke of wealth long forgotten; strobe lights and fast, hard beats dominated the dance floor. Only here could electronic music correspond with such architecture—the senses were left equally numbed and brutalised.[7]

Hegemann opened Tresor in March 1991. A record label of the same name followed in September 1991. As a venue for performances and a forum for record production and distribution, the two entities were central to the development of Berlin's techno scene. Perhaps more surprisingly, they were also essential to the continuation and promulgation of Detroit techno. Berliners such as Hegemann revered the musicians of the early Detroit sound, who were frequent performers at Tresor from the outset. The record label Tresor also became a principal site of musical collaboration between the two cities. A sound emerged, clearly steeped in Detroit's four-on-the-floor origins, but with an increasingly hard and rough aesthetic. Tresor's first release, an EP entitled *X-101*, was by the iconic collective of Detroit musicians known as Underground Resistance; aptly enough, its most successful track was called "Sonic Destroyer." At the time, Underground Resistance included Jeff Mills, the DJ and producer whose "fast, hard beats" might be considered the epitome of the new Detroit/Berlin hybrid. For many Germans in this scene, Detroit functioned as an imagined sister city, a parallel metropolis characterized by dystopian urban life, empty architectural relics, and a love for technologized music.[8] This attitude is captured most succinctly in the phrase "Berlin—Detroit: A Techno Alliance"—the title of a 1993 Tresor compilation,[9] and now a slogan appearing on Tresor t-shirts.

The flow of techno music from Detroit to Berlin constitutes a particularly striking example of electronic dance music in motion. In only a few years, a highly localized EDM style had found a new home across the globe. Once situated, Berlin's techno scene began to exert a gradually increasing centripetal force, drawing musicians, infrastructure, and clubbers toward it. In Tresor's case, the pull was toward the very center of the city itself, to a place underground. Events aboveground did not bode well for the club in the long run, however. The newly reopened space near Potsdamer Platz was not only attractive to counter-cultural entrepreneurs seeking to create interesting musical experiences within liminal spaces. It was also immensely appealing to large businesses interested in centrally located real estate. In 2005, the city sold the land on which the club was located to an investment group, who subsequently constructed an office building on the site. Over the course of the next two years, the club Maria hosted a weekly event entitled "Tresor im Exil." On May 24, 2007, Tresor reopened in its current location, an enormous former power plant at Köpenickerstraße 70 in the eastern part of Mitte. Legendary Detroit artists continue to perform there on a regular basis, although they seldom draw the large crowds that they would have attracted in the 1990s.

One of the most distinctive and well-known examples of musical mobility associated with Berlin is the Love Parade. The event began in West Berlin in 1989, prior to the fall of the Wall. Organized by Dr. Motte (Matthias Roenigh, a West German DJ who also performed at Tresor during its early years), it was initially a small, countercultural event with less than two hundred participants. It maintained this basic demeanor over the next several years, although its popularity increased as the reputation of the event grew throughout Germany and eventually across the world. Each year the number of attendees doubled or tripled—a development that eventually necessitated a move from its original location on the Kurfürstendamm (a primary commercial thoroughfare) to an even larger and wider street. In 1996 the parade was relocated to the Straße des 17. Juni, one of the principal routes connecting the main city park known as the Tiergarten to the center of Berlin.[10] Attendance subsequently reached a peak of about 1.5 million participants in 1999. During the second half of the 1990s the parade stopped being part of anything that might rightfully be considered a Berlin EDM "scene," having instead become a trans-European pop-cultural event. In 2001, things began to go downhill: the parade had become a bone of contention for many Berliners due to the large amounts of trash, urine, and other detritus left behind by partiers, and it lost its protected legal and economic status as an officially sanctioned "demonstration."[11] The 2004 and 2005 events in Berlin were canceled, and the 2006 parade (which I attended) was the last. Most recently, the event has been scheduled for various small cities along the Ruhr River, from Essen in 2007 to Gelsenkirchen in 2011, and the organizers have secured a multiyear contract with German health-club chain McFit.[12]

The basic premise of the event as it developed during the Berlin years is as follows: the "parade" itself consists of floats, which are trucks sponsored by particular clubs, record labels, and other musical outlets.[13] Each truck has its own sound system and a platform upon which DJs perform, accompanied by dancers who encourage the surrounding crowds. The parade moves through the city along a predetermined route, concluding with an *Abschlusskundgebung* (closing rally): a final concert in which very famous DJs perform short sets (e.g., thirty minutes) while the sound systems of all of the trucks are connected.

The mobility that characterizes the Love Parade is in fact its most distinctive attribute. A performance that moves as it unfolds is a radical departure from the club-oriented traditions of EDM, in which sound is strongly associated with—and indeed often tailored to meet the needs of—particular fixed locations. This aspect of EDM praxis is very well established, dating back to the origins of club music in the discothèques of the 1970s. In the late 1980s, an alternative approach began to develop in association with Europe's emergent rave culture, which in certain ways functioned as an antecedent for the Love Parade. The rave concept introduces a degree of mobility with respect to the overall landscape in which it occurs, since each event takes place in a unique location. Ideally, the organizers should be able to move into the space, set up quickly, and leave when they are done; they should also be able to quickly shift to an alternate location if necessary. Nevertheless, raves retain a strong site-specific dimension; although only used for one-time events, venues are chosen for their distinctive, particular qualities.

The Love Parade can be understood as both an extension of and a departure from the raving practices that formed its context.[14] The mobility inherent within the rave experience is now the core component of the event, unfolding on several levels. First, there is the centripetal attraction that draws participants toward Berlin. This force is also approximately cyclical, as the event occurs once per year (usually in summer, though not on the same date every year). Within Berlin, the parade takes on additional circular aspects—most notably in relation to the Siegessäule, the column topped by a golden angel that serves as the site of the closing performances. In physical terms the Siegessäule is the center of the traffic circle known as the Großer Stern, from which five streets radiate outward. The partiers who fill the surrounding park are free to orient themselves toward the parade in any way they wish, of course. Two common approaches are to follow one truck through the parade or, by contrast, to remain in one place and observe the various trucks as they pass by. Within the space immediately surrounding the Siegessäule itself, ravers often ascend streetlights and other smaller poles (see Figure 10.1). In so doing they reveal a kind of excess momentum, as the parade pushes its surfeit of bodies upward into space.

The actual route of the event, meanwhile, follows a decidedly linear and horizontal trajectory. Its path along the Straße des 17. Juni connects two major intersections, each with its own architectural markers and historical resonances. On the western side is the Siegessäule or "Victory Column" (built 1871–73), which was erected as a symbol of Prussian victories over Denmark, Austria, and France. At the eastern limit of the parade route, meanwhile, lies the Brandenburger Tor: the enormous columned gate that forms the symbolic center of the city and of Germany itself. Like Potsdamer Platz, the Brandenburg Gate fell within the path of the Wall; in fact, it was physically enclosed within the two sides of the barrier. Today, of course, it functions as one of the chief symbols of reunification, the parade-goers circulating across its plaza indexing the larger freedoms of movement that Germans and Europeans now enjoy. Yet the Gate, like the Victory Column to the west, also has strong associations with past oppressive regimes and the declaration and preservation of state power. These connections are most obvious via the proximity of the Reichstag immediately to the northwest of the Gate; the seat of government has been reconstructed with a modern glass dome, but still displays its historic façade. Notably, the Siegessäule was originally located in front of the Reichstag; it was moved to its current location by Hitler, as part of a plan to turn the street now known as the Straße des 17. Juni into a grand avenue connecting the center of power in Mitte to West Berlin. Ironically, the current name of the street has a decidedly anti-establishment gloss: it refers to the date of a major uprising of East German workers against the government in 1953. (The uprising was subsequently violently crushed on the same day.) In traversing this route and its resonant sites, the Love Parade therefore visibly and sonically adumbrates the contradictory forces that have shaped Berlin's geography.

The fall of the Wall demarcates the origins of both the Love Parade and Tresor: the former began just prior to this event, while the latter arose within its immediate aftermath. As this heady time gradually gave way to the realities of reconstruction, Berlin's

FIGURE 10.1 Berlin Love Parade 2006, vicinity of Siegessäule and Tiergarten (photograph by author).

electronic musicians continued their collaboration with Detroit, while also developing a significant techno infrastructure of their own. In 1993, for instance, Mark Ernestus and Moritz von Oswald founded the record label Basic Channel, which soon became the basis for various EDM-related activities. Under a variety of aliases (Octagon, Radiance, etc.), Ernestus and Oswald released a series of highly influential tracks. Oswald in particular also worked with several prominent Detroit musicians, including Juan Atkins, Eddie Fowlkes, and Carl Craig.[15] In nearly all respects, Basic Channel was a thoroughly minimal operation: their sound was slower in tempo, lower in frequency, and less abrasive than that of Tresor (although both labels were equally characterized by purist aesthetic attitudes). One of the chief influences for their work—and one that opened a further stream of transatlantic interaction—was Jamaican dub.[16] Only nine releases were issued under the Basic Channel name, although the duo continued to form sublabels for various projects (among the most highly regarded of these being Chain Reaction and Rhythm & Sound). Ernestus also ran a record store, Hard Wax, in an edgy part of the Kreuzberg district near the Kottbusser Tor U-Bahn station; it remains there to this day, along with the affiliated recording studio Dubplates and Mastering.

In sum, Berlin during the 1990s reveals several distinctive (and often dichotomous) trends in its emergence as a center of EDM. On the one hand, its most visible event, the Love Parade, became a major tourist attraction and received a great deal of press coverage. Although it was hardly representative of anything local by the end of the decade, it became a powerful symbol of the city's relationship with EDM. On the other hand, club culture during this era had a strongly underground flavor. Many clubs were set up in abandoned sites, in areas that were previously neglected or off-limits, and illegal events and venues were extremely common.[17] There seems to have been an awareness of the early post-Wall era as a special time that would not last forever, as Sean Nye indicates in the following description of clubs such as Tresor: "The old designs were innovative and playful, but also provisional. The owners knew the locations were likely to be bought out by developers."[18] Most of these venues were located in the newly reestablished central district, Mitte; with the exception of the Love Parade, the participants were primarily German. The most prominent sounds were the hard techno of Tresor and related labels and the pop techno that developed in conjunction with the Parade.

Within Europe, 1990s Berlin was not yet the undisputed capital of EDM that it is today. Rather, it was one of a number of leading urban centers. Tobias Rapp situates its role within this decade as follows: "[I]n the nineties... the scene was more polycentric. It was all over the place: in Sheffield, Manchester and London in the UK, in Chicago and Detroit in the US. In Germany, cities like Cologne and Frankfurt were also more important" (Rapp 2009b). In Frankfurt, for instance, the labels Force Inc and Mille Plateaux were founded in 1991 and 1994, respectively (Reynolds 1999:363–64), while Cologne's club scene eventually became an important base for the "minimal" sound.

After the turn of the millennium, the draw of Berlin for those interested in EDM began to intensify. By 2004, the city had clearly emerged as the center of a burgeoning mass-cultural phenomenon. The first broadly visible signs appeared in the popular press, which during that year began to widely document a very particular form of immigration: leading EDM producers were moving to Berlin, in ever-increasing numbers. Of the many newspaper and magazine articles that appeared, the one that has received the most attention (at least among English-speaking techno fans) is an essay from the *Detroit Metro-Times* narrating the 2003 relocation of recording artist and performer Richie Hawtin to the city, along with protégé Madga Hojnacka.[19] Hawtin and Hojnacka both specialize in minimal techno (also known simply as "minimal"), a style that quickly became the dominant soundtrack of the new decade in Berlin. Moreover, Hawtin's move clearly took on symbolic significance, as his distinctive history and image place him squarely at the intersection of two competing forces within EDM culture. On the one hand, he is widely recognized as a pioneer of second-wave Detroit techno, with important productions dating back to the early 1990s. For these achievements he has achieved enduring respect from other techno musicians and "serious" fans. On the other hand, Hawtin is also a massively popular performer among the EDM proletariat; he is easily the most famous North American DJ. This combination of serious artistic credentials with mainstream success is uncommon among figures from the techno underground; while EDM purists may have become suspicious of Hawtin's subcultural capital, they have to pay attention to him nonetheless.

Other musicians had preceded Hawtin: his label-mate Daniel Bell had moved to Berlin in 2000, and Jeff Mills had also lived in the city. Moreover, most of the German musicians cited in the following section had been based in Berlin since the '90s. The post-millennial acceleration, however, brought a much larger international influx. Many American musicians, ranging from the internationally known to the aspiring, moved to the city beginning around 2004, as did growing numbers of European techno musicians and record labels.[20] In the "zero years," as Rapp describes the new era (2009a), Berlin has increasingly become a key site from which electronic sounds and practices are dispersed.

The reasons for this centralization are many. While a full accounting thereof is beyond the scope of this paper, the most widely cited set of factors is economic. In brief: Berlin is cheap. Rents for both housing and commercial space remain significantly lower than in other large European cities; the amount of buildings present in the city exceeds the needs of the population, which (outside of EDM and artistic communities) is declining. Unemployment presently stands near 16%—approximately 260,000 people[21]—and about 40% of residents receive some sort of government subsidy in the form of pensions, welfare, or unemployment (Theil 2006). The city government, which was largely subsidized by the competing Germanys during the Wall era, is now in debt by billions of Euros. Reconstruction-era hopes for the city were high: one author remarks upon the "post-unification speculation that the city, as a rising Germany's new capital, would metamorphose from a gritty outpost of the cold war into yet another homogenized, prosperous Eurotropolis" (Theil 2006). But Berlin has not become a major economic center; indeed, the German capital only relocated from Bonn—and then incompletely—in 1999.

The absence of work and wealth has not dampened residents' enjoyment of life, however. Rather, they have continued to take advantage of a low cost of living and significant amounts of free time. The club life of Berlin has become famous for its unrestricted hours and extreme durations. Clubs and bars are not legally required to shut down at a particular hour, such that even small neighborhood venues are frequently well populated until 5 a.m. on weeknights. All nights except Tuesday are popular for going out, and the "weekend" offers continuous clubbing from Friday evening through Monday morning. Some institutions become most crowded on Sunday mornings between 6 a.m. and noon (Berghain/Panorama Bar), while others fill up on Sunday afternoons (Bar 25).

In geographic terms, the clubs of post-millennial Berlin have slowly crept eastward. While the immediate post-Wall era was focused on the rediscovery of Mitte, the strongest trend since 2000 has been the opening of numerous club spaces on or near the Spree River. On the east side, most clubs are in the student-ish Friedrichshain district (Maria, Berghain, Bar 25); on the west side, they are in Kreuzberg (Watergate, Club der Visionäre, 103 Club) or the eastern part of Mitte (Golden Gate, the new Tresor) (see Figure 10.2). This riverside region coincides, of course, with the location of another former border strip—the only part of Berlin in which the Wall ran alongside the Spree.[22] Not surprisingly, the area is currently the focus of yet another land debate; as documented by Tobias Rapp in his recent book on the Berlin club phenomenon, investors are trying to gain access to the area, while club owners and others oppose development. Though presently unresolved, the matter has been petitioned for referendum (Rapp 2009a and 2009b).

FIGURE 10.2 View of the Spree and Schillingbrücke from the patio of club Maria, July 16, 2006, 7 a.m. (photograph by author).

Meanwhile, Berliners continue to organize and distribute club space in highly creative ways. In 2006, for instance, I attended a club called Kubik. It was a temporary installation, erected only during the summer in a vacant lot on the western side of the Spree near the Schillingbrücke.[23] The walls of the club were formed entirely from large plastic cubes that slowly blinked on and off, emitting glowing green light in seemingly random patterns. The club was open-air, having no ceiling, and the area along the riverbanks was covered with sand to form a "Strand." Another memorable venue, which I visited in fall 2007, was a former brewery. From the outside it appeared unremarkable, a non-descript single-story warehouse. The ground floor functioned as an entryway, lit solely by a single disco ball. Clubbers rode their bicycles across this large and empty space up to the doorman. The actual dance area was reached by descending a staircase five floors underground; here the club was situated within a network of rooms, with large circular holes in the walls where the brewery's pipes had once been. This club was also open for a limited period of time. Notably, it was located in the decidedly unglamorous district of Neukölln, thus revealing the ongoing tendency of the club scene to push ever forward into "edgier" spaces.

One of the most important factors facilitating these changing patterns of consuming and performing EDM has been the emergence of budget airlines within Europe.

"Techno tourists" from across Europe are now able to fly to Berlin for the weekend at minimal cost, and they are doing so in record numbers. One mainstream publication notes a 22% increase in tourist numbers in 2006, "driven, officials say, mainly by young Europeans coming to play in the city's ever-cool club scene" (Theil 2006). In the course of three annual stays in Berlin over the course of 2005–7, I saw the lines outside Berghain grow to feature regular wait times of more than an hour; while waiting, one hears Spanish, Italian, French, and English spoken as much as (if not more than) German. Rapp, who has dubbed these travelers the "Easyjetset," epitomizes the phenomenon as follows: "Every weekend thousands of techno tourists fly to Berlin, in order to party in a way that they are unable to at home. Numerous DJs and producers have been drawn here. The discount airline traveler has revolutionized going out" (2009b:78).[24] Citing an advertising slogan, Rapp also speaks of the "airplane as taxi" (*"Ein Flugzeug als Taxi"*) (78). Notably, there is one other major demographic taking these taxis: the musicians who have moved to Berlin. Through short-run flights to virtually any city large enough to have an airport, performers have access to steady work—a situation that is certainly not feasible in the presently diminished US EDM scene, in which the market for club performances is much more limited as well as geographically disparate. For example, a visit to the website of record label Minus reveals the following schedule for Richie Hawtin over the course of three weeks in July 2009: July 10—Novi Sad, July 11—Kiev, July 12—Budapest, July 18—Fraga, July 19—Amsterdam, July 24—Stratford upon Avon, July 25—Pirovac, July 27—Gent, July 29—Mykonos.[25] Label-mate Magda maintains a similar schedule, as do numerous lesser-known performers.

In sum, the club-cultural practices of Berlin during the zero years reveal at least three distinctive forms of musical mobility. First, there is the immigration of musicians, characterized by a unidirectional flow toward an increasingly attractive urban center. Second, there is the shifting spatialization of nightlife throughout the urban landscape, which demonstrates both the temporary use of distinctive spaces (after the rave tradition) as well as a steadier eastward drift. Third, there is the flow of clubbers and performers—"the Easyjetset"—both to and from the city. As these clubbing patterns developed, so did certain influential musical practices. It is toward these trends that I direct my attention in the second half of this chapter.

# MOBILITY AND PRESENCE IN EDM PERFORMANCE: THE RISE OF THE LAPTOP SET

The increasingly prevalent mode of performance known as the "laptop set" has especially strong roots in Berlin. Like its club-cultural counterparts, the laptop set also demonstrates a growing emphasis on mobility. The first and most obvious way in which it does so is through making it easier for musicians to transport recordings for use in performance. Quite simply, the vinyl records that DJs play—and which continue to form the core of EDM production and performance in spite of the frequent introduction of newer technologies—are heavy. When DJs travel to performances, they bring with them only a small fraction of the records they own. They are usually limited to the amount that will fit in about two "crates" designed for this purpose, and even this moderate amount has a substantial weight. With a laptop, by contrast, performers can play DJ sets using mp3 files, a possibility that enables them to access much larger musical collections. Laptop sets also allow EDM musicians—almost all of whom are recording artists as well as performers—to construct sets from their own compositional material. Crucially, this material does not have to be in a final form, as is the case with produced tracks; performance components may be drawn from any stage of the compositional process and do not have to be complete.

Laptop-based approaches can also functionally enhance mobility by reducing the amount of gear that a musician must carry to a performance. Instead, equipment may be subsumed into virtual forms on the computer itself. In the following remarks, for instance, DJane Aroma links the creative possibilities afforded by this reduction to a particular kind of mobility:

> I make a lot of music outside, in the nature, because I love nature. With my laptop I produced a lot of tracks sitting on the beach, just having the sea beneath me, and I have some good headphones....So, I can sit in the forest, where I go quite often with my bicycle, or at the sea, wherever I am on this planet I can produce music.[26]

Notably, she associates the laptop with nature and the self. As she continues this train of thought, she further places this mode of music-making in a dialectical relationship with the city:

> And that's also what inspires my work very much. I really love sitting in nature and getting away from the city thing. Because I love living in the city; I've always lived in the city all my life, but...it's like traveling and finding out who you are, you know—you have to always go back and forth to see who you are and to see what your picture in the mirror is. That's for example why I call the album *Skyline*. Because it's about what happens in the city, and it's about the promise the city makes. The city is a promise for sex, and for meeting people and whatever, and for alcohol and excess and everything. Then you have the countryside where you see the skyline, and you have this promise, you know? But since you're sitting in a totally different environment, you can just think about the city in different terms. And this is the freedom my laptop gives me.[27]

At this point, some basic explanation of the technologies and techniques involved in laptop performance are in order. In general, the term "laptop set" as it is used today denotes any sort of EDM performance in which a portable computer functions as a primary source of musical material. (In most cases it is *the* primary source of this material.) It is possible for the laptop to be used in conjunction with turntables as a source of mp3 files (as mentioned earlier), an approach that is supported by a number of competing technologies.[28] In general, however, most laptop performers play their own music rather than recordings by others. The material they use, which is stored on the computer, may take a variety of forms: short loops consisting of just one or two instrumental sounds; four- to sixteen-bar sequences involving combinations of several patterns; longer sections; or complete recorded tracks. Some elements of the set may be preliminary—in "sketch" form, to be tested for effectiveness within performance—while others may be drawn from the producer's own commercially released recordings. Within performance, the musician treats these elements as raw material, selecting, combining, and transforming them in improvisational ways. As with a DJ set, the duration of a laptop performance is expansive; a set almost always lasts for at least one hour, and may last for several. In addition to the laptop itself, most performers incorporate one or more pieces of supplementary hardware, although the amount and types of technology used vary widely.[29]

The roots of the laptop set date back to the 1990s, when various performers, departing from the DJ-centric traditions of EDM, began to perform on-stage with equipment normally reserved for the recording studio. Frequently called "live PAs" (for "public appearance" or "personal appearance"), these performances were thought of as different from DJ sets since they involved playing one's own rather than someone else's music; even today, laptop performers tend to bristle if someone describes them as a "laptop DJ." At least three factors motivated the development of live PAs during this decade: first, musicians looking for different modes of performance chose to explore new technological possibilities; second, the live PA foregrounded musicians' status as composers and helped promote their records; third, certain emerging EDM super-groups (e.g., Prodigy, Chemical Brothers) were promoted according to rock-based models in which it was desirable to go on tour and perform on stage with clearly visible "instruments."

While personal computers had become an important part of studio production for EDM during the 1990s, they did not have the capacity to function as centerpieces for performance during this time. Instead, live PAs drew upon hardware designed for music production. In stage-oriented approaches (as with the super-groups mentioned earlier, or at large EDM festivals) these would typically be keyboard-based synthesizers, drum machines, and sequencers. In club contexts performers were more likely to use fewer devices, focusing instead on multipurpose machines with hands-on functionality. One widely employed device, for instance, was the Akai MPC-2000 sampler-sequencer.[30]

Going back even further in time, to the early 1970s, brings us to the original and still primary mode of EDM performance: the interplay of DJ and dancers. All participants in this communal experience are musical performers, including the audience (whom I have elsewhere described as the "performing audience"[31]) as well as the person behind the decks. Most relevant to the present context is the fact that the basis for this performance is *recorded* music.[32] While recording practices have had far-reaching effects on the ways in which we experience and perform all forms of music, club music brings tensions between recording and performance into especially sharp relief.

Considered individually, an EDM record cannot be said to imply some sort of "virtual" performance underlying it; one does not imagine its sounds as having been produced by a group of musicians playing together. Nor is any further performative re-creation implied *after* it is recorded. Instead, the recording itself is the ultimate product of composition. The experiential gaps that recordings open for listeners—who produced these sounds, and how?—intensify when the music involved is also electronic. With synthesized sounds that cannot be traced to familiar instruments, it can become difficult or even impossible to imagine or understand how the sounds one hears are produced. Moreover, when recordings are the formative material of performance, the musician must prove to the audience that something other than playback is involved.

In response to these vacuums, performance assumes an even more central role within EDM. The DJ takes records and transforms them in the context of a real-time event, while the audience performs their role as listeners by enacting the music through dance. In these capacities participants cultivate an enhanced awareness of the here and now—an experiential goal of clubbing that arises, paradoxically, from the very primacy of recordings within the experience. The "now" component of this aesthetic configuration is often described as "vibe"—a particular kind of collective energy between a performing musician and dancers that has long been considered an essential aspect of an effective EDM event.[33] For vibe to emerge, one must feel part of a unique, one-time occasion; a technically proficient performance is not enough. The "here" involved in this criterion, meanwhile, can be understood in relation to the site-specificity highlighted earlier. The powerful sense of presence that arises within an EDM event can only develop in a special place, one designed for this purpose and set apart from the everyday world.

Within both EDM and other styles, the word most frequently used to describe this enhanced awareness of the here-and-now is as "liveness." Although this term is now so commonplace that its meaning might seem transparent, it reflects a thoroughly modern perception of performance, one that derives from the pervasive production and distribution of music in recorded form. When we experience a performance as "live," we are experiencing it as "im-mediate" in a literal sense—that is, unmediated by the technologies of sound reproduction. Indeed, it is only as we become aware of the opposing possibility—that musical performances can be played back without human intervention—that certain kinds of performances begin to seem live.

Integral to the preceding description is an emphasis on liveness as a perceived attribute: I seek to frame immediacy not as a fundamental ontological condition of performance—as argued most famously by Peggy Phelan (1993)[34]—but rather as but as a culturally and historically determined perception that shapes the way participants experience and describe music. In this regard I follow Philip Auslander, who argues that "the historical relationship of liveness and mediatization must be seen as a relation of dependence and imbrication rather than opposition" (1999:53). More specifically, he contends that "the history of live performance is bound up with the history of recording media; it extends over no more than the past 100 to 150 years" (52). According to this argument, it would be anachronistic to describe a performance from the early nineteenth century as "live"; in fact, as Auslander points out, the definitive *Oxford English Dictionary* did not even use this word in relation to performance until the mid-1930s (52–53).

As the technologies involved in EDM performance have diversified within the twenty-first century, liveness has become an increasingly important aesthetic value. Since the advent of the laptop set it has become especially common to frame EDM performances as "live." Terms such as "live set," "live PA," and "live performance"—or simply the musician's name followed by "live" in parentheses—are used interchangeably to describe laptop-based approaches; notably, all of these labels use liveness as a criterion to differentiate these newer modes of performance from DJ sets. Although this distinction is suspect in at least two respects—laptop sets are also centered around recordings (albeit in digital rather than physical form), and liveness is essential to DJ performance as well (as I have shown)—it does significantly register the ongoing presence of anxieties around liveness within discursive practice.

During the years in which non-DJed performance first emerged in EDM, such anxieties were clearly difficult to address. Some performers altogether abandoned attempts at authenticity in their live shows; instead of attempting to overcome the technological "problem," they chose to foreground it ironically by simply "pressing play" and directing their energies toward dancing, lights, and other visual displays for the audience.[35] The increasing prevalence of the laptop set, by contrast, reveals the emergence of a new historical moment—one in which the issues surrounding mediated performance are both more acutely manifested and increasingly solvable. With regard to the former, the following section will reveal a number of ways in which musicians have responded to the particular concerns about liveness raised by laptop performance. With regard to the latter, I will explain how the proliferation of laptop sets has also been facilitated by new kinds of software that support flexible, real-time control of musical parameters. The most widely used of these programs, produced in and distributed from Berlin by the software company Ableton, is named—appropriately enough—"Live."

## INTERFACE DESIGN AND (IN)VISIBLE MEDIATION

As the most general-purpose of the devices involved in EDM performance, the laptop seems innocent enough—yet it provokes more intense manifestations of anxiety than any other device, for both performers and audiences alike. As such, it highlights the communicative issues at stake in technologically mediated performance in a particularly striking fashion. The following description from an interview with Pacou illustrates a very common way in which musicians characterized the problems associated with performing with laptops:

> I know a lot people that are also using Ableton, but in a very boring way. They are just clicking the parts on, in a sequential order, and from an audience point of view it looks like they are checking emails or playing Tetris or things like that. Very boring presentation. And these guys are charging money for this?[36]

In conversations with performers, negative comparisons to "checking email" came up time and time again. This image evokes several key dimensions around which musicians' concerns coalesce. The first involves the perceived purpose of the laptop: while devices such as turntables, drum machines, synthesizers, and sequencers are clearly designed for music-making, if not of a traditional sort, the computer is associated primarily with nonmusical pursuits and is certainly not thought of first as a performance instrument. The second focal point of anxiety concerns the visual appearance of the performer to the audience (in Pacou's description, this appearance is expressed as imagined by the performer). The latter point is broad, involving several distinct subpoints.

First, the interface elements of a laptop, which include virtual elements on the screen as well as the mouse, keyboard, and physical display, are for the most part invisible to the audience. This is partly due to size—they are too small to be seen clearly from a distance—but more significantly due to the orientation of the computer, which faces the musician. Second, the only visible controller, the mouse, is itself used to manipulate onscreen elements; as a result, there is a lack of perceptible connections between the musician's physical gestures (specifically, hand and arm movements) and the sounds that arise. Third, whenever the mouse comes into play, the musician must devote his or her full attention to the screen; this precludes the performer from making contact with the audience, particularly eye contact, suggesting instead the self-involvement intrinsic to the "personal" computer.[37]

One significant consequence of these issues is that rarely if ever is a "laptop set" *only* a laptop set. Instead, the internal, digital elements of the laptop environment are externalized—made physical and visible in the form of MIDI controllers and other hardware devices. As MIDI, or "Musical Instrument Digital Interface," is really just an agreed-upon design protocol for facilitating communication between instruments, a "MIDI controller" in theory could be almost any kind of device that meets these specifications. Reflecting practice, however, I use the term to describe a particular class of devices that have arisen since the turn of the century in association with the laptop set. Although some performers design their own controllers (as I describe in further detail later), the majority of those in use are mass-produced for commercial markets.

During the period in which fieldwork was conducted (2005–2007), the UC-33 controller by the company Evolution was one of several widely used devices of this type. Like most commercially produced controllers, the UC-33 is designed for variety and generality of function. Its interface contains a fairly even mix of sliders, knobs, and buttons, which allows musicians to interact with it according to their preferred method.[38] Although it can be employed for production as well as performance, the manufacturers' descriptions of the product emphasize its functionality within performance-oriented programs such as Live.[39] In its division of musical space into channels, each of which has controllable frequency bands, it is similar in design to DJ mixing boards.

The Micromodul series of controllers from the German company Faderfox is comparable to the UC-33 in terms of its variety of control organs: it also presents knobs, sliders, and buttons, as well as a joystick and LEDs for visual feedback.[40] The Faderfox series, however, is even more expressly oriented toward performance; the manufacturers have explicitly stated that these controllers are "designed primarily for use with Live from Ableton."[41] For this reason, the Faderfox interface is simpler than that of other MIDI controllers, with a noticeable emphasis on tactility: while the LV2 itself is rather small (thereby promoting portability), its knobs and sliders are large and made of soft, touch-inviting plastic. In addition, as indicated by the name of the series ("Micromodul"), the Faderfox controllers are markedly modular. This aspect of design is intended to facilitate customization: the LV2 is the base unit for a network of up to three additional auxiliary units, which are specialized according to the type of control organ involved (for instance, the LX2 features buttons exclusively, and the LD2 knobs). The basic premise of the overall system is that musician can assemble a configuration of performance controllers using one or more LVs as the core unit(s) and other units according to their individual needs and preferences.

The manual for the FaderFox MicroModul LV1 provides an interesting gloss on the attitudes behind the emergence of these types of interfaces:

> It is 2004. Music is being made with electronic instruments that were originally intended to replace the typewriter. PC's and Mac's are replacing more and more synthesizers, pianos, CD players and LP turntables in the inventory of today's musician.... Since computer music should also thrive from improvisation, we... designed a controller to support the playful use of loops.... Let's face it, who wants to drive a car with a computer keyboard or a mouse? Fact is, slide controls, knobs, joysticks, buttons, and LEDs are as much a part of electronic music as a steering wheel is to a car.[42]

Providing an unusually explicit explanation of their intent, the designers of the MicroModul contrast the mouse and keyboard of the computer (which they relate to the typewriter) with slide controls, joysticks, buttons, and LEDs. In an ironic twist, interface elements that are more typically associated with the technical and functional come to seem warm, live, and human. In a traditional rock performance these bits of gadgetry would be emblems of *in*authenticity—if they were associated with performance at all—but in this context they serve as a way of grounding performance, of locating something physical that one can manipulate in a visible, visceral manner. The knobs and levers of MIDI controllers, drum machines, and mixing boards—all of which originated as recording or playback equipment—become conveyors of liveness. An increase in the amount, variety, and presence of technology addresses a problem that itself originated in technological mediation.

One of the most significant interfaces for contemporary laptop performance—more properly, a *set* of interfaces—is that found in the program Live, which was developed in Berlin by Gerhard Behles and Robert Henke, members of the EDM duo Monolake.[43] Live's distinctive characteristic is its performance orientation: it is a software sequencing program that allows users to change any of its parameters instantaneously. Prior to its introduction in 2001, musicians sometimes incorporated other available sequencing programs into performance, but these technologies were of limited functionality in a real-time context. Their interfaces and other features were designed first and foremost for studio production; to process a sound with an effect such as reverb or delay, for instance, could involve considerable lag time or "latency." (Also relevant, though less interesting for the point at hand, is the fact that computers had less memory, processing power, and portability.) After Live was released it increased steadily in popularity; today it is so widespread that almost all laptop performers use it.[44]

Musicians interact with Live through two main "views." The arrangement view (not shown) is basically a piano-roll notation: it proceeds through the piece from left to right, marking the music in measures and seconds. In this regard it is similar in design to a number of other widely used sequencing programs. As an interface, it is intended primarily for studio functions such as composition, production, and recording. It is Live's other principal interface, the "session" view, that is a real distinguishing feature of the program; it is designed expressly for use in performance. The primary elements of the session view are short instrumental patterns called "clips," which are normally set to repeat in cyclical patterns (loops). Represented by small colored blocks, clips form a grid of vertical columns and horizontal rows (see Figure 10.3). In this example (drawn from one of the program's demo tracks), clips are arranged into five columns and three rows. Rows contain formal sections or "scenes," which hold a mixture of different textural elements; here the scenes are labeled A, B, and B2 (see the "Master" column). The columns, meanwhile, consist of categories of timbrally or instrumentally related sounds, such as "bass," "pad," and "drums."

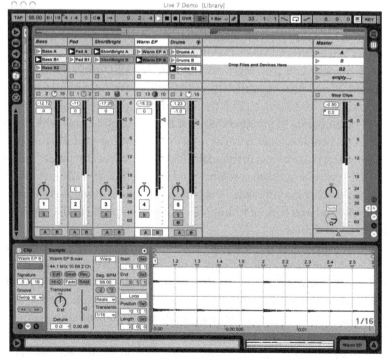

FIGURE 10.3 Session View in Live.

It is possible to move through the session view in a prearranged, linear fashion, treating the scenes as formal sections and proceeding in order from top to bottom. However, the interface is deliberately designed in a way that facilitates nonsequential, extemporaneous navigation through the grid. The text accompanying the demo notes, "The Session View offers an improvisational approach to music-making, allowing you record, play and combine ideas **on the fly**" (original emphasis). Clips can be switched on and off at will, independently of their arrangement in rows; in Figure 10.3, for instance, patterns from three different rows are playing, as indicated by the lit-up triangles on the clips of Bass B1, Pad A, ShortBright A, Warm EP B, and Drums B2.

The range of performance interactions that the design of this interface invites or allows suggests a conceptualization in terms of "affordance," a term originating in psychologist J. J. Gibson's ecological theory of perception (1977, 1979). Briefly, Gibson defined "affordance" as the possibilities for physical action inherent in an environment in relation to the capabilities of an actor. The concept was subsequently adapted within the areas of research described as "human-machine interaction" (HMI) and "human-computer interaction" (HCI), particularly by Donald Norman (1988). Here affordance is useful as a way of imagining interfaces as sites of possibilities rather than as fixed elements generating outcomes predetermined by their physical properties. While the preceding examples derive from environments found within Live, this view of interfaces is equally applicable to individual hardware devices as well as to assemblies of different machines, extending all the way up to the complete array of technology used by a particular performer at any given time.

Within this perspective, two particular emphases are notable. First, the interface is conceived of in spatial terms: technologies are described as "environments" and "sites" through which performers move. Electronic musician John Bowers, for instance, characterizes his performance configurations as follows: "In most of my performance work, I have adopted the strategy of *having a varied set of musical resources* before me which I have structured as an arena for activity, *a performance ecology*" (2002:57, original emphases). To the degree that motion is involved, this spatial dimension is also temporal, for the performer's actions involve a sequence of behaviors unfolding in time. Second, the way in which I have applied affordance also foregrounds the agency of the performer. Although technologies inevitably contain certain invariant features, it is the creative way in which a performer interacts with an interface that ultimately determines the course of a musical event.

Indeed, performers who use Live vary greatly in their utilization of its technological capacities. When Pole performs with his band, for example, he employs the program in a highly organized and relatively prearranged way: clips are organized according to color, with degrees of timbral similarity indicated by the palette, and several rows of scenes form a track. This organization, along with the use of one or more empty rows as spacers, clearly delineates each track from the ones that surround it. In the course of performance, Pole mostly moves in descending order, activating rows as he proceeds through his set. These features are evident in Figure 10.4, a screen close-up from a performance in Montreal in June 2006; here, a band of orange and reddish clips represent the track currently in play (see rows 3–8 in Figure 10.4).

FIGURE 10.4 Screen close-up from performance of Pole and band at the Mutek festival, Montreal, June 4, 2006 (still image from video recording by author).

Pacou's approach represents the opposite extreme. There is little if any organization by track in his set; instead, it is largely loop-based. In Live, this fact translates into a screen densely packed with clips, with many different colors and no apparent systematization (Figure 10.5). Pacou moves through this grid in various directions, turning loops on and off in a highly extemporized manner.

Henrik Schwarz's approach is somewhere in between that of Pole and Pacou. Visual organization is readily apparent, as columns of the same color represent families of loops. Some of these are copies (duplication allows them to be placed into diverse textural configurations more rapidly), while others are variants.[45] His source material comes from his tracks, but these larger entities are broken down into many short loops. These modular elements form the basis of improvisation, though which Schwarz reconfigures his compositions (to the extent that their identities can be specified) in significant ways. In general, he uses drastically fewer loops than Pacou; a significant amount of blank space is usually visible on the screen. At the same time, he works with individual sounds much more intensively; he devotes a significant amount of attention to the manipulation of parameters within individual samples.

In these performers' approaches, interesting intersections emerge between the intent of the designers toward specific elements of the interface and the diverse ways in which musicians use them. Some musicians follow the leads suggested by particular program

FIGURE **10.5** Screen close-up from performance by Pacou, Tresor night at S036, Berlin, July 15, 2006 (still image from video recording by author).

features: they use colors to indicate timbre, or they arrange tracks in series of textural "scenes." Others, however, disregard these elements entirely or even work against them (as when Schwarz arranges his set loosely into scenes and then moves freely between them in order to focus on individual loops). The way in which the interface suggests actions to performers accordingly reveals itself not as a deterministic case of feature $x$ resulting in action $y$, but rather as a series of affordances or possibilities of varying specificity that musicians encounter and negotiate within the performance environment.

Live facilitates variety among performers in part because it is customizable. Indeed, when musicians use the program to create clips and tracks, they are also producing the specific graphical interface they will use in performance. In this way, the "data" they record in preparation for performance can be understood as both text and context: these musical facts constitute the formative matter of performance (musical patterns) *and* the interface through which it is encountered (manipulable graphic representations of those patterns). Customizability was also seen as an advantage in the Faderfox controllers, although in that case the musician can only effect variability as a consumer (one can purchase and arrange different configurations of controller units according to one's preference).

Even as software and hardware companies have responded to musicians' desires for adaptable interfaces, performers have chafed against the perceived limitations of commercially available products. In response, a number of musicians have literally taken matters into their own hands and designed their own devices. Robert Henke provides one of the best examples. Since 2003 he has performed with a unique controller, the "Monodeck," which he designed and built himself. On his website he explains the motivations behind his decision:

> In 2003 I decided to build my first own [*sic*] MIDI controller, the Monodeck. A MIDI controller is a hardware unit made for controlling a computer in a musical way, turning a general problem solving machine into a true musical instrument. For my live performances I needed a very specific device. No commercial product matched, so I finally built my own one, a box with knobs, LEDs and buttons, with a layout optimised for my performance. It worked much better for me than expected, my concerts became more spontaneous and I became quite skilled playing it.[46]

The resulting device, a photograph of which appears in Figure 10.6, features twenty-six binary controls (buttons), as well as continuous controllers in the form of knobs (there are no sliders). The buttons can provide visual feedback and stimulation by lighting up. The interface contains three main parts or regions. The central part determines which sounds are present and their volume. Like a DJ mixer, it divides the texture into a number of channels (in this case, six), with volume controls and a three-band EQ for each. It also contains several features specific to Live, however, such as buttons for turning clips

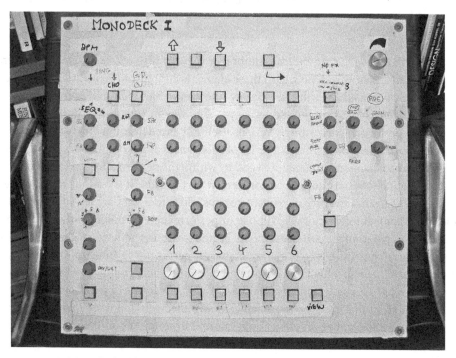

FIGURE 10.6 Monodeck (first version). Photo courtesy of Robert Henke. Used with permission.

on or off and scrolling up or down through the grid. To the left and right of the central six channels are the other two regions of the Monodeck, which control effects.[47] When I observed Henke using the Monodeck in performance, however, he alternated between periods focused on the controller and segments in which he scrolled and clicked on screen. Although this is a common way of using a MIDI controller, Henke clearly regarded it as a limitation: "the first Monodeck still only served as an additional interface and could not replace operating the computer with the mouse and staring at the screen during my concerts."[48] As a result, he developed a new Monodeck, which he calls "Monodeck II." With several assistants, he completed the Monodeck II in 2005–2006 and began to perform with it in late 2006; it remains his principal controller.

As is evident in Figure 10.7, the Monodeck II expands the features of its predecessor considerably. It is larger, and it contains many more control elements. The basic layout of the interface is the same, with a central section focused on the control and manipulation of texture and peripheral sections dedicated to effects; the number of channels, however, has increased to eight. The effects areas are more elaborate and hierarchized, containing small subsections for controlling individual parameters within each overall effect. Lighting is also noticeably more complex; the interface now includes ninety-two LED lights, each capable of seven different colors. According to Henke, their purpose is to "provide constant optical feedback and facilitate navigation" through his set.[49]

Henke's work on the Monodecks complicates issues of determinism, intent, and agency in interesting ways. Scholarship on the design of interfaces and instruments has

FIGURE **10.7** Monodeck II

generally assumed a separation between makers and users, such that a device intended to function in a certain way might "determine" its resultant uses, or users might be seen to assert their creative agency in the face of apparent technical constraints or specific intended uses. These circuits of power begin to break down, however, when controllers are self-designed. Furthermore, while such self-designed interfaces are an ever-increasing trend in recent years, Henke represents a special case above and beyond this development, in that he is also the creator of the software that the controller is meant to manipulate. In particular, his work with the Monodecks and Live shows a striking convergence between software, controller, and music, in which all three elements are linked through specific design correlations.

These correspondences are most visible on the central part of the interface. In Figure 10.7, note the way in which the eight channels are grouped into five rows (counting up from the bottom of the machine).[50] Each button in this grid controls a clip in the software, which in musical terms represents a loop. When a loop is playing, an LED beside the button is lit to display its status. Each loop is categorized in two ways. First, it is part of a textural configuration (a "scene" in Live), which corresponds to a row on the Monodeck; second, it is a member of a timbral category, which in turn relates to a column in Live and a channel on the Monodeck. The matrix on the controller always corresponds to a virtual matrix in the software, which as a whole represents one track in Henke's live set. In other words, Henke has developed an approach in which tracks consistently form structures of five scenes and eight columns, and the controller he has designed matches this organization exactly. Figure 10.8, which shows a screen in Live from an interview in which Henke explained this approach to me, reveals this patterning within the software. At the top of the screen, four rows (80%) of a light-orange track are visible; below this follow two complete tracks, colored dark orange and fuchsia. The musical structure of a performed track thus has two visual analogs—the on-screen graphical interface and the grid of buttons and LEDs—one of which is physical in form as well. In Henke's words, "You cannot separate the instrument and the composition."

According to Henke, the constrained structure of his interface design facilitates performative freedom. It does not force him, as one might assume, to follow an obvious or predetermined route through his set, proceeding in descending order from scene to scene and track to track. Rather, he moves through the highly controlled environment of five-by-eight tracks in a decidedly nonlinear fashion, combining clips from multiple scenes and even different tracks. Except in cases where he wishes to make a stark textural change quite suddenly, he rarely uses the prearranged scenes as wholes. Instead, the scenes function in a trifold manner: as strata of visual information, as documentation of the way in which the track has been arranged up to the point of performance, and as starting points for musical reconfiguration.

Another kind of performative freedom engendered by the Monodeck II is liberation from the computer: specifically, from the twin attachments of hand and eye to mouse and screen to which Henke objected in his previously quoted criticism of the original Monodeck. When I observed him performing with the Monodeck II at the 2007 Detroit Electronic Music Festival, for instance, I was stunned to see that he never once touched or looked at the computer after beginning his performance. Never before have I seen

FIGURE 10.8 Screenshot of Live in relation to Monodeck II (still image from video recording by author).

a musician refrain from at least periodically manipulating the computer. Henke relies instead solely on the physical interface; his laptop only serves as a source of data and of the program that the Monodeck controls.

It is remarkably ironic that a musician who has played such a pivotal role in the popularization of the laptop set should himself design a controller that problematizes the very notion of what a "laptop set" is. Furthermore, it is equally ironic that someone who designed a program oriented specifically toward performance with laptops should be part of a trend *away from* laptop computers in favor of physical performance tools. As part of a performance environment that is self-designed to an unprecedented degree, "Live" remains in dynamic tension with the ideals of "liveness," provoking unexpected results in the context of performance. Paradoxically, it is through waves of technological mediation (electronic music, computer software, an intricate hardware controller) that Henke approaches an unmediated ideal, one in which he plays music only with his hands.

## CONCLUSION

Throughout this chapter I have described a quite diverse range of musical flows. The first set of these was broadly geographical: from three American cities (Detroit, Chicago, and New York), electronic dance music spread to the United Kingdom and the rest of Europe, and then onward throughout the world (including the United States more generally). Second, with regard to Berlin I have shown how one pioneering club and label (Tresor) drew inspiration from Detroit to the center of the once-divided city; how the Love Parade drew throngs of celebrants to Berlin and moved them along a resonant route; and how patterns of techno tourism, immigration, and club geography have transformed the present-day city. Third and finally, I have discussed the variety of flows that characterize the increasingly common performance approach known as the laptop set. These include the mobility of musicians—for laptop performance, in contrast to the DJ set, is actually distinguished by its mobile nature—as well as that of the software (now also flowing from Berlin) and the overall approach itself. Understood as environments that performers navigate, interfaces appear as sites of mobility. Notably, this mobility is not just about place, but also, crucially, about *time*. The success of the program Live is not just a matter of its effective interaction with mobile computers; above and beyond this, it allows a temporal fluidity that was not previously possible. The compositional acts of the recording studio now take place in real time, in performance. Live mediates between recording and performance.

In so doing—and in parallel to the very idea of liveness itself—this mediation hinges upon an axis of visibility/invisibility. M. Norton Wise, constructing a theory of knowledge frameworks, effectively characterizes this operation as follows: "The work of mediation is successful only if it makes the mediator disappear, so that the agreement connects the two parties directly. Similarly, mediating technologies, to the degree that they function well as mediators between theory and reality, make themselves transparent" (1993:246–47). This further suggests a kind of merger between technologies and subjects: "In performing their function,…the technologies themselves faded into the background, projecting their action into the subjects they related" (240). Within modern EDM performance, "liveness" likewise folds into space through the temporal mobility noted previously. Presence emerges in the specific sites in which this music continually anchors itself, which it reaches by traversing great distances to disparate locales. Thus, while electronic dance music may be fluid, digital, abstract, and mobile in all the ways I have mentioned, it is important to realize that it is not rootless. It grounds itself again and again in particular spaces and places, and the same adaptability that enables its fluidity facilitates these affiliations.

## NOTES

¹ Following on this point, it should be noted that I use the term "electronic dance music" (and the abbreviation "EDM") as a broad term encompassing all genres that might be considered to fall within this category. This is in keeping with the way in which the term has been employed in both popular and academic writing since the late 1990s (and throughout my own work). In the past few years, "EDM" (and "Electronic Dance Music," often but not always capitalized) has also emerged as a label for recent, commercially popular genres such as dubstep. My own usage should not be confused with this narrower one.

2. The historical information presented in this section is derived from the accounts given in Brewster and Broughton (2000), Fikentscher (2000), Reynolds (1999), and Sicko (1999). Because these books, although valuable, are not historiographically oriented—and no critical historiography of EDM currently exists—the narrative here should be understood as a summation of the key historical developments as they are most commonly traced. See also Butler (2006:32–47) for further discussion.

3. Although the Warehouse changed its name to the Music Box in 1982, the genre term "house" remained. The best-known DJs of the Music Box period, which lasted until 1987, were Ron Hardy and Marshall Jefferson.

4. The most comprehensive and thorough account of the events described in this paragraph appears in Tim Lawrence's excellent *Love Saves the Day* (2003). Based in particular on numerous interviews with original participants, this work documents the history and institutions of disco in exhaustive detail.

5. Cross-fertilization between New York and Chicago also took place fluidly during this time. Larry Levan was originally sought after as a DJ for the Warehouse, but he declined; instead, Frankie Knuckles moved to Chicago to take the position. Accounts of Levan's DJing also frequently speak of him playing house music.

6. A current map of Berlin (searchable by address) is available at http://www.berlin.de/stadt-plan/. Also of interest are the aerial photographs of the Wall's former course available at http://www.berlin.de/mauer/luftbilder/1989/index.en.php. (Both sites accessed August 13, 2012.)

7. Available at www.tresorberlin.de (accessed May 23, 2009).

8. Notably, it was the music and image of Detroit, rather than Chicago or New York, that captured the attention of these Berliners.

9. Various Artists, *Tresor II: Berlin—Detroit: A Techno Alliance* (Tresor 013LP/12 NoMu 14, 1993). The tracks on the album are by a mixture of Detroit- and Berlin-based artists.

10. This institutionalization was met with a countercultural reaction of its own: the birth of a new parade, known as the Fuck Parade, in opposition to the increasingly popular and commercial event.

11. During the same period, however, the Love Parade model began to be transplanted to other cities worldwide. Locales that have held Love Parade events since 2001 include San Francisco, Mexico City, Santiago, Cape Town, Sydney, Budapest, and Tel Aviv.

12. The most recent parades have been hugely popular; the 2008 event in Dortmund broke a record with 1.6 million participants. Once again, however, the parade appears to have been a victim of its own success: the 2009 event in Bochum was canceled, after city authorities declared that they were unable to handle such an enormous influx of visitors. See "Loveparade 2009 fällt komplett aus (Love Parade 2009 completely cancelled)," *WDR*, <http://www.wdr.de/themen/freizeit/freizeitgestaltung/loveparade_bochum_09/index.jhtml> (accessed May 27, 2009).

13. In the discussion that follows I speak of the Berlin Love Parade in the present tense, in order to highlight the cultural forces at work without linguistic awkwardness.

14. In fact, the two phenomena developed in very close temporal proximity—the Love Parade following the first major explosion of European raving by just about a year. Hence one should not overemphasize raves as an "influence" for the parade. One obvious connection is the way in which parade attendees continue to preserve "old-school" rave traditions in their appearance and behavior; many participants still sport fake-fur angel wings, fuzzy pants, blinking jewelry, and Ecstasy-induced grins long after the fading of these practices from the EDM mainstream.

15. The collaborations with Fowlkes and Atkins were released under the name 3MB and also involved West Berliner Thomas Fehlmann, while Craig recorded a remix of Oswald's track "Domina" on a twelve-inch along with the original.

16. Discussion of the dub/techno connection is beyond the scope of this paper; see Veal (2007:235–39) for further information.

17. By "illegal," I refer to situations in which promoters did not possess permits and/or occupied buildings without permission. In Berlin such actions have not typically generated the strongly punitive responses that they have met in the United States; at the time the government was focused on much more pressing issues, and there was already a well-established squatter counterculture in the city.

18. Nye (2009); see also van Heur (2008:177–79).

19. See Wasacz (2004), "Losing Your Mind in Berlin: Hawtin, Magda, and the Berlin Scene." Hawtin hails from Windsor, Canada (part of the Detroit metropolitan area), while Hojnacka is from Detroit. Wasacz's article, with its sometimes over-the-top prose, was famously parodied on the now-defunct site www.ubercoolische.com and through t-shirts referencing the article with phrases such as "Time and place exist in blurry indistinct partnership" and "Magda make the tea."

20. Other events demarcating a shift around this time include the cancellation of the Love Parade in 2004 and 2005 and the closing of Tresor in 2005. However, the trends described here and in the following paragraphs had already begun to develop during the preceding years.

21. See http://www.berlin.de/berlin-im-ueberblick/zahlenfakten/index.en.html (accessed June 10, 2009).

22. More precisely, the Wall began to meet the Spree at the Schillingbrücke, currently the site of Maria, and continued in a southeasterly direction to the Oberbaumbrücke, current site of Watergate. (The Oberbaumbrücke was also one of the eight official border crossings.) From there, the East German side of the Wall continued to the next bridge, the Elsenbrücke, before returning to land.

23. The former location of Kubik is nearly visible in Figure 10.2; its lot lay just to the right of the large office building on the left side of the picture.

24. "Jedes Wochenende fliegen Tausende Technotouristen nach Berlin, um hier so zu feiern, wie sie es zu Hause nicht können. Zahlreiche DJs und Produzenten sind hergezogen. Die Billigflieger haben das Ausgehen umgewälzt." Translation by author.

25. Available at www.m-nus.com (accessed June 12, 2009).

26. Interview with the author, August 9, 2006. In Germany, female DJs such as Aroma sometimes use the appellation "DJane" to highlight their gender and to problematize the fact that the "DJ" is normatively defined as a masculine figure. This practice also reflects the grammatical structure of German, in which feminine gender in professions is denoted through the addition of the suffix –in.

27. Ibid.

28. The most widely used programs for MP3-based DJing are Final Scratch and Serato Scratch Live. Each type of software involves a setup in which the laptop is connected to a traditional analog mixing board and turntables; a special vinyl interface shaped like a record affords physical manipulation of the sound files using standard DJ techniques. See Butler (2006:58–59) for further discussion of Final Scratch.

29. I comment further on both external hardware and internal software later in the chapter.

30. For further discussion see Butler (2006:65–67). The MPC-2000 has also been widely used in hip hop; for example, it appears in the cover photo for *Making Beats*, Joseph Schloss's 2004 monograph on hip-hop sampling.

31. Butler (2006:47–49).

32. As indicated by the key term "discothèque," a combination of "disc" and "bibliothèque."

33. See Fikentscher (2000) for an extended discussion of "vibe." Also see Thornton, who connects vibe to authenticity through a reconfiguration of Benjamin's "aura": "What authenticates contemporary dance cultures is the buzz or energy which results from the interaction of records, DJ, and crowd" (1996:29).

34. See especially chapter 7 of *Unmarked* ("The Ontology of Performance: Representation without Reproduction"), in which Phelan strongly opposes performance and technologies of reproduction: "To the degree that performance attempts to enter the economy of reproduction it betrays and lessens the promise of its own ontology" (1993:146).

35. An interesting and quite self-aware example from the pop side of the EDM continuum would be the Pet Shop Boys, whose tours have most commonly emphasized dramatic staging, elaborate costumes, and other effects in conjunction with prerecorded backing instrumentals.

36. Interview with the author, July 26, 2005.

37. This paragraph's emphases on visibility might rightly raise certain affiliated questions—in particular, to what extent can the performer be seen by the audience, and how concerned is the audience with actually watching him or her? With regard to the former, my experience in Berlin has been that the performer is almost always visible within the dance-floor area, even in very large clubs such as Berghain. In a culture in which musicians are expected to demonstrate authenticity through performance, it would be unacceptable to sequester them in a hidden DJ booth. Moreover, as musicians repeatedly expressed to me in interviews, audience feedback is extremely important to the direction of their performance, and they want to be well positioned to receive it. As for the degree of audience engagement with this process, the norms of club-cultural praxis allow this to vary tremendously from one person to the next over the course of an evening. In general, however, a successful performance will generate and sustain a dance floor full of musically engaged individuals, a significant percentage of whom will periodically direct their attention toward the processes being displayed on stage. (A further question, which will certainly require substantial ethnographic and historical research to be answered definitively, involves the extent to which the orientation of audience members toward performers has varied within different historical periods and club cultures; sources on earlier clubbing practices seem to suggest that audiences were more inwardly directed than they are today.) Finally, it should also be noted that performers convey involvement, expressivity, exertion, agency, and other factors crucial to the perception of liveness through additional techniques such as physically demonstrative use of their interfaces, dancing, and facial expressions. Questions of space prevent me from developing these points further in the present context; however, I treat them in depth in the book-length project from which the current work is derived.

38. Although space limitations prevent me from including a photo of the UC-33, images of it can be obtained by searching for "Evolution UC-33" on sites such as Google Images. In addition, there are a number of YouTube videos of musicians using the device.

39. See, for instance, http://www.evolution-i.net/products/evo_uc33e.htm (accessed April 9, 2008).

40. At the time of writing, photos of these controllers were available through the manufacturer's website. See http://www.faderfox.de/mark/index.php?option=com_content&view=article&id=111&Itemid=176 (accessed September 26, 2011). They are also accessible through Google Images; search for Faderfox LV2, LX2, and/or LD2.

41. Faderfox LV1 User Manual (2004), p. 6; available from http://www.faderfox.de/html/download_page.html (accessed April 9, 2008).

42. No author cited: 3. Available from http://www.faderfox.de/html/download_page.html (accessed April 28, 2008).

43. Behles has since left the duo to focus on running the company that distributes Live, Ableton. Henke, who was interviewed for this project and who will shortly be discussed at length, continues to record and perform under the Monolake name. Although his work as Monolake and his development of Live fall within a generally "popular" realm of electronic-music practices, he also regularly creates sound installations and other performances of a decidedly experimental ilk in venues such as the Centre Pompidou and the Tate Modern. In this regard he is among a number of musicians and interface designers whose work inhabits an increasingly porous zone of overlap between popular and academic electronic music. Thus, while the technologies and practices that I discuss here center around popular EDM, the reader should note that issues of interface design and mediated performance have received increasing amounts of attention within the academy as well. Particularly relevant sources include the journal *Leonardo* (I have cited four articles apposite to EDM and/or performance in the reference list for this chapter) as well as the proceedings of the annual conference "New Interfaces for Musical Expression" (first held in 2002), available from www.nime.org.

44. In addition, many musicians who formerly shunned laptops within their live sets have been drawn to the program in recent years. Examples include Pacou, discussed later, and Adam Jay, mentioned in Butler (2006).

45. In all of the examples I have presented, musicians assign colors to instruments arbitrarily; there is no fixed association between color and timbre in Live. This is evident even in the demo (Figure 10.3), in which timbrally identical sounds within the same column are assigned different colors.

46. Available at http://www.monolake.de/monodeck/ (accessed March 14, 2008).

47. Henke has indicated the specific effects involved, along with various other details, using handmade masking-tape labels. Apropos of customizability, it appears that the effects assigned to particular knobs or buttons are variable. In various photos of the Monodeck I that Henke has shared with me, the labels differ significantly—and they also change in images that I recorded in an August 2005 interview.

48. Available at http://www.monolake.de/monodeck/ (accessed March 14, 2008).

49. Ibid.

50. The five-by-eight matrix at the bottom of the Monodeck II is separated from the other control organs by a row of double LEDs, above which is another row of buttons (labeled 1–8 to show the eight channels) that act as master on/off switches for each channel.

## References

Auslander, Philip. 1999. *Liveness: Performance in a Mediatized Culture*. New York: Routledge.

Born, Georgina. 2005. "On Musical Mediation: Ontology, Technology, and Creativity." *Twentieth-Century Music* 2(1):7–36.

Bowers, John. 2002. "Improvising Machines: Ethnographically Informed Design for Improvised Electro-Acoustic Music." MA Thesis, University of East Anglia.

Brewster, Bill, and Frank Broughton. 2000. *Last Night a DJ Saved My Life: The History of the Disc Jockey*. New York: Grove Press.

Butler, Mark J. 2006. *Unlocking the Groove: Rhythm, Meter, and Musical Design in Electronic Dance Music*. Bloomington: Indiana University Press.

Fikentscher, Kai. 2000. *"You Better Work!" Underground Dance Music in New York City*. Hanover, NH: Wesleyan University Press.

Gibson, James J. 1977. "The Theory of Affordances." In *Perceiving, Acting, and Knowing: Toward an Ecological Psychology*, ed. Robert Shaw and John Bransford, 67–82. Hillsdale, NJ: Lawrence Erlbaum Associates.

——. 1979. *The Ecological Approach to Visual Perception*. Boston: Houghton Mifflin.

Lawrence, Tim. 2003. *Love Saves the Day: A History of American Dance Music Culture, 1970–1979*. Durham, NC: Duke University Press.

Norman, Donald A. [1988] 2002. *The Design of Everyday Things* [originally printed as *The Psychology of Everyday Things*]. New York: Basic Books.

Nye, Sean. 2009. Review of *Lost and Sound: Berlin, Techno, und der Easyjetset*, by Tobias Rapp. *Dancecult: Journal of Electronic Dance Music Culture* 1(1), http://dj.dancecult.net/index.php/journal/index.

Phelan, Peggy. 1993. *Unmarked: The Politics of Performance*. London: Routledge.

Rapp, Tobias. 2009a. *Lost and Sound: Berlin, Techno, und der Easyjetset*. Frankfurt am Main: Suhrkamp.

——. 2009b. "'Lost and Sound': A Book about Berlin's Techno Scene." Interview by Ulrich Gutmair. http://www.goethe.de/kue/mus/thm/wmr/en4315121.htm (accessed June 10, 2009).

Reynolds, Simon. 1999. *Generation Ecstasy: Into the World of Techno and Rave Culture*. New York: Routledge.

Sicko, Dan. 1999. *Techno Rebels: The Renegades of Electronic Funk*. New York: Billboard Books.

Theil, Stefan. 2006. "Poor but Sexy." *Newsweek*, September 18.

Thornton, Sarah. 1996. *Club Cultures: Music, Media, and Subcultural Capital*. Hanover, NH: Wesleyan University Press.

van Heur, Bas. 2008. "Networks of Aesthetic Production and the Urban Political Economy." PhD diss., Freie Universität Berlin.

Veal, Michael. 2007. *Dub: Soundscapes and Shattered Songs in Jamaican Reggae*. Middletown, CT: Wesleyan University Press.

Wasacz, Walter. 2004. "Losing Your Mind in Berlin." *Detroit Metro-Times*, November 10. http://www2.metrotimes.com/arts/story.asp?id=6949 (accessed August 22, 2013).

Wise, M. Norton. 1993. "Mediations: Enlightenment Balancing Acts, or the Technologies of Rationalism." In *World Changes: Thomas Kuhn and the Nature of Science*, ed. Paul Horwich, 207–56. Cambridge: MIT Press.

CHAPTER 11

# TURNING THE TABLES: DIGITAL TECHNOLOGIES AND THE REMIXING OF DJ CULTURE

## CHRISTINA ZANFAGNA AND KATE LEVITT

WAVING goodbye to their turntables, the London club DreamBagsJaguarShoes began hosting an iPod DJ night in 2003 called *No Wax*—a title that celebrates the ease of compiling and mixing MP3s instead of lugging heavy crates of vinyl records. A review of the event reads, "Somewhere in East London the turntables are motionless. The only thing spinning is a chorus of iPod hard drives, or the ceiling (if you're friends with the bartender)" (J.LOVE). There is no celebrity DJ headlining the night; patrons are encouraged to bring their own iPods to the club and "plug-n-play." Just thirty years prior, legendary hip-hop DJ Grandmaster Flash was cutting up his father's wax (old LPs) at block parties in New York City. *No Wax*, and dozens of similar events, signal the ways in which DJing, as both a practice and cultural movement, has been significantly changed and challenged in the last several decades by the transition to digital and now portable media—a turn about as smooth as a chorus of hard drives might sound.

This chapter tells the still unfolding story of DJ media—from ad hoc analog setups to state-of-the-art iPod mixers to the burst of smartphone and tablet DJ apps in 2011—through both its uses and perceptions, hoping to contribute not only to the history of music media but also to ways in which musical meanings change as new media emerge. In exploring these changes, this chapter aims to debunk a few common assumptions and myths about DJ culture and practice in relation to proliferating sound technologies, the widespread use of digital, handheld playback devices and the pervasiveness of DJ-inspired music in various realms of culture and commerce.

Myth #1: Digital media has made the DJ obsolete.
Myth #2: Increased access to DJ technologies is breaking down hierarchies of musical taste and value.
Myth #3: Music is becoming more mobile.

To understand these myths and assess the impact of digital, portable technology on DJ culture, we begin with the most basic of questions: What is DJing? Who constitutes a DJ?[1] The emergence of new digital DJing tools in particular raises questions around how we define the work of the DJ. Furthermore, the instruments of the DJ—turntables—function as playback devices as well as technologies of musical composition, lending them openness and flexibility. This, along with the relative newness of DJing as a vocation and practice, renders the DJ difficult to define, and it is this ambiguity that makes the emergence of digital, portable DJ technologies so contested.

We ground our analysis in the history of DJing, placing emergent media forms in a longer trajectory of musical collecting, mixing, and DJing. DJing as a culture was borne of innovation and boundary crossing, yet remains anachronistically attached to a nostalgic sense of its past: often referring to "keeping it real" by "diggin' in the crates." We outline three significant shifts in DJing over the last 30–40 years. The first phase focuses on DJ culture as it emerged in the 1970s, outlining the work of the DJ in these early years as a combination of both song selection and technical skills. In addition, it examines the role of remix as it contributed to the development of what has now become a cross-cutting DJ culture in many electronic music genres—a practice grounded in its movement from bedroom to block party to nightclub.

Moving into the 1990s and 2000s, the second shift reflects the uneven transition to digital playback technologies by professional DJs, or the emergence of the laptop DJ. While these technologies certainly eased portability, they are most significant in the questions they raise around the authenticity and sound quality of digital media. The new advances challenged tradition—the analog setup and its crate of vinyl—with the increased capabilities and convenience of digital music technology. Again, we see the work of the DJ called into question as the materials of the DJ's practice change, thus producing differences in sound quality between digital and analog media.

The third phase is initiated by portable MP3 players such as the iPod—introduced in 2001—and continues into the present moment with the iPad and computing tablets. The increasing portability and decreasing size of the technologies has vastly changed participation—who gets to be a DJ, who calls themselves a DJ, and what these DJs do. The tension has shifted to a question of access and the effects of the supposed democratization of DJ culture on the quality of music in club scenes, the uses of sound technologies, and the role of the DJ in popular culture. When less exclusively the domain of virtuosos and professionals, what happens to DJing?

These phases tend to map onto discrete moments, although we emphasize that they are not chronologically distinct; rather, they are overlapping and interrelated periods of DJ/remix culture. While the distinction between the three typologies underlines changes wrought by technological developments and digital media, it is not meant to reify these categories or oversimplify the process of sound production and consumption into a teleological narrative. Furthermore, mobility has long played a central role in DJing; the transition to more easily portable digital technologies does not necessarily signify deterministic changes in music's mobility. DJ culture has always produced mobile, multiplex, and transitory soundscapes through new uses and forms of technology. Instead, handheld devices and digital software programs for DJing complicate hierarchies of music performance and participation—who gets to play music and what gets played—thereby posing questions about what the labor of a DJ actually means. And while some may argue that the transposition of DJ practices from turntables to iPods represents a degradation of "authentic" DJ performance, digital sound media in fact offer exciting new opportunities and platforms for engaging with DJ culture and its various practices. There are more possibilities and expanded potentials for sound collecting, mixing and sharing—empowering users to engage in remix and imagine DJing in all kinds of places and spaces.

Across these three phases we have interrogated the different tactile experiences associated with new DJ technologies as well as the specific aural changes in the soundscapes, particularly as DJs and listeners understand these changes. Undoubtedly some of these technological developments affect certain musical scenes differently than others: for instance, digital turntable interfaces may be embraced more unevenly in hip-hop due to its celebration of vinyl, while a subgenre like dubstep, which allies itself with digital effects, may utilize digital media more readily. However, in the spirit of remix, we do not focus on one particular genre of music and instead look at the implications of digital developments across DJ culture(s). Throughout shifts in media, no matter the music scene, the work of the DJ remains to rock the party. How the party is rocked is up for debate.

# Phase 1: In the Beginning There Was ... Analog

"There's not a problem that I can't fix/cause I can do it in the mix," proclaimed Indeep's 1982 hit "Last Night a DJ Saved My Life." A decade into the disco club craze and a handful of years after early hip-hop heads first started experimenting with turntables and reconfiguring mixers, this now iconic message attests to the promise of a new sonic relationship. The DJ mix not only rocked dance floors for hours on end, but also dynamically recuperated and recomposed sound through innovative layering, sampling, and scratching. A relatively small group of committed practitioners with access to bulky equipment and expansive record collections reinterpreted the world around them, mixing up vinyl, machines, and sound systems in relation to new modes of dancing and different uses of public and private space. Records, turntables, mixing boards, and speakers became tools for experiments in sound, the mechanical building blocks of an emergent culture that combined with innovations in body movements and responded to changes in urban environments.

Many musical movements contributed to the evolution of the DJ from radio jockey to dance floor grandwizard, including sock hops in the United States and northern soul in England, but it was a combination of Jamaican music practices and New York's underground disco scene in the 1960s and 1970s that laid the foundation for the DJ as selector and, eventually, remixer. In the 1960s, dub reggae's "versioning" deconstructed the record, using it as a tool rather than a finished product, a technique appropriated in disco clubs in the 1970s, hip-hop in the 1980s, and just about every other music genre thereafter. In addition to highlighting the music selector in the latter decades of the twentieth century, DJ culture explored ways of making music more mobile, bringing the party to the people. Mobile speaker units in both Jamaica and the Bronx in this early era allowed DJs to create dance floors in a wide range of spaces, from the schoolyard to the street to the community center. It would not be a stretch to argue that these sound systems foreshadowed the boombox, Walkman, and MP3 players in terms of their emphasis on music's mobility and portability.

The history of DJing has been well documented in numerous accounts (Brewster and Broughton 2000; Chang 2005; Hebdige 1987; Keyes 2002; Lawrence 2004), which pay necessary tribute to the figures and events that have come to define it as a musical practice. These texts tend to construct two competing and yet complementary DJing philosophies to define the labor of the DJ: musical selection and technical ability. In the former, DJs function as archaeologists and archivists, diggin' in the crates for obscure and high-quality tracks and playing them in such a way that creates a musical "journey" for the audience. The power of this mix lies in its ability to build a musical narrative as well as maximize the sonic qualities of each track. The latter approach prioritizes technical skill and precision, making a science of dexterity, speed, and sound innovation. However, the division between these two styles is largely artificial; as anyone who has listened to a DJ Premier track can attest, the best DJs can hone technical skill while still crafting a unique and well-planned song selection.

The first decade of DJing, roughly the 1980s, defined itself in relation to the physical materials of recorded sound. Vinyl became the instrument and basis from which a number of new meanings and uses arose. DJ culture shifted the emphasis of recorded music playback from a one-way flow of information to a multifaceted conversation between DJ and vinyl, turntables, mixer, dancers, and the urban environment. As a consequence, the significance of DJ culture was not merely the ability to weave recorded songs, but the fact that it connected bodies, sounds, and technology in an urban ecology. More important, it underscored the parameters of what the work of the DJ should be in the first place—the credibility of a curated archive of breaks combined with the technical mastery reflected by hours of practice. Music crowds encountered DJs in very specific locales—mainly clubs and other organized parties—and predominantly viewed them as masters of their trade, specialists in the art of the mix and the dance floor.

The first phase of DJing is also significant in that it introduced and popularized the idea of remix, helping to propel it into a far-reaching cultural movement. As a theory unto itself, the remix refers not only to the practice of rearranging, but also the *idea* that we can take things apart and reorganize them. It grants the ability to change and play with representation, not only an enhancement but also a product relevant on its own terms. Vinyl, as a music text, is not a "fixed and immutable creation, but rather raw material that must be recast through its insertion into a flow of texts" (Hadley 1993:58). More generally, remix culture can be defined as a global practice of creative exchange made possible by advancing digital technologies that often results in the reinterpretation of preexisting visual and sonic media. The concept of remix that became popularized in this early phase of DJing also laid the foundation for approaches to iPoding and new methods of DJing and music-sharing in the present day. And yet the celebration of the remix in itself also obscured the more tedious aspects of the labor of the DJ, expanding DJ culture to anyone and everyone with a pair of turntables and a love of continuous music.

## PHASE 2: THE DIGITAL TURN AND GETTING LOST IN THE SAUCE

Today, it is surely stating the obvious to note that digital technologies emerging in the mid-1980s have had a huge impact on the sound and methods of producing and listening to music. While digital recording became more common in the late-1970s, the first CDs were not marketed until 1982 and their popularity did not surpass vinyl until 1988. Years after DJs had been manually matching songs together with pause-button cassette players, or sampling and remixing with only records, turntables and a mixer,[2] digital samplers reproduced these techniques on a much more exact and efficient level. By the mid-1980s relatively affordable sampling machines, along with improvements in synthesizers, led to an upsurge in dance music records made of entirely electronic sounds, the explosion of innumerable dance and electronic music subgenres, and the mainstream popularity of electronica as a formal musical genre by the mid-1990s. Digital production of the music played by DJs on their analog setups was important long before any means of digital playback worked its way into common DJing practices. Paradoxically, despite the fact that most music in a DJ's set tends to be digitally produced, many performers express a tepid acceptance of non-analog playback technologies.

The ways in which professional DJs adopt digital playback technologies while embracing the digital production of music reveals a complicated and contested relationship with new media and digital sound. Rather than a smooth evolution to infinitely improved ways of playing music, the adoption of digital DJ equipment is fraught with little scratches and warps, or the debates around what constitutes professional DJ practice as it relates to sound technologies. Hesitation with regard to the digital turn is caught in struggles of authenticity and "the real," a DJ history tied to vinyl records and digging for music in obscure stores. Although digital playback media is convenient, highly mobile and lower-cost—in some ways a logical extension of DJing's history of innovation and mobile sound units—the analog sound and feel of vinyl remains DJing's soul, its mythologized root. In an era when the remix has become common to the point of banality and almost anyone has the tools to try their hand at DJing, distinction and authenticity become critical modes of evaluation. Consequently, vinyl symbolizes the "grain" of authenticity (Barthes 1991) as well as the physical manifestation of subcultural capital (Thornton 1996).

This section focuses on how two specific technologies, CDs and digital audio files like MP3s, have changed DJing and reflect the disputed effects of the digital turn. CD turntables, popularly known as CDJs, were first introduced in 1994, designed to mimic turntables and provide more extensive "tools" for manipulating music. The small "platter" on the top of the CD player does allow the DJ to move it similar to a turntable, and the pitch control expands the range in which the DJ can control the song's speed. Both allow for beat matching and scratching, although on a different tactile interface. The CDJ also includes functions for looping and sampling, playing the record in reverse, and even measuring beats per minute.

Digital audio interface technologies, like Final Scratch Pro and Rane's collaboration with Serato Scratch Live, first emerged in 1999, although they were not embraced immediately. Still, less than a decade later most clubs provide an interface connection and a laptop stand to accommodate the growing number of DJs using these media. The programs emulate traditional DJ set-ups, allowing DJs to play MP3s (and similar sound files) from their laptop on turntables using specific software and digitally time-coded vinyl records. The computer reads a signal encoded on custom-made vinyl via the stylus, accounts for information about speed, direction and location, and accordingly maps an MP3 audio file onto the vinyl for playback. These programs also provide beat counters, looping functions, cue markers, and a number of other features designed to aid the work of the DJ.

Digital technologies impact professional DJing in a number of ways. First, and most obviously, they allow DJs to play digital song formats, which fit by the thousands on a tiny hard drive or hundreds in a small book, rather than by the dozens in bulky crate, as with records. Second, they make tasks like beat matching and cuing immeasurably easier and faster, mainly resulting in quick song transitions and more precise mixing. Third, they include technical aids, in which DJs can sample specific sections of songs and play them in ways and at rates that are close to, if not entirely, impossible in the traditional setup of a turntable, mixer and record.

Despite the presence and even centrality of digitally *produced* music in DJ culture, these changes in the "instruments" of the DJ have created tensions around its sounds and styles. The ways in which DJs negotiate the conflict that has arisen between analog and digital, or past and future, reveals insights into how turntable musicians define themselves and their work, as well as how they defend hierarchies of musical taste and value. Yet as Jonathan Sterne points out in *The Audible Past* (2003), concerns over sound fidelity and format have long dogged musical production. DJ culture, born amidst debates over rare selection and technical ability, and as equally tied to its twelve-inches as it is to technological innovation, enters into this debate with a mix of enthusiasm and contention.

## Wax on? Professional DJ Perspectives

The majority of the professional DJs we interviewed have transitioned to some form of digital audio format.[3] They largely cite its convenience in easing mobility, as carrying heavy record bags to multiple gigs in a week takes a physical toll on both the body and the albums. Brooklyn-based DJ Center admits that in addition to its convenience, programs like Serato offer an alternative to some of the most annoying qualities of vinyl—the bass hum, warped or scratched records. "I'm not going to romanticize vinyl like it was perfect," he quips, revealing that Serato's digital format has also helped him listen and use music more efficiently. Furthermore, it gives him access to songs he otherwise could not find or afford on vinyl, such as imports that rarely make it to the United States.[4] But the technology is not flawless. Frequent accounts cite Serato freezing or shutting down in the middle of a set, given glitches in the software or corrupted MP3 files. Still, these digital DJing technologies are most contentious not in terms of their technical capabilities, but rather in the sense that they facilitate "cheating" in live and recorded performances, enable impoverished collecting practices, and often result in poor sound quality.

Constructions of distinction between analog and digital sound media produce an authenticity specific to DJ culture. Its realness often lies in vinyl records, traditional techniques, and non-digital sound, even among those who have transitioned to digital media and equipment. For example, internationally known DJs like Z-Trip and Lee Burridge hesitantly adopted Serato as a more convenient way to tour, but miss "cool, groovy record stores" (*Las Vegas Weekly* 2008). Others frown on laptop DJing's aesthetics, which makes performers look as if they are answering e-mails or writing a paper, an image that does not add to the vibe of the dance floor. Furthermore, a persistent concern about "killing vinyl," or the disappearance of record stores, points to the mythical or symbolic violence of technology on analog's historical "roots." As "Sixxx" states on the Serato message boards, "There's NOT ONE THING IN PARTICULAR that can kill vinyl. If you really want to get technical . . . YOU AND ME ARE KILLING VINYL. Because if it wasn't for people like us who can accept new technology, then Serato or Final Scratch or whatever, would never sell."[5] Sixxx's comment illustrates a consensual vision of technologically determined progress, in which DJs are complicit in the violent transition from analog to digital.

The warmth, richness or feeling of vinyl reappears time and again in discussions with professional DJs.[6] In Serato's online message boards, vinyl recalls "getting fingers dusty," "warmth," and "remembering where we came from," a tangible root grounding DJ culture in its mythologized analog history. DJ Tabu reflects, "there's a certain thrill to hearing when the needle hits the record, that little crackling." She continues,

> there is a lot of fun in the surprise when you find a record that's in mint, pristine condition and you can smell, and touch it and it has that sound on it. [Serato] takes away from the beauty of it. It's like looking at a beautiful painting but the reproduction is on a computer. You'll never get that depth of color or see the strokes of the painter.[7]

Tabu invokes the persistence of an artistic "aura," a notion of originality in a world of incessant reproduction. The aura of the original version is devalued in subsequent copies, which become sensory degradations and therefore less powerful tools of the DJ trade. Particularly in an era when the digital production and reproduction of almost anything is possible, the analog-digital dichotomy tends to reinforce certain musical hierarchies of taste and value. In addition, a DJ can prove her value and commitment to the trade through attention to a depth of sound, a sense of sonic "care" that digital formats do not allow.

In other arguments, DJs cite scientific evidence of digital sound's fractured sonic qualities, its very structure a fatal flaw. Here, analog sound waves produce a continuous sonic experience, whereas digital files break sound into samples. By definition, you are listening to fragments of music that do not account for ambient sound, air, inflection, and the other components of white noise that help produce analog's "richness." MP3s further remove sound information; their small size results from a compression that essentially discards sound extremities. Digital sound is therefore sensory deprivation, although some suggest MP3 sound files preemptively remove data that the ear would likely discard anyway (Sterne 2006:832).

Bob Garcia, aka Bobbito, is a notable critic of the digital turn in DJ culture. Famous for his long-running hip-hop radio show, music journalism and residencies in many of New York's nightclubs, he has been involved in hip-hop culture and DJing since its early years. He comments, "I appreciate vinyl for its intrinsic physical qualities...an analog recording will hit the width and the sound wave and it will give you that warmth." Continuing, he argues that, "my ear appreciates that warm sound, that once in a while little crackle, that signifier that it's wax and not so perfectly compressed. I don't need to walk around with 5,000 songs on my waist that I'm not going to listen to in even five years."[8] If sound is inherently physical and music immersive, as Ken Jordan (2008) has written, then wouldn't more sound data travel more fully through our bodies and immerse us more deeply in the musical experience?

However, if "sound is a product of perception, not a thing 'out there'" (Sterne 2006:834), its purity and the feeling it produces is never fixed. The debate over sound fidelity here is culturally determined by the aesthetic tastes of DJs and temporally determined by the defense and preservation of a disappearing history. Importantly, it is also located in the confusion over what the true work of the DJ should be in the first place— what lends professional clout to their performance? Not only do records possess more "feeling," but also record shopping itself connects to a larger community, and it gives a "high" or lets people "relax." Nonetheless, DJs have a professional stake in preserving fidelity, as it determines their performance and crowd reception. Many MP3 files do in fact sound much worse than an original, analog recording, so transitioning to digital audio media requires close attention to compression rates and other factors affecting quality. DJs play on large high-fidelity sound systems, not the MP3 players and lo-fi headphones on which MP3s are meant to be listened; they simply need a fuller sound.

Bobbito's aversion to digital music is not entirely ideological or sound-based. Rather, it emerges from the material consequences of the turn to cheap, easily accessible music files, which have drastically reduced the demand for vinyl. Philip Sherburne terms this the "micromaterialization of music," as record collections have come to exist in silicon rather than on shelves (2003:46). In a matter of two to three years, Bobbito notes, most of New York City's most popular and established record stores have closed, a reality that runs counter to "trends" reported in recent press.[9] More critically, the vinyl plants pressing these records are dying out, making vinyl harder to come by. "Their choice [to use digital media] affects my ability to choose," Bobbito asserts. He continues, saying it's a loss of "the whole digging experience, and having a personal relationship with the record, and knowing where the break is, and knowing when it ends. Not a computer telling you all that. And that's not nostalgia. That's pure. This is our history. It's losing a part of history." For Bobbito, then, the work of the DJ is rooted in its use of a certain kind of instrument—one that is definitively not digital. To understand his point, imagine if the iPad offered "violin" apps, where a user could rub the screen in a particular way to create a violin sound. Yes, the iPad then becomes an instrument, but does it really replace the violin? Distinguishing between these two different types of materiality comes down to the politics of mediation, or the ways in which we assess the amount of distance between the user or musician and their instrument.

Bobbito is not alone in expressing fears of a digital technology-driven DJ culture. The expanded access to music that downloading offers is "a gift and a curse," in DJ Center's words, "because you can get lost. It's kind of like less is more, because before what you brought was what you played and you made the most of that. Now, it's like in this ocean of music and sometimes it's like, damn, I'm lost in the sauce." The very shift from the massive expanse of a record library to the compact cache of data files causes insecurity in a trade that has always existed in its sense of ownership of discrete objects (Sterne 2006). Like media consumers' anxiety about the inundation of information in the internet age, DJs are experiencing the overwhelming effects of infinitely expandable music collections. In a matter of years, there is suddenly more "stuff" to play with, and it exists in an entirely different format; it is not a surprise that the transition can feel overwhelming.

As Pingree and Gitelman affirm, "all media were once 'new media'" (2003, xi). Here, the authors point out that all new forms of media pass through a phase of identity crisis precipitated by the uncertain status of the medium in relation to known media. A slow process of adaptation between existing habits and desires for new uses ultimately shapes the meanings and functions of new media (xii). This conceptualization helps to situate the digital turn in DJ culture, which finds itself caught between its analog history and the promise of technological developments. Digital DJ equipment and audio files tend to mediate an understanding of the past (xiv), placing the digital playback devices in negotiation with their analog counterparts. Laptops, then, create interfaces that look like a traditional turntable DJ setup while offering expanded mixing functions and the ease of a more portable music collection. The quality of digital sound files has improved, approaching the fullness of a vinyl recording. Ultimately, the patterns of adoption, adaptation and hesitation expressed by the DJs in this section reveal the paradoxically controversial role of digital technologies in DJ culture. While forward-thinking and dependent on mixing the new and old, DJ culture's attachment to its non-digital instruments may also signal the ways in which these musicians defend their work, as well as enduring hierarchies of musical taste and ability. If this is the case, it is not surprising that the increasing use of not only digital, but also handheld, music devices to mix music heightens some of the disputes over what DJing is and should be.

# PHASE 3: THE PORTABLE TURN AND DANCE FLOOR DEMOCRACY?

While other DJing technologies and practices persist, this section examines the emergence and proliferation of iPod DJing and how such transportable modalities of digital sound-sharing further complicate long-standing debates around access, amateurism, authenticity, and authority within DJ culture. This phase marks an emphasis on hyper-portability and miniaturization with the widespread use of handheld, pocket-size devices such as the iPod, iPhone and iPad. As portability assumes a greater value in DJ scenes around the world, many practitioners and listeners are critical of what has become the DJ's labor and domain of expertise.

Since the iPod's initial release in October 2001, Apple has continued to develop increasingly affordable and user-friendly new models and programs, allowing people to carry their entire music collections in the palm of their hand. In April 2003, iTunes Music Store opened with its 99-cent downloads, focusing musical consumption around the individual track and the instant purchase. The size of the iPod continued to shrink in 2004 with the iPod mini (35% smaller), in 2005 as the iPod nano replaced mini, and again in 2006 with the second generation iPod nano—a persistent minimizing of playback machines extending from the jukebox, boom box, walkman, and portable MP3 player (first released in 1998). Finally, the iPhone arrived on the market in 2007 with an iPod in it. And the iPad, Apple's almost-handheld tablet computing device, was released in April 2010. It is important to note that all of these products were initially created and promoted as devices for personal listening, not for DJing in a collective arena. iPod billboards clearly illustrate the individualism of such sound machines through the image of the lone dancing silhouette absorbed in the sonic world of his or her white earplugs.

iPod DJs point to the unlikely uses and outcomes of turning interactive digital media into things it may not have been initially intended for. The inventive and resourceful deployment of iPods and mobile phones toward DJing echoes early hip-hop practices and tactics (see Phase 1).[10] In light of such everyday manipulations of digital devices, this phase is also marked by an increased accessibility and visibility of DJing as both a profession and an amateur practice. Specifically, the recent fad of playlist parties and iPod DJ nights—where anyone can DJ—aided by technologies like (the admittedly little-known) Djammer (a hand-held device that allows you to scratch and mix on your iPod or MP3 player), complicates and dismantles existing regimes of who controls and produces public soundscapes. This expansion of who is participating in the everyday "work" of the DJ may have started with the advent of CDJs, but it is furthered by the ongoing ubiquity of DJs in many sectors of social life and the continued affordability and simplicity of new musical media. The growing popularity of mash-up and remix cultures (Danger Mouse's 2004 release of the Grey Album acting as a kind of zenith) offers a fertile terrain for iPod DJ parties to take root, giving traction and currency to the musical eclecticism and randomness prized at iPod DJ events. Not only do we see the literal physical portability of ever-shrinking devices (from two turntables to a laptop, iPod, iPhone), music (from vinyl LPs to digital files, iTunes libraries), and the micropractices of DJing (selecting and mixing music), but also an increased circulation of the symbolic economy of DJ culture—the ethics, aesthetics, and general mythologies percolating within it, however contested they may be. To what extent has the hypermobilization and massification of DJ culture actually changed the music we hear in clubs and other public spaces and who gets to participate?

## IPod DJing and Playlist Personas

Returning to the *noWax* event—a title that clearly celebrates the lack of analog weight and physical sensuousness in iPod DJing (also known as MP3-jing or iPoding), MP3-Js bring their iPods and wait for their number to appear above the DJ booth. They plug their iPods into a mixer and mix three songs back to back. Similar in nature to hip-hop freestyle battles, where unknown rappers can "taste the glory" of the spotlight with the successful delivery of a biting and clever "on the spot" rhyme, the audience determines the winner. The originators of the event, Raj Panjwani and Charlie Gower, warn participants to expect a very eclectic night of sounds, as anyone has the chance to DJ and play *their* music. Anything from Chuck Berry to Steely Dan to Brittany Spears can be heard within a 10-minute span. Panjwani and Gower explain the essence of noWax,

> The basis of noWax is democracy. Anyone can step up and play their tune. Now and again you can have some friction when people play things that others don't want to hear, but try not to censor their music as this is at the heart of the concept. Also, sometimes people think that they'll get up there and play something obtuse, but when confronted by a merry throng they play something more crowd friendly. Very few DJs want to be hated by the crowd they are playing to.

Drawing on the spirit and ethics of DiY culture, this kind of liberatory or democratic rhetoric is pervasive in iPod DJing scenes with the use of phrases like "digital diversity" and "dance floor democracy." These phrases of social and sonic harmony may gloss over the live aural tensions and dissonances occurring between different styles and genres of music on these nights. Furthermore, such celebratory, community-based discourses about the inclusivity of iPod DJing are often in tension with some of the skepticism, hesitancy, and nostalgia articulated by vinyl DJs in Phase 2. While iPod DJ nights are certainly cheaper to produce than hiring a celebrity DJ to rock the crowd for several hours, the benefits of increased access, ease, and pocket portability are accompanied by the costs of amateurism, the lack of control club owners and promoters have over the musical identity of a given night, and the technological and aesthetic limits of new media forms. As one club attendee states, "I paid $25 one night for some DJ I didn't even know. DJ MegaByte or something stupid and computerized like that" (quoted in J.LOVE). She complained that all the DJ did was push buttons. Her comments reflect concerns about what constitutes the skilled labor of a digital or iPod DJ. Is pushing buttons musicianship? To what extent do people's expectations of the DJ have more to do with the physical labor of DJ practices than the actual sounds that the DJ produces? Certainly, the exact musical work of the iPod DJ is a contested terrain, where many clubgoers are questioning whether it is the technology or the individual that is doing the *performing*.

A similar night called iParty began in 2002 at the club APT in New York City's meatpacking district.[11] In an effort to subtly manage the kinds of music played at the club, DJ Andrew Andrew (two guys both named Andrew who decline to reveal their last names), create a 3,000 song (and growing) playlist every week; patrons then select tracks from this pre-selected list. Anyone can sign up by grabbing a ticket from a deli dispenser next to the DJ desk and then they wait for their number to be displayed on the "Now Serving" sign. Each DJ gets seven minutes to create a set using two iPods. Printouts of the playlist are available for patrons to read over in preparation for their set, much like a list of karaoke songs. The printouts also include a quick guide to DJ etiquette, which include the cardinal rule, "Playing of any heavy metal ballads will result in immediate expulsion from the premises." The bar started a request list for customers to add their favorite songs; the manager or staff takes the iPods home to upload the newly requested tracks. APT regulars who have proved their good taste and technical skill are allowed to bring their own iPods. In an interview with the *New York Times*, DJ Andrew Andrew justifies this kind of musical regulation, stating, "APT has a really strong musical identity, and we want to make sure there is a certain type of music playing" (Vance 2005). This level of control allows the event promoters to guarantee a certain character and quality of the soundscapes produced and heard at APT while still allowing patrons to choose their own music—a kind of freedom within limits. In this light, the event is more akin to a "do it yourself jukebox/Karaoke system for the crowd" (J.LOVE).

Furthermore, the mixing capacities of the iPod are limited. Matt Maland, who has played at APT three or four times states, "It's fun. It's different. It's a challenge. You have to think what songs go together more than vinyl because you can't beat-match" (Kahney 2002). In this way, DJing on iPods as opposed to turntables privileges the selection or playlist over technical mixing and beat-matching skills. Despite Panjwani and Gower's claim that iPod DJs will generally attempt to please the crowd, the technology itself shifts the DJ's work from "reading the crowd" to assessing the flow from one song to the next on a purely aesthetic level. This emphasis seems to reflect the practice of making mixtapes more than it does performing a live remix on turntables. Often at these parties, the song remains intact, unlike the live remixing and layering that can be achieved with a turntable DJ setup.

Playlist Parties constitute another major iPod DJing phenomenon of recent years—a multi-sited international network of iPod DJ nights that began in London in 2004. Playlist Parties were also started in Luzerne, Switzerland, Beijing, China, and Philadelphia, and have inspired similar events throughout the globe. As at other iPod DJ nights, aspiring DJs are judged on their selection of songs—the quality of their playlist. The Playlist Party Myspace page states,

> Playlist is the club for music lovers in the digital age. We believe the days of superstar DJs are over. Playlist takes power over what tunes are played away from the elite and into the hands of the people. People like us. Fed up being dictated to? At Playlist we give you 15 minutes to play a set of your top tunes, mixes, mash-ups, and random weirdnesses from your iPod, MP3 player, laptop, or any digital music player. The best DJs on the night win prizes, or at least endless adulation, but most important of all we all create the club together. We make it happen. It's not easy pleasing a crowd (as some aspiring DJs have found out) but it's always fun.[12]

Once again, reverberating through these lines is the anti-celebrity and communal rhetoric associated with digital DJing events, where everybody has the right to decide what will be gracing the airwaves. Such rhetoric is in stark contrast to the tone of the DJs in the previous section, who seem deeply wedded to their status as an artist/professional musician as they are encroached upon by hordes of amateurs without regard for the skills, tactics, and tastes that previously defined DJ culture. The case for the democratization of DJing calls into the question the extent to which DJing is a precise and artful labor or simply the act of providing music for the people.

Although Playlist Parties promote the collective *making* of the club experience through patron participation, the sharing of playlists sometimes feels more like the display of pre-made products than an active process. Audience reaction is critical to who gets to stay on the pods, but the musical mixes at these parties are perhaps more like one-off statements than a feedback loop between DJ and crowd. A quick perusal of the winning playlists at their website www.ipod-dj.com reveals an eclectic mix of music where randomness and the juxtaposition of divergent kinds of music are valued. In an article about Playlist Parties, the Philadelphia City Paper says: "If compact discs are going the way of cassettes, then MP3 playlists are the new mix tape."[13] In a certain way, the rise of iPod DJing and its emphasis on playlist is more of a return to the concepts and values associated with making and sharing mixtapes than it is an expansion of turntablism and DJing practices on vinyl. The focus on playlist evokes a self conscious, premeditated approach to the DJ set, where bedroom DJs get a chance to share the minutia of their personal collections, tastes, and sonic musings in a public venue in hopes of "endless adulation"—the personal made public. The phrases "Playlist as character" (Levy 2007:23) and "Fame is an iPod" reveal how playlists can be more telling badges of identity than gender, race, or hometown as well as how musical selection has the potential to diminish or confer status on individuals. (Some iPod DJs have admitted that iPoding at clubs is a way of flirting with and picking up members of the opposite sex, which reveals how these nights are sometimes more about persona than practice, more about the performance of identity than the fostering of community). Some refer to iPod and playlist scenes as *geekchic*, simultaneously nerdy and cool (traits that high-level skill DJing has taken on with the likes of the Invisibl Skratch Picklz and DJ Shadow). In their efforts to carve out a space in opposition to the singular control of professional DJ nights, these parties may in fact do little to create an egalitarian music culture; rather, they assert certain musical tastes and values over others, directed by the party organizers rather than the DJ herself.

The technology and language of the iPod has also sparked a fascination with the playlists and music collections of celebrities. Beck and George Bush's iPods have been the subject of much public interest and debate. In playlist mythology, the iTunes library or playlist gives us a porthole into the depths of a person's character. In what ways are iPod DJs rebuking the concept of "celebrity DJ" as they seek their five seconds of fame? How are practices of iPod DJing both borrowing from and redefining the language of DJ culture? Certainly, such events signal a shift from the "remix" to the "playlist" as the format of the DJ's work. Here, in the world of Playlist parties, authenticity hinges more on the presentation of one's "authentic" self in music as opposed to the "authentic" practice of using vinyl and turntables.

## iPod/iPad DJ Technologies and the Rise of Professionalism

Despite the emphasis on playlist and selection, many iPod DJs are invested in advancing the technical capabilities and skill involved in the practice. Such practitioners have an interest in approaching iPods and, more recently, iPads like turntables—as a musical instrument—and transferring the aesthetics of the craft from *wax* to *no wax*. For instance, daring iPoders can attempt a kind of faux scratching by tapping the center button of the iPod and gently jogging back a second or two, thus making the music pause. It actually sounds more like a CD is skipping, but what else is an iPod DJ to do? In the wake of iPod parties and club nights, technology industries have responded by creating new devices that continue to change the nature and physical labor of iPod DJing. The phrase "pure pod," which refers to the use of just two iPods with a mixer (no laptop or auxiliary equipment or programs), already implies the beginnings of a burgeoning discourse of authenticity *within* iPod DJ circles as opposed to *in relation to* other forms of earlier DJing. Furthermore, the development of new iPod DJ technologies such as Djammer and the Numark iDJ iPod mixer point toward a growing professionalism and distinction between different levels of expertise in iPod DJing's supposed open field of cultural production.

iPod DJs often complain about sound quality, low sound levels, and the lack of pitch control, which is what allows for beat-matching. The Numark iDJ is a mixer that aims to address these issues, with two iPod docks, neon-lit buttons and a scroll wheel and has certain features that distinguish it from the "pure pod" set-up. While the mixer is mostly made out of plastic, which raises questions around the longevity of such a device, users say that it is a lot lighter and more portable than most mixers. Furthermore, a reviewer on the Playlist Party website says, "I have also noticed a little more warmth to the sound that comes out of the pods using iDJ. There's a reason for this: the sound doesn't come out of the headphone connection, oh no—that wouldn't be elegant enough. What iDJ does is suck the sounds out using the iPod's Dock connectors, which makes for a better bandwidth of sound—so it's richer, warmer and more defined."[14] Again, listeners invoke the rhetoric of "warmth," illustrating the ways in which sound authenticity is discursively produced vis-à-vis technology. In this case, the debate is not between analog and digital setups but rather about how certain kinds of technology are deemed higher-quality or higher-fidelity than others—how dock connectors are preferred over a 1/8" jack. The mixer also includes a fader start button that helps create smooth transitions between songs. This feature keeps one iPod on pause as another track is selected, and automatically unpauses it as the crossfader is activated. Mixing tracks together must be done by ear with a little practice, as the device still lacks pitch control capabilities necessary for beat-matching.

iPads and digital tablets are also making inroads into traditional DJ practices in ways that mirror the use of laptops. The iPad featured the app "Djay" in the opening few seconds of its 2011 commercial, emphasizing the device's function as a musical instrument in a DJ's lineup. Applications such as the Sonorasaurus Rex, Baby Decks, DJDECKX and Mixr, among others, also offer DJs opportunities to try out new digital—*glass*—interfaces. The touch screen has been a particularly interesting development, as it captures the tactile and hands-on nature of DJing in a way that the iPod wheel and even the smaller screens of iPods and iPhones (or touch-MP3 players and smartphones) do not. In fact, the "return to touch" may be the best synthesis of digital and analog to date, incorporating the benefits of more portable music collections and improved performance technologies with the tactile.

Other emergent technologies aim to make DJ practices more easily portable and less bulky, from iPhone sound-mixing apps to the wearable DJammer. Though still an experimental piece of technology that is not commonly used, the main draw of HP's DJammer is its size and scratching simulation. This technology places the emphasis of digital DJing back on mixing instead of selection. HP Labs Researcher, April Slayden, calls the device "a new musical instrument."[15] It contains three programmable buttons that can be set for specific features. DJs can hold a track in the same way they hold vinyl on a turntable and a built-in motion sensor monitors the DJs hand movements, allowing them to effectively and wirelessly "scratch" on a track. The Discovery Channel describes the essence of the DJammer technology: "DJammer takes all the technology of conventional DJ equipment and puts it into the palm of the DJ's hand."[16] The product's engineers want to be able to accommodate the flexibility and creativity of users and encourage customers to play with the technology in new and unexpected ways. Here we see the trend of iPod DJing altering the ways in which technology industries approach product design, preemptively creating possibilities for users to turn technology toward musical ends. With the proliferation of iPod DJs and playlist parties, not only are these types technologies facilitating an increased physical portability of music in terms of the ease of carrying smaller and more manageable digital DJ friendly devices but also an increased circulation of the discourses and practices of DJing—the mythology of mix and remix, the meaning of the dance club or DJed party. Celebratory discourses hail the remix as a questioning and dismantling of hierarchies more broadly—hierarchies of taste and authority. In particular, the cultural capital most commonly associated with the realm of early black hip-hop DJs and Asian American turntablists is now more widely available to other social groups, undermining the professional DJ as god. While iPod DJs often promote a politics of inclusion, boundary blurring, and participation in the name of digital democracy, who and how many people are actually participating in this scene? Although iPod use is rampant and DJing continues to go digital, iPod parties and DJ nights are certainly not dominating the club world. Playlist and remix may reflect a democratic philosophy but it does not necessarily mean that DJ club cultures are becoming less elitist and hierarchical.

On an obvious level, there are clear changes in the materiality and physical labor of DJ practice as iPods (as opposed to turntables, laptops, and CD players) become more popular as technologies of DJing. New opportunities continue to open up for amateur DJs to perform and participate in the *making* of the club experience. The increased portability of music and equipment does not necessarily eclipse older forms and practices of vinyl DJing; in fact, the nostalgia for wax is heightened in the same moment as the lack of wax is applauded. Sound quality debates and issues of fidelity are still paramount. The twin goals of musical selection and technical skill continue to be important aspects of gaining respect as a DJ; DJing, it seems, will continue to be about both *what* and *how* music is being played. With the increased emphasis on playlist and persona there appears to be less focus on technical skill and mixing, but developments such as the Numark iDJ and the Djammer point toward a critical interest in elevating and legitimizing iPod DJing as viable and respected cultural practice. Further, the enhanced touch screen capabilities of iPad DJ technologies may signal a return to some of the sensuousness that characterized early practices of DJing with vinyl. Certainly, new technologies will continue to be developed; how people creatively approach and manipulate these technologies will expand and complicate our notions of the DJ's labor and the role of DJing in the production of both private and public soundscapes.

## CONCLUSION

From its incipient years through the digital transition and into a highly portable era, DJing continues to find itself in a negotiation between old and new media. DJ culture is a rich example of how users construct discourses around technology, invoking hierarchies of sound fidelity, authenticity, and participation. The celebration of technological development often confronts issues of history and tradition, all of which impact DJs' relationship to their practice. For example, a strong sense of the past in DJ culture renders older technology authentic as opposed to obsolete, as the use of analog vinyl retains an aura of warmth that the digital format simply does not convey. The perception of this difference, and its concomitant valuation of sound, nonetheless occurs in tandem with a growing excitement about new technological forms, such as the digital interface program Serato and accessible mobile devices like the iPod and the iPad. These media developments allow DJs to shed some of the weight of the past both literally and figuratively, thereby easing access to music and reshaping performance styles.

Specifically, changes in digital and mobile sound media have affected the labor of the DJ, from its materials to the techniques used to mix, scratch, juggle, and blend music. Professional DJs often bemoan the proliferation of "average Joes" now entering the field, who have learned the trade with digital technologies that perform much of the work formerly done manually, such as beat-counting. MP3-Js and their iPod/iPad comrades also suffer from criticism that their practice is nothing more than a playlist made public, with none of the technical skill and flair that characterize turntable-based forms of DJing. However, as noted previously, the "MP3-Js" or iPod DJs, celebrate their approach, where song selection trumps technical ability and access to DJ performance is more inclusive. The expansion of DJ culture into the digital realm allows those who may not have the time, money, or—let's face it—skills to learn to become professional DJs.[17] Still, some critics argue that the increase of both DJs and DJ-based media through digital, portable devices often signals the devaluation or banalization of the work of the DJ rather than a revolution in music participation.

Both sides of the argument around digital and MP3-based DJing are problematic. First, hyperportable MP3-DJing has not necessarily flattened hierarchies of taste and opened unrestricted access to the DJ booth. The mostly esoteric, often incredibly random, music mixes played in iPod parties and similar events may actually exclude some audiences; further, in certain instances the gatekeepers of these parties subtly assert their own musical tastes while restricting others'. Second, digital developments such as the iPod DJ party do not devalue the work of the DJ. Instead, such events constitute one mode in a proliferating constellation of modes of DJing and possibilities for remix culture. The expansion of DJ culture through mobile and handheld devices can invigorate DJing, creating more interest and connection to practices of sound mixing. It simply makes DJing more deeply woven into the fabric of everyday life, which ultimately can only raise the bar on what this musical practice will become.

Furthermore, some of the new digital and portable developments in DJ culture actually draw heavily on original analog sound technologies and equipment. For example, CDJs mimic turntable functions, while Serato and FinalScratch interface with traditional turntable set-ups and reproduce the feel of vinyl. Most iPad DJ apps also visually replicate turntables and mixers, and some also allow users to scratch the 'record' by touching the screen the same way you would to scratch a piece of vinyl.[18] In addition, iPod parties do not necessarily change the relationship between music selectors and dancers, and they predominantly take place in spaces like bars and nightclubs that have long been home to DJs. What these examples tell us is that while the technology has changed and the devices have become more easily portable, DJing in its many analog and digital formats still remains bound to the practices and environments in which it emerged. DJ culture has been expanded and reshaped through digital, portable media, but it has not fundamentally changed. Equally as important is the fact that DJing has always been a mobile practice, from its origins in parks and streets and its movement through nightclubs and entertainment venues. iPods, smartphones, and iPads reproduce many of the same functions of mobile sound systems in a different format. The digital devices do grant certain flexibilities—quantity of songs, compatibility with other media, portability to a larger range of spaces—but the basic premise of music's mobility remains intact throughout these technological changes.

As technological developments seek to create new consumers and modes of consumption, users are able to work and play with technologies that also create different musical subjectivities. Like Jamaican sound systems and the linking of two turntables to a mixer, the intersection of music and technology creates dynamic interfaces that have been used to produce social and artistic possibilities. Further, in a culture predicated on the philosophy of remix, play with digital and portable media forms remains intrinsically unstable. The value of these new technologies only emerges through practice and perception, negotiated in the hands of DJs and on the screens of their machines. One thing can be certain, however: even if the turntables are still, there is nothing motionless about this process.

## NOTES

1. The term *disc jockey* developed in tandem with the rise of the radio in the early twentieth century. However, the concept of selecting records from one's collection and playing them live for a dance floor in fact began in England in the 1940s, laying a foundation for the jukebox and dancing to recorded rather than live music in clubs and early discotheques. These original disc jockeys were the backdrop of the evening; it was not until the growth of disco that the DJ would become the focus of the night, a musician in his or her own right.

2. "The Adventures of Grandmaster Flash on the Wheels of Steel," which in 1981 was the first recorded song composed entirely of samples of other songs and scratches, was produced in one analog take.

3. We conducted interviews with fifteen DJs between January and March 2009.

4. DJ Center, interview with author, February 20, 2009.

5. Scratchlive Message Boards, http://www.scratchlive.net/forum/discussion/?discussion_id=24672 (accessed March 3, 2009).

6. See Thornton (1996).

7. DJ Tabu, interview with author, February 18, 2009.

8. Bob Garcia, interview with author, February 17, 2009.

9. An article in the January 10, 2008 issue of *Time* magazine reports, "vinyl records...are suddenly cool again...to the surprise and delight of music executives, increasing numbers of the iPod generation are also purchasing turntables (or dusting off Dad's), buying long-playing vinyl records and giving them a spin" (Dell 2008).

10. Most recently, groups of young people have been gathering in parks and train stations to dance collectively to the same song at the same time. To the average passerby, these mobs appear as a mass of dancers moving together in silence.

11. Other iPod DJ nights have been held at the Tonic Room in Chicago and 21st Amendment in San Francisco.

12. http://www.myspace.com/playlistclub (accessed March 7, 2009).

13. Quoted on the Playlist website http://www.ipod-dj.com (accessed January 25, 2009).

14. Article by Lisa Rocket, "Numark iDJ iPod Mixer," *Playlist*, http://www.ipod-dj.com/NumarkiDJ.html (accessed January 25, 2009).
15. Article by Jonny Rocket, "Playlist's exclusive interview with the HP team developing an all-new instrument for digital DJs, the DJammer," *Playlist*, http://www.ipod-dj.com/djammer.html (accessed January 25, 2009).
16. Ibid.
17. And yet, the costs of these products range in the hundreds if not thousands of dollars, which while still cheaper than a pair of high-quality turntables and a massive record collection, require significant financial investment. In addition, the built-in obsolescence of these products guarantees a continued re-investment in order to stay current.
18. "DJ Scratch" app, released via iTunes in April 2010.

## REFERENCES

Barthes, Roland. 1991. *The Grain of the Voice*. Berkeley, CA: University of California Press.
Brewster, Bill, and Frank Broughton. 2000. *Last Night a DJ Saved My Life*. New York: Grove Press.
Chang, Jeff. 2005. *Can't Stop Won't Stop: A history of the hip-hop generation*. New York: Macmillan.
Dell, Christina. 2008. "Vinyl Gets Its Groove Back." *Time International*, Issue 2, January 12: 47.
Hadley, Daniel J. 1993. "Ride the Rhythm: Two Approaches to DJ Practice." *Journal of Popular Music Studies* 5(1):58–67.
Hebdige, Dick. 1987. *Cut "n" Mix: Culture, Identity and Caribbean Music*. New York and London: Routledge.
J.LOVE. "Goodbye Turntables: The iPod DJ Revolution." http://www.methodshop.com/gadgets/tutorials/mp3j/mp3j.shtml (accessed January 14, 2009).
Jordan, Ken. 2008. "Stop. Hey. What's That Sound?" in *Sound Unbound: Sampling Digital Music and Culture*. Cambridge, MA: MIT Press.
Kahney, Leander. 2002. "With IPod, Who Needs a Turntable." *Wired*, July 18, http://www.wired.com/gadgets/mac/news/2002/07/53938.
Keyes, Cheryl. 2002. *Rap Music and Street Consciousness*. Chicago: University of Illinois Press.
*Las Vegas Weekly*. 2008. "The Great DJ Debate." June 12.
Lawrence, Tim. 2004. *Love Saves the Day: A History of American Dance Music Culture, 1970–1979*. Durham, NC: Duke University Press.
Levy, Steven. 2007. *The Perfect Thing: How the IPod Shuffles Commerce, Culture, and Coolness*. New York: Simon & Schuster.
Pingree, Geoffrey B., and Lisa Gitelman. 2003. *New Media 1740–1915*. Cambridge, MA: MIT Press.
Sherburne, Philip. 2003. "Digital DJing App that Pulls You In." *Grooves* 10:46–47.
Sterne, Jonathan. 2003. *The Audible Past*. Durham and London: Duke University Press.
——. 2006. "The mp3 as Cultural Artifact." *New Media and Society* 8(5):825–42.
Thornton, Sarah. 1996. *Club Cultures*. Middletown, CT: Wesleyan University Press.
Vance, Ashlee. 2005. "IPODS act as D.J.'s at Clubs Where Patrons Call the Tunes." *New York Times*, January 27: G.8.

# CHAPTER 12

.........................................................................................

# DANCING SILHOUETTES: THE MOBILE FREEDOM OF iPOD COMMERCIALS

.........................................................................................

## JUSTIN D BURTON

CLICKING keys.

We see the Apple logo emblazoned on a laptop computer and centered in the frame. Over the top of the computer screen, we see a man's forehead with a shock of dark hair atop black-rimmed glasses. His brow is furrowed; he is working at something. The clicking stops, and a bass-heavy dance track—"Take California," by the Propellerheads—kicks in. The man glances to the side, as if contemplating what he hears, slightly nodding his head in time. After two bars of music, the man gives himself over to the Propellerheads, bobbing his head more vigorously now and flailing his limbs in a comedic but endearing chair dance. This marks the first of many camera cuts (roughly one every three seconds) and allows us to see our subject in his native setting (Figure 12.1).[1]

It is a fairly spacious, multi-room apartment. We can see a filled-in fireplace on the back wall and a leather reading chair in front of it. The walls and mantle are covered with knick-knacks, and the desk where the man is working is cluttered, too. It is situated just below two windows and extends from the side wall into the middle of the room.

The man is really grooving now. A close-up of his face shows him removing his glasses to allow his head more fervent thrashing. His attention turns to his computer as he uses his mouse to drag "Take California" across the interface of a software application labeled iTunes. He presses a button on his keyboard, and the camera pans, finally, to the star of this scene. It is a white electronic device, about the size of a deck of cards, attached to the computer by a firewire chord. The man unplugs it, stands to replace his glasses, and . . . the music stops.

He places earphones in his ears and retrieves his device. The silence is jarring. The only soundtrack remaining is the ambient noise of the man's actions. As he runs his thumb along the circular pad on the front of the device, we hear clicking noises, followed by a single, emphatic *clack* emitted when he presses the center button. It has been

FIGURE 12.1 The man from the first iPod commercial, dancing in his apartment.

four seconds since music last played, and "Take California" rushes lustily into the sonic void, louder and with a deeper bass than before.

The man's dancelike movements are now practically exultant. The first downbeat of the music's return is prepped with a silent uptick from his head and punctuated by his plunge into a headbanger's bow. He moves from behind the desk to dance in the open space of his living room. Whereas the camera featured close-ups of the man's head in the first half of the scene, the shots now are of his feet sliding and kicking across his slick wooden floor. We watch as he reaches for and dons a lightweight jacket, slides his device into his front jacket pocket, and leaves the apartment, dancing all the way. The door slams shut, the Propellerheads fall silent, and a voice-over tenor intones, "iPod. A thousand songs, in your pocket." The word "iPod" appears on the screen, followed by the Apple logo and the company's ungrammatical slogan, "Think different."

This was the first iPod commercial, originally aired in October 2001, and it ran a full minute—twice the length of many subsequent iPod spots. Apple used the extra time to emphasize that the iPod would provide a "different" music experience, and this first commercial introduces an invisible slogan—words neither written nor spoken that nonetheless form the foundation of every iPod advertisement since: the iPod sets you free.

The form of the commercial underscores this theme, with the break in the music neatly dividing the ad into two halves. In the first half, the man is tethered. His movement is restricted by the chair and desk, and he must remain in the immediate vicinity of his computer to properly hear his music. Though he can manage a crude dance from this posture, our attention is repeatedly directed toward his head, marking his experience as aural but little else. He hears, but his body is limited, and the inadequacy of this listening scenario is acted out through the man's ultimately unsatisfying chair lurches.

In the second half of the commercial, the man is freed by his iPod. The furrowed brow is exchanged for effusive footwork; the music is fuller, more resonant; the man can not only leave his desk, but his apartment, too, without leaving the Propellerheads behind. Though the iPod attaches to the man at his head, this is much more than simply an aural experience. With the iPod, the man can hear music—*his* music (a cursory glance at his iTunes library reveals the names of several electronica musicians who represent the periphery of the early 2000s mainstream music scene)—and he can also allow it to course through his entire body as he moves in any manner he wishes, wherever he wants. The iPod grants the man mobile freedom, and this first commercial promises viewers the same.

The promise of freedom through a portable listening device is not new to the iPod. Michael Bull describes the experience of personal stereos in much the same way:

> Personal stereos might be conceived of as an urban tool used by "urban" dwellers enabling users to extend their mediated behavior into many environments previously inaccessible to privatized listening. Personal stereos often migrate with users to other non-urban places such as the beach, the mountain, or the sky. They are invariably used on the move: on foot, bicycle, or on buses, trains, tubes, and sometimes even in cars.... Structurally, personal stereos allow users to take their own "personalized" sounds with them virtually anywhere and this distinguishes it from any other form of music reception. It is invariably a private experience yet paradoxically represents one that is invariably "floodlit" in its interpersonal resonance. (2000:17–18)

Whereas the Sony Walkman, the previous iconic personal stereo, invested little in advertising, Apple has relied on heavy advertising saturation to sell the iPod, and their commercials have consistently featured mobile freedom as a central theme (5).

Two years would pass before another iPod commercial aired.[2] In the meantime, the iPod evolved from a puzzling and seemingly futile Apple side-project to a sleek device on the cusp of becoming a necessary accessory and cultural icon. It was now compatible across both Mac and PC platforms, more powerful, smaller, lighter, and cheaper. The right ad campaign could launch it beyond the techie and internet crowd and into the public consciousness. Enter the dancing silhouettes.

Since October 2003, the iPod has been primarily advertised using dancing silhouettes—shadowy figures with few defining features, all with the iPod's signature white earbuds dangling from their ears—on billboards, in print, and in commercials.[3] These silhouettes continue the theme of mobile freedom defined by the original iPod commercial, but they are able to extend it to a much broader audience. By looking closely at the commercials released between October 2003 and October 2004—the period during which the iPod attained iconic status—I track the extension of mobile freedom via three key changes: (1) The image of the silhouettes themselves invites more viewers to project themselves into the ads than the dancing man does, expanding the target audience beyond the limits of the first commercial while also evoking racialized images and histories. (2) A broader campaign allows for greater diversity in music choices, allowing Apple to target fans of many different genres. (3) The October 2004 U2 ad was the first to feature visual images of the musicians whose song provides the soundtrack for the commercial. The introduction of recognizable artists into the world of the silhouettes makes the connection that the iPod forges between listener and artist seem even closer, and it extends the depiction of mobile freedom even further.

To best understand the vision of mobile freedom Apple sells through its iPod ads, I start with an account of the ways the original commercial targeted only a very small, already devoted audience in order to better highlight the changes that have made the dancing silhouette campaign successful even as it acts as a variation on the original ad's main theme: mobile freedom.

# THE DANCING (YOUNG, WHITE, AFFLUENT, FREE-THINKING, MAC-LOVING) MAN

The introduction of the iPod was not greeted as enthusiastically as one might imagine. More than a decade later, having experienced a slew of hotly anticipated and much-discussed biannual rollouts of the iPod and its sister devices, it is difficult not to be surprised by the tepid reception of the inaugural model. "Most people were indifferent at best. Some were even outraged," notes Leander Kahney in the opening chapter of his book *The Cult of iPod*. Kahney also compiles the following complaints from the popular tech media just after the iPod's introduction:

> Writing for *Wired News*, MacCommunist columnist Luka Hauser, said "smash the iPod…Apple had been claiming we were going to be treated to a 'breakthrough' device with the iPod's release. But the only 'breakthrough' here is a growing desire to break a 2-by-4 over Steve Jobs' skull," Hauser wrote. "iPod. iYawn," wrote the popular Mac columnist Rodney O. Lain on the Mac Observer site. "The name is stupid, and the price is too high," added the site's editor, Bryan Chaffin. (2005:13)

It is no surprise, then, that the first iPod commercial targeted an already existing consumer base of Mac users and lovers. The iPod's future (much less its market dominance) was not guaranteed, and the support of Apple's own constituency would be needed to ensure the device's success.

Looking again at the original iPod commercial, we can see that its intended audience is narrow. Consider what we know about the dancing man. He is white and in his late twenties or early thirties. He also seems to have a good deal of disposable income, as evidenced by the spaciousness of his apartment and the items he has lining his shelves and decorating his walls, including some furniture that looks as if it were bought at an antique store and a couple of musical instruments. Above all, his technological setup is expensive: he has a Macintosh laptop computer, an iPod (the first iPod cost $400), and a healthy digital music collection.

The dancing man is probably single. He wears no visible wedding ring, and his apartment is decorated in dark earth tones using mismatched pieces of art and furniture, with every flat surface topped by a good bit of clutter. The windows are covered with blinds but have no curtains or drapery. None of this precludes a partner, of course, but the apartment is decorated to signal "bachelor" to viewers who have seen other single man habitats on television and in movies. Any markings of femininity—even stereotypical ones—are absent here.

Finally, the man is dressed casually in khaki pants with a long-sleeved t-shirt and short-sleeved unbuttoned collared shirt on top. His attire is an echo of the grunge look codified by Kurt Cobain and other early 1990s Pacific Northwest rockers, who layered multiple shirts atop baggy, holey pants. By 2001, when the iPod commercial aired, the grunge scene was a memory, a dated genre that new bands might cite as influential without trying to emulate its sound. The style functions the same way. The man's clothes no longer represent the same spirit of rebellion that Cobain's outfits did, and they are no longer even relegated to the world of grunge, as made evident by the dance track that accompanies this particular commercial and the electronica collection on the man's Mac. A decade after the grunge explosion, the man's style operates beyond the limits of a single genre and signals a general air of aloof coolness. In this way, the dancing man exactly matches the persona of Apple Corporation, which has long billed itself as a smart alternative to Microsoft. Instead of selling Macintosh computers with a bandwagon campaign—"Everybody's doing it!"— Apple acknowledges that the majority of consumers actually use Microsoft's products. The Apple sales pitch instead characterizes Mac users as knowledgeable and technologically savvy; the company concedes the majority and claims to service the attractive minority. Even the slogan, "Think different," highlights the image Apple has constructed for itself— just outside the mainstream, coolly observing the drooling masses of Microsoft users.[4]

The drooling masses, in fact, were early foils in Apple's efforts to define its brand. The company first introduced its Macintosh computer in a 1984 Super Bowl ad conceptualized by the marketing firm Chiat/Day. The commercial features a world of PC and IBM drones freed by a woman who hurls a sledgehammer through the computerized Big Brother controlling them. David Aaker, in *Building Strong Brands*, stresses the importance of the *1984* commercial in establishing Apple's "brand personality," a measurable and powerful aspect of marketing that ascribes human characteristics to brands. The effect of the commercial and much of Chiat/Day's and TBWA/Chiat/Day's advertising of Apple since 1984 has been to brand the company as "friendly, unpretentious, irreverent, and willing to go against the grain. The use of Apple, for some," concludes Aaker, "expresses a personal identity of being non-corporate and creative" (1996:154).

Not surprisingly, another advertising campaign for Mac in the 2000s—"Get a Mac"— features a self-satisfied twenty-something personification of Mac computers who dresses much like the dancing man from the original iPod commercial. He wryly antagonizes PC, a frumpy late-thirties suit who tries desperately to compensate for his many shortcomings. The dancing man fits neatly into this archetype. While there is no direct attack on Microsoft in the original iPod ad, the dancing man exudes confidence in his quirkiness. From his dancing to his music preferences to his Apple technology, he is different, and that, the commercial tells us, is a good thing.

Nearly every component of the original iPod commercial presses together to form a mirror that reflects Apple's own consumer base back to itself. "Do you have money? Do you know good technology when you see it? Are you an independent thinker? Are you a white man? Do you already own Apple products? Then the iPod is for you!" We've seen that the commercial portrays the iPod as a freeing device, one that offers its users greater choice while they are mobile. But, as constructed, freedom is offered to a very few in this commercial.

Apple has consistently relied on its core consumers to ensure the initial survival of new products, and the iPod was no different. Margaret Kane, writing within a week of the iPod's introduction, noted that the MP3 player was "generating buzz among Mac devotees," but speculated that such interest would "not translate into strong sales," not least of all because the iPod still required a Mac computer to function (2001). Kane was not the only one to doubt Apple's ability to sell the device, as I've noted previously. A Mac Rumors discussion forum that features a chat happening as Steve Jobs first introduced the iPod includes several remarks that are humorously pessimistic in hindsight.

> ELITEMACOR:    "iPoop...iCry. I was so hoping for something more. $400 for an mp3 player! I'd call it the Cube 2.0, as it won't sell, and [sic] be killed off in a short time...and it's not really functional."
>
> WEEZERX80:    "Great [sic] just what the world needs, another freaking mp3 player. Go Steve!"
>
> NOBODY SPECIAL:    "All that hype for an mp3 player? Break-thru digital device? The Reality Distortion Field is starting to warp Steve's mind if he thinks for one second that this thing is gonna take off."[5]

Apple had to work, then, to win over even its most loyal consumers (i.e., the kind who chat on the internet while watching Steve Jobs at a Macworld Expo). But in its first two years on the market, the iPod could be considered a definitive success. In the fourth quarter of 2002, the iPod owned 27% of the dollar market share for MP3 players (including much cheaper and readily available flash-based players), while its closest competitor, Rio, lagged behind at 10% (Gibson 2003). When restricted to hard-drive based players (whose prices would be much closer to the iPod's price), the iPod held 33% of the market (Smith 2004). By October 2003, Apple had sold a total of 1.3 million iPods and seized 31% of the entire market for MP3 players and 64% of the hard-drive market (Fried and Borland 2004; ibid.).[6] Still, though the iPod dominated its competitors, the potential market for mobile music consumers remained largely untapped in 2003, and Apple would require a new campaign to extend the promise of the iPod's mobile freedom from the confines of their existing consumer base to a much broader audience.

# DANCING SILHOUETTES

Some of the growth in iPod sales after 2003 is certainly attributable to improvements and upgrades Apple made to the device itself, as well as to its companion software iTunes. By late 2003, the iPod had evolved into a more robust product than the original had been. Its hard drive had grown from five gigabytes (5GB) to 30GB, yet it was slightly thinner and lighter than the original. The interface no longer featured moving parts (the first scroll wheel actually moved), favoring touch-sensitive controls instead. Most importantly, though, Apple had expanded its reach via two iPod additions: in early 2002, the iPod was updated for compatibility with Windows, and in summer 2003, the iTunes Music Store was launched.

Fashioning the iPod to function with the Windows operating system removed a significant barrier for many potential iPod owners. In early 2002, the Mac operating system held a scant 4% market share in the United States (Quittner 2002:2). Windows compatibility meant that the number of computer users who could purchase and use an iPod (without having to also purchase a Mac) grew exponentially. The iPod was no longer for Mac enthusiasts only.

The iTunes Music Store (iTMS) would not expand the potential consumer base as profoundly as Windows compatibility, but it was meant to enrich the iPod experience. Users could now purchase (iTMS), manage (iTunes), then carry their music with them (iPod), all through an integrated digital music system operated by Apple. This was MP3 for the masses. With a few clicks of the mouse, an entire world of music was available to any iTMS/iTunes/iPod consumer. And with this expansion of the iPod's functions came a new advertising campaign meant to universalize the mobile freedom promised by the iPod.

Just as in the original iPod commercial, the opening seconds of "Hey Mama" (October 2003) feature a partial view of a person's head and a piece of Apple technology. This time, however, our iPodder is a woman shown in profile, and we see only from the tip of her nose to her chin as she mouths the Black Eyed Peas lyrics that mark the beginning of the ad: "La la la la laaaa." The camera cuts to a wider view midway through her line, and we see white headphones, shaped unmistakably like the iPod's earbuds, dangling from her ears. It is a striking visual. The background is monochrome but vibrant pink, and the woman is a silhouette, the contours of her visage cutting a sharp line down the center of the screen, rendering one side entirely black, save those white earbuds (Figure 12.2).

The portrayal of mobile freedom begins with elements of the original ad's portrayal, then amplifies them. Just as the dancing man commercial depicts the iPod as a full-bodied listening experience, so, too, does "Hey Mama," after an establishing head shot, feature

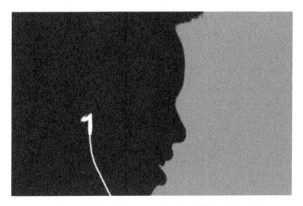

FIGURE 12.2 The opening shot of the silhouette in the "Hey Mama" commercial.

FIGURE 12.3  Dancing silhouette from the "Hey Mama" commercial.

quick cuts to hands, feet, and torsos to highlight the full engagement of the dancing bodies. Throughout the advertisement, the white earbud cords partner with the dancers,
twisting and turning in response to the silhouettes' movements and reminding viewers
exactly what is the source of this crazed dance party that Steven Levy terms "an aural bac-
chanalia" (2006:84). The earbud cords, it turns out, serve too great a purpose in the commercial for their movements to be left to chance, so Alex Brodie and a team of artists from
the postproduction firm Company 3 added them after the shoot. "They wanted the wires
to have a specific look and thickness, so I drew them in frame by frame. That allowed me
to give them a smooth movement that would have been impossible to achieve with real
wires" (Digital Producer 2004). The smoothness of movement gives the earbud cords their
own sleek persona, and they neatly complement the impossibly cool dancers on screen.

While only a single dancing man was featured in the original iPod commercial, in
"Hey Mama" we see four different silhouettes against four colored backgrounds (pink,
green, yellow, purple), each with more impressive skills than the dancing man. The
heightened energy of the silhouettes' dancing is coupled with a more rapid rate of cuts
(thirty-nine shots in forty-five seconds) than the original commercial (twenty-four shots
in one minute) to propel the ad forward with a greater sense of urgency (Figure 12.3).

While some elements of the new ad campaign are simply intensified remnants of
the original, the dancing silhouettes also feature three new components that are meant
to extend the idea of mobile freedom beyond Apple's narrow consumer base and into
the imagination of a much broader viewership. Specifically, these new components
are (1) the silhouettes themselves, (2) the commercials' soundtracks, and (3) the use of
celebrity endorsements.

## SILHOUETTES

The charm of the dancing man in the first iPod commercial is also a glaring limitation: his uniqueness. He is likeable and drawn in fairly broad strokes—affluent,

masculine, quirky with eclectic taste—but he still represents only a small portion of the ad's potential audience, and a product offering a lifestyle (mobile freedom) should ideally appeal to as many different lives as possible. These shortcomings are largely addressed by the silhouettes, which function as shadowy voids that invite viewers to project themselves into the commercials while simultaneously tapping into historical and artistic images of blackness. Because the silhouettes are at once empty vessels and racial ciphers, they offer viewers the freedom to step into new and alternate identities by simply plugging into an iPod.

Naomi Klein, in her book *No Logo*, discusses the rise of branding in the late twentieth century, detailing the public's disenchantment with overt advertising and corporations' subsequent reimagining of branding possibilities. One creative advertising model that appeared in the 1990s was Absolut Vodka's "cultural sponge" campaign:

> Its product disappeared and its brand was nothing but a blank bottle-shaped space that could be filled with whatever content a particular audience most wanted from its brands: intellectual in *Harper's*, futuristic in *Wired*, alternative in *Spin*, loud and proud in *Out* and "Absolut Centerfold" in *Playboy*. (2000:17)

It requires only a slight revision of Klein's text to see that the dancing silhouette ads work much the same way: "the [dancers] were blank [human]-shaped spaces that could be filled with whatever [identity] a particular audience most wanted from [the iPod]."

The Absolut bottle and dancing silhouettes are extensions of the intertextuality integral to postmodern advertising. "Advertising," Leiss, Kline, and Jhally write in *Social Communication in Advertising*, "borrows its ideas, its language, and its visual representations from literature and design, from other media content and forms, from history and the future, and from its own experience" (1990:193). The result is a fusion of products with ready-made cultural references. In the case of the dancing silhouettes, the intertextual material that fuses with the product can be the consumers themselves, who are soaked up by the silhouettes, filling the dancers with their own identities.

At the same time, the leaky intertextual boundaries of the silhouettes that allow consumers to pour themselves into the shadowy dancers also allow Apple's own brand personality to flow in the other direction—from silhouette to viewer. As discussed earlier, Apple, with the help of Chiat/Day (and later TBWA/Chiat/Day), has created a resilient brand personality that is displayed in commercials for Apple's projects, including the 1984 Super Bowl ad, the "Get a Mac" campaign, and the original dancing man commercial. The silhouettes maintain much of this identity—the dancing is sometimes quirky, the music of the commercials is eclectic, and the dancers are, above all, self-assured. And all of this is achieved without the narrowly conceived physical trappings of the dancing man. As consumers are invited to imagine themselves in the place of the silhouettes, they are also subsumed in Apple's overarching brand personality. In this way, the dancing man from the original commercial transforms into a dancing every/wo/man in the silhouette ads, a nearly blank space in which any viewer might construct a persona alongside Apple's own brand identity.

Of course, shadowy figures are not always good things. It isn't simply the silhouettes themselves that prompt positive associations in viewers but the silhouettes in their context. That context is a lively aural and visual environment. As noted earlier, the silhouettes dance against vibrant pink, green, yellow, and purple backgrounds with upbeat tunes providing the soundtrack. Just as the silhouettes can be empty bodies that invite viewers to project themselves into the ads, the background is an empty locale that, partly because of its energetic colors, invites viewers to imagine an ideal backdrop for themselves. Where are the silhouettes? Who knows—what matters is that wherever it is, it certainly looks fun.

TBWA/Chiat/Day's silhouette concept was executed by production company @radical.media and yielded three separate iPod commercials in October 2003, one of which features the song "Are You Gonna Be My Girl," by the Australian rock band Jet, and illustrates well the enticing void of the silhouettes. From the opening shot of the green dancer—bent at the waist, knees buckled, hair flying in all directions—to the final shot of the yellow dancer—back turned, head cocked, fist punched in the air—the commercial depicts an array of tireless silhouettes grooving to an infectious tune.

After the establishing shot of the female green dancer, a quick camera cut shows us the male yellow dancer's face as he mimes a yell from the band. Just as in "Hey Mama," then, one of the earliest shots of the commercial features a lip sync, and, in fact, the first four shots of the yellow dancer in "Be My Girl" show him mouthing lyrics or "playing" air guitar or air drums (Figure 12.4). His mimicry of the song fits into the larger pattern of the commercial, which is shown in Table 12.1. The ad is organized so that pairs or groups of shots are assembled around which of the dancers' limbs are featured, and the yellow dancer's "performance" unfolds in conjunction with the other three silhouettes (Table 12.1).

The yellow dancer is not the only one with a unique persona. Each silhouette has a distinct style—yellow "performs" the song, green is a full-body dancer, pink poses, and purple works hands and feet. Each dancer, though silhouetted, also bears identifying features. Green and purple are women; green has long straight hair and wears a skirt, while purple has shorter curly hair and wears capris. Pink and yellow are men; pink has

FIGURE 12.4 The yellow silhouette from the "Be My Girl" commercial playing air guitar.

Table 12.1 "Are You Gonna Be My Girl" Body Part Timeline

| Body Part | Dancer | Time |
| --- | --- | --- |
| Full Body | Green | 0:00 |
| Face (Yell) | Yellow | 0:02 |
| Full Body | Pink | 0:03 |
| Feet | Pink | 0:04 |
| Feet | Purple | 0:06 |
| Hands and Waist (Twist) | Purple | 0:07 |
| Hands and Waist (Air Guitar) | Yellow | 0:08 |
| Hands and Waist (Spin) | Green | 0:09 |
| Full Body | Green | 0:10 |
| Full Body | Pink | 0:11 |
| Hands (clutching Head) | Purple | 0:12 |
| Hands (counting to 3) | Green | 0:13 |
| Hands (holding iPod) | Yellow | 0:14 |
| Head (thrusting) | Green | 0:15 |
| Head | Pink | 0:19 |
| Head and Hands | Green | 0:20 |
| Head and Hands (pose) | Pink | 0:20 |
| Hands (air drums) | Yellow | 0:22 |
| "iPod" against green background | | |
| Full Body (jump) | Yellow | 0:24 |
| Head and Hands | Green | 0:25 |
| "Mac or PC" against pink background | | |
| Full Body | Yellow | 0:28 |
| Apple logo against purple background | | |

straight hair and wears shoes that resemble Chuck Taylors, while yellow has wavy hair and wears a jacket. Despite the markings of individual personae, though, the silhouettes still bleed together, in part because their defining features are so few and also because the commercial's edits layer the dancers' bodies atop each other. As successive shots feature the same body parts of different silhouettes, the dancers become an amalgam of hands, feet, and heads moving as one.

The Jet ad highlights the way Apples maintains its brand identity with unique, confident, savvy characters while also forfeiting some of that uniqueness in favor of a mass audience that is more vaguely defined. To sell the iPod to PC users, Apple has abandoned the specificity of the dancing man and replaced him with silhouettes who can only barely be discerned from one another. The result is a cultural sponge campaign that attempts to soak up the personae of all potential consumers, whoever they may be (and whatever operating systems they may use), while branding the whole experience with Apple's easily recognizable personality.

While the dancing silhouettes can be convincingly read as blank voids that take on the personalities of viewers, they are also (whether intentional on the part of TBWA/Chiat/Day and Apple or not) figures that are racially charged. The color of the silhouettes is, obviously, black. While some of the dancers appear to be white (based on the little bit of identifying characteristics available), the image of black silhouettes dancing across the screen can be a striking juxtaposition to the white dancing man from the original iPod commercial. And beyond the superficial lies a much deeper connection between the silhouettes and blackness.

Kara Walker, a contemporary black artist, is probably best known for her work portraying the antebellum South using paper cut-out silhouettes.[7] Her silhouettes, just like the ones in the iPod ads, are entirely black even though they portray both white and black characters. Walker makes the distinction between black and white by appropriating the exaggerated physical characteristics of racist stereotypes in her black subjects. Posteriors bubble, lips protrude, postures slouch.[8] Walker uses the grotesque trappings of racism to depict a complex interracial history that mixes oppression and irony, as the title of her 2007–2008 Whitney Museum exhibition suggests: *Kara Walker: My Complement, My Enemy, My Oppressor, My Love.*[9]

The silhouette is a powerful image in Walker's hands in part for the same reason TBWA/Chiat/Day was able to envision it resonating across a broad viewing public. It is flat, indistinct, allowing Walker to assemble tableaux that are about no one in particular and everyone at the same time. It is also powerful in Walker's hands because of its playful and horrific treatment of the unique slave history of African Americans. The silhouettes clearly evoke the antebellum South through a variety of stylistic elements, including but not limited to the images of chattel slavery, the style of dress of both blacks and whites, and the silhouette cutouts themselves, which are echoes of an artistic medium whose heyday came and went more than a century ago (Copjec 2002:83).

But, when examined more closely, the historical nature of the silhouettes fades into absurdity, as the characters—black and white alike—engage in all manner of the most deviant behaviors imaginable, blurring the line between victim and victimizer, civilized and animalistic, and even, ironically, black and white. Hamza Walker calls Walker's silhouettes "a freak scene á la de Sade. Lick, suck, devour. Prod, poke, puncture. Shit, fuck, bludgeon. They are a psycho-sexual mess of Looney Toons proportion" (1997:2). It's a compliment. Elsewhere, Hamza Walker summarizes Walker's ahistorical approach to history: "The work smacks of history in order to smack history, which, needless to say, are two very different things" (2006:277).

Beyond the history of the antebellum South, Walker's work also smacks the racist history of the silhouette itself. From the physiognomy of Johann Caspar Lavater to the phrenology of nineteenth and twentieth century pseudo-scientists, the silhouette has been called on to ratify white racial superiority by claiming that the deficiencies of blackness are evident in even the broadest, least distinct portraits of a people. Physiognomic silhouettes, Gwendolyn Dubois Shaw observes, "were a space whose margins contained all pertinent information and whose centers were spaces of blank, yet readable, negative interiority" (2004:20–21). The shocking taboos performed by Walker's silhouettes are the logical conclusion of an illogical history; they are stereotypes rendered larger than life, parading through exhibition spaces apparently oblivious to their onlookers' gazes but demanding active engagement from their audience nonetheless. Calling on the cyclorama—a medium Walker herself conjures when describing her work—Glenda R. Carpio notes that viewers of Walker's silhouettes are positioned disorientingly inside her displays, with silhouettes prancing and posing all around, "denying [the audience] the usual coordinates for interpretation" (2008:184). Viewers of Walker's silhouettes, then, are invited—commanded, even—to somehow find themselves within the absurdist narrative that she has constructed, as if the shadow figures merely soaked up the most secret desires and terrors of their audience in order to spit, slit, and shit them back out.

Whether TBWA/Chiat/Day intended to lead Apple into the kind of murky racial politics that characterize Walker's work is unclear, but the silhouette iPod ads are certainly meant to touch potential black consumers in a way the original iPod commercial was not. "Hey Mama," released in tandem with "Be My Girl," features the requisite four dancers, all of whom appear to be people of color. The pink and green dancers sport an afro and dreadlocks, respectively, while the purple and green dancer, in the manner of cultural sponge advertising, absorb their surrounding environment so that any racial ambiguity yields to the multicultural nature of the pink and green dancers, as well as the diverse Black Eyed Peas, who provide the commercial's soundtrack.

To be sure, iPod ads do not employ the sort of stereotypical visuals that form the foundation of Kara Walker's work. Rather, iPod commercials traffic first in the general emptiness of the silhouettes that invites viewers to cast themselves in the ads' starring roles with very few visual cues to restrict access for any particular race. Apple also airs a great number of silhouette commercials, allowing the few visual cues available to rather neutrally depict a range of dancers across many boundaries, including race. An ad like "Hey Mama" is likely meant to appeal to black consumers through both of these means, but the same leaky boundaries that allow it to function as benignly multicultural also admit Walker's superficially similar imagery as well as the silhouettes of pseudo-sciences past. Given the ill repute and racist foundation of physiognomy and phrenology, it's perhaps surprising that no significant racial controversy has stirred around the iPod silhouettes and that, in fact, the silhouette campaign has been judged a definitive marketing success by the industry.[10] Though the silhouettes carry racial connotations, they seem to strike viewers as generally positive or desirable images,[11] and this, perhaps, is in part the fruit of Kara Walker and other African American humorists who dredge up epithets and stereotypes, dress them in darkly comedic garb, and ultimately rob them of some (though certainly not all) of their venom.

Because its history includes many uses beyond racist pseudo-science, the silhouette can be salvaged for benign ends more easily than epithets and other markers of racial discrimination. The iPod dancing silhouettes, for their part, are able to evoke racialized images—mostly white, black, Latina/o, and Asian—in a way that invites viewers—whether white, black, Latina/o, or Asian—to step into the dancing shoes of any of the silhouettes. The racialized nature of the silhouettes combines with their sponge-like nature and Apple's brand personality to suggest a transformability that is available to viewers if only they plug into an iPod.

# MUSIC

The dancing silhouettes are meant to extend the promise of mobile freedom to a larger audience than the original commercial did by absorbing the personae of a wide variety of people across race and gender boundaries. Unsurprisingly, the music in these ads works much the same way.

As mentioned in the previous section, the dancing silhouette campaign was launched with separate commercials that were running in ad spots simultaneously. As new commercials were released every few months, Apple continued the trend of airing several at once. This practice expands the soundtrack used for iPod commercials so that, during each iPod ad cycle, viewers will hear a greater variety of music. More dancers plus more commercials equals more diversity.

The first silhouette commercial cycle included songs by Jet (rock) and the Black Eyed Peas (hip hop), as already noted, as well as N.E.R.D. (poppy hip hop). In mid-2004, when Apple released its new-look fourth generation (4G) iPod, the commercial cycle featured songs by Ozomatli (jazz-infused hip hop) and Steriogram (rock), and the trend continued throughout the decade.[12] This is not, to be sure, the widest possible music net the commercials could cast (there are no commercials set to country or classical music, for instance). Still, the ads draw from multiple genres, and within each genre, the songs chosen tend to meld a variety of styles so that instead of just hip hop, for instance, the viewer will hear jazz and pop laced into the music's texture. Dance tracks are common, too, and these numbers typically blend elements from several different genres.

Using a multiplicity of song tracks ensures that viewers will not associate the iPod with only a single genre, and it increases the possibility of catching a potential consumer's ear with a preferred musical sound or style. The iPod is able to offer mobile freedom to its audience because it exists in an aural context that encourages viewers to conclude that it's the perfect device for any musical style; iPodders will be freed to listen to whatever pleases them most.

Beyond the mixing of genres, even the musicians whose songs are featured in iPod commercials often represent a diverse background, both culturally and, as already mentioned, musically. The last piece of the first troika of ads displays the eclectic nature of the dancing silhouettes' soundtrack. The commercial is set to N.E.R.D's "Rock Star," a song that is the product of collaboration across racial, ethnic, and genre boundaries. N.E.R.D, the group responsible for "Rock Star," is the side project of Pharrell Williams and Chad Hugo, whose primary musical identity is the production duo The Neptunes.

Pharrell and Hugo have formed an integral part of hip hop and pop since the late-1990s, producing hits ranging from Britney Spears' "Boys" and "I'm a Slave 4 U" (2003) to Ludacris' "Southern Hospitality" (2000) and Ol Dirty Bastard's "Got Your Money" (1999). When the "Rock Star" commercial first aired in late 2003, Pharrell and Hugo were beginning to experience a greater level of exposure, thanks to the debut of their first N.E.R.D. album, *In Search Of...* (2002), the release of an album bearing their production name, *The Neptunes Present...Clones* (2003), Pharrell's frequent cameos, including with Snoop Dogg, Busta Rhymes, and Jay-Z (who now calls himself Jay Z), and even a Pharrell solo release, "Frontin" (2003).

The Neptunes' growing reputation ensured that many viewers would recognize Pharrell's voice and that the slippery nature of the duo's genre status could become emblematic of the new direction of iPod advertising. And just as the ambiguity of the dancing silhouettes' identities is meant to appeal to audiences across various racial and ethnic boundaries, Pharrell, an African American, and Hugo, a Filipino American, embody the new multiracial audience Apple seeks. Added to the cross-genre and multiracial cache of the Neptunes is the third part of the original N.E.R.D. song, a white, four-piece rock band from Minneapolis called Spymob. Finally, the version of "Rock Star" heard in the commercial is the product of Jason Nevins, a white producer who specializes in house mixes. In this forty-five second spot, then, the listener encounters a handful of racial and ethnic identities, as well as three distinct genres via a group of musicians who perform at the crossroads of many more.

Moreover, N.E.R.D. aligns closely with the shift from the dancing man's uniqueness to the dancing silhouettes' combination of uniqueness with broad appeal. Pharrell and Hugo have a distinctive sound. No matter which artist sings along with a Neptunes production, it bears the duo's sonic signature—futuristic, minimalist, syncopated, and funky. But this uniqueness is no barrier to widespread success. "Boys" and "Slave 4 U" defined the adult fantasy world at the heart of circa 2003 Britney Spears, while "Got Your Money" is still Ol Dirty Bastard's best known song, and "Southern Hospitality" was the launching pad for Ludacris' remarkable career. Like the dancing silhouettes, Pharrell and Hugo bear identifying marks that set them apart from whomever is around them. And, also like the dancing silhouettes, everyone seems to be able to imagine themselves dancing to their tunes.

The formula for choosing songs for iPod ads is not quite as easy as just finding a catchy popular tune and plugging it in, however. A balance must be achieved between popular appeal and slight obscurity, which requires an expert's touch. For the commercials featuring Jet and the Black Eyed Peas, Stimmüng, a Los Angeles based music-licensing group, handled music production. Specifically, Liza Richardson, a Dallas native and film and television music producer, worked on the two commercials. Richardson, who has produced music for the television show *Friday Night Lights* and movies such as *Y Tu Mamá También, Dogtown, Push*, and *Nacho Libre*, began her career in the music business on a late night show, "The Mad Doll," on a Dallas radio station. The show was known for its eclectic playlist, and Richardson prizes her broad taste in music: "I'm so grateful for the time I've spent on the air at KNON and KERA because I learned so much about all of the Texas-based songwriters: folk, rock, music from Deep Ellum, polka, you name it" (Liles 2008). Richardson brings the same ethos to the projects she produces for larger audiences, including the iPod ads. She is, in fact, widely credited with launching Jet's career by licensing "Are You Gonna Be My Girl" for the iPod spot. By hiring a firm like Stimmüng and a producer like Richardson to license music for the original silhouette ads, Apple ensured that the commercials' soundtracks would be set to catchy but relatively obscure songs.

The soundtrack to the second round of silhouette commercials (June 2004) continues the trend started by Richardson by featuring bands with rabid but small followings: Ozomatli and Steriogram. iPod commercials employ catchy, danceable tunes by these bands that are meant to be infectious whether one is aware of the bands playing them or not. Songs by little known artists are susceptible to few of the preconceived notions viewers might hold about more popular tunes. One would not expect to hear, for instance, a Britney Spears hit, or the latest number one single on the Billboard charts in an iPod commercial. Once songs have risen to the height of popularity, they do not appear in iPod ads, which keeps the balance between unique and popular from tipping decisively toward the latter. Again, this continues a trend that started with the dancing man commercial. Propellerheads, too, is a little known band, but "Take California" is quite catchy. Replace the dancing man with silhouettes, and now both music and image invite a broader consumer base.

Even when the silhouettes dance along with well known artists, the songs used are often not yet hits. When "Hey Mama" aired, the Black Eyed Peas' "Where is the Love" was still in the top 20 of Billboard's Hot 100 (it peaked at #8), but "Hey Mama" would not be released until April 2004 (it peaked at #23). Jet, likewise, experienced success with "Are You Gonna Be My Girl," but the song appeared in the iPod commercial two months before it entered the Hot 100, and it would be April before it peaked (at #29). "Feel Good Inc.," a song by Gorillaz featured in a 2005 commercial, appeared on the Billboard Hot 100 roughly simultaneously with the commercial's airing, though the height of its sustained success would not happen for two more months.[13]

For all of the care dedicated to selecting music for dancing silhouette commercials, the soundless iPod print and billboard advertisements may actually most closely match the empty, spongy nature of the silhouettes, as viewers are free to provide any soundtrack they choose. For commercials with backing tracks, the billboards' ability to absorb viewers' soundtracks can be approximated with songs that are infectiously danceable but not particularly well known. In the original iPod commercial, the man's intrinsic need to dance was integral to defining the mobility the iPod affords. This same musical feeling animates the silhouette ads and expands it into many different genres in order to better capture the spirit of mobile freedom being sold to viewers.

# Musicians' Endorsements

The company that best exemplifies the marriage of technology and pop culture is Apple.... The iPod is probably the greatest pop object since the electric guitar. We—as a band—feel strongly about the iPod. We—as a band—talked about the idea for an iPod years ago. We—as a band—are

fans of Apple...We want to work with them. The Edge wants to work with
their scientists. We want to play with their design team. We want to be in
their commercial.[14] (Klosterman 2006:25–26)

And, indeed, U2 were in an iPod commercial. The first silhouette ad to include distin-
guishable people featured the iconic Irish rock group performing their most recent hit,
"Vertigo." The U2 commercial differed from other silhouette ads in subtle but significant
ways. For starters, the song "Vertigo" had already entered the Billboard Hot 100 by the
time the commercial aired (October 2004), and it would peak (at #32) only three weeks
later. The song was not the only recognizable part of the ad: atop solid black silhouetted
bodies were the faces of U2's members, shadowy but distinct (Figure 12.5). Whereas previous, anonymous silhouettes mimed performances of commercials' songs, the U2 ad
was the first to include the actual musicians on screen. The introduction of artists to the
silhouette ads extends the idea of mobile freedom in a number of ways.

Because U2 is performing "Vertigo" instead of listening to it, the band is not wearing the traditional earbuds that are always inserted into silhouettes' ears. Instead, we
see earbud-white cords snaking across the vibrant backgrounds and plugging into the
band's instruments (or, in Bono's case, plugging into his microphone). Shots of the band
are interspersed with dancing silhouettes, all of whom sport the requisite white earbuds,
as the music courses directly from U2 to listener via the iPod.

The opening ten seconds recall previous iPod commercials. "Vertigo" begins, as "Are
You Gonna Be My Girl" does, with a count-off from the lead singer (in Bono's case, the
rather bizarre "Uno, dos, tres, quatorze"), and, as already seen in the Jet commercial, a
dancing silhouette is mouthing the numbers. For "Vertigo," however, the counting silhouette is an African American woman whose afro is reminiscent of the first shot of
"Hey Mama." Between "tres" and "quatorze," the camera cuts to Bono, who finishes the
count-off as the band launches into the song.

We have already noted that the rapid succession of silhouetted dancers has the
effect of fusing multiple silhouettes into one, and, especially when combined with
the way the earbuds flow from band to dancers, the joint count mouthed by both

FIGURE 12.5 The shadowy face of the Bono silhouette from the "Vertigo" ad.

the silhouette and Bono ties the listener even closer to the music source. The theme of mobile freedom is established in the original iPod commercial by demonstrating how little constriction the dancing man experiences while listening to his iPod, which pumps music directly into his ears, when compared to the limited range of movement he is allowed at his desk, where music emanates from a distance. The same theme undergirds every silhouette ad, as dancers stretch and splay across the screen as loud music pumps from their earbuds. With the U2 commercial, the distance collapses further, as musicians and listeners form a single string of shadowy dance, held together by a white iPod cord.

This enhanced mobile freedom yields changes in the silhouettes' landscape. The extended two-minute version of the "Vertigo" ad begins with the same color scheme as previous silhouette commercials. Each silhouette is attached to one of the four background colors: Larry Mullen, Jr. (drums) is yellow, The Edge (guitar) is blue, Bono (vocals) is purple, and Adam Clayton (bass) is green. Meanwhile, the African American woman who counts along with Bono is green, while an air-guitar-playing dreadlocked man is yellow, a frizzy-haired woman is blue, and another woman in a cowboy hat is also green. Just after the appearance of this second green dancer, the color scheme is disrupted. It happens at the twenty second mark, as Bono sings the last half of the first verse:

A feeling so much strong/er than/a thought your eyes are wide and though your soul/ it can't/be bought your mind can wander

And U2 wanders. First each member of the band appears in succession against the purple background at the end of the first verse, then reverts to his original color at the beginning of the chorus ("Hello, hello!"), spins in tandem against the yellow background as Bono shouts, "I'm at a place called vertigo," and returns once more to his original hue. From this point in the ad, the members of U2 are free to roam across any of the available background colors.

They are not the only ones. The chorus of "Vertigo:"

Hello, hello! (¡Hola!)
I'm at a place called vertigo (¿Dónde está?)
It's everything I wish I didn't know
Except you
Give me something
I can feel
Feeeeeeeel

At the word "you," a new dancer—male, with short hair and tassels on his pants—appears against the green background, as the African American counting woman has moved from green to yellow. The dancing silhouettes, like U2, spend the remainder of the commercial grooving in front of any background, no longer attached to a single color, and at least four new silhouettes are introduced.

Again, the feeling of mobile freedom is heightened as the iPod is portrayed as the ideal conduit for music. In addition to the immediate connection from U2's instruments to silhouettes' ears via the earbud cords, the band now grants greater mobility to the dancers, sending them—"you"—roving about the commercial's landscape, untethered from color in the same way the original dancing man was freed from his computer desk. At the moment of emancipation, Bono sings, "You give me something I can feel," making explicit the nearness of listeners to musicians in iPod ads.

This nearness allows for an alternate reading, as well. Just as the leaky boundaries of the silhouettes permit both viewers' identities to flow in and Apple's brand identity to flow out, the white earbud cords and wires suggest that as freedom is flowing from U2 to the silhouettes, the silhouettes are able to transmit via those same wires.

At the moment of color disruption mentioned earlier (the line that begins "A feeling so much…"), the style in which the band is filmed shifts. The early shots of Bono, The Edge, Mullen, and Clayton feature each member of the band performing for the camera, which is a style that meets the expectations of a generic rock music video. For the last half of the first verse, though, the band members are pulled up in rapid succession while the purple background remains static. The effect of the band members being shuffled past the screen is similar to the "Album Flow" feature Apple would later add to the iPhone and iPod Touch, allowing iPodders to view the album covers for their music while swiping the screen to advance from one cover to the next. This mode of viewing information is stylistically uniform across Apple platforms, as the company has long favored a display format that tiles pieces of information and allows users to shift from one icon, image, or window to the next with a click of the mouse or, increasingly, swipe of the finger.

As the chorus begins, the band is filmed from a roving camera point-of-view, much like the first-person perspective of many video games (Figure 12.6). So, at roughly the same time that the silhouettes are freed to move from one background color to another, the viewer is given the sense of freedom to roam among the band members or to call them up individually. U2 has become a manipulatable, virtual band, as control flows

FIGURE 12.6 A screen shot of the roving, video-game angle of U2 from the "Vertigo" ad.

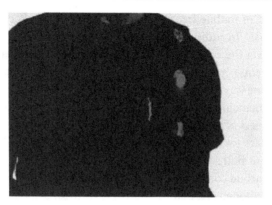

FIGURE 12.7 Blue silhouette originating from The Edge's heart.

through the white earbud cords and wires from the silhouettes to the band. For the remainder of the commercial, the band is seen alternately through the more direct, traditional camera shots as well as the virtual, roving angles. As freedom pumps from U2 to listener and control flows from listener to U2, silhouette and band fold into one another to create a feedback loop. The standard camera shots depict U2's performance of their song, while the video-game angles display the silhouettes' virtual experience of controlling the band at the click of a button.

The feedback loop created between dancers and U2 is displayed vividly at the 1:09 mark of the commercial. As Bono repeats the line, "Swinging to the music" just before the second chorus, shots of the band are interspersed with the dancing silhouettes. Now, however, the silhouettes appear in vivid colors while the background turns to black. The effect is accomplished by zooming into the blackness of the band's silhouettes to discover a vibrant silhouette dancing there. Another zoom into the silhouette uncovers the next band member. The progression begins with the Edge, performing against a yellow backdrop. As the camera zooms toward his heart, we see the blue silhouette of a woman dancing (Figure 12.7), and The Edge's silhouette becomes her backdrop. The camera then zooms toward her torso so that the black silhouette of Clayton fills the screen, with the woman's blue becoming his background. From the edge of Clayton's bass, held just below his waist, emerges the green silhouette of a dancing man. The succession climaxes with Mullen and his drum set shooting from the green silhouette's crotch and playing the final measures of the second verse against the green background (Figure 12.8). In this short sequence, band begets dancer begets band, as listener and performer become seamlessly integrated via the iPod's signature earbud cords.

The hyper-subjectivity of the U2 "Vertigo" commercial becomes more pronounced when compared with the later U2 iPod ad used to introduce the fifth generation iPod, whose new feature was video capability. The majority of the latter commercial is a live performance of the song "Original of the Species." The band is not depicted as silhouettes, and it isn't until close to the end of the ad that the camera zooms out from the video to reveal that it has been playing on an iPod screen all along. "Watch your music," the

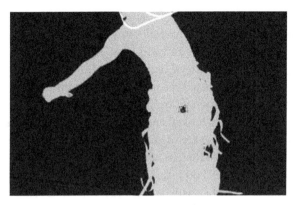

FIGURE 12.8  U2 drummer Larry Mullen, Jr. emerging from a green silhouette.

tag tells us. Here U2 is rendered at a distance, as the commercial's focus on the fidelity of the video quality on the new iPod forfeits the participatory feedback loop formed in the "Vertigo" spot.

The intimacy of the "Vertigo" loop capitalizes on the nature of the mobile freedom the silhouette campaign offers consumers. The music coursing through the iPod's headphones is meant to offer the physical freedom for one to hear music while moving through space, unencumbered by computers or stereo systems. As a result of this mobility, the listener is also offered the powerful freedom of control over one's soundscape, and this control, as depicted in the U2 "Vertigo" commercial, extends beyond sound so that iPodders are offered a sense of control over all of their surroundings. The ability to manipulate music becomes the ability to shape one's world to fit one's own desires.

> With its enveloping acoustics iPod users move through space in their auditory
> bubble, on the street, in their automobiles, on public transport. In tune with their
> body, their world becomes one with their "soundtracked" movements; moving to
> the rhythm of their music rather than to the rhythm of the street. In tune with their
> thoughts—their chosen music enables them to focus on their feelings, desires, and
> auditory memories. (Bull 2007:3)

# CONCLUSION

By October 2004, when the U2 ad first appeared on television, the iPod had amassed an 82% share of the hard-drive based MP3 market in the United States and 42% of the entire MP3 player market (Smith 2004). This number represented an increase of eighteen percentage points from the previous year's hard-drive market share and eleven percentage points from the previous year's full market share. The remarkable growth occurred despite the fact that the iPod's price was undercut by nearly every major rival.

In the coming years, though the market share would slip a bit, iPod sales would increase dramatically.[15] The silhouette ads appeared two years into the iPod's existence, when Apple had sold a total of 1.3 million units. In 2004 alone, 8 million iPods were sold; in 2005, Apple sold 32 million (Kingsley-Hughes 2008; Darlin 2006). As the MP3 market swelled, Apple experienced repeated record sales figures. In fact, the iPod's staggering numbers suggest that it did not benefit from an MP3 player boom so much as it actually created that boom. New devices looked and functioned much like the iPod, and Apple CEO Steve Jobs noted the device's trend-setting ways in a 2004 *New York Times* article, calling the iPod "the Walkman of the 21st century" (Hansell).

Certainly a good deal of the iPod's success can be attributed to its attractive design and smooth integration with the easily accessible iTunes and iTunes Music Store. But TBWA/Chiat/Day's silhouette concept seems equally responsible for the iPod's market domination. Just as the iPod became a more robust device in 2003—compatible across both Mac and PC platforms, integrated with iTunes and iTMS, and expansive enough to hold tens of thousands of songs—it was marketed to a more robust audience. From sponge-like silhouettes that absorbed the personae of viewers to diverse musical choices that encompassed many genre categories to the inclusion of music celebrities bound up with the dancing silhouettes, the new commercials included devices that were meant to attract a broader audience than the original iPod ad could. Sales figures indicate that the silhouette campaign was wildly successful.

After the 2004 U2 ad, Apple began to diversify its iPod offerings. A flash-drive option, the shuffle, became available, as did a smaller hard-drive model, the nano. In 2007, Apple partnered with AT&T to offer the iPhone, which also begat the iPod Touch, a device with functions similar to the iPhone but without cellular capability. With these new products came new commercials, many of which focus on each model's particular functionality (similar to the "Original of the Species" ad). But the silhouettes have not disappeared entirely. The monochromatic backgrounds have evolved into abstract shapes and cityscapes, and the silhouettes have conceded airtime to more music celebrities as well as their cousin devices, but the shadowy dancers remained the backbone of iPod marketing, even as the iPod itself surrendered advertisement space to its sister products, especially the iPhone. And it is little wonder why. The dancing silhouettes mark a transformative moment in the marketing of mobility. The silhouettes are emptied, and viewers are encouraged to take on Apple's brand personality so that they may fill the silhouettes with the promise of mobile freedom that was not quite fulfilled by the original dancing man: any (good) music, any (good) time, any (good) place.

## Notes

1. For all of the iPod commercials mentioned here, I place the release dates using the Internet Archive. The Archive, available at http://www.archive.org (accessed August 17, 2011), keeps a log of past websites that can be viewed as they appeared on a particular date. By visiting the iPod section of Apple's site—which always includes the latest commercials—through

the Archive's collection, I was able to roughly pinpoint when each advertisement first aired. I used a 2007 article from MACSUPPORT (available at http://www.macsupport. ca/2007/02/04/songs-from-ipod-commercials/, accessed 30 September 2010) to guide my search, which sometimes turned up results that differed from the MACSUPPORT article. In many cases, the archived commercials are actually unviewable because they are formatted for an outdated version of Quicktime, but some identifying mark, whether the names of the song and artists or a still shot from the commercial itself, will be visible on the page. For viewing the ads, youtube is quite helpful. The following is a list of all commercials discussed in this chapter with links to the Internet Archive and youtube.

Propellerheads, "Take California" (October 2001). http://web.archive.org/web/20011106230256/www.apple.com/hardware/ads/ (accessed August 17, 2011). http://www.youtube.com/watch?v=nWqj6OQQOHA (accessed August 17, 2011).

Black Eyed Peas, "Hey Mama" (October 2003). http://web.archive.org/ web/20031202025418/ www.apple.com/ipod/ads/large45.html (accessed August 17, 2011). http://www.youtube.com/watch?v=iqxS2hILO8s&feature=PlayList&p=3A2D8D559 9F11148&pplaynex=1&playnext_from=PL&index=36 (accessed August 17, 2011).

Jet, "Are You Gonna Be My Girl" (October 2003). http://web.archive.org/web/20031204044556/www.apple.com/ipod/ads/ad2large45. html (accessed August 17, 2011). http://www.youtube.com/watch?v=TaVFCdwTohk&feature=PlayList&p=ED59159 E2CD24680&playnext=1&playnext_from=PL&index=36 (accessed August 17, 2011). Steriogram, "Walkie Talkie Man" (July 2004) http://web.archive.org/web/20040710074431/www.apple.com/itunes/video/240. html (accessed August 17, 2011). http://www.youtube.com/watch?v=UH5ZTvmHaIk (accessed August 17, 2011).

The Vines, "Ride" (August 2004) http://web.archive.org/web/20040910022515/www.apple.com/ipod/ads/ (accessed August 17, 2011). http://www.youtube.com/watch?v=YCanu4LjYIA (accessed August 17, 2011).

Ozomatli, "Saturday Night" (September 2004) http://web.archive.org/web/20040918035706/www.apple.com/ipod/ads/ (accessed August 17, 2011). http://www.youtube.com/watch?v=wEiZBQZY_3Y (accessed August 17, 2011). U2, "Vertigo," (October 2004). http://web.archive.org/web/20041014074841/http://www.apple.com/ (accessed August 17, 2011). http://www.youtube.com/watch?v=r5vhgqmyVzw (accessed August 17, 2011).

2. This is verified by Steven Levy in his brief discussion of the silhouette campaign in *The Perfect Thing* (2006:83), as well as by the absence of any video content on the archived Apple site during this period.

3. As Apple diversified its offerings and funneled money into the marketing of the nano (a smaller version of the iPod), the iPhone, and the iPod Touch (a device with most of the features of the iPhone—including wireless internet access and the ability to play games or run web-based applications—except the cellular connection), fewer commercials were produced that featured what is now known as the "classic" iPod, which is the primary focus

of this chapter. Nano, Touch, and iPhone commercials largely diverge from the silhouette model, focusing instead on the specific features of these devices and functioning as thirty second tutorials. Still, commercials for these devices will often include visual imagery evocative of the silhouette ads, including dancing iPodders and the incorporation of the silhouettes' vibrant background colors. Even iPod commercials appearing after 2006 rely more heavily on music stars while incorporating stylistic elements introduced in the silhouette ads, and I discuss the beginning of this trend later in the chapter.

4.  A 2002 editorial posted at *The Mac Observer* reflects the perception of the Mac as chic and mildly counter-cultural. Michael Munger admits that the main reason he owns a Mac is because he likes its "industrial design, it looks good in my apartment and it makes a favorable impression on my visitors; I like the operating system's eccentricity, friendliness and distinctiveness."

5.  Posts from http://forums.macrumors.com/showthread.php?t=500 (accessed August 17, 2011).

6.  Apple keeps an archive of its press releases (http://www.apple.com/pr/library/, accessed August 17, 2011) and quarterly sales statements (http://www.apple.com/investor/, accessed August 17, 2011) online, but the press releases currently only extend as far back as 2004, and the quarterly statements only extend to 2007. For graphs that chart iPod sales during the years unavailable on Apple's website, one can consult Charles Gaba's website, *Mac vs PC System Shootouts*, http://www.systemshootouts.org/ipod_sales.html (accessed August 17, 2011).

7.  Thanks to Sumanth Gopinath and Jason Stanyek for suggesting Walker's work as a useful cipher for understanding the racial implications of the dancing silhouettes.

8.  Photos of Walker's exhibition, *Kara Walker: My Complement, My Enemy, My Oppressor, My Love*, displayed at the Whitney Museum of Modern American Art from 11 October 2007 to 3 February 2008, can be viewed at the museum's website, http://www.whitney.org/www/exhibition/kara_walker/exhibition.html (accessed 24 October 2009).

9.  Walker is not the only artist that toys with stereotypes in the interest of telling an anti-racist story. The trickster figure in much black art is unraveled most famously in Henry Louis Gates's *The Signifying Monkey: A Theory of African-American Literary Criticism* (New York: Oxford University Press, 1988).

10. TBWA/Chiat/Day won the 2004 Grand Prize Kelly Award as well as the Grand EFFIE for the silhouette campaign, and Apple was named *Advertising Age*'s Marketer of the Year in 2003, in no small part because of the dancing silhouettes.

11. The commercials received favorable reviews in a study conducted by *USA Today* in 2004 (Howard).

12. The rollout for the summer 2004 commercials was staggered. The Steriogram ad first appeared on the apple website in July, and Ozomatli followed in early September. In August, Apple released a commercial featuring "Ride," by the rock group the Vines, where a young, male iPodder walks by a bank of silhouette posters, which begin to dance when he passes. This commercial, obviously, is different from the other early silhouette ads, and, while it appeared on the Apple website for a time alongside the Steriogram and Ozomatli spots, it had disappeared from the site by the end of September (http://web.archive.org/web/20041001040553/www.apple.com/ipod/ads/, accessed August 17, 2011), though the other two remained well into 2005. Because of the oddities of the Vines ad, it is not analyzed in detail here. Several websites include lists from users that include a commercial featuring "Channel Surfing," by Feature Cast, among the summer 2004 crop, but the archived Apple

website does not corroborate this. These same lists often also place the Vines ad at January 2005, though it appears alongside Steriogram and Ozomatli in September 2004 (http://web.archive.org/web/20040916014047/www.apple.com/ipod/ads/, accessed August 17, 2011) and must have been recorded in the first half of 2004, as the iPodder is using a third generation iPod, which was replaced by the fourth generation in July 2004 (http://web.archive.org/web/20040720082743/http://www.apple.com/, accessed August 17, 2011).

13. Information on songs' performance on the Hot 100 and other charts can be found by searching the artists' names at billboard.com.

14. In early 2009, U2 announced a partnership with Research in Motion, the producers of the Blackberry, and Bono himself was involved with the production of the Palm Pre, an iPhone rival (Spence 2009).

15. One reason the iPod's market share for hard-drive based MP3 players has decreased is because the iPod is in competition with itself in other markets. The iPod nano competes in the flash-drive market, and the iPhone in the cellular phone market. As consumers purchase these other devices, Apple's sales and profits actually increase as its market shares suffer from being spread over three different areas (Arthur 2005).

## REFERENCES

Aaker, David. 1996. *Building Strong Brands*. New York: The Free Press.

Arthur, Charles. 2005. "Apple Share of mp3 Player Market to *Shrink*... Sort of," *The Register*, September 15, http://www.theregister.co.uk/2005/09/15/apple_nano_analysis/ (accessed October 24, 2009).

Bull, Michael. 2000. *Sounding Out the City: Personal Stereos and the Management of Everyday Life*. Oxford: Berg.

——. 2007. *Sound Moves: iPod Culture and Urban Experience*. New York: Routledge.

Carpio, Glenda R. 2008. *Laughter Fit to Kill: Black Humor in the Fictions of Slavery*. New York: Oxford University Press.

Copjec, Joan. 2002. *Imagine There's No Woman: Ethics and Sublimation*. Boston: MIT.

Darlin, Damon. 2006. "The iPod Ecosystem," *The New York Times*, February 3, http://www.nytimes.com/2006/02/03/technology/03ipod.html?ei=5090&en=a1164823d8486931&ex=1296622800&partner=rssuserland&emc=rss&pagewanted=all (accessed October 23, 2009).

Digital Producer. 2004. "Company 3's Alex Brodie Rocks with Apple's iPod," *Digital Producer*, January 5, http://www.digitalproducer.com/2004/01_jan/news/01_05/company3015.htm (accessed September 30, 2010).

Fried, Ina, and John Borland. 2004. "Apple Shrinks iPod's Size and Price," *ZDNet*, January 7, http://www.zdnet.co.uk/news/desktop-hardware/2004/01/07/apple-shrinks-ipods-size-and-price-39118920/ (accessed September 27, 2010).

Gaba, Charles. 2008. *Mac vs PC System Shootouts*, March, http://www.systemshootouts.org/ipod_sales.html (accessed September 27, 2010).

Gibson, Brad. 2003. "Apple iPod Number One in Music Player Market," *The Mac Observer*, March 12, http://www.macobserver.com/tmo/article/Apple_iPod_Number_One_In_Music_Player_Market/ (accessed September 27, 2010).

Hansell, Saul. 2004. "Gates vs Jobs: The Rematch," *The New York Times*, November 14, http://www.nytimes.com/2004/11/14/business/yourmoney/14music.html (accessed October 24, 2009).

Howard, Theresa. 2004. "Ads for iPods Offer Big Music Gift in Small Package," *USA Today*, January 5, http://www.usatoday.com/tech/news/2004-01-05-ipod_x.htm (accessed September 29, 2010).

Kahney, Leander. 2005. *The Cult of iPod*. San Francisco: No Starch Press.

Kane, Margaret. 2001. "Retailers: Apple iPod demand iffy," *CNET News*, October 29, http://news.cnet.com/2100-1040-275054.html (accessed September 27, 2010).

Kingsley-Hughes, Adrian. 2008. "Taking a Look at iPod and iPhone Sales Date," *ZDNet*, April 24, http://blogs.zdnet.com/hardware/?page_id=1729&tag=col1;post-1736 (accessed October 24, 2009).

Klein, Naomi. 2000. *No Logo: No Space, No Choice, No Jobs*. New York: Picador.

Klosterman, Chuck. 2006. *IV: A Decade of Curious People and Dangerous Ideas*. New York: Scribner.

Leiss, W., S. Kline, and S. Jhally. 1990. *Social Communication in Advertising*. London: Methuen.

Levy, Steven. 2006. *The Perfect Thing: How the iPod Shuffles Commerce, Culture, and Coolness*. New York: Simon & Schuster.

Liles, Jeff. 2008. "Echoes and Reverberations: Liza Richardson's Infinite Axis of Influence," *Dallas Observer*, December 12, http://blogs.dallasobserver.com/dc9/2008/12/echoes_and_reverberations_liza.php (accessed September 30, 2010).

Munger, Michael. 2002. "On the Flip Side," *The Mac Observer*, April 2, http://www.macobserver.com/columns/flipside/2002/20020402.shtml (accessed October 7, 2009).

Quittner, Josh, and Rebecca Winters. 2002. "Apple's New Core." *Time* 159:2, January 14: 46–52.

Shaw, Gwendolyn Dubois. 2004. *Seeing the Unspeakable: The Art of Kara Walker*. Durham, NC: Duke University Press.

Smith, Tony. 2004. "Apple Grabs 82% US Retail Market Share, *The Register*, October 12, http://www.theregister.co.uk/2004/10/12/ipod_us_share/ (accessed October 23, 2009).

Spence, Nick. 2009. "U2 Dumps Apple for RIM, Palm," *Network World*, March 11, http://www.networkworld.com/news/2009/031109-u2-dumps-apple-for-rim.html (accessed March 12, 2009).

Walker, Hamza. 1997. "Cut It Out," *Nka: Journal of Contemporary African Art* Fall/Winter 2000:11–12 (2000):108–113.

——. 2006. "A Mind is a Terrible Thing to Waste." In *Witness to Her Art*, ed. Rhea Anastas and Michael Brenson, 273–79. New York: Distributed Art Publishers.

# PART V

## POPULAR MUSIC PRODUCTION

CHAPTER 13

# MUSIC, MOBILITY, AND DISTRIBUTED RECORDING PRODUCTION IN TURKISH POLITICAL MUSIC

ELIOT BATES

THE music industry of Turkey, symbolically centered in the Unkapanı and Beyoğlu neighborhoods of Istanbul, has increasingly come to rely on work performed outside of Istanbul and often outside of Turkey. Numerous studios and record labels in North America and Central and Western Europe cater to Turkish, Kurdish, and Zazaki-language markets, and they maintain ties with Istanbul in myriad cultural, economic, and artistic ways. However, the mobility of musicians is hampered by political boundaries, as Turkish citizens face difficulties in obtaining overseas travel visas, and thousands live in political exile in Europe and elsewhere, unable to return to their homeland.

A cluster of technologies for creating, manipulating, duplicating, and transmitting digitized audio now enables diverse, geographically distributed sites to be connected in a veritable transnational production network. Moreover, these technologies have made *distributed production* feasible, meaning that musicians who cannot physically be together are able to simultaneously (although not synchronously) work on albums or films. Despite the limits musicians face in physical mobility, their music is mobile, as is the digital data that they use as a technology of collaboration with other musicians.

In this chapter I focus on the creation of Grup Yorum's twentieth anniversary album, *Yıldızlar Kuşandık*, released by the large independent record label Kalan Müzik Yapım in 2006. An ambitious work, it consumed over five hundred studio hours, employed dozens of studio musicians, and featured some arrangements with well over one hundred distinct simultaneous parts. The group, which since its inception in 1985 has had over fifty core members (called Yorumcular) and many ancillary ones, is one of the longest-running musical *groups* in Turkey, and it is famous for its socialist political activism. Many members have been (and continue to be) jailed for participation in demonstrations, or for performing or recording songs in the Kurdish language. Other members have lived in exile in Germany, unable to enter Turkey. Yet, members local and abroad—those in F-Type prisons and those free—collaborated toward creating this album.[1] Production and collaboration were made possible by a host of mobile technologies: flash memory MP3 players brought arrangements and test mixes to those without studio access, hard drives and DVD-Rs transported digital audio workstation sessions on a daily basis between studios in Istanbul and Germany, and CD-Rs and flash drives connected Yorum with their record label.

Two factors come to shape the mechanics of distributed production networks: technological capacity and the connections between nodes within a network, particularly the ability for people, objects, and data to flow. As I show later in this chapter, distributed music production as a paradigm became possible due to the confluence of particular digital technologies, but technological capacity limited the ways in which work could simultaneously be done at disparate sites within the production network. It was with great effort that hard drives moved across the tightly secured border and flash drives were brought to members in prison, but nevertheless there was a veritable ongoing trafficking of digital data. However, this flow was only possible when people were able to transport devices between sites. This research, therefore, is a study of the mechanics of the mobility of music, even when the musicians and consumers may be limited in their mobility.

## RESEARCHING DISTRIBUTED PRODUCTION

The bulk of my research for this project stems from an intensive three-month period when I interacted with Grup Yorum as one of the tracking and mixing engineers for their nineteenth studio album, *Yıldızlar Kuşandık*. ZB Stüdyo, located in the Galata-Tünel neighborhood of Istanbul, was one of the major sites for recording and mixing, and I engineered all the instrumental and vocal recordings that were made at ZB.[2] I also performed most of the digital editing for the album and mixed three of the album's songs. During the same period, I was frequently in phone or internet chat contact with the recording/mixing team based in Germany, as files and arrangement ideas were frequently shared between the two spaces, and during the mixing phase I was in regular contact with the other two mixing engineers.

Being an "insider" in the project made the research possible while also introducing a host of potential representational issues. It is likely that I observed more of the work that transpired for the album project than anyone else, including the members of Grup Yorum themselves. I was able to collect a large amount of primary data, observe repeat interactions, and notice moments that an occasional visitor to the studio would likely have not been able to see. The content of this study of music and mobility is the culmination of these fleeting moments, as much of the recording transpired in a fashion that, superficially, resembled other, less "mobile" projects. I was concerned at the start of my embedded ethnography project that my own aesthetic preferences as an engineer would unduly affect the object of my study. However, it became quickly apparent that Yorum had a clear audible aesthetic in mind, that my purpose was to facilitate this aesthetic, and that group members and hired studio musicians had no hesitation to intervene if anything (aesthetic or otherwise) was moving in what they perceived to be the wrong direction.[3] When I interviewed Yorum following the album release, group member İnan Altın indicated that the primary difference in having me as an engineer (compared to other engineers) was not aesthetic, but rather the extent of conversation that transpired during work itself, as there was additional need to explain to me what it was they wanted. Occasional "misunderstandings," as İnan termed them, may have delayed the recording process, but in retrospect they were probably essential for my resulting field notes, because processes, aesthetics, and issues that would have normally been unvoiced ended up being openly discussed.

# GRUP YORUM, POLITICAL MUSIC, AND DANCE

In Turkey, the name Grup Yorum is inextricably linked with political activism. For their fans, Yorum is a voice of Turkey's active revolutionary socialist movement.[4] Yorum is the only long-term musical group advocating for prisoners' rights; singing against war, imperialism, and foreign aggression; and being willing to publicly protest in the name of causes they believe in, regardless of potential negative consequences to them as individuals. Members of Yorum can often be found at public demonstrations, most notably anti-war marches, thus resulting in many members of Yorum serving extended terms in prison or becoming exiled outside Turkey. As many as four hundred lawsuits have been filed against the group (Korpe 2007:40). İnan explains the relation of Grup Yorum to other political organizations:

> Grup Yorum's members emerged in opposition to the September 12, 1980 coup d'état, silently, but in reaction to September 12 they were the sound of the youth. Besides their concerts, they helped thousands of university students participate in forums, meetings, and direct action. It is possible at some Grup Yorum concerts to hear slogans of organizations such as DHKP-C (formerly named Devrimci Sol). However, Grup Yorum members make it very clear in every interview they give that they are not members of any illegal organizations. Instead, they oppose imperialist exploitation, occupation, and torture; and state that they exist in order to establish a socialist country and world from within a democratic struggle. As a means to rid the world of these [imperialist exploitation and so on], they invite all peoples' organizations. They explain that they have an organization themselves, and are situated within a democratic struggle.[5]

For Yorum's detractors, the group's championing of Kurdish rights and singing of Kurdish-language songs is viewed as highly problematic. For some, the very idea of

Kurdish language rights itself amounts to a fundamental assault on the foundations and values of the Turkish Republic.[6] One translation of the word *yorum* is "commentary," and regardless of an individual listener's sociopolitical orientation the songs Grup Yorum sing are a substantial commentary on how contemporary Turkish society *is* polarized around numerous issues: ethnic rights, socialist and populist ideologies, and Turkey's foreign, domestic, and military policy.

Political music has a long and complex history in Anatolia, extending back at least as far as Pir Sultan Abdal, a prominent Alevi Turcoman musician and poet born in the fifteenth century in Sivas. Pir Sultan's poetry continues to be used in contemporary songs (including in new compositions by Grup Yorum) and influences the prosody of contemporary Turkish-language poets. Other folk poets, including Köroğlu (sixteenth century) and Dadaloğlu (nineteenth century) wrote critically of the sultanate, later becoming part of a new canon of "anti-divan folk literature" championed by educators in the nascent Turkish Republic in the early twentieth century (Öztürkmen 2005:200; Holbrook 1994:22). The lyrics of Pir Sultan, Köroğlu, Dadaloğlu, and more contemporary poets such as Aşık Mahzuni Şerif and the exiled Nazim Hikmet share the bizarre distinction of being officially recognized as among the most significant Turkish-language poetry, while inspiring music that is routinely banned or censored for having political meanings.

However, the long history of political music has not meant that political music has always been championed. The September 12, 1980 military coup d'état, for example, inaugurated a six-year period when political music was effectively silenced, causing formerly political groups such as Yeni Türkü to abruptly shift focus to wholly uncontroversial themes (Özer 2003). Cem Karaca, an Anadolu rock singer who set the often-political lyrics of Pir Sultan, Dadaloğlu and other *aşık* poets to psychedelic rock influenced music, lived in exile in Germany until 1987 (Stokes 2002a). Grup Yorum was one of the first political groups to emerge in Turkey following the 1980 coup.

A second category of political music is Kurdish, Zaza, and other Anatolian "ethnic" music. It is the public prominence and deep contestation of ethnopolitics itself within the modern nation-state of Turkey, and the prominent role of musical performance in the expression of ethnicity, that today defines music in Anatolian ethnic languages as *siyasal* (political). Thus, the performance of any song in Kurdish (regardless of lyrical content) is to an extent political. Language plays a big role in the political perception of ethnic music, but it is not entirely a linguistic matter. Alevi music has increasingly become perceived as political as well, yet it is sung in Modern Turkish and many Alevis could be considered ethnically Turkish.[7] The expression of an ethnic identity other than Turkish is a political act, perceived as such by performers, audiences, and the nation at large.

Not all music that is regarded as *siyasal* today contains resistance narratives, overt references to centralized authority, or ethnopolitical leanings. Another form of political music sings praises or support of political parties or of great leaders. Âşık Veysel Şatıroğlu composed "Atatürk'e Ağıt" (lament for Atatürk) shortly after the death of the visionary general and founder of the Turkish Republic, which is a song about the great

deeds of Mustafa Kemal Atatürk as well as the profound loss the nation felt for the passing of this great leader. Âşık Veysel continued to champion the CHP (Cümhuriyet Halk
Partisi, or Republican People's Party) at official functions, and other musicians since
have been prominently associated with particular political parties (Yılmaz 1996). The
links between music and governance continue to characterize Turkey's political landscape, as within the past decade several popular singers have become members of parliament, including Zülfü Livaneli (CHP), Tolga Çandar (CHP), and İlkay Akkaya—a
former member of Yorum and co-founder of the Yeşiller, or Greens Party.

The music of Grup Yorum is most commonly categorized as *protest* or *özgün* (authentic) music by fans and the music industry, referencing a genre of leftist political music
that Martin Stokes describes as having "much in common with Anatolian rock" and
features lyrics that are "complex and often were taken from major leftist poets such
as Nazim Hikmet" (2002b:251). Ahmet Kaya (1957–2000) is widely regarded as the
founder of this genre. *Protest* or *özgün* are political in the first sense (protest against state
policies) and second (expression of ethnicity other than Turkish), but not in the third
(support of a political party). However, in the same way that Grup Yorum is a largely
self-contained organization and is not affiliated with other political associations, they
do not self-describe their music as *protest* or situate their work in relation to Ahmet
Kaya, instead describing their music as *devrimci* (revolutionary) music.

Grup Yorum may be best known for their protest songs (particularly their hundreds
of numerous newly composed marches as well as their innovative adaptations of traditional political folk poetry), but this does not accurately encapsulate their opus. Many
fans attend their shows to dance, and the primary dance at Yorum concerts is the *halay*,
a line or circle dance found throughout Turkey but particularly important in localities of
Eastern and Southeastern Anatolia. Fans from specific localities usually dance together,
thus one will find a *Sivas sarı kız halayı* line next to a *Diyarbakır halayı* next to a *Batman
govend* next to circles from different localities within the Tunceli Province. For as many
protest songs as they have authored, Yorum has composed an equal number of love
songs, lullabies and works in other song genres. For their twentieth-anniversary album,
from the project's inception onward it was clear that protest, *halay*, love songs, and lullabies would obligatorily be included.

The lyrics to the most overt protest songs, "Felluce" and "Sıra Neferi," tell in graphic
terms of the horrors of the second Iraq war and leave no doubt to their specific political themes and message. But what of the *halay* line dances, which are typically done to
instrumental music, or of the love songs or lullabies that Yorum sings? On the popular social dictionary website Ekşi Sözlük,[8] the newly coined term *ideolojik halay* has
thirty-one entries, ranging from descriptions of *halay* dancing at Communist gatherings at Istanbul University, to suggestions that the meaning of *halay* in the Eastern
Anatolian (and predominantly Kurdish) city of Diyarbakır is inseparable from its
political-ideological associations. *Halay* dancing thematically appears in Grup Yorum's
lyrics themselves. Their most famous composition, "Cemo," ends with the lyrics "o
büyük günün görkeminde çocuklar halaya duracak" (in the glory of that big day, the
children will line up to dance the *halay*). This is not to say that dance is always political

or that *halay* in particular has a singular, prescribed political meaning. However, in the milieu of Grup Yorum's concerts and albums, *halay* dance has come to have a particular constellation of political meanings inseparable from those of the more overtly political songs. Yorum's concerts create a liminal space where the performance of multiple kinds of identities—local, regional, ethnic, and even religious—is itself a political act, and *halay* serves as a galvanizing force of this performance and the multiplicity of identities.

For the creation of *Yıldızlar Kuşandık*, the *halay* concept was important from the project's inception:

> *Halay* is definitely one of the things we are thinking about. *Halay* of course has a cultural dimension, I mean in Anatolia, this is the music that accompanies people's dances, this is a kind of dance music and for hundreds of years *this* tradition has existed. Everywhere you go in this land there's a distinctive dance style, and this *halay* concept, for Yorum, is really one and the same. I mean, Yorum also sings heavy songs and such but always one of the first things really to come to mind when you think of Yorum is *halay*, the *halay*-s danced at concerts. Hundreds of people, thousands of people excitedly dancing, I mean this sight has come to be very much synonymous with Grup Yorum.[9]

In addition to the century-old associations of *halay*, traditional line dancing was part of the overall rhythm of concerts:

> A concert generally has a rhythm to it. Certainly it begins with this heavy sit-down kind of a thing, later we pick up the energy. I mean, standing in place and singing is accompanied by applause, later [people] begin to get up, *halay* dancing begins and later, marches, singing accompanied strictly by fists [waved in the air] begins, they even march around while stomping with their feet, that increases in intensity quite a bit.[10]

## Censorship and "Emerging Markets"

> Throughout the period of the state monopoly on broadcasts (1925–2000) political censorship and self-censorship always existed, changing only its form or framework.
>
> —Yurdatapan (2004:190)

Music entrepreneurs, particularly those who explore emerging and untapped potential markets (such as Kurdish-language music, the production of which was officially banned from 1928–1991), work in a legal environment characterized by substantial risk. Access to television and radio continues to be tightly controlled by RTÜK,[11] an agency that answers to the Turkish Ministry of Culture; songs can be banned for any reason, particularly if they contain any kind of political critique or could be perceived to be morally problematic, a sentiment which shifts with each successive ruling government.[12] Even for "approved" songs the corresponding videos may be banned for similar reasons. Regional governments also have the capability to ban songs or albums that were nationally approved. Thus, labels and artists alike work with the knowledge that their efforts may be greatly curtailed, and suddenly so, through censorship. Many independent labels and artists simply write off the possibility of radio or TV exposure and utilize other less regulated means to promote their creative work, including overseas performances.

Although the period in which I conducted research exhibited perhaps the greatest extent of artistic freedom ever seen in Turkish recording history, decades of censorship had resulted in a situation where artists such as Grup Yorum assumed that their work would be censored.

> Some groups and singers, such as Grup Yorum, [Grup] Kızılırmak, Koma Amed, Koma Denge Jiyane, Koma Asmin, Şivan [Perwer], Ciwan Xeco, Ferhat Tunç, Suavi and Ahmet Kaya—who died in exile—are automatically non grata for private radio and TV stations, for they know that the state does not like them. It is almost the same with the press. Many journals and TV and radio stations belong to just a few bosses. The editors and programmers know what not to do, so direct censorship is not necessary at all. (Yurdatapan 2004:192)

This passage was written by Şanar Yurdatapan, a prolific songwriter and producer who himself was jailed for performing with the seminal Kurdish pop group Koma Asmin. To situate two of these artists in the recording industry context, Ahmet Kaya was the number seven top-selling artist in Turkey in the 1990s, with combined total pressings of 4,940,000 units (*Milliyet* 2000). Grup Yorum has likely sold an equivalent number of units, but there has not been accurate reporting of their sales or manufacturing statistics.[13] These artists managed to succeed despite their near-complete lack of access to mainstream magazine, newspaper, TV, and radio exposure.

It is in light of this risk that everyone operates in the Turkish recording industry. The post-1991 Turkish music industry has experienced "a Catch-22": there is a glut of poor-selling Turkish-language material on the market, yet it is the Anatolian ethnic language material (most notably Kurmancı, Lazuri and Zazaki) that appears poised for financial growth, as those markets are not yet saturated. The less saturated the market, the greater the risk, at least from a legal perspective. However, risk is not exclusively linked with governmental or state concerns. In January 2009, the Turkish government began Kurdish language broadcast on the state-controlled TV station TRT 6. Even though TRT 6 employees receive government paychecks, most use pseudonyms, fearing that they may become the target of assassinations by right-wing nationalist militias. Additionally, program guest lists and content are controlled, to the extent that famed Kurdish singer Rojin quit TRT 6 two months after launching a daily TV show focused on women's issues, claiming she was treated as a "criminal" and not allowed to invite her own guests onto the show (*Hürriyet Daily News* 2009). And, despite the technical legality of broadcasting in Kurdish in 2009, Grup Yorum *still* cannot be heard on the radio nor seen on TV.

# DISTRIBUTED PRODUCTION

For this chapter, I define *production* to include all work that leads up to the tangible creation of a cultural product, including studio performances, evaluative stages that lead to further work, and the approval of work done (but not the marketing of the work, or any work done after the completion of the final duplication master). A particular aspect of the production of this album was the manner in which work transpired simultaneously at multiple sites. However, I do not believe that the term "multi-sited production" best describes this work, as "multi-sited" does not tell us anything about the relation between different sites. Instead, I term this manner of work as *distributed production*, in order to draw attention to the mechanics of the sharing and the techniques facilitating the movement of work between sites.

Motivating a study of distributed production is the assumption that cultural production no longer happens at a single site. But, if not a single site, on what (or where) exactly should such a study be focused? Four questions help define a framework for finding a focal point and assisting the analysis of distributed production systems. First, what work is conducted at each site? Second, how do products, production, and cultural producers move between sites, what constraints exist on the movement, and what is done to overcome these constraints? Third, what is the temporality of the particular distribution, and how does the technological capacity limit the kinds of work that can be done simultaneously at multiple sites? Fourth, what are the politics of and affecting distribution?

Distributed production analysis is not the first attempt to understand those cultural production systems that cannot be adequately studied through single-sited analysis. Arjun Appadurai's oft-used theory of a multiplicity of "scapes" (Appadurai suggested the terms mediascape, technoscape, ideoscape, finanscape, and ethnoscape, and similar constructions were coined by other scholars) has been particularly influential in the study of the transnational flows of culture (Appadurai 1990). While "scapes" turn attention away from singular, bounded field sites, they do so without critically investigating the character of or the mechanisms behind the flows themselves. Precisely what flows, and how does it flow? What processes and systems enable certain flows to happen, restrict the occurrence of other flows, and thus come to define the actual mechanism of the flow that we perceive to be a smooth, undifferentiated "scape"? What is the temporality of the flow? As I will show later in this chapter, music and digital data were able to flow, but those flows still required human agency, and were neither smooth nor undifferentiated, nor was their roughness accurately described as simply a "disjuncture." It was not through an undifferentiated technoscape or mediascape that distributed production happened, but through a specific, strategically created, temporary network of a multitude of sites with differing kinds and degrees of connection to each other.

# THE MECHANICS OF DISTRIBUTED RECORDING PRODUCTION

In electronic circuits, computer programs, neurophysiology, and systems design, a primary distinction is made between two kinds of processes: *serial* and *parallel* (see Figure 13.1). The same distinction can be made in organized production systems of a social nature, such as audio or video recording. A serial process is one whereby work happens sequentially at a series of sites or nodes, and describes the common mode of multi-sited production in analog and early digital production workflows. In a workflow using serial processes, tapes recorded at one studio are transported to another studio for mixing, and the resulting analog master brought to a third facility for mastering. However, work does not happen simultaneously on the same tapes at multiple facilities, but rather sequentially, as it was not technologically feasible to coordinate disparate work done at multiple sites. An analysis of serial multi-sited production is always focused on a single site, with a shifting focal point when production moves between nodes.

With the advent of non-linear digital recording and standardized digital audio work-station sessions, which became commercially widespread starting in the mid-1990s and common in Turkey around 2000, it was possible for identical copies of sessions to exist at multiple locations, and therefore for project work to be shared between and happen simultaneously at multiple sites. Therefore, it was technologically feasible to implement parallel processes. However, the ability to easily implement parallel work on an album of the scope of *Yıldızlar Kuşandık*, where some songs exceeded one hundred simultaneous parts, did not exist until roughly 2002. Hard drive and optical media capacities were too low, storage interfaces did not allow sufficient throughput to run a session off of a single hard drive, and digital audio workstations had limited track counts.[14] Immediately after the technology became available it remained infrequently used, as seasoned engineers

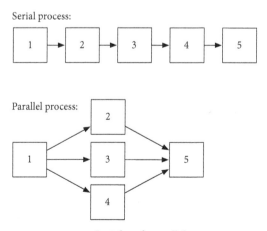

FIGURE 13.1 Serial and parallel processes

were more experienced and comfortable with serial processes. However, in the early 2000s it has become more commonplace, sometimes for economic reasons (the bulk of the work can be done at home studios, which incur no hourly use fee, and later integrated with work done at professional facilities), sometimes for creative reasons,[15] and sometimes (as in this case study) for personal and political reasons. Whatever the reasons, the ease of implementing serial *and* parallel processing is a technological requirement and precursor to distributed album production. The nature of digital audio workstation sessions—portable, copyable, archivable, infinitely expandable, and extendable—*encourages* the moving and sharing of production between sites.

For distributed production and parallel processing to take place, the strategic use of numerous technologies is imperative. In some cases, this necessitates a rethinking of what the particular technology actually is, what kinds of work technologies enable, and the mechanics of how they enable particular kinds of work. For example, a technical definition of a hard drive might focus on certain physical characteristics (its solid exterior protects an interior filled with delicate moving parts; it interfaces to computers via a serial buss, stores X gigabytes of digital data, and allows random write and read-access to data). Hard drives are normally invisible, residing inside a single computer, and due to the integrated appearance of computers and the graphical interface of operating systems are rarely perceived as a discrete entity that warrants attention (unless they stop working or are full, at which point they become visible due to their deficiencies). But what happens when the very same hard drive is covertly transported across national boundaries, repeatedly, by those few individuals free enough to be legally allowed to make the trip itself? What happens when this same hard drive contains several albums' worth of music, storing not only the rough mixes of songs, but also a record of the entire compositional process itself, and the capability of generating new arrangements and versions of those album songs? How does our perception of hard driveness change when we learn that the actual path that the physical hard drive takes is one that many of the band's members could never take?

My questions point to the precariousness of the flow itself between sites. I draw particular attention to the transport of physical devices, as the primary flow of digital media for this project occurred through physical means rather than through internet-assisted file transfer. It is important to consider the state of internet access in Turkey at the time of this album project. Although ADSL internet was available, it was expensive and much slower than European or American internet connectivity, particularly in transferring data in and out of Turkey.[16] The sheer amount of data in a multitrack album project, coupled with slow internet speeds, meant that DAW sessions could not be readily shared via P2P, FTP, or other file transfer protocols. MP3 test mixes were small enough to be emailed or uploaded, but many sites within the production network in question (members in prison, for example) were not connected to the internet, therefore requiring the transport of devices which stored digital audio. Therefore, the mobility of music, at least for this particular project, depended upon physical objects and human travel.

Technological limitations curtail the kinds of simultaneity that can be implemented within parallel processes. For example, it was neither possible for musicians to perform "together" in real-time, nor for individuals to fully participate, remotely, in real-time mixing or editing work happening at a different studio. Ostensibly, with different technological capabilities in place (video conferencing, or remote access that allowed real-time synchronization between computers over a network connection), other kinds of simultaneity could be achieved and impact the nature of how distributed, parallel production is undertaken and managed.

# CASE STUDY: *YILDIZLAR KUŞANDIK*

For their twentieth anniversary album, Grup Yorum wished to create their most elaborate, orchestrated, and dynamic album to date. Well before any recording began, the group had agreed on song themes, general musical aesthetic ideas, and a plan for approaching the task of arrangement. Music for the album was composed by a geographically dispersed network of lyricists and songwriters, several of whom were, at the time the album was created, in Turkish prisons for political charges or in exile in Europe. Two de facto project arrangers—İnan Altın in Istanbul, and Ufuk Lüker in Köln, Germany—managed the recording and arrangement process, and group and studio musician performances were recorded at three professional studios (ZB and Sistem in Istanbul and Per Sound in Köln), mixed at three studios, and finally mastered by Michael Schwabe at Monoposto, a mastering facility in Düsseldorf, Germany. Up until the mastering stage, music charts, lyrics, mixes (on CD-R, flash drive, and MP3 player), session files (on hard disk and DVD-R), and ideas were continuously moving between spaces.

The arrangements realized in Istanbul and Germany first manifested as a set of four to twelve MIDI plot tracks outlining the most important melodies, chordal sequences, and rhythmic layers. Yorum created these on basic home computers with Cubase software and, in Istanbul, with the help of İnan's Roland Fantom LE keyboard workstation synthesizer. The MIDI plot tracks for these arrangements contained only the information one might find on a simple musical score—note durations, pitches, and dynamics values. Unlike a musical score, MIDI data can trigger sounds in synthesizers or samplers and thus make audible the musical information through a variety of timbres. However, MIDI data is useless without either a computer or a hardware sequencer that can parse the data. MIDI data is portable, but its creation and audition both require bulky and relatively expensive hardware.

Following a several-month rehearsal process at İdil Kültür Merkezi,[17] Grup Yorum brought their MIDI parts to Stüdyo Sistem in Istanbul in order to track percussion parts (played by İnan and by studio musician Ömer Avcı, and recorded by Hasan Karakılıç), *bağlama and cura* (the ubiquitous long-necked Anatolian lutes with movable frets), acoustic guitar, and silver flute. Yorum also hired the famous studio drummer Turgut Alp Bekoğlu, electric bassist Emrah Günaydın, and guitarist Gürsoy Tanç to record foundational drum rhythms, bass lines and electric guitar textures for seventeen songs during a two day recording marathon. The result of this was a Cubase session file containing WAV format audio files, along with the MIDI plot parts. All of the audio, MIDI, and session files were copied onto two hard drives, one which went to Per Sound/ Köln and the other which was brought to ZB Stüdyo/ Istanbul, where the remainder of work was done in the Protools HD platform.

One of the first complications we encountered at ZB Stüdyo was that the MIDI parts had been created with particular sounds in mind that were found only on İnan's Roland Fantom keyboard (which was on loan to a friend). We did not have the same sounds available via the sampler plugin for ZB's Protools system (IK Multimedia's Sampletank), but we could "map" each MIDI part to any sound on hand and "hear" what the parts might sound like played on different virtual instruments. The MIDI standard allows for basic musical data to be stored in a very compact file. The entirety of *Yıldızlar Kuşandık*, in MIDI form, took up less than 50k worth of memory, which is significant as the MIDI data was exchanged regularly during the early stages of the album project, with studio musicians, between studios, and once with a friend of the group who used a digital piano to render one of the MIDI parts into actual digital audio.

From this point on, the bulk of the arrangement, soloist and session musician recording, and editing work for the album technically happened at two studios, though a considerable amount of activity happened at other spaces and in moving data between spaces. Every day, progress and test mixes were made and shared between the two studios and auditioned for group members in both countries. After these audition sessions group members or friends then transported digital copies to more distant nodes throughout the geographically distributed network. Music, in various digital formats, moved around on a daily basis, brought from here to there on flash drives and hard drives, shipped from one location to another on CD-R or DVD-R, emailed as MP3s, and/or uploaded to and downloaded from web servers (although the latter was only infrequently used). On many occasions multitrack Protools sessions (the session format in common to ZB and Per Sound) on hard drives and DVD-Rs were transported by a friend of Grup Yorum from Istanbul to Germany or vice versa, overdubs were recorded, the sessions were copied onto the hard drive or onto a new DVD-R, and sent back the other direction. Evaluation of an arrangement's progress, discussions of future work to be done, and arrangement changes were done by group consensus even though the group in its entirety was never able to meet face-to-face.[18] This social structure mirrored the broader social movement in which the Yorumcular participated, one that was similarly distributed and used similar communication methods to enable the temporary connection of nodes in a larger, but hard-to-define network.

It is impossible to document every moment when music, data, ideas, and people moved between spaces. In part, this is due to the nature of the number of sites, besides studios, that were temporarily a part of the production network for this album. However, specific kinds of flows consistently occurred between specific locations. Figure 13.2 depicts a diagram of sites, individuals, and groups that participated in the production process, with line arrows specifying the direction and frequency of inter-node interaction. The figure also depicts, roughly, the temporal flow of production from the pre-production stage (top) to the finished CD master (bottom). At the

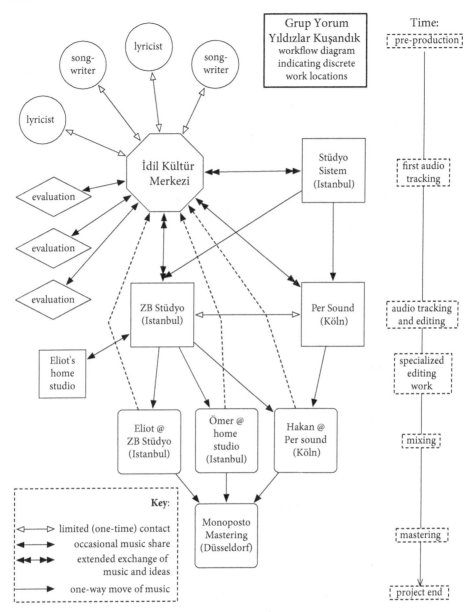

FIGURE 13.2 Moving music between spaces

top are songwriters and lyricists, who only had occasional, limited contact (one or two instances) with İdil Kültür Merkezi, but with no other nodes. It is impossible to say how many songwriters or lyricists were actually involved in the process; I estimate that up to a dozen individuals might have been involved in that capacity.

The diamonds to the left represent "evaluations"—moments when individuals or groups not located at any of the studios or at İdil Kültür Merkezi approved, rejected, or suggested changes to song ideas, arrangements, and mixes. It is possible that certain lyricists and/or songwriters also performed evaluations, but I separate them here, as evaluation stages involved different technologies and kinds of connections between nodes than studio-sited content creation. The evaluation nodes are important since they signify specific moments when digital audio moved between locations, moments that allowed individuals to participate in aesthetic decision-making for the album. Again, the number of evaluation nodes is impossible to estimate, as Yorum has approximately fifty former core Yorumcular and hundreds of past and present ancillary members. I observed two evaluation sessions myself, during which I was struck by the extent to which input from the evaluator(s) produced tangible, meaningful effects on the outcome of the song in question. Often, the recording process would be held up as we waited for input from some unspecified but essential evaluation.

How did evaluations happen? From what I was able to ascertain, CD-Rs filled with progress mixes that were burned at ZB were brought to İdil, subsequently "ripped" to MP3s, put on portable flash drives or flash-based MP3 players, which were transported by hand to evaluators. The smallest flash-based MP3 players, some of which in Turkey masquerade as cigarette lighters, are apparently small enough that they can reach individuals who are in prison.[19] Other evaluators were located too far away (physically) for flash players to help; their distance was overcome through the same MP3s being emailed or shared through an internet-based file server.[20] Music, in the form of compressed digital audio files stored on ultra-portable devices, was able, somehow, to get to everyone who needed to hear it, and for critique to be generated from within a maximally sized social network.

Yorumcular working in the German and Istanbul studios could readily audition mixes, but were constantly faced with a larger problem—the impossibility of being all together, simultaneously, in the same studio. Larger-capacity storage media—hard drives and DVD-Rs—were essential technologies for minimizing the extent to which collaboration was lost due to physical distance and for maximizing the potential complexity of arrangements and track counts. The capability to create an album in the manner of *Yıldızlar Kuşandık* (and here I refer both to a homology between technologies, engineering practices, workflows, and audible aesthetics) had only existed for a few years prior to the creation of this album; therefore, we could consider Grup Yorum to be "early adopters" of a nascent mode of music production.

Whether specific work done for *Yıldızlar Kuşandık* was done in series or parallel appeared to unduly affect neither technical processes nor the resulting musical aesthetic. Parallel work required one additional step—the establishment of a single sync-point through setting a "zero-point" in the DAW session timeline—but with that established, work *from* any of the sites could be integrated into the session *at* any of the sites. Parallel processing was also used in editing work that was initially done at other sites. For example, at ZB Stüdyo we "fixed" some *bağlama* parts that had been tracked in Köln on the same day that Per Sound was "replacing" a piano solo done earlier at ZB with a guitar solo that had just been tracked in Köln. Thus, parallel processing enabled not just additive processes (contributing new parts), but the collective distribution of the recording, editing, and mixing stages of album production work.

However, the distributed nature of production did generate audible aesthetic effects. As acoustic instrumental parts and vocals were tracked at three studios with different acoustic characteristics and equipment selections, the resulting recordings sounded disparate rather than cohesive. ZB Stüdyo's tracking room (where microphones are placed and studio musicians or singers perform) was small, consisting of a rectangular concrete structure to which was nailed an inch-thick panel of fabric-covered insulation, leading to flutter echoes and low-frequency buildup but an overall acoustically dead character.[21] Stüdyo Sistem's tracking room was much larger, but had thicker sound-deadening materials on the walls than ZB Stüdyo and no flutter echo. Based on anecdotal evidence and my own analysis of the recordings, Per Sound in Köln featured a substantially more "live" tracking room, which provided a bright-sounding natural room ambience to the *bağlama* tracked there that was not present on the parts tracked in Turkey. Therefore, by the mixing stage of the project, songs featured a combination of tracks recorded in different spaces with different acoustic characteristics. Digital reverberation ended up being used on many parts in an attempt to compensate for the mismatch in recorded ambience and create the illusion of a singular acoustic space in which the recorded performances had transpired, but audible traces of the original acoustic spaces still remained.

Distributed production resulted in one phenomenon that could not be entirely compensated for: the differences in studio musician performances that resulted from extended, synchronous, interpersonal interaction between specific Grup Yorum members, an engineer, and a studio musician. This became most apparent during tracking sessions featuring well-known studio musician Çetin Akdeniz, a self-proclaimed "bağlama virtüözü." Although most Yorumcular are competent *bağlama* players (and many album parts were played by group members based in Turkey and Germany), unlike the Yorumcular, Çetin is famous for Aegean-region repertoire knowledge and super-fast execution of complex ornaments. Although there had been transnational group consensus about which parts he was to record, the content of his *bağlama* parts for songs like "Davet" and "Kavuşma" arose through a fairly extensive studio-situated interaction at ZB Stüdyo, where he demonstrated several options and the final ornamentation and timing choices were approved collectively by Cihan Keşkek and İnan (of Yorum), myself, and Çetin.[22] In contrast, *bağlama*-playing on pieces managed by Ufuk in collaboration with Hakan Akay (the engineer at Per Sound) consistently employed different ornamentation conventions and had a much more relaxed relation to the beat. This suggests that had Çetin tracked in Köln, through the interactive process with different engineers and group members, the resulting timing and ornamentation aesthetic might have been considerably different.

In sum, nine Yorumcular, thirty-two studio musicians and professional singers, four recording engineers, and one mastering engineer contributed directly to the sound of *Yıldızlar Kuşandık*, and dozens of others contributed indirectly, as evaluators or content creators. Perhaps two hundred CD-Rs, twenty five DVD-Rs, four hard drives, dozens of flash drives or flash media-based MP3 players, and hundreds of MP3s, all told encompassing hundreds of gigabytes worth of data, were in motion during the production phase of the album.

# Mobility and Turkish-Speaking Diasporas

In this chapter I have focused on one case study; however, the phenomenon of distributed production is not isolated, but rather, one instance of music mobility within a transnational production economy. A similar case can be seen in the creative work of Zaza/Alevi brothers Metin and Kemal Kahraman.[23] Metin was one of the founders of Grup Yorum in 1985 and, like many migrants from the Tunceli Province to Istanbul, was attracted to the leftist movement he found there. His brother Kemal followed a similar path, but following several years of imprisonment and torture in Turkey, became a refugee in Germany in 1991. The two brothers have been recording music together in 1991, and like Grup Yorum, attempt to operate in what Leyla Neyzi terms a "transnational space" (Neyzi 2003:118)—a nebulous space encompassing Germany, Turkey, Metin and Kemal's shared homeland of Dersim, and routes that connect these territorial sites.

While national borders can function as barriers toward collaboration, for other Turkish citizens, the increased economic opportunities available in Europe, greater ease in procuring visas, and decrease in airfare costs from increasing competition and budget carriers, has led to a new generation of musicians whose livelihood depends on the festival and concert tour economy. While foreign concerts are the most obvious manifestation, many of these musicians end up doing recording work in European-based studios that are run by and cater to the Turkish diaspora in continental Europe.[24] Some Turkish-based engineers and session musicians emigrated to Germany to provide services to the Turkish diasporic recording industry.[25] However, albums produced in Amsterdam, Hamburg, and other continental locations are often released through labels based in Turkey. The Turkish music sector still revolves around Unkapanı, the production hub of the transnational Turkish recording industry, but increasingly relies on work done outside of Turkey.

Even with this newfound mobility of musicians, mobile media are still central to production. In 2007, toward the end of my primary research period in Turkey, I observed many situations where someone involved in a German-based recording production would come to ZB Stüdyo or another studio with an MP3 of an arrangement in progress, hire a studio musician to play a specific part, burn the resulting WAV file to a CD-R, and bring it to a studio in Germany to be incorporated into a recording. I would guess that when internet upload speeds increase in Turkey, the need for the physical transportation of media will probably wane, and internet file hosting services (or a similar technology) will serve as the medium for music's mobility.

# Conclusion

In 2009 I visited Grup Yorum at the İdil Kültür Merkezi in Okmeydanı (Figure 13.3). They had just released their twentieth studio album—*Başeğmeden* (Kalan Müzik

FIGURE 13.3   İdil Kültür Merkezi. Photograph by Ladi Dell'aira.

Yapım, 2008)—which unlike *Yıldızlar Kuşandık* was made at a time when none of the group members were in prison. There were several other significant changes. Ufuk Lüker, the long-standing group member and political exile who had coordinated the German recording efforts, was no longer with the group, and therefore Yorum's newest album did not involve the same kind of back-and-forth digital media exchange between Germany and Turkey. Perhaps most significant, much of the album was recorded (but not mixed) at a brand new, small, project studio that Yorum had created inside İdil (Figure 13.4). İnan, who had been a primary arranger for *Yıldızlar Kuşandık* and had attended every recording session for that album, did much of the engineering himself for the new album. However, mixes still happened elsewhere, as well as some of the recording itself. Hard drives were still moving around, if at a less frenetic rate and traveling shorter distances. The *Başeğmeden* project was notable for the increasing use of cellular phones, iPhones, and instant messaging/ online chat technologies, all of which enabled İnan's personal transformation from group member/musician into a recording engineer, but those mobile communications technologies are the subject of another story.

In comparing the making of *Yıldızlar Kuşandık* and *Başeğmeden*, it is apparent that Grup Yorum did *not* choose distributed production due to an aesthetic preference or because it was easier or preferable to another extant production workflow alternative. To the contrary, challenging circumstances (imprisonment, inability to travel) led to

FIGURE 13.4  Music-arranging workstation at İdil. Photograph by Ladi Dell'aira.

creative and innovative solutions. The portability of digital media—MIDI files, MP3s, and multitrack digital audio sessions—was what enabled all of these solutions.

## Acknowledgments

My research was facilitated by a State Department Fellowship, generously provided by ARIT (American Research Institute in Turkey) (2006–2007), and a Fulbright IIE grant (2005–2006). All interviews were conducted in Turkish, and translations appearing here were made by the author. I wish to thank İnan Altın and the other members of Grup Yorum, Yeliz Keskin (for helping with interview transcription), Ulaş Özdemir and Hasan Saltık at Kalan Müzik Yapım, and Ladi Dell'aira (for photographs and moral support).

## Notes

1. F-Type prisons are single-cell, high-security prisons that have largely replaced the preceding norm of dormitory-style prisons. Their adoption led to the largest prison hunger strike

in modern history, claiming over one hundred deaths. See Green (2002) and Anderson (2004).

2. See Bates (2008) for a more extensive ethnography of ZB Stüdyo and the recording studio culture of Istanbul.

3. It also helped that I was familiar with the sound of their previous albums.

4. For a contextualization of 1970s to 1990s socialism in Turkey, see Karpat (2004).

5. "Grup Yorum'cular 12 Eylül darbesine karşı ortaya çıkıp, sessiz ama 12 Eylül'e tepkili gençliğin sesi oldular. Konserlerinin yanısıra, binlerce üniversite öğrencisinin katıldığı forumlara, mitinglere ve eylemlere katılarak destek verdiler. Bazen Grup Yorum konserlerinde önceki ismi Devrimci Sol olan, sonra adını DHKP-C olarak değiştiren örgütün sloganlarını işitmek mümkün. Fakat Grup Yorum üyeleri her söyleşide, açıklamalarında hiçbir illegal örgüte üye olmadıklarını belirtiyorlar. Emperyalist sömürüye, işgallere, işkenceye karşı çıkıp sosyalist bir ülke ve dünya kurulması için demokratik bir mücadele içinde olduklarını söylüyorlar. Tüm bunlardan kurtulmanın yolu olarak halkı örgütlenmeye davet ediyorlar. Kendilerinin de örgütlü olduklarını, demokratik mücadele içinde yer aldıklarını açıklıyorlar." İnan Altın, personal communication with author, January 13, 2010.

6. In an article about the performing ensemble Kardeş Türküler, a group inspired by Grup Yorum that performs music of many Anatolian ethnicities but eschews blatantly political lyrics, Orhan Kahyaoğlu notes that simply asserting a discourse of multiculturalism makes music, or musicians, "automatically political" in Turkey (2008:206).

7. Alevis are a hereditary heterodox order that live throughout Turkey and Azerbaijan and are closely affiliated with the Bektaşi Sufi order. Although some Alevi music has long had a political bent, the Sivas hotel fire of 1993, where Sunni extremists murdered thirty-seven prominent Alevi writers and musicians, is frequently cited as the primary event after which Alevi cultural expression was unambiguously regarded as political (Sökefeld 2008:118).

8. Ekşi Sözlük (www.sourtimes.org), which translates to "sour dictionary," was launched by Murat Arslan and Sedat Kapanoğlu in 1999, and is arguably the most widely used and significant Turkish language social media website. It is a "social dictionary," meaning that the focus of user activity is on creating multiple, often competing definitions of words and phrases. The social dictionary phenomenon is popular among Turkish speakers in Turkey and abroad, and clones of Ekşi Sözlük were started by students at Istanbul Technical, Bilgi, and Uludağ Universities. Several hundred thousand Turkish speakers participate in this social media form.

9. İnan Altın, personal communication with author, June 4, 2006.

10. Ibid.

11. RTÜK (Radyo Televizyon Üst Kurulu), which stands for the Radio Television High Council, was established in 1994 out of an extant set of laws that regulated private broadcast media (Algan 2003:182).

12. See Hassanpour 1998 for examples of the myriad legal reasons provided by the government for censorship. It should be noted that censorship sometimes transpires with no overtly stated reason, as was the case with Grup Yorum's 2001 album *Feda* (Kahyaoğlu 2003:334).

13. Anecdotal evidence supplied by Hasan Saltık, the owner of Kalan Müzik Yapım, suggests that prior to the industry-wide collapse of sales in 2005, most Grup Yorum albums each sold at least 250,000 legitimate copies and countless more bootleg copies.

14. Regarding technologies, the first consumer hard drive with a 40 gb capacity was released in 2000; the first sub-$1000 DVD-R burner (the Pioneer DVR-103) was released in 2001,

and in the same year, Protools TDM 5.1 software with MIXplus hardware was still limited to sixty-four tracks of simultaneous playback (Digidesign 2001).

15. Several online forums have initiated international song production competitions, where musicians, engineers, and producers in different countries collaborate toward the creation of new recordings. One such competition is CAPE (Composers, Artists, Producers, Engineers), which was launched in 2004 on the website ProSoundWeb, later relocated to other music industry forums, and by 2012 had completed ten rounds, enlisting the talents of several hundred different musicians (http://thewombforums.com/forumdisplay.php?f=7).

16. From late 2005 to early 2006, the most common home or office internet connection was a 512 kbit download/128 kbit upload, which cost approximately $60 a month for a 6 gb a month bandwidth-limited account, and $100 a month for an unlimited account. Internet cafes typically had a faster 2048 kbit connection, but one that was shared by sixteen or more computers. Rated speeds were only attainable between two peers within Turkey. As the internet was a government-controlled monopoly and there was only a single backbone entering Turkey, bandwidth between Turkey and other countries was very limited, particularly during peak usage times.

17. İdil Kültür Merkezi (İdil Cultural Center), now located in the Okmeydanı neighborhood of Istanbul, is a licensed association that provides low-cost education, a small concert venue, and a library in addition to housing the offices of *Tavır* magazine and the Anadolu Sesi (Anatolian Sound) radio station.

18. The Grup Yorum project was the only group project I saw during my research in Turkey where every aspect of arrangement, recording, and mixing was decided by democratic group consensus without the direction of a single producer or band leader.

19. I was not able to obtain data about exactly how flash media devices were transported into prisons and how feedback made it back to Grup Yorum.

20. Although the portability of MP3s allows for a distributed network of individuals to be more extensively involved with the production stage of an album, similar circuits of production have existed with Grup Yorum for at least fifteen years. One former group member I interviewed, who wished to remain nameless, recounted tales about being imprisoned in the mid-1990s, routinely smuggling musical scores and lyrics sheets out of prison, and fabricating makeshift flutes out of water pipes. What is new, therefore, is the ability for recorded audio media—in digital form—to move through similar circuits.

21. "Dead" and "live" are non-rigorous terms that tend to refer to two characteristics of room sound: the reverberation time (the time it takes for a source signal to decay to 60 dB below its original value), and the overall frequency response curve for room reflections. "Dead" rooms have shorter reverberation time (less than a second) and less high frequency energy in room reflections, while live rooms have a longer reverberation time and more high frequency energy in the reflected sound. Flutter echoes, typically considered undesirable for recording studios, are a property of rooms where the reverberation, rather than having a linear decay, has a pulsating, rhythmic echo effect.

22. For more on the story of the song "Kavuşma," see Bates (2011:101–3).

23. Zaza Alevis are Zazaki-speaking Alevis, and hence have two ethnic identity distinctions in addition to their identities as Turkish subjects.

24. The development of Turkish performing and recording culture in Germany from the 1950s until 1999 is well documented in Greve (2006).

25. While I was conducting research in Turkey, Gürsoy Tanç (a studio guitarist and arranger who had performed on Grup Yorum's album and many other projects at ZB Stüdyo) and Metin Kalaç (an engineer who is best known for his Karadeniz popular music engineering, see Bates 2010) both temporarily emigrated to Germany.

# REFERENCES

*Hürriyet Daily News.* 2009. "State TV, Singer Disagree on Finale." Domestic section, 15 April.

*Milliyet.* 2000. "10 Yılın Tiraj Rekortmenleri." Magazin section, 12 April.

Algan, Ece. 2003. "Privatization of Radio and Media Hegemony in Turkey." In *The Globalization of Corporate Media Hegemony*, ed. Lee Artz and Yahya Kamalipour. Albany: SUNY Press, 169–194.

Anderson, Patrick. 2004. " 'To Lie Down to Death for Days': The Turkish Hunger Strike, 2000–2003." *Cultural Studies* 18(6):816–46.

Appadurai, Arjun. 1990. "Disjuncture and Difference in the Global Cultural Economy." *Theory, Culture & Society* 7:295–310.

Bates, Eliot. 2008. "Social Interactions, Musical Arrangement, and the Production of Digital Audio in Istanbul Recording Studios." PhD diss., University of California Berkeley.

——. 2010. "Mixing for *Parlak* and Bowing for a *Büyük Ses*: The Aesthetics of Arranged Traditional Music in Turkey." *Ethnomusicology* 54(1):81–105.

——. 2011. *Music in Turkey: Experiencing Music, Expressing Culture.* New York: Oxford University Press.

Digidesign. 2001. "Pro Tools Reference Guide: Version 5.1 for Macintosh and Windows." Palo Alto: Digidesign Inc.

Green, Penny. 2002. "Turkish Jails, Hunger Strikes and the European Drive for Prison Reform." *Punishment & Society* 4(1):97–101.

Greve, Martin. 2006. *Almanya'da "Hayali Türkiye"nin Müziği.* Trans. Selin Dingiloğlu. Istanbul: Bilgi Üniversitesi Yayınları.

Hassanpour, Amir. 1998. "Satellite Footprints as National Borders: MED-TV and the Extraterritoriality of State Sovereignty." *Journal of Muslim Minority Affairs* 18(1):53–72.

Holbrook, Victoria R. 1994. *The Unreadable Shores of Love: Turkish Modernity and Mystic Love.* Austin: University of Texas.

Kahyaoğlu, Orhan. 2003. *"Sıyrılıp Gelen": Grup Yorum.* Istanbul: neKitaplar.

——. 2008. "Kendiliğinden Politik bir Müzik Tavrı." In *Kardeş Türküler: 15 Yılın Öyküsü.* Istanbul: bgst yayınları.

Karpat, Kemal H. 2004. *Studies on Turkish Politics and Society: Selected Articles and Essays.* Leiden: Brill.

Korpe, Marie. 2007. *Music Will Not Be Silenced: 3rd Freemuse World Conference on Music & Censorship.* Copenhagen: Freemuse.

Neyzi, Leyla. 2003. "Zazaname: The Alevi Renaissance, Media and Music in the Nineties." In *Turkey's Alevi Enigma*, ed. Paul White and Joost Jongerden. Leiden: Brill, 111–124.

Özer, Yetkin. 2003. "Crossing the Boundaries: The Akdeniz Scene and Mediterraneanness." In *Mediterranean Mosaic: Popular Music and Global Sounds*, ed. Goffredo Plastino. New York: Routledge, 199–220.

Öztürkmen, Arzu. 2005. "Folklore on Trial: Pertev Naili Boratav and the Denationalization of Turkish Folklore." *Journal of Folklore Research* 42(2):185–216.

Sökefeld, Martin. 2008. *Struggling for Recognition: The Alevi Movement in Germany and in Transnational Space*. New York: Berghahn Books.

Stokes, Martin. 2002a. "Music in Performance: Cem Karaca, Live." In *Garland Encyclopedia of World Music Volume 6: The Middle East*, ed. Virginia Danielson, Scott Marcus and Dwight Reynolds. New York: Routledge, 243–245.

——. 2002b. "Turkish Rock and Pop." In *Garland Encyclopedia of World Music Volume 6: The Middle East*, ed. Virginia Danielson, Scott Marcus and Dwight Reynolds. New York: Routledge, 247–253.

Yılmaz, Niyazi. 1996. *Aşık Veysel: Milli Kültürümüzdeki Yeri*. Ankara: Ocak.

Yurdatapan, Şanar. 2004. "Turkey: Censorship Past and Present." In *Shoot the Singer! Music Censorship Today*, ed. Marie Korpe. London: Zed Books.

## Discography

Grup Yorum. *Yıldızlar Kuşandık*. Kalan Müzik Yapım CD 374, 2006, compact disc/audiocassette.

Grup Yorum. *Başeğmeden*. Kalan Müzik Yapım CD 461, 2008, compact disc.

# CHAPTER 14

# RHYTHMS OF RELATION: BLACK POPULAR MUSIC AND MOBILE TECHNOLOGIES

## ALEXANDER G. WEHELIYE

In this chapter I focus on the singular performances of the interface between (black) subjectivity and informational technologies in popular music, asking how these performances impact current definitions of the technological. After a brief examination of those aspects of mobile technologies that gesture beyond disembodied communication, I turn to the multifarious manifestations of techno-informational gadgets (especially cellular/mobile telephones) in contemporary R&B, a genre that is acutely concerned, both in content and form, with the conjuring of interiority, emotion, and affect. The genre's emphasis on these aspects provides an occasion to analyze how technology thoroughly permeates spheres that are thought to represent the hallmarks of humanist hallucinations of humanity. I outline the extensive and intensive interdependence of contemporary (black) popular music and mobile technologies in order to ascertain how these sonic formations refract communication and embodiment and ask how this impacts ruling definitions of the technological. The first group of musical examples surveyed consists of recordings released between 1999 and 2001; the second set are recordings from years 2009–2010. Since ten years is almost an eternity in the constantly changing universes of popular music and mobile technologies, analyzing the sonic archives from two different historical moments allows me to stress the general co-dependence of mobiles and music without silencing the breaks that separate these "epochs." Finally, I gloss a visual example that stages overlooked dimensions of mobile technologies so as to amplify the rhythmic flow between the scopic and the sonic. The artifacts in question boost the singular corporeal sensations of informational technologies without resorting to a naturalization of these machines. In other words, black musical formations relish the synthetic artificiality of cell phones and other mobile gadgets as much as making these a vital component of the performed body. They achieve this by transforming the sounds of mobile telephones into rhythmic patterns vital to their musical texts, which make audible how humans and mobile machines form a relational continuum.

I frequently return to Samuel R. Delany's constructive differentiation between "the white boxes of computer technology" and "the black boxes of modern street technology," because it highlights the racialized core of the very definition of technology (cited in Dery 1994:192). Although things have changed somewhat—Delany made this statement in 1994—due to the proliferation of mobile devices (laptops, netbooks, smart phones, portable music players with web capabilities, tablet computers, etc.), and the move away from "white boxes" as the de facto model for personal computing, Delany's pithy distinction still holds, both in its general implications and in the racialized provenances of this split. As recent studies have shown, most youth of color in the United States log on the internet from mobile devices or public personal computer terminals, and thus still only have access to the "the black boxes of modern street technology" (Schiffer 1991; Black Digerati 2009; Contreras 2009; Lang 2009; Watkins 2009; Wortham 2009; Brustein 2010). Moreover, black and Latino youth have been early adopters of "street technologies," especially portable music players such as the boom box and Walkman. The culture of using boom boxes and other portable music devices to occupy public space continues today in "sodcasting": "the public playing of trebly MP3s off mobile phones on British public transport—mostly buses, mostly in London, mostly by teenagers, often non-white teenagers…" (Hancox 2009; Marshall 2009). Generally, the pioneering use of mobile "black boxes" such as pagers and boom boxes in non-mainstream cultures does not figure into the histories cellular telephones, MP3 players, or current internet-enabled mobile devices, showing how the inclusion in or exclusion of particular machines determines how technology is defined (Araujo n.d.; Schiffer 1991; Heckman 2006).[1]

Much of the critical literature about cellular telephones tends to focus on how radically this technology has altered communicative patterns at the node of public and private through its mobility and how people use cell phones to distinguish themselves from others or project images of themselves as hip teenagers or successful businessmen in a Veblenesque or Bourdiuesque fashion. Communications studies scholars James Katz and Mark Aakhus, for instance, propose a theory of "Apparatgeist" that encapsulates the particular historical instantiation of cell phones as well as other social technologies; they write: "We coin the neologism Apparatgeist to suggest the spirit of the machine that influences both the designs of the technology as well as the initial and subsequent significance accorded to them by users, non-users and anti-users" (2002:307). This approach is useful for locating the significance of technologies in the interstices between the apparatus and a variety of attendant practices, rather than accenting one at the cost of the other. Writing more specifically about the cell phone, Katz and Aakhus argue that the machine's Apparatgeist follows the logic of "perpetual contact" that combines mobile communication, private talk, and public performance. Still, the notion of "perpetual contact" leaves intact the largely communicative and content centered bias in

many theories of information technologies. While those aspects clearly remain important in any considerations of technology, too often the tactile or haptic dimensions of
these machines remain muted. How can we think about cell phones as communicative
devices without losing sight and sound of their ringtones, vibrate modes, visual displays,
touch screens, keypads, and so forth, as well as the feel and color of the material the
machines are made of?

Many critics have noted how mobile communication reduces the non-linguistic
aspects of the communicative performance between the two or more speakers given
that they appear to each other only as disembodied voices and/or snippets of text (email,
SMS, mobile chat, for example), including Leopoldina Fortunati, who asserts: "mediated communication lowers the quality of communicative performance, as far as to
deprive it of the support by non-verbal language, proxemics, kinesics, etc." (2002:517).[2]
Nevertheless, these forms of interaction also buttress the non-face-to-face tête-à-tête,
for instance through the different environments (temporal, geographic, social, etc.) the
speakers inhabit and the various textures (sonic, haptic, visual, olfactory, etc.) of the
mobile devices. Accordingly, body-to-body communication does not vanish in mobile
communication but (re)materializes in both the participants' respective location and
in the apparatus itself (Fortunati 2005). Put simply, mobile devices are bodies too, even
if they exist chiefly in relation to and in symbiosis with humans. Given the ubiquity of
mobile devices in the western world and across the globe, it would behoove us to conceptualize them not merely as disembodied tools that facilitate pure communication but
also devise languages that allow for the analysis of the "fuzzy" and textural dimensions
of mobile communication and the different apparatuses in which it is bodied forth.[3]

For my purposes, contemporary black popular music not only presents sonic redac-
tions of techno-ecologies, but more importantly their transposition into the realms of
sensation via rhythm. These musical formations stage the "rush" of itinerant information technologies, what Anna Everett has referred to as "digital plentitude" (2003:14).
Instead of merely focusing on the communicational dimensions of these machines,
contemporary R&B unearths the aspects of technology above, beyond, and between the
transmission of zeros and ones, highlighting, for instance, a body registering a pager
set to vibrate mode. Brian Massumi elucidates the different modalities through which
humans experience the world, differentiating "perception," "[which refers] to object
oriented experience" from "sensation," "[which refers to] 'the perception of perception,'
or self-referential experience. Sensation pertains to the stoppage- and stasis-tending
dimension of reality.... Sensation pertains to the dimension of passage, or the continuity of immediate experience.... Perception is segmenting and capable of precision; sensation is unfolding and constitutively vague" (2002:258–59, n11). Conveying sensation
is crucial for it locates the import of technologies not merely in the contents they transmit or their socio-political significance, but also in the textural provenances of these
machines, which are a considerable part of their allure and utility while oftentimes elud-
ing the grip of critical discourse. In this regard, the sonic represents an ideal venue for
hearing and being affected by "the constitutive vagueness" of information technologies
due to its non-linguistic qualities such as timbre and rhythm that resonate throughout

the body. Whereas scholarly discussions tend to focus on the perception of mobile technologies, (black) popular music intensifies their sensation: the textural relay and relation between human bodies and machines.

I will now make a few points about the generic parameters of R&B, particularly its overdetermined relationship to hip-hop. Although recent post- or hyper-soul manifestations of R&B have imported certain masculinist tendencies from hip-hop, it still remains a "feminine" genre (Bat 2001). While hip-hop routinely transacts black "masculine" exterior braggadocio in its obsessions with guns, hypersexuality, and conspicuous consumption, R&B might be said to stage a more "feminine" version of the (black) subject that traffics in love and sex stories without hip-hop's hardened outer shield. I am not, however, suggesting any strict correlation between biology and the performative body, although R&B is the only musical category in which black female performers dominate; I merely wish to register some broad discursive markers.[4] Modern R&B is also the popular musical field most concerned with interpersonal relationships, and while it is considered a particularly 'black' genre due to the racial identity of most of its performers, obvious socio-political overtones remain a rarity. For every "I'm Black and Proud," there are numerous invocations of "Will You Satisfy?," "Turn Off the Lights," or "Where Is the Love?" Even in some of the more politically inspired soul of the 1960s and 1970s explicit political messages appear in a rather oblique fashion, hence song titles like "A Change Is Going to Come," "Respect," and "People Get Ready." This tendency to circumvent the strictly political and the genre's "femininity" might explain the absence of any sustained critical discourse about R&B (particularly when contrasted with the sizeable archive of hip-hop criticism), or discussions that do not reduce the genre to the musical manifestation of the Civil Rights Movement. In this way, R&B figures in scholarly debates primarily through its manifest (political) content, echoing the functionalist Cartesianism found in so many considerations of technology.[5]

When not fettered to benchmark of political content R&B emerges as the deterritorialization of hip-hop, especially in the genre's differently tuned configuration of the black (female) voice. In the wake of hip-hop, singing appears as "softer" and less assertive than rapping, which has now become the standard against which black musical expressivity is measured. Hence, the statements by many rappers, who claim that they feature R&B singers to sing hooks on their records to "appeal to the ladies." While contemporary hip-hop is engulfed by and has in some sense been superseded by R&B in popularity, its femininity is often kept at bay by masculinist retrenchment. Because R&B centers on a variety of interpersonal intimacies, it creates a complex rhythmic arrangement for the sensation of human-machine enmeshments.

Communications and other technologies have been a steady presence on R&B recordings as lyrical topics and as structural components for some time. At the moment, lyrically, nary a hit song exists without the mention of cellular phones, beepers, two-way pagers, iPhones, Blackberry's, answering machines, various surveillance gadgets, email messages, the internet, Twitter, etc., stressing the interdependence of contemporary interpersonal communication and informational technologies.[6] This penchant for machines in R&B can also be found in the genre's use of cellular telephones both as a voice alteration apparatus and as part of the sonic tapestry. In fact, the uses of the "cell phone effect" have recalibrated conceptions of the voice and soul within the contemporary popular musical landscape. Lately, a plethora of mainstream R&B productions feature parts of the lead or background vocal performance sounding as if they were called in over a cell phone as opposed to produced in a state of the art recording studio.[7] The increased prominence of these technological artifacts in R&B indicates the enculturation of informational technologies in practices that are customarily relegated to the dominion of the non- and/or pre-technological, as well as amplifying some neglected attributes of current techno-informational flows.

Instead of trying to downplay the technological mediation of the recording, the "cell phone effect" does away with any notion of the self-same presence of the voice. Jeremy Gilbert and Ewan Pearson explain that in majority popular musical practices newer technologies are considered artificial and inartistic, creating a hierarchy of counts as technological:

> Some items are considered *more* technological in status than others. In this scheme, a drum machine is more technological than a drum…Such considerations are founded on an order of the real within which aesthetic preferences are transformed into ontological distinctions…. Such distinctions almost always proceed by rendering the technological components utilized in their favored forms invisible as technologies—they are more 'real' or 'natural', absorbed wholly into those that play them as expressive extensions of the performing body. (1999:112)

The "cell phone effect" resists such principles of the "real," choosing instead to stage voice processing devices as both technological *and* expressive "extensions of the performing body." More importantly, the "cell phone effect" makes audible the sensation of hearing the human voice distributed across the digits of binary code. In addition, cell phones appear not as cumbersome synthetic obstructions of "authentic" and "natural" human speech at either end, but as integral to post-millennial interpersonal communication, while also rhythmifying their acoustic properties. The mobile "black boxes" of street technology break through the sound barrier between humans and machines; their mobility allows for a relational engagement with the technological.

R&B features numerous lyric incantations of cell phone use qua social interaction, often positioning this ubiquitous feature of current life worlds as the embodiment of interpersonal relations. On her 2000 track "Hey Kandi," Kandi, one of the only prominent female R&B song writers and producers, responsible for such hits as Destiny's Child's "Bills, Bills, Bill" and TLC's "No Scrubs," deploys a variety of voice processing maneuvers to almost baroque extremes.[8] "Hey Kandi" is structured around a cell phone heart-to-heart between the artist and a friend concerning Kandi's new beau. All the background vocals are sung and/or spoken through the phone, we often hear a dial tone, and the track makes ample usage of the popular auto-tune voice alteration software.[9] Here, the cell phone functions as the conduit for interpersonal communication as well as aiding the creation of intimacy. This particular track also renders audible quite a few sounds associated with cell phones (voice at the other end of the "line," busy/free signal, and ringing), producing a technological intimacy that arises from both the content and mode of transmission.

Aaron Soul's "Ring, Ring, Ring" (2001), which echoes the previous recordings that bear similar names by ABBA and De La Soul, begins with a shout out to "one to one Erickson," and then tells a sad story about the hurtful words he uttered to his girlfriend "when [they] were last face-to-face," leading the couples' subsequent estrangement.[10] By the time we get to the chorus, Aaron's cell phone has transmogrified into a prime indicator of his amorous woes: "ring, ring, ring, my cell phone's not ringing," and apparently his girlfriend's "cell phone keeps ringing," because the caller ID feature on her phone allows her to ignore his persistent calls. What strikes the ear here is that Aaron Soul's voice almost shapeshifts into a cell phone through the incessant chanting of "ring, ring, ring," in what initially sounds like a musical figuration of onomatopoeia.

Nevertheless, the repetition of *ring* fails to dissolve into a mimetic ocean since it sounds nothing like the "real world" ringing of a cell phone. Instead, the track imagines a sonico-linguistic modality of hearing mobile technologies that traverse the fields of desire and are embodied in the recorded human voice. Later in the song, Soul tells us that he wishes his mobile would sing, thus affecting a reversal in which the singer transforms into a cell phone, and the machine takes on the singer's attributes. Rather than accurately reproducing cell phone sounds, Aaron Soul channels and seems possessed by its ring-tones. The song brings to mind Sadie Plant's comments regarding the cell phone's significant realignment of contemporary acoustic bionetworks:

> The warbles, beeps and tunes of the mobile have become so common that their calls have begun to constitute a new kind of electronic bird song, changing the soundtrack of cities and altering the background noise in regions as varied as the forests of Finland and the deserts of Dubai. [In fact,] many urban song birds have become adept at impersonating mobile tones and melodies." (2002:29)

Perhaps we can think of Aaron Soul's sonic redaction of his cell phone as the emergence of a different sort of urban songbird, one that codes humans and machines not as separate entities but both as components of a constitutive relation, which performs the technicity of the human via rhythm and the humanity of machines through vocalization.

On "Call Me" (2000) Soul's compatriot Jamelia tells a different story.[11] Accompanied by the ringing of a cell phone and the sounds of an ultra-modern clavichord, Jamelia instructs her own man and, by extension, all other men, "don't forget to call your boo tonight, baby is waiting for your call." This track differs most manifestly from "Ring, Ring, Ring" by weaving cell phone ring tones into its rhythmic fabric, albeit only during its final minutes. Rather than hearing these tones as similitude, I want to ask how we might understand the effects of their rhythmic recurrence within the confines of black musical formations? These musical examples equate verbal communication with mobile technologies by merging the supposedly deeply personal with technological gadgets. In this way, the technological appears not so much in the Nokia's and Erickson's as it does in the spaces between the apparatus and social practices, what Edouard Glissant (1997) calls "a poetics of relation." In these songs mobile phones are so much more than mere facilitators for the intricacies of intimate affairs, they serve as sonic indices of desire and as machines of longing.

Ginuwine's "2Way" (2001) revolves around the two-way pager, which, as opposed to regular pagers (only numeric and one-way) allows its users to exchange text messages.[12] When this song was released over ten years ago two-way pagers and similar devices were widespread in the United States, while cell phone text messaging was already hugely popular in Europe and the rest of the world.[13] The track begins with the ring tones of a pager, which give way to a cascade of strings and Ginuwine's introductory speech and is followed by the chorus: "It's a two-way street, it a two-way door/It's a two-way life (Pick it up and two way me)/It's a two-way sky it's a two-way tel/It's a two-way life, pick it up girl and hit me." This passage is striking because it only references the pager implicitly, choosing instead to signify on the interpersonal connotations of the two-way moniker. Ginuwine equates the give and take of an intimate relationship with the machine's reciprocal attributes so as to sound the constitutive technicity of "human communication." As the song continues Ginuwine offers a cornucopia of sensations through the aural lens of the two-way pager: the auditory "Now I got mine on loud/ if you get at me I'll hear you;" the visual: "If it's dark light it up, put 'em up. Put 'em up/If it's closed, flip it up/ in the club, beam me up;" and the haptic "I got mine on vibe, so if you get me/I'll feel you/I'll call you back real quick/no lie better yet, I'll just reply." While communication surely represents one of main functions of the two-way pager, Ginuwine's track is more interested in exploring the "constitutively vague" dimensions of this machine. In this context, sound performs the sensation of communicational technologies by virtue of its a-signifying signifying properties; those aspects of the sonic that exceed linguistic content, but nonetheless engender strong tactile and aural responses.

All the recordings I have discussed thus far were released at the dawn of the millennium when ringtones were primarily monophonic and could easily be differentiated from music.[14] While early mobile ringtones consisted of a particular sequence of tones and did not differ significantly from the functional sounds of a ringing landline, mobile phone ringtones are now largely MP3 clips (usually around 15 seconds in duration) of existing musical recordings. Besides featuring only parts of songs, these clips attain ringtone character by virtue of their repetition, which blurs the line between their utility as sonic indicators of incoming calls and musical consumption. Moreover, just as the previous examples musicalize functional ringtones via rhythmification, using excerpts of songs as ringtones embeds them in a different rhythmic context (Gopinath 2005; Licoppe 2008:139–52; Goggin 2011:55–79). In fact, the incorporation of monophonic or polyphonic ringtones into popular musical recordings is now largely a historical relic given the almost complete disappearance of these types of ringtones specifically designed to alert users to incoming calls, which have largely been replaced a with ringtone sounds culled from musical recordings. For, in order to achieve the same effects as Jamelia, Ginuwine, or Kandi, current artists would have to interpolate, repeat and rhythmify other pieces of music, which would be akin to the practice of sampling and require a completely different set of musical and legal practices. In 2000 consumers used the functional ringtones that were preinstalled on their mobile, now users either acquire bits and pieces of preexisting songs or create ringtones from their own MP3 collection, if they use ringtones at all.[15] Despite this virtually total move to using digital audio recordings as indicators of incoming voice calls and the absence of actual ringing sounds, these sonic marks still carry the name and operate as ringtones. Due to the steep decline in ringtone sales since 2009, alternative modes of the interanimation between mobile devices and popular music have flourished: the immensely popular app by musician T-Pain that allows everyone to emulate the musician's trademark auto-tuned voice, or the purchase of songs for the massively popular rhythmic iPhone game Tap Tap Revenge, for instance.[16] More generally, with the advent of Apple's iPhone and similar devices, mobile phones and portable music players are no longer separate physical entities but housed in the same gadget. Recorded music and mobiles enjoy an unprecedented symbiotic relationship in term of content and at the hardware level. Furthermore, mobile devices have become the embodiment of "convergence culture," since they now also include calendars, alarm clocks, notebooks, compasses, e-readers, still and video cameras, voice recorders, flash lights, calculators, navigation devices, answering machines, and video players.[17]

In another instance of the continual blending of popular music and mobile technologies, hip-hop star Drake proclaims that he can only write his rhymes on his BlackBerry mobile device. In a MTV documentary (Mack and Warren 2010) Drake's producer describes the artist's process thus: "All Drake's raps for eternity have been written inside of a Blackberry.... I've had dummy Blackberrys around that I just pull out for him to write on, like if he needs one...that don't actually even work!" This is how Drake portrays how he works: "I can't write my raps on paper. The Blackberry keys—my thumbs were made for touching them" (quoted in Ziegbe 2010). The documentary then cuts to a shot of Drake in the sound booth of a recording studio, reading his raps from a BlackBerry. It bears noting that of all the functions contained in such a device, Drake singles out the haptic sensation of the keyboard in the portrayal of his compositional process. Ringtones and mobile technologies have become an essential part of composing, recording, distributing, and commodifying contemporary popular music: all musical recordings can potentially be used or sold as ringtones, all ringtones can possibly become songs, but only some of them are currently used in this way.

In addition, the success of ringtones has lead to the creation of a (almost universally derided) sub-genre of hip-hop dubbed "ringtone rap." The recordings by artists such as Soulja Boy, Mims, Dem Franchize Boyz that fall into the purview of ringtone rap are generally written/produced (catchy short sing-song hooks, tinny beats, non-sensical rhymes) so as to sound best when heard through cell phone speakers, and, therefore sell as many ringtones as possible (Moody 2007). Hence, ringtone rap reverses the absorption of monophonic ringtones into popular music that occurred at the turn of the millennium by transmogrifying songs into extended ringtones. Although Trey Songz's "Lol:-)" (2009) is sung rather than rapped, it features a prominent ringtone rapper Soulja Boy, and bears the sonic hallmarks of the subgenre, sounding like a crunk version of the children's song "Frère Jacques."[18] The lyrics further compound the interweaving of popular music and mobile technologies: "Cruisin' in that Benz around the city (round tha city Yup!)/Then I felt my phone buzz, I know that she like thugz/ . . . Then she sent a text that had read, 'baby, I'm at home'/Then she sent another one that said she's all alone/ So I texted her a smiley face and said, 'let's do the grown' She said, 'lol boy you crazy, come on'/Sent that lil' face with the tongue 'cause I'm nasty/I'm on my way (way), girl I can't wait (wait) Twitter me a picture, lemme see that okay." Songz song narrates his mobile interaction with a female love/lust object via text messaging, which is why his phone does not ring but buzzes.[19] In response to her initial written missive, Songz sends an SMS that contains a "smiley face'" emoticon, and later he includes another emoticon a face with its tongue sticking out—":-P"—, which is usually used to indicate playful defiance. Here, it presumably works as an indicator of Songz's willingness to engage in cunnilingus ("cause I'm nasty").[20] The "smiley face," like other emoticons, is a pictogram, which can be formed either by combining punctuation marks [:-)] so that they visually approximate the shape of a smiling face or by using a graphic image (☺). The emoticon's power of signification does not rely on the sound of the graphic marks, it is solely based on the iconic shape of its signifiers. In this way, pictograms operate in diametrical opposition to logograms (u = you, 2nite = tonight, etc.), which depend entirely upon the sound of the letters and numbers (Crystal 2008:37–62). Instead of substituting a short series of punctuation marks or an image for two words for the sake of brevity, the "smiley face" symbolizes a particular sentiment (happiness). Conversely, this pictogram enters the phonetic record as a linguistic approximation of an image ("smiley face") and not a description of a sentiment, otherwise Songz's would sing the words "happy" or "happiness" instead of "smiley face." Songz's rendition of the "smiley face"—translating the emoticon to words and ensconcing this alphabetic amalgam in his rhythmically stylized vocalization—extends the sign's reach into the realm of the sonic, albeit only insofar as it refers back to the graphic image of a "smiley face."

The chorus of "Lol:-)" introduces another composite that hails from the land of electronically mediated communication: "Shawty just text me, say she wanna sex me (LOL smiley face, lol smiley face)/Shawty sent a Twit pic saying come and get this (LOL smiley face, lol smiley face)." LOL is one of the most common abbreviations used in internet and mobile written communication, and it also represents one of the few instances in which initialisms from this jurisdiction have successfully crossed over to spoken English.[21] As with "smiley face," the LOL (initially a contraction of three words: laughing out loud) makes the jump from written to spoken language not by simply restoring the acronym to its original three word glory but by giving voice to the letters: L O L. Thus, the invocation of LOL and smiley face, both of which were initially used to append affect to written communication, achieve their effects in the context of the song, because they have already transitioned from electronic script/image to oral communication. They have become a part conversational spoken English as noticeable symbols of and for (mobile) electronic communication. In addition, the backing track—expressly designed to sound like a simulacrum of a now historical monophonic ringtone—as well as the singing and repetition further accent the sonorous dimensions of these traditionally silent signs/ phrases. Rhythm, which is defined by recurring patterns of sound, sets in motion a conversion of the expressive signification that has accrued to "LOL" and "smiley face."

Accordingly, "LOL" and "smiley face" cease connoting humor and happiness, they are now phonic signifiers for the rhythmic relationality of mobile technologies.

In a slightly different vein, Monica's "Blackberry" (2010) track begins with a non-musical sonic indicator for an incoming text message and goes on to narrate the singer's powers of electronic detection (her willingness to check his phone and her ability to crack the device's lock code).[22] These powers impart warnings to Monica's boyfriend, whom she accuses of infidelity (Who you sneakin' wit 'cause I already got the code to ya phone), and the "other woman" (Get yo hands off my man/Girl you already know). Monica's beau conducts his affairs on a BlackBerry smartphone, which was launched in 1999 as a two-way pager, took on its current smartphone capabilities in 2002 (email, web browsing, SMS, etc.) and owes its success primarily its outstanding emailing capabilities.[23] At the outset BlackBerrys were pitted against similar devices produced by Motorola: BlackBerrys were used by the elite personalities such as Bill Gates or Al Gore while Motorola pagers were allied with rappers and sports figures, Jay-Z and Shaquille O'Neal, for instance (Century 2001). Rapper Jay-Z's immensely popular "I Just Wanna Love U (Give It 2 Me)" (2000) includes the following lines: "Only way to roll, Jigga and two ladies/I'm too cold, Motorola, two way page me, c'mon," which cemented the gadget's place in the popular imagination.[24] According to Howard Rheingold, "Hip-hop culture, streetwise and fashion-conscious fans of rap music, favor Motorola's two-way pagers, while young stockbrokers, suits, and geeks in the information technology industry favor the BlackBerry wireless pagers from Research in Motion" (2003:23). BlackBerrys have until recently been associated almost exclusively with white-collar work, the corporate world, masculinity, and whiteness, Motorola two-way pagers (and subsequent devices such as the Sidekick), on the other hand, have signaled leisure, sexuality, youth, femininity, blackness, etc., thus rescripting the black/white boxes of technology partition for the era of ubiquitous mobile communication and computing (Sage 2009).[25]

As a consequence of the widespread dissemination of smartphones, the BlackBerry has since traveled beyond its early professional stomping ground, yet it still registers in the cultural imagination primarily as a professional and masculine tool. All these factors contribute to how Monica mobilizes the BlackBerry, since the device stands in for her male love object as well as his infidelity. On the one hand, this provides a reference to the pivotal role of the BlackBerry in the public spectacle of Tiger Woods' extramarital affairs: Monica, like Woods' wife, will uncover his dalliances by monitoring his mobile phone.[26] On the other hand, the BlackBerry, as a signifier for the business world and masculinity, magnifies the lover's transgression, since he is using the device to conduct personal and illicit communication. Monica's "untrustworthy boo" does not appear in the song, he is personified by the repurposed BlackBerry and the singer's affective relationship with the machine.

Akin to Aaron Soul's "ring, ring, ring" chant, the word "blackberry" materializes in this song in such an interrupted, rhythmic, and digitally altered way that it barely registers any relation to the linguistic unit that it is based on: "I'm the one that checks (checks), check the (chicks) Black (black) ber (ber) ry (ry)/Yep that's me/I'm the one that checks his phone when he falls asleep early in the morn/You better have a call, go to your phone, ring leave it on with the black (black) ber (ber) ry (ry)." In fact, if the song were not named "Blackberry" the listeners would probably not be able to decipher the signification of the word through the auto-tune haze, and, accordingly, it signifies chiefly in the domain of sensation. While the verses concentrate on the intricacies of intimate relationships as refracted through mobile technologies, the scat-like singing and auto-tuning of "blackberry" in the chorus locate it beyond the grasp of wordness and meaning. The chorus is the only part of "Blackberry" in which Monica intonates in this scat-like fashion (emphasizing rhythm and sonority rather melody or meaning) and her voice appears audibly digitally altered, providing a stark contrast to the naturalistic and melismatic grain of the singer's voice throughout the rest of the track. Thus, Monica's particular staging of the word "blackberry" relies on its cultural meanings (mobile device and attendant practices) at the same time as it recodes this linguistic unit as a sonic emoticon. The way Monica vocalizes "blackberry" in the chorus supplements the song's narrative with non-linguistic affect. Monica's "Blackberry" takes a different path than Trey Songz's "LOL:-)" to the aural rendering of emoticons: Songz takes written electronic signs, sounding them out through song while fully retaining their sociolinguistic signification, Monica, however, transforms a word into a sonic affective sign that almost leaves behind linguistic meaning altogether. In both cases R&B allows for the rhythmic ensnaring of machines and emotions, because the genre possesses an expansive repertoire—in lyrical content, available styles of "emotive" singing, and musical gestalt—for the sonic transaction of interpersonal affairs.

I will now turn to the British TV series *Metrosexuality* (1999) to draw attention to the rhythmic representation of mobile technologies in a chiefly ocular medium.[27] In *Metrosexuality* much of the social interaction between the characters takes place on mobile and sedentary telephones, and phone conversations constitute at least half of the screen time. In the very first scene after the opening credits, we are introduced to teenager Kwame, who is desperately trying to reunite his divorced fathers Max and Jordan. Before Kwame makes a visual entrance on the screen, we witness a fast paced montage of the telephone call Kwame places on his mobile. Rather than showing Kwame dialing his father's number, however, the screen is taken up by a series of accelerated motion images featuring city streets and buildings that are soundtracked by swishing sounds and accelerated recordings of mobile dial and ringing tones. Moreover, the camera angles are frequently irregular, which only adds to the perplexity engendered by these shots, especially since these shots also function as an introduction to *Metrosexuality*. The expedited noises and visual montage come to an abrupt halt with the tone of Max's mobile as he answers Kwame's call while sitting in a hair salon. Then, the editing crosscuts between Kwame's position on the streets of Noting Hill (the lettering on screen reads "In the heart of Noting Hill…") and Max's location at the salon as up-tempo dance music plays in the background. In this part of the sequence the camera circles restlessly around Kwame as he moves around and speaks to his father, while a stable camera frames a medium close-up of Max's face.

Once the phone conversation between the two has ended, we cut to a close-up of Kwame's hands as he dials papa Jordan's number, which is followed by another fast-motion montage that depicts the rapid travel of information over cellular networks via the rhythmic editing of image and sound. Jordan takes Kwame's call on a grey cordless phone whilst working in a recording studio with mid-tempo bass heavy music emanating from the studio speakers. In his conversations with his fathers, Kwame tells both that the other parent has failed to pick him up from soccer practice, and, as a result, Max and Jordan arrive at Kwame's location at the same time, while Kwame and his two best friends watch the them interact at a distance. Sadly, Max and Jordan do not reconcile as Kwame had hoped in devising this elaborate ruse. In Jordan's portion of this tripartite interaction, the diegetic music, the telephone, and Jordan's clothing provide a muted contrast (monochrome, largely grey clothing, enclosed space, only the bass of the music is audible, etc.) to the brash, colorful, and buoyant sounds and colors that structure the shots featuring Kwame (canary yellow hip-hop outfit, electric blue cellular phone, lots of movement, etc.) and Max (red mobile phone, blond dreadlocks, red flowery outfit, etc.). There are many instances like this over the course of the show's narrative that imagine how aural information traverses space via the deployment of highly accelerated and rapidly intercut images accompanied by swishing and ringing noises to accentuate the velocity of the montage. Here, velocity registers as the intensification of sensation, because the viewer is forced to bear witness to the duration of its escalation. The collages of the telephone calls in *Metrosexuality* punctuate the triangulated visual and sonic flow between the different locales/characters, channeling the rush mobile communication in ways that are specific to the medium of television; they also set in motion a rhythmic "poetics of relation" at the juncture of mobile devices and humans.

Nicola Green's treatment of rhythm accents the different temporal structures of mobile technology use, distinguishing between three modalities of mobile rhythm: "the rhythms of mobile use; the rhythms of integrating mobile use into everyday life; and the rhythms of relation between use in everyday life and institutional social change" (2002:285). The examples discussed in this chapter add another rhythmic layer to the relational complexities of mobile time by initially removing mobile technologies from everyday life. Wrested from the vagaries of the quotidian and interfaced with pop songs or televisual narratives, these machines have radically different functions, moving, to put it in schematic terms, from practical use to aesthetic sensation. Surely, both of these aspects already commingle before their musicalization, and in this way, it is a shift not in kind but in degree and intensity that amplifies those rhythmic dimensions beside and below routine information transmission. Moreover, once they have entered into rhythmic relations with other matters and forces, the textural facets of mobile technologies reenter the annals of every day life, becoming integral to these devices' allure and functionality. According to Gilles Deleuze, "rhythm...is more profound than vision, hearing, etc....What is ultimate is thus the relation between sensation and rhythm, which places in each sensation the levels and domains through which it passes.... Sensation is not qualitative and qualified, but has only an intensive reality, which no longer determines within itself representative elements, but allotropic variations" (2003:37–39).[28]

The instances of mobile rhythm analyzed above produce the polymorph variations mentioned by Deleuze in their emphasis on the diverse rhythms of the technological and the human, hinting at an embodied relational theory of mobile technologies that accents their communicative *and* aesthetic facets.

As a conceptual tool and a mode of apprehending the world "rhythm" mobilizes "the processes of bringing-into-relation" that are fundamental to any social formation and/or object but are habitually neglected in favor of their stagnant counterparts (Glissant 1997:95). Still, these models of rhythm (and Glissant's notion of relation) do not simply replace the metronomic beat of the inert and unchanging with sheer flux; instead they dwell in the uneven territory at the junction of mobile use, everyday life, institutional social change, and aesthetics. Indeed, rhythm names and transacts the dialectical liaison of these at times opposing forces, making them constitutive of the objects or practices they envelop. Therefore, rhythm produces the multifaceted processes through which mobile technologies (along with a host of other technologies and rituals) come into being as consuming textural, sonic, and haptic relations, or in Henri Lefebvre's phrasing: "To grasp a rhythm it is necessary to have been **grasped** by it.." (2004:27, original emphasis). Taken together, the cell phone rings, the pager sounds, Drake's BlackBerry authorship, ringtone rap, the repeated sung vociferations of ring, ring, ring, call me, 2-way, LOL, smiley face, and blackberry, as well as the optico-sonic overflow of *Metrosexuality* boost the mobile sensations of communication technologies through the conduit of rhythm. The aforementioned rhythmifications might appear auxiliary, but they tap into facets central to the existence and utility of mobile technologies that do not register on the metronomic radar of many critical dialects. If, as John Urry remarks, "humans are sensuous, corporeal, technologically extended and *mobile* beings," then cellular telephones, because they are highly mobile and facilitate interpersonal contact, operate as prime indicators of what it means to be human at this point in history (2007:51, original emphasis). The sonic incorporation of mobile technologies into popular music extends and remixes these machines' anthropomorphic bass line, and, as a result embodies the rhythmic relation of all technologies.

## NOTES

1. These "facts" should not be construed as providing sociological evidence for the musical examples I will discuss later but contextualize the pivotal place of mobile technologies and sound in black culture.
2. See also Urry (2007:177).
3. According to the 2009 ICT (information and communication technologies) Development Index there were four billion mobile subscriptions worldwide (61% penetration rate) while there existed 1.3 billion land-lines (19% penetration rate). Given that these numbers only include subscriptions and exclude various modes of mobile sharing that are prevalent in the poorer parts of the globe, the overall penetration rate is likely higher. See International Telecommunication Union (2009). On mobile sharing, see, for instance, Steenson and Donner (2009).

4. These tendencies have shifted somewhat in recent years with the growing popularity of rappers (Kanye West and Drake, for instance) that do not conform to hip-hop's masculinist template.

5. See Ward (1998); Werner (2006). The problem here is not R&B's inherently apolitical nature but that critics value the genre if the lyrics 'transcend' the interpersonal and putatively private domain by espousing recognizably political themes, which rehashes the long-standing gendered qualities of the public/private divide. For a general consideration of the public/private split and gender, see Elshtain (1993).

6. Here is a partial list of contemporary songs (1995–2010) that devote a significant part of their lyrics and sounds to mobile technologies. R. Kelly: "3-Way Call," "Remote Control," and "Text Me." Soulja Boy: "Kiss Me Through the Phone." Ludacris: "Sexting." Christina Milian: "Call Me, Beep Me! (The Kim Possible Song)." Hi Town DJs:"Ding-A-Ling." Jackie Boyz. "Callin' Me." The Firm: "Phone Tap." Field Mob:"Stop Callin." Vybz Kartel: "Video Recorder" and "U Nuh Have a Phone (Hello Moto U)." Three 6 Mafia: "2 Way Freak." J-Luv: "Telefon Liebe." Romeo: "Romeo Dunn." Beyonce & Lady Gaga: "Video Phone." Trina: "Phone Sexx." The Game: "Camera Phone." Ciara: "Pick Up the Phone." Adina Howard: "Phone Sex." Next: "Phone Sex." Rayvon: "2-Way." Teairra Marí: "Phone Booth." Lil' Romeo: "2 Way." Destiny's Child: "Bug-A-Boo." Sammie: "Twitter Freak." Big Boi: "Ringtone." The following songs contain references to previous communication technologies: Skyy: "Call Me." Blondie. "Call Me." Missy Elliott: "Beep Me 911." De La Soul: "Ring, Ring, Ring." ABBA: "Ring Ring." Jodeci: "My Phone." A Tribe Called Quest: "Skypager."

7. See Woods (2000); Weheliye (2002).

8. Kandi, *Hey Kandi...*, CD (Columbia Records, 2000), http://www.discogs.com/Kandi-Hey-Kandi/release/1486224.

9. Auto-Tune software was initially designed to correct the pitch of a singer's voice in the recording process, it was, however, taken up primarily by popular musicians as a voice distortion mechanism that rendered the human voice robotic. This altered use of Auto-Tuning, which has now become the defining feature of the software for the majority of pop music audiences, was initially popularized by its prominence in R&B at the end of the 1990s. See Tyrangiel (2009). For a general consideration of voice altering techniques in black popular music, see Weheliye (2002).

10. Aaron Soul, *Ring, Ring, Ring*, CD (Def Soul, 2001), http://www.discogs.com/Aaron-Soul-Ring-Ring-Ring/release/465459.

11. Jamelia, *Call Me*, CD (Rhythm Series, 2000), http://www.discogs.com/Jamelia-Call-Me/release/1108420.

12. Ginuwine, "2 Way" *The Life*, CD (Sony Music, 2001), http://www.discogs.com/Ginuwine-The-Life/master/258621. Two-way pagers were en vogue popular communicational devices when Ginuwine's song was released in 2001. They have since been replaced by text messaging on mobile phones. See "Pager," in *Wikipedia, the free encyclopedia*, http://en.wikipedia.org/wiki/Pager (accessed July 27, 2010); and the 1999 entry "Paging" in *Focal Dictionary of Telecommunications*, Focal Press. Oxford: Elsevier Science & Technology, http://www.credoreference.com/entry/bhfidt/paging (accessed July 27, 2010).

13. On the history of text messaging, see Goggin (2006:65–88). There are a variety of reasons for the initial slow adoption of text messages in the United States; however, as of 2008 US mobile subscribers send and receive more written messages than they do voice calls. See Reardon (2008).

14. Sumanth Gopinath describes different mobile ringtones thus: "the commodification of the ringtone has occurred in several stages. These stages provide the outline of a model for ringtone development, whereby functional tones become: (1) monophonic ringtones or simple melodies; (2) polyphonic tones (MIDI synthesizer music); and (3) digital sound files (True Tones or other company–specific formats, and ultimately MP3 files)" (2005). In the earlier period around 2000, ringtones were primarily monophonic and slowly being replaced by polyphonic ringers, now digital sound files have all but eclipsed the other two forms. Nonetheless, non-musical sounds (beeps, chirps, and so on) are still prevalent in signaling incoming text messages, Twitter alerts, instant messages, emails, calendar reminders, etc.

15. Due to the increasing demand for these recordings, Billboard Magazine introduced its "Hot RingTones" chart, which tracked the sales of polyphonic ringtones, in the November 6, 2004 issue. The "Hot RingMasters" chart that tabulates the sales for all ringtone species superseded this chart in December 2006 (see *Billboard* 2006). Even though ringtones based on popular hits still represent a significant portion of digital musical sales in the United States, it has become quite easy to produce ringtones from digital music files in iTunes or smartphone apps such as Ringdroid. See May and Hearn (2005); Bull (2007).

16. The "I Am T-Pain" iPhone app sold 300,000 in its first three weeks of release and continues to average 10,000 downloads per day. The game requires players to tap a series of colored balls in accordance with the rhythm of a particular song. As of June 2010, Tap Tap Revenge had sold more than five million tracks through its in-game music store. See Johnson (2009); Dredge (2010).

17. See Goggin (2006:143–211); Jenkins (2006).

18. Trey Songz, *LOL:-),* CD (Atlantic Recording Corporation, 2009), http://www.discogs.com/Trey-Songz-LOL---The-Remixes/release/2044187.

19. Even though musical ringtones are now used for voice calls, incoming text messages, and emails, IMs are frequently signaled by a buzz, a beep, or other "non-musical" noises.

20. Wikipedia defines emoticon as "a textual expression representing the face of a writer's mood or facial expression. Emoticons are often used to alert a responder to the tenor or temper of a statement, and can change and improve interpretation of plain text." "Emoticon," in *Wikipedia, the free encyclopedia,* http://en.wikipedia.org/wiki/Emoticon (accessed July 12, 2010). In instant messaging, email, and text messaging images such as these ☹ ☺ are used rather than punctuation marks. For instance, whenever I typed the title of Songz's song while writing this chapter, MS Word autocorrected the punctuation marks to look like this ☺.

21. The abbreviations ROFL (rolling on the floor laughing), TTYL, (talk to you later), and OMG (oh my god) have also made the jump to spoken English. See Crystal (2006); Ulaby (2006); Tagliamonte and Denis (2008). LOL also plays a crucial role in the codification of a sociolect ("lolspeak" or "kitty pidgin") particular to the internet phenomenon Lolcats, which combines images of cats with witty captions. See Dash (2007). In her discussion of "cyberpunctutation," Jennifer Brody (2008) shows how emoticons are mobilized in contemporary cinema, which suggests another modality for the cultural logics I have been outlining here. Finally, the transposition of LOL into face-to-face communication has a precedent in the "air quotes" (using one's fingers to make quotation marks in the air during conversation) that are now synonymous with the "ironic 1990's" (Beers 2001). Although "air quotes" are not spoken per se, they are written characters that are at present used to punctuate verbal communication with affect (irony).

22. Monica, "Blackberry" *Still Standing*, CD (J Records, 2010), http://www.discogs.com/Monica-Still-Standing/release/2279141.

23. Barack Obama's avowed dependency on his BlackBerry and the public discourse about Obama's relationship with this device epitomize the apex of BlackBerry's cultural omnipresence in the United States. See Clifford (2009); Hauser (2009).

24. Jay-Z, *I Just Wanna Love U (Give It 2 Me)*, CD (Roc-A-Fella Records, 2000), http://www.discogs.com/Jay-Z-I-Just-Wanna-Love-U-Give-It-2-Me/release/781701.

25. The now discontinued Sidekick (introduced in 2002) was the precursor to today's smartphones, featuring an LCD screen, a full QWERTY keyboard, email, IM, and web capacity. The gadget entered the annals of popular culture in 2005 when a group of hackers appropriated the private information from Paris Hilton's Sidekick and posted it on the Web.

26. In the aftermath of Woods' much publicized text message conversations with his mistresses, there is now an iPhone app (TigerMail: Tigers don't always leave tracks) that promises to erase the traces of potentially incriminating notes once they have been received. As Gerard Goggin shows, mobile technologies have acquired cultural meaning in part by being associated with the uncovering and making public of illicit celebrity romances (Prince Charles' taped phone conversations with Camilla or the text messages found on Paris Hilton's stolen Motorola Sidekick) (2006:126–40).

27. Rikki Beadle Blair, dir., "Metrosexuality," DVD, 1999, http://www.imdb.com/title/tt0212216/. For an extended consideration of mobile music players in the cinematic construction of urban space, see Weheliye (2005:123–44).

28. I am not advocating the privileging of rhythm as a sign of Afro-diasporic alterity as occurs frequently but attempting to make its formal properties usable for a conceptualization of mobile technologies. For a critical genealogy of how rhythm came to be heard as an enactment of radical black difference, see Radano (2003), especially chapter five.

## References

Araujo, Luiz. n.d. "History of Pagers and Beepers." *LafaCity.Info*, http://lafacity.info/index.php/cell-phones-history/3-history-of-pagers-and-beepers.

Bat. 2001. "What Is Hypersoul?" *riddim dot ca*, http://www.riddim.ca/?p=180 (accessed July 20, 2010).

Beadle Blair, Rikki, dir. 1999. "Metrosexuality," DVD, http://www.imdb.com/title/tt0212216/

Beers, David. 2001. "Irony Is Dead! Long Live Irony!" *Salon.com*, September 25, http://www.salon.com/life/feature/2001/09/25/irony_lives/print.html (accessed July 27, 2010).

*Billboard.* 2006. "Ringmasters Chart Debuts." December 9.

Black Digerati. 2009. "I Use My T-Mobile Sidekick to Get Online More Than My Computer!" *Black Web 2.0*, September 4, http://www.blackweb20.com/2009/09/04/i-use-my-t-mobile-sidekick-to-get-online-more-than-my-computer/ (accessed July 13, 2010).

Brody, Jennifer DeVere. 2008. *Punctuation: Art, Politics, and Play*. Durham, NC: Duke University Press.

Brustein, Joshua. 2010. "Mobile Web Use and the Digital Divide." *Bits: NYTimes.com*, July 7, http://bits.blogs.nytimes.com/2010/07/07/increased-mobile-web-use-and-the-digital-divide/ (accessed July 13, 2010).

Bull, Michael. 2007. *Sound Moves: Ipod Culture and Urban Experience*. New York: Routledge.

Century, Douglas. 2001. "A World Divided Into Two-Way-Pager Camps." *New York Times,* January 14. http://www.nytimes.com/2001/01/14/style/noticed-a-world-divided-into-two-way-pager-camps.html?pagewanted=all&src=pm (accessed August 16, 2013).

Clifford, Stephanie. 2009. "For BlackBerry, Obama's Devotion Is Priceless." *New York Times,* January 8 http://www.nytimes.com/2009/01/09/business/media/09blackberry.html?_r=0 (accessed August 16, 2013).

Contreras, Felix. 2009. "Young Latinos, Blacks Answer Call Of Mobile Devices." *NPR.org,* December 1, http://www.npr.org/templates/story/story.php?storyId=120852934#comment Block (accessed July 13, 2010).

Crystal, David. 2006. *Language and the Internet.* New York: Cambridge University Press.

——. 2008. *Txtng: the Gr8 Db8.* New York: Oxford University Press.

Dash, Anil. 2007. "Cats Can Has Grammar." *AnilDash,* April 23, http://dashes.com/anil/2007/04/cats-can-has-gr.html (accessed July 27, 2010).

Deleuze, Gilles. 2003. *Francis Bacon: The Logic of Sensation.* Trans. Daniel W. Smith Minneapolis: University of Minnesota Press.

Dery, Mark. 1994. "Black to the Future: Interviews with Samuel R. Delany, Greg Tate, and Tricia Rose." In *Flame Wars: The Discourse of Cyberculture,* ed. Mark Dery, 179–222 Durham, NC: Duke University Press.

Dredge, Stuart. 2010. "5m Song Sales Milestone for Tap Tap Revenge Games." *Mobile Entertainment News,* June 4, http://www.mobile-ent.biz/news/37390/5m-song-sales-milestone-for-Tap-Tap-Revenge-games (accessed July 27, 2010).

Elshtain, Jean Bethke. 1993. *Public Man, Private Woman: Women in Social and Political Thought.* Princeton, NJ: Princeton University Press.

Everett, Anna. 2003. "Digitextuality and Click Theory: Theses on Convergence Media in the Digital Age." In *New Media: Theories and Practices of Digitextuality,* ed. Anna Everett and John Thornton Caldwell, 3–28. New York: Routledge.

Fortunati, Leopoldina. 2005. "Is Body-to-Body Communication Still the Prototype?" *The Information Society* 21(1):53–61.

——. 2002. "The Mobile Phone: Towards New Categories and Social Relations." *Information, Communication & Society* 5(4):513–28.

Gilbert, Jeremy, and Ewan Pearson. 1999. *Discographies: Dance Music, Culture and the Politics of Sound.* New York: Routledge.

Glissant, Édouard. 1997. *Poetics of Relation.* Trans. Betsy Wing. Ann Arbor: University of Michigan Press.

Goggin, Gerard. 2006. *Cell Phone Culture: Mobile Technology in Everyday Life.* New York: Routledge.

——. 2011. *Global Mobile Media.* New York: Routledge.

Gopinath, Sumanth. 2005. "Ringtones, or the Auditory Logic of Globalization." *First Monday* 10(12), http://firstmonday.org/issues/issue10_12/gopinath/index.html.

Green, Nicola. 2002. "On the Move: Technology, Mobility, and the Mediation of Social Time and Space." *The Information Society* 18(4):281–92.

Hancox, Dan. 2009. "On the Buses: Sodcasting and Mobile Music Culture." *dan hancox: a miasma of lunatic alibis,* October 23, http://dan-hancox.blogspot.com/2009/10/on-buses-sodcasting-and-mobile-music.html (accessed July 17, 2010).

Hauser, Kasper. 2009. *Obama's BlackBerry.* New York: Little, Brown and Company.

Heckman, Davin. 2006. " 'Do You Know the Importance of a Skypager?': Telecommunications, African Americans, and Popular Culture." In *The Cell Phone Reader: Essays in Social Transformation,* ed. Anandam Kavoori and Noah Arceneaux, 173–86. New York: Peter Lang.

International Telecommunication Union. 2009. "Measuring the Information Society-ICT Development Index 2009," www.itu.int/net/pressoffice/backgrounders/general/pdf/5.pdf (accessed July 19, 2010).

Jenkins, Henry. 2006. *Convergence Culture: Where Old and New Media Collide.* New York: NYU Press.

Johnson, Lynne D. 2009. "Sorry Jay-Z Auto Tune Isn't Dead, T-Pain Has an iPhone App to Spread It to the Masses." *Fast Company,* September 4, http://www.fastcompany.com/blog/lynne-d-johnson/digital-media-diva/sorry-jay-z-auto-tune-isnt-dead-t-pain-has-iphone-app-spread (accessed July 27, 2010).

Katz, James Everett, and Mark A. Aakhus. 2002. *Perpetual Contact: Mobile Communication, Private Talk, Public Performance.* Cambridge: Cambridge University Press.

Lang, Michael. 2009. "Young Blacks and Latinos Are Labeled the 'hyerusers' of Mobile Devices." *Noire Digerati—The Future Face of Technology,* November 30, http://www.noiredigerati.com/articles/2009/11/30/young-blacks-and-latinos-are-labeled-the-hyerusers-of-mobile.html (accessed July 13, 2010).

Lefebvre, Henri. 2004. *Rhythmanalysis: Space, Time and Everyday Life.* Trans. Stuart Elden and Gerald Moore. New York: Continuum.

Licoppe, Christian. 2008. "The Mobile Phone's Ring." In *Handbook of Mobile Communication Studies,* ed. James Katz, 139–52. Cambridge, MA: MIT Press.

Mack, Tim, and Michael John Warren, dir. 2010. "Drake: Better Than Good Enough." *MTV,* June 23, http://www.imdb.com/title/tt1686457/.

Marshall, Wayne. 2009. "Mobile Music & Treble Culture." *wayneandwax.com,* September 1, http://wayneandwax.com/?p=2332 (accessed July 17, 2010).

Massumi, Brian. 2002. *Parables for the Virtual: Movement, Affect, Sensation.* Durham, NC: Duke University Press.

May, Harvey, and Greg Hearn. 2005. "The Mobile Phone as Media." *International Journal of Cultural Studies* 8(2):195–211.

Moody, Nekesa Mumbi. 2007. "Rappers Aim for Ringtones." *News & Observer | newsobserver.com,* November 2, http://www.newsobserver.com/105/story/757666.html.

Plant, Sadie. 2002. "On the Mobile." *The Effects of Mobile Telephones on Social and Individual Life, classes.dma.ucla.edu/Winter03/104/docs/splant.pdf* (accessed September 24, 2011).

Radano, Ronald M. 2003. *Lying up a Nation: Race and Black Music.* Chicago: University of Chicago Press.

Reardon, Marguerite. 2008. "Americans Text More Than They Talk." *Wireless—CNET News,* September 22, http://news.cnet.com/8301-1035_3-10048257-94.html?tag=newsLatestHeadlinesArea.0 (accessed July 27, 2010).

Rheingold, Howard. 2003. *Smart Mobs: The Next Social Revolution.* Basic Books.

Sage, Simon. 2009. "Study: BlackBerry Adds 15 Hours to Work Week." *intomobile.com,* August 24, http://www.intomobile.com/2009/08/24/study-blackberry-adds-15-hours-to-work-week/ (accessed July 27, 2010).

Schiffer, Michael B. 1991. *The Portable Radio in American Life.* Tucson: University of Arizona Press.

Steenson, Molly, and Jonathan Donner. 2009. "Beyond the Personal and Private: Modes of Mobile Phone Sharing in Urban India." In *The Reconstruction of Space and Time: Mobile Communication Practices,* ed. R. Ling and S. Campbell, 231–50. Piscataway, NJ: Transaction Publishers.

Tagliamonte, Sali, and Derek Denis. 2008. "Linguistic Ruin? Lol! Instant Messaging and Teen Language." *American Speech* 83(1):3–34.

Tyrangiel, Josh. 2009. "Auto-Tune: Why Pop Music Sounds Perfect." *Time*, February 5. http://www.time.com/time/magazine/article/0,9171,1877372,00.html (accessed August 16, 2013).

Ulaby, Neda. 2006. "OMG: IM Slang Is Invading Everyday English." *NPR.org*, February 18, http://www.npr.org/templates/story/story.php?storyId=5221618 (accessed July 27, 2010).

Urry, John. 2007. *Mobilities*. Cambridge: Polity.

Ward, Brian. 1998. *Just My Soul Responding: Rhythm and Blues, Black Consciousness, and Race Relations*. Berkeley, CA: University of California Press.

Watkins, S. Craig. 2009. *The Young and the Digital: What the Migration to Social-Network Sites, Games, and Anytime, Anywhere Media Means for Our Future*. Boston: Beacon Press.

Weheliye, Alexander G. 2002. "'Feenin': Posthuman Voices in Contemporary Black Popular Music." *Social Text* 20.2(71):21–47.

——. 2005. *Phonographies: Grooves in Sonic Afro-Modernity*. Durham, NC: Duke University Press.

Werner, Craig Hansen. 2006. *A Change Is Gonna Come: Music, Race & the Soul of America*. Ann Arbor: University of Michigan Press.

Woods, Scott. 2000. "Will You Scrub Me Tomorrow." *Village Voice*, December 12, http://www.villagevoice.com/2000-12-12/music/will-you-scrub-me-tomorrow/.

Wortham, Jenna. 2009. "Mobile Internet Use Shrinks Digital Divide," *Bits Blog—NYTimes.com*, July 22, http://bits.blogs.nytimes.com/2009/07/22/mobile-internet-use-shrinks-digital-divide/ (accessed July 13, 2010).

Ziegbe, Mawuse. 2010. "Drake Reveals Songwriting Process In 'Better Than Good Enough' Documentary." *MTV.COM*, June 21, http://www.mtv.com/news/articles/1642017/ 20100621/drake.jhtml.

PART VI

GAMING AESTHETICS

# CHAPTER 15

# A HISTORY OF HANDHELD AND MOBILE VIDEO GAME SOUND

KAREN COLLINS

## INTRODUCTION

THE history of handheld gaming is an interesting one for many reasons: it represents a constant battle of technological constraint against aesthetic choice; it has echoed the development of home game consoles and arcades in its progress and approach to these constraints; and it illustrates an ongoing desire for consumers to be able to play games anywhere, anytime. Of particular importance is that there are several distinctions between console and handheld gaming that have impacted the way that handheld games—and their sound—have developed. The portability of handhelds has meant that these games are often played in a public space, and thus designers are conscious of the fact that sound may become intrusive, rather than an aid to gameplay. However, this does not mean that sound does not play an important role. In fact, the development of headphones designed for handheld gaming, as well as rhythm-action and sound- or music-based games for handhelds indicates that these devices are by no means meant to be played silently. Rather, the consideration has to be made at the design stage what role sound will play, and how to give an alternative to sound in the event that it is switched off. For instance, speech balloons can be used to indicate events that have been typically used to represent sound effects, such as in *Legend of Zelda: Phantom Compass* (Phantom Hourglass, 2007; Nintendo 2006), in which a balloon is used in conjunction with a sound change to indicate approaching enemy. This *Zelda* game, for Nintendo DS (a portable device), is highly effective in integrating speech balloons so that the user can play the game with the sound off and still be cued to important changes.

A second major distinction is, of course, the processing and memory capabilities of portable devices. This directly influences the type of games that get built, since large games (particularly in the downloadable space) can create processing problems. Likewise, the fact that these games are often played in public spaces means that there is an expectation that the player may be interrupted, or just play for a short time (e.g., on the bus on the way to school or work, waiting in line at an event, and so on). As such, casual games have risen to the forefront of the handheld market. The International Game Developers Association (IGDA) defines casual games as "games that generally involve less complicated game controls and overall complexity in terms of gameplay or investment required to get through [the] game" (IGDA 2006). This idea of *investment* is particularly important to the development of games for the devices: players generally invest less time, invest less emotion, as well as invest less money in these types of games. A market report on causal games notes that the games are

> fun, quick to access, easy to learn, and require no previous special video game skills, expertise, or regular time commitment to play. Many of these games are based around familiar game concepts that consumers played in arcades or the family Atari from childhood. In addition, casual games are usually easy to pause, stop and restart with little consequence to the player's enjoyment. (Casual Games Association 2007)

A consequence of the casual nature of the games and lower price-point of handheld games has meant that audio has in many cases been developed by non-professional sound designers and composers, as the games are often developed by an individual or very small team. Many of the largest mobile phone developers, for instance, still have no in-house sound designers or composers. Rather, sound is either contracted out at best, or assigned to a team member whose primary function is not sound-related. Typically, contracting out would take place after the game is already developed, and so audio can play only a limited role, whereas with console games, it is increasingly the case that the sound team gets involved early on in the design process in order to play a more significant role.

The history and development of sound in handheld devices is interesting, there-fore, because it highlights some of these distinctions between the handheld and home console markets. This chapter explores this history of sound in handheld and mobile games, focusing on how the sound development has been shaped by both the techno-logical constraints, and the constraints of the portability and functions of gaming on the devices. I first introduce the market for handhelds, before delving into this history. I divide the history into several sections: the pre-digital era, early digital games, the rise of systems with dedicated sound chips, more recent handheld systems, and then finally games on mobile phones and convergent media devices.

## An Introduction to the Mobile Market

The fastest growing area of the video game industry today is undoubtedly that of mobile and handheld games. Having a consumer base now at ease with carrying a mobile phone, MP3 player, and other electronic portable devices like digital cameras, portable DVD players, and GPS units means that game developers can expect that we are now accustomed to constant uninterrupted access to our media, whether it be music, the internet, movies, or games. Although handheld portable electronic game devices have been around for three decades, the convergence of these different portable hardware units into smartphones and multimedia players has pushed the portable game market into the mainstream, particularly as adults are no longer embarrassed to be carrying around a catalogue of games in the guise of a work-related device. Some experts predict that the industry, currently worth $1 billion a year in the United States, will soar to $6.8 billion by 2013 (Duryee 2008).[1]

Mobile smart phones are now cutting into the dedicated handheld gaming market. Nintendo currently has a base of about 70 million users for its DS/DSLite/DSi, and Sony has about half that for their Playstation Portable (PSP). However, Apple's iPod Touch is growing at a faster rate than each of these devices and has a base of about thirty million users, and the iPhone an estimated twenty million (Wagner 2009).[2] Some forecasts suggest that in the next few years, the iPhone and iPod Touch will account for 24% of total handheld games sold (Graft 2009). In fact, the iPhone has shown mobile phone developers that it is the applications, not the hardware, that will drive mobile sales in the future (El Akkad 2009).

The audience for mobile gaming is incredibly diverse. Currently, the Asia Pacific region dominates the market for mobile games at about 38% of the market-share, with Europe following at about 31% and North America 22% (the rest of the world making up the remainder).[3] Statistics on gender from 2005 show a near even distribution of women and men playing mobile games, although males tend to play for longer lengths of time, and men tended to download more games (67% of downloads) (*The Online Reporter* 2005). However, more recent reports suggest that this is changing, and that women now account for more than half of mobile game purchases (Hetherington 2008). Likewise, Nintendo DS reported a near even split on sales to women and men in 2008, and has begun targeting women with pink hardware, as well as advertising aimed at female gamers, such as the "I Play for Me" campaign that used Liv Tyler and Carrie Underwood (O'Connor and Breckon 2009).

# THE BIRTH OF DIGITAL HANDHELD GAMES

Before delving into a history of digital handheld games, it is worth mentioning a few pre-digital precursors. Some of the concepts that were and still are a part of the handheld game console market—particularly the way that users interact with the devices—can be found in much older non-electronic toys and games. Small mechanical wind-up clockwork tableau, other clock-work toys in the late nineteenth century, and later electric toys introduced elements of player interactivity with some form of built-in animated, automatic (mechanical or electro-mechanical) response. More recently,

*Etch-A-Sketch* introduced an interface resembling a handheld television with a screen and turning knobs (Ohio Art Company 1960) that brought the idea of a screen-based toy to children.[4] The *Tickle Bee* (Endless Games 1956) preschool game used magnets and a magnetic wand to guide a bee around through a park without getting "stung" (touching the edges), a game play element that has been mimicked often in the Nintendo DS touch-screen stylus, for instance in mini-games incorporated into the latest *Zelda* game, *Phantom Hourglass* (Nintendo 2007). At times, some spring-driven or mechanical handheld toys like handheld pinball machines and automata would have had small bells or, later, piezo-electric buzzers and beepers, but the real contribution made was the tools or devices of player interaction in a handheld device, including winding keys, wands, turning knobs and buttons. The simple pleasure and tactility of these interactions undoubtedly helped to open up the market for the later digital games.

In addition to handhelds, of course, it is also necessary to point out that home video-game consoles and arcades were an important precursor to their mobile cousins. The Magnavox Odyssey, the Atari VCS, various *Pong* games, and popular arcade games helped to drive the desire for handhelds. Many of these early games were and still are reproduced in a handheld—Namco Bandai has re-released their classic games on the Nintendo DS (as Namco Museum DS 2008) and for various mobile phone platforms. Their list of top selling games currently includes *Pac-Man* (originally 1980), *Dig-Dug* (originally 1982) and *Galaga* (originally 1981).[5]

Finally, it is worth mentioning musical toys as precursors to the music-based and rhythm-action handheld games in particular. Although musical toys have existed since at least the eighteenth century with tiny bird-shaped whistles for children, the more likely precursors to music-based video games are 1960s toys like the Fisher-Price Giant Screen Music box TV of 1964, which played melodies while pictures scrolled across a small screen, and *Stylophone* (1967) and other pocket synthesizers and experimental synthesizer-based toys like General Electric's *Tote-A-Tune* (1971) and Ohio Art's *Sketch-a-Tune* (1975). It is also worth mentioning *Speak & Spell* and other electronic puzzle/learning games, some of whose ideas are found in games like Nintendo's *Brain Age*. Lastly, electronic virtual toys and pets like *Tamagotchi* cross over into the video game realm and have been adapted for new simulation animal games on the Nintendo DS. Of course, toys that make sound are always popular with children, and it's likely that the developers of the very first handheld games were well aware that the addition of sound would be an important element in the adoption and popularity of these devices, and help to distinguish them from existing portable electronics, which were largely confined at the time to business devices.

# EARLY DIGITAL HANDHELD GAMES

Mattel's LED-based *Auto Race*,[6] which came out in 1976, was the first all-electronic handheld videogame. Using a simple variation of a calculator chip, it had just 512 bytes of memory. Programmed by Mark Lesser, he noted in an interview, "The sound was implemented using a single output and a piezo-ceramic speaker—one output line to generate sounds and music, such as it was, without any sound driver hardware. The toggling of the speaker had to occur within the program loop, with variable timing to produce tones" (Stilphen n.d.). What this means was that the speaker itself was a simple tone generator. The frequency of a tone, measured in Hertz, is the cycles per second of a waveform. To generate a 10 Hz tone through a speaker, a waveform can be created by toggling a voltage wave ten times per second. For a 2000 Hz tone, the wave would need to be toggled at 2000 times per second. In other words, the speaker, sometimes referred to as a "beeper" or "bipper," could only make one tone at a time and in only a primitive fashion. Games, therefore, would have simple beeping sounds, or basic monophonic melodies made out of these beeps for just a few notes at a time. Although *Auto Race* may have been the first, it was Mattel's *Football* game of 1978 that was probably Mattel's most popular seller. Right from these early days, sound was nearly always used as a selling point. A description in the 1978 Mattel Toy Fair Catalogue advertised, "Cut back, avoid tacklers, run for daylight! Score and hear the Victory Sound!" (83). *Football II*, released the following year, boasted "Simulated game sounds include whistle and the victory tune for those hard-fought touchdowns and field goals" (Mattel Toy Fair Catalogue 1979:95). A simple monophonic melody of six notes was about all the game's processor could handle for its theme song. Although these early Mattel LED games primarily had just simple, quite abstract square wave and noise sound effects, a few did have such short melodies at the start or end of the game. *Missile Attack* (1976; later released as *Battlestar Galactica Space Alert*) for instance played "Taps" when the player lost.

Another toy company, Milton Bradley, was also quick to get in on the handheld market in the late 1970s with their LCD Microvision, which had been designed by Jay Smith, previously the creator of the Vectrex home console game system. The most significant difference between the Microvision and Mattel's predecessors was that the handheld could use interchangeable cartridges of games such as *Star Trek: Phaser Strike*, *Bowling*, and *Pinball*. Like the Mattel systems, sound was created with a piezoelectric speaker beeper, and was limited to simple sound effects of hisses and buzzes, with the occasional very brief monophonic melody at best.

Taking advantage of the basic sound capabilities of early handhelds, Atari was one of the first to release an electronic musical-memory game with their *Touch Me*, released as a coin-operated arcade machine in 1974 and later as a handheld in 1978. *Touch Me*'s original 1974 flyer discussed the use of sound: " 'Beep' or 'Bleep'? *Touch Me* challenges the player to remember the sequence of sight and sound, and correctly repeat the pattern.... When the sound occurs, the corresponding button lights to give a visual clue.... Did you correctly repeat those sounds when the button lit?"[7] There were four colored buttons that lit up, and four tones on the machine whose patterns would get progressively more difficult. Ralph Baer recalled:

> I was in Chicago attending an MOA (Music Operators of America) show of coin-op devices. I went to these shows routinely on Sanders' and Magnavox's behalf to check

on the presence of games that might infringe our patents, for which Magnavox was our primary licensee. Atari had several coin-op units at the show. One of these was 'Touch-Me'.... Howard Morrison also saw 'Touch Me' and played it.... Some time later, we discussed the game. We both came to the same conclusion: Nice game idea, terrible execution... visually lousy, miserable sounds! (n.d.)

*Touch Me* did not catch on, however, until it was redesigned by Baer for Milton Bradley and released as *Simon* in 1977. Similar to *Touch Me*, each button on *Simon* had a corresponding sound and color, and increasingly difficult melodies had to be memorized. This time, Baer improved on the sounds, as he describes here:

I took on the job of selecting the four tones, which was a non-trivial matter because the tones actually define much of *Simon's* character. Looking through my kid's Compton Encyclopedia for an instrument that can play a variety of tunes with only four notes, I found what I was looking for: The bugle! Henceforth, *Simon* was programmed to beep G, C, E and G...the bugle sounds that can be played in any sequence and still sound pleasant! (n.d.)

*Simon,* of course, perhaps because of its improvement over *Touch Me's* tones, became a huge success. In the wake of *Simon's* sales, a wave of copy-cat games followed, including *Super Simon* (a two-player version by Milton Bradley in 1980), Parker Brothers' *Merlin* (1978), the Tiger *Copy Cat* (1979), and Castle's *Einstein* (1979). More complex was the *Logix T.E.A.M.M.A.T.E* (Parker Bros 1980), a tabletop console, which had a speaker and a primitive sequencer that allowed the user to create their own melodies, described in a November 1980 *Consumer Reports* magazine: "By way of introduction to this musical entertainment, the toy provides a preprogrammed version of 'Oh, Susanna'. It didn't really encourage us to proceed, since it was rhythmically faulty. Persevering, though, we found music-writing rather a challenge—at first. But we became frustrated when our laborious compositions were erased when the toy was turned off" (655).[8] *Simon* had perhaps paved the way for the success of handheld electronic games, proving to toy manufacturers that handhelds could enjoy tremendous profits. It is interesting that *Simon,* one of the most popular early handheld games, was sound-based. While other games rarely yet had an off switch for the sound, sound was nevertheless often treated like an afterthought, and certainly played second fiddle to graphics. *Simon* managed to propel sound to the forefront of the handheld gaming industry for a time. Finally, handheld manufacturers realized the important role that sound could play in games, and the technology was soon to enable the advance of sound beyond monophonic beeping.

As the video game industry's first wave of real successes propelled it beyond mere novelty and into homes with the rise of home consoles like the Atari VCS, the Intellivision and the Colecovision, handhelds also witnessed increasing sales and popularity. It was a company which was not yet a household name in the Western world that would introduce one of the most important early handheld systems: Nintendo. Nintendo's Game and Watch series, an LCD-based system featuring a clock timer and alarm (perhaps the first handheld game device to include non-game functions), went through a series of different incarnations. The first was the Silver series of 1980, with the game *Ball*. Other games could be had, including *Flagman, Vermin*, and *Fire*. The Gold version followed a year later, along with a widescreen version, and then a multi-screen in 1982. These games had a simple piezoelectric speaker, like the Microvision and Mattel handhelds, and so undemanding sound effects were the norm; sine-wave beeps of varying pitch and white noises used for crashing sounds, gunshots, and explosions. The first really significant change, however, was the Tabletop editions in 1983, with VFD color screens, and improved use of the simple beeper to include some minimal music. These were "mini arcade" consoles of single games and were soon copied or licensed by competitors. Coleco, for instance, licensed the popular *Donkey Kong* game from Nintendo. The manuals for the tabletop games often advertised that they played and sounded like the original arcade versions of games like *Frogger, Donkey Kong, Pac-Man*, and *Galaxian*, indicating that the goal was clearly to emulate the success of the arcade by mimicking (albeit in a more limited fashion) its game play, graphics, and sound. The games could manage monophonic square wave or sine wave music as introduction and game over music, but during gameplay it was still rare to have music, due to the demands of the music on the processor.

It is interesting to note that the *Consumer Reports* November 1980 report on these games mentions sound in a few cases, indicating that the sound played an important role even this early on, although its effectiveness was questionable. The description of Vanity Fair's *Computer Matician 3010* tabletop model for instance, which asked a series of math questions, included sound: "The correct answer elicits a high-pitched, repeating beep and the word "right" flashing at the top of the screen. An incorrect answer is punished by a penetrating low buzz and the word "wrong" flashing at the bottom of the screen...most of the children were unnerved and annoyed by the strident beeping and buzzing" (654). Indeed, it was the lack of an understanding of the use of sound as a feedback device that often led to the acoustic frustration of the early days. Since players could trigger the sounds, yet memory was limited, the sounds would repeat endlessly with often no control over volume. Moreover, the technology of the time meant that harsh, abstract square wave sounds and white noise were the norm when it came to sound, and though children may have enjoyed button-mashing to make noise, those around them rarely did.

The first to introduce cartridge-based handheld "tabletops" was the Entex Adventure Vision (Entex has previously made a variety of handheld tabletops like *Pac-Man* and *Galaxian*). It also improved sound quality over its predecessors, even including a headphone jack. Instructions for the hardware advertised, "Your Adventure Vision game unit has a special internal sound effects generator and a full speaker to furnish the user with full fidelity sound effects" (Entex Industries Inc. 1982). More critical to advancing sound capabilities was a new hardware advance: a sound co-processor chip.[9] The chip in the Adventure Vision was capable of creating pure tones of about an octave and a half (fifteen tones), as well as thirteen different sound effects created from noise. The chip, however, like that of the early Atari VCS home console was not precise, and the frequency could vary by about 15% (Boris 2005; Collins 2006). With these advances, it's perhaps not surprising, then, that along with hardware innovations came some important changes in the use of sound. Not merely sound effects, sound had a new function in requiring the listener to actively listen. *Electronic Games* magazine from July 1983 tells the player of Adventure Vision's *Super Cobra*, a game that resembled *Venture*: "Super Cobra makes use of a range of sound effects to enhance the play. Listen to these special tones since they frequently warn you of what type of enemy the helicopter will face next" (Electronic Games 1983:112). Of Adventure Vision's *Space Force*, the same guide notes "Pay close attention to the sound effects. The approach of alien ships are signaled by alien cannon fire. This alerts you to be prepared to shoot. Since the small spacecraft is worth 1000 points, you don't want to let it slip past you" (112). *Space Force*, however, was suspiciously similar in sound to the arcade game *Asteroids*, with a simple two-note descending A to B-flat repeated motif, with very similar laser-like space ship sounds. On the other hand, perhaps for the first time in handheld sound, the sound *effects* became an integral part of the game experience, and turning sound off (as was capable on the Adventure Vision though not most of its predecessors) could be detrimental to game play. As sound played more important alerting functions in games, sound was less likely to be turned off by the player, and on-going advances followed to improve quality of sound through headphones and speaker, and the rise of dedicated sound chips.

# The Game Boy and Dedicated Sound Chips in Handhelds

The Nintendo Game Boy was a significant advance in handheld game sound, having a dedicated polyphonic sound chip.[10] The original system was released in 1989, and it went through several changes (Pocket in 1996, Light in 1997, Color in 1998), eventually selling over 100 million units. Though each of the models improved upon the graphics and increasingly streamlined the hardware, the sound remained the same until the Game Boy Advance. Also, although the sound chip was similar to that of the Nintendo Entertainment System home console, the Game Boy had a very distinct sound, which is perhaps one of the reasons why it has been so popular with chiptune musicians. The chip had three 4-bit semi-analog tone channels and one noise channel pseudo-stereo programmable sound generator. The first channels were square waves, which were commonly used for chords or melody. There were four duty cycle options for the square waves, which set the timbre of the wave sound (12.5%, 25%, 50%, and 75%). The first channel had volume and frequency sweep, while the second was limited to volume control, which meant the first channel was more commonly used for melodies (Gevaryahu 2004). Channel three was a variable wave channel with 32 4-bit programmable samples, and was commonly used for bass-lines. Channel four was a white noise generator, most often used for percussion sounds. A simple 4-bit digital to analogue converter with high pass and low pass filter options output the sound to the amplifier. With Game Boy, therefore, polyphonic music could be created, and for the first time complete songs were heard during game play, such as in *Tetris*. Sound effects were still synthesized sounds, mostly from the white noise generator, however, and so Game Boy helped to create its own aesthetic, one which is still popular with chip-tune composers today.

The first major challenger to the Game Boy was the Atari Lynx, released the same year (1989). It was more expensive than the Game Boy, with an original US sales tag of $189.95 versus $90 for the Game Boy (*Console Passion* 2009), and so despite the advanced sound and graphics, did not fare as well in terms of consumer sales. The Lynx sound was controlled by the 16-bit CPU, although it had a separate sound engine and an 8-bit digital to analogue converter (DAC). There were four channels of 8-bit sound available (mono in its original, and stereo in a 1991 redesign). Each channel had a programmable base frequency, programmable sequence generator, volume control and a wave shape selector (including square, triangle, pseudo-random noise and sine waveforms). The Lynx could, like the Game Boy, handle polyphonic music and play background music during game play, but like the Game Boy, the sound effects were most often white noise. The documentation for the Lynx explains the choice of sound hardware:

What in the world were we thinking when we designed the sound hardware? The original design goals were that the circuits

1. Be cheap
2. Require relatively little CPU to make useful game noises
3. Have sufficient range and accuracy for tolerable music
4. Have four channels
5. Have direct access to the DACs
6. Be cheap (Domin and Schick 1987)

Clearly, then, cost was a primary driving factor for the sound technology. Music was at best an afterthought (note only the reference to the goal of "tolerable music"). In these early days of games, sound effects were viewed as more important than music, and the ways that sound could be used in games were not fully realized.

Even less successful commercially (likely due to its cost) though equally important in terms of advances in audio capabilities was the NEC Turbo Express, basically a portable version of the home console Turbografx16. In fact, the Turbo Express could play the home console cartridges (called Hucards), making it convenient for those who purchased the home version. It was, however, released at a prohibitively expensive original price-point ($250), and so despite advanced capabilities was not widely adopted. The Turbo Express featured a separate sound CPU (a Z80, popular in the arcades), and a six-channel programmable sound generator. Compared to other handhelds, therefore, the possibilities for polyphonic music were far superior. The first two channels were capable of simulating a low frequency oscillator to create FM-synthesis-like sounds. Channels five and six could generate noise and so were used frequently for sound effects. The channels could even use direct memory access to stream up to 10-bit sampled sound into any channel.

# HANDHELD GAME AUDIO IN THE 1990S

Sega's Game Gear was released in 1991 at a price of US$150, going backward in sound quality from the relatively progressive six-channel PSG of the Turbo Express. The Game Gear was fairly successful despite the lesser sound capabilities, partly due to the large repertoire of games at Sega's disposal. The console featured a simple Texas Instruments SN76489 programmable sound generator.[11] This sound chip had been popular in the arcades in the early 1980s, and was the same chip found in the ColecoVision, and BBC Micro.[12] It had three channels of square wave sound generators, one noise generator, and output to a mono speaker (stereo sound could be had via headphones). Although Game Gear's sonic capabilities did not represent an advance, its reduced price, along with Sega's large catalogue of games, ensured the success of the handheld.

Sega improved on the Game Gear's sound with the 1995 release of their Nomad, a handheld version of the popular Genesis/MegaDrive. This included the same SN76489 chip, but it was peripheral to the main sound chip, a Yamaha YM2612 FM synthesis chip that had six channels of digitized stereo sound, and one PCM 8-bit sample channel (the same chip used in the popular Yamaha DX27 and DX100 music keyboards). Just as on the Genesis, instrument sounds and sound effects had to be coded by hand in a cumbersome format, and thus sounds and instruments were used many times in different games to save coding new ones. Each FM channel had four "operators" (waveforms) assigned, each with a frequency and an envelope with which to modify the input. Operator One (the oscillator, or carrier wave) could feed back into itself, creating a more complex waveform, and thus, a different instrument sound. The other operators served as modulating waveforms (known as "slots"). The oscillator would produce a basic sine-wave tone, and the modulators could then affect the output waveform, altering the complexity of the waveform, and therefore, its timbre. There were eight different algorithmic configurations of these four operators, presented with suggested instrument uses in Sega's technical manual. Although they could be used for other instrument sounds, these suggested sounds became the most common. The result of the assembly programming and the eight algorithms meant that many of the same types of sounds were used over and over in games. Typically, one channel handled percussion, one bass, one melody, and others were used for filler chords, or arpeggios. The multiple channels were also used to create various effects, including phasing and double tracking (Collins 2008:40).

Although Sega and Nintendo were the clear leaders in the handheld market in the 1990s, there were a few other systems that had some moderate success. The SNK Neo Geo Pocket and Pocket Color of 1998–1999, a 16-bit handheld version of the Neo Geo home console, with essentially two of the SN76489 chips seen on the Game Gear, but with just 4 kB of RAM available for the sound processor (a Z80) to access, and as a result was similar to the Game Gear in its use of music and sound. The Bandai Wonderswan series, designed by Nintendo's Game Boy creator Gunpei Yokoi, released in 1999–2000 with a four-channel digital sound chip also attempted to nudge in on the handheld market without much success, although it managed to exclusively license the *Final Fantasy* games for a time, leading to some moderate sales in Japan.

It was to be the successor to Yokoi's popular Game Boy that would dominate the handheld market for a time. The Game Boy Advance, released in 2001, was the first of the Game Boy series to upgrade the sound, by adding two 8-bit DACs to the original configuration. Not only the hardware, but the software was also improved: the Advance BIOS contained many sound-related functions for converting MIDI to Game Boy data, although it is worth noting that Nintendo did not even bother to release information about sound in their press release specifications, suggesting that sound was not considered as relevant on handheld games as it was on home consoles.

# CURRENT POPULAR HANDHELD
# GAME CONSOLES

The Nintendo DS (and later DS Lite and DSi) was originally released in 2004 with a few very innovative ideas integrated, including built-in WiFi, microphone, and the DS stylus. The DS has virtual surround sound and a sixteen-channel Direct Memory Access sound chip. The DS has also become a popular sound toy and has a wide series of home-brewed music software available. These include sequencers such as *BlipTracker, Nitrotracker, DSstep, glitchDS, DStar*; samplers such as *Protein[DS], repeaterDS*, and *Sampling Keyboard*; and synthesizers, including *Midipad, Soundcells, Monome DS, KaosDS* (which converts X/Y touch-screen information into synthesized sound), and *Pulse DS* (which can use the DS's PSG chip to produce sounds similar to Game Boy).[13] What is unique about the DS is the use of the stylus, and thus the Kaos pad can be treated much like a *Stylophone*.

There are also several notable uses of sound in DS games, including in the *Legend of Zelda: Phantom Hourglass* (music by Kenta Nagata and Toru Minegishi; sound effects by Toru Asakawa and Sanae Susaki). The game features several places where the user is required to make noise (via the microphone) in order to advance, even at one place having to shout at the machine. Sound has, therefore, become an input device for some recent games.

Another innovative game in which sound plays an important role is *Electroplankton*, a kind of art-piece by media artist Toshio Iwai, who is the creator of a new handheld instrument by Yamaha called Tenori-on. When players draw on the *Electroplankton* game screen, plankton react and create unusual sounds. A rather Brian Eno-esque ambient soundscape is created as a result. One mini-game inside *Electroplankton* called *Beatnes* uses tracks from Nintendo's early NES games, such as *Super Mario Bros*, and allows the user to "remix" these tracks in real time by adjusting the plankton to make the sound effects from the game over the music.

The Sony PlayStation Portable (PSP) was originally released in 2004 and remains the primary competitor to Nintendo's DS. More a full multimedia device than merely a game machine, the PSP is designed for music and movie playback, and so supports Dolby 7.1 multi-channel sound and integrated stereo speakers. Because the PSP supports MP3 and MP4 playback, there are fewer limitations in terms of audio capabilities for games beyond the memory/CPU footprint. It even has a built-in equalizer for music playback. Although not quite as popular for music-makers as the DS, the PSP does have a few music-making options, including a homebrew wireless X/Y MIDI and mouse control with software to control music sequencing software Ableton Live from the PSP called *playLive*. There is also *PSPSeq*, another Ableton Live controller, and *PSP Rhythm*. The rise of popularity in music-based applications in particular has meant that handheld devices are increasingly improving sound technology for the devices. This is particularly the case with the recent explosion of rhythm-action games, which are helping to drive improvements in sound technologies and interface devices for handhelds.

# RHYTHM-ACTION GAMES ON HANDHELDS

Rhythm-action games, in which the player must directly interact with the music and/or sound as the main game play element, to some extent have been incorporated into some other types of video games—in several of the *Legend of Zelda* games for the Game Boy Advance, for instance, the player is required to memorize short melodies and play them back (*Ocarina of Time*), or have their character "dance" to various rhythms (*Oracle of Ages*, Nintendo 2001). Full rhythm-action games have become far more popular in the wake of the success of *Guitar Hero* and *Rock Band. Guitar Hero*, of course, has been released for the DS as *Guitar Hero: On Tour* (Activision 2008), which used a special add-on hardware unit called the Guitar Grip. *Elite Beat Agents* (for the Nintendo DS 2006), a sequel to the Japanese-only *Ouendon*, had a similar concept, asking players to tap the screen with the stylus according to the beat of a song. Cross-over music training games have also been released, including *Rhythm N' Notes* (Agetec, Inc. 2007), offering tonal and rhythmic music training.

The PSP also has a series of rhythm-action games, including *Gitaroo Man Lives!* (Koei 2006), a game of bizarre brilliance that uses the PSP stick to mimic pitch shifting on a guitar. *Lumines* (Q Entertainment 2004) is a popular puzzle game based on patterns of sound and light, created by Tetsuya Mizuguchi, who was behind the innovative music-based *Rez* game for the Playstation. A block-like game vaguely similar to *Tetris, Lumines* (pronounced "luminous") integrated the music right into the game play. Blocks move in time to the beat, and elements of game play change the music (which includes Japanese acid jazz stars like Mondo Grosso) as you play. Moving or rotating blocks or creating combinations add layers of sound to the soundtrack in real time. Another highly notable rhythm-action game for the PSP is *Patapon* (Sony 2007), a 2D platform action-adventure in which players must use musical beats to lead tribal armies. Different drumbeats are used to signal marching, defending, retreating, and attacking.[14]

A very recent interesting development in the handheld rhythm-action genre is the incorporation of user-generated playlists into rhythm-action games by pulling a user's MP3 files off the device, turning their playlist into an interactive music game. Harmonix (who created *Guitar Hero*) developed a game called *Phase* for the iPod Touch to do precisely this. The complexity of the music maps in the game, therefore, can depend on the type of music the user listens to, and there is a never-ending possibility of new game play.

# Crossing Over into Mobile Phone Territory

Before delving into mobile phone/personal digital assistant (smart phone) gaming, it is worth taking a minute to examine a few systems that attempted to bring together phone or smart phone capabilities to gaming systems. These game systems all failed to achieve any degree of success and with the arrival of smartphones are likely to never be attempted again. Tiger Electronics' game.com system released in 1997 was perhaps the first game console aimed at an older audience. It featured a touch screen and stylus like the smart phone systems of the time and could be connected to a modem (although it was limited to text-only access to the Web). Only a few games were ever released for the system, although some of its innovations were incorporated into the Nintendo DS. Nokia similarly achieved little success with their N-Gage, released in 2003. It was essentially a game system with cell phone functionality, MP3 playback, and Bluetooth connectivity. What is interesting about the N-Gage is that Nokia (previously a phone company) attempted to get in on the gaming market by launching their own gaming division, producing a few games and licensing some other successful games. Tiger Telematics (not to be confused with Tiger Electronics) also tried to bring smart phone functionality to a game system with the Gizmondo in 2005. The Gizmondo had GPS, Bluetooth, and WiFi, but unfortunately the system was so unsuccessful the company was forced to file for bankruptcy.

# Mobile Phone Games

The history of mobile phone games (distinguished from handheld gaming in that games are not the primary intended use of the machines) in many ways echoes the history of consoles and handhelds. The earliest mobile phone game, *Snake*, written by Taneli Armanto on the Nokia 6110 in 1997, was black and white and lacked sound. The phone also featured basic *Memory* and *Logic* games. These games were originally installed on phones by the phone companies, but are now commonly purchased through mobile networks or through internet download. Furthermore, mobile phones are increasingly becoming small computers, known as smartphones, allowing for more complex games, and opening up a whole new market in the mobile game territory.

One of the most important elements of mobile gaming has been network capabilities. Even many early games had multiplayer modes, so simple games like checkers could be played with live competitors. Real-time network play on mobile phones has become increasingly popular, particularly with games like *Bejeweled Multiplayer* (Jamdat 2006). Some games can also interface with their PC counterparts, such as *Ragnarok Mobile Mage* (Skyzone Mobile 2006), so players can continue their game after they have left their house.

Mobile gaming is rapidly becoming an important part of the games industry as the technology converges, with publishers like Jamdat joining forces with Electronic Arts. Some companies that have been in the business a long time are now re-releasing their classic arcade games for the mobile community, such as Namco, Capcom, Konami, and Vivendi Games.

Mobile games today are increasing at a tremendous rate. However, considering that one of the purposes of such devices is to communicate through sound, it is ironic that audio capabilities lag behind graphics. Many of the same difficulties and constraints that plagued early computer games have been seen in the mobile game audio world. Audio resources on some phones can be as small as 100 kB, and as such, many of the same techniques of the 8-bit era have been reproduced to save space. As ringtone composer Peter Drescher elaborated a few years ago, "The most important trick is to be as ruthlessly efficient as possible. You want to squeeze every last drop of variation out of each and every byte of audio data at your disposal. Repetition is the enemy, compression is your ally, and creative use of limited resources is your battle cry" (2006). A developer at Glu Mobile elaborates: "The challenge with mobile games is that we have sound size limitations... While we don't use voice actors, we do use music a lot. We have to think about what will take up the majority of space. We have to think about the visuals and the sound—what will create the richer experience" (Hetherington 2008). A constant balance is struck, therefore, between what is needed and what can be technically accomplished.

This problem with technological constraints is rapidly changing as phones move into the smartphone territory and MP3 sampling for the games. The Apple iPhone for instance can record and play back audio in a variety of formats. Many popular games for the iPhone are old games revisited, including *Tetris* (Electronic Arts), Sega *Columns, Ms Pac-Man*, and *Frogger*. Of course, there are also many other games available. Rhythm-action games like *Guitar Rock Tour* and *Tap Tap Revenge* have also been released. But along with traditional games have also come a series of very innovative changes to the nature of games that grew out of the technology. *Soul Trapper Episode 1*, for example, is a game from Realtime Audio Adventures, a kind of cross between a radio drama and old-fashioned Choose Your Own Adventure game. The company promises "Realtime Audio Adventures take your mind deeply into the spectrums of sound and imagination for a truly unique gaming experience."[15] David Warhol, who runs the company, noted "Everyone seems to appreciate that we pulled out all the stops to make the audio as compelling as possible" (*iPhone Footprint* 2008). Despite the desire for good audio, though, hardware limitations in terms of processing power and memory remain. *Soul Trapper*, for instance, is an enormous 264 MB, a massive download size for a phone. The result means heavily compressed samples that significantly reduce sound fidelity. In other cases, some platforms don't support simultaneous layering of audio tracks, meaning there can be sound effects or music, but not both at the same time.

The iPhone and iPod Touch have more recently become musical instruments with the development of sequencers and sound tools/sound toys. *Looptastic* and *Sound Warp* (both by Sound Trends) for instance, allow users to mix loops, manipulate sound effects, record music, and play back songs. Perhaps even more interesting is, due to the accelerometer available on the device, the development of gestural music applications, like *Bravo Gustavo*, a conductor game in which the player swings the phone, released by the LA Philharmonic.

Despite a seeming desire, then, at least amongst some companies, to create quality audio for mobile games, even as the technology catches up, there are still distinct differences between mobile games and home console counterparts. Mobile audio has different requirements than other games due to the casual nature of the games—people playing mobile games are, at present, primarily using their phone to play games while they "kill time," and games are secondary to the other functions of these machines. Nokia's guide to sound for phone games, for instance, warns, "The game should be playable without the sounds. Allow silent starting of games. If intro music is implemented, there must be a way to switch it off. Prompt for sound settings at the start of the game....Do not include loud or high-pitched sounds, have sounds on as the default, [or] use sounds that are similar to ring tones and alert tones" (Nokia Corporation 2005).

Some mobile games do not even include sound or have minimal sound effects at best. *Fieldrunners,* an iPod/iPhone game listed by *Time* magazine as one of the top 10 mobile games of 2008, did not initially have any sound, although the 1.1 upgrade included sound effects and a theme song (Grossman 2008). One article on game sound for the iPhone asks, "Can you hear that? Probably not, if like most gamers you flick the silent switch on your iPhone before playing a game. Of the hundreds of games populating the App Store, few earn the prestigious honour of having the volume turned up" (Erickson 2008). Magmic's Joshua Ostrowalker described to me: "The first thing you want is a screen that gives the options to turn on or off the sound."[16] It is interesting, then, that there is a growing number of audio-based and rhythm-action games for the mobile phone market. It appears that as gaming on phones increases, people are more inclined to carry around headphones to play games and use sound.

# THE FUTURE OF HANDHELD GAME AUDIO

Now that smartphone mobile games are at about the same technical level as gaming handhelds, the desire for better mobile audio is increasing. Where previously games on mobile phones could get away with little or no audio, the demand for better games—and better game audio—on mobiles is increasing as these platforms converge. Nevertheless, there remain some difficulties and constraints that are holding back audio advancements on both handhelds and mobiles.

One significant problem primarily affecting mobiles but also affecting handhelds is the lack of standards between devices. For game developers, this means generally focusing on a single manufacturer or platform, thus shrinking their potential market size. Developers of iPhone games, for instance, cannot easily convert these games to work on a Blackberry, just as PSP games cannot be easily ported to the Nintendo DS. Another significant problem is size of audio files, particularly for mobile games, since these games are downloaded rather than cartridge-based and, therefore, players may not want to pay for the bandwidth or be able to download the massive file sizes required.

There have also been several advances that have come in the last year or so that will help to make handheld and mobile video games a much better audio experience. Mobile DLS (Downloadable Sounds) is a standardization specification that defines a wavetable instrument format for mobiles. This is essentially a sound bank of instruments for MIDI enabled devices that improve sound quality of MIDI for mobiles. Packaged with Mobile DLS is usually Mobile XMF (eXtensible Music Format), another specification that enables users to use sampled sounds without large file sizes by bundling Mobile DLS sounds into one file (MIDI Manufacturer's Association 2008). There are also DSP (sound processing) capabilities in some systems now, with the result that simulating environments in games is becoming easier with reverb and other effects. Finally, there is also the use of 3D positional audio in headphones which will also give the games a sense of space or environment by creating the illusion that sound are emanating from or heading to anywhere in the three-dimensional space.[17]

Perhaps most importantly, mobile game systems offer some advantages for unique gameplay. Location-aware technologies such as GPS have led to location-based mobile multiplayer games, for instance, in which social interaction, virtual game worlds, and real locations merge, as well as augmented reality games that combine the real world with a game world.[18] Customized content based on player location can be integrated into a game, and alternate reality games have been created that require the player to take photographs of particular locations and upload these to the game, relying further on functionality of smartphone devices.

## Notes

1. While experts chosen for these predictions may be from dubiously biased sources (with the industry often hyping itself), thus far the predictions have been on the conservative side, and all indications are that the mobile market will continue to grow at a rapid rate.
2. The iPhone sales number is an estimate based on quarterly sales numbers. Allegedly, there have been fifty million iPod Touch and iPhone sales combined. See also Norris (2009).

3. These are estimates based on projected revenues. See: "Global Mobile Games Market to reach $17bn by 2011" (2006), and "Projected Mobile Gaming Revenues in North America, Europe and Asia Pacific" (2008).

4. It is interesting to note that *Etch-A-Sketch* has more recently converged with the game market and released digital games, with sound effects, such as *Etch-A-Sketch: Knobby's Quest* game for PC and Mac.

5. From the Namco Mobile website, https://www.namcogames.com/mobile/ (accessed March 11, 2009).

6. Not relevant to our discussion of sound, but an LED is an array of light-emitting diodes, whereas an LCD is a liquid crystal display. A VFD, mentioned later, is a Vacuum Flourescent display, closer in technology to LEDs than LCDs. LEDs and VFDs are familiar to consumers through VCR and microwave displays, digital clocks and watches, and so on.

7. For a copy of the flyer, see http://www.atarihq.com/dedicated/touchme.php (access March 11, 2009).

8. Elements of this section are drawn from Collins (2008).

9. A National Semiconductor COP411 4-bit microcontroller with 512 bytes of internal ROM and 32 4-bit internal RAM locations.

10. Technically, it is referred to as a PAPU, a pseudo-audio-processing unit. It is not a separate circuit or unit from the main processor, although for programming purposes it is separate.

11. An emulator to convert Sega MOD files to PSG sound using this chip can be found on the Kontechs website, http://mod2psg.kontechs.de/ (accessed March 11, 2009).

12. See Collins (2008:15).

13. See *Synthopia* (2008).

14. A playable web version "Beat Camp" demo is on http://www.patapon-game.com/ (accessed March 11, 2009).

15. From the Real Time Audio Adventures website, http://www.rtaudioadventures.com/About.html (accessed March 11, 2009).

16. Joshua Ostrowalker, interview with author, Ottawa, Ontario, October 14, 2009.

17. See Curtes (2007).

18. See Vanhanen (2008).

## References

Baer, Ralph H. n.d. "The Simon Story," http://www.dieterkoenig.at/ccc/english/se_story_simon.htm (accessed March 11, 2009).

Boris, Daniel. 2005. "Entex Adventurevision Technical Specs V1.2," http://www.atarihq.com/danb/files/AdvTechSpecs.pdf (accessed March 11, 2009).

Casual Games Association. 2007. "2007 Casual Games Market Report," http://www.casual-gamesassociation.org/research_news.php (accessed October 20, 2009).

Collins, Karen. 2006. "Flat Twos and the Musical Aesthetic of the Atari VCS." Popular Musicology Online, http://www.popular-musicology-online.com/ (accessed March 11, 2009).

——. 2008. *Game Sound: An Introduction to the History, Theory and Practice of Video Game Music and Sound Design.* Cambridge: MIT Press.

*Console Passion.* 2009. "Atari Lynx." http://www.consolepassion.co.uk/atari-lynx.htm (accessed October 13, 2009).

Curtes, Mike. 2007. "Editorial: Why Mobile Games Need Better Audio," *Games on Deck*, http://www.gamesondeck.com/feature/1516/editorial_why_mobile_games_need_.php (accessed March 11, 2009).

Domin, M. and Schick, Bastian. 1987. "Lynx-Documentation," http://www.geocities.com/SiliconValley/Byte/4242/lynx/lynxdoc.html (accessed March 11, 2009).

Drescher, Peter. 2006. "Could Mobile Game Audio BE More Annoying?!" O'Reilly Digital Media, http://digitalmedia.oreilly.com/2006/04/26/could-mobile-game-audio-be-more-annoying.html (accessed March 11, 2009).

Duryee, Tricia. 2008. "U.S. Mobile Game Industry Worth $1 Billion; Will Soar to $6.8 Billion in 2013," *Moco News Net*, October 15, http://www.moconews.net/entry/419-us-mobile-game-industry-worth-1-billion-will-soar-to-68-billion-in-2013/ (accessed March 11, 2009).

El Akkad, Omar. 2009. "Apple, RIM wage app wars," *Globe and Mail*, October 18, http://www.theglobeandmail.com/report-on-business/apple-rim-wage-app-wars/article1328535/ (accessed October 22, 2009).

Electronic Games. 1983. "Stand-Alone Preview." *Handheld Museum*, http://www.handheldmuseum.com/BooksMagazines/Mag-EG_0783/EG0783_16.htm (accessed March 11, 2009).

Entex Industries Inc. 1982. "Adventure Vision (original manual)," http://zappa.brainiac.com/cdyer/instructions/adv.pdf (accessed March 11, 2009).

Erickson, Tracy. 2008. "Sound off: iPhone gaming's audio problem," Pocket Gamer, http://www.pocketgamer.co.uk/r/iPhone/iPhone/feature.asp?c=10446 (accessed March 11, 2009).

Gevaryahu, Jonathan. 2004. "Nintendo(TM) Gameboy sound system (PAPU) guide," http://www.joshuawise.com/~nightmare/GBSOUND.txt (accessed March 11, 2009).

"Global Mobile Games Market to reach $17bn by 2011." 2006. *Indiantelevision.com*, July 10, http://www.indiantelevision.com/headlines/y2k6/july/july87.htm (accessed October 3, 2009).

Graft, Kris. 2009. "Analyst: iPhone To Drive Mobile Game Market Sales To $11.7 Billion By 2014," *Gamasutra*, October 22, http://www.gamasutra.com/php-bin/news_index.php?story=25766 (accessed October 23, 2009).

Grossman, Lev. 2008. "The Top 10 Everything of 2008." *Time Magazine*, November 3, http://www.time.com/time/specials/2008/top10/article/0,30583,1855948_1863763_1863777,00.html (accessed March 11, 2009).

Hetherington, Janet. 2008. "Upwardly Mobile Gaming," http://www.awn.com/articles/gaming/upwardly-mobile-gaming (accessed October 23, 2009).

IGDA Casual Games Special Interest Group. 2006. "2006 Casual Games White Paper," http://www.igda.org/casual/IGDA_CasualGames_Whitepaper_2006.pdf (accessed October 20, 2009).

*iPhone Footprint*. 2008. "Sound of Joy: Audio Content and iPhone Games." November 30, http://www.iphonefootprint.com/2008/11/sound-of-joy-audio-content-and-iphone-games/ (accessed March 11, 2009).

Mattel Toy Fair Catalogue. 1978. *Handheld Museum*, http://www.handheldmuseum.com/Mattel/Cat1978/1978Cat3.htm (accessed March 11, 2009).

——. 1979. *Handheld Museum*, http://www.handheldmuseum.com/Mattel/Mattel1979/Mattel79_5.htm (accessed March 11, 2009).

MIDI Manufacturer's Association. 2008. "About DLS Format for Mobile Devices," http://www.midi.org/about-midi/dls/abtmdls.shtml (accessed March 11, 2009).

Nokia Corporation. 2005. "From Beeps to Soundscapes: Designing Mobile Game Audio," http://sw.nokia.com/id/e2b3d80a-5ea7-453b-978e-1814310b4639/From_

Beeps_To_Soundscapes_Designing_Mobile_Game_Audio_v1_0_en.pdf    (accessed March 11, 2009).

Norris, Ashley. 2009. "Two Billion Apps Downloaded, 50 million iPhone/touches sold—landmark day for Apple," *Tech Digest*, September 28. http://www.techdigest.tv/2009/09/two_billion_app.html (accessed October 23, 2009).

O'Connor, Alice, and Nick Breckon. 2009. "Nintendo DS Reaching Gender Harmony," *ShackNews*, March 25, http://www.shacknews.com/onearticle.x/57838 (accessed October 23, 2009).

*The Online Reporter*. 2005. "Men twice as likely to download mobile games but game play is gender neutral." May 21, http://www.theinternetpatrol.com/males-are-twice-as-likely-to-download-a-game-than-women (accessed October 20, 2009).

"Projected Mobile Gaming Revenues in North America, Europe and Asia Pacific." 2008. *GoRumors.com*, March 5, http://techcrunchies.com/projected-mobile-gaming-revenues-in-north-america-europe-and-asia-pacific/ (accessed October 3, 2009).

Stilphen, Scott. n.d. "DP Interviews Mark Lesser," *Digitpress*, http://www.digitpress.com/library/interviews/interview_mark_lesser.html

*Synthopia*. 2008. "24 Nintendo DS Music Programs." June 30, http://www.synthtopia.com/content/2008/06/30/24-nintendo-ds-music-programs/ (accessed March 11, 2009).

Vanhanen, Anssi. 2008. "Mobile Games Business." In *Topical Evolution Paths of Mobile Multimedia Services: Proceedings of the Research Seminar on Telecommunications Business (ed. Sakari Luukkainen) Helsinki University of Technology Publications in Telecommunications Software and Multimedia*, http://www.tml.hut.fi/Opinnot/T-109.7510/2007/Proceedings_2007.pdf (accessed March 11, 2009).

Wagner, James Au. 2009. "iPod Touch Cutting Into Handheld Game Market, Top Analyst Says." *The Apple Blog*, August 12, http://theappleblog.com/2009/08/12/ipod-touch-cutting-into-handheld-game-market-top-analyst-says/ (accessed October 12, 2009).

# CHAPTER 16

# THE CHIPTUNING OF THE WORLD: GAME BOYS, IMAGINED TRAVEL, AND MUSICAL MEANING

## CHRIS TONELLI

Structure and mobility are opposites—in the realm of the imagination as in so many others. It is easier to describe forms than motion, which is why psychology has begun with forms. Motion, however, is the more important. In a truly complete psychology, imagination is primarily a kind of spiritual mobility of the greatest, liveliest, and most exhilarating kind.

—Gaston Bachelard ([1943] 1988:2)

*Little Sound DJ* brought trackers into the mainstream and the Game Boy came to be a popular symbol for the art of chip music composing and performance.

—Anders Carlsson (2008:159)

GASTON Bachelard's *Air and Dreams* questioned and attempted to expand the ways we understand motion. In his thinking about poetry and embodiment he asked: Can we be mobile while our bodies are perfectly motionless? His answer was a qualified yes. Insisting that spiritual mobility was not to be trivialized as a metaphor for movement, Bachelard argued for what he called the "realism of unreality" ([1943] 1988:5) and chastised those who were quick to draw distinctions between the "real" and the "imagined."[1]

This chapter is an attempt to theorize the ways in which real mobility and imagined mobility participate in the articulation of meaning with sounds, but it is also an attempt to employ this theorization to examine the aesthetics of a music scene fueled by a portable gaming device, the Nintendo Game Boy.[2] In the musicologies, articulation is often thought of only in terms of the union of the discursive with the sounds of music. In this chapter, however, I take "imagined" movement as a form of meaning that is articulated with the sounds of music, and argue that Bachelard's observations on mobility and his correction of errors in our thinking about motion have implications for understanding music. The scene I am concerned with here, known as the chip music or the chiptune scene, is significant for many reasons, including the unique dynamics of its transnationalism, the ways it misuses commercial technology, and the ravenous aesthetic of re-presentation it champions.[3] Though I will comment on the issues of transnationalism and misuse of commercial technology, its aesthetic of re-presentation will be my main concern.

From re-presentations of classic jazz albums, to pieces from the Western art music canon, to popular music both "commercial" and "underground," chip music's aesthetic of re-presentation is uniquely far-reaching in what it incorporates. Many popular musical practices are invested in an aesthetic of re-presentation, but few compare to the almost imperialist spirit chip music brings to the practice. I want to think through this "imperialist" spirit and argue that it is structurally connected to the incidental effect portable gaming had in transforming the way gamers experienced public space. I will try to argue that recognition of such a connection is warranted, that the sudden and radical ability placed, quite literally, into the hands of gamers to rearticulate public space with the sounds of gaming marked those sounds as tools of transformation. In an initial stage, I will argue, those sounds acted on public space in a libratory manner, articulating the materiality of that space with the pleasure and imagined mobility of the gamer. Following this, and, in some sense, because of this, I will contend, chip musicians used these same sounds not just to create, but to transform.

## DYNAMIC INDUCTIONS

Bachelard's discussion of spiritual mobility, which he also referred to as dynamic induction, came out of his attempt to understand the experiential aspects of poetry reading. He was interested in the ways different uses of language would or would not cause a state of spiritual motion in their readers. The term *induction* was meant to refer to "a truly active participation" ([1943] 1988:8) involving the reader in the dynamism/mobility afforded by a particular poetic image.[4] For Bachelard, the poetic image merely invites us into embodied experiences of motion; we choose, on some level, whether or not to accept this invitation.

Reading poetry and playing video games are vastly different experiences, but, to most, the notion of spiritual mobility is probably less obscure in gaming than in poetry. Video gaming almost always involves an on-screen representation of motion corresponding with the real motion of the gamer as they manipulate a keyboard or joystick or, more recently, as his or her body as is tracked by velocity or motion sensitive devices. Unlike the standard, relatively static body of the reader, the gamer is usually in motion to varying degrees. With traditional/early game controllers, the actual motion of the gamer is, arguably, secondary to the on-screen representation of motion and their felt sympathy with that motion.[5] On-screen avatars are, in most games, travelling vast distances through imagined worlds, leaping, flying, dropping, and executing spectacular feats of martial arts while the gamer traditionally moved little more than his/her arms, fingers, neck, and eyes. As such, in traditional/early gaming imagined motion is always as or more important than actual motion to the experience of gaming. This is truer still for game players who might only be watching while they wait for their turn to play.

Video gaming requires a great deal of supplementary imaginative work; gamers are not merely tracking motion visually, but are committing to navigating and sympathizing with the motion of an avatar as that avatar moves in fantastical ways through fantastical worlds. The projections of light that represent those worlds and that motion are insufficient in themselves and beg for the gamer to imagine the tactility of the action represented and to use their own embodied experiences to translate the represented distances, buoyancies, speeds, and slownesses of the avatars into the language of the gamer's embodied experience. The ways in which our bodies can and do participate in the representations of motion that video games involve, the pleasures that we derive from imagining ourselves moving as the avatars we control move, the movement of the spirit that can arise as we commit our minds and bodies to the act of gaming bear resemblance to what Bachelard is concerned with in *Air and Dreams*.[6]

But, despite Bachelard's insistence on their equivalence, real motion, it must be acknowledged, differs from dynamic induction. To acknowledge this is not to devalue Bachelard's intervention; the distinction we need to make here is less categorical than universal. Instances of real motion differ from instances of dynamic induction in the same way real motion differs from other real motion—in terms of actual materiality. As material moves in and out of perception, meanings associated with that material manifest and decay in the mind of the moving individual. At the same time, the nature of the motion itself may affect the way the material environment that is passed through is understood; new meanings may be articulated with that material, affording new experiences.

Handheld gaming devices have played a role in these articulations; they introduced the practice of engaging in the imaginary motion of gaming simultaneously with "real" motion/travel. I am interested here in thinking through the implications of this copresence of real and imaginary motion. I am interested in asking: What occurs when the combination of imagined motion and real motion that video gaming always involves occurs with the movement of gamers through space? How do the imaginary worlds that games manifest act upon the experience of the real worlds that they become copresent with and vice-versa? How do the sounds of gaming affect the relationship between the bodies of gamers and the imagined and real worlds they experience? And, how does the experience of imagined motion affect the meanings and experience of game sound?

Chip music, a genre that re-presents elements of game music outside the experience of gaming, allows us to critically approach some of these questions. By looking at trends within the genre, we can observe aspects of how the imagined mobility characteristic of video game play remains articulated to the sounds of gaming, even in the absence of the game. The Gramscian/Althusserian notion of *articulation*, in the sense found in the work of Stuart Hall (1980:69) and adapted in the musicological work of Richard Middleton (1990:8) and of John Shepherd and Peter Wicke (1997:117), is a term describing the process of meaning making as the result of a contingent and temporary joining of materiality and meaning. Articulation is a key process through which musical meaning arises. When chip music appropriates the sounds of early gaming it can be, I argue, in part, because they carry, articulated with them, embodied memories of the imagined travel gaming fosters. Through articulation, I contend, the sounds of early gaming have, for a significant body of listeners, come to "mean" the spiritual mobility they once accompanied. Therein lies the first layer of the argument I am forwarding here. In the second layer, I want to suggest that those sounds articulated with the experience of that mobility have, through handheld devices, played a role in the way gamers have experienced real world spaces. The symbolic role of the handheld gaming device in the chip music scene is due, in part, I feel, to the way they allowed chip sound articulated with the experiential aspects of imagined travel to act upon a variety of real world spaces. Beyond this, in the final layer of my argument I contend that the experience of chip sound being made copresent with the act of moving through public space is essentially connected to the aesthetic of re-presentation that chip music forwards. With the rise of handheld gaming devices, the libratory "imaginary" travel that gaming affords began to mediate the experience of public space, inscribing the mobility of the gamer into the experience and meaning of that space. The aesthetic of re-presentation that chip music forwards is a kind of rewriting of the public sphere in the form of the musical collective unconscious isomorphically akin to the rewriting of public space that occurred with the rise of handheld gaming. Both represent a renegotiation of the public sphere through chip sound. More importantly, both represent an inscription of the pleasure and mobility of the gamer into structures, materiality, and a world over which they have limited control.

In other words, the affordances of both handheld and home video gaming seem to have played a role in forming the aesthetic of chip music. The handheld gaming device allowed sounds articulated with those affordances to transform public space, to enact a kind of chiptuning of the world. The rewriting of the musical collective unconscious occurring in the chip music genre is coextensive with this, it is a rewriting of a scape—here a soundscape rather than a landscape. It is an inscription of the pleasure, mobility, and presence of the gamer into all that once failed to speak their name.

## INTRODUCING CHIP MUSIC AND THE DEMO SCENE

Chip music is a relatively new musical genre and has been troublesome to define, largely because of this aesthetic of re-presentation adopted by its practitioners, but also because of the distinction, important to members of the chip music scene, between chip music and game music. In one of the only academic articles on the genre to date,

Anders Carlsson addresses this difficulty by discussing how neither a technological nor a pure stylistic definition works to draw lines between what is and is not chip music. He observes: "For the most part, more recent chip songs have been short and happy-sounding loops in 4/4, often flirting with C64 music from the 1980s, but composers have used chip sounds to make songs sounding like jazz, noise, death metal or even hip-hop" (2008:160).[7] A generic definition seems, thus, more useful than a stylistic definition; though the musical styles of chip music songs are derived from a variety of stylistic realms they are presented together in live performances, on CD compilations, or on websites devoted to chip music.[8] However, no matter how varied the styles of chip music may be, what unites them is their incorporation of elements of the limited sound world of early video game systems; Carlsson refers to the essential element of chip music as "bleepy C64 nostalgia" (2008:160).[9]

The C64 home computer was remarkably popular, dominating the home computer market from 1983–86. Carlsson's invoking of the C64 reflects that popularity, but is somewhat misleading as the music chip music composers "flirt with" can be music from any one of the unique but related video gaming devices that have, since the late 1970s, provided music as an element of the gaming experience.[10] In her book *Game Sound: An Introduction to the History, Theory, and Practice of Video Game Music and Sound Design*, Karen Collins notes that "[i]n the arcades, sound varied considerably from machine to machine" (2008:9) and provides specifics about the considerable diversity of the sound chips incorporated into home and handheld consoles. Indeed, each of the early arcade, home, and handheld video gaming devices had its own distinct sound producing capabilities. But, despite the technological diversity recognizable in the world of early video game sound, what fuels the chip music genre is the fact that many of these devices shared the same limitations, limitations which ensured that the word "bleepy" could be a sufficient adjective to summarize and celebrate the dominant aesthetic feature of early video game sound and video game music.

"Blippiness" or "bleepiness" is capable of describing both the sound effects these games incorporated and key features of the aesthetic of game music. Collins argues that "the first real arcade hit," Atari's 1972 game *Pong*, "was to some extent responsible for making the sound of video games famous" (2008:8). The audio element of *Pong* consisted entirely of isolated tones whose primary function was to provide information to the game player about the status of events occurring within the table-tennis style game. These tones occurred frequently during gameplay, with different pitches indicating the completion of different events (the "paddle" successfully connecting with the "ball," the "paddle" failing to connect with the "ball" and the scoring of a point, and the "ball" connecting with and deflecting off the side boundaries toward one of the "paddles"). When the "ball" is deflected by the "paddle" at an angle, it often quickly bounces off the two side boundaries (the top and bottom of the screen), causing a series of the same pitch to be sounded and silenced in a regular rhythm before the "paddle" either connects with or misses the "ball," ending with a different pitch this regular rhythm and a phrase or section of sonic activity. At other times, the "ball" is deflected more slowly causing relatively long silences between the appearances of these indicator tones. In the latter type of sequence, the listener is likely to parse the tones differently from the busier rhythmic sequences. These brief, isolated "blips" shatter the silence with an assertive but harmonically impoverished sonic interruption that decays back into silence.[11] Both in the era before continuous music became a common feature of video games (pre-1978) and after that era, the omnipresence of these types of isolated sound events/effects that convey information to the gamer about action occurring within the game contributes to the idea that early video game sound is best described as "bleepy."[12]

Though "blip" or "bleep" may most immediately refer to these isolated sonic events, it also seems clear that uses of these terms in relation to chip music also invoke the aesthetic particularities of the way early game consoles and home computers synthesized pitches and sequences of pitches in the formation of game music. Above all, it was the timbral limitations of early game sound that made early game music universally bleepy. The spectral content of the pitches synthesized by the sound chips was limited because the chips employed simple periodic waveforms (pulse waves, triangle waves, sawtooth waves) to produce them. More importantly, the spectral envelope stayed consistent over time while those periodic waveforms were employed to synthesize pitched material. These chips generally had the capacity to produce three to five channels of sound and they usually dedicated three of those channels to the production of pitched musical content. In most cases, alongside these three channels a noise-producing channel served as accompanying percussive content. The pitched musical content usually consisted of one channel producing a melody, a second channel harmonizing that melody, and a third that provided a bass line.[13] All three of these channels were engaged in the production of pitches with these even spectral envelopes. Though the individual pitches of game music are not isolated blips sandwiched with silence like the sounds of *Pong*, as they shift from pitch to pitch in their melodic or harmonic function with their static timbral simplicity, strict metrical durations, and the clarity afforded to events within the thin four channel texture, each pitch of the music conveys a kind of isolation and uniformity deserving of the adjective bleepy.

The sound chip of the Commodore 64, the SID, provided it with sonic capability that was both state of the art for home computer technology of the time and timbrally and texturally similar to the sound producing capacity of other gaming devices. The SID chip shared essential sonic characteristics with the sound generators of other canonic devices such as the five-channel Ricoh 2A03 chip used in the Nintendo Entertainment System and the four-channel system of the Nintendo Game Boy.[14] When discussing these sounds, Carlsson invokes "nostalgia" due to the fact that chip musicians are not concerned with celebrating all video game music; rather, they concern themselves exclusively with the limited, blippy sound worlds described earlier. The limited sonic capabilities of home computers and gaming systems were drastically expanded with the introduction of FM synthesis into game sound in the late 1980s, and came to a definitive end as the memory capacity for these technologies and the media they employed reached a level where they could reasonably support the inclusion of recorded music rather than rely on these earlier forms of synthesis. Home computers and video game consoles first appeared on the commercial market in the late 1970s; by the early 1990s game music composers and sound designers had an unlimited sonic palette to work with.

Carlsson argues that technological definitions of the chip music genre fail for two reasons. The first has to do with chip music's roots in a subculture of game crackers and rogue programmers known as the demoscene. From the early days of computer gaming, game manufacturers realized that their potential to profit in their industry was being compromised by piracy. These companies invested energy into creating more and more intricate copy protection for their games. A subculture developed around the sport of "cracking" those copy protections and distributing illegal versions of these games. The "crackers" who broke through these copy protections began to create short advertisements for themselves called "crack intros."[15] These "ads" were comprised of graphics and music and they became more intricate as crackers competed with one another, flaunting their programming skills to the transnational group of peers they shared their cracks with through the mail or, faster still, through their modems. The practice of creating these crack intros eventually mutated into the practice of creating "demos."

Rather than appearing as short introductions before games, "demos" were self-contained works of art. Their visual and audio content was generated in real-time by the computer in the same way a game is, but, unlike a game, the demo audience was a passive spectator to the images and sounds being generated. Demo creators and fans began creating events where they would gather in person to watch/hear and celebrate these works of art. In the 1980s, these events began as small informal parties, and in the 1990s they grew into gatherings large enough to be held in arenas like the Vikingship in Hamar.[16]

To be clear, *chip music,* in my use of the term, is not game music. The date of origin of chip music as a separate musical genre is difficult to pinpoint as it involves resolving debates over whether music composed for "demos" should be considered part of the same category as chip music, which, unlike demos, is not intended as accompaniment to specific visual material.[17] Regardless, the majority of chip music emerged in the era when game music became dominated by recorded music rather than earlier modes of synthesis and after the home computing and gaming technologies discussed here became commercially obsolete. As such, the term *chip music composers* should only refer to those composers that employ/re-present a specific variety of obsolete game sound outside of the realm of the games they were formerly isolated in.

To reiterate, the demo scene and the chip music scene are related but distinct. The practice of creating demos and crack intros involves the composition of chip-based music; yet, while demo appreciation revolves largely around the admiration of the ability of the programmer to create complex graphics and music in the limited programming environments of early computer systems, chip music appreciation has more to do with musical invention and sound itself than with programming skill. The composition of chip music certainly has its roots in the demo scene and many of its practitioners occupy both worlds. The chip music scene, however, has been established as a distinct realm with its own values and practices. Both in the demo scene and in the chip music scene, the sounds of game music are appropriated and presented in instantiations separated from the experience of gaming. Yet, the implications of their differing methods of valuation separate the scenes; the valuation of programming on early computer systems active in demo culture, but less important in chip music culture, places limits on the ways in which music is created in the demo scene that do not exist in the chip music scene.

In the demo scene, the generation of sound and image in real-time by hardware authentic to early computer systems with their limited memories and the restrictions of their programming languages is valued. Because of this ethic, the sounds themselves are limited to those made available by the capabilities of these systems, which become the sounds of demo music by default. In the chip music scene, however, the sounds of early game systems are not present by default but because of the significance of these sounds to the composers and audiences in the scene. Chip music in the chip music scene is not always created through the composer programming early home computer systems to generate sound in real-time. There are a variety of other ways chip music composers make those sounds present, including emulation of the sounds on more advanced computer systems and sound chips, sampling, and the use of software interfaces that make computer and game systems generate sound in real-time but that do not require the composer to use programming language to compose. Describing Little Sound DJ, tracker software many chip musicians use to make music, Vblank, a visualist active in the various chip music scenes on the American East Coast, explains: "it's hard to come by and it's hard to install, but a lot of time musicians here call it the great equalizer, because everyone can use it."[18]

This brings us back to the first reason Carlsson gives for the failure of a technological definition of chip music. A technological definition of chip music fails in the chip music scene, as opposed to the demo scene, because the presence of the sounds of early gaming is more important than the means through which those sounds become present. The second reason Carlsson gives for the failure of a technological definition of chip music is his observation that there are musicians who employ the early computer chips central to the demo scene but whose "music is not generally considered chip music" (2008:160).[19] He explains that their music is made with the tracker software developed within and for chip music making communities, but doesn't contain the "bleepy" timbres that accompanied the imagined travels of the users of early game systems. By ignoring certain aspects of the limited sound world of these early systems, by, for instance, using the noise channels heavily and not creating melodic material with pulse wave producing channels, these sound chips can produce music that does not reflect the dominant timbres and textures of early game music. This second reason supports the logic of the first; it also shows that the defining element of chip music as a style is, simply, the substantial presence of the "bleepy" timbres dominant in early gaming.[20]

# Handheld Gaming: Resetting Game Sound

While the chip music scene does not require that composers program on early computer systems to be included, the symbolic value of both early home computers and game systems is a central feature of chip music in its various manifestations to date. Currently, more than any other, the Nintendo Game Boy, particularly in the forms available before the 1998 release of the Game Boy Color, serves as a, perhaps the, central symbol of the genre. There are a number of reasons for its centrality. The most practical of these reasons is that many of the artists in the scene create their music on the Game Boy with a variety of software programs, like Little Sound DJ, that members of the scene have developed. Like the guitar in rock music or the turntable in hip-hop music, the Game Boy is a valuable symbol because it is an instrument essential to composers in the genre. Yet, I believe, the Game Boy's symbolic value also has much to do with the experiences the game system afforded after coming on the market in 1989.

The Game Boy was not the first handheld gaming system, nor was it the first handheld gaming system to have interchangeable cartridges (Milton Bradley's Microvision preceded the Game Boy by a decade), but it was the first handheld gaming system with interchangeable cartridges to be commercially successful.[21] It is widely recognized that "it was Nintendo that popularized the hand-held console concept with the release of the Game Boy" and that "the hand-held Game Boy [built] a historical sales record" (Steinblock 2005:150). The Game Boy was the first means through which a sophisticated and diverse variety of portable handheld games became available to game players. Handheld video games were popular throughout the 1980s, but these games differed fundamentally from Game Boy games in terms of the duration of time they could sustain a gamer's attention and the kinds of gaming experiences they afforded.

The goal-oriented pleasures of video gaming are central. Video games are usually built around the pursuit of a task, and achieving that task is almost always the purpose of playing the game. However, games like the iconic Super Mario Bros series afforded a great deal of non-purposive action. A player could spend time as a kind of flâneur, moving back and forth and up and down through the surreal spaces of the game world, controlling purposeless interaction between their avatar and the objects in their world. The Game Boy was unique in 1989 for being a portable gaming device that offered interchangeable games and games, like Super Mario Bros, that allowed players to navigate their avatars in purposeless ways through imagined space. Earlier handhelds usually offered only one game wherein the gamer could only navigate their avatar in ways that furthered the progress of the game. Though it is true that the non-purposive aspects of video games are almost always mixed with purposive action, it is also certain that the Game Boy was able to keep gamers aimlessly exploring imagined worlds for much longer durations than any previous portable gaming system.

With the portable Game Boy system, imagined worlds could be navigated by gamers while their own bodies were in motion. It was undoubtedly common for gamers to be enjoying non-purposive "imagined" movement with their Game Boys while experiencing purposive "actual" movement in a vehicle, or perhaps even on foot, on route to a specific destination. It was also undoubtedly common for gamers to enjoy purposive "imagined" movement at intervals as they wandered non-purposively through "actual" space. In either scenario, the gamer is able to engage in a form of imagined motion whose aesthetico-political affordances are distinct from those of the actual motion they are engaged in. While we may be inclined to conceptualize gaming as an escape into another world, it is also a making copresent of an imagined world, and of the light and sound that facilitates that imagination, with innumerable experiences of space and place; escaping into is always also transformation of that we imagine one to be escaping from. Not only did handheld gaming offer gamers a degree of autonomy over the aesthetico-political implications of the motion they engaged in, it mediated/transformed their experiences of the various "actual" spaces and places they moved through.

There is no way to distill the transformations that gaming has afforded down into words, no way to quantify them and compare them with other ways additions of sound and light have mediated/transformed our experiences of space and place. Yet, it seems safe to say that gamers play video games because the experience is, for the most part, pleasurable. It also seems safe to assume that the forms of imagined movement the gamers are afforded by the games are libratory to some degree when compared the kinds of mobility they are afforded in "the real." It follows that the sounds of gaming come, in time, to be articulated with memories of this pleasure and this autonomy and that the transformative effect they have had on spaces and places becomes viewed on some level as the "meaning" and the utility of those sounds.

The sounds of music are often experienced as belonging to particular social groups, geographic locations, and historical eras. Most often, these forms of belongingness are generated from perceptions of a music's origins; the idea of the place and people from which a music emerges is articulated with the sounds of that music. When the sound worlds afforded by early programmable sound generators became widespread globally through the consumption of arcade games and, later, home computer and gaming systems, those sounds arrived, in the ears of many listeners, relatively undercoded.[22] The bleepy sounds produced by the early forms of game sound synthesis likely would not, in the early days of video gaming, have evoked belongingness to any "real" cultural group or any bygone cultural era. As well, though a practice of listener acknowledgement of game music composers and sound designers has emerged more recently, in the early days of gaming few gamers would have been likely to attend to game sound and music as "works" and assign them belongingness to any world outside of the world of the game. To many gamers, the sound worlds made audible by their gaming devices would have belonged exclusively to now, and to them. The ubiquity of the limited timbral and textural signature described earlier combined with the experience of these sounds as undercoded affords a sonic materiality ripe to be coded with the powerful feelings of imagined movement games fostered. The significance of their reappearance in the chip music scene seems as much a result of those articulations remaining active as any pleasures the materiality of the sounds themselves, without these articulations, give rise to.

The Game Boy allowed the gamer to go out into nearly any worldly environment and force it into copresence with game sound. Unavoidably, the game sound acted on these new environments. If heard by others, the game sound could assert a kind of violence, forcing the pleasures and the autonomy of the gamer into the environment around them. If heard only by the gamer, these sounds mediated the experience of the material world and, articulated with the pleasures and liberties generated in the gaming experience, forced innumerable material environments to become temporary containers for those feelings. Writing about sound's role in film, Fred Camper notes, "sound gives the action it accompanies a spatial presence; the image gains the illusion of filling the air around one, as the sound itself does" (1985:371). If video game sound is the element that allows the game space to act on the body of the player creating embodied sympathy with their avatar, when they are experiencing actual motion while handheld gaming their body moving through space bathed in chip sound bears some equivalence to their avatar, the world they move through some equivalence to the game world.

Thanks to the Game Boy's portability, game sound became a tool for mediating the materiality of the environment outside of the game world. The sounds of pulse waves and triangle waves, which were already articulated with powerful, pleasurable dreams of movement, became sounds that could intrude on the public sphere and/or act on and transformatively mediate real world environments. Now, in the chip music community, the same sounds are being employed to act upon, re-presenting and timbrally transforming, a variety of musical styles and the Game Boy is serving as the symbolic centre of the genre at large. The portability of the Game Boy, the way in which it allowed game sound to move into and act on the materiality of virtually any space, seems to be one key source of an almost imperialistic desire in chip music to transform, through re-presentation and timbral alteration, any and all existing musical material. The musical timbres that define chip music have become a tool in support of the aesthetic of re-presentation I am concerned with here.

## CHIPTUNE AND RE-PRESENTATION

Nostalgia comes up often in the discourse around chip music. Yet discussions of re-presentation in chip music need to transcend this topic. Carlsson refers to chip musickers[23] as nostalgics and, certainly, they display such tendencies; there is a longing perceptible in the discourse around the scene for the pleasures of their collective youths and a revisitation of its symbols and sounds. But when one looks closely at chip music itself, it also becomes clear that much of its re-presentation is not best understood as nostalgic in character. This is because very little of its re-presentation is direct re-presentation of game music.

We have established that the "bleepy" timbres that comprised the limited sonic vocabulary of early game systems are the defining element of chip music. Now we must ask: Given their ubiquity and necessity within the genre, when, if at all, do these sounds function as re-presentations of early game sound and when, if at all, do they function in non-referential manners? I suggest that the timbres in themselves cease to function as *strongly* referential the moment one has acclimatized to the chip music style at large. Listeners familiar with the sound world of early gaming devices will be likely to experience chip music, upon first encountering it, as music that appropriates a sonic palette from those devices. They are likely to notice that chip music has taken game sound outside of the realm of the game. But this meaning is likely to fade when that same listener is immersed in chip music for sustained periods. This is because all chip music uses these timbres; as the appropriation becomes established as normative in the mind of the individual listener, the timbres cannot function as *strongly* referential. My qualifier 'strongly' exists here to make a distinction between referentiality that remains in the foreground of meaning from referentiality that has become normative and fades from the attention of the listener, but which is still residually present and may occasionally rise to the foreground. The timbres come to belong to the chip music genre rather than to game music; they remain coded as "game timbres," but do not assert a consistent aesthetic of re-presentation because their use is so normative within the genre.

As such, the experience of nostalgia for game music and sound does not necessarily characterize the experience of sustained participation as a listener or fan of the chip music genre. However, the re-presentations that never fade from re-presentation into "first-order" normativity are those that Carlsson refers to as "songs sounding like jazz, noise, death metal or even hip-hop" (2008:160). The aesthetic of re-presentation that I want to identify here has more to do with re-presentations of other musical styles in the language of game music than with nostalgic re-presentations of game music itself.[24]

## GAINING CONTROL AND REFORMATTING THE PLANET

Richard Dyer (2008) defines pastiche as textually signaled, evaluatively open imitation. Textual signaling refers to the perception that an imitation is overtly marking its status as imitation, while evaluative openness refers to a perception of ambiguity in the imitator's relationship to the imitated. Forms of imitation like nostalgia, parody, or homage are textually signaled, evaluatively *predetermined* forms of imitation. Other forms of imitation like "straight genre work" (Dyer 2008:35), versions, or copies are not textually signaled forms of imitation, yet they, like pastiche, are perceived to be evaluatively *open* toward the material they re-present. Chip music's aesthetic of re-presentation is quite wide and includes works more likely to be received as tribute, others more likely to be received as parody, and others that may not be perceived as signaled imitation and would be received as unsignaled "versions" of their hypotext.[25] From entire recreations of classic jazz albums like Miles Davis' *Kind of Blue*, to chip sound translations of classical works, to covers of pop and hip-hop numbers, re-presentation in the genre comes in a variety of forms. Yet, arguably, the event most likely to occur when a listener encounters a chiptune re-presentation is the event of pastiche.[26] Most of the music re-presented in chip sound is being, at once, violated and celebrated. This copresence of violation of and celebration of the imitated makes manifest the evaluative openness Dyer uses to define pastiche. Re-presentations in chip sound both offer the imitated music in question to the chiptune listener and subject that music to the violence of timbral alteration through the re-presentation of that music in the language of pulse waves, triangle waves, and white noise.

This timbral alteration often feels like an imaginary colonization of the music being imitated, yet, its translation into chip sound also opens that music and its affordances to the chip music fan, encouraging an embodiment of that which has been colonized. Tracks like "Classical Favorites" by Virt, which re-presents fragments of well-known classical melodies in chip timbres, or "Remix Medley" by Tugboat, which does the same for well-known hip-hop songs, seem to neither be homages to nor parodies of the music they re-present.[27] They seem less interested in making clear evaluative statements about that music than simply asserting their right to appropriate and transform it. Commenting on "Classical Favorites," Virt refers to this appropriation in terms of violence, writing: "You'll probably recognize the original pieces, and upon hearing what I've done to them, mail a bomb to my house."[28] This kind of language is recurrent in the discourse around chip music re-presentations. Describing another of his re-presentations, a re-presentation of Christina Aguilera's "Genie in a Bottle" entitled "Game Genie in a Bottle," Virt metaphorizes his re-presentation as a narrative of violence: "Christina Aguilera gets mutilated by a farm combine, but wait! They can reanimate her and give her singing ability back! Only it comes out as square waves!!!! Ha! Ha! Ha! Ha!"[29] Again, this violence belies the fact that the music being re-presented is music chip musicians and fans are choosing to consume and to derive pleasure from. In its timbrally transformed state, the re-presented music is often divorced from aspects of the meanings articulated with it in its original context and becomes, to some degree, an object of affection in ways the original cannot. Again, this copresence of violence and affection qualifies this signaled imitation as evaluatively open.

We can appeal to the visual culture of chiptune to help underscore this point. DJ Scotch Egg's "Scotch Bach" provides an example of the evaluative openness of chip sound re-presentation through a music video version of the song which visualizes the copresent violence and affection recurrent in the genre.[30] The black and white video directed by Steve Glashier begins with shots from multiple angles of around 40 individuals in three arced rows facing the same direction (See Figure 16.1).

They are dressed identically in pixilated tuxedo pattern t-shirts and are seated behind stands holding sheet music. The audio track consists, at first, of room tone and quiet murmurs of conversation, which are eventually accompanied by a single set of footsteps. Upon hearing these footsteps we see a figure walk around and in front of the group of individuals and up onto a podium. The figure, DJ Scotch Egg, raises his arms and begins to conduct what appears at this point, because of the absence of musical instruments, to be a choral ensemble (See Figure 16.2).

FIGURE **16.1** "Scotch Bach" Opening Image (0:01) Director: Steve Glashier

FIGURE **16.2** "Scotch Bach" DJ Scotch Egg (0:18)

The next shot of the ensemble accompanies the introduction of the music; it is a tight shot of three members. It becomes clear that this is not, in fact, a choral ensemble, as the three now each hold a Game Boy (See Figure 16.3) and we hear the opening melodic gesture of J.S. Bach's *Toccata and Fugue in D Minor* in a chip sound timbre.

The video continues to oscillate between shots of the conductor and the Game Boy ensemble while the music re-presents various fragments of the *Toccata* in chip sound while the texture gets denser and noise elements are added. At one point, the first 8 notes of the *Toccata* recur and begin to loop. Shortly after this occurs, a sampled vocal scream underscores the rhythm of the looping melody as the song reaches its thickest density. At this point in the visuals, the ensemble cease playing their Game Boys and begin to mosh, knocking over each other, the seats, and the music stands as DJ Scotch Egg continues to conduct. Musically throughout the piece, the *Toccata* is violated; besides being translated to chip sound, the piece is fragmented. Similarly visually, the mosh pit at the end of the video violates the structure of the orchestra. The conductor seems to want this to occur; he continues to conduct throughout the moshing and, conducting with his

FIGURE 16.3 "Scotch Bach" Game Boy in Hand (similar shots from 0:23 onward)

hands, he brings the visuals and the music to a close at their ends. The imitated elements, both musical and visual, are violated but also celebrated. It is significant that they are no more violated than celebrated; the relationship of imitator to imitated remains evaluatively open. Bach is neither deified nor detested.

Turning back to the "imperialist" rhetoric active in the genre following this example is instructive. In a bio they used in 2008, Argentinian duo 8GB describe themselves as "pretending to gain 'world audiovisual domination.'"[31] They describe their "mission" in steps:

> Infiltrate a 3rd world nation—Settle into the local music and multimedia scenario—Spread 8-bit propaganda by means of an audiovisual set created with a mix of seemingly harmless 8-bit technology and modern weaponry—Gain control of the population with live setups and record releases—Completely dominate local scenario and expand to other countries by own means or by recruitment—World audiovisual domination.[32]

While this kind of language is both somewhat ironic and referential of the narratives of certain kinds of video games, it also seems reflective of the feeling chip music is giving rise to in its current manifestations. This kind of language appears in the most central nodes in the scene. The title of a documentary on the rise of one of the key chip music events, New York's Blip Festival, is called *Reformat the Planet*.[33] This title captures a structure of feeling active in contemporary manifestations of the chiptune scene internationally, one that both informs the choices of artists in the scene and is reinforced by their artistic choices.

If chiptune's goal is to "reformat the planet," reformatting of individual pieces or styles of music would be less likely understood to be due to the imitator's particular valuation of the imitated and more likely to be understood as a part of a total generic mechanism or mission that has been set into action. Re-presentations of particular hip-hop pieces or the style at large, of sections of classical works or of particular European art music styles, and of well-known and obscure pop songs are the dominant forms of re-presentation in the genre. Yet they exist alongside re-presentations of forms of metal, reggae, disco, electronic dance music, various forms of jazz, the Japanese "city pops" genre, college folk, Cuban son, and other styles. It can often seem as if re-presentations in the chip music genre are part of a ravenous force seeking to blindly consume and transform all that it encounters, turning the world into a game world, reformatting the planet.

# CONCLUSION

Not all chip music is oriented toward re-presentation. However, re-presentation makes up an atypically large portion of chip music practice and is common internationally among established artists in all, or almost all, of the local and translocal chip music scenes.

The transnational chip music community is unique amongst transnational popular music communities because of game space. When recorded sounds travel across cultural borders, or even within cultural borders, key shared articulations generated by particular individuals or communities who first "used" that music, meanings that depend upon the experience of that music from within physical space or cultural place, often do not survive the voyage. With chip music, one key space in which meaning is generated is available to listeners despite their physical and cultural distances; game players in different locations across the globe share certain contextual meanings important to the sounds and music of early game systems. Foremost, they share the experiential affordances of gaming itself. Thus, it is not merely the sounds of early game systems that unite the members of the global chip music community; what unites them is also their participation in a process by which those sounds became articulated with particular varieties of meaning. In some way, they experience the process of articulation in a manner similar to a community in physical proximity. Cultural differences between members of the chip music community may seem secondary to the contexts they have shared as gamers, at least when it comes to the "meanings" of the sounds and music celebrated in all local or translocal chip music scenes.

However, this observation, it must be noted, excludes certain important members of the chip music community. Not all of the creators of chip music are or ever were gamers and there is a prominent discourse in the community on the differences between "chip music" and "game music." Certain creators of chip music feel that their work has been drastically misunderstood by journalists and other newcomers to the chip music scene.[34] They complain that chip music events have been mistakenly described as gatherings at which music from video games is re-presented and celebrated. Journalists who describe chip music events in this way fail to hear that the compositions performed at these events are compositions that were never intended to accompany game play. There are differences between the music that accompanies early video games and most chip music, differences that are lost on these listeners. Game music must serve as the accompaniment to an undetermined duration of game play, whereas most chip music has a set duration. They therefore can, and do, incorporate a formal trajectory that most game music compositions cannot. Game music must repeat itself as it accompanies varying durations of game play, and it must terminate with the game player's completion of a segment of play. Its formal manifestations are, subsequently, varied and dependent on the game player. Though chip music pieces in performance may similarly exist in multiple forms, in almost all cases this variation would depend on the aesthetic judgment of the composer/performer and not on the contingency of durations of game play. As well, many of the ideas and much of the musical invention of chip music bears little connection to music intended to accompany early video games; quite simply, chip music is not game music.[35]

This distinction aside, chip music composers who have never been game players exist, but are, at present, a minority within the chip music scene.[36] The same can safely be claimed is true for chip music fans, although the proportions may be different and will continue to change with time.[37] This minority is important and would clearly be exempt from the category of chip musickers that I am theorizing here. For these individuals, the sounds of chip music cannot "mean" in the same ways that chip music "means" to gamers for the simple reason that they are not as familiar with the game worlds and the ways gaming experience has contributed to the meaning of game sound for gamers. The pleasures these listeners derive from the timbres central to the genre are, to an extent, different varieties of pleasure. However, given the dominance of gamers in the scene, it is plausible that these "meanings" are communicated to some extent to non-gamers and become part of their experience of the sounds of game music that chip music incorporates.[38] That the sounds of music are differently articulated for individuals and groups of individuals within particular music scenes is an inevitable fact that makes the study of popular music so methodologically difficult. My theory of the importance of "imagined" motion to the genre as it currently exists does not claim to be a total theory of the meanings circulating in the genre; no discussion of music can ever reasonably claim to be such a theory. Yet I do feel that chip music is a unique example of a popular music subgenre wherein the dominant forms of meaning currently articulated with the music are graspable through the fairly easy access a great deal of us have to the game systems valued and referenced in the chip music scene. The practice of re-presentation discussed here arose in a period where most of the artists involved were gamers and were subject to the articulation of the sounds of gaming with the experiential affordances of gaming. It will be interesting to see what becomes of chip music and its approach to re-presentation when the generation for whom the game music of their youth was not a unique timbral and textural sphere distinct from other major forms of popular music starts to dominate the scene.

Undoubtedly, there are many reasons for the emphasis on re-presentation in chip-tune music. Surely it can, in part, be attributed to the technology standard to the creation of chip music and to the learning curve required to master that technology.[39] Just as painting students often attempt to reproduce "masterworks" as part of their studies, users of music software sometimes try to reproduce existing recorded music in the early stages of teaching themselves that software. A quick scan of user forums of non-chip related music software like *Vocaloid* confirms that re-presentation commonly serves a pedagogical function in the world of software based music composition.[40] Also, the act of re-presenting well-known musical works in styles at a remove from the stylistic language in which the music was originally presented serves the practical purpose of drawing attention to a project that it might not otherwise have gotten. These two practical purposes are likely to explain much of the re-presentation that occurs in chip music.

However, the experiential aspects of gaming also deserve consideration. With a unique and limited timbral vocabulary undercoded enough to be rearticulated in game space, early game sound has been able to act as a vehicle for the experiences of mobility that gaming affords. The sounds of chips act not only upon the game worlds, but upon the real-world environments gaming occurs within. With the commercial success of the Nintendo Game Boy, the scope of those environments changed dramatically; game sound and game music, already articulated with the pleasures of the dynamic induction game play gave rise to, acted transformatively on the world in spaces across the globe. It is not just the possibility that this music has become articulated with Bachelardian experiential states that is important, also essential to understanding this music's significance is the recognition that those transformations of space also have become articulated to the sounds of early game music. Through its articulation with experiences of imagined travel, the sounds of early gaming acted on and with spaces in ways that articulated the mobility of the game player with the materiality of those environments. In turn, those sounds gained a utility that also became a part of their meaning—these were sounds capable of acting on materiality, transforming its meaning, inscribing not only the pleasure of the gamer but his or her experiences of mobility and autonomy into materiality that might not previously have served as containers of that pleasure. What I am suggesting in this chapter is that this utility has played a significant role in the aesthetic forms chip music has taken. Chip music has manifested as music that re-presents, and thus acts upon, other music. It has been fundamental to the scene, in all of its manifestations, that chip sound becomes a tool for the mediation of preexisting materiality, a means of reformatting the planet. That utility began with chip sound's copresence with dreams of movement; it continued with those sounds (that now "mean" dreams of movement) inscribing the pleasure and mobility of the gamer onto public space at large via the mobility afforded by the handheld game device; and it continues with the memory of those sonic transformations of space informing chip music practice by coding those sounds as tools of transformation.

The character of chip music's aesthetic of re-presentation bespeaks that these previous two levels of articulation are still part of the meaning of chip sound. Josh Davis, known as Bit Shifter in the chip music scene, explains:

> There is something intrinsic to the sound of really primitive synthesis which is really the defining characteristic of chip music. There's something intrinsic to that sound or that quality of sound…It does, I think, evoke something that is very visceral, whether it's a memory of childhood experiences or a memory of a particular sound that we have not heard since childhood…I can't put my finger on what it is that

creates that hook for people, and I think that it may differ from person to person, but I think it's there and I think it will never be fully divorced from gaming.[41]

Perhaps what Bit Shifter can't put his finger on here is the way these sounds carry memories of spiritual mobility and/or memories of moments when they have acted transformatively on material space. What seems clear to him is that the power of the sounds has something to do with the act of gaming itself, and, at least to my mind, mobility, both imagined and real, seems a worthy candidate for the "hook" he was trying to identify.

The idea that sound can mediate our relationship to space is nothing new; the Sony Walkman, the portable "ghetto blaster," car stereos, harmonicas, marching bands, and many other portable sound technologies have afforded listeners the mobility to act upon a wide variety of spaces with a wide variety of sounds. One of the goals of this volume is certainly to emphasize the importance of the study of copresence of sound and space and to theorize the implications increases and reductions in the mobility of varieties of sound have in our lives. What is new about the way the Nintendo Game Boy fits into this list is the articulation of imaginations of movement with its sounds. With the "meanings" of imagined mobility and autonomy of movement articulated with it, the sounds of game music have acted on or with material environments to, temporarily, force them to be containers of those feelings. The rise of chip music out of the demoscene at the moment when the first generation of gamers reached young adulthood represents the reclamation of these sounds *and* of the functionality they once possessed. All music acts on or with the materiality of spaces; game music inscribes feelings of autonomy and mobility on the world, temporarily "reformatting" the world to speak the pleasure of the gamer. The Game Boy's sonic transformation of space can be seen as connected and comparable to chip music's approach to re-presentation. Both hold the potential for a thorough plundering, a reformatting of the planet, a chiptuning of the world.

## NOTES

1. Bachelard explains he is not describing "a simple metaphor. We will really feel it within ourselves.... It effects in us a dynamic induction" ([1943] 1988:4).
2. I am using *scene* in the sense defined by Bennett and Peterson in the introduction to their 2004 volume *Music Scenes: Local, Translocal, and Virtual*. They define *scenes* as "the contexts in which clusters of producers, musicians, and fans collectively share their common musical tastes and collectively distinguish themselves from others" (1). They point out that contemporary musical scenes exist in local, translocal, and virtual forms. The first and last are self-explanatory; the *translocal scene* refers to "widely scattered local scenes drawn into regular communication around a distinctive form of music and lifestyle" (6). The chiptune musician and fan frequently moves fluidly between all three of these varieties of musical scene.
3. I use the terms *chip music* and *chiptune* interchangeably throughout.
4. *Affordance* is, as well, a term that implies collaboration between our mind/body and other materiality. For a discussion of musical affordance, see DeNora (2000:38–44).

5. An exception can be found in the recent development of video games for the blind.

6. It must be noted that Bachelard argued that visual perceptions of movement were not like poetic images and did not give rise to dynamic induction. Using the opposition of dynamics and kinematics in a rather idiosyncratic manner he writes, "we must realize that movement perceived visually is not *dynamized*. Motion perceived visually remains purely kinematic. Because sight follows movement so effortlessly, it cannot help us to make that movement an integral part of our inner lives" ([1943] 1988:8). By extension, he might have argued that visual perceptions of representations of movement also fail in this regard. While it seems true that not all visual perceptions of mobility amount to dynamic induction, it does not seem difficult to me, as I look out at the eucalyptus grove in front of me on this unusually blustery day, to sympathize with a particular tree branch or cluster of treetops such that visual perception of them brings me to a embodiment of that movement as profound and "real" as "actual" motion. It may be more accurate to say that the visual perception of movement might only rarely prompt our collaboration with that movement in the creation of inner dynamisms. This is not only because of the effortlessness of sight, but also because of its temporality (consumption of the poetic image moves us outside our naturalized sense of the 'actual' duration of events), its commonality (in all our waking hours we are subject to visual perception of objects in motion), and our tendency not to ritualize the everyday (the reading of poetry is treated as an event or ritual in a way that everyday visual encounters with objects in motion are not). Bachelard's insistence on the participatory nature of dynamic induction seems to require that we leave open the question of dynamic induction's potential sources. As he suggests, dynamic induction is not an inevitable or constant experiential process; the individual plays a role in its creation. Subsequently, it seems shortsighted to privilege poetry as the solitary site of a kind of spiritual mobility that is comparable to "real" motion. If the individual plays a role in dynamic induction's manifestation, Bachelard should not confidently assert that dynamization of the visual does not ever occur. However, again, it is not visual perception of movement we are dealing with when we are speaking of video gaming but, rather, visual perception of representations of movement. Bachelard died in 1962, roughly a decade before the beginnings of the commercial video gaming market. We cannot know whether he would have seen gaming as a special category of visual perception of movement wherein the supplementation of representation of movements with imaginations of movements qualified as dynamized.

7. C64 here refers to the Commodore 64 personal computer that appeared on the market in 1982. For more on the Commodore 64 see Bagnall (2005).

8. Websites like 8 bit collective (www.8bitcollective.com) foster the virtual element of the chip music scene and host large libraries of free and legally downloadable chip music.

9. "Bleepy" and "blippy" seem to be the preferred adjectives characterizing the aesthetic of early game sound. Karen Collins also employs this language, referring to "low-fidelity blips and bleeps" (2008:9) to summarize the sound effects of early arcade games. See Collins' *Game Sound* for more a more detailed history of sound production in this era of video gaming history.

10. Carlsson's use of the term music here may well imply the ideas of both video game sound and music. Certainly, the "non-musical" sound effects of early gaming are "flirted with" in chip music alongside the "music."

11. Further on in this paragraph I discuss how it is that these early forms of synthesis are "harmonically impoverished."

12. Collins describes how "The first IBM PCs and clones contained. . . a tiny speaker that could produce simple tones of varying pitch but of a fixed volume, designed to indicate errors or other messages," and how this indicator tone producing speaker was "sometimes referred to as a *bipper* or a *beeper*" (2008:29).

13. As an example, we can consider the Ricoh 2A03 with its five channel capacity. A typical game music piece composed for this chip would see the chip's two pulse wave producing channels generating a melodic line and a complimentary line harmonically supporting that melody. A third channel on the chip synthesized triangle waves. Commonly, triangle waves were employed in the production of bass lines in game music. The fourth channel produced noise which, again, generally served a percussive function. The fifth channel employed differential pulse-code modulation which can be understood as a rudimentary form of sampling. The additional timbres added by uses of this channel were generally used for sound effects rather than music.

14. See Tomczak (2007) for more information on the technical specifications for Nintendo Game Boy audio. Tomczak explains: "The Game Boy does not have an individual sound chip as such. Instead, the main processor handles sound routines, including sound output. The pseudo audio processing unit of a Game Boy has a total of four channels. Channels 1 and 2 are pulse wave oscillators. Channel 3 is a programmable waveform channel capable of playing back samples and synthesizing more complex waveforms. The last channel is a noise channel."

15. For a more detailed history of the demoscene see Tasajärvi (2004).

16. Stamnes (2004) provides an overview of the history "The Gathering," one of the largest of these "computer parties."

17. Live performances of chip music almost always involve the combination of music and projected visual content. In fact, visualists are often given equal billing with musicians in the promotion of shows. However, these visualists often generate their material improvisationally and the music and visuals share an aleatoric relationship. Of course, in the age of YouTube, music videos are produced to accompany certain chip music pieces, but this too should be considered categorically distinct from the demo where sound and visuals are created together as part of a total artwork and would not be consumed in isolation from one another in the way music videos supplement a musical work that can stand on its own as a work.

18. Interview with author, December 5, 2008. In the course of my research, the majority of chip musicians I spoke with made their music using Little Sound DJ (LSDJ). This program, created by Johan Kotlinski, who performs and records in the chip music scene under the name Role Model, has at times been available for sale in the form of a game cartridge that can be inserted into a Game Boy. However, Kotlinski has no associations with Nintendo and has never mass produced these cartridges. Each cartridge is made individually and only a relatively small number of Kotlinski produced cartridges exist. However, Kotlinski has also made the software available for purchase online and has provided instructions on how to install the program on a Game Boy cartridge. Further, the software will also run on certain computer Game Boy emulator programs. For more information on Little Sound DJ, visit www.littlesounddj.com/lsd/. Other software programs musicians use with various models of the Nintendo Game Boy include, among others, Nanoloop (www.nanoloop.de) and Pixelh8 Music Tech (pixelh8.co.uk/software).

19. The artists that serve as his examples are Dutch gabber artist Neophyte, Australian artists Nasenbluten and Xylocaine, and German artists Patric Catani, e18or, and Christoph de Babalon. The technology in question here is the Protracker software for the Commodore Amiga. Protracker is one of a number of tracker software programs that serve as popular means for the creation of chip music. A tracker program is a software interface that manifests an x-y axis tool for music composition. The y axis represents time divided into a sequence of metrical units and the x axis represents the sounds triggered on each beat and the parameters affecting the shape of those sounds. Each sequence is called a pattern. Tracker programs store a number of these patterns and songs are generally created by alternating between and repeating these patterns with variations to the sounds and parameters of the patterns. Tracker programs are relatively easy to use and do not require that their users be knowledgeable about programming languages. Still, tracker software often allows the user to view the code the software produces and demo creators often altered the code itself and/or produced their own tracker programs (Carlsson 2008:158).

20. My qualifier "substantial" here refers to the fact that some music that incorporates these timbres in minor or ornamental ways exists without being considered chip music by members of the chip music community; these timbres need to be dominant aesthetic elements for the music to be considered chip music.

21. The Milton Bradley Microvision lasted a mere three years on the market and very few games were produced for the system.

22. For a discussion of "coding" in popular music see Brackett (1995:7–14). Brackett re-presents the framework set out by Middleton in *Studying Popular Music* (1990). What I find particularly useful in Brackett's re-presentation of Middleton's framework are his examples of "overcoded" sounds. I find the idea of "overcoding" useful to describe musical encounters wherein the listener experiences a sound as being so strongly articulated with particular meanings that the idea that those sounds could be rearticulated with new meanings (that either coexist with or erase previous meanings) becomes unthinkable. By claiming the sounds of video gaming were "relatively undercoded" I mean to imply the opposite, that sounds are experienced without the presence of such meanings. This does not mean that the sounds are not articulated with meaning; it means that the meanings that do manifest are far from contributing to the perception I am referring to as overcoding.

23. The term "musicker" here is derived from Christopher Small's *Musicking* (1998). Small's term, an intervention into the field of musicology intended to make the discipline recognize that the study of all forms of participation in music cultures are necessary areas of music research, is a valuable contribution to the field that I hope to reinforce by employing his term.

24. However, alongside and overlapping with the chip music scene exists a widespread practice of nostalgic re-presentation of game music. For the most part, re-presentation in this practice does not involve the production of imitative works, but instead involves the re-presentation, outside of the game environment, of works that are ontologically identical to the 'works' that first appeared as part of the gaming experience. As I asserted earlier, chip music and game music must be considered distinct despite their obvious connections. Contemporary practices of nostalgic re-presentation of game music should also be considered apart from chip music practices. This having been said, chip music composers will make direct reference to particular pieces of game music from time to time by quoting snippets of familiar game melodies or by including samples of some of the most iconic sonic moments from popular games. Yet, these usually amount to isolated moments of

nostalgic re-presentation that occur from within constant incorporation of game derived timbres. These moments are important; they function like in-jokes amongst a group of old friends. But they are, in most cases, ornamental to the genre. There are occasions when chip music re-presents game music, but it is a mistake to allow these isolated re-presentations to obscure the wider functions and concerns of the genre at large. My conclusion continues this line of thought and explains how I am following the lead of my interviewees from the chip music scene in insisting on the distinction between these two practices.

25. Gerard Genette, whose book *Palimpsests: Literature in the Second Degree* has became a central text in the study of literary imitation, established the use of the term hypotext to refer to that which is imitated. Hypertext, in turn, is used to refer to the imitation itself. I follow scholars like Serge Lacasse in his "Intertextuality and Hypertextuality in Recorded Popular Music" in employing these terms in the discussion of musical imitation.

26. Tribute is certainly a contender for the dominant imitative mode in the genre. Many chiptune artists are invested in the re-presentation of works that they are fans of and use the word tribute to categorize their re-presentation. When I argue that most function as pastiche, I am separating pastiche as an imitative process from pastiche as an effect that arises when a listener encounters an imitative work. I am arguing here that some of the evaluative predeterminedness motivating the creation of certain individual chiptune re-presentations is obscured by the way re-presentation is practiced and framed at large within the genre. In other words, much of the work that may have been created as tribute would shift toward being received as evaluatively open to some degree due to its participation in a genre-wide project of "reformatting the planet" in chip sound. Of course, at the same time, much of what was created as tribute has also surely functioned as such.

27. At the time of writing, both of these tracks were available free online. For "Classical Favorites" see the URL in the following note. For "Remix Medley" see www.myspace.com/tugboat.

28. Virt (Jake Kaufman), Big Lion Music: the Various Projects of Jake "Virt" Kaufman, "Chiptunes," http://www.biglionmusic.com/category/music/chiptunes (accessed April 22, 2009).

29. At the time of writing, "Game Genie in a Bottle" was available at the URL listed in the previous note.

30. At the time of writing, the video version of "Scotch Bach" was available online on the director's webpage at http://www.steveglashier.com/index.php/dj-scotch-egg-scotch-bach (with director's commentary), as well as the Nothing To See Here webpage at http://www.ntsh.co.uk/scotchegg-hausen.php (with full production credits).

31. This bio was included on the My Space page for the group as well as the online biographies used to promote the 2007 Blip Festival. See www.myspace.com/8gb.

32. See previous endnote.

33. *Reformat the Planet*, directed by Paul Owens (New York: 2 Player Productions, 2008).

34. This point was emphasized by a number of artists I have spoken with, including: Disassembler (Will Collier), interview with author, December 5, 2008; Lo-Gain (Logan Erikson), interview with author, December 5, 2008; Stealthopera (Suzan Eraslan), interview with author, December 6, 2008; Bitshifter (Josh Davis), interview with author, December 6, 2008.

35. By some definitions of chip music, game music may fall under the umbrella of the term. Here, I am not trying to label such usages as incorrect; I am, however, following the lead of my interviewees in distinguishing the two in this manner (see previous endnote) and

pointing to the categorical misunderstanding that may ensue when this distinction is not made.

36. All of the performers I have discussed the topic with played video games before beginning to make chip music. In the *Reformat the Planet* documentary, the New York based artist Bubblyfish (Haeyoung Kim) explains she is an exception: "Yes, I am from that generation but I've never really played a video game. So, I don't have this association of playing 8bit music as video game music. It depends on the background of the artist."

37. These comments are based on interviews I have conducted with performers and fans in the scene. Both Peter Swimm, who I interviewed December 10, 2008, and Low-Gain (Logan Erickson), who I interviewed on December 5, 2008, discussed how listeners too young to have grown up with the early game consoles have been starting to attend chip music performances.

38. This may occur in a variety of ways. For instance, images like the cover of chiptune artist Arcadecoma's album *The Game Boy Tree Adventures*, which places the viewer into the visual perspective of a gamer playing a Game Boy while sitting on the branch of a tree they have climbed, can cause a non-gamer to understand the ways portable game devices have mediated the experience of real world spaces for gamers.

39. The Tin Foil Hat Brigade (James Bentley) impressed this point upon me in an interview on December 7, 2008.

40. *Vocaloid* is vocal synthesis software. A user forum for the software can be found at http://www.vocaloid-user.net/modules.php?name=Forums. A survey of recent music posted to the site usually reveals imitative tendencies amongst the software's users. For example, on March 28, 2008, the user "vocamonster" posted a version of the rock band Queen's song "Bohemian Rhapsody."

41. Bitshifter (Josh Davis), interview with author, December 6, 2008.


## REFERENCES

Bachelard, Gaston. [1943] 1988. *Air and Dreams: An Essay on the Imagination of Movement.* Dallas: The Dallas Institute Publications.

Bagnall, Brian. 2005. *On the Edge: The Spectacular Rise and Fall of Commodore.* Winnipeg: Variant Press.

Bennett, Andy, and Richard A. Peterson, eds. 2004. *Music Scenes: Local, Translocal, and Virtual.* Nashville: Vanderbilt University Press.

Brackett, David. 1995. *Interpreting Popular Music.* New York: Cambridge University Press.

Camper, Fred. 1985. "Sound and Silence in Narrative and Non-narrative Cinema." In *Film Sound*, ed. Elizabeth Weis and John Belton, 369–81. New York: Columbia University Press.

Carlsson, Anders. 2008. "Chip Music: Low-Tech Data Music Sharing." In *From Pac-Man to Pop Music: Interactive Audio in Games and New Media*, ed. Karen Collins, 153–62. Burlington: Ashgate Publishing.

Collins, Karen. 2008. *Game Sound: An Introduction to the History, Theory, and Practice of Video Game Music and Sound Design.* Cambridge, MA: MIT Press.

DeNora, Tia. 2000. *Music in Everyday Life.* New York: Cambridge University Press.

Dyer, Richard. 2007. *Pastiche.* New York: Routledge.

Genette, Gerard. 1997. *Palimpsests: Literature in the Second Degree.* Lincoln: University of Nebraska Press.

Hall, Stuart. 1980. "Cultural Studies: Two Paradigms.'" *Media Culture and Society* 2(2): 57–72.

Lacasse, Serge. 2007. "Intertextuality and Hypertextuality in Recorded Popular Music." In *Critical Essays in Popular Musicology*, ed. Allan F. Moore, 147–84. Burlington, VT: Ashgate.

Middleton, Richard. 1990. *Studying Popular Music*. Bristol, PA: Open University Press.

Shepherd, John, and Peter Wicke. 1997. *Music and Cultural Theory*. Malden, MA: Blackwell Publishers.

Small, Christopher. 1998. *Musicking: The Meanings of Performing and Listening*. Hanover: University Press of New England.

Stamnes, Bent. 2004. "Case: The Gathering." In *Demoscene: The Art of Real-time*, ed. Lassi Tasajärvi, 44–52. Helsinki: Even Lake Studios.

Steinblock, Dan. 2005. *The Mobile Revolution: The Making of Mobile Services Worldwide*. Sterling, VA: Kogan Page.

Tasajärvi, Lassi. 2004. "A Brief History of the Demoscene." In *Demoscene: The Art of Real-time*, ed. Lassi Tasajärvi, 10–31. Helsinki: Even Lake Studios.

Tomczak, Sebastian. 2007. "Handheld Console Comparisons: Lateral Consumer Machines as Musical Instruments." Paper delivered at the Australian Computer Music Conference. Online version available on author's homepage at http://milkcrate.com.au/_other/downloads/writing_stuff/tomczak.acmc2007.pdf (accessed April 15, 2009).

# CHAPTER 17

·····························································································

# RHYTHM HEAVEN: VIDEO GAMES, IDOLS, AND OTHER EXPERIENCES OF PLAY

·····························································································

## MIKI KANEDA

> A groove is a comfortable place to be.
> —Steven Feld

THE Nintendo video game *Rhythm Heaven* was released in Japan in 2006 for the hand-held portable video game console, Game Boy Advance (GBA).[1] In the game, the user is asked to "groove" along to the beat of the music and press the appropriate button on the Game Boy following aural cues. The game topped the charts, far exceeding expectations in sales figures, and was released for the newer Nintendo DS portable gaming console in July 2008, renamed *Rhythm Heaven Gold*. With over 1,594,000 units sold in Japan by January 2009, within the category of music-based video games, *Rhythm Heaven Gold* became the first game to exceed sales of the popular hit, Sony Playstation's Parappa *Rappa,* in twelve years since Parappa's release (Iketani 2009). Both versions of the game collected accolades in the fields of game development and new media design: In 2006, *Rhythm Heaven* received an award in the entertainment category at the annual Media Arts Festival sponsored by the Japanese Agency of Cultural Affairs. In 2009, *Rhythm Heaven Gold* was awarded the grand prize in the category of sound design at the Computer Entertainment Supplier's Association Developers Conference, and another award for excellence at the Japan Game Awards alongside games such as *Dissidia Final Fantasy* and *Mario Kart Wii.*

Advertisements for the game present the game as fun, easy to play, and, most of all, an entertaining experience that allows users to acquire a better sense of rhythm—which, according to the game's chief producer, Tsunku (also a celebrity pop star and J-Pop producer), is not a quality very highly developed in the millennial Japanese body.[2]

What does that even mean? What makes rhythm such a desirable asset according to Tsunku, and how are notions of rhythm mobilized in relation to specific notions of

Japaneseness and Tsunku's version of the Japanese body? Does *Rhythm Heaven* articulate the fetishized rhythmic body through, or against, perceived notions of "Japanese" bodies? My argument is two-fold: first, from the producers' and creators' side, the discourse surrounding the game capitalizes on a racialized ideology about the uniqueness of millennial Japanese bodies. Yet focusing on the modes of game play I show that users of the game do not necessarily concern themselves with this ideology and, instead, create other spaces of pleasure and intimacy. In this way, the game becomes a part of everyday lives in other satisfying and surprising ways.

But why study a GBA game now? By 2009, the GBA was no longer being manufactured and had long been replaced by the newer DSi and DS game modules, which had already been on the market since 2004. In other words, it was already an obsolete technology by the time I even began work on this project. Nevertheless, old technology can still shed light on more recent issues about new media use and practices. My job as a scholar is different from that of a game reviewer's, to whom perhaps *Rhythm Heaven* would be old news and not worth writing about. While this chapter includes a description of the game, I do not make judgments about whether the game is a "good" one or a "bad" one; nor do I make recommendations to readers on why or why not they should play the game. I also believe that new media studies must come to terms with, but need not be fixated on just chasing, as new media scholar Abigail de Kosnik puts it, the "parade of new media objects" that flow incessantly.[3] In this chapter, I am concerned with the question of what it means when Japanese consumers are able to purchase a gaming device and software for less than $100 total and are supposedly able to attain new rhythmic bodies.

*Rhythm Heaven* also presents a curious contradiction. While on the one hand, the medium of the video game abstracts the physical act of dancing, on the other hand, the game claims to reinvigorate the millennial Japanese public with this very thing, which the technology of the game seems to take away. When video games and digital toys are under attack by adults for alienating play and moving bodies, *Rhythm Heaven* reinserts the body into the picture. I do not mean to present *Rhythm Heaven* as a digital utopia that somehow reunites disembodied selves. Still, I do want to make a case against a dystopian technological determinism that would simply dismiss the game as a manipulative toy of capitalism that has managed to extract body and work, packaging it into a consumable object. In a rare moment of technological redemption, Adorno wrote: "As music is removed by the phonograph record from the realm of live production and from the imperative of artistic activity and becomes petrified, it absorbs into itself, in this process of petrification, the very life that would otherwise vanish" (2002: 279). Maybe Adorno's comment on what the phonograph did to sound in 1934 can offer the possibility of hope to those who lament the disappearance of the body with the advent of video game. Working from Walter Benjamin, anthropologist Anne Allison writes, through the mimetic process, "technical production can give back to humanity that capacity for experience that technical production threatens to take away" (2006:29). Allison continues, "The enchantment held by consumer/techno goods work on people in specific ways, even if (or precisely because) they come linked to a socioeconomic system that is also alienating" (86). Following Allison, I want to believe that this "toy of capitalism" has more to offer than sucking the rhythm and soul out of our bodies.

As sold, the Game Boy Advance is not a networked gaming device that connects users over the internet. However, an internet-based ethnography that focuses on users sharing their tips, experiences, and feelings with other consumers provides insight into the personal engagement with the game of a loosely tied community of amateur game shoppers and reviewers.[4] Online shopping sites and forums constitute a crucial part of the knowledge and product-circulating world of the Game Boy. Forum users share tricks about playing the game, tips on software and hardware, and information about the myriad illegal copies, hacks, and emulators that allow users to subvert standard practices. As a casual consumer of the game myself, the internet—not the video game store—was the first place I turned to. Transactions such as purchasing the game from Amazon Japan and bidding on a used Game Boy on eBay took place on the internet. I also drew on sites like Wikipedia for information from fans and specialists far better versed than I am in the technical and historical life of Game Boy. Moreover, I visited Amazon Japan again and again to read individual responses and reviews of the game.

As with almost any research project, the methodology used was based on a combination of practical and theoretical interests. From a practical point of view, internet ethnography allowed me to conduct research without extensive travel to survey families all over Japan. In the process, it became more and more clear to me that modes of engagement with what are called "virtual technologies" or "digital technologies" are hardly merely virtual or digital. They involve, engage, and affect the fleshy, analogue, and the mental in very direct ways. My eyes get blurry from playing *Rhythm Heaven* one too many times, and my thumbs feel sore from the repeated motion of pressing the buttons on the Game Boy unit. eBay seller Tracy of Texas carefully packaged the Game Boy unit in a padded manila envelope and took it to the post office to mail off to me in Berkeley, California. Amazon Japan reviews were written by individuals, perhaps hearing the sound of the TV, children playing, and the garbage truck coming around the corner—in a real physical space.

In the following section, I provide a description of the physical, visual, and sonic properties of the Game Boy that are interconnected with the bits and pixels of the moving onscreen objects inside the world of *Rhythm Heaven*.

# Hardware

First hitting the market in 2001, the GBA follows a line of handheld game consoles released by Nintendo. As of March 31, 2008, Nintendo reported that the GBA had sold over 80 million units world wide, with 16.96 million of those in Japan, and 41.64 million in the Americas. Prior to the Nintendo DS system's release (which sold 113.48 million copies by September 2009), it was the most popular handheld game console in history (*Wikipedia*).

FIGURE 17.1 Hardware and Software. Game Boy Advance and software packaging for *Rhythm Heaven*. Photo by author.

The GBA console is considerably bulky compared to devices like the Apple iPod, but at approximately 5.5 inches long, 1 inch wide, and 3 inches high, it is still small enough to fit in a large coat pocket (see Figure 17.1). The screen is about 3 inches wide—just large enough to keep track of a number of moving characters and text. The images are in color, but the weak backlighting makes the colors much duller than a computer screen. The screen is hard to see without enough light shining on the apparatus. The hardware is capable of displaying 511 simultaneous colors in "character mode" and 32,768 ($2^{15}$) simultaneous colors in "bitmap mode." Still, the light, contrast, and size of the screen makes it better suited for viewing images with flat blocks of color, rather than those with more subtle shading and detail (Nintendo 2001). The GBA takes two standard AA batteries, which gives it a life of about fifteen hours of gaming pleasure. The sound is far from CD quality, but nonetheless, capable of polyphony and stereo sound, enough to have pop tunes as accompanying music to the game.

## SOFTWARE AND GAME PLAY

Format: *Rhythm Heaven* consists of six stages each comprised of six games, plus a dozen "expert-level" games for a total of forty-eight different mini-games. The duration of each of the mini-games ranges from less than a minute and a half to just under four minutes long—about the length of a radio-edit pop song. In this chapter, I use the phrase "the game" to refer the collection of these many mini-games that comprise *Rhythm Heaven*. The concept behind each of the mini-games is simple. To reinforce this aspect, there is no manual—both a strategy and a proof from the creators' part to demonstrate the game's simplicity. In *Rhythm Heaven*, the user is asked to "groove"[5] along to the beat of the music and press the appropriate button on the Game Boy following aural cues. The game rates users based on their rhythmic prowess judged by their ability to respond in sync with the music while following onscreen visual cues. In order to advance to the next level, all the mini-games in the lower stages must be completed successfully.

Characters: All the mini-games have their own unique set of characters, challenges, and songs. Though the animation style changes from mini-game to mini-game, the general theme hints at a comic/disco era style. Graphics using flat, bright colors are kept fairly simple, in keeping with a retro/cute aesthetic. Many of the characters are anthropomorphized animals or space-creatures; others are cartoon people. With the exception of the stock "traditional" Japanese figures such as the ninja, samurai, and *bon-odori* dancers, it's hard to tell the characters' ethnicity, but through sound bytes, speech bubbles, and commentary, they all communicate in Japanese, though some of the songs include English words (see Figure 17.2).

Sounds and Rhythm: All of the songs accompanying the mini-games in *Rhythm Heaven* are original tunes. Tsunku personally crafted around thirty of these tunes just for the game. The soundtrack can be purchased separately from the game online and in stores. The length of the tune determines the length of the mini-game associated with the tune. The music keeps going whether the user makes the correct moves or not, but sound effects and angry or disappointed facial expressions in the on screen characters let the user know when he or she has messed up.

As with many video games, in addition to the main theme song for each mini-game, there are also sound effects that vary based on the user's and player's actions. Most of the tunes rely exclusively on synthesized keys, strings, and winds sounds. In the case of a few exceptions, a small number of tunes sound as if live instruments and human voices were used (the credits to the game list names of people who provided the sampled voices for the game). Still, the limitations of the 8-bit sound card basically reduces any sampled sounds to a less-than-CD-quality synth sound, blurring the difference between a sampled live instrument and a good synth approximation of the live instrument.

Stylistically, the music makes references to various genres, including funk, disco, and rap, as well as traditional Japanese genres through *bon-odori* dance drums and *enka* style melodies. The soundtrack also includes old school video game music sounds from the microchip-based audio of the late 1970s and early 1980s. It also samples instruments like the stringed instrument, the *shamisen*, and *tsuzumi* drum from traditional Japanese music, and employs a stock melodic minor flourish with a Taj-Mahal-like building in the background to stereotypically signify the "Oriental" sound.

In terms of rhythm, the greatest difference between the sense of flexible rhythm required in musical performance and the sense of rhythm encoded in the game is

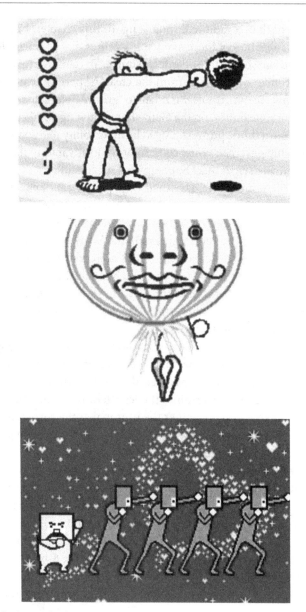

FIGURE 17.2 Stills from *Rhythm Heaven*. From the top, the main characters in the mini-games, (a) "Karate-dude," (*karate-ya*) and (b) "Rhythmic depilation" (*rizumu datsumo*) from stage 1, and (c) "Space Dancers" (*supesu dansu*) from stage 3.

that the musical cues flow exclusively one way, from the game to the user. The kind of rhythm presented in the game is based on a metronomic time, rigidly attached to a pulse, bound by meter (all the songs are in duple or triple meter), and offers little room for gradual speeding up or slowing down of tempo, or interactive adjustments of time. This notion of rhythm is at odds with the notion of "groove," which is an aspect of rhythm that is the result of social interactions according to Bonnie Wade (2009) and Steve Feld's (1994) definitions.[6] Except for a few games, all of the tunes have a fixed beat and tempo. It might be worth noting that in the 2006 version three of the four games that do include tempo changes involve some kind of stock Japanese figure—a samurai, karate player, and a rice ball (I ask if this should be read as a hint that the musical direction of the game is equating Japanese rhythm with unsteadiness?). The game's programming software enables measurements of rhythmic precision only. Outside of the small allowable margin of error that is based on the accuracy of the timing in relation to metronomic time, the scoring system of the game does not account for the senses of pushing and pulling against the beat, which make groove so precarious and playful at the same time.

Rhythm Heaven and Pop Music: Two pop songs performed by the recording artists Tokito Ami and Tanaka Soshi are used in the game.[7] Both artists are pop idols who record for Tsunku's label, TNX. Tokito's song is a cute synth-pop ditty called "*Koi no* Honey Sweet Angel," and her song fits in nicely with the pop sci-fi/fantasy visual elements of *Rhythm Heaven*. The mini-game that her song accompanies is the "remix" mini-game that users are allowed to play after completing the mini-games in stage 3. Visually, the video that comes with the song shows flashbacks to the various games in stage 3, intercut into the main action of a bunny bouncing off whales and rocks in a rainbow-colored ocean. Stage 3 games include the Space Dancers (*supesu dansu*), a flower-planting fairy (*mahotsukai*), balloon catching show penguins (*sho taimu*), and the circus performer boy and girl duo, Tran and Poline (*Toran to Porin*). Tanaka's song, which accompanies the "remix" after completing all stage 5 games, is an up-tempo rock ballad love song called "Wish—*kimi o matenakute*," which roughly translates to "wish—I just can't wait for you."

In addition to the mashed up flashbacks to previous games, like a typical music video, these two songs show images that thematically correspond to the lyrics. "Honey Sweet Angel" has heart motifs that appear in the background, and "Wish" has silhouette images of brokenhearted lovers in motorcycle jackets and rockabilly hairdos as a backdrop to the game. At the end of the tune, the song title appears at the top left corner of the screen. The credits for the singer (Tanaka Soshi / Tokito Ami), lyricist/composer (Tsunku), arranger (Hideyuki "*Daichi*" Suzuki for "Honey Sweet Angel" or Yuasa Koichi for "Wish"), and the agency with the rights to the song (J.P. Room) also follow (see Figures 17.3 and 17.4).[8]

Along with the dozens of other tunes for the game, Tsunku wrote Tokito and Tanaka's songs explicitly for the purpose of inclusion in the game. Both Tokito and Tanaka then also released singles of the tunes separately from the video game soundtrack, so fans could become familiar with the tunes either through the game, or through separately released CDs. In this sense, *Rhythm Heaven* has direct and robust ties to the musical world of commercial J-pop.[9] Later in this chapter, I will examine how the work ethic and discipline grounded in the rules and logic of the game might also be tied to the particular form of popular music that Tsunku produces.

FIGURE 17.3 Still from *Rhythm Heaven*: a scene from "3rd Remix" accompanied by Tokito's song, "Honey Sweet Angel."

FIGURE 17.4 Still from *Rhythm Heaven*: a scene from the end of the mini-game, "5th Remix." An animated Tanaka Soshi (with guitar in hand) appears with the volleyball-playing trio, the "Toss Boys." The text on the top left corner credits Tanaka as the singer.

## CONTROLS AND GAME PLAY

Taking advantage of the mini-game format, a user can engage with the game very briefly to occupy himself or herself—a few stops on the subway, or waiting for the bus to arrive, for example.[10] Another option is to play with the specific motive of mastering the game by completing all the levels with the highest scores possible. Because the duration of each mini-game is determined by the length of the tune, rather than the actions of the players, modes of play that alter the course of the game are more difficult to attain without altering the software first. Additionally, if the user wishes to move beyond the very first mini-game, he or she must first go along with the rules of the game in order to "graduate" from each stage to the next.[11]

FIGURE 17.5 High Level Pass! The user is rewarded by words of congratulations for playing through a mini-game with high accuracy. Translation of the text: "a message from the mysterious rhythm organization" (top left), "pretty amazing" (center), "high level!" and "you get a medal!" (bottom right).

For each of the mini-games, there are usually between one and three moves the user can make by pressing the "A," "B," or ":" buttons. The most important thing is to repeat the required action at the correct timing corresponding to the beat of the music. Before most of the games, there is a practice run where the user learns the correct timing to press the buttons. At the end of each game, the user is given a high pass, pass, or fail rating. After the first thirty-six mini-games have been mastered, the Drum Samurai appears on screen and congratulates the user. "I hope your rhythm has gotten better," he says, making an instructional purpose of the game explicit. A high-level pass earns the user a "medal." These accumulate and after a certain number of medals, the user gains access to locked bonus games and "toys" such as the "rap machine" (see Figure 17.5).[12]

Unlike many other music-based games like *Guitar Hero* or *Rock Band*, which rely mostly on the users' ability to coordinate *visual* cues with the music in order to succeed in the game, *aural* cues are much more significant in *Rhythm Heaven*. There are some games that can be played almost entirely without looking at the screen without extensive memorization, but none that can be played without listening. The visual imagery often supports game play, but at times, the timing must be so precise that listening proves more helpful than watching. For example, in one of the mini-games called The Fab Three (*baribari sannin-shu*), set in a country-western scene with saloons in the background, three fabulous clapping lions in matching blue suits and white gloves stand in a row facing the user. Pressing the "A" button, the user is responsible for manipulating the clapping of the lion closest to the right hand side of the screen (see Figure 17.6). The tempo of the Dixieland/Western Swing-inspired march with an oom-pah bass line is

FIGURE 17.6 Still from *Rhythm Heaven*: "The Fab Three" (*baribari sannin-shu*), from stage 6. The user is able to manipulate the timing that the lion on the right-hand side claps by pressing the "A" button.

around 112 half-notes a minute. Periodically, the lions clap to the music. The clapping is initiated by the first of the three lions (from the user's perspective, the one closest to the left side of the screen). The timing of the clapping varies, sometimes falling on the beat, but at other times falling on the up-beats or a combination of the two. All three lions must clap according to an established pattern. After the first lion claps, the clapping of the second lion determines the pattern for each sequence. The third lion (controlled by the user) must clap at the most appropriate moment based on the first two claps, keeping time with the music. Usually, but not always, the pattern is in even intervals. Following the lead of the first two lions, the pattern must be discerned by picking up on rhythmic patterns in the musical melody or accompaniment. Toward the end of the mini-game, the user must make the third lion "clap" on the downbeat after two speedy eighth-note triplets leading up to it. Visually, the clapping goes by in a blur. However, sonically, the individual claps are clearly articulated, and the pattern that ends in an accented downbeat comes quite easily, if the user is able to keep a beat. Figure 17.7 shows a transcription of the process of this fast clapping sequence.

In playing the game, I experienced that timing and the motile relationship between music and body are essential, and the more ways I was attuned to the sonic element by tapping or humming along, the better focus I could attain. Users who I observed playing the game also commented that they found it easier to play when they moved their bodies to the beat.

Over the course of writing this chapter, my "rhythmic sensibility" game score improved. (I began in the low sixties, but now I'm up to eighty-three!) However, I have no way of measuring how that translates onto the dance floor. I am not convinced that my sense of dealing with rhythm has improved outside of playing the game. Nevertheless, what I did find were insights about the relationship between consumers and games that were not necessarily questions that I had formulated prior to beginning research.

𝅗𝅥 = 112
(Half Note = 112 beats / minute - "March Tempo")

Downbeat ↓

| | | | | | | | | | | | | | | | | | | | | | | | | |
|---|---|---|---|---|---|---|---|---|---|---|---|---|---|---|---|---|---|---|---|---|---|---|---|---|
| Beat | 1 | | | | | | 2 | | | | | | 1 | | | | | | 2 | | | | | |
| Triplet Subdivision | 1 | 2 | 3 | 1 | 2 | 3 | 1 | 2 | 3 | 1 | 2 | 3 | 1 | 2 | 3 | 1 | 2 | 3 | 1 | 2 | 3 | 1 | 2 | 3 |
| Claps | | | | | | | | | | | $X_1$ | $X_2$ | $X_3$ | | | | | | | | | | | |
| Bass line | 𝅗𝅥 | | | | | | 𝅗𝅥 | | | | | | 𝅗𝅥 | | | | | | 𝅗𝅥 | | | | | |
| Button | | | | | | | | | | | | | Press A | | | | | | | | | | | |

FIGURE 17.7 Transcription of the fast clapping sequence from the mini-game, "The Fab Three." In the diagram, $X_1$ represents the timing that the first lion initiates the clapping, $X_2$ the clap by the second. The shaded box with the large $X_3$ represents the down beat on which the third lion must clap. By pressing the "A" button on the downbeat, the user makes the third lion successfully completely the three-note clapping sequence. If the user misses the "clapping" at the correct timing, it prompts the first and second lion to give mean and dismayed sideways glances toward the third lion for ruining the performance.

## Discourses Around the Game

A wider gap also emerged between promotional statements by the producer, Tsunku, and users' interactions with the game. By looking at discourses behind game production and promotion, I problematize the discourse of cultural essentialism that the game plays in to. At the same time, I hope to also show the contradictions, or limits of such deterministic modes of thinking.

According to Tsunku, who played an extensive role in pitching, developing, and promoting *Rhythm Heaven*, having rhythm matters tremendously. Through his role as producer of the game and as a producer/songwriter for pop idols such as the immensely popular all-girl group Morning Musume and the culture that surrounds his business of producing pop stars, Tsunku's views figure deeply in the discourses of the game.

The main tenets of Tsunku's treatise called "Teachings on Rhythm" (*rizumukun*) available on his personal website can be broadly summarized as follows:

- Rhythmic sensibility (*rizumukan*) is something innate to all people
- Rhythm is inscribed onto the body around the time that people learn to speak
- Rhythmic sensibility can be enhanced through training (Tsunku 2008)

According to Tsunku, as in language, rhythmic accents or habits are difficult to shed after the age of three. However, rhythmic ability may still be learned, and "like a businessman who speaks a foreign language with an accent, but with the fluency to accomplish his work," so can one acquire rhythmic proficiency. His treatise also suggests routines to hone rhythmic sensibility: "with 1-2 hours of dedicated and specific practice a day, rhythmic sensibility can be improved most effectively." He explains that rhythmic sensibility is not the same thing as "rhythm," which can be written down. Rhythmic sensibility is better (*kakkoii*) if it grooves (*nori ga ii*). Other reasons to improve rhythmically, he suggests, are "it seems that a better rhythmic sensibility makes one more sexually attractive," and "dance practice, with an understanding of rhythmic sensibility, allows one to develop ways of expression that depart from the Japanese person's movements" (*nihonjin banare shita hyogen ga dansu de dekiru*). He continues: "The concept of rhythm hasn't taken root in Japan yet. Now is the time to get out of this rut" (*nihon niwa rizumu to iu gainen wa mada nezuitenainode nukedasu nara imada*). Similar viewpoints are expressed in a promotional interview conducted by Nintendo president Iwata Satoru and Tsunku linked from the Japanese website for *Rhythm Heaven Gold*:

> IWATA:    For both *Rhythm Heaven* and *Rhythm Heaven Gold*, the concept that you really emphasized was the idea that rhythmic sensibility can be learned through training. Can you tell us a little more about that?
>
> TSUNKU:    Sure. Well, for example, many Japanese people harbor the complex, "I can't speak English. Similarly, many feel that "I can't dance," or "I can't groove to a rhythm." I always think, it's not possible for those people to learn English like a native speaker, but with practice, they can reach a certain level of proficiency. Especially with regards to rhythm, I think everyone can achieve some degree of competence.
>
> IWATA:    Is that something you came to believe as you train the performers in the group Morning Musume?[13]
>
> TSUNKU:    I believe so. I mean, in the beginning, the newbies [who newly enter the rotating cast of Morning Musume] can't do anything. But after a while, they manage to be able to dance.
>
> IWATA:    In other words, for you, the idea that "rhythmic sensibility can be learned" is something that you have proven evidence for.
>
> TSUNKU:    I guess you could say so. I do have a proven record. It's much easier to improve rhythmic sensibility than become better at singing in tune. It was my hope that everyone, including grown-ups—not just kids—could take a stab at trying to improve their rhythmic sensibility with the same kind of casual attitude that people have when they think, "hmm ... maybe I'll take English conversation lessons."[14]
> (Nintendo 2009)

These comments, like the cultural nationalist discourses of *nihonjinron*, which posit the biological and cultural uniqueness of the Japanese, are easy to ridicule.[15] But even though Japanese artists have been practicing and interfacing with Western music (classical, popular, and experimental) for a long time, the discourse of inferior "Japanese rhythm" remains to this day.[16] As Inagaki Masayuki, son of Japanese jazz trombonist Inagaki Jiro, claims, the "Japanese rhythmic sense is impaired: they cannot play behind the beat or the chord for fear of 'messing up'" (Atkins 2001: 41). Through an investigation of the meanings and values attributed to the notion of authenticity of jazz in Japan, historian E. Taylor Atkins makes it clear that this notion of Japanese rhythmic sensibility has been expressed by many musicians, critics (Japanese, black and white American, and European), and fans. The voices overseas re-circulate in Japan and are then used to reinforce statements by Japanese commentators. But if this "authenticity complex" (to borrow a term from Atkins) uses racialized aesthetic criteria to evaluate innate musical abilities, this argument is just as easily reversed to make a claim for Japanese exceptionalism. If Japanese musicians are unable to perform to American standards simply because of a biologically or ethnically determined quality, then it also follows that no one else can access the essence of Japanese performance, and in extension, culture.

Tsunku's theories are presented as knowledge gained through personal experience and years of practice. No statistical or scientific evidence is given to support his statements. Yet Tsunku's assessment of Japanese rhythm has potency because he validates his authority to speak about rhythmic sensibility as a successful musician with a long career. In the 1980s and 1990s, he played in the popular Japanese rock group Sharam Q. As a celebrated producer, he oversees the recruiting and training of countless young "idols" including the all-girl group Morning Musume, who boast the most albums sold by a female group in the history of Japanese popular music (Oricon 2007).[17] Notably, their performances feature coordinated dance routines that incorporate various styles including Broadway, hip hop, Bollywood, and more.

An important common characteristic of the appeal of the "idol" groups such as those produced by Tsunku, are their paths to fame through auditions and hard work. These life stories are made public, and shared by fans as part of the idol worshiping ritual. As anthropologist and idol scholar Aoyagi Hiroshi points out, the "pure" and "ordinary" origins of idols are highlighted as part of the "charm," and one of the expected aspects of the commercial packaging of idols (Aoyagi 2005:20). The logic then goes that these girls may come from anywhere—often from rural parts of the country—but they become stars through dedication and rigorous training. Enter Tsunku, mega-producer of idols, who possesses the skill and knowledge to train these plain country girls to become glamorous pop stars.

Advertisements for *Rhythm Heaven* support this fantasy that "anyone can play" and improve his or her rhythmic sensibility by learning to pay attention to rhythm (Nintendo E3 Website 2008). Coupled with Tsunku's teaching that practice makes, not perfect, but perfectly fluent, users are encouraged to play along with this idea of self-improvement through disciplined practice. The structured game play thus follows the logic of what philosopher Susan Bordo calls the "pedagogy of defect," where women in Bordo's case, or Japanese subjects in the case of *Rhythm Heaven*, "learn that various parts of their bodies are faulty [and] unacceptable" (1999:37).

The game offers the possibility for its consumers to obtain more desirable bodies through practice, self-discipline, and repetition. But this mimetic process of repeating after the teacher is *not* the same thing as a one-way model of imitation based on the notion of a Japanese "lack" that can be fulfilled by imitating the Western other. Notably, nowhere in Tsunku's treatise does he encourage listening to Western music (American or other) as a way to learn about good rhythm. Nor does he prescribe observing and studying dance performances by non-Japanese masters. The notion of *kata*, or form, that permeates Japanese aesthetic and social practices offers insight into the learning processes that the form of the game prescribes. Laura Miller, in her study of consumption practices around beauty in Japan, explains that "*kata* in the traditional arts makes it possible to study precise, exact movements" (2006:10). *Kata* can also be understood as "a way of acquiring one's social role by submerging oneself into the socially-constructed model" (Aoyagi 1999:25). Tsunku's idol understudies spend hours in the dance studio practicing moves to fit the *kata* of commercially successful pop idols, following the model set by Tsunku and other teachers. In *Rhythm Heaven* then, users can study the *kata* of pop-star approved rhythm first by buying the game, and then by practicing to fit the *kata* of the empty rhythmic spaces that demand the user to press the A button at the precisely correct instance. The game invites the user to fill the mold of the *kata* through self discipline, with the goal of achieving a more refined and rhythmically sensitive form. However, Bordo's notion of "self-normalization" underscores the fact that it is neither Tsunku nor users alone who hold the power to dictate what rhythmic, or desirable bodies move like (despite his authority honed in the entertainment industry). To paraphrase Bordo, consumers may contribute to the perpetuation of the notion of racialized Japanese rhythmic sensibilities, but "without this meaning that they have power in the production and reproduction of cultural nationalist views" (1993: 262). Meanings and ideals are thus formed and reproduced in the process of the circulation of the product.

## Rhythm Heaven in the Home

Yet the personal practices of individual consumers both reinforce and contradict the discourses presented in the sales and creative logic of the game. Rather than focusing on the disciplining aspects of the game, users seem keen on sharing their experiences about the game as an opportunity for social activity. New media theorist Dominick Chen has described this process as the "socialization of the game" (2006: 164). This aspect of the game deserves some attention because it shows how users find deeper meaning in the game that goes beyond a one-on-one master-student relationship to the game. At the same time, a kind of meaningful "groove" that is very different from the one that the game measures based on a point system is allowed to emerge from the social interactions taking place not *in* the game, but *around* it.

Comments by users of *Rhythm Heaven* confirm the ideas and goals about rhythmic training presented by the creators of the game. On Amazon Japan's reviews of *Rhythm Heaven*, Yohei from Chiba testifies to the increased level of musicianship that his band experienced thanks to the game. Monsuke and Onnel from Osaka point out that their favorite part of the game is the bonus drum lesson feature, where users are invited to learn different drum patterns by imitating the Drum Samurai. Sakurako from Aichi gushes her praise about the benefits of the game to the entire family:

> I bought the game so that my 6-y.o. could develop his rhythmic sensibility, but it's really a great game ... There are some games that even adults might find challenging,

but it can really be enjoyed many times over. One game only lasts for about 2–3 minutes, so you can play it very casually. It's a nice break, and I think it might be good a good workout for my brain as well... We use it in our home... and I think it's something that can be enjoyed by old and young, male and female for a long time to come. I think everyone would find this a good buy. Oh, and my child's rhythmic sensibility has gotten pretty good. I mean, it's a lot more fun than playing piano with a metronome!

For Sakurako, *Rhythm Heaven* not only teaches her child. It also offers Sakurako herself a fun "brain workout." She sees the game as an asset that might be part of the family's life for a long time to come, perhaps even something that could be shared with the grandparents![18]

Besides Sakurako, other users' testimonies of their experience with *Rhythm Heaven* also mention the communal nature of their interactions with the game. These often refer to domestic contexts within the home, sharing their enjoyment by watching and laughing at each other's hilarious play. Tico, who first bought the "simple game" for his wife "so she could entertain herself" in her spare time, soon found himself completely absorbed. Finally, he came to the conclusion that it was fun enough to play alone, but that things could get "really heated" when he played with his wife, his kids, or friends. Tico's and others' comments suggest that the individual experience of playing alone with the game is just one of the many modes of play.[19]

While my own ethnographic work is very limited, such comments resonate with the findings of the large-scale Digital Youth Project published in *Hanging Out, Messing Around, and Geeking Out: Kids Living and Learning with New Media* (Ito et al. 2010). The project was conducted over three years, led by principal investigators Peter Lyman, Mizuko Ito, Michael Carter, and Barrie Thorne. For example, the white paper, *Living and Learning with New Media* submitted by the team to the MacArthur Foundation, includes a section on cross-generation mediation through video games in the home. The main findings that the researchers present in this section are the following:

1. Family members casually use media together at home.
2. Some family members enjoy talking while others played different games.
3. Parents use new media to keep up with and stay in touch with their kids.
4. Kids often play the role of technology expert in the home. (Ito et al. 2009: 19–10)

Although the Digital Youth Project is a US-based study, many of the tools and social contexts observed by the researchers resonates very strongly with the comments made by users of *Rhythm Heaven* in Japan.[20]

Contrary to commonly held beliefs by skeptics about how personal electronic devices alienate individuals from the social, a significant number of users described experiences of playing *Rhythm Heaven* with others. The notion of video gaming as a form of "participatory culture" is no news, as studies and practices of group- or performance-oriented games like *Guitar Hero, Rock Band, Dance Dance Revolution, Grand Theft Auto*, and various Nintendo Wii games have demonstrated (Smith 2004; Jenkins 2006; Taylor 2006;

Miller 2007). However, the evidence that this communal mode of play is so widespread, even for games played on a portable, personal gaming device is striking.

Promotional campaigns around the game focused on a fun but self-deprecating ethos revolving around a mythologized notion of groove for the rhythmically deficient Japanese. Perhaps what makes the game most successful is not the consumer's desire to conform to a model or to fix a lack, but rather, the new spaces of intimacy that the game helps to create by triggering the production of energy accompanying sound and movement in the home.

Personal and individualized uses of portable entertainment systems are but one mode of potential engagement with *Rhythm Heaven*. An exploration of game play through *Rhythm Heaven* contests assumptions that portable video games devices create private experiences in public spaces by means of a "virtual reality" that alienates, or that "virtuality . . . separates the subject from the body [and that] digital media are supposed to be the most radical form of mediated disembodiment yet invented" (Sterne 2006:836). The alienation-model is quite difficult to realize in the case of *Rhythm Heaven*. A January 2010 subway poster for the Tokyo Metro shows a young man wearing big headphones and playing a video game. Blocking the door, he is far too absorbed in his game to be mindful of riders' comfort. Physically and sonically obtrusive portable gaming and audio entertainment is officially disdained upon by one of the largest subway systems in the world: "Let's do this at home," says the caption (see Figure 17.8).

Through play, Yohei becomes a better musician. Tico's daughter may ridicule her father for failing a level in the game without facing any disciplinary consequences. This reversal of roles is not so much disruption of the father's authority, as it is the very essence of play: a suspension of the quotidian. In play, I become lion, fox, alien, penguin, fairy, male, female, and samurai. I feel no awkwardness in temporarily suspending my understanding of my corporeal body because I know I'm "only playing." But as Huizinga suggested in *Homo Ludens*, play in everyday life is important precisely because it takes us out of it (1950:9). But play, including video game play, is not just an escape, but also a very productive means of exploring new alignments of relationships between people, and with the technologies that mediate.

In video game play, human-technology relationships do not operate exclusively in terms of relations of dominance and alienation, but in more complex and unpredictable relationships of possibilities, accommodation, and adaptation. According to the testimony of *Rhythm Heaven* users, communities are formed, and family ties are strengthened in coming together in a space distinct from the everyday, by "mutually withdrawing from the rest of the world and rejecting the usual norms" (Huizinga 1950:12). But it is a withdrawal and rejection of norms that also produces new norms and senses of the everyday. *Rhythm Heaven* becomes a part of family life. It can be educational as well as fun, as Sakurako observed. Games and gaming devices multiply the possibilities of social use. *Rhythm Heaven* shows how the purpose and meaning of video games have changed from entertainment for young boys, to now integrate various forms of social functions for a much broader audience.[21]

FIGURE 17.8 Framed public service announcement poster at the Suitengūmae subway station in the Tokyo Metro. The poster, called a "manner poster" by the Tokyo Metro Company, is part of an ongoing series that comes out with a new poster each month. Through humorous illustrations, the posters give tips to subway riders on subway car etiquette.

Despite the ostensible form of the hardware as a "personal" entertainment system, users playing at home, and around others, became part of a shared experience of playing, watching and commenting on each other's performance. An investigation of users' testimonies reveals that through particular contexts and modes of play, a personal, portable sound-reproducing device can enable intimate moments in the Japanese home. In fact, if we are to understand "groove" as a kind of socialized, anticipatory listening accompanied by a sense of "feelingful participation, a positive physical and emotional attachment" (Feld 1994:111), the Japanese living room filled with moving bodies, shared laughter, and affixed gazes surrounding a tiny Game Boy unit has its own kind of groove. After all, is this not an embodied way of experiencing socialized rhythm as groove, albeit, a very different one from notion of groove that we are perhaps more used to thinking of? As Steve Feld says, "a groove is a comfortable place to be" (111). Then, Tico's family room is that comfortable place, the site of a multidimensional, "intimate understanding of what is generally true in the locally obvious" (Casey 1996:44–45). Groove is emplaced through the mediating living bodies at play.

Play absorbs, magically transforms, and permits the absurd, hilarious, impossible, ridiculous, and cruel to coexist in the same place. Discourses of power including cultural nationalist arguments may systemically shape beliefs about racialized bodies and the limits of their essentialized bodily qualities. Yet there is a multiplicity of actual and potential configurations of modes of play that are contingent on the alignment of users and the spaces and places of play in relation to one another. The success and popularity of the game thus undermines any unitary message associated with the game. This assemblage of elements at play provides not just the conditions of possibility, but an "unprescribed potential" for the emergence of new means and meanings about rhythm, about the game, about rhythmic bodies, and about Japanese bodies.[22] That is, unprescribed both by the producers of the game, and by the consumers at the time of purchase, and un*scripted* in terms of the many other potential stories of experience of play that may be told.

## NOTES

1. The Japanese title for the game is *rizumu tengoku* (リズム天国), which translates to "rhythm heaven." In this paper, I refer to the game as *Rhythm Heaven*. All translations in this chapter are the author's.

2. Tsunku is the professional name that the producer uses publicly. A Mars Symbol frequently follows his name as in: Tsunku ♂ His given name is Terada Mitsuo. Terada is the family name, Mitsuo the given name. All Japanese names in this chapter appear in the order of family name, followed by given name, as is customary in Japanese.

3. Abigail De Kosnik, email message to author, December 20, 2009.

4. I say "as sold" because there are countless ways that users have hacked software, as well as gaming device emulators that they share with others on line. However, this is a topic that is beyond the scope of this chapter.

5. In Japanese the term *noru* is used. *Noru* refers to the physical act of riding something (a bus, horse), but is also used to refer to "going along" with a social situation, as well as in the sense of getting into, or grooving to a rhythm, as in this case.

6. In Bonnie Wade's textbook *Thinking Musically*, terms related to musical durations are defined as follows (2009:205–15):

Pulse: Equal length durations.
Rhythm: Any succession of durations. "A rhythm" is a particular set of durations.
Beat: In rhythm, equal-length durations or long or short subgroup in some systems of rhythmic grouping.
Meter: Regular grouping of beats.
Syncopation: In terms of beat, stress between beats, offbeat; in terms of meter, accenting a beat where stress is not expected.
Polyrhythm: Musical texture of multiple rhythmic patterns performed simultaneously.
Tempo: The rate of basic beats.
Groove: The way ensemble musicians react during performance.

Feld's definition of groove takes an even wider context into consideration, conceptualizing "groove" as a "feelingful participation, a positive physical and emotional attachment"

(1994:111). Groove, for Feld, becomes not just an interaction between performers, but a form of affective sensibility shared by the whole set of engaged participants present. By extension, these participants may be physically present in the same space, or connected by a larger affective network.

7. In his solo career, Tanaka goes by the name Kurei Soshi, whose family name sounds more exotic than the very common name, Tanaka. He was the winner of the 18th Junon Superboy Contest, where he was "discovered" by Tsunku.

8. Originally, J.P. Room was a management company responsible for producing music and stage productions of projects by Tsunku. Since Tsunku founded his own record label TNX in 2006 for his personal projects and others, J.P. Room continues to represent artists and groups that Tsunku oversees.

9. For the 2008 version of *Rhythm Heaven Gold,* the single "Koi no rung rung paradise" (La la love paradise) by the group Za Posshibo (The Possible), one of the tunes for the 2008 Japanese version of *Rhythm Heaven Gold*, eventually achieved a number 10 ranking on the Oricon J-pop charts. Oricon is a company that compiles information on sales and other information on the Japanese music industry.

10. It goes without saying there are a large number of possible ways that individuals can creatively engage with the game. However, the ways of playing that I outline here are those that would be consistent with the modes of play suggested by the instructions given on-screen in the course of game play without using hacks to crack the code.

11. There are, however, bonus games, which move away from the more standard conquer-and-progress model of teleological game play. The bonus games include those referred to as "endless games." As the name suggests, in these mini-games the user is invited to play as long as he or she wishes, and there is no single "goal" or finality. One example is the horseback riding mini-game, where the speed of the horse can be increased through continuous smooth manipulation of the game's control buttons. As the tempo changes, the background landscape also changes. If the user stops or slows down, the tempo stops or slows down and the horse simply rests or trots, but the mini-game doesn't end. There are two additional bonus-games that are only made available to users after they collect a certain number of "medals" for attaining high scores in the regular mini-games. One is the "rap machine," an on-screen sampler, which contains beats and sound effects from the "rap men" mini-game. With the rap machine, the users are free to create their own tunes using the samples on the rap machine. Another kind of bonus game is the "songs" that the user is awarded. When a song is awarded, the user can accompany the song by controlling an on-screen drum set, choosing to follow (or divert from) a song used in the mini-game.

12. See previous footnote for a description of the "rap machine" and other bonus games.

13. Morning Musume is the most successful of the pop groups operating under the Hello! Project, with Tsunku acting as the primary producer. An ongoing group since 1997, Morning Musume is an all-girl pop idol group that features a rotating cast. As of January 2010, the members ranged in age from sixteen to twenty-three. After a number of years with the group, the older members "graduate" and often form new groups, pursue careers as solo artists, or a combination.

14. Language lessons, especially English conversation lessons, are a very popular activity for people of a wide range of age groups in Japan. Subway cars, newspapers, and magazines for various readerships are plastered with ads for language schools and language programs for a variety of purposes. They take the form of supporting early childhood education,

study abroad programs, career advancement, or a practical hobby that will enable students to have more fun during their overseas vacations.

The conversation between Iwata and Tsunku was translated from the following Japanese text on the Japanese Nintendo website for *Rhythm Heaven Gold*:

岩田　　『リズム天国』、あるいは『リズム天国ゴールド』においてつんく♂さんが強く打ち出してらっしゃったコンセプトというのは「リズム感は鍛えられる」というものでした。そのあたりについて、教えていただけますか。

つんく♂　　そうですね、たとえば、「英語がしゃべれない」というのは、日本人が抱きがちなコンプレックスですよね。それと同じように、「踊れない」とか、「リズムにのれない」というのもあると思うんです。で、これは、いつもぼくが思うことなんですけど、いまからネイティブな英語をしゃべるのは無理かもしれないけど、鍛えればある程度まではたどり着けるんじゃないかと。

とくに、リズムに関しては、鍛えればある程度の領域には、全員、行けるんじゃないかなと思うんです。

岩田　　それは、やっぱり、モーニング娘。の人たちをレッスンしていくうえではっきりと確信したことなんでしょうか。

つんく♂　　そうですね。もう、みんな、最初はぜんぜんできないですからね。それでもなんとか踊れるようになりますから。

岩田　　つまり、つんく♂さんには、「リズム感は鍛えられる」ということについてはすでに実績があるわけですね。

つんく♂　　そうですね。ぼくのなかでは証拠も実績もある。歌のピッチをよくするよりも、リズム感をよくするほうがよっぽど簡単です。ですから、若い子だけではなく、おじさんやおばちゃんも含めて、「英会話でも習ってみようか」という気持ちと同じくらいの感覚で、リズム感を鍛えてもらえればなと。

15. *Nihonjinron*, or "theories of the Japanese person," refers broadly to a body of theories that have circulated in Japan mostly since 1945. However, the roots of the discourses go back to at least the beginning of the nineteenth century by thinkers such as Motoori Norinaga. Key tenets of these theories include a belief in cultural homogeneity and shared subjecthood across Japanese people. Although many of these theories were initiated in academic and economic spheres, by the 1970s and 1980s, ideas about essentialized uniqueness circulated widely in popular discourse as well.

16. For example, Tokyo Ongaku Gakko, the first Japanese conservatory of Western music was founded in 1887. Jazz became hugely popular practice in Japan in the 1920s, almost immediately along with its popularity in the United States. The first Japanese electronic music research lab opened in 1955 at NHK Radio in Tokyo, only three years after the German WDR was established in 1952–1953.

17. By 2007, album sales reached eleven million, surpassing a record set by the duo Pink Lady in the late 1970s (Oricon 2007).

18. On another level, Sakurako's comment shows how "playing" a musical instrument has become reduced to a chore, an expected requisite for social status as "cultured" rather than a vehicle for lifelong creativity and pleasure that many others find in musical practice, while "playing" the game comes to present more "fun" rewards than playing the piano. Many thanks to Chelsea Spangler for pointing this out.

19. Reviews of the game by Yohei, Monsuke, Onnel, Sakurako, and Tico were accessed February 24, 2009 through the amazon.co.jp website. Links to each of their reviews are as follows:

    Yohei: http://www.amazon.co.jp/review/R2C3942PR7I2SU

    Monsuke: http://www.amazon.co.jp/gp/cdp/member-reviews/A2V0EU8QVYN5QS/

    Onnel: http://www.amazon.co.jp/gp/cdp/member-reviews/A2RM6T4SSC8RV4/

    Sakurako: http://www.amazon.co.jp/gp/cdp/member-reviews/A1BTPNY31S8EQI/

    Tico: http://www.amazon.co.jp/gp/cdp/member-reviews/A1D94N44ISU3M7/

20. For specific ethnographic studies in Japan, cultural anthropologist Ito Mizuko has published several studies on new media and youth in Japan, including *Engineering Play: A Cultural History of Children's Software* (2009), and *Personal, Portable, Pedestrian: Mobile Phones in Japanese Life* (Ito Mizuko, Okabe Daisuke, Matsuda Misa 2005).

21. This change is also reflected in Nintendo's marketing strategy as the Game Boy units transitioned to the Nintendo DS system in 2005, and most recently, the DSi in 2009. Nintendo's portable device no longer refers exclusively to games or boys. Fittingly, after the Game Boy Advance, it shed the gendered and age-specified naming of the gaming console, and by extension, its implied users, and takes on a name that refers directly to the system itself (DS stands for both "dual screen" and "developer's system"), rather than an assumed set of users and uses.

    The new innovation that sets the DSi from the DS is that users can now take pictures with the integrated camera, and also upload their own music onto the system. It also allows users to then distort and edit those pictures using the editing application that comes with the unit (Schiessel 2009). To me, the 'i' in DSi resonates with the same letter in Apple's iPod, calling forth notions of the empowered, active user's role in controlling his or her customizable interactive device. *Rhythm Heaven* is relatively non-interactive in the sense that the user cannot create avatars, or call shots about different combinations of characters. Yet it somehow foreshadowed and integrated the notion of the video game as social utility into its software long before the inventions of the Apple iPhone or Nintendo DSi entered the market.

22. In the introduction to *Parables of the Virtual*, calling for a playful and processural mode of doing scholarship on movement, affect, and sensation, Massumi writes on the difference between the "possible and the potential" that draws on the work of Deleuze, Guattari, Bergson, and Spinoza:

    > That there is a difference between the possible and the potential needs to be attended to ... Possibility is back-formed from potential's unfolding. But once it is formed, it also effectively feeds in. Fed back, it prescripts: implicit in the determination of a thing or body's positionality is a certain set of transformations that can be expected of it by definition and that it can therefore undergo without qualitatively changing enough to warrant a new name. These possibilities delineate a region of nominally defining—that is, normative variation. Potential is unprescripted. It only feeds forward, unfolding toward the registering of an event: bull's-eye. Possibility is a variation *implicit in* what a thing can be said to be when it is on target. Potential is the *immanence* of a thing to its still indeterminate variation, under way ... Implication is a code word. Immanence is process. (2002:9)

## References

Adorno, Theodor. 2002. "The Form of the Phonograph Record." In *Essays on Music*, ed. Richard Leppert, 277–82. Berkeley: University of California Press.

Allison, Anne. 2006. *Millennial Monsters: Japanese Toys and the Global Imagination*. Berkeley and Los Angeles: University of California Press.

Atkins, E. Taylor. 2001. *Blue Nippon: Authenticating Jazz in Japan*. Durham, NC: Duke University Press.

Aoyagi Hiroshi. 2005. *Islands of Eight Million Smiles: Idol Performance and Symbolic Production in Contemporary Japan*. Cambridge: Harvard University Press.

Bordo, Susan. 1993. *Unbearable Weight: Feminism, Western Culture, and the Body*. Berkeley: University of California Press.

———. 1999. *Twilight Zones: The Hidden Life of Cultural Images from Plato to O.J.* Berkeley: University of California Press.

Casey, Edward. 1996. "How to Get From Space to Place in a Fairly Short Stretch of Time: Phenomenological Prolegomena." In *Senses of Place*, ed. Steven Feld and Keith Basso, 13–52. Santa Fe, NM: School of American Research Press.

Chen, Dominick. 2006. "Gemu no choetsu ni tsuite" (On the new era of gaming). *Eureka: Shi to hyōron* 38(6):159–64.

Feld, Steven. 1994. "Aesthetics as Iconicity of Style (uptown title); or, (downtown title) 'Lift-up-over Sounding': Getting into the Kaluli Groove." In *Music Grooves*, ed. Steven Feld and Charles Keil, 109–50. Chicago: University of Chicago Press.

Huizinga, Johan. 1950. *Homo Ludens: A Study of the Play Element in Culture*. Boston: Beacon Press.

Iketani Hayato. 2009. "Tomaranai rizumu tengoku gorudo, 12-nen buri ni oto-gei uriage saiko kiroku o nurikaeru" (Rhythm Heaven Nonstop: First new record for music games in 12 years), +D Games Website, http://plusd.itmedia.co.jp/games/articles/0901/26/news087.html (accessed May 1, 2009).

Ito, Mizuko. 2009. *Engineering Play: A Cultural History of Children's Software*. Cambridge, MA: MIT Press.

Ito, Mizuko, et al. 2010. *Hanging Out, Messing Around, and Geeking Out: Kids Living and Learning with New Media*. Cambridge, MA: MIT Press.

Ito, Mizuko, et al. 2009. *Living and Learning with New Media: Summary of Findings From the Digital Youth Project*. Cambridge, MA: MIT Press.

Ito, Mizuko, Daisuke Okabe, and Misa Matsuda. 2005. *Personal, Portable, Pedestrian: Mobile Phones in Japanese Life*. Cambridge, MA: MIT Press.

Jenkins, Henry. 2006. *Fans, Bloggers, and Gamers: Exploring Participatory Culture*. New York: New York University Press.

Massumi, Brian. 2002. *Parables for the Virtual: Movement, Affect, Sensation*. Durham, NC: Duke University Press.

Miller, Kiri. 2007. "Jacking the Dial: Radio, Race, and Place in *Grand Theft Auto*." *Ethnomusicology* 51(3):402–38.

Miller, Laura. 2006. *Beauty Up: Exploring Contemporary Japanese Body Aesthetics*. Berkeley: University of California Press.

Nintendo. 2001. GBA Specifications and Information. http://www.nintendoworldreport.com/specialArt.cfm?artid=1739 (accessed December 15, 2009).

———. 2008. E3 website, e3.nintendo.com/ds/rythmheaven/index.html (accessed December 12, 2008).

——. "Shacho ga kiku rizumu tengoku" (*Rhythm Heaven Gold* as heard by the CEO) http://touch-ds.jp/mfs/st95/interview8.html (accessed December 15, 2009).

Oricon. 2007. "Morning Musume, Pink Lady koe, josei gokan" (Morning Musume surpasses Pink Lady to achieve 5 titles). http://contents.oricon.co.jp/news/rankmusic/44224/ (accessed November 15, 2009).

*Rhythm Heaven.* 2006. Prod. Tsunku and Yoshio Sakamoto. Kyoto, Japan: Nintendo.

Smith, Jacob. 2004. "I Can See Tomorrow in Your Dance: *A Study of Dance Dance* Revolution and Music Video Games. *Journal of Popular Music Studies* 16(1): 58–84.

Sterne, Jonathan. 2006. "The MP3 as Cultural Artifact," *New Media and Society* 8(5): 825–42.

Taylor, T. L. 2006. *Play Between Worlds: Exploring Online Game Culture.* Cambridge: MIT Press.

Tsunku. 2008. "Tsunku Rizumukun" (Tsunku teachings on rhythm). http://www.tsunku.net/riq_rithmkun.htm#0718 (accessed May 30, 2008).

Wade, Bonnie C. 2009. *Thinking Musically: Experiencing Music, Expressing Culture.* New York and Oxford: Oxford University Press.

*Wikipedia, The Free Encyclopedia.* "Nintendo DS." http://en.wikipedia.org/wiki/Nintendo_DS (accessed December 20, 2009).

# PART VII

## MOBILE MUSIC INSTRUMENTS

# CHAPTER 18

........................................................................................................

# THE MOBILE PHONE
# ORCHESTRA

........................................................................................................

## GE WANG, GEORG ESSL, AND
## HENRI PENTTINEN

THE Mobile Phone Orchestra (MoPhO) is a repertoire-based ensemble that uses mobile phones as the primary musical instrument. While mobile phones have been used for artistic expression before, MoPhO is the first ensemble of its kind and scale, employing more than a dozen players and mobile phones that serve as compositional, research, performance, and educational platforms. MoPhO was founded in Fall 2007 at Stanford University's Center for Computer Research in Music and Acoustics (CCRMA) and performed its debut concert in January 2008. Since then it has spawned new ensembles at the University of Michigan, as well as in Berlin and Helsinki, and has performed in Genoa, Belfast, Helsinki, San Francisco, and Berlin. We chronicle the motivation and the process of creating such an ensemble and the repertoire of MoPhO's first performances. MoPhO aims to demonstrate that mobile phone orchestras are exciting technological and artistic opportunities for new types of music-making (Figure 18.1).

Mobile phones are growing in sheer numbers and computational power. Hyper-ubiquitous and deeply entrenched in the lifestyles of people around the world, they transcend cultural and economic barriers that other general computing devices such as laptops have failed to penetrate. Computationally, the mobile phones of today offer speed and storage capabilities comparable to desktop computers from less than ten years ago, rendering them suitable for real-time sound synthesis/analysis and other musical applications. Like traditional acoustic instruments, mobile phones are intimate sound producing devices. These devices also have the advantages of strength in numbers and ultramobility, making them attractive for holding jam sessions, rehearsals, and even performances in both formal as well as ad hoc settings. A goal of MoPhO is to explore these possibilities as a research and music-making environment, fusing technological artifact and human musicianship.

The notion of a mobile phone orchestra bears many similarities with that of a laptop orchestra (Trueman 2007; Smallwood et al. 2008:9–25; Wang et al. 2008:26–37;

FIGURE 18.1 The Mobile Phone Orchestra in action.

Fiebrink, Wang, and Cook 2007:164–67; Wang, Essl, and Penttinen 2008). The idea of phones as intimate sound sources leads to our notion of "mobile electronic chamber music." MoPhO presents a well-defined context for researchers and composers to craft new music tailored to mobile instruments and ensembles. As in the laptop orchestra, the combination of technology, aesthetics, and instrument building presents a powerful pedagogical opportunity. At the same time, the mobile phone orchestra is differentiated by its unique limitations (i.e., computational power) and opportunities, such as its extreme mobility and potential for wide-area social interactions.

# RELATED WORK

## Mobile Phones as Musical Interfaces

The transformation of mobile computing devices into musical instruments has been explored in several bodies of research. Tanaka (2004) presented an accelerometer-based custom augmented PDA that could control streaming audio. Geiger (2003, 2006) designed a touch-screen based interaction paradigm with integrated synthesis on the mobile device using a port of Pure Data (Pd) for Linux-enabled portable devices like iPAQs. Various GPS-based interactions have also been proposed (Strachan, et al. 2005;

Tanaka, Valadon, and Berger 2007). Many of these systems used an external computer for sound generation.

Using a mobile phone as a physical musical instrument in live performance has been explored by Schiemer and Havryliv (2006:37–42) in their *Pocket Gamelan* instrument. Meanwhile, other research investigated how to transform commodity mobile phones more broadly into musical instruments. A project called CaMus presents a system that uses the camera of mobile phones for tracking visual references for musical interaction (Rohs, Essl, and Roth 2006:31–36). CaMus2 extends this to allow multiple mobile phones to communicate with each other and with a PC via ad hoc Bluetooth networking (Rohs and Essl 2007:160–63). In both cases an external PC was still used to generate the sound.

MobileSTK (Essl and Rohs 2006:278–81) ports the Synthesis ToolKit (STK) (Cook and Scavone 1999) to Symbian OS, and is the first fully parametric synthesis environment available on mobile phones. It is used in combination with accelerometer and magnetometer data in ShaMus (Essl and Rohs 2007) to allow purely on-the-phone performance without any laptop. More recently, a system called *SpeedDial* explored interactive mapping and editing of mobile phone instruments during live performance (Essl 2009). In particular, the availability of accelerometers in programmable mobile phones such as Nokia's N95 and Apple's iPhone has enabled these devices to serve as meta-instruments for gesture-driven musical performance, allowing physical motion to be expressively mapped to sound.

The emergence of the iPhone has catalyzed mobile phones as a mature programmable multimedia platform. Popular commercial musical interfaces like Smule's *Ocarina* (Wang et al. 2009; Wang 2014a), *RjDj* (2009), and *ZooZBeat* (Weinberg, Beck, and Godfrey 2009) have opened up mobile performance to a broad audience. For example, *Ocarina* transforms the iPhone into a physical flute-like wind instrument co-opting multi-touch, microphone, and accelerometer control of real-time sound synthesis, and has gained a user base exceeding ten million in size. A social component of *Ocarina* allows its users to hear one another around the world while displaying their GPS locations, enabling a type of semi-anonymous, geographically diverse music-making. Another work explored gesture-based interfaces with tactile feedback (Gillian, O'Modhrain, and Essl 2009). Overall, the iPhone is an attractive platform for research, offering a blend of fast computational power, rich sensory capabilities, and a clean and low-latency audio architecture (Essl and Rohs 2009:197–207; Wang 2014b).

## Locative Performances

Several researchers have employed mobile devices as part of artistic performances, leveraging the personal and portable nature of mobile phones, as well as their everyday ubiquity. In these works, although mobile phones did not play the role of traditional instruments in ensemble settings, they demonstrate the versatility of phones and the significance of location.

Golan Levin's *Dialtones (A Telesymphony)* is one of the earliest concert concepts that used mobile devices as part of the performance (Levin 2001). In *Dialtones*, the audience itself served as the primary sound sources, and the localization of people in the concert hall is part of the performance. Audience members registered their phone numbers upon entering the concert venue. A precomposed piece was rendered by calling various audience members while simultaneously placing spotlights on those receiving the call. A large mirror above the stage and a visual projection displayed the spatialized call patterns. The conceptual use of mobile phones in *Dialtones* was passive yet spatial in nature, blurring the performer and audience boundary.

The art group Ligna and Jens Röhm created an installation performance called "Wählt die Signale" (German for "Dial the Signals"). The performance used 144 mobile phones that were arranged in an installation space. People called the publicized phone numbers and the resulting piece was broadcasted over radio. Unlike Levin's piece, the compositional concept is aleatoric—the randomness of the calling participants is an intended part of the concept (Behrendt 2005).

A performance installation that used mobile technology indirectly, and predates both Levin's and Ligna's work, is Wagenaar's "Kadoum" (2005). Heart-rate sensors were attached to twenty-four Australians. The signals were sent via mobile phones to other international locations where electric motors excited water buckets as part of an installation that displayed the heart-rate activities. In this case, mobile technology was not an inherent part of the artistic concept, but instead it served as a means of wide-area communication. Wagenaar's piece is an example of what we will call "locative music."

It is worth noting the distinction between what we term the broader category of "mobile music" and the notion of "locative music." The latter refers to using mobility as an inherent concept in a performance—for example, pieces that require moving in an urban setting. The former is a broader term that refers to any use of mobile technology for music making, but can also be used in a static and localized performance. According to Gaye, Holmquist, Behrendt, and Tanaka: "mobile music is a new field concerned with musical interaction in mobile settings, using portable technology" (2006:22–25). Atau Tanaka and Lalya Gaye offered the term "locative media" (2006), and provided several prominent instantiations.

A further example of locative music, *Sonic City* (Gaye, Maze, and Holmquist 2003), used a variety of sensors attached to a special jacket. These sensors picked up environmental information as well as body-related signals that in turn modified music heard by the wearer of the jacket through headphones. For example, the jacket would be able to track signals such as heart-rate, arm motion, pace and compass heading. Sensed environmental data included brightness, noise level, pollution level, temperature, and electromagnetic activity. As the location and the environment changed, the sonic experience varied with it.

A project called Malleable Mobile Music (Tanaka 2004:154–56) explored the ability to turn passive networked music sharing into an active endeavor. Tanaka's installation piece *Net_Dérive* (Tanaka and Gemeinboeck 2009) took this performance concept further. The installation consisted of two settings: one taking place in a gallery with large-scale video projections, and the other, using mobile phones embedded in scarves, in the streets of the city. Through headphones, participants heard instructions guiding them through the city, while the phones took pictures and recorded sounds of the environment. Through GPS and wireless communication, their position and information were traced and displayed in the gallery space where the visuals and sounds changed with the choices made by the moving audience (Tanaka and Gemeinboeck 2006:26–30).

The concepts, ideas, and realization of these works have inspired and influenced the development of the MoPhO, which is deeply interested in exploring all of these aspects of mobile music—gestural, creative, locative, and social. We believe that the mobile phone has great potential in serving as an omnibus device to adopt all these practice due to its increasing ubiquity as a commodity.

## THE MOPHO ENSEMBLE

The original MoPhO consisted of sixteen mobile phones and players, and contained a repertoire of publicly premiered pieces ranging from scored compositions and sonic sculptures, to structured and free improvisations. So far, all works have used a combination of the phones' onboard speakers, custom-made glove-speakers (Figure 18.2), and

FIGURE 18.2 Mobile phones and speaker gloves.

occasional human vocalization for sound production, combining a certain sonic intimacy found in traditional chamber music ensembles with the potential of new forms of electronic expression—a notion we'd like to call "mobile electronic chamber music."

MoPhO performs with Apple iPhones, iPod Touches, and Nokia N95 smart phones, and, in principle, is open to leverage the creative potential of any mobile computing device.

There are various mechanisms by which one can envision forming mobile phone orchestras along these same lines. For one, many people can simply bring their own device and form ad hoc groups. In our case, we were supported by the industry, notably Nokia who provided numerous device for the first ensemble and Deutsche Telekom Laboratories, academic institutions (School of Humanities at Stanford University and College of Engineering at University of Michigan), and funding agencies, such as the National Science Foundation.

It is worth noting the onboard features of the iPhone and the N95 to provide an assessment of the capabilities of contemporary phones. The iPhone offers (1) a microphone; (2) onboard loudspeakers; (3) headphone output; (4) multi-touch (up to five points) screen at 480x320 pixel resolution; (5) 3-axis accelerometers; (6) 412 MHz (or faster) CPU; (7) a dedicated graphics processing unit (GPU); (8) location via GPS, cell-tower triangulation, and Wi-Fi access point; (9) Bluetooth; and (10) persistent data connection via 3G, Edge, or 802.11. Newer iPhones also contain a compass sensor.

In terms of software, the iPhone and iPod Touch run iPhone OS, a mobile version of MacOS, sharing the same XCode development environment as other Apple platforms. It supports a simulator as well as on-device debugging. The iPhone offers a clean and fast audio architecture that allows for real-time musical interactions. The Nokia N95 does not support multi-touch, provides a smaller screen resolution, but offers an additional front-side camera, as well as stereo onboard speakers. It runs Symbian OS with an SDK in C++.

In terms of software, the ensemble uses a combination of custom programs and also some commercial musical applications for iPhones, including Smule's *Ocarina, Leaf Trombone*, and Normalware's *BeBot*. On the N95, MoPhO makes use of audio synthesis engines in C++ combined with Python front-end GUIs.

The acoustical radiation power of typical mobile devices is somewhat limited. They are powerful enough to play chamber-sized concert venues but can encounter difficulties filling larger or open performance spaces. Hence we have designed portable, wearable speakers units to amplify the phones while preserving both the localized nature of the radiating sound as well as the mobility of the devices themselves. In the first version, a pair of battery-powered speakers was sown onto finger-free sport gloves. This design affords the performer comfortable control over the device and its touch screen, as well as over the directionality of the sound radiation (see Figure 18.3). The second version used wrist-bands, which put less weight on the hands but also reduces directional control. We are also exploring other forms of wearable speaker configurations (e.g., on neck, head, waist, ankle). These solutions help overcome the challenge of amplifying most venues.

FIGURE 18.3 Gloves providing local amplification and versatility for performance.

FIGURE 18.4 New ensembles lead to new conducting styles.

## Performance Practice

MoPhO performed its first public concert on January 11, 2008 to a packed audience at the CCRMA Stage at Stanford University. It featured eight initial pieces of the MoPhO repertoire, all composed especially for mobile phones. Since then new repertoire has been added and concerts have been performed in Genoa, Belfast, Helsinki, San Francisco, and Berlin.

Mobile phone ensembles pose unique new challenges to performance practices due to the characteristics of both the ensemble and the instruments played. Mobile phone instruments can utilize a wide range of sensor technology, and these sensors can relate to physical motions or actions of the performer. They allow for diverse and rich expressive control that often is not well covered by traditional ensemble communication traditions and conducting. Hence, along with inventing the instruments and composing the pieces, an additional creative step is often the formation of suitable ensemble communication for each piece (Figure 18.4).

We use a range of communication methods, which sometimes closely resemble direct information exchange such as signaling gestures to for others to mirror, keys to press, or volume levels to adjust. The conductor often leverages arm and hand gestures designed for good visibility.

# ORIGINAL REPERTOIRE

## *Drone In/Drone Out*

*Drone In/Drone Out* (Figure 18.1) is a structured improvisation for eight or (many) more players/phones, composed and programmed by Ge Wang. Based on the laptop orchestra piece *Droner* by Dan Trueman (see Smallwood et al. 2008), *Drone In/ Drone Out* explores both individual and emergent timbres synthesized by the phones and controlled by the human players. The phone generates sound via a real-time version of a classic sound-synthesis technique known as FM-synthesis (Chowning 1973:536–34), and maps the two-accelerometer axes to spectral richness (via index of modulation, up/down axis) and subtle detuning of the fundamental frequency (left/ right axis). The result is rich in controllable low-frequency interference between partials, and creates a saturated sonic texture that permeates even large performance spaces despite the limited output power of onboard speakers. Additionally, preprogrammed pitches and modulation ratios (selectable via the phone's number pad) allow the ensemble to move through a variety of harmonies and timbre-scapes, as directed by a human conductor. Furthermore, by experimenting with modulation ratios and spectral richness, the resulting partials can suggest the perception of low fundamental frequencies well beyond the limited bass response of the phone speakers.

Due to the extreme mobile nature of phones, players may be placed almost anywhere throughout the performance area, and furthermore, are able to easily move during a performance and even play from the audience, further underscoring the "every-day" nature of using this technology for creative ends. For example, during the MoPhO debut performance at the CCRMA Stage, we began the concert with members of the ensemble sitting, disguised among the audience. The remaining players marched in with phones droning, as the disguised players revealed themselves and moved to surround the audience (resulting in 12 players/phones). A reprise of the piece (Drone Out) closed the concert, exploring additional spatial configurations of phones before the players exited the stage or returned to the audience.

## *TamaG*

*TamaG* by Georg Essl is a piece that explores the boundary of projecting the humane onto mobile devices, and at the same time displays the fact that they are deeply mechanical and artificial. It explores the question: how much control do we have in the interaction with these devices or do the device itself at times controls us? The piece works with the tension between these positions and crosses the desirable and the alarming, the human voice with mechanical noise. The alarming effect has a social quality and spreads between the performers. The sounding algorithm is called a circle map (Essl 2006a, 2006b), which is a non-linear algorithm offering easy-to-control and hard-to-control regimes. These in turn evoke in the performer and audience an experience of the meaning of control and desirability on the one hand, and the loss of control and mechanistic function on the other hand. The first regime consists of single-pitch-like sounds that resemble the human voice. When the performer approaches the hard-to-control regime the sound starts to resemble a stuttering voice. The second regime is mechanistic noise that too can be manipulated, but only with great difficulty.

## *The Phones and the Fury*

*The phones and the fury* by Jeff Cooper and Henri Penttinen is a DJ-style one-performer table-top piece in which multiple phones play looped music. The playback rate can be controlled by tilting the devices. By interweaving looped patterns it references the cross-mixing of a DJ performance. Fast movements result in quickly changing timbres. The piece was played by one person, but more players can be easily introduced.

## *Circular Transformations*

*Circular Transformations* is a collaborative and experimental work by Jonathan Middleton and Henri Penttinen. The piece is composed for a mobile phone ensemble of five to ten players and is structured in the same manner as an organum with four clausula sections. The title gets its name from the circular patterns of a harmonograph (Anthony 2003) set to the ratio 5:3 (major sixth). From the rotary shapes Jonathan was able to translate the lines into musical patterns by mapping the actual forms of the lines into number representations. The post-production of the notes and numbers was done in the software called music algorithms (Middleton and Dowd 2008:128–35). The tones were created using FM-synthesis as well as circle maps (Essl 2006a, 2006b), and controlled by a simple sequencer. The piece can be either played with a collective synchronization and letting the players control the timbres of their part, or with a conductor who gives timing cues for each part. The spatialization was formed as a semi-circle with one bass player at both ends and the other players situated in pairs.

## Phoning It In

Chris Warren's *phoning it in* is a mobile phone "tape piece" performance, where the performers act as diffusers in space. The piece is spatialized and each phone carries a different component of the composition. By positioning and orienting the phones, the players diffuse the piece through the performance space. The tape composition is tailored specifically to the bandwidth of the mobile phone play-back by using compression and other techniques.

## The MoPhive Quintet: Cellphone Quartet in C Major, op. 24

Adnan Marquez-Borbon's *MoPhive Quintet* (Figure 18.5) is a free-form improvisation for four or five players exploring live sampling via onboard phone microphones and speakers. At any time, players are encouraged to vocalize, capture the sound of other human players or phones, and/or playback a previously recorded clip. As the piece evolves, new vocalizations are intertwined with samples potentially passed from phone to phone via live, on-the-fly recording. This piece is carried out with the default sound recorder software provided with the phone, and playfully suggests new group musical possibilities using common phone features.

FIGURE 18.5 The MoPhive Quintet in performance.

## Chatter

Ge Wang's *Chatter* is a conducted improvisation for twelve or more players and phones, and employs a simple software buffer playback that maps an axis of the phone accelerometer to playback rate. The players are distributed throughout the audience in an effort to immerse the audience in a sonic web of cell phone conversational clouds. The source material consists of greetings, short sentences, laughter, and various guttural utterances (courtesy of Georg Essl and Ge Wang) that are triggered via the phones' number pads, easily permitting rhythmic interplay between phones (when desired). More recent instantiations of the piece contain utterances of nine additional speakers, most German, but some also in Portuguese, Hindi, Dutch, and French (courtesy of Berlin members of the ensemble).

## Botz Groove

*Botz Groove* is a two-part call and response riff piece played using a pentatonic scale with the *BeBot* instrument, written by Georg Essl. It features a backdrop over which individuals play solos in various voices provided by the BeBot instrument. The piece explores more traditional pitch worlds, yet conventional syncopated rhythms combine with flexible free-form improvisation. In particular, BeBot's PWM voice is used to evoke resemblance of an electronic guitar solo.

## T-Fare

*T-Fare*, by Georg Essl, is a two-part, two-voice *Ocarina* piece with prerecorded sound. It is a variation on commercial mobile phone ring tone of T-Mobile, played and reharmonized for the *Ocarina*. While playing intervals of thirds and fourths, the base of the phrases uses the full range of the twelve-tone diatonic scale. The piece is designed to reenact traditional voiced diatonic polyphonic performance in a mobile phone ensemble. The piece starts with a few members of the ensemble planted in the audience and accidentally having their mobile phone ring with the well-recognized ring tone, the ensemble then responds by playing the phrase, which slowly morphs into variations on the theme, hence playing humorously with the boundary between the expectation associated with a ring tone and musical performance. Custom music stands attached to the iPhones are used to help performers keep track of the score (Figures 18.6, 18.7).

# CONCLUSION

The Mobile Phone Orchestra uses programmable commodity mobile devices as its primary means of musical expression. The modern phones' computational power allows

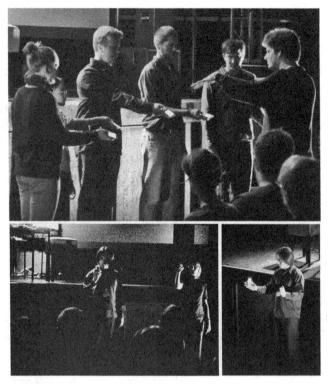

FIGURE 18.6 The Mobile Phone Orchestra in Belfast 2008.

FIGURE 18.7 The program notes of the first mobile phone orchestra concert at Stanford University in January 2008. Note that these show an early ensemble name, which was later shortened to MoPhO.

for rich interactive sound synthesis and the platform offers a diverse set of interactions—gestures via accelerometers, multi-touch and key input, built-in camera as vision-based sensor, microphone, and location-based social interactions Figure 18.8).

The technology is stable enough to both form a well-defined ensemble and to create a persistent repertoire. The development of a mobile phone ensemble parallels and diverges from that of laptop orchestras. Mobile phones, like laptops, provide a technological basis that can serve as instruments of new music performance, where the engagement with the programmable device itself constitutes the instrument and fuses the teaching of technology and art, and allows new forms of ensemble expression. Some of the properties of the mobile phone orchestra are rather distinct from laptop ensembles. They are extremely easy to transport and set up. Mobile phone performances can easily be moved, performed on-the-go, and spontaneously organized. The typical power of the speakers of these devices allows for a chamber music quality of the performance: strong enough for adequately quiet spaces while preserving the intimate instrumental qualities of these devices. Portable speakers attached to gloves, neck, or belt can overcome even this limitation and allow for intimate yet potent performance in large concert venues or outdoors.

Perhaps a deeper question to ask is "why a mobile phone orchestra?" In addition to our desire to explore new technology as means for artistic expression, we believe that entrenched in the mass adoption of this type of mobile personal technology lies potential for radically new paradigms of creative and social exchange. The structure of an

FIGURE 18.8 How to best interact with mobile musical instruments?

FIGURE 18.9 Members of the first Mobile Phone Orchestra ensemble.

orchestra serves as a foundation for unifying research, artistic exploration, and social organization, allowing for new and robust repertoire to emerge and evolve.

This type of ensemble is still in its infancy. The first concert in January 2008 provided credence that the technology is mature enough to explore the concept of the ensemble. Since then a number of concerts have been presented in Genoa, Belfast, Helsinki, San Francisco and Berlin. But there are still many pieces yet to be defined and many open questions remain: How to best make use of sensor data mapping? What new performance paradigms might be afforded by the mobile nature of the phones, and how might we take advantage of the ubiquity of smart phones? What new types of music can we make? As the MoPhOs at Stanford, Michigan, and elsewhere mature, how can we exploit the possibility of wide-area remote performances? Furthermore, how can we engage with the mobile devices in the hands of millions of people around the world?

On the artistic side, these are only the first steps within the MoPhO setting (Figure 18.9). The complexity of pieces is quite open-ended, as location, interconnection, and mapping of gestures to musical sound can all diversely contribute to mobile phone ensemble play. We also look forward to exploring performances with other instruments—acoustic, electronic, or otherwise. We believe that this is only the beginning for mobile phone orchestras and are excitedly looking forward to diverse developments of this new emerging medium.

# ACKNOWLEDGMENTS

This project was possible thanks to the support and enthusiasm of Jyri Huopaniemi of Nokia Research Center, Palo Alto, and thanks to Nokia for providing a sizeable number of mobile phones. Jarno Seppanen provided invaluable input into mobile phone programming during a workshop taught at CCRMA in November 2007. Many thanks to Chryssie Nanou, Artistic Coordinator of CCRMA, for guidance and support throughout the project and for setting up the first concert at CCRMA. Many thanks to Brett Ascarelli and Yungshen Hsiao for documentation in the form of pictures and video footage of rehearsals and concerts, and to Rob Hamilton for his excellent support. Thanks to Smule. Last but never least, hearty thanks to all the great MoPhO performers and co-composers: Steinunn Arnardottir, Mark Branscom, Nick Bryan, Jeff Cooper, Lawrence Fyfe, Gina Gu, Ethan Hartman, Turner Kirk, Adnan Marquez-Borbon, Jonathan Middleton, Diana Siwiak, Kyle Spratt, and Chris Warren. For Belfast, Genova we also featured Ajay Kapur, Adam Tindale, Ian Knopke and Ananya Misra. In Berlin we were joined by Alex Müller, Fabian Hemmert, Michael Rohs, Sven Kratz, Nicole Weber, Matthias Rath, Constanze Kettliz-Profe, Susann Hamann.

## REFERENCES

Anthony, Anthony. 2003. *Harmonograph: A Visual Guide to the Mathematics of Music.* New York: Walker & Company.

Behrendt, Frauke. 2005. *Handymusik. Klangkunst und 'mobile devices.'* Osnabrück: Epos. Available: www.epos.uos.de/music/templates/buch.php?id=57.

Chowning, J. 1973. "The synthesis of complex audio spectra by means of frequency modulation." *Journal of the Audio Engineering Society* 21(7):526–34.

Cook, Perry, and Gary Scavone. 1999. "The Synthesis ToolKit (STK)." In *Proceedings of the International Computer Music Conference*, 164–66. Beijing: ICMA.

Essl, Georg. 2006a. "Circle maps as a simple oscillators for complex behavior: I. basics." In *Proceedings of the International Computer Music Conference (ICMC)*, 356–59. New Orleans: ICMA.

——. 2006b. "Circle maps as a simple oscillators for complex behavior: II. experiments." In *Proceedings of the International Conference on Digital Audio Effects (DAFx)*. Montreal: McGill.

——. 2009. "SpeedDial: Rapid and On-The-Fly Mapping of Mobile Phone Instruments." In *Proceedings of the International Conference on New Interfaces for Musical Expression (NIME09)*, 270–3. Pittsburgh: Carnegie Mellon University.

Essl, Georg, and Michael Rohs. 2006. "Mobile STK for Symbian OS." In *Proceedings of the International Computer Music Conference*, 278–81. New Orleans: ICMA.

——. 2007. "ShaMus—A Sensor-Based Integrated Mobile Phone Instrument." In *Proceedings of the International Computer Music Conference*, 200–3. Copenhagen: ICMA.

——. 2009. "Interactivity for Mobile Music Making." *Organised Sound*, 14(2):197–207.

Fiebrink, Rebecca, Ge Wang, and Perry R. Cook. 2007. "Don't forget the laptop: Using native input capabilities for expressive musical control." In *Proceedings of the International Conference on New Interfaces for Musical Expression*, 164–67. New York: New York University.

Gaye, Lalya, Lars E. Holmquist, Frauke Behrendt, and Atau Tanaka. 2006. "Mobile music technology: Report on an emerging community." In *NIME '06: Proceedings of the 2006 conference on New Interfaces for Musical Expression*, 22–25. Paris: IRCAM.

Gaye, Lalya, Ramia Maze, and Lars E. Holmquist. 2003. "Sonic City: The Urban Environment as a Musical Interface." In *Proceedings of the International Conference on New Interfaces for Musical Expression*, 109–15. Montreal: McGill.

Geiger, Günther. 2003. "PDa: Real Time Signal Processing and Sound Generation on Handheld Devices." In *Proceedings of the International Computer Music Conference*. Singapore: ICMA.

——. 2006. "Using the Touch Screen as a Controller for Portable Computer Music Instruments." In *Proceedings of the International Conference on New Interfaces for Musical Expression*, 61–64. Paris: IRCAM.

Gillian, Nicholas, Sile O'Modhrain, and Georg Essl. 2009. "Scratch-Off: A gesture based mobile music game with tactile feedback." In *Proceedings of the International Conference on New Interfaces for Musical Expression (NIME09)*, 308–11. Pittsburgh: Carnegie Mellon University.

Levin, Golan. 2001. *Dialtones—(A Telesymphony)*, www.flong.com/telesymphony (accessed April 1, 2007).

Middleton, Jonathan, and Diane Dowd. 2008. "Web-based algorithmic composition from extramusical resources." *Leonardo* 41(2):128–35.

RjDj: A Mind-twisting Hearing Sensation, http://rjdj.me/ (accessed August 2009).

Rohs, Michael, Georg Essl. 2007. "CaMus2: Optical Flow and Collaboration in Camera Phone Music." In *Proceedings of the International Conference on New Interfaces for Musical Expression (NIME)*, 160–63. New York: New York University.

Rohs, Michael, Georg Essl, and Martin Roth. 2006. "CaMus: Live Music Performance using Camera Phones and Visual Grid Tracking." In *Proceedings of the International Conference on New Instruments for Musical Expression (NIME)*, 31–36. Paris: IRCAM.

Schiemer, Greg, and Mark Havryliv. 2006. "Pocket Gamelan: Tuneable trajectories for flying sources in Mandala 3 and Mandala 4." In *Proceedings of the International Conference on New Interfaces for Musical Expression (NIME)*, 37–42. Paris: IRCAM.

Smallwood, Scott, Dan Trueman, Perry R. Cook, and Ge Wang. 2008. "Composing for laptop orchestra." *Computer Music Journal* 32(1):9–25.

Strachan, Steven, Parisa Eslambolchilar, Roderick Murray-Smith, Stephen Hughes, and Sile O'Modhrain. 2005. "GpsTunes: Controlling Navigation via Audio Feedback." In *Proceedings of the 7th International Conference on Human Computer Interaction with Mobile Devices & Services*, 275–78. Salzburg, Austria: ACM.

Tanaka, Atau. 2004. "Mobile Music Making." In *Proceedings of the International Conference on New Interfaces for Musical Expression*, 154–56. Hamamatsu: Shizuoka University.

Tanaka, Atau and Petra Gemeinboeck. 2006. "A framework for spatial interaction in locative media." In *Proceedings of the International Conference on New Interfaces for Musical Expression*, 26–30. Paris: IRCAM.

——. 2009 "Net_Dérive: Conceiving and Producing a Locative Media Artwork." In *Mobile Technologies: From Telecommunications to Media*, ed. Gerard Goggin and Larissa Hjorth, 174–86. London: Routledge.

Tanaka, Atau, Guillame Valadon, and Christophe Berger. 2007. "Social Mobile Music Navigation using the Compass." In *Proceedings of the International Mobile Music Workshop*. Amsterdam: STEIM.

Trueman, Dan. 2007. "Why a laptop orchestra?" *Organised Sound* 12(2):171–79.

Wang, Ge. 2014a. "Ocarina: Designing the iPhone's Magic Flute." *Computer Music Journal.* 38(2).

——. 2014b. "The World is Your Stage: Making Music on the iPhone." *Oxford Handbook of Mobile Music Studies*, ed. Gopinath and Stanyek. Oxford University Press.

Wang, Ge, Georg Essl, and Henri Penttinen. 2008. "MoPho: Do Mobile Phones Dream of Electric Orchestras?" In *Proceedings of the International Computer Music Conference (ICMC08)*. Belfast: ICMA.

Wang, Ge, Dan Trueman, Scott Smallwood, and Perry R. Cook. 2008. "The laptop orchestra as classroom." *Computer Music Journal* 32(1):26–37.

Wang, Ge, et al. 2009. "Smule = Sonic Media: An Intersection of the Mobile, Musical, and Social." In *Proceedings of the International Computer Music Conference*, 283–86. Montreal: ICMA.

Weinberg, Gil, Andrew Beck, and Mark Godfrey. 2009. "ZooZBeat: a Gesture-based Mobile Music Studio." In *Proceedings of the International Conference on New Interfaces for Musical Expression (NIME09)*, 312–5. Pittsburgh: Carnegie Mellon University.

# CHAPTER 19

# CREATIVE APPLICATIONS OF INTERACTIVE MOBILE MUSIC

ATAU TANAKA

THE past decade has seen enormous development in the portability and mobility of musical content, aided by advances in mobile wireless networks and the miniaturization of data storage. This chapter reviews foundational research conducted in this period at Sony Computer Science Laboratory Paris (CSL), a noncommercial industry laboratory for fundamental research, and at Culture Lab Newcastle. The work draws upon methods from creative practice and reexamines the forms and formats that music can taken on when deployed on mobile devices and wireless infrastructures. It takes as a fundamental point of departure the notion of music as an emergent, fluid form that is expressive and contextual rather than a fixed media industry commodity. With this, the chapter covers a range of contexts, including domestic environments, scenarios of socializing, locative media, and interactive music performance. Taken together, the body of work presented here provides insight into the development of conceptual thinking of mobile music creation that is outside the sphere of commercial applications and consumer markets.

## CONVERGENCE AND INTEGRATION: FROM WALKMAN TO iPHONE

It is natural today to imagine, and utilize, advanced portable devices that are at once mobile telephone, personal music player, and digital camera. These devices, symbolized by the Apple iPhone and a range of smartphones built on the Android and other operating systems, are for the most part also connected to mobile broadband networks, and provide location sensing by means of the Global Positioning System (GPS). It is interesting to note that these products are almost all referred to as mobile *phones*. This implies that their communications functions take primacy and that their musical and imaging functions are secondary. As a composer, I was interested in turning around this relationship to conceive of advanced musical scenarios that could be supported by wireless content streaming, gesture detection, and location awareness.

Whether music takes the fore or not, the coexistence of such functionality on a single device represents not only a high level of technology integration but also forms of conceptual convergence. While the technology exists in an integrated manner on a single piece of hardware, less attention has been paid to the actual integration of usage. Music playing, telephoning, messaging, photo taking, location mapping are separate applications that change the mode the device is in. To date, there have been no forward-looking apps that might, for example, pipe one's current MP3 playlist as background music to a telephone conversation, or allow associations of music and photographic image. Raskin's notion of modelessness in screen-based interface design allows users to more productively manage multiple tasks. Moving from modal interfaces to modeless interaction is less trivial on portable devices, given their limited screen size and in-the-while use contexts, but tackling these challenges might contribute to more imaginative use integration of the different media functions on mobile devices.

Jenkins extends the mechanics of simple feature integration to propose the concept of *technological convergence*. Beyond the functionalities of sound, image, location, and communications is a higher level convergence of consumer electronics hardware, media content, network data and other services. Convergence products have seen enormous development in recent years, most notably by Apple's iTunes system that couples entertainment content and application software catalogues to their hardware line up. This convergence, however, has taken place at a commercial level and has not resulted in a fundamental change in the actual content, its form and format, to otherwise exploit the new possibilities afforded by personalized, context aware network distribution. In online music distribution, a single is still a single, and an album is still an album. In the work described here, we adapt existing music into new, malleable formats specific to the infrastructures on which they reside, and imagine entirely new forms of music created specially for these systems.

The idea to combine a personal music player with a mobile telephone seems a natural fit. Besides the challenge of technology integration and conceptual convergence, there are underlying differences in the cultural contexts of music listening and communications that render this combination nontrivial. Bull notes the isolating experience of headphone listening, while Ito and Matsuda report on the constant contact that mobiles provide. While MP3 players and cell phones share many qualities—they are portable devices, they are audio devices, they are highly personal devices—in the end they each serve very different social functions. The work presented here seeks out ways in which to bridge these differences to imagine what a true convergence device might be like. We shall call upon notions of social computing to see how music can serve the new social dynamics that mobile networks allow. We will see from an audio processing perspective how participative, flexible content forms can be supported. Finally, we will look at real world issues of deploying such systems on off-the-shelf mobile phones and commercial cellular telecommunications networks.

# LOCATION SENSING

Dynamic geographic location is one of the fundamental characteristics of a user in a mobile environment. Mobile use implies that the user can access the same universe of information wherever he might be—*anytime, anywhere*. Designing information systems for mobile use, however, entails more than just porting a web page meant to be viewed on a desktop computer to display on a mobile phone screen. Not only do the screen dimensions and device form-factor change, but the usage dynamic. Here, we focus less on providing a single information stream when in movement but rather on shifting needs when location changes. Commercial location based services exist in many flavors—from the simplicity of geo-tagging Twitter photo uploads to broadcasting location updates to "check in" on Foursquare, to GPS city tours guided by movie stars, but the killer location-aware app has yet to arrive. Much in the way that the challenges of creating information spaces for mobile environments is distinct from those meant to serve stationary settings, I argue that imagining music for mobile environments should go beyond the act of putting one's whole album collection in the shirt pocket. Here we look at ways in which location sensing can be used in a musical way to create new, contextual musical experiences.

Artists in the field of *locative media art* have seized on the creative potential of geographic information. This includes the visualization of movement across geographic space in the form of drawings, to tagging of physical space by sound as in Mark Shepherd's Tactical Sound Garden. Theatrical choreography linked to displacements of participants is seen in the seminal work of Blast Theory. In sound based projects, the city can become interface to a generative electronic music system in systems like Sonic City. Yolande Harris's projects meanwhile undo assumptions of multi-user connectedness typically associated with systems to focus on the data jitter of stasis.

The Global Positioning System is the technology most commonly associated with location tracking but is not the only solution. The projects described there have used motion capture techniques, Bluetooth signal reception, GSM antenna strength, as well as GPS to sense user location. Each technology has its advantages and disadvantages with each approach having distinct characteristics, such as accuracy and response time, that have an effect on the musicality when used as an input to sound processes. In this way, we take a view that geographic localization is not one thing, but a form of information that can be captured in different musical ways.

# DOMESTIC ENVIRONMENTS

While GPS location tracking assumes, and operates only in, outdoor environments, indoor location sensing continues to be a highly relevant task and nontrivial technical challenge. Starting in 2002 with the *SoundLiving* project, we used low power Bluetooth base stations to arm a domestic environment in order to create personalized spheres of sound that could follow a user throughout the home (Figure 19.1). It resulted in a working prototype designed to augment a home stereo system where, in place of the traditional remote control for the hi-fi system, the user had a Bluetooth probe that could communicate with receivers in each room. The listener would use the touchscreen on the device to select what music to play. Once the music was playing, if the listener moved to another room in the house, for example from the living room to the kitchen, the probe announced his presence to the room he just entered, and caused the system to re-route the network data stream carrying the music, in a seamless manner, from the living room to the kitchen. From the listener's vantage point, the music simply continued uninterrupted, and just naturally started coming out of the speaker system in the kitchen and stopped playing in the living room stereo. It was as if the music he was listening to constituted his personal audio sphere that followed him around the house.

The design of this first system separated the mobile device (in this case the personal location probe) from sound production (the speakers of the stereo systems). Hidden behind what otherwise looked like a common hi-fi system were localization

FIGURE **19.1** Example in SoundLiving of sound following user from selection made in bedroom from the stereo next to the bed down the stairs to the stereo in the kitchen.

and network routing services that integrated the different speaker systems throughout the house.

Products for wireless broadcast of audio throughout the home have since been introduced, including Apple's AirPlay. However they are for the most part cable replacements, and at best based on a broadcast model where a single source can broadcast to multiple wireless speakers. Technically they do not perform location sensing, and more important, conceptually, they do not broach the personal nature of music that can take on embodied qualities as it is co-located around, and relocates according to the listener's movements. The SoundLiving system was unique in providing a continuity of music delivery, creating the sense of a location-aware personal audio bubble.

## MALLEABLE CONTENT

In moving from an indoor, domestic space to imagining how music might be deployed across a multi-user, geographic space, we conceived a music remix software engine to generate continuous variations on well known popular music based on location. The idea was that each participant in a group would be represented by a part, or an instrument, in the music, and that their relative proximity would be mapped to the amplitude of that part in the total mix. The user's gestures and actions on the mobile device (the personal context) would modulate effects on his own part, and give the others in the group an idea of his behavior—whether he was running, dancing, or just sitting still. Meanwhile the mix of parts would reflect the social context reflected in the location data. The resulting mix was streamed from the server side engine back over wireless broadband networks to each of the mobile devices. All members of the group heard the same stream, thus creating a shared experience. The notion that the remix of a song could reflect the behavior of each participant as well as the global state of the group, creates what we term a *social remix*.

We implemented the Malleable Mobile Music system using a familiar pop song by the artist, Björk. We detected the global tempo of the recording, and used it to build a temporal map of the song. In this map we identified large scale structure (such as verse and chorus), and the appearance of different musical parts in each section (voice, percussion, horn section). The Malleable Music engine then used the song map as an index into the original recording, instantly seeking to any measure in the song, and looping on a certain loop length for a certain number of iterations. The server instantiated multiple voices of this engine (as many voices as there were participants in the system), and was able to synchronize them. In a three user system for example, three voices were independently playing on arbitrary sections of the original song, were synchronized in rhythm, and mixed to an output streamed to all the mobile devices. In this way, with the map and the original recording, a kind of live cut/paste remixing took place.

In this example, music became a direct carrier of social information. The part in the music that represented each user became their *musical avatar* (Figure 19.2). The remix

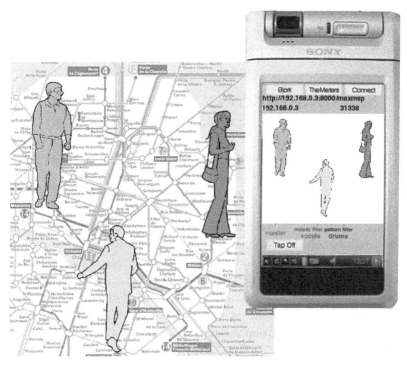

FIGURE 19.2 Malleable Mobile Music—with client device displaying 3 visual avatars (right) and a location service simulator (left) interface for testing location-dependent social music remixes.

unfolded following the movements of the participants. One user could hear the proximity of another by noticing the volume of their part in the mix. One could guess at their activity through the filtering and delay effects that were heard on their part. This points to the use of music in the area of ambient information displays where the user does not need to take any explicit action (such as making a phone call or sending a text message) to gain relevant information on their friends' relative proximity and activity. This social information is embedded into the musical content itself, and perceived through the otherwise normal activity of music listening.

This work builds on a long tradition of rendering existing music interactive. Early examples included Peter Gabriel's CD-ROM, *Xplora 1* originally published in 1995. Since the original malleable music research was conducted in 2004, the technology company MXP4 has introduced a new file format in 2006 separating component tracks of a musical composition for playback in a synchronized interactive manner to facilitate listener remixing. Artists like Trent Reznor have published web-based remix systems in 2007. While all these systems and formats are similar in that they permit music to be deconstructed and reconstituted, the commercial products cited here focus on a single user actively engaging in the remix process. With Malleable Mobile Music, we were interested not just in deploying such an interactive music system in geographic space, but to re-contextualize music following Erickson's notion of *social translucence* to become a location-aware and responsive media form that could reflect back to the listener the state of her immediate social group.

# SENSING THE SELF WITHIN A GROUP

A perceptual challenge exists in decoding fluid changes in abstract forms such as music when they are meant to represent concrete phenomena such as physical proximity. Social translucence describes the representation of social dynamic in information displays and is a term used in social computing to describe the use of social information to support collective action. A key element in the decoding process is the task of situating oneself within the whole. In a location based remix, the instrument that represents the listener may stay at a constant volume with respect to other, dynamic voices. Giving local context to the listener's own part may provide reflexive understanding of the situation that may aid that listener to decode the wider context of other users. We extended Erickson's original term to coin the term *reflexive translucence* to include the user's own sense of agency and place in a group situation.

In order to heighten the listener's sense of agency, we implemented two ways in which the system responded to local context. One was through a sensor subsystem on the handheld device that detected grip pressure, rotation, and shaking, and the second was a localized audio display. This research took place in 2005, two years before the release of the iPhone popularized the integration of accelerometers in mobile devices to detect rotation for user interface features. In our system the local sensors (Figure 19.3) detected gestures that the listener performed, consciously or subconsciously, while listening to music. The gesture as captured by pressure and accelerometer sensors in turn affected the music being listened to, creating a feedback loop of perception, reaction, and enaction. In a multiuser musical environment such as a social remix, the sensors local to one listener gave that listener interactive feedback on his own part, creating a different and identifiable immediacy relative to the more slowly modulated mix of part representing the other users.

The local sound output of the mobile devices could be directed to a built-in speaker on the device, or to its headphone output creating a separate audio stream from the whole mix that might be playing in a room. This helped to situate the device and its listener in a physical space and himself in the midst of a music that projected multiple users' states. This acoustically placed a sound source in the space and differed markedly in effect compared to the virtual surround sound panning representing the group. The use of local outputs or network as audio destinations and the possibility to render audio in the public space or locally to headphones constitutes a multifaceted, hybrid audio space. This hybrid model supports the two social contexts, personal and community.

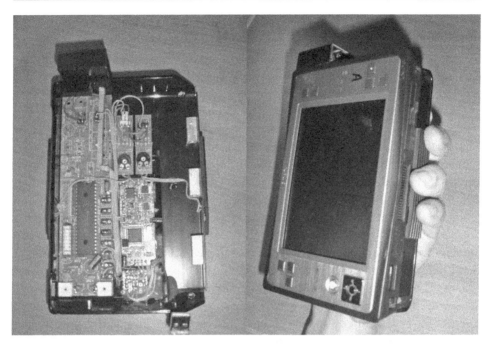

FIGURE 19.3 Visceral Mobile Music device—a palmtop PC with custom sensor acquisition card capable of sending two pressure sensors, two tilt sensors, and a gyroscope to pick up the personal context of the listener.

# INTO THE WILD—THE REAL WORLD AND REAL MOBILES

In the social remix example, we were concentrating on how generative music content and delivery could respond to personal and community contexts. Community context was derived from geographic data generated by a location simulator module that placed three visual avatars on a city map. By dragging the avatars across the screen, the simulator generated geographic data. With this the Malleable Mobile Music engine was set up to receive geographic data as control input from the network. It helped us conceive of ways in which the music would evolve as community members moved around. The next step was to move beyond the simulator and look at location tracking techniques that would work out on the streets. This work, originally conducted in 2003, was done in anticipation of the broad mass-market deployment of 3G/UMTS mobile broadband in Europe around that time. With the arrival of 3G and handsets supporting these infrastructures, these early experiments led to real world implementations.

First generation 3G mobile phones in 2005 were beginning to be multimedia capable. They had high resolution color screens, built-in mega-pixel digital cameras, and could be programmed using Flash and Java J2ME. If the mobile's capabilities were limited, the 3G networks were even more so. The Malleable engine works over live MP3 streaming over the network. Signal coverage was and continues to be a problem for persistent connections such as audio streaming. Moreover, advanced control over ports and network protocols such as RTSP remained in the hands of the telecommunications network operators. While the internet is governed by an international series of committees and standards defending openness, 3G networks are governed by private entities who decide what parts of the network are accessible based on their own commercial interests.

The reality of implementing a streaming mobile system is non-trivial. The mass market mobile internet applications available today are for the most part based on web services, and reduce the scope of network communications mostly to the HTTP protocol. To this day, fixed line streaming music services, like Spotify, operate on a download-based model for their mobile version. Meanwhile in our research, conceptual development of possibilities of locative media interaction continued to develop. Despite the technical limitations of 3G networks, GPS, and the capabilities of mobile phones, the goal of these projects was to create a community-based, location aware music system. While the initial prototypes ran on various non-telephone devices, it was imperative to make the system run on mobile phones—to bring to a logical end the initial concepts, to validate them on the true target device, one that is already charged with cultural associations and common usage patterns. How could we implement a new music listening experience on mobile phones, and what were the requirements to create an engaging experience within the practical constraints of contemporary infrastructure and technology?

Conceptually we accompanied movements of the time in the area of locative media arts that drew upon radical ideas of the Situationist International movement in the 1960s. Festivals like Conflux in New York were dedicated to the notion of *psychogeography*. Many mobile media projects drew upon the related concept of the dérive. *Net_ Dérive* was a collaborative work with Petra Gemeinboeck and Ali Momeni that sought to create a mobile audiovisual derive through a work of locative music.

While we wished to utilize commonly available mobile telephone technology, we were interested to push beyond the typical cultural associations and musical contexts linked to those associations. We created a hollow scarf-like structure out of neoprene fabric that housed two phones and a then necessary external GPS device. There was one phone on each end of the scarf, and the GPS mobile in the middle, behind the neck. The result was an object inspired by research in wearable computing, where computing functionality is integrated into clothing (Figure 19.4). The user donned the scarf, and wore the headphones that came out of one of the ends. On the other end was the second phone whose display was visible. Only the buttons relevant to use in the project (the 5-way button) was accessible. Other controls on the phones (the numeric keypad in particular) were covered by the scarf to prevent unintentional button pushes.

GPS coordinates were reported to a location server automatically every five seconds. A photo was taken by one of the phones every 20 seconds and uploaded to the server, tagged with GPS coordinates, thus leaving a visual trace. The server logged all this data in

FIGURE 19.4 Net_Dérive wearable device—two Symbia S60 devices and Bluetooth GPS module enclosed in a scarf-like garment.

XML files, keeping a separate record for each user, the path they took, and the images that were taken during their walk. Meanwhile one of the phones captured audio and streamed it up to the server, as a live input feed to the media content engine. The server-side content engine had several modes of visualizing the users' walks based on the GPS data and the photos taken along the way. The walks were *sonified*, generating rhythmic sounds based on the relative proximity of the users, and mixing that with live processing on the audio feeds coming from each phone. The resulting graphics and soundscape were streamed back down to each mobile device, heard on its headphones and seen on its color display.

The content in this case was not based on existing music as had been the case in the previous example. Instead here we were interested in looking at whether sound and image could work together to sonify/visualize the state of the community to each of the users while on the move. The goal was to create a satisfactory experience for the user within the technical constraints described earlier.

## AGGREGATION AND META-DATA TAGGING

In 2008 a major sporting event provided us the opportunity to explore the effects of mass numbers. The Great North Run half-marathon commissioned the artist group, NAME,

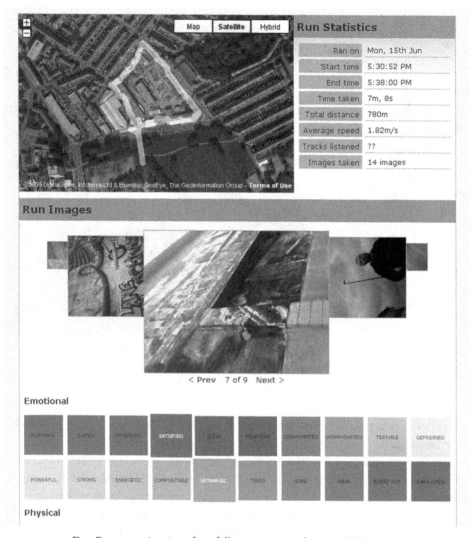

FIGURE 19.5 Dry Run—tagging interface following a run showing GPS trace, statistics, and photo trace for tagging by emotional and physical descriptors.

using technology from Culture Lab for a mobile, to create an online project tracing the emotional trajectory of a long distance run. The result was *Dry Run*, a prototype that tracked ten runners over one month of training for the event. Using the logging functionality from Net_Dérive, the run was automatically documented in geo-tagged photographs, generating an image bank that re-traced each training session. Photos from each run were additionally tagged post-facto by meta-data from the runner. This geographically and emotionally tagged visual trace of the run was designed to be correlated to the playlists of music that had been listened to by the athlete during the training. While unfinished, the project brought a different perspective to mobile music than the continuous, personal creative streams that had been explored in the previous projects. The sequence of events, outlined here, included capture, tagging, aggregation, and visualization.

During the run, a mobile device running custom Symbian software was used to replace the MP3 player commonly used by runners to listen to music during training. On this device, the runner had, in the classic manner, loaded a playlist of music to accompany this run. Upon starting the run, she initiates software on the mobile which plays the playlist, and activates the GPS module, built-in camera, and 3G broadband network. Similar to Net_Dérive, the journey is documented by an automatic series of photographs taken once per minute that are geo-tagged with the latitude and longitude data, and uploaded live over 3G mobile broadband to a fixed line server. Additional functionality not found in Net_Dérive include associating the current music with the photo. In essence, each photo was time-stamped, geo-tagged, and music-tagged.

Following the run, the runner completed the process by meta-data tagging photos from the run using a post-training interface (Figure 19.5). A series of descriptors drawn from sports science studies that describe physical and emotional exertion during sport were proposed in drop-down menus as possible meta-data tags for the runner to select and associate with each photograph retracing the run. This created a topologically correlated physical and emotional trajectory characterizing a run which could then be visualized in different ways (Figures 19.6 and 19.7).

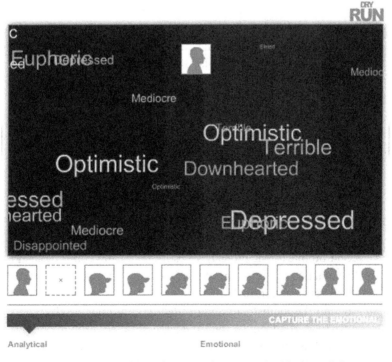

FIGURE **19.6** Dry Run—tag cloud visualization of emotional and physical descriptors.

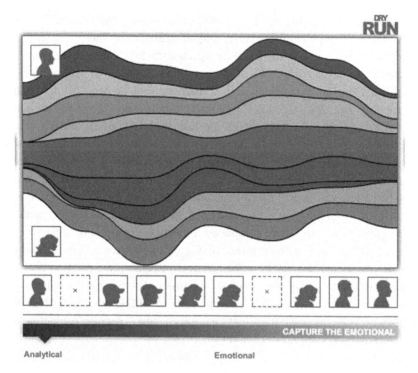

FIGURE 19.7 Dry Run—exertion curve visualization of emotional and physical descriptors.

The aggregation of multiple runs by any single runner, then of multiple runners, created an accumulation of statistically significant data across time and across a number of participants. With the association of the playlist track being played at each data point, it becomes possible to begin to understand the role of music in the training process. While products like Nike + iPod connect music listening to sports training, Dry Run situates music in both the geographic and emotional trajectories of a training session. By aggregating across training sessions and runners, the idea, to be completed in a future version of the project, would be to extract from the data set the "ideal playlist."

## THE MOBILE MUSICAL INSTRUMENT

In our most recent mobile music project, we adopt the by now ubiquitous iPhone and focus on creative practice and live concert performance. Throughout the time that the research described here was conducted, technologies from the laboratory have steadily found their way into the mainstream, embedded in consumer products. The iPhone represented the arrival of advanced multimedia, embodied, mobile computing. This has triggered the publishing of numerous music apps, some of which are discussed elsewhere in this volume. One of these music apps for iPhone and Android mobile phones to emerge from the open source community is the free software RJDJ, standing for *Reality DJ*. RJDJ is a mobile interactive music playback engine based on Pure Data (PD), the open source branch of the family of graphical music programming environments that also includes Max MSP, originally developed at IRCAM by Miller Puckette. RJDJ deploys a simplified version of PD on mobile processors, and facilitates interactivity through microphone input, and the accelerometers and touch screens found on advanced smartphones. The developers of RJDJ publish a catalogue of what they term "reactive music"—different forms of generative and interactive music that extend traditional Walkman-style music listening from one of fixed music assets to one that is continuously context aware. With this, some of the vision originally articulated in research projects such as Gaye's Sonic City have arrived in the marketplace.

It is noteworthy that the dissemination of these technologies and concepts to broader audiences are built on the same software platforms that have been at the root of interactive computer music composition and performance since the 1980s. Beginning with the Patcher at IRCAM, the graphical programming paradigm of programmatic function represented onscreen as objects interconnected by virtual wires, started as a way to control computer music synthesis on mainframe computers. With Max/MSP and PD, real time computer music on personal computers and laptops became pervasive. The port of PD to iPhone and Android in many ways has put the IRCAM studio of the 1980s in one's pocket. Along with this transposition from mainframe to mobile comes a fundamental shift of the social contexts in which computer music can take place.

My own musical output has paralleled this development, with the formation of different music ensembles that reflect the musical and technological contexts in live concert performance. This included Sensorband, formed in 1993 and Sensors_Sonics_Sights formed in 2003. With the move to RJDJ on iPhone, the duo of Adam Parkinson and this author, 4 Hands iPhone, continues the live computer music tradition with the use of mobile music technology.

In the duo, we exploit the iPhone, a commonly available consumer electronics device, as an expressive, gestural musical instrument (Figure 19.8). The device is well known an iconic object of desire in our society of consumption. While the iPhone can play music as a commodity, we re-appropriate the device and exploit its advanced technical capabilities to transform the consumer object into an expressive musical instrument for concert performance. In a duo, with one device in each hand, we create a chamber music, four hands for iPhone. The accelerometers which typically serve as tilt sensors to rotate photos are reutilized for high precision capture of the performer's free space gestures. The multitouch screen, otherwise used for scrolling and pinch-zooming text, becomes a reconfigurable graphic user interface akin to the JazzMutant Lemur, with programmable faders, buttons, and 2D controllers that control synthesis parameters in real time. We have ported Nobuyasu Sakonda's advanced granular synthesis implementation of from MaxMSP to RJDJ and use it as the single process by which a battery of sounds are stretched, frozen, scattered, and restitched. Source sounds include, among other things, excerpts and loops from popular music—the very music that is commodified and typically listened to in fixed form on iPods, as well as natural sounds—artificially processing

FIGURE **19.8** Adam Parkinson and Atau Tanaka: 4 Hands iPhone in concert.

and re-contextualizing the kinds of experience associated with standard, ambulatory personal music player use. The fact that all system components—sensor input, signal processing and sound synthesis, and audio output, are embodied in a single device make the RJDJ enabled iPhone very different than the controller + laptop setup typically seen in contemporary digital music performance. The encapsulation of all instrumental qualities from gestural input to expressive sound output in a self-contained, manipulable object take the mobile phone beyond consumer icon to become a powerful musical instrument.

# CONCLUSION

The goal of the systems described here were to leverage the possibilities of contextual sensing, from location tracking to gestural capture, coupled with dynamic media delivery systems to create new musical experiences that could be shared by groups of performers and listeners. Each of these topics—localization, musical expression, content delivery, association, and community dynamic—were developed step by step over a number of technology iterations. Content delivery began with SoundLiving as a single user experience, with a fixed piece of music seamlessly being redirected on the fly. This developed into a group experience with Malleable Mobile Music where we looked at how each respective participant could maintain a sense of agency for their contribution to the musical whole and used the term reflexive translucence to describe this effect. Net_Dérive focused more closely on the music and ways music could be a carrier of social information. Moving from questions of how music could convey information on human presence, we concentrated on a tight association between the sonification and visualization of community dynamic. This was extended to a broader group dynamic in a non-musical context with Dry Run. Finally, 4 Hands iPhone brings contextual sensing back to a pure musical performance, exploring the potential of the mobile phone as expressive, holistic musical instrument.

Throughout these projects is a working method that considers music an emergent form to be sculpted rather than a fixed media commodity to be consumed. While this position may be natural for musical performance seen in 4 Hands iPhone, we apply this notion of the malleability of music to the very consumer formats of popular song in SoundLiving and Malleable Mobile Music to demonstrate how music otherwise recorded and produced to be a commodity can be rendered interactive and context sensitive, to define personal spatial spheres and signal human presence. Small's notion of *musicking* describes forms of engagement with music that overcome traditional boundaries between the playing and listening of music. Here we have created musical systems built on mobile technologies that perhaps represent musicking machines.

## Bibliography

Bongers, Bert. 1998. "An Interview with Sensorband." *Computer Music Journal.* 22(1):13–24.

Bull, Michael. 2000. *Sounding Out the City, Personal Stereos and the Management of Everyday Life.* Oxford: Berg.

Casas, Roberto, et al. 2007. "Hidden Issues in Deploying an Indoor Location System." *IEEE Pervasive Computing* 6(2):62–9.

Erickson, Thomas, and Wendy A. Kellogg. 2000. "Social Translucence: An Approach to Designing Systems that Mesh with Social Processes." *ACM Transactions on Human Computer Interaction* 7(1):59–83.

Galloway, Anne, and Matthew Ward. 2006. "Locative Media As Socialising and Spatializing Practice: Learning from Archaeology." *Leonardo Electronic Almanac* 14(3). Cambridge, MA: MIT Press.

Gaye, Lalya, R. Maize, L. E. Holmquist. 2003. "Sonic City: The Urban Environment as a Musical Interface." In *Proceedings of New Interfaces for Musical Expression (NIME)*, National University of Singapore:109–15.

Harris, Yolande. 2007. "Taking Soundings—Investigating Coastal Navigations and Orientations in Sound." *Proc. Mobile Music Workshop.*

Hemment, Drew. Locative Arts, http://www.drewhemment.com/2004/locative_arts.html (accessed December 17, 2010).

Ito, Mizuko, Daisuke Okabe, and Misa Matsuda, ed. 2005. *Personal, Portable, Pedestrian: Mobile Phones in Japanese Life.* Cambridge, MA: MIT Press.

Jenkins, Henry. 2006. *Convergence Culture: Where Old and New Media Collide.* New York: New York University Press.

Koleva, Boriana, et al. 2001. "Orchestrating a Mixed Reality Performance." In *Proceedings of the SIGCHI conference on Human Factors in Computing Systems.*

Loubet, Emmanuelle. 2000. "Laptop Performers, Compact Disc Designers, and No-Beat Techno Artists in Japan: Music from Nowhere." *Computer Music Journal* 24(4):19–32.

Nine Inch Nails. http://remix.nin.com (accessed December 17, 2010).

Puckette, Miller. 1996. "Pure Data: Another Integrated Computer Music Environment." In *Proceedings, Second Intercollege Computer Music Concerts*, 37–41. Tachikawa, Japan.

Raskin, Jef. 2000. *The Humane Interface.* Boston: Addison-Wesley.

Shepard, Mark. 2008. "Tactical Sound Garden [TSG] Toolkit." In *Creative Interactions—The Mobile Music Workshops 2004–2008*, ed. N. Kirisits, F. Behrendt, L. Gaye, A. Tanaka, 92–93. Vienna: Di'Angewandte.

Small, Christopher. 1998. *Musicking: The Meanings of Performing and Listening.* Middletown: Wesleyan University Press.

Tanaka, Atau. 2004. "Malleable Mobile Music." In *Adjunct Proceedings of the Sixth International Conference on Ubiquitous Computing (UBICOMP).*

——. 2008. "Visceral Mobile Music Systems." In *Transdisciplinary Digital Art: Sound, Vision and the New Screen*, ed. R. Adams, S. Gibson, and S. Müller Arisona, 155–170. Berlin: Springer-Verlag.

——. 2009. "Sensor-Based Musical Instruments and Interactive Music." In *The Oxford Handbook of Computer Music*, ed. R. Dean, 233–57. Oxford: Oxford University Press.

Tanaka, Atau, and Petra Gemeinboeck. 2008. "Net_Dérive: Conceiving and Producing a Locative Media Artwork." In *Mobile Technologies: From Telecommunications to Media*, ed. Gerard Goggin and Larissa Hjorth, 174–86. Oxford: Routledge.

Zicarelli, David. 1998. "An extensible real-time signal processing environment for Max." In *Proceedings of the International Computer Music Conference (ICMC).*

....................

# CHAPTER 20

# THE WORLD IS YOUR STAGE: MAKING MUSIC ON THE iPHONE

....................

GE WANG

DUE to their mobility, intimacy, and sheer strength in numbers, mobile phones have become much more than "portable miniature computers," increasingly serving as personal extensions of ourselves. Therein lies immense potential to reshape the way we think and act, especially in how we engage one another socially, creatively, and musically. This chapter explores the emergence of the iPhone as a unique platform for creating new expressive and social mediums. In my dual role as an Assistant Professor at Stanford University's Center for Computer Research in Music and Acoustics (CCRMA) and the co-founder of Smule—a startup company devoted to music-making on the iPhone—I chronicle the beginnings of the iPhone for musical expression and first-hand experience in co-founding Smule in 2008, designing its products, and reflecting on the ramifications (so far). Three case studies examine how Smule's early "social musical artifacts" are able to take deep advantage of the iPhone's intersection of technologies (multi-touch, powerful mobile CPU and GPU, full audio pipeline, GPS and location, persistent data connection) and its human factors (mobility, ubiquity, and intimacy) to provide experiences that seek to be expressive on a personal level, and social on a global scale. These case studies demonstrate a potential for new types of creative communities and look ahead into a possible future of global music-making via personal computing devices.

The mobile music evolution has been catalyzed by the advancement and proliferation of the smartphone, portable and compact computing devices with built-in physical sensors, persistent connectivity, and location awareness. In particular, the iPhone brought about an inflection point in mobile devices, and transformed the notion of the mobile device into a general computing platform. Looking back only five short years (to 2008), we might attribute the success of the iPhone to several reasons. First reason: "*killer hardware*." The iPhone presented users with a unique intersection of technologies, integrated

FIGURE 20.1 Playing Ocarina, an expressive wind instrument for the iPhone.

into a single personal device: CPU, GPU, multi-touch (up to five points), dual-axis accel-erometer, high quality audio pipeline (two speaker outputs, microphone headset, high fidelity digital audio), location, and persistent data (via 3G, Edge, or Wi-Fi). Second reason: *software platform.* Deployed in spring 2008, the iPhone OS (now iOS) Software Development Kit (SDK) provided developers access to the myriad of iPhone hardware and software features, remarkable in its ease of programming. Third reason: *critical mass.* By 2010, the iPhone/iPod Touch/iPad has an install base exceeding one hundred million devices worldwide in over one hundred countries, with more than 250,000 third party applications in the iPhone's App Store sharing over six billion downloads. This has triggered a revolution in software for smartphones, and the critical mass is poised to increase. Fourth reason: *distribution.* Apple's App Store provided an easy way to deliver mobile software from developers and researchers to users around the world.

The arrival of such new technology and its wide adoption present exciting opportuni-ties to explore new uses that change the way people make music and relate socially. In this chapter, we explore the potential for and implications of musical (or proto-musical) social interaction and collaboration using currently available technologies embedded into mobile phones. The dynamics of this particular brand of social intercourse and the emergence of an associated aesthetic is described. The clichéd concept of a global village is made a vibrant reality by introducing instruments with inherent communal and collaborative properties. A proximate sonic connection encouraging social linkage within a microcosm is coupled with a global communal music network. As case studies, I describe a series of commercial iPhone applications that introduce a unique aspect of music-mediated community building. The research mission that pervades this work is simple: to change how people think, do, and play through technology and music.

Perhaps by setting the conditions right, we can explore a fundamentally more global and social music-making paradigm and mindset.

# BACKGROUND

## Mobile and Locative Music

The field of mobile music has been explored in several bodies of research, much of which has informed and inspired this essay. Tanaka (2004) gives an overview of how the control of streaming audio could be achieved via an accelerometer based custom-augmented PDA. Geiger (2003, 2006) designed a touch-screen based interaction paradigm with integrated synthesis on the mobile device using a port of Pure Data (Pd) for Linux-enabled portal devices like iPAQs. Schiemer and Havryliv (2006) explored mobile phones as physical musical instruments in *Pocket Gamelan*. Meanwhile, CaMus and CaMus2 introduced systems that use the onboard cameras on mobile phones for tracking visual references for musical interaction (Rohs, Essl, and Roth 2006; Essl and Rohs 2007a). The MobileSTK (Essl and Rohs 2006) port of Perry Cook's and Gary Scavone's Synthesis Toolkit (STK) (Cook and Scavone 1999) to Symbian OS is the first full parametric synthesis environment available on mobile phones. It was used in combination with accelerometer and magnetometer data in ShaMus (Essl and Rohs 2007b) to allow purely on-the-phone performance without any laptop. Golan Levin's *Dialtones (A Telesymphony)* performance is one of the earliest concert concepts that used mobile devices as part of the performance (2001).

Location and global positioning play a significant role in the work presented in this chapter. This notion of "locative media," a term used by Tanaka and Gaye (Gaye et al. 2006), has been explored in various installations, performance, and other projects. These include Wagenaar's *Kadoum*, which featured GPS sensor sonified heart-rate information from twenty-four participants and across two continents. Gaye, Maze, and Holmquist (2003) explored this idea in *Sonic City* with location-aware body sensors that crafted personal musical experiences from the urban city surrounding. Tanaka has pioneered a number of projects on this topic, including *Malleable Mobile Music* and *Net Dérive*, the latter leveraging a centralized installation that tracked and interacted with off-site participants with mobile devices embedded into scarves (Tanaka 2006). Locative performances have also been explored by Ligna and Jens Röhm in *Wählt die Signale* (Behrendt 2005), involving sensors and mobile phones in wide area settings.

More recently, the Mobile Phone Orchestra (Wang, Essl, and Penttinen 2008; see Chapter 18, "The Mobile Phone Orchestra," in this volume) is exploring the combination of real-time sound synthesis, interaction design, and musical performance in an ensemble setting, extending the notion of "electronic chamber music" of the Princeton Laptop Orchestra and Stanford Laptop Orchestra (Trueman 2007; Wang, Bryan, Oh, and Hamilton 2009; Fiebrink, Wang, and Cook 2007) by adding mobility and potential for locative interactions. The Stanford Mobile Phone Orchestra (MoPhO), founded in 2007 by the author, Georg Essl, and Henri Penttinen at the CCRMA, and more recently the Michigan Mobile Phone Orchestra, explore the mobility of phones to create a new form of ensemble and classroom experience.

The emergence of the iPhone has evolved the mobile phone into a mature programmable multimedia platform. Popular commercial musical interfaces like RjDj (2009), ZooZBeat (Weinberg, Beck, and Godfrey 2009), Bloom (2009), LaDiDa (Khu.sh 2009), SHAZAM (2009), as well as artifacts analyzed in this work, including *Ocarina* (Wang 2014, Figure 20.1), have originated from ideas and technique in computer music research and opened up mobile music to a broad audience. Additional work explored gesture-based interfaces with tactile feedback (Gillian, O'Modhrain, and Essl 2009). Overall, the iPhone's offering of fast computational power, rich sensory capabilities, and a clean and low-latency audio architecture, is attractive for new music research.

## Founding Smule

In the remainder of this chapter, I focus on three social/musical artifacts by Smule and a vision that binds them. Smule, founded in 2008, is a start-up company creating technology and experiences to explore social music making. It provides a unique platform for research and development of this paradigm, combining computer music research with a unique potential to bring its visions to a wide population (Wang et al. 2009). In five years since its inception, Smule has reached more than one hundred million users on iPhones, iPod Touches, and iPads, demonstrating that—through mobile, expressive, social means—it is possible to effect penetration on a massive scale, fostering semblances of global communities in a short timespan.

How did Smule get off the ground, and how did I find myself in the concurrent role of an academic, as well as a rather "accidental" entrepreneur? The idea of starting a company exploring music-making around mobile phones began in Spring 2008, shortly following Apple's announcement of the iPhone OS SDK and the App Store (this gesture opened the iPhone to developers in a way that insulated them from the mobile carriers, making it much easier to build and distribute mobile applications). I had never intended to start a company, but I had helped create the first instantiation of the Mobile Phone Orchestra at Stanford and witnessed first-hand the power of the modern smartphone. It seemed that devices like the iPhone held the potential to change the way people made music and interacted socially on a massive scale. From a research perspective, I felt that to carry out the investigation, we fundamentally needed mass adoption (hence the intersection of academic research and a startup aiming to bring music-making to the masses made sense to me). I have come to appreciate that no one in their right mind should ever want to start a company—unless one is so determined to try something different that one cannot afford *not* to do it. This turned out to be the clinching reason to co-found Smule while embracing my academic role and mission: to explore a new music-making paradigm and bring it to many people.

Our research and development on mobile music at both Smule and Stanford University's CCRMA explore a type of new social music-making, sometimes referred to as *interactive social music*, that touches on three primary ideas. First, it explores real-time expressive audio and physical interaction design on personal mobile devices. Second, it explores the belief that everyone has an innate desire to express themselves and the ability to be creative, and by setting the conditions right through technology, we can unlock this type of creativity. Finally, the research seeks to explore new social interactions through music. The physical instantiations of social music are here referred to as *sonic artifacts*. Aesthetically, these artifacts seek not to simulate, but to transform the mobile device into visceral musical experiences. This design approach views mobile computing devices as personal and intimate, rendering new activities and interactions uniquely feasible on mobile phones.

# FROM LIGHTER TO LEAF TROMBONE: THREE CASE STUDIES

Having defined interactive social music in this context, I present and analyze three sonic artifacts from Smule that are all commercial products with origin in computer music research. These artifacts, *Sonic Lighter, Ocarina*, and *Leaf Trombone: World Stage,* each take into account human factors, and are cognizant of the mobility, physicality, and social potential of the iPhone platform. They encourage new uses and interactions between people, and build on each other to articulate a vision that seeks to connect people through the personal, mobile, and social.

It is worth noting that while these three artifacts are the subjects of case studies here, Smule is but one of many entities, researchers, and developers exploring music-making on the iPhone. Along with Smule apps, many music-oriented applications (some of which are mentioned above in section 2) continue to be created for the iPhone and, more recently, the iPad. In fact, the "Music" category in the App Store is a vibrant and growing catalog of mobile, musical interactions.

## *Sonic Lighter*

Our first sonic artifact, *Sonic Lighter*, is not a musical instrument (in fact, it is barely audible). Nonetheless, it is a fitting starting point in that it is somehow expressive, leverages computer audio for expressive physical interactions, and presents a unique wide-area social mechanism. It also serves as a foundation for later experiments.

At first glance, the *Sonic Lighter* is a fairly "standard" virtual lighter for the iPhone (there were dozens in the iPhone's App Store when the app was launched), whose animated flame responds to tilt via accelerometer and multi-touch (simulating the effect of running one's fingers through a candle flame). What differentiates *Sonic Lighter* are its sonic and social features.

A simple aesthetic statement is expressed in allowing the virtual flame to "scorch" the side of the iPhone when tilted too far, as if to say the device actually *is* a lighter, rather than merely simulating one. This shifts from a purely virtual mentality to one that recognizes physicality, a metaphor that is extended by two sonic (and perhaps more poetic) gestures. By blowing gently into the microphone (located at the bottom of the device), the user causes the virtual flame to dance. Blowing with sufficient intensity extinguishes the flame. This gesture further treats the device as a physical artifact, leveraging the microphone as a breath sensor by tracking the amplitude of the incoming audio signal generated by air molecules hitting the microphone (Hoffman 2007; Misra, Essl, and Rohs 2008).

A second sonic (and equally physical) gesture requires two or more devices equipped with *Sonic Lighters*. By toggling an onscreen control on one *Sonic Lighter*, the flame can "spread" to nearby phones. This simple near-field communication is mediated through a sonic modem—the transmitting phone emits a special pair of tones, while the receiver continuously analyzes the incoming audio stream, scanning for the special encoded signals.

In addition to the physical interactions described above, there is a parallel social side to the artifact. By navigating to a globe view in the *Sonic Lighter*, the user is presented with a visualization that shows where other *Sonic Lighter* users recently ignited around the world (Figure 20.2). This is achieved by making use of the devices' location-awareness

FIGURE **20.2** The Sonic Lighter and visualization of ignitions around the world.

(via GPS) and persistent connectivity (e.g., WiFi, 3G, Edge, etc.). If the phone-to-phone ignitions constitute a type of *local* social interaction (requiring its participants to be in close physical proximity with each other), then this social interaction is wide-area and *global* in nature. Furthermore, it is *anonymous*. One does not know *who* the other points of light represent, only *where* they are and that they have ignited the lighter recently. The idea is to provide a small sense of connection with others through the knowledge that they have performed a similar gesture, and knowing *where* somehow provides a powerful context (e.g., seeing an ignition in Paris somehow feels different than an ignition from Beijing). In contrast to the existing social communities on the Internet (Facebook, the blogosphere, Twitter, etc.), this is a much more anonymous interaction, providing a "someone somewhere out there" effect, where one does not actually know who is participating but that someone nonetheless is.

I chose the *Sonic Lighter* as the first artifact to analyze because it explores physicality, mobility, and a type of anonymous social interaction that seems feasible at this intersection of new mobile technology and a critical mass of global users connected via a constantly shifting mobile network topology. In the next case study, we add musical expression and a more intimate social mechanism to create a whimsical and magical personal musical instrument that allows its users to listen to one another.

## Ocarina

*Ocarina* transforms the iPhone into an expressive wind instrument, while adding a somewhat "voyeuristic" social music feature that allows users to listen to one another play around the world (Figure 20.1, Figure 20.3). Designed and built in only six weeks, *Ocarina* was first released for iPhone in November of 2008, where it became a #1 application in the United States, United Kingdom, and twenty other countries. At the time of this writing, *Ocarina* has been downloaded to more than ten million devices worldwide, and its users have listened to each other in over forty million sessions.

### The Instrument

Smule's *Ocarina* instrument is a re-imagining of the ancient acoustic clay ocarina while radically transforming it in the "kiln" of modern technology (Wang 2014). *Ocarina* is sensitive to breath (gently blowing into the microphone controls articulation and intensity), touch (via a multi-touch interface based on the four-hole English Pendant ocarina), and movement (dual axis accelerometer controls vibrato rate and depth). It also extends the traditional instrument by providing precise intonation, extended pitch range, and key/mode mappings. As one plays, the finger holes respond sonically and onscreen the breath is visualized in pulsing waves. Sound synthesis takes place in real-time on the iPhone via Smule's audio engine, using the ChucK programming language (Wang 2008). The accelerometer's up/down tilt is mapped to vibrato depth, while the left/right tilt is mapped to vibrato rate. This allows expressive control, and

FIGURE 20.3 An ensemble of 5 Ocarinas and guitar plays the introduction to Led Zeppelin's "Stairway to Heaven." Like the *Theme from Legend of Zelda*, this online video was created to capture the magic of the iPhone Ocarina through the rendition of an iconic piece of popular music. This video was shot and edited overnight at Smule HQ (the rug actually came from the living room of CEO Jeff Smith, who is also the middle Ocarina player, sporting a wig). Ocarina was launched with the Zelda theme and this video, and have since been viewed a combined three millions times on YouTube.

contributes to the visual aspect of playing the instrument, requiring the player to physically move the device.

The traditional acoustic ocarina produces sound as a Helmholtz resonator, where sound results from the vibration of air volumes inside a container with one or more holes. The size of the finger holes on acoustic ocarinas are carefully chosen to affect the amount of total uncovered area as a ratio to the enclosed volume and thickness of the ocarina—this relationship directly affects the resulting frequency. The pitch range of a four-hole English Pendant ocarina is typically one octave, the lowest note played by covering all four finger holes, and the highest played by uncovering all finger holes. Some chromatic pitches are played by partially covering certain holes. Since the iPhone *Ocarina* digitally synthesizes its audio, a certain amount of flexibility becomes available. No longer coupled to the physical parameters, the digital ocarina offers accurate intonation, and is able to remap and extend the fingering. For example, *Ocarina* allows the player to choose the root key and mode (e.g., Ionian, Dorian, Phrygian, etc.), the latter offering alternate mappings to the fingering (A whimsical "Zeldarian" mode is also offered, facilitating playing music from *The Legend of Zelda*, a video game series that helped to popularize the ocarina in mainstream culture).

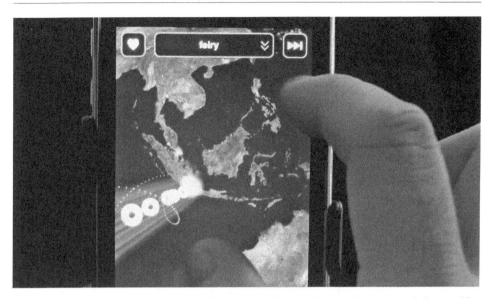

FIGURE 20.4 Browsing the globe, and listening to Ocarina being played around the world.

## Listening to the World

As a social artifact, *Ocarina* is perhaps the first instrument in history that allows its players to hear (somewhat voyeuristically) one another on a global scale (Figure 20.4). Achieved through gesture tracking, GPS position, and the persistent data connection on the iPhone, *Ocarina* captures salient gestural information (timing, key, melody) that can be compactly transmitted, stored, and precisely rendered into sound in the instrument's "World Listener," presenting a different way to play and share music. In the first year since its release, over 40 millions snippets have been created and shared.

If the listener likes the snippet, he or she can "heart" the snippet by tapping the heart icon. Each snippet being heard is chosen via an algorithm at a central *Ocarina* server, and takes into account recentness, popularity, geographic diversity, and filter selections by the user. The listener can choose to listen to (1) the world, (2) a specific region, (3) snippets that he or she has loved, and (4) snippets he or she has played. This is truly an anonymous social activity—everyone is only identified via a self-chosen handle, their GPS location, and through one's music.

This rather voyeuristic social interaction, first featured in the *Sonic Lighter* and now extended to hearing others' playing, is a fascinating (and potentially disturbing) feature of the *Ocarina* (I had no idea how this would be received when designing it). Over time, the response from our users has been overwhelmingly positive. An iTunes review of the *Ocarina* on the iPhone App Store from 2009 expresses one user's reaction:

> This is my peace on earth. I am currently deployed in Iraq, and hell on earth is an every day occurrence. The few nights I may have off I am deeply engaged in this app.

The globe feature that lets you hear everyone else in the world playing in the most calming art I have ever been introduced to. It brings the entire world together without politics or war. It is the EXACT opposite of my life. I completely love this app. ("Deployed U.S. Soldier")

## Inside-Out Design

*Ocarina* was designed with an approach that I call *inside-out design,* which argues against deciding what to build ahead of time, and instead begins with the capabilities and limitations of the device itself, asking "what is *it* good at doing?", and then designing backwards and outward from there. For example, instead of "porting" a larger instrument, such as a piano or guitar, and shrinking it down to the size (capabilities) of the iPhone, *Ocarina* originates from the phone's small form factor, and aims to naturally leverage multi-touch, accelerometer, microphone, and GPS. The design follows the device and the aesthetics it affords, not the other way around. This approach feels more consistent with the aforementioned physicality and newness of the technology, as well as encourages a discipline that experiments, embracing both the advantages and limitations of the platform.

For every product, the design process we have taken at Smule strives for short development cycles (no more than a few months) and focuses on providing experiences that invite musicians and non-musicians alike into the product. To such end, creatively bringing the mobile experiences to many users is very much an integral part of experiential design (for example, all else being equal, we prefer features that translate well to grassroots, user-generated videos on YouTube, trying to encourage word-of-mouth spreading of the apps).

## Leaf Trombone: World Stage

*Leaf Trombone: World Stage* extends the expressive and social experience in *Sonic Lighter* and *Ocarina* into a game-like instrument and introduces a crowd-based social music experience for the iPhone (Wang et al 2011). The physical aspect of *Leaf Trombone* is a whimsical wind instrument that consists of a leaf-like trombone slide, accompanied by an animated "Music Box" (Figure 20.5). In free-play mode, the *Leaf Trombone* can be used to play melodies, taking advantage of the expressive instrument, capable of portamento and a pitch range of three octaves. In game-play mode, players perform a particular musical selection, with scrolling leaf markers prompting where to position the Leaf trombone slide next. The interpretation and embellishment is open for the player to express, and enables freedom at various levels for the performer.

Following the trajectory of *Sonic Lighter* and *Ocarina,* there is a unique social element to *Leaf Trombone.* After a player performs a song, he or she can submit it to the "World Stage," where it will be judged and scored by a live panel of juries consisting of other *Leaf Trombone* players from around the world (Figure 20.6). In its judging of the quality of

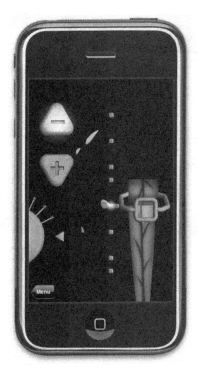

FIGURE 20.5 Leaf Trombone instrument. Leafs hint where to position the trombone slide, expression is left to the user.

a performance, which may contain expressions and nuances at many levels, the World Stage explores the notion that distributed, multi-user assessments of performance quality can represent a powerful form of sociality.

In each judging session, three judges are selected from the pool of *Leaf Trombone* users. They are to listen, comment, and rate a particular performance. While the performance takes place before it is judged, the three judges participate in real-time relative to each other. Each judge is able to comment (via text, and in their preferred language) and display a particular emoticon, ranging from enthusiastic approval to boredom or bafflement. At the end of each performance, each judge gives a score of 1 (weak) to 10 (strong). The judging sessions are fully recorded, stored on the central *Leaf Trombone* server, and available to the performer for playback. Additionally, observers on the "World Stage" can randomly access any existing judging session (of which there are more than half a million to date). This combination of instrument (Leaf trombone) and massive social interaction ("World Stage") investigates the notion of a global musical community mediated by technology and facilitates unique interactions between its denizens.

*Leaf Trombone: World Stage*'s musical content was designed to be "crowd-sourced" and created by its users. Each *Leaf Trombone* selection consists of a score for the Leaf trombone instrument with accompaniment from its "Music Box." To date, more than 6,000 user-generated scores have been published to the game. These scores are created

FIGURE 20.6 A panel of live users judge Leaf Trombone performances.

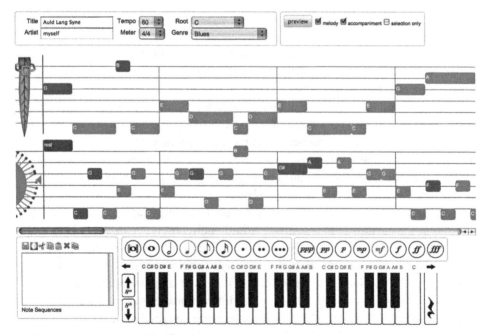

FIGURE 20.7 Composing interface for Leaf Trombone. This web-based application publishes directly to the app.

using a web interface (Figure 20.7), which presents a notation system created specifically for the instrument. A user can compose by entering notes for the melodic trombone part as well as the background accompaniment to be played on the "Music Box." Scores can be previewed and saved to the author's online account. When a score is completed to satisfaction, a user publishes and instantly makes the score available to all instances of the game around the world.

## Global Communities

These sonic artifacts have their similarities and differences, but the common thread is a social awareness centered around expressive sonic/musical interactions and manifested in ad hoc, grassroots global user communities. As an early example of a user-generated, wide-area interaction, *Sonic Lighter* users have literally taken to the streets to create messages by igniting in specific places and patterns, such as the "hi" message spelled out in the city of Pasadena, California spanning multiple city blocks (Figure 20.8).

For *Ocarina*, in addition to the social experience on the mobile device, there is a web portal dedicated for users to generate and share musical scores. Since November 2008, users of the *Ocarina* have authored more than 1500 online scores using a custom *Ocarina*

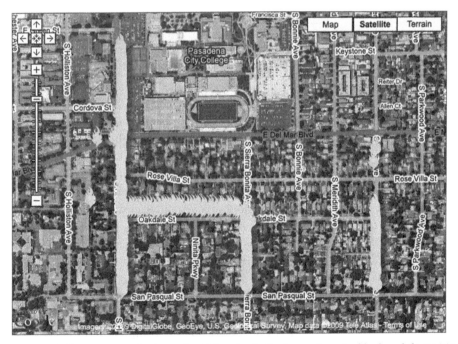

FIGURE 20.8 User-generated art produced by physically traversing city blocks while igniting the Sonic Lighter.

Amazing Grace

D Ionian

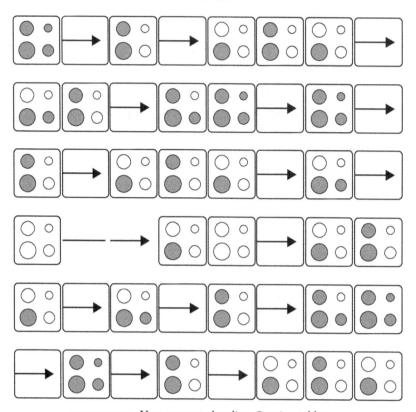

FIGURE 20.9 User-generated online Ocarina tablature.

tablature (Figure 20.9), serving millions of views. User-generated scores include video game music (e.g., "Legend of Zelda Theme Song," "Super Mario Bros. Theme"), Western classical melodies (e.g., "Ode to Joy," "Blue Danube," "Adagio for Strings"), rock classics (e.g., "Yesterday" by The Beatles, "Final Countdown" by Europe), and movie music ("Star Wars Imperial March," "Superman Theme), as well as show tunes, holiday music, and more. These tablatures require no prior musical training or score-reading abilities to use, and in fact may appear as a game to its user. In the first year of *Ocarina*'s release, we have observed (from user feedback, reviews, and YouTube/twitter) that most *Ocarina* users are not "musicians," and yet they are musically expressive.

Thousands of user-generated *Ocarina* videos have appeared on the Internet, many of them via YouTube (Figure 20.10). Many videos capture users at home, holiday and birthday parties, in demos, and performances. Many subjects are seen and heard performing in front of the camera, presumably using the computer both for video capture, as well as score and even as a music stand. In this context, *Ocarina* resembles a traditional instrument (e.g., a recorder) in that players are practicing (or learning) in

FIGURE 20.10 A sampling of publicly online user-generated Ocarina video performances.

front of scores while playing a physical artifact. What these artifacts and user communities have shown is that it is possible to build social musical experiences that foster organic, global communities, leveraging both the geography and critical mass of mobile user bases.

More recently, new social music artifacts have built on the ideas described here. They include *Magic Piano*, which presents a real-time anonymous duet interaction that randomly pairs users to play music together. *I Am T-Pain* auto-tunes the user's voice and broadcasts the result to others in the application. The social feature in Smule's *Glee Karaoke* allows anonymous users to add their voice to songs sung by others around the world (one instance of this collaborative singing has forty different voices from more than twenty countries creating a single rendition of John Lennon's "Imagine"; the largest collaboration to date has 3000 users worldwide jointly creating a rendition of "Lean on Me").

# Looking to the Future

What lies ahead for the future of mobile music? We don't know yet—but the time seems ripe to take the next step and explore. The mobile artifacts and experiences described here have only become possible through the recent mass adoption of powerful mobile computing technologies. They touch on design, aesthetics, physical interaction, physical proximity, global social participation, as well as community building. While these are only beginnings in an increasingly mobile, personal, and connected world, we have begun learning how take advantage of this new medium of mobile computing.

The move from simply *ringtones* to mobile *apps* has signaled a degree of interactivity previously not possible (though the early the ringtones were often composed by users, and even polyphonic ringtones were complemented by ring tone remix engines). One significant consequence of this shift is that people are *making* music on mobile devices, in addition to consuming it.

It is worth noting that, despite its mass popularity, iPhones (and smartphones in general), when viewed in a global frame, are still a relatively rare commodity that has higher adoption for those with higher income. While the semblance of community described in this chapter is intended for everyone, this disparity has ramifications on the participants in such global musical communities. At the same time, mobile technology is advancing rapidly, and it may not be long before powerful mobile computing devices become ubiquitous as commodity items.

The iPhone has created an inflection point in mobile computing, putting an unprecedented combination of hardware sensors and software features in the hands of hundreds of millions. The persistent network connectivity and location-awareness makes it possible to create expressive experiences both locally (i.e., on device) and globally (i.e., with other users, in communities). Designing experiences and products around new technology, especially musical ones, can fundamentally benefit from a "blank-slate" approach that rethinks and transforms the platform.

There is a sense of magic in wide-area, massive-scale location-aware activities. In many of these interactions described in this work, identity is not crucial, and anonymity can be just as powerful as it encourages different types of social interactions. On a more personal level, the sheer number of *Ocarina* and *Leaf Trombone* users at large shows that perhaps with the right approach and settings (e.g., mobile, personal, easy), we can encourage a large population to engage in expressive music making, and even create new wide-area communities quickly.

Our community of mobile music researchers and developers has a long way to go in terms of truly unlocking the potential of the technology. In this context, it is useful to never forget that it is people we are ultimately designing for. Technology, almost by definition, will evolve, rise, become obsolete, and be replaced, while human nature changes much more slowly (if at all). So while we embrace cutting-edge technology, we believe it is crucial that we relentlessly design for people.

The space for social music applications is wide open and we expect many of the ideas presented here to mature into new applications, new interactions, and better contexts for expressive social exchange. There is much work to be done to invent new mobile-mediated instruments and experiences that harness the specific features of this technology to the fullest and for people. We are excited to be part of this ongoing evolution.

# References

Behrendt, Frauke. 2005. *Handymusik. Klangkunst und 'mobile devices.'* Osnabrück: Epos. Available: www.epos.uos.de/music/templates/buch.php?id=57.

Bloom: Generative Music, http://www.generativemusic.com/ (accessed December 2008).

Cook, Perry, and Gary Scavone. 1999. "The Synthesis ToolKit (STK)." In *Proceedings of the International Computer Music Conference*, 164–66. Beijing: ICMA.

Essl, Georg, and Michael Rohs. 2006. "Mobile STK for Symbian OS." In *Proceedings of the International Computer Music Conference*, 278–81. New Orleans: ICMA.

——. 2007a. "CaMus2: Optical Flow and Collaboration in Camera Phone Music." In *Proceedings of the International Conference on New Interfaces for Musical Expression (NIME)*, 160–63. New York: New York University.

——. 2007b. "ShaMus—A Sensor-Based Integrated Mobile Phone Instrument." In *Proceedings of the International Computer Music Conference*, 200–3. Copenhagen: ICMA.

——. 2009. "Interactivity for Mobile Music Making." *Organised Sound* 14(2):197–207.

Fiebrink, Rebecca, Ge Wang, and Perry R. Cook. 2007. "Don't Forget the Laptop: Using native Input Capabilities for Expressive Musical Control." In *Proceedings of the International Conference on New Interfaces for Musical Expression*, 164–67. New York: New York University.

Gaye, Lalya, Lars E. Holmquist, Frauke Behrendt, and Atau Tanaka. 2006. "Mobile Music technology: Report on an Emerging Community." In *NIME '06: Proceedings of the 2006 Conference on New Interfaces for Musical Expression*, 22–25. Paris: IRCAM.

Gaye, Lalya, Ramia Maze, and Lars E. Holmquist. 2003. "Sonic City: The Urban Environment as a Musical Interface." In *Proceedings of the International Conference on New Interfaces for Musical Expression*, 109–15. Montreal: McGill.

Geiger, Günther. 2003. "PDa: Real Time Signal Processing and Sound Generation on Handheld Devices." In *Proceedings of the International Computer Music Conference*. Singapore: ICMA.

——. 2006. "Using the Touch Screen as a Controller for Portable Computer Music Instruments." In *Proceedings of the International Conference on New Interfaces for Musical Expression*, 61–64. Paris: IRCAM.

Gillian, Nicholas, Sile O'Modhrain, and Georg Essl. 2009. "Scratch-Off: A Gesture Based Mobile Music Game with Tactile Feedback." In *Proceedings of the International Conference on New Interfaces for Musical Expression (NIME09)*, 308–11. Pittsburgh: Carnegie Mellon University.

Hoffman, M. 2007. "*Breathlyzer?*" Performance for Princeton Laptop Orchestra.

Khu.sh: Intelligent Music Applications, http://khu.sh/ (accessed December 2009).

Levin, Golan. 2001. *Dialtones (A Telesymphony)*, www.flong.com/telesymphony (accessed April 1, 2007). (This site is no longer available.)

Misra, Ananya, Georg Essl, and Michael Rohs. 2008. "Microphone as Sensor in Mobile Phone Performance." In *Proceedings of the International Conference on New Interfaces for Musical Expression*. Genova, Italy.

RjDj: A Mind-twisting Hearing Sensation, http://rjdj.me/ (accessed August 2009).

Rohs, Michael, Georg Essl, and Martin Roth. 2006. "CaMus: Live Music Performance Using Camera Phones and Visual Grid Tracking." In *Proceedings of the International Conference on New Instruments for Musical Expression (NIME)*, 31–36. Paris: IRCAM.

Schiemer, Greg, and Mark Havryliv. 2006. "Pocket Gamelan: Tuneable trajectories for flying sources in Mandala 3 and Mandala 4." In *Proceedings of the International Conference on New Interfaces for Musical Expression (NIME)*, 37–42. Paris: IRCAM.

Shazam on iPhone, http://www.shazam.com/iphone/ (accessed December 2009).

Tanaka, Atau. 2004. "Mobile Music Making." In *Proceedings of the International Conference on New Interfaces for Musical Expression*, 154–56. Hamamatsu: Shizuoka University.

Tanaka, Atau, and P. Gemeinboeck. 2006a. "A framework for spatial interaction in locative media." In *Proceedings of the International Conference on New Interfaces for Musical Expression*, 26–30. Paris: IRCAM.

——. 2006b. "Net_Dérive: Locative music for 3 mobile phones and gps." http://www.ataut.net/site/Net-Derive (accessed?).

Tanaka, Atau, Guillame Valadon, and Christophe Berger. 2007. "Social Mobile Music Navigation Using the Compass." In *Proceedings of the International Mobile Music Workshop*. Amsterdam: STEIM.

Trueman, Dan., 2007. "Why a Laptop Orchestra?" *Organised Sound*, 12(2):171–79.

Wang, Ge. 2008. *The ChucK Audio Programming Language: A Strongly-timed, On-the-fly Environ/mentality*. PhD diss., Princeton University.

——. 2014. "Ocarina: Designing the iPhone's Magic Flute." *Computer Music Journal*. 38(2).

Wang, Ge, G. Essl, J. Smith, S. Salazar, P. Cook, R. Hamilton, R. Fiebrink, J. Berger, D. Zhu, M. Ljungstrom, A. Berry, J. Wu, T. Kirk, E. Berger, J. Segal. 2009. "Smule = Sonic Media: An Intersection of the Mobile, Musical, and Social." In *Proceedings of the International Computer Music Conference*. Montreal: ICMA.

Wang, Ge, Georg Essl, and Henri Penttinen. Forthcoming. "The Mobile Phone Orchestra." *Oxford Handbook of Mobile Music Studies*, ed. Gopinath and Stanyek. Oxford University Press.

——. 2008. "MoPho: Do Mobile Phones Dream of Electric Orchestras?" In *Proceedings of the International Computer Music Conference (ICMC08)*. Belfast: ICMA.

Wang, Ge, Nicholas J. Bryan, Jieun Oh, and Robert Hamilton. 2009. "Stanford Laptop Orchestra (SLOrk)." In Proceedings of the International Computer Music Conference, 505–8. Montreal: ICMA.

Wang, Ge, Jieun Oh, S. Salazar, and Robert Hamilton. 2011. "World Stage: A Crowdsourcing Paradigm for Social Mobile Music." In *Proceedings of the International Computer Music Conference*. Huddersfield, UK.

Weinberg, Gil, Andrew Beck, and Mark Godfrey. 2009. "ZooZBeat: A Gesture-based Mobile Music Studio." In *Proceedings of the International Conference on New Interfaces for Musical Expression (NIME09)*, 312–15. Pittsburgh: Carnegie Mellon University.

# INDEX

Note: Page numbers in italics indicate figures or tables.